DICTIONARY
OF
LABOUR BIOGRAPHY

Volume V

DICTIONARY
OF
LABOUR BIOGRAPHY

Volume V

JOYCE M. BELLAMY
Senior Research Officer, University of Hull

and

JOHN SAVILLE
Professor of Economic and Social History, University of Hull

First published 1979 by
THE MACMILLAN PRESS LTD
London and Basingstoke
Associated companies in Delhi
Dublin Hong Kong Johannesburg Lagos
Melbourne New York Singapore Tokyo

Typeset and printed in Great Britain by
UNWIN BROTHERS LIMITED
The Gresham Press, Old Woking, Surrey
A member of the Staples Printing Group

British Library Cataloguing in Publication Data

Dictionary of Labour Biography,
  Vol. 5
  1. Labor and laboring classes—Great
  Britain—Biography
  I. Bellamy, Joyce Margaret   II. Saville, John
  335' . 1'0922   HD8393.A1

  ISBN 0–333–22015–3

Contents

Acknowledgements

This present volume continues along the same lines and upon the same principles as the previous volumes. We have included, however, a new feature which is intended to become a permanent constituent of all future volumes. This is the publication of Special Notes relating to aspects of general labour history, or movements, which have tended to be somewhat or mostly neglected in historical writing: a neglect which is probably due to the fact that the items we have in mind are not perhaps sufficiently important in themselves for an independent article in the periodical literature or for a separate chapter in a book. In the present volume we have chosen three subjects for Special Notes, and our readers will appreciate from their titles the reasons for this decision. These three subjects are: the Mosely Industrial Commission of 1902; the First World War Parliamentary and Joint Labour Recruiting Committees; and the 1917 Club. Each Special Note has its own bibliography; and we shall be interested to hear from our readers any suggestions for similar items in future volumes. We would also like to remind our readers that we are proposing in volume VI to include Addenda and Corrigenda to the first five volumes and we shall be grateful to receive any additions or corrections to our entries that they may have.

The research for this volume has been made possible by a generous grant from the Social Science Research Council. Our debts to many individuals are considerable. We particularly wish to thank the members of our research group: Mrs Margaret 'Espinasse, Ms Ann Holt and Mrs Barbara Nield in Hull, and Mrs Vivien Morton for work in London. From our former colleague, Dr David E. Martin, now of the University of Sheffield, we have received growing assistance, and we are especially grateful for his editorial skills and care in reading MS entries. We have been much helped and encouraged, as we have been from the beginning of this project, by Dame Margaret Cole. We also wish to record our appreciation of the advice and help we have received from Dr R. Page Arnot, Dr P. S. Bagwell, Dr C. Baier, the late Harold Bing, Edmund and Ruth Frow, Mrs Margaret Gibb, OBE, Dr Marion Kozak, Mr G. I. Lewis, Mr R. A. McKinlay, Dr K. O. Morgan, David and Naomi Reid, Dr Eric Taylor, and Mrs Irene Wagner and Mrs Judith Woods (both of the Labour Party). We also wish to thank our contributors and those whose names are listed in the Sources section of the biographies.

Our debt to many librarians and their staffs is immense. To Dr Philip Larkin and his colleagues of the Brynmor Jones Library, Hull University we are especially grateful, and we also wish to record our thanks to the staff of other university libraries including those at Bradford, Girton College, Cambridge, Edinburgh, Institute of Germanic Studies of London University, Nottingham, Oxford and Sussex. We have also received much assistance from the British Library, London and Boston Spa, and the Newspaper Library, Colindale; the British Library of

viii ACKNOWLEDGEMENTS

Political and Economic Science and members of the former Historical Records Project at LSE; Miss J. Elise Bayley, librarian of the Plunkett Foundation for Co-operative Studies, Oxford; Miss Christine Coates, TUC librarian; Mr Roy Garratt, information officer and librarian of the Co-operative Union; Mr Gordon Phillips, archivist of *The Times*; Mr R. A. Storey, archivist, Modern Record Centre, Warwick University and Ms Janet Druker, formerly of the MRC; Dr Hywel Francis of the South Wales Miners' Library and Mr S. Tongue, archivist, London Borough of Hackney. Among the public libraries we wish to thank are those in Birmingham (including the City Museum and Art Gallery), Blackpool, Bradford, Bristol, Bolton, Boston, Cardiff, Corby, Coventry, Croydon, Glasgow, Hereford, Ipswich, Kingston upon Hull, London Boroughs of Camden, Ealing, Finsbury, Greenwich, Hackney, Hillingdon, Islington, Lambeth, Lewisham, Newham, Tower Hamlets, Wandsworth and Westminster, Manchester, New York, Newcastle upon Tyne, Northampton, Norwich, Peterborough, Portsmouth, Preston, Stirling and Sunderland. We are much indebted also to staff in the General Register Offices in Belfast, Dublin, Edinburgh and London, in the House of Commons Library, the National Libraries of Scotland and Wales, the Record Offices in Bristol, Doncaster, Edinburgh, Hereford and Warwick and the Royal Commission on Historical Manuscripts.

The trade union offices consulted were: AEUW, APEX, ASW (now UCATT), ISTC, Miners' International Federation, NUJ, NUM, NUS, National Union of Sheet Metal Workers, Coppersmiths, Heating and Domestic Engineers, NUT, TGWU and TSSA. We have also been helped by the Ancient Order of Foresters in Birmingham and the Independent Order of Odd Fellows, Manchester. We are indebted to staff on the following journals and newspapers: *Bournville Reporter*, East Midland Allied Press Archives, *Middlesex Advertiser*, *New Statesman*, *Northamptonshire Evening Telegraph*, *North-Eastern Evening Gazette*, and *Tribune*.

We further acknowledge the help received from a number of other organisations: BBC News Information Service and Written Archives Centre; Central Chancery of the Orders of Knighthood; CCAHC; Co-operative Societies of Chesterfield and District and Coventry and District; Devon and Cornwall Constabulary; Gray's Inn Library; Hull Fisherman's Trust Fund; India House; ICFC; Industrial Society; Labour Party; LRD; National Society for Clean Air, N.W. Division; Nene College, Northampton; Save the Children Fund; Society of Friends Library; University Tutorial College.

We also wish to record our thanks to all those in the University of Hull and outside who have given typing and photo-copying assistance. We further acknowledge the help given in proof reading by John Atkins, Jan Crowther, Ann Holt, Don Major, Joy Marshall, Dr David E. Martin, Barbara Nield, Richard Saville and Jill Ward and the work undertaken on the index by Barbara Nield, assisted by V. J. Morris and G. D. Weston of the Brynmor Jones Library. Finally we wish to thank our publishers and in particular Mr T. M. Farmiloe in the London office of Macmillan and Mr A. Aslett, Mr A. Bathe and Mr H. W. Bawden at Basingstoke.

JMB
JS

University of Hull
February 1978

IN MEMORIAM ANTHONY ELLIOTT
1921-1976

Anthony Elliott was an unexpected and unusual contributor to a biographical *Dictionary* of the British labour movement. The son of Sir Ivo Elliott and his wife Margery (née Carey), his social origins and education were conventional for the high servant of State which he became. He was educated at the Dragon School, Oxford, then at Eton and Balliol College, his university career being interrupted by war service, mostly with the King's Shropshire Light Infantry in East Africa, where he finished with the rank of Captain. After graduating in 1946 he joined the Foreign Service and held various positions in Belgrade, Peking, Hong Kong, and then in Washington, where he was Minister and Head of Chancery. In 1972 he was appointed Ambassador in Helsinki, and in 1975 he moved in the same rank to Tel Aviv. Not quite a year later, on 28 August 1976, he died while swimming near Caesarea. He left a much-loved wife and four children.

During his undergraduate years—or it might even have been when he was still at Eton – he read Simon Haxey's *Tory M.P.*, published as a Left Book Club volume in 1939; and from that time he conceived a passion for political biography. During all the years of his professional career he built up, patiently and carefully, a huge amount of detailed biographical material on all parliamentary members of the House of Commons of all parties. The time period he worked in was from about 1918 to 1951. He first contacted the editors of the *DLB* after the publication of Volume I, and from that time we sent him drafts of MPs on whom we were working. His information was always extraordinarily detailed, and we never ceased to be impressed with the range of his sources, which were often of the most recondite kind. It must be rare in the history of the British Foreign Office for a newly appointed ambassador, in this case to Israel, to write with great satisfaction: 'I have just heard that there are complete files of the 19th-century *Jewish Chronicle* in Tel Aviv so, in what spare time I have, I may be able to do a little original research on Jewish members there' [letter, 15 Nov 1975].

The obituary notices at the time of Anthony Elliott's death underlined his professional skill and dedication. They also emphasised what an extraordinarily nice man he was. As a friend wrote in the *Times* of 13 September 1976: 'Behind [the] front of professional achievement lay a personality of great depth and unostentatious warmth. His sense of fun, not least at his own expense, and total lack of pomposity, above all about himself, made him, I believe, tremendously endearing to those who worked with him.'

Joyce Bellamy and I say Amen to these words. He enjoyed working with us, using the detailed material he had collected over the years, and he was obviously happy to have found one outlet for part of his own meticulous research. From our side he was invaluable, and in the technical sense we shall not find a successor. But more than this, as a man, a contributor and a friend, we loved him; whatever the pressures upon him, and they must have been many, his letters were always helpful, courteous and pleasant; and until he had provided his comments, our entries for MPs were never finalised. We salute his memory as a scholar; to a colleague we offer this brief tribute to a rare spirit.

JOHN SAVILLE

Notes to Readers

1. Place-names are usually quoted according to contemporary usage relating to the particular entry.
2. Where the amount of a will, estate value or effects is quoted, the particular form used is normally that given in *The Times*, or the records of Somerset House, London, or the Scottish Record Office, Edinburgh. For dates before 1860 the source will usually be the Public Record Office.
3. Under the heading **Sources,** personal information relates to details obtained from relatives, friends or colleagues of the individual in question; biographical information refers to other sources.
4. The place of publication in bibliographical references is London, unless otherwise stated.
5. P indicates a pamphlet whose pagination could not be verified. Where it is known, the number of pages is quoted if under sixty.
6. The *See also* column which follows biographical entries includes names marked with a dagger and these refer to biographies already published in Volumes I, II, III, or IV of the *Dictionary*; those with no marking are included in the present volume, and those with an asterisk refer to entries to be included in later volumes.
7. A consolidated name list of entries in Volumes I–V will be found at the end of this volume before the general index.

List of Contributors

David Barton Esq. — Branch Librarian, County Branch Library, Matlock

The late Harold F. Bing Esq. — Formerly Lecturer, Co-operative College, Loughborough

Mrs Margaret Blunden — Aynho, Banbury

Ian Britain Esq. — Research Student, Corpus Christi College, Oxford

Dr Kenneth D. Brown — Reader in Economic History, The Queen's University of Belfast

Raymond Brown, Esq. — Lecturer, Department of Economic and Social History, Hull University

Dr Raymond Challinor — Principal Lecturer and Head of History Group, Newcastle upon Tyne Polytechnic

Miss Doris N. Chew — Burnley

Dame Margaret Cole — London

Fergus D'Arcy Esq. — Lecturer, Department of Modern History, University College, Dublin

Peter D. Drake Esq. — Social Sciences Department, Birmingham Reference Library

Ms Janet Druker — School of Industrial and Business Studies, Warwick University; formerly at Modern Records Centre, Warwick University

Mrs Margaret 'Espinasse — Formerly Reader in English Language, Hull University

Edmund Frow Esq. — Manchester

Mrs Ruth Frow — Manchester

Professor Janet Fyfe — School of Library and Information Science, University of Western Ontario, London, Canada

Kenneth L. Goodall Esq. — Watford

Stephen Gosling Esq. — Chorlton-cum-Hardy

Ms Ann Holt — Research Assistant, Department of Economic and Social History, Hull University

Dr David Howell — Lecturer, Department of Government, Manchester University

Seán Hutton Esq. — Bridlington School, North Humberside

Dr Beverley Kingston — Senior Lecturer, School of History, University of New South Wales, Australia

Dr Marion Kozak — London

Professor Judith Fincher Laird — Department of History, Denison University, Ohio, U.S.A.

Dr David E. Martin	Lecturer, Department of Economic and Social History, Sheffield University
Dr Robert G. Neville	Associate Editor, Historical Abstracts, European Bibliographical Centre, Oxford
Mrs Barbara Nield	Research Assistant, Department of Economic and Social History, Hull University
Frederick C. Padley Esq.	Formerly chief technician, Department of Zoology, Reading University
Archie Potts Esq.	Principal Lecturer in Economics, Department of Economics, Newcastle upon Tyne Polytechnic
Norman W. Robinson Esq.	King James I School, Bishop Auckland
John J. Rowley Esq.	Lecturer, Liberal Studies and English, Dudley Technical College
Dr Edward Royle	Lecturer, Department of History, University of York
Dr David Rubinstein	Senior Lecturer and Head of Department of Economic and Social History, Hull University
Bryan H. Sadler Esq.	Lecturer, Department of Economics, Warwick University
Professor James A. Schmiechen	Department of History, Illinois State University, Bloomington-Normal, U.S.A.
John B. Smethurst Esq.	Eccles
Eric L. Taplin Esq.	Head of Department of Social Studies, Liverpool Polytechnic
Dr Eric Taylor	Senior Lecturer in Modern History, Wolverhampton Polytechnic
Professor George F. Thomason	Department of Industrial Relations and Management Studies, University College, Cardiff
Adrian Tranter Esq.	Research Student, Emmanuel College, Cambridge
Bob Whitfield Esq.	Withywood Comprehensive School, Bristol
Professor Martin J. Wiener	Department of History, Rice University, Houston, Texas, U.S.A.

List of Abbreviations

AACAN	Association of All Classes of All Nations
ACA	Agricultural Co-operative Association
ACCA	Agricultural Central Co-operative Association
Add.	Additional
AEU	Amalgamated Engineering Union
AGM	Annual General Meeting
AIMS	Associated Iron Moulders of Scotland
Ald.	Alderman
Anon.	Anonymous
APEX	Association of Professional, Executive, Clerical and Computer Staff
App.(s)	Appendix (Appendices)
ARWS	Associate of the Royal Society of Painters in Water Colours
ASCJ	Amalgamated Society of Carpenters and Joiners
ASE	Amalgamated Society of Engineers
ASLEF	Amalgamated Society of Locomotive Engineers and Firemen
ASRS	Amalgamated Society of Railway Servants
ASW	Amalgamated Society of Woodworkers
AUEW	Amalgamated Union of Engineering Workers
AUT	Association of University Teachers
BBC	British Broadcasting Corporation
BL	British Library
BLPES	British Library of Political and Economic Science, LSE
BM	British Museum (now British Library)
Brit. J. Soc.	*British Journal of Sociology*
BSP	British Socialist Party
BSSA	British Steel Smelters' Association
Bull.	*Bulletin*
Bull. Soc. Lab. Hist.	*Bulletin of the Society for the Study of Labour History*
BWL	British Workers' League
C./Cd/Cmd	Command Paper
CAWU	Clerical and Administrative Workers' Union
CC	County Council
CCAHC	Central Council for Agricultural and Horticultural Co-operation

CI	Communist International
CLC	Central Labour College
Cllr	Councillor
CMG	Commander of the Order of St Michael and St George
CNAA	Council for National Academic Awards
CND	Campaign for Nuclear Disarmament
CO	Conscientious Objector
Coll.	Collection
Comisco	Committee of the International Socialist Conference
Cont. Rev.	*Contemporary Review*
Co-op.	Co-operative
CP	Communist Party
CPGB	Communist Party of Great Britain
CPI	Communist Party of India
CRO	County Record Office
Cttee	Committee
CWS	Co-operative Wholesale Society
d	old pence
DATI	Department of Agriculture and Technical Instruction
DLB	*Dictionary of Labour Biography*
DNB	*Dictionary of National Biography*
Dod	*Dod's Parliamentary Companion*
DWRGLU	Dock, Wharf, Riverside and General Labourers' Union
EC	Executive Committee/Council
ECCI	Executive Committee of the Communist International
Econ. Hist. Rev.	*Economic History Review*
Econ. J.	*Economic Journal*
Econ. Rev.	*Economic Review*
ed.(s)	edited, edition, editor(s)
et al.	*et alia/et alii* (Lat.): and others
ETU	Electrical Trades Union
FAO	Food and Agriculture Organisation
FC	Football Club
ff.	pages following
Fortn. Rev.	*Fortnightly Review*
GER	Great Eastern Railway
GFTU	General Federation of Trade Unions
GMC	General Management Committee
GNR	Great Northern Railway
HPF	Horace Plunkett Foundation
IAOS	Irish Agricultural Organisation Society

ibid.	*ibidem* (Lat.): in the same place
ICA	International Co-operative Alliance
ICFC	Industrial and Commercial Finance Corporation
idem	(Lat.): the same; author as mentioned in previous entry
ILO	International Labour Office/Organisation
ILP	Independent Labour Party
imp.	impression
Int. Affairs	*International Affairs*
Int. Rev. of Missions	*International Review of Missions*
Int. Rev. Social Hist.	*International Review of Social History*
ISF	International Socialist Forum
ISTC	Iron and Steel Trades Confederation
J.	Journal
J. Cont. Hist.	*Journal of Contemporary History*
J. Mod. Hist.	*Journal of Modern History*
J. of Econ. Hist.	*Journal of Economic History*
JP	Justice of the Peace
JPE	*Journal of Political Economy*
Jr	Junior
Kelly	*Kelly's Handbook to the Titled, Landed and Official Classes*
Lab. Mon.	*Labour Monthly*
LCC	London County Council
LCMF	Lancashire and Cheshire Miners' Federation
LEA	Labour Electoral Association
LGB	Local Government Board
Lib-Lab	Liberal–Labour
LNER	London and North Eastern Railway
LNWR	London and North Western Railway
LP	Labour Party
LRC	Labour Representation Committee
LRD	Labour Research Department
LSC	London Society of Compositors
LSE	London School of Economics
LSI	Labour and Socialist International
LTC	London Trades Council
Mag.	*Magazine*
Mass.	Massachusetts
MFGB	Miners' Federation of Great Britain
misc.	miscellaneous
MMM	Miners' Minority Movement
M of E	Minutes of Evidence
MP	Member of Parliament

MRC	Modern Records Centre, Warwick Univ.
MS(S)/ms.	manuscripts
M S & L	Manchester, Sheffield and Lincolnshire Railway
NAC	National Administrative Council
NAGRC	National Association of General Railway Clerks
N. Amer. Rev.	*North American Review*
NAPSS	National Association for the Promotion of Social Science
NCA	National Clerks' Association
NCB	National Coal Board
NCF	No-Conscription Fellowship
NCLC	National Council of Labour Colleges
NCMA	Northumberland Colliery Mechanics' Association
NCWW	National Council of Women Workers
n.d.	no date
NEC	National Executive Committee
NFBTO	National Federation of Building Trade Operatives
NFWW	National Federation of Women Workers
19th C.	*Nineteenth Century*
NJC	National Joint Council
NLA	National Library of Australia
NLP	National Labour Press
NLS	National Library of Scotland
NMA	Northumberland Miners' Association
NMWM	No More War Movement
non-parl.	non-parliamentary
NORAD	North American Air Defence Command
Notts	Nottinghamshire
n.s.	new series
NSFU	National Sailors' and Firemen's Union
NTWF	National Transport Workers' Federation
NUAW	National Union of Agricultural Workers
NUC	National Union of Clerks
NUDL	National Union of Dock Labourers
NUFW	National Union of Foundry Workers
NUGMW	National Union of General and Municipal Workers
NUJ	National Union of Journalists
NUM	National Union of Mineworkers
NUR	National Union of Railwaymen
NUS	National Union of Seamen
NUT	National Union of Teachers
NUWSS	National Union of Women's Suffrage Societies
NUWW	National Union of Women Workers
NWC	National Workers' Committee
NY	New York

Obit.	Obituary
o.s.	old series
OUP	Oxford University Press
P	Pamphlet
p.a.	per annum
PC	Privy Councillor
PFCS	Plunkett Foundation for Co-operative Studies
PL	Public Library
PLP	Parliamentary Labour Party
Pol. Q.	*Political Quarterly*
POUM	Partido Obrero de Unificación Marxista
PPU	Peace Pledge Union
Proc.	Proceedings
pseud.	pseudonym
pt	part
Q.	*Quarterly*
QJE	*Quarterly Journal of Economics*
Q(s)	Question(s)
RAF	Royal Air Force
RASC	Royal Army Service Corps
R.C.	Royal Commission
RCA	Railway Clerks' Association
RDC	Rural District Council
Ref.	Reference
repr.	reprinted
rev.	revised
Rev.	Reverend
Rev.	*Review*
Rev. of Revs	*Review of Reviews*
RILU	Red International of Labour Unions
s	shilling(s)
S.C.	Select Committee
SDF	Social Democratic Federation
ser.	series
SJC	Standing Joint Committee
SLP	Socialist Labour Party
Soc.	Society
Soc. Rev.	*Socialist Review*
SPCK	Society for the Propagation of Christian Knowledge
SPE	Society for Pure English
Spec.	*Spectator*

SSAFA	Soldiers, Sailors and Air Force Families' Association
SWMF	South Wales Miners' Federation
TGWU	Transport and General Workers' Union
TLS	*Times Literary Supplement*
Trans.	*Transactions*
TSSA	Transport Salaried Staffs Association
TUC	Trades Union Congress
UCATT	Union of Construction, Allied Trades and Technicians
UDC	Union of Democratic Control
UKA	United Kingdom Alliance
UN	United Nations
Univ.	University
UPW	Union of Post Office Workers
v.	versus
VAD	Voluntary Aid Detachment
vol.(s)	volume(s)
WAOS	Welsh Agricultural Organisation Society
WCG	Women's Co-operative Guild
WEA	Workers' Educational Association
West. Rev.	*Westminster Review*
WHNC	Workmen's National Housing Council
WPPL	Women's Protective and Provident League
WSA	Women's Suffrage Association
WSPU	Women's Social and Political Union
WTUL	Women's Trade Union League
WU	Workers' Union
WW	*Who's Who*
WWW	*Who Was Who*
YMA	Yorkshire Mineworkers' Association
YMCA	Young Men's Christian Association
Yorkshire Mine-workers' Q.J.	*Yorkshire Mine-workers' Quarterly Journal*

List of Bibliographies and Special Notes

Bibliographies

The subject bibliographies attached to certain entries are the responsibility of the editors. The entries under which they will be found in Volumes I–V are as follows:

British Labour Party		
1900–13	LANSBURY, George	II
1914–31	HENDERSON, Arthur	I
Christian Socialism, 1848–54	LUDLOW, John Malcolm Forbes	II
Co-operation		
Agricultural		
Co-operation	PLUNKETT, Sir Horace Curzon	V
Co-operative Education	HALL, Fred	I
Co-operative Party	ALEXANDER, Albert Victor	I
Co-operative Production	JONES, Benjamin	I
Co-operative Union	HAYWARD, Fred	I
Co-operative Wholesaling	REDFERN, Percy	I
Co-partnership	GREENING, Edward Owen	I
International Co-operative		
Alliance	MAY, Henry John	I
Irish Co-operation	GALLAGHER, Patrick	I
Retail Co-operation		
Nineteenth Century	HOLYOAKE, George Jacob	I
1900–45	BROWN, William Henry	I
1945–70	BONNER, Arnold	I
Scottish Co-operation	MAXWELL, William	I
Guild Socialism	SPARKES, Malcolm	II
Mining Trade Unionism		
1850–79	MACDONALD, Alexander	I
1880–99	PICKARD, Benjamin	I
1900–14	ASHTON, Thomas	I
1915–26	COOK, Arthur James	III
1927–44	LEE, Peter	II
Scottish Mining Trade Unionism	SMILLIE, Robert	III
Welsh Mining Trade Unionism	ABRAHAM, William (Mabon)	I
New Model Unionism	ALLAN, William	I
New Unionism, 1889–93	TILLETT, Benjamin (Ben)	IV

Special Notes in Volume V

The Parliamentary Recruiting Committee and the Joint Labour Recruiting Committee in the First World War *see* **BOWERMAN, Charles William**

The 1917 Club *see* **HAMILTON, Mary Agnes**

The Mosely Industrial Commission *see* **STEADMAN, William (Will) Charles**

ADAMS, Francis William Lauderdale (1862-93)

POLITICAL JOURNALIST, POET, NOVELIST, AND LITERARY CRITIC

Adams was born on 27 September 1862 in Malta, where his father, Andrew Leith Adams, was at the time a surgeon in the British Army contingent stationed on the island. Francis's grandfather (also called Francis) was a distinguished Scottish physician and classical scholar, who had risen from fairly humble origins, his family having run a small farm at Lumphanan, Aberdeenshire. Francis's father later took up an academic career; he was a professional colleague and supporter of Charles Darwin, and became professor of zoology and of natural science at the university colleges of Dublin and Cork respectively. Francis spent a part of his early boyhood in Ireland, as well as in England and Canada.

The years 1869 to 1879 were devoted to his formal education, which he received at a number of schools in the Midlands. During 1879 he was in the sixth form at Shrewsbury, where he perhaps showed the first signs of the rebellious streak in his nature by developing a strong reaction to the school's cripplingly pedantic methods of instruction, and its general atmosphere of dullness and sterility (see his description of school life in his first novel, *Leicester*, published in 1885, republished as *A Child of the Age*, 1894). He was never to oppose the public school system in principle, however, always concentrating his attacks on its vices as an educational, rather than as a social, institution.

The influence of his mother, Bertha Jane Adams (née Grundy), was perhaps the initial divisive factor in the shaping of his views on contemporary society. She was a fashionable novelist, whose works, in the words of Sydney Jephcott, the Australian poet and disciple of Adams, 'epitomised all the ineffable English worship of "Society" '. From Francis's relationship with her as a child he may have imbibed the fascination he reveals in his own novels and stories with the trappings of the upper-class world. On the other hand, there is evidence to suggest that her infidelities to his father – a father he adored – aroused in him a certain repugnance for his mother and for all her social values. Jephcott quotes Adams as saying harshly: 'A lifelong prostitute to "Society" as my mother was, does not find it hard to prostitute herself to any man who stirs her blood.'

The fact that Adams's father accepted the radical scientific ideas of the day (even if he did not apply these outside the field of natural science) created an intellectual atmosphere at home which enabled the son to develop a turn of mind which was open to new ideas in general and sceptical of the received notions of the Victorian era. It may have been in such an environment, with its easy access to books and its fund of learned talk, that Adams first came into contact with the ideas of Matthew Arnold, which were to exercise a dominant, if at times fiercely resisted, influence over his thought.

The years Adams spent, immediately after leaving school, mixing in the literary and artistic circles of London and Paris, may also have served to introduce him to the ideas of Arnold as well as those of the other 'modern men' in the field of letters, among whom he included Goethe, Heine, Carlyle and Walt Whitman. It was in the early 1880s that Adams formed a warm friendship with Sarah Bernhardt, and was invited to the 'bachelor "at homes" ' of Oscar Wilde and his circle. His contact with writers like Wilde and those in other semi-Bohemian groups nurtured the strong distaste he was to show for Victorian ethical and literary conventions.

During these years in London and Paris Adams not only hobnobbed with Bohemians and aesthetes in studios and salons, he also trudged the slums of these two cities, as a social observer, and learned their tale of squalor and misery and hard, grinding poverty. With his naturally questioning turn of mind, and a social conscience stirred by such experiences, it was not surprising that he was caught up in the Socialist revival in Britain in the early 1880s. His plans for a diplomatic career falling through, he took up school-teaching at Ventnor College on the Isle of Wight; and on one of the occasions that he returned to the mainland, he joined H.M. Hyndman's Democratic Federation. Although he made a lasting impression on Frank Harris, to whom he had introduced himself after hearing a Socialist address delivered by this notorious journalist at Hyde

Park, Adams failed to make any conspicuous contribution at this stage to the germination of the Socialist movement in England. The state of his health ruled this out.

From early adolescence he had suffered from pulmonary tuberculosis – which carried off his father in 1882 and his brother, Henry, ten years later. This illness had such a grip on him by 1884 that he was advised by the doctor at Ventnor to seek out a warmer climate. At the end of the summer of that year, he sailed for Australia, accompanied by Helen Elizabeth Uttley, whom he had married in London a few months earlier.

He left England before the Democratic Federation had even changed its name to the Social Democratic Federation. From his brief connection with this organisation, however, Adams seems to have imbibed some rudimentary knowledge of Marxist theory. The first substantial work which he published after arriving in his new home (*Australian Essays*, 1886) was dedicated to Matthew Arnold; but it is interesting to note, alongside the customary obeisance to the ideal of 'Culture' and lamentations about the shortcomings of middle-class education, certain passages of socio-political analysis which are strongly reminiscent of Marxist pronouncements on the role of the class struggle in contemporary society. (An interesting example of Adams's view of the class struggle working historically can be found in his verse drama, *Tiberius*, which was written over a long period of time, and finally published only after his death.) Adams's acquaintance with Marxist notions was to lead him further and further away from the Arnoldian gospel, though he never completely deserted it.

A year after the appearance of the *Australian Essays*, a volume of *Poetical Works* by Adams was published in Brisbane and London which included, among much new material, all of the poems he had collected in his first book of verse, *Henry. And other Tales* [1884]. The rather insipid love-lyrics and world-weary elegies which appear in both these volumes stand in conspicuous contrast with the angry, militant verse that dominated his next collection, *Songs of the Army of the Night*, published in Sydney in 1888, and in four later editions in London. 'The Army of the Night' refers to the working classes of Britain and Australia, oppressed by the forces of capitalism and imperialism, and the songs themselves show how the main focus of Adams's social concerns had now shifted to these oppressed, and away from his own 'dear Middle-class', which was now seen to be among the oppressors. As he indicated in his preface to the *Songs*, Adams now suspected Matthew Arnold, for all his assaults on the philistinism and pseudo-liberalism of the middle class, of sharing the lofty complacency of that class in his attitude to the whole problem of the socially depressed. Adams could not acquiesce in such an attitude. Throughout the *Songs*, he exhorted the working classes to rise up and create a new classless society. His stress on the fact that only by their own efforts could they emancipate themselves from the oppression of the upper and middle classes, and his belief that violent revolution would be the inevitable means of emancipation, showed his predilection for 'Scientific', rather than 'Utopian', Socialism. Adams made explicit criticisms of the rather tame political stance of 'Utopian Socialists' like Edward Bellamy in America and William Lane in Australia.

The militancy of Adams's *Songs*, however, was of a curiously compulsive, almost involuntary, kind; and his later writings on the labour movement in England and Australia showed that his acceptance of the necessity of violent revolution was basically more in the nature of resignation to the inevitable than of outright commitment.

There is no evidence that the *Songs* had an extensive impact on the labour movement. The fact that the book went through five editions may be attributed less to its intrinsic popularity than to the vigorous championship of its author by his colleague and fellow-Socialist, Henry Stephens Salt, who edited the two posthumous editions of the *Songs*, in the hope of remedying the neglect which Adams had suffered at the hands of Socialist groups in England. Nonetheless, among the individuals and groups that are known to have read the *Songs* – ranging, in England, from anarchist journalists to readers of Robert Blatchford's *Clarion*, and including fellow poets of revolt such as Walt Whitman in America and Bernard O'Dowd in Australia – Adams's collection seems to have made a potent and lasting impression.

It has been suggested that Adams may have done some political and union organising for the labour movement in Australia in the late 1880s, but this is hard to verify, as the chronology and details of his six years' sojourn in the antipodes are nowhere precisely documented. He seems to have supported the idea of setting up a Labour Federation, but this body (the immediate precursor of the colonial labour parties) did not have its first general meeting till August 1890, five months after Adams had left the country. Any influence he may have had in the sphere of active and direct involvement in politics was probably small compared with the impact of his journalistic writings in labour newspapers, and of his personal relations with a number of leading activists and literary figures in the labour movement.

When he was in Queensland, Adams became through his work in journalism a close colleague and friend of William Lane, one of the most prominent figures in Australian labour history. The constant tendency of Lane to back away from the full implications of a revolutionary solution to social problems would often infuriate Adams and result in a heated argument between the two men. Though Adams never succeeded in converting Lane from his utopian position, the latter was sufficiently impressed by his fiery young friend to invite him to become intellectual mentor to the 'New Australia' community about to be set up in Paraguay. Adams, though amused at the offer rather than indignant, felt bound to reject it.

In Queensland, where he seems to have spent the bulk of his time in Australia, Adams also came into personal contact with the conservative political leader, Thomas McIlwraith. While admitting that the latter was an 'unashamed capitalist and speculator', Adams felt he was the 'only public man in Australia whom one could call great'. This strange attraction to McIlwraith was based partly on the belief that the Queensland politician was one of the few thoroughgoing champions of the idea of 'an Australian nationality' completely independent of shackling British influences. But Adams was also taken in by the bluff and genial personality of the man, who was very hospitable to his young admirer at times when he was extremely ill. It would appear that these kindnesses tended to blind Adams to the hypocrisies and authoritarian excesses of McIlwraith which were emphasised by the radical press. Ironically enough, the two papers to which Adams contributed most regularly during his stay in Australia, the *Bulletin* in Sydney and the *Boomerang* in Brisbane, proved to be among the most vociferous in their denunciations of McIlwraith.

Adams's contributions to such newspapers consisted of short stories (many of which he later republished in a book called *Australian Life*), poems, political squibs and letters to the editor on current social and political topics. During the last half of 1887, he travelled as the *Boomerang*'s special correspondent to Indonesia, Malaya and various Pacific Islands and there is evidence to suggest that he also made brief visits to China and Japan during these months.

Apart from doing some private tutoring in country homesteads in his early days in Australia, Adams lived solely by his pen, and this entailed many lean periods in which he was reduced almost to destitution. To eke out his living, he sometimes contributed to more conservative newspapers, such as the Brisbane *Courier*, which even employed him as a leader-writer on occasions. His other writings in Australia included literary criticism for various colonial periodicals, a serialised tale about bushrangers (later published in book form as *John Webb's End*) and two novels dealing with aspects of urban life in Australia: *Madeline Brown's Murderer* (published in Sydney in 1888) and *The Melbournians* (not published till 1892).

Disease afflicted Adams even more than poverty, and it was not only his own suffering with which he had to contend. His wife died of rheumatic fever in July 1886 and their baby son a few months later. Adams was married again in 1887 – to Edith Goldstone, a nurse and former actress. There is evidence that he had at least two children by Edith and that they also died in infancy.

The Australian climate, however soothing to consumptive lungs, could afford no protection against the ravages of a cancerous growth which now began to develop in Adams's throat. More and more regularly he was subjected to fits of violent choking, which usually culminated in a haemorrhage. It was with a sense of fatalism that he left Australia in 1890 to return to England.

He departed on 7 March, accompanied by his second wife. He had an accident on board which hastened his decline into complete invalidism, but this did not prevent him from completing on the voyage the manuscript of a novel which explored the theme of women's rights. Tentatively entitled *The Mills of the Gods*, it was later published as *Lady Lovan*, and ascribed pseudonymously to 'Agnes Farrell'.

Once Adams was back in England, a combination of poverty and bad weather contrived to aggravate his plight. A boarding-house which he and his wife attempted to run in Bournemouth failed to attract any boarders; and the unusually severe winter of 1890-1 forced him to seek retreat in the Isle of Wight. His wife went to London, where on the return of warmer weather, he was eventually able to rejoin her. Through the offices of his old friend, Frank Harris, who was then editor of the *Fortnightly Review*, Adams managed to ease his financial problems by submitting a series of political and literary essays to that journal. (Much of the material he wrote at this stage formed the basis of later collections of his work, such as *The Australians: a social sketch*, and *Essays in Modernity*.)

His remaining days were spent mainly at resorts in England or on the Riviera, though his last winter (1892-3) was partly taken up with a trip to Egypt as correspondent of the *Westminster Gazette*. Harris was again responsible for getting him this commission, and it resulted in a series of remarkable interviews with Egyptian leaders, and in yet another book, *The New Egypt*, in which Adams expressed great sympathy with the grievances of these leaders against British imperial rule as it was exercised by the administration of Lord Cromer.

While Adams was in Egypt, he heard the news of his brother's death. The details of the acute suffering which had preceded it made him determined not to die in the same way. In May 1893 he returned to England, and settled finally in Margate. On the morning of 4 September he suffered a particularly severe haemorrhage, and, having mustered sufficient strength to fetch his revolver, he shot himself. The inquest into his death returned a verdict of 'suicide while in a state of temporary insanity'. Though medical evidence made it plain that Adams would have died in any case within a few minutes, regret was expressed that Mrs Adams, who had been present throughout the whole scene, had not tried to prevent his fatal act. He was buried at Margate Cemetery. He left effects valued at £193.

Writings: *Henry. And other Tales* [1884]; *Leicester: an autobiography* 2 vols (1885); *Australian Essays* (Melbourne, 1886 & London, 1892); *Madeline Brown's Murderer* (Melbourne, 1887); *Poetical Works* (Brisbane & London, 1887); *Songs of the Army of the Night* (Sydney, 1888 & London, 1890, 1892, 1894 & 1910); *John Webb's End* (1891); *Australian Life* (1892); *The Melbournians* (1892); *The Australians: a social sketch* (1893); *The New Egypt* (1893); *A Child of the Age* (1894); *Tiberius: a drama* (1894); *Lady Lovan* (1895, written under pseudonym 'Agnes Farrell'); *Essays in Modernity* (1899); various articles, reviews, short stories, poems and letters [c. 1885-94] in the *Boomerang* (Brisbane); the *Bulletin* (Sydney); *Centennial Mag.* (Sydney); the *Courier* (Brisbane); *Fortn. Rev.*; *Melbourne Rev.*; *New Rev.* (London); *Queensland Rev.* (Brisbane); *Sydney Morning Herald*; *Sydney Quarterly Mag.*; *Victorian Rev.* (Melbourne); *Westminster Gazette* (London); the *Worker* (Brisbane).

Sources: (1) MSS: Angeli papers, Special Colls, Univ. of British Columbia Library, Vancouver; E.M. Miller papers, MS. 87, National Library of Australia, Canberra; Vance and Nettie Palmer papers, MS. 1174, NLA; J.B. Stephens papers, MS. 3271, NLA. (2) Other: Newspaper Cuttings, vol. 7, A.G. Stephens Coll., Mitchell Library, Sydney. (3) Thesis: I.M. Britain, 'The Political and Social Thought of Francis Adams' (Australian National Univ. BA, 1971). (4) Secondary: *DNB 22*; 'Sirius' (pseud.), 'Francis Adams', *Free Rev. 1* (Mar 1894) 551; *Labour Annual* (1895) 161; B. O'Dowd, 'Francis Adams. The Trumpeter of the Army of the Night', in *This World and the Next* (Melbourne, 15 May 1896) 167-9 and the *Tocsin* (Melbourne, 23 June 1908) 7, written under the pseudonyms 'Delmer Fenton' and 'Gavah the Blacksmith' respectively; P.I. O'Leary, 'The Neglect of Francis Adams', *Australia 3* (Feb

1920) 58-9; H.S. Salt, *Seventy Years among Savages* (1921); R.S. Browne, *A Journalist's Memories* (Brisbane, 1927); H.A. Kellow, *Queensland Poets* (1930); H.S. Salt, *Company I have kept* (1930); E.H. Lane, *Dawn to Dusk. Reminiscences of a Rebel* (Brisbane, 1939): E.M. Miller, *Australian Literature, 1* (Melbourne, 1940); C. Turnbull, *These Tears of Fire. The Story of Francis Adams* (Melbourne, 1949; repr. in Turnbull's *Australian Lives*, Melbourne, 1965); S. Winsten, *Salt and his Circle* (1951); V. Palmer, 'Life and Death of Francis Adams', *Southerly 15* (Sydney, 1954) 102-6; S. Murray-Smith, 'Francis Adams. Forerunner of Socialist World Literature', *Yi-Wen 57* (Peking, Mar 1958) 151-4; F. Harris, *My Life and Loves* (1964); L. Arinshtein, 'A Francis William Lauderdale Adams Unknown Poem', *Victorian Poetry 7* (1969) 55-6; *Australian Dictionary of Biography 3* (Melbourne, 1969); I.M. Britain, 'Francis Adams: the Arnoldian as socialist', *Historical Studies 15* (Oct 1972) 401-23. OBIT. *Daily Chronicle*, 5 and 6 Sep 1893; *Clarion*, 9 Sep 1893; *Table Talk* (Melbourne), 15 and 22 Sep 1893; the *Bulletin* and the *Commonweal*, 16 Sep 1893; *Freedom*, Oct 1893; *Athenaeum*, no. 3445, 4 Nov 1893.

IAN BRITAIN

See also: *Henry Stephens SALT.

ADAMSON, William (Billy) Murdoch (1881-1945)
TRADE UNIONIST AND LABOUR MP

William Adamson was born in Kilmarnock, Ayrshire, on 12 April 1881, the son of William Adamson, an iron moulder, and his wife Annabella (née Findlay). William was the next to youngest child in a family of five. His father had something of a radical political background. The young Adamson was named after William Murdoch, the family having some distant connection with the man who pioneered gas lighting.

After an elementary and secondary education, he was first employed in a large jewellery business before being apprenticed to pattern making. When he had served his time he became a member of the United Pattern Makers' Association; but the failure of a strike forced the family to leave Kilmarnock. He had married Jennie Johnston in 1902, and it was shortly after the birth of their first child that they left Scotland. Adamson worked in various towns in the Midlands and the North of England, including Preston, Sheffield, Barrow, Rugby and Manchester. In this last town he became so well known for his political activities that he was blacklisted at his own trade; and for a period of sixteen months he worked for only six weeks. He took part in unemployed agitations. On occasions he could find work only as a commercial traveller or a cinematograph operator. At a later date he was engaged in political work for the Labour Party in North and North-East Manchester, at both municipal and parliamentary elections.

In 1910 or 1911 he went to Birmingham where he came into contact with John Beard of the Workers' Union. Adamson then accepted an appointment as organiser for the Coventry ILP and secretary to the Labour Party; and during his time in Coventry he acted as chairman of a strike committee of pattern-makers (he always retained his membership of the union) in a long-drawn-out struggle of some six months. In 1912 Beard offered him an organising job for the Workers' Union in the Black Country district; Julia Varley was appointed in the same year. The Workers' Union was growing fast in the area and the demand for a general minimum wage of twenty-three shillings a week was now revived as a main union objective.

Adamson quickly established his reputation as a capable and effective organiser, and in the great Black Country strike of 1913 he was in charge of the Wednesbury and Walsall areas. The successful conclusion to the strike in early July 1913 was followed by a massive increase in union membership. By the outbreak of the war in August 1914 Birmingham and the Black Country had six full-time organisers, with a quarter of the union's total membership. In late July 1914 Adamson had been accused of assaulting a blackleg during a strike in Walsall. The case was heard on 24 July before two local magistrates who fined Adamson £5, including costs, with the alternative of one month's hard labour. Adamson, who strenuously denied the charge, chose to go to prison in Stafford Gaol. The case aroused enormous interest, nationally as well as locally, and the labour movement in the Midlands united in protest against the decision. The bias of the magistrates was vigorously attacked at the many protest meetings which were held; questions were asked in the Commons; and within a week the Home Secretary advised the Crown to offer a Royal Pardon and reduce the sentence imposed. The whole incident was an interesting example of the effectiveness of political pressure from below. A few days later war was declared.

In 1915 Adamson, still a Workers' Union organiser, was sent to Belfast in order to encourage unionisation in what hitherto had been a backward region. He returned to England at the end of the war and became district organiser of the new East Midland area. The Adamsons made their home in Lincoln where both he and his wife were active in the local Labour Party.

In 1922 Adamson was elected MP for the Cannock division of Staffordshire and he won all subsequent elections, with steadily increased majorities, until the Labour débâcle of 1931. He was a good constituency MP and a lively backbencher. In December 1925 he was suspended from the Commons for persisting in a question relating to a pensions case, but after expressing his regret for his behaviour, the motion for termination of his suspension was moved by Stanley Baldwin, the Prime Minister. Adamson was a committed supporter of equal suffrage – his wife had always worked for the cause – and in 1923 he had introduced a Bill to give women the vote on equal terms with men. He was a vice-president of the Workers' Birth Control Group which was founded in 1924.

The amalgamation of the Workers' Union with Bevin's Transport Workers in 1929 left him a national officer, concentrating mainly on fishermen and merchant seamen. He was re-elected for Cannock in 1935, and his wife joined him in the Commons three years later, having won Dartford at a by-election by a narrow majority. During the years of war Adamson served as a Lord Commissioner of the Treasury. By this time his ideas had become less radical and towards the end of his time in Parliament he was beginning to be severely criticised by certain groups among his constituents for what they thought was neglect of their interests. Miners' groups in particular were vocal in their opposition to his continuation as their MP. Adamson had been suffering from ill-health for some time and there is no doubt it was because of ill-health as well as for other reasons that he decided not to stand again at the general election of 1945.

He died on 25 October 1945 at his home in Forest Hill, south-east London, and the funeral was at Honor Oak Crematorium. At the time of his death his wife was MP for Bexley and parliamentary secretary to the Minister of Pensions. A younger son had been killed in action in 1944, but three other children survived him. He left an estate valued at £3788.

Sources: *Walsall Observer and South Staffordshire Chronicle*, 25 July, 1 and 8 Aug 1914; *Workers' Union Record* (Aug and Sep 1914) and (Aug 1915); *Labour Personalities in the House of Commons 1922-3*, ed. E.G. Yates [1923?]; S.V. Bracher, *The Herald Book of Labour Members* (1923); *Dod* (1923); *Hansard* (1923-31, 1936-45); *Labour Who's Who* (1924); *Times House of Commons* (1929); *Cannock Chase Advertiser*, 8 Mar 1941; *WWW* (1941-50); *Cannock Chase Courier*, 6 Oct 1944 and 26 Jan 1945; J. Leask and P. Bellars, *"Nor shall the Sword sleep . . .": an account of industrial struggle* [1953?] 32 pp.; R. Hyman, *The Workers' Union* (Oxford, 1971); biographical information: the late T.A.K. Elliott, CMG; Dr E. Taylor, Wolverhampton; personal information: Mrs A. Redgrave, London, daughter; Mrs E. Kemp, Surbiton, daughter. OBIT. *Daily Express, Daily Herald*, and *News Chronicle*, 26 Oct 1945; *Daily Herald* and *Times*, 27 Oct 1945; *Kentish Mercury*, 2 Nov 1945; *Lewisham Borough News*, 6 Nov 1945; *Labour Party Report* (1946).

JOHN SAVILLE

See also: †Jennie Laurel ADAMSON.

ALDERSON, Lilian (1885-1976)
LABOUR AND CO-OPERATIVE PARTY COUNCILLOR

Lilian Alderson was born in Hull on 22 January 1885, the daughter of Frederick Haste, a seaman, and Sarah Ann Haste (née Dennis). When Lilian was six, her father was drowned at sea, leaving her mother with three children and no means of support. Lilian and her four-year-old brother went to Hull Seamen's and General Orphanage in Spring Bank, Hull, and Sarah Haste took in washing to support herself and her baby of six weeks.

The girls in the Orphanage were trained for domestic service, and very little academic education was considered necessary for them; the boys were trained for the sea and received rather more. Lilian used to try to get a seat near the screen dividing the boys' and girls' lessons so that she could listen to what the boys were being taught. Throughout the rest of her long life she loved books and had a passionate interest in education.

After leaving the Orphanage she went into domestic service with a family in Hornsea. While there she met her husband, Thomas Anthony Alderson, formerly a regular soldier, who had left the Army in 1901. They were married in 1907 and settled in Hull. At the time Thomas Alderson was working as a dock labourer, but after twelve years' army service in India his health was not good, and he later went into a less physically taxing job in the Hull Museum Service. He was eleven years older than his wife and not involved in politics himself, but he always encouraged her in her political work, which began in 1916 when she joined the Women's Co-operative Guild. She later became secretary of the North Hull branch and in 1921 secretary of the joint executive committee of the ten branches of the Guild in the Hull Co-operative Society, a position she held until 1930. She served on the East Yorkshire District Committee from 1928 to 1933. She had joined the Hull Society's education committee in 1924 and served as vice-president, and from 1926 she taught in women's and intermediate classes. She was also for some time president of the South Yorkshire and Lincolnshire Federation of Co-operative Parties. In 1933 she attended the Women's Co-operative Guild Jubilee Demonstration at the Crystal Palace, where a Jubilee Song was sung for which she had composed the words.

In the local government elections of 1 November 1929 Labour representatives gained control of the Hull Council and displaced five opposition aldermen by nominating their own. In the by-election which followed in the same month, Mrs Alderson, who had stood for Botanic ward in the election, was elected for East Central ward. She had been on the maternity and child welfare committee as a co-opted member from 1927 until 1929, and after her election to the Council was a member from 1931 until her retirement. At a Leeds District Conference of the Women's Co-operative Guild in October 1933 Mrs Alderson criticised the recommendations of the Ray Committee on local government expenditure during a lecture she gave on 'Social Services and what they mean to us'. She was chairman of the maternity and child welfare committee from 1934 to 1938, and during her period of office the North Hull Clinic was opened, in 1936, to provide maternity, child welfare and school medical services. Mrs Alderson also laid the foundation stone, in October 1938, of the Margaret McMillan Nursery School, Hull's first purpose-built nursery school. She served on several other committees, including health and public assistance, education, electricity and care of the blind. She was also on the Northern Counties Committee for the Blind. She was always a passionate supporter of women's rights and abilities: in the early days of the Second World War it is said that she even succeeded in having an ARP poster withdrawn because it showed a woman and child cowering behind 'a great big he-man' [*Hull Daily Mail*, 14 Apr 1939 and 10 Oct 1976 and Alderson papers]. From 1939 to 1943 she was a JP.

Lilian Alderson was a tall, attractive woman, with a bright-eyed and eager expression. She was originally dark-haired, but at an early age her hair became white. She always dressed elegantly, in clothes of her own making and, in the early days of her family, she had undertaken dressmaking to increase the family budget. Her ideals seem to have been formed by her own political reading and the co-operative movement. She was not particularly religious, although she regarded herself as a Methodist and sent her children to Methodist Sunday School. As a councillor she aimed at a humane and high-spending administration to provide a decent and healthy standard of living for all.

She resigned from the Council in 1941 when her husband became ill and they went to live with their daughter in York; when he died in 1948 she returned to Hull. Always independent, she lived alone until 1965, when she went to the newly-opened Highfield House, a local old people's home. Her interest in education remained active to the end of her life. The year before she died an award for spoken English was instituted in her name at the Hull primary school where her daughter, Mrs J.H. Mather, was the headmistress until 1977. Her other daughter, Florence Crawforth, trained as a nurse at the Victoria Children's Hospital in Hull. Mrs Alderson died on 27 October 1976, aged ninety-one, and the funeral service was held at Hull Crematorium. She left no will.

Sources: *Hull Daily Mail*, 27, 28 and 29 Nov 1929; *Kingston upon Hull Year Books* (1930-43); Women's Co-operative Guild, *Of Whole Heart cometh Hope* [Jubilee Demonstration Programme] (1933) 3 pp.; *Co-op. News*, 11 Nov 1933; *Election Addresses* (1934) and (1937); *The North Hull Clinic* [Opening Ceremony Programme] (1936) 8 pp.; 'Safeguarding Childhood's Health', *Public Assistance J. and Health and Hospital Rev.*, 30 Oct 1936, 1194; *Hull Daily Mail*, 14 Apr 1939; *Hull Times*, 15 July 1939; *Hull Daily Mail*, 7 Sep 1972; Alderson papers and personal information: Mrs J.H. Mather, Kirkella, North Humberside, daughter. OBIT. *Hull Daily Mail*, 30 Oct 1976.

ANN HOLT

ARMSTRONG, William John (1870-1950)
TRADE UNIONIST AND LABOUR ALDERMAN

William Armstrong was born in Belfast on 1 December 1870, but spent almost all his life in Leeds, a town to which his family migrated before he was two. His father was a platelayer on the Midland Railway, and Will was educated at the Leeds Parish School. He began to earn his living as a clerk but later advanced to become manager of a woollen merchant's firm. At some point in his career he owned a small business, the nature of which has not been discovered. It was his early employment as a clerk that inspired his lifelong involvement in white-collar trade unionism. He was one of the sponsors – Joe Hazelip being another – of a meeting called on Friday, 26 May 1893, at 24 Blenheim Place, Leeds, to establish what became known as the Clerks' Union. There were about a hundred people present at this first meeting, which was followed by a public meeting on 2 June at the YMCA, South Parade.

The new union went on to establish branches at Hull, Bradford, Manchester and Liverpool, and in 1895 it changed its name to the National Clerks' Association. Five years earlier, in May 1890, a clerks' union had been established in London, to be known later in the same year as the National Union of Clerks. It developed branches in other parts of the country, and in 1898 amalgamated with the Leeds-based NCA, retaining its own name. In these developments Armstrong played a leading part. The union always maintained a strong base in Leeds, and Armstrong himself became a national executive member, and president in 1911.

At the same time as Armstrong developed his union work he became active in the political life of Leeds. We know little of his specific interests until the years just before the outbreak of the First World War. He was probably a member of the ILP at least in the early years of the century, but it is definitely known that he was president of the Leeds Labour Party from 1910 to 1912. In the latter year it is on record that he was issued with a permit allowing him to make collections and sell literature in the Leeds parks and recreation grounds; and in the same year he was a member of the trading and finance committee of the Leeds Labour Party. In early May 1914, D.B. Foster, who was secretary of the Leeds Labour Party, suggested that Armstrong should become part-time secretary in order to help especially with the recruitment of individuals and of trade unions to the Party, and also to take charge of the growing clerical work in the office. Foster wrote in the letter to the EC which made this suggestion that 'having a small business of his own he [Armstrong] would be able to devote nearly the whole of his time for 25/-a week'. The new arrangement was agreed to although it is not known how long Armstrong continued in his new position; but he certainly continued in Labour politics.

In November 1917 he was elected councillor for Holbeck ward (in which he lived), and he held this seat until his nomination as alderman in 1926, a position he retained until 1933. His activities also involved him in the work of the local Labour paper, the *Leeds Weekly Citizen*; and at some time in the 1920s he became secretary of the Leeds Labour Party. It was, however, as a Labour representative on the Leeds Council, and from 1928 as chairman of the finance and parliamentary committee, that he began to enjoy a wider reputation in the general life of Leeds. His pet scheme was a plan to build a large Civic Hall behind the existing Town Hall. He began developing the idea in 1930 and was successful in obtaining a large government grant, in the negotiation of which his personal friendship with Philip Snowden was important. The total cost was to be £360,000 and government funds were offered to the amount of £270,000. Armstrong himself insisted that the scheme, apart from the benefits to the general life of Leeds, would be of considerable help to the local unemployed. Work began in October 1930, and the completed building was opened by George V and Queen Mary in August 1933.

Before this, however, Armstrong had resigned from the secretaryship of the Labour Party, in September 1932. He was noted for a 'hasty and irascible temper' [Hughes (1953) 15] and he had a marked propensity to quarrel with those with whom he worked. He himself said that he resigned because he was not receiving adequate assistance from the assistant secretary, Clara Adams, who had been ill for twenty-two weeks. But there were perhaps other reasons on his side: he was supposedly dissatisfied with the absence of discipline among Party representatives on the Council, and disheartened by the lack of support for the Civic Hall scheme. His version of events, however, was not confirmed by the evidence of the minutes of the Labour Party at this time. In November 1932 the EC accused him of non-attendance at council and committee meetings, and he was asked to resign his aldermanic seat; but this he refused to do. He left Leeds at the end of 1932 for Lincoln, where he kept a small grocery store in Swanpool, a suburb of the town. He returned to Leeds in 1934, and little is heard of him after that date.

It is difficult to be precise about Armstrong's political attitudes. He strongly supported the Leeds Corporation strike of 1913. He seems to have been in favour of the First World War, but critical of its impact upon the working class. In this he was following the general attitude of the Leeds Labour Party, which tended to distance itself from the war effort on the grounds that certain basic injustices ought to be remedied before wholehearted support could be given, especially on the issue of conscription. Armstrong was most vociferous when it was a matter of local problems, and he always insisted that work ought to be, and could be, found for the unemployed – by a public works programme, for example. He was in general terms probably middle-of-the-road, and we cannot get much further than that on present information.

He had been appointed to the magistrates' bench in 1924 and in 1934 was awarded the MBE. He died in St James Hospital, Leeds, on 26 February 1950, leaving a widow and two daughters. His estate was valued at £1435.

Sources: (1) MSS: Leeds Labour Party archives, minutes and correspondence: Leeds Central Library. (2) Other: *Leeds Weekly Citizen*, 8 Apr and 19 Aug 1932, 22 Mar 1940; F. Hughes, *By Hand and Brain: the story of the Clerical and Administrative Workers' Union* (1953); J.E. Williams, 'The Leeds Corporation Strike in 1913', in *Essays in Labour History* vol. *2: 1886-1923*, ed. A. Briggs and J. Saville (1971) 70-95; biographical information: A.I. Marsh, St

Edmund Hall, Oxford. OBIT. *Yorkshire Post* and *Yorkshire Evening Post*, 27 Feb 1950; *Leeds Weekly Citizen*, 3 Mar 1950; *Clerk* (May-June 1950) 64.

MARION KOZAK
JOHN SAVILLE

See also: [Mark] Revis BARBER.

AYLES, Walter Henry (1879-1953)
TRADE UNIONIST, PACIFIST AND LABOUR MP

Walter Henry Ayles was born at 26 Thorne Street, Wandsworth Road, London, on 24 March 1879, the son of Percy Walter Ayles, a railway porter, and his wife Elizabeth (née Little). He received only an elementary education, but supplemented this by what he was able to teach himself. At the age of thirteen he found a job in a cardboard box factory; and two years later he was apprenticed to the engineering trade in the London workshops of the London and South Western Railway Company. He was dismissed from the workshops in 1897 for refusal to blackleg, and he then went to work in a newsagents. In 1899 he moved to Birmingham, where he worked again in engineering. He became active in the ASE and between 1903 and 1907 served as the Birmingham district secretary of the union. Later he carried on his union activities in an honorary capacity, when he was elected honorary treasurer of several ASE branches, including the Bristol no. 1 branch. In Birmingham he achieved notoriety in local radical politics for his vigorous opposition to the Boer War. He joined the ILP in 1904 and as a Labour candidate he won a seat on the Birmingham Board of Guardians, serving for one three-year term, 1904-7.

In the summer of 1910, he and his wife moved to Bristol, where he was to take up the post of full-time general secretary of the Bristol ILP. The ILP was by that time well established there as the leading political group within the Labour movement, with a membership of over 500; and Ayles turned his considerable organisational talents to the task of consolidating and strengthening that position. Under his direction organisation was improved, membership increased and new premises – the Kingsley Hall – were acquired. In 1912 he entered the City Council as Labour member for Easton ward, a seat he retained until 1922. His absence from the council after this defeat was brief, for within a few months he had been returned on 27 February 1923 at a by-election for the St Philip and Jacob South wards.

In 1912 also he began his pamphleteering career with the publication of *Bristol's Next Step*, in which he outlined a programme of reforms for a future Labour-controlled council; this became the basis of the Labour Party's municipal programme in Bristol over the years to come. Thus, within a very short space of time, Ayles had established himself as a leading political figure within the locality. He was a member of the NAC of the ILP from 1912 to 1927, adopted as an ILP candidate for Bristol in 1913, and was chairman of the Bristol Labour Party from 1915 to 1923.

During the First World War Ayles achieved national prominence as a leading conscientious objector. A Quaker by religion, he based his opposition to war on the Christian doctrine of the sanctity of human life; and he was one of the founders of the No-Conscription Fellowship. He was one of five members of the national committee of the NCF (there were eight members in all) who refused to pay their share of a fine of £800 imposed at the Mansion House, London, on 17 May 1916 for publishing and disseminating a leaflet, *Repeal the Act*, which demanded the repeal of the Military Service Act. On 17 July 1916 the defaulting five members surrendered to the police at the Mansion House. The five were A. Fenner Brockway, W.J. Chamberlain, A. Barratt Brown, John P. Fletcher and Walter Ayles. The sentence was 112 days' hard labour in Pentonville. On his release Ayles failed to secure absolute exemption from military service and, refusing to perform work of national importance, he spent the next two years in a number of different prisons. His speech at a Bristol Court in November 1916 – a classic statement of the Christian pacifist argument – was later published as a pamphlet by the ILP and the NCF under the title *My Higher Duty to Conscience, Humanity and God*. He was finally released in the summer of 1919. During the months between the end of the war in 1918 and his release, Ayles had been at the centre of the agitation for the release of the wartime conscientious objectors. Following the Armistice on 11 November 1918, a great wave of unrest had swept through the prisons in which the COs were kept. In an attempt to calm the situation the Government moved all objectors who had served more than two years' hard labour to Wakefield Prison: the intention being to offer a new scheme of working conditions in somewhat improved conditions. There was a marked lack of communication between the Home Office and the Governor of Wakefield, and the COs, making a quick appreciation of the situation, organised themselves into an advisory committee under the chairmanship of Ayles; and for a short period the advisory committee controlled the internal working of the prison. When the new Home Office proposals finally arrived, and were put to the now officially recognised advisory committee, they were rejected. The Home Office then abandoned its scheme, and the 'Wakefield Absolutists' were returned to their former prisons to continue what were still indefinite sentences [Boulton (1967) 260-2].

Ayles returned to Bristol and immediately became active in ILP politics. His candidature for Bristol East had had to be withdrawn in 1918 (because he was in prison, and because the ILP were short of funds), but he was adopted as Labour candidate for Bristol North in 1919. He stood unsuccessfully in the general election of 1922, but won the constituency in the following year and was thus a back-bencher during the period of office of the first minority Labour Government. By this time Ayles had re-established himself at the national level of the ILP. He also remained continuously active in the pacifist movement. He was a member of the NCF drafting committee at Jordans in July 1919. Ayles and W.J. Chamberlain wanted the continuation of an organisation which would stand for absolute pacifism and internationalism, while the majority followed Clifford Allen in supporting a union of all who opposed conscription as such. Late in November 1919 the NCF disbanded and established two committees representative of these different views. The No More War Movement was established in 1920, with Ayles a member of its national committee, and five years later, in 1925, he became its financial and organising secretary. The secretary of the NMWM was Miss Lucy Cox, formerly a teacher, who had worked with Ayles in the South Western Division of the ILP. Ayles and Miss Cox (who later married Jim Middleton, national secretary of the Labour Party) were the official NMWM delegates to the Third Triennial Conference of the War Resisters' International at Lyons in 1931. They resigned together from the No More War Movement in the following year, on issues mainly of practical politics and tactics. Ayles was also chairman of the Fellowship of Reconciliation from 1923 to 1924, and earlier, from 1920 to 1923, he had been British representative on the Christian International – an organisation established after the end of the First World War to bring together into a loose international grouping people and organisations whose pacifism was based on Christian beliefs.

By the end of the twenties, when he was again elected MP for Bristol North, Ayles had been for some years pretty permanently resident in London, and had lost interest in Bristol local politics. In 1924 he had resigned from the secretaryship of the Bristol ILP and in 1926 he did not seek re-election to the Bristol City Council. In the following year he resigned as the region's representative on the national council of the ILP. In the 1929-31 Parliament he followed the practice of his earlier membership by asking questions on an extraordinary range of subjects, although the Christian pacifist argument remained at the centre of his political thinking. After the defection of Ramsay MacDonald in August 1931 the PLP passed an important resolution – which became known, from its proposer, as the 'Ayles' resolution – asking for an inquiry into the future relations between the PLP and the Labour Party with regard to the choice of Prime Minister, members of the Government and policies to be followed. The NEC gave considerable attention to the difficult constitutional questions involved, and reported at length to the 1933 Annual LP Conference [*Labour Party Report* (1933) 8-10, 166-8; Cole (1948) 288ff.].

By this time Ayles was out of Parliament once more – he had been defeated in the 1931 election. He fought Bristol North – for the seventh time – in the general election of 1935, but failed, as in 1931, and the local Party decided to seek a new candidate. His long association with

Bristol was at an end. After his resignation from the No More War Movement in 1932, Ayles had established in the same year, and was secretary of, the Commonwealth Peace Committee, which sought to unite groups within the Commonwealth in the pursuit of international peace. He became a member of the Orpington District Council in 1937. In the general election of 1945 he was candidate for Southall (which later became Hayes and Harlington). He had been nursing the constituency for eight years, and his election speeches were as vigorous and radical as ever. He attacked Winston Churchill for his pre-war record, argued strongly for nationalisation of the basic industries, and warmly commended an international policy based upon the Charter of the United Nations. Ayles won the seat with 37,404 votes and a majority over the Conservative candidate of 24,057. The Liberal polled 7598. Ayles held the seat (by that time the new constituency of Hayes and Harlington) in 1950 and 1951 though with reduced majorities.

In the post 1945 Parliaments Ayles took an active part on the Labour back-benches, although he rarely spoke at any length. He signed a parliamentary motion opposing peacetime conscription in 1946, and voted against the National Service Bill in the following year. He was one of forty-five signatories to an Open Letter to Ernest Bevin, in late July 1948, following the serious deterioration in international relations signalled by the Berlin blockade. The letter urged the Government to make a 'bold effort' to avert the threat of a new war; and it called for a policy which would include disarmament, unilateral repudiation of all atomic weapons, destruction of all existing atomic stocks and plants, and an international system of inspection and control of all atomic plants and materials. Ayles retired from the Commons in February 1953, and left Southall, where he was living, to settle in Scotland.

He was a big-built man, with dark hair, a dark complexion, and a heavy square jaw. He had great energy together with considerable ability, and was an impressive public speaker. He was a Rechabite for sixty years; and a member of the Society of Friends. Ayles aroused quite different emotions in different people. For some he was a powerful, attractive personality, of great moral courage and stamina. In others he aroused considerable antagonism, and for some he was objectionable. Certainly, no one was indifferent to him.

He was married twice: on the first occasion in 1904, to Bertha Winifred Batt. Bertha was a political personality in her own right. For several years she worked for the Women's Labour League in the Bristol and South Wales region, and it was only the birth of her son and, later, an impaired heart, that curtailed her political activities. There was only one son of the marriage, who was killed on active service in 1943. His second marriage was in 1944, to Jean Ogilvie Middleton, who survived him. Ayles died on 6 July 1953 at his home in Kingussie, Inverness-shire. He left an estate valued at £2463.

Writings: *Bristol's Next Step* [1912?] P.; (with others) *Why I am a Conscientious Objector* [1916] P.; *Repeal the Act* [handbill] (1916) 1 pp. [copy in Bristol Archives Office]; *My Higher Duty to Conscience, Humanity and God* [a speech] (ILP and NCF, [1917?]) 2 pp. [copy in Bristol Archives Office]; *Coalition Hypocrisy* (ILP, 1921) 16 pp.; *The Hell of Unemployment: the only way out* (ILP, 1921) 12 pp.; *What a Socialist Town Council would do* (ILP, [1923/4?]) 16 pp.; *Why I worked for Peace in the Great War* (NMWM, 1928) P; *Militarism unmasked* (NMWM, 1928) P; *The Case for Disarmament* (n.d., n.p.)

Sources: (1) MSS: Minute books and papers, Bristol ILP. (2) Other: S.V. Bracher, *The Herald Book of Labour Members* (1923); *Dod* (1924); *Hansard*, 13 Feb 1924; *Labour Who's Who* (1924) and (1927); S. Bryher, *An Account of the Labour and Socialist Movement in Bristol* (Bristol, 1929-31); *Hansard* (1929-31); *Times Guide to the House of Commons* (1929); Debrett, *House of Commons* (1929); *Labour Party Report* (1933); *Election Address*, (1935); *Hansard* (1945-50); *Middlesex County Times*, 2, 16, 23 and 30 June and 7 July 1945; C. Bunker, *Who's Who in Parliament* (1946); G.D.H. Cole, *A History of the Labour Party from 1914* (1948); R.W. Lyman, *The First Labour Government 1924* [1957]; E.J. Meehan, *The British Left Wing and Foreign Policy* (Rutgers Univ. Press, 1960); A. Marwick, *Clifford Allen: the open*

conspirator (Edinburgh, 1964); R.E. Dowse, *Left in the Centre* (1966); D. Boulton, *Objection Overruled* (1967); biographical information: the late T.A.K. Elliott, CMG; personal information: the late H.F. Bing, Loughborough; Mrs Lucy Middleton, London. OBIT. *Times,* 7 July 1953; *Middlesex County Times,* 11 July 1953.   JOHN SAVILLE
                                                                                         BOB WHITFIELD

See also: †Reginald Clifford ALLEN; †Herbert Runham BROWN.

BALFOUR, William Campbell (1919-73)
LABOUR PARTY INTELLECTUAL AND ACTIVIST

William Campbell Balfour was born in Berry Street, Aberdeen, on 18 July 1919, the first child of William Campbell Balfour and his wife Henrietta (née Mitchell). There were three other children of the marriage: one daughter and two sons. Balfour's father had begun his working life as a lithographer but for medical reasons had to change to outdoor employment. During the First World War he had been a member of the Army Service Corps and at the time of his son's birth he was working as a carter. The family were poor. The house in which they lived with a number of other families was a typical Aberdeen granite structure; the one lavatory in the basement was used by the twenty-seven occupants. The young Campbell began attending the Aberdeen Demonstration School at the age of four. His father, a dedicated Socialist, took a keen interest in his son's education, and encouraged him to regard 'pleasure' as a synonym for reading books. But the father died in 1930, and the family found themselves in even more difficult circumstances. Campbell's mother took work as a cleaner (on the early morning and late afternoon shift), and a month before his fourteenth birthday he himself found a job as a grocer's delivery boy. He soon moved to a better-paid job as a cart boy in a chemical works, and then one of his uncles helped him to secure employment as a messenger boy in the Post Office – an employment much prized among unskilled workers in the 1930s. The job required him to attend night-school and thus extend his education to a limited extent, but he was still showing no signs of academic ambitions of any kind. By this time he was already a Socialist, but he took little part in political activities, although he had joined his appropriate trade union in both the chemical factory and the Post Office (not surprisingly, since three of his uncles were prominent union officers in the town). His main interests in his teens were sport, and to a lesser extent general social activities. By the outbreak of war in 1939 he was a very strong and physically very fit young man.

In February 1940 he was called up for military service, and after basic training went with the Gordon Highlanders to France. After Dunkirk he got back to Britain through Cherbourg, and immediately volunteered for the Commandos, with which unit he spent the rest of the war, seeing action in the Dieppe and St Nazaire raids, in Tunisia, Sicily, Italy, Yugoslavia and Greece. He was wounded in the leg at Monte Cassino in Italy, and spent a short time in hospital at Molfetta. When the Commandos were disbanded he was posted to the Royal Scots Fusiliers and finished his service in Germany, having transferred to the Army Education Corps a year before his demobilisation.

He spent his year in the Education Corps in Hamburg, as a sergeant, teaching economics and history. He sat the LSE entrance examination and began his undergraduate career there in 1948, reading for the BSc(Econ.) honours degree with sociology as his special subject. It was from the time of his entry into LSE that he became involved in active politics. He was chairman of the student Labour Society at a time when the conflicts between Communists and Labour Party supporters were at their most intense, and outside LSE he was active in the Marylebone constituency party, becoming vice-chairman in 1950. John Silkin fought this seat unsuccessfully in 1950 and in the following year's general election, Campbell Balfour was the Labour candidate. He increased the Labour poll and won 13,964 votes against Sir W. Wavell Wakefield's total of 28,783.

LSE was of major importance in his personal development. The School was full of ex-servicemen, eager to discuss and debate, and his years there deepened and broadened his political convictions. He graduated in 1951 and was appointed research assistant in the Department of Industrial Relations in University College, Cardiff. Michael P. Fogarty had just been appointed to the Montague Burton chair in industrial relations. Campbell Balfour was expected to teach as well as research, and he also taught classes outside the University, in the Cardiff Technical College, the Extra-Mural department, the WEA and the NCLC. Apart from temporary teaching positions abroad, he was to spend the rest of his academic life at Cardiff.

He always took a lively interest in university affairs. He was an active member of the Non-Professorial Staff Committee and represented it at various times on Senate, Council and the Court of Governors. He played a prominent part in the AUT: he was president of the Cardiff Association in 1966-7, and at the national level he became a member of the AUT's national salaries committee in 1965, was elected national vice-president in 1972, and took office as president on 1 September 1973. At his first meeting with the National Union of Students after he became president, he invited the student representatives to join him in what the press labelled the 'Balfour Declaration'. This was a suggestion that together they might issue a Code of Conduct to govern certain forms of public behaviour, particularly those to be expected of students when controversial figures were invited to speak on a university campus. Balfour had always taken a strong interest in student affairs, and with vivid memories of the era of McCarthyism in the United States, he was anxious that no individual left-wing student or teacher should be vulnerable to attack from the right wing in Britain.

His active involvement in local politics began almost as soon as he arrived in Cardiff in 1951. At that time, the city was dominated by Conservatives. Balfour joined the Penylan ward and was quickly elected to the North Constituency Party. In May 1952 he contested the Gabalfa ward against a Ratepayers' candidate and missed election by only 186 votes. During the next few years he did not stand again but remained extremely active in the local party. His academic research interests were, however, growing and coming to occupy most of his time. In the summer of 1952 he joined an international seminar at Harvard. Among those also invited were Fred Mulley, MP, and Dennis Walters from Britain, Dominic de Grunne of Belgium, and Herman Volle of Germany, with whom he maintained a close contact for the rest of his life. The executive director of the seminar programme was Henry Kissinger, and this contact was the beginning of a firm friendship between Kissinger and Balfour.

In the following year Balfour secured a Fulbright fellowship to visit the US and a Smith-Mundt grant to enable him to read for a PhD at the University of Chicago – which his own interests in community and occupational sociology made an obvious choice. In Chicago he met his future wife, Jewel Elaine Feldman, a graduate in physiotherapy and the daughter of a Chicago real estate agent. They were married early in 1955. Balfour went back to Cardiff on tenure at the beginning of the session of 1954-5, and soon became active again in Labour Party politics. He found himself embroiled in the debate around the threatened expulsion of Nye Bevan from the Labour Party – a step which Balfour himself vigorously opposed. His general political attitudes during the fifties were like those of many Labour intellectuals. He wrote a revealing letter to a friend on 24 October 1955 which, whether accurate or not, certainly reflected a wide spectrum of opinion among them at this time:

> The Labour Party had its conference two weeks ago and I went as delegate from Cardiff. The struggle between Left and Right is now over and we are all members of the Extreme Centre now. Bevan still provides the emotional goad, the old crusading spirit, but conditions have cut the ground from under his feet. There is no longer a militant, impoverished working class of the kind he grew up in. Today the scramble is for a higher standard of living after the austerity of the war years and the rationing which followed them. So the amount of overtime

being worked amounts to two or three evenings a week and the people doing this were the active workers of the past. So Labour is an ageing party and there is little replacement from youth for the Welfare State, with its widespread opportunity, is producing masses of students who are not in the least grateful to the State for their opportunity as the old pioneers used to hope, but who grumble and turn right wing as their professional rewards are undercut by organised workers. So if they're political at all they just turn Tory. Weh ist mir.

Balfour made other visits to the United States during the remainder of his life but from the late fifties he became increasingly interested in, and involved in, closer contacts with Europe. He supported Britain's entry into the Common Market and had links with a number of European organisations, including a few months' secondment to the ILO in Geneva. He greatly widened his range of contacts in Europe and in 1971 he was asked to join the ILO-NORAD mission to South-East Asia – it was at the beginning of a similar mission that he died in October 1973. His academic interests moved over a wide area of the social sciences: industrial relations were always a central interest, but he researched and wrote in the field of Labour history and in the late fifties and early sixties was closely associated with the European Commission for Social Structure and Social Movements. He was a good speaker, and became well known as a lecturer in trade union circles. He was by now a senior lecturer in his department.

Throughout the last decade of his life he continued active in Cardiff politics. In 1965 a serious attempt was made to persuade him to stand as parliamentary candidate for Cardiff North, but in the end he refused. He was, however, elected as a local Labour councillor for Plasmawr ward in 1966, and he served for three years, being especially active on educational committees. His public life by this time was a busy one: he had been appointed to the Cardiff Bench in 1961, was a member of the Cardiff Industrial Tribunal, and served for many years on the board of governors of various educational institutions (including, from 1961, the Welsh College of Advanced Technology).

In politics he moved to the Right as he got older. Never a Bevanite, he retained affinities with the group around Bevan – he had characteristically opposed Bevan's expulsion mainly on the grounds that dialogue must be maintained. This was typical of his stance in the 1950s and early 1960s. On the Gaitskell issue, he tried to hold the middle position in the interests of keeping a strong debate going on all sides. When CND became a matter of intense Labour Party discussion he was reluctant to allow either of the factions which formed around positions for and against the conference resolution a free hand to guide the destinies of the Labour Party. The old Left saw this as evidence of a shift in his political position to the Right. But whether that was really so or not, it was probably his increasing immersion in academic affairs and a tendency to see 'all sides of an issue' that led him to attempt the 'honest broker' stance. In this transition period, however, he continued writing for a number of years on industrial issues for *Tribune*.

At the beginning of 1959 it was discovered that he had developed high blood pressure, and he spent a period in hospital. In the summer of the same year he was involved in a car accident in which both he and his wife were injured, and his blood pressure was again affected; but for the rest of his life he seems to have learnt to live with his hypertension. His wife became ill in 1970; her condition deteriorated very quickly from the New Year, and she died on 3 April 1971.

Balfour was now forced to reduce some of his evening activities in the interests of his family. In the next two years he produced four books. By the summer of 1973 he may be said to have reached the height of his second career. He was widely respected as a teacher, research worker and public figure, within and outside the university world, in Britain and elsewhere. He died at the age of fifty-four in Oslo on 28 October 1973, at the beginning of his second ILO-NORAD mission to South-East Asia. Two daughters survived him.

His remains were cremated in Oslo, flown back to Cardiff, and buried in Cardiff Cemetery after a short memorial service there at 3 p.m. on Wednesday, 7 November 1973. The service was attended by family, friends, and colleagues, from the University, the Local Authority and the various City Parties. Councillor David Seligman spoke on behalf of the Labour Party and the

City Council, and Professor George Thomason on behalf of colleagues in the University; a short prayer was offered up by Rabbi Graf.

The outstanding thing about Campbell Balfour was his concern for his fellow men, regardless of their station in life or their politics. It was this which led him to his academic career as a means of helping others, to his involvement in politics, both nationally and locally, in order to influence policies, and to the help he gave more privately to many colleagues and students, and to ordinary people who came to him in his representative or magisterial capacity. His basic sincerity in all these activities distinguished him, but so also did his ability to be quite devastating in the political debate in which he so delighted. A great wit and an engaging personality, he made many friends quite literally all over the world.

Writings: 'Productivity and the Worker', *Brit. J. Soc. 4*, no. 3 (Sep 1953) 257-65; 'British Unions: a cultural analysis', *Relations Industrielles 13*, no. 3 (July 1958) 313-29; 'British Labour Attitudes to the Common Market', in *Marché Commun: Institutions Commun*, ed. Arrango-Ruiz (Librairie de Droit et de Jurisprudence, Paris 1960); 'British Attitude to the Common Market', *Rev. Militaire Générale* (Feb 1962) 224-35; 'British Labour from the Great Depression to the Second World War' and 'Union Management Relations in the Steel Industries from the Great Depression to the Second World War' in *Mouvements ouvriers et Dépression économique de 1929 à 1939*, ed. Mme Fauvel-Rouif (International Instituut voor Sociale Geschiedenis, Amsterdam, 1966) 234-44 and 245-61; 'Captain Tupper and the 1911 Seamen's Strike in Cardiff', *Morgannwg 14* (1971) 62-80; *Industrial Relations and the Common Market* (1972); *Incomes Policy and the Public Sector* (1972); (with I.G. Smith), 'How real are the Pilot's Problems', *New Scientist*, 22 Mar 1973, 672-3; *Unions and the Law* (NY, 1973); Editor of *Participation in Industry* (1973). Campbell Balfour also wrote a number of political articles in *Europa Archiv* between 1960 and 1971 and several in *Cymric Democrat*, 1954-6, *Plebs*, 1957-8, *Tribune*, 1960-1. He also contributed articles to the *Western Mail*, and other periodicals.

Sources: Personal knowledge. OBIT. *Times*, 31 Oct 1973; *AUT Bull.* no. 53 (Nov 1973).

GEORGE F. THOMASON

BARBER, [Mark] Revis (1895-1965)
TRADE UNIONIST AND LABOUR ALDERMAN

Revis Barber (the name by which he was later known) was born on 16 December 1895 at Bradford, the son of Walter Barber, a cotton dyer's labourer, and his wife Alice (née Armitage), both ardent Socialists. Revis Barber was awarded a scholarship to the Belle Vue Secondary School, Bradford, which he attended until he was sixteen. He then worked for about two years with the Bradford Electricity Department and extended his education through evening classes organised by the WEA and the Central Labour College. An avid reader of literature on Socialist philosophy and trade unionism, he took a post in 1912 as assistant secretary to the Bradford Trades Council, of which his father, a founder-member of the ILP, had been the secretary since 1907. About the same time he joined the National Union of Clerks and began his lifelong trade union career.

He was a conscientious objector during the First World War and served two years in various prisons including the Dartmoor Work Centre. On his release he returned to Bradford in 1919 to rejoin his father at the Bradford Trades Council. Their office was the HQ of the local Council of Action during the General Strike and Barber succeeded his father as secretary of the Trades Council on the latter's death in 1930. For twenty years he was secretary of the Yorkshire Federation of Trades Councils and for a similar period was secretary of the May Day Committee. A severe illness in 1949 compelled him to retire from the Trades Council in the following year.

The Bradford branch of the NUC, of which Barber became secretary, had a chequered early career – like others in Yorkshire and Lancashire – but whereas most of the latter were short-lived, the Bradford one under Barber's leadership survived [Hughes (1953) 15-16]. In 1930 Barber was elected to the union's north-eastern area council, of which he was chairman for many years. In 1940-1 the NUC amalgamated with the Women Clerks' and Secretaries' Association to form the Clerical and Administrative Workers' Union (subsequently to become part of APEX). During the Second World War Barber was the north-eastern area's representative on the union executive council and worked for a more centralised control of the union – in which he was supported by John Kerr and also two Scottish representatives, R.E. (Bob) Scouller and Dan Fraser. Barber's influence '. . . set going a movement that had far-reaching effects in Union administration' [Hughes (1953) 117]. From 1946 to 1949 he was the union's vice-president and in 1950 he received the TUC Silver Medal for twenty-one years' service. When he resigned, on health grounds, from the union's national executive in 1963 he was awarded the CAWU Gold Badge for meritorious service – which he displayed with pride in his coat lapel.

Revis Barber also followed his father's example of service to the Labour Party and the Bradford City Council. A member of the LP for about fifty years, he was secretary of the Bradford North division for a number of years and treasurer of the city's LP for thirteen years. He was an ardent supporter of the Republican side in the Spanish Civil War. A number of refugee Spanish children were placed with Bradford families and there were many local efforts to raise money for their care.

Elected to the Bradford City Council in 1942, Barber was made an alderman in 1945. He was leader of the Labour group and had served as chairman of the finance committee for three years but his special interest was in education – he served for twenty-three years on the education committee (four as chairman) and was chairman of the further education sub-committee. He will be particularly remembered as one of the pioneers who pressed for university status for the Bradford Institute of Technology. From 1957 to 1962 he was chairman of the Institute's board of governors and in 1963 one of the halls of residence of the Institute – now Bradford University – was given his name. He also received a medallion for work associated with the establishment of the Margaret McMillan Training College [now (1977) Bradford College] on whose committee he served from 1954 to 1965 and of which he was chairman from 1954 to 1957. He declined nomination as Lord Mayor – although his father had served in that capacity – but among his other activities were membership of the local Bench from 1949 and service on the Yorkshire Electricity Board's Consultative Council. For a number of years, prior to nationalisation, Barber had been chairman of the Bradford Electricity Committee. He was awarded the OBE in the 1965 New Year Honours for his political and public services in the City.

He had married in 1919 Alice Graham whose parents, like his own, were members of the ILP, and they shared the same ideals throughout their married life – serving together on the Bradford City Council, as magistrates, and in all spheres of political and public life. They were both bitter opponents of nuclear armament. At the 1950 and 1951 general elections Mrs Barber was election agent for Bradford North. They had two children – a son, who died in early childhood, and a daughter, who trained as a nursery nurse, and, after the war, worked as a teacher and also for the Red Cross.

Dame Anne Godwin, general secretary of the CAWU, 1956-62, gave the following appreciation:

> Revis Barber was what is regarded as a typical Yorkshireman, direct of speech, outspoken but never talking unless he had something to say, wasting no time on pleasantries. He was an excellent committee-man with a practical down to earth approach to trade union problems . . . on a matter of principle he never compromised. 'You've sold the pass', he said to me on an occasion when I had given support to an educational development of which he disapproved, 'You've allowed the workers to be fobbed off with the second best' [personal letter, 31 Jan 1977].

Revis Barber died on 23 July 1965 at the Duke of York's Nursing Home, Bradford, only a few months before the charter for Bradford University was confirmed. On the day of his cremation, a memorial service, attended by over 400 people, including the Lord Mayor, was held at Eastbrook Hall, Bradford. His wife and daughter survived him.

Sources: F. Hughes, *By Hand and Brain : the story of the Clerical and Adminstrative Workers' Union* (1953); *Telegraph and Argus* [Bradford], 16 July 1959, 16 June and 14 Dec 1960, 26 July, 1 and 24 Nov 1961, 17 Apr 1962, 26 and 28 Nov 1963; M. Ashraf, *Bradford Trades Council 1872-1972* (Bradford, 1972); J. Reynolds and K. Laybourn, 'The Emergence of the Independent Labour Party in Bradford', *Int. Rev. Social Hist. 20*, pt 3 (1975) 313-46; biographical information: Dr K. Laybourn, Huddersfield Polytechnic; T. Ferguson, APEX, London; F. Earnshaw, Librarian, Bradford Univ.; personal information: Mrs Alice Barber, JP, Rainham, widow; Dame Anne Godwin, Worcester Park, Surrey; R.A. McKinlay, Pro-Vice-Chancellor, Bradford Univ.; Mrs D. Milne, JP, Manchester, A.A. Wallis, MBE, Bradford. OBIT. *Telegraph and Argus* [Bradford] and *Yorkshire Post*, 24 July 1965; *Clerk* (Aug-Sep 1965).

JOYCE BELLAMY

See also: Walter BARBER.

BARBER, Walter (1864-1930)
TRADE UNIONIST AND LABOUR ALDERMAN

Walter Barber was born on 16 March 1864 at Bradford, the son of Charles Barber, a stuff presser and his wife Sarah (née Jowett). He began work at the age of six-and-a-half as a messenger boy and later became a dyer's labourer and warehouseman. According to one account he joined the Amalgamated Society of Dyers in 1880, following a strike, and he undoubtedly became actively involved in trade union affairs early in his career. Bradford was a lively political town in the late 1880s and early 1890s – the Manningham Mills strike of 1890-1 radicalised the attitudes of many workers – and it is in keeping with local tradition that Barber should have joined the ILP in its early days, and he was involved in organising 'demonstrations, protests and social activities' [Barker (1973) 7]. Henceforth the Party was to be at the centre of his political loyalties.

By the early 1900s Barber had become a leading personality in the Bradford labour movement and in the wider sphere of Bradford civic life in general. In 1907 he became secretary of the Bradford Trades Council and remained in office until his death in 1930. He concentrated his industrial interests particularly on the workmen's compensation legislation, and he became known for this and other legal interests affecting working-class conditions as 'the working man's lawyer'. He was especially concerned with the disease of anthrax and played an important part in the passing of legislation which made compulsory the disinfecting of imported wools likely to be dangerous to the health of those who worked with them. When the National Insurance Act was introduced in 1911 Barber was responsible for the establishment of the Bradford Trades Council Approved Society – the only one of its kind in the country – and which had, by the end of the First World War, a membership of 6000.

In the same year, 1907, that he became secretary of the Trades Council he stood, unsuccessfully, for the local Board of Guardians; but was elected to the Town Council a few months later for the Allerton ward. At this and subsequent elections up to the First World War, Barber stood as a Workers' Municipal Federation candidate, an organisation formed in the early years of the twentieth century to unite the various factions of the Labour movement and to enable trade unionists who were not ILP members to vote for a Labour candidate. Barber served until 1910, then again from 1913 – for Bradford Moor ward – until 1921. He was made a JP in 1915, an alderman in 1918 and deputy to Bradford's first Labour Lord Mayor, Joseph Hayhurst. On the latter's death in July 1919 Barber served as acting Lord Mayor until the following November. He remained an alderman until 1923. During the General Strike of 1926 the Council of Action had its headquarters at the offices of the Bradford Trades Council and Barber's son, Revis, was secretary of the combined Councils of Action formed by the local Councils of Action of the textile unions in each town in the West Riding of Yorkshire.

For eleven years until shortly before his death Walter Barber was secretary of the Yorkshire Federation of Trades Councils; for thirty years he was associated with the Independent Order of Odd Fellows (Manchester Unity) and became a member of the Past Grands Lodge. He possessed a fine bass voice and sang in churches of almost every denomination in the city. In his younger days he sang solos from the *Messiah* and the *Creation*. He died on 7 March 1930 and was buried at Scholemoor Cemetery. He left effects valued at £818. His wife Alice predeceased him. One of his three sons, Revis had become assistant secretary of the Trades Council in 1912 and succeeded his father as secretary in 1930.

Writings: *Notes and Explanations of Workmen's Compensation Act 1906* (n.d.); *Defects and Suggested Amendments to Workmen's Compensation Act* (n.d.).

Sources: (1) MSS: papers of the National Union of Textile Workers, Huddersfield PL. (2) Other: *Yorkshire Observer*, 8 July 1919; Bradford Trades Council, *Year Book* [for 1921] (1922) and *Year Book* [for 1926] (1927); W. Bateson, *The Way we came; an historical retrospect of the adventures of the pioneers of the Amalgamated Society of Dyers* (Bradford, 1928); M. Ashraf, *Bradford Trades Council 1872-1972* (Bradford, 1972); B. Barker, 'Anatomy of Reformism: the social and political ideas of the Labour leadership in Yorkshire', *Int. Rev. Social Hist. 18* (1973) 1-27; biographical information: Dr K. Laybourn, Huddersfield Polytechnic; Cllr A. Lightowler, Bradford; Mrs N. Reid, Stockport; personal information: Mrs A. Barber, JP, Rainham, daughter-in-law. OBIT. *Yorkshire Observer*, 8 Mar 1930; *Bradford Pioneer*, 14 Mar 1930; *Labour Party Report* (1930).

JOYCE BELLAMY
JOHN SAVILLE

See also: [Mark] Revis BARBER; †John Henry PALIN.

BARROW, Harrison (1868-1953)
BIRMINGHAM BUSINESS MAN, QUAKER AND LABOUR PARTY COUNCILLOR

Harrison Barrow was born on 8 August 1868, in Birmingham, into a Quaker family already prominent in the public life of the town. His father, Richard Cadbury Barrow, had been a member of the Board of Guardians since 1859 and was to become mayor in 1889. The Barrows were originally a north Lancashire family who, by the late eighteenth century, had become extensive shipowners and traders. A double marriage connection with the Cadbury family made Birmingham, in particular, a second home. Richard Barrow had travelled widely in England and France before, in 1849, he came to Birmingham to help his uncle, John Cadbury, in a tea and coffee business. In 1864 he married a fellow-Quaker, Jane Harrison from Stourbridge; Harrison was the third of their five children.

After attending elementary school in Birmingham, Harrison Barrow was sent to live with an aunt in Lille, where he attended the Lycée. At eighteen he returned to Birmingham to complete his education at Mason College and then to join his father's business. When Richard Barrow died in 1894 the business was formed into a limited private company with Harrison Barrow as managing director. His two brothers, Louis, an engineer, and Walter, a solicitor, joined him on the board. The business prospered, expanding into the field of general provisions and becoming one of Birmingham's best-known stores. Like his father, Harrison Barrow was regarded as a benevolent employer; he was particularly active before 1914 in campaigning for reductions in the working hours of shop assistants, becoming president of the Birmingham and District Early Closing Association as well as introducing a Wednesday half-day closing in his own store.

In May 1898 he took his first steps into local politics by winning a municipal by-election in Ladywood for the Liberals. He became the council's youngest member. Apart from two periods, 1898-9 and 1902-4, Barrow served as a Liberal councillor until 1918. During these years he built up a considerable reputation for fair-mindedness and independence among the numerically small group of Labour councillors. His main interest was in the city's tramway system whose administration was then the most contentious issue in Birmingham politics. Barrow was a strong advocate of municipal ownership of the entire system. His first vote on the council had been cast against a proposal to cede one of the tramways to a Canadian-owned syndicate. The defeat of this proposal in June 1898 effectively opened the way to municipal ownership. Barrow's abilities were recognised in 1907 when he was appointed chairman of the tramway committee.

Apart from his commitment to municipal ownership Barrow's pacificism was the other major strand in his political life. He was at the centre of the opposition in Birmingham to the Boer War. He was on the platform at the notorious Town Hall meeting attended by Lloyd George in 1902, and he subsequently opposed the granting of the freedom of the city to Lord Roberts. Neither of these actions endeared him to his Ladywood constituents, who rejected him at the 1902 municipal elections. He was re-elected, however, in 1904 and, shortly before the outbreak of the First World War, had been offered and had accepted the Lord Mayoralty. The war was to be for Barrow, as it was for many Liberals, the turning-point in his political career. The first consequence was that he withdrew from the Lord Mayoralty, recognising that, in his own words, 'the duties of the Lord Mayor must include those of a distinctly military character. As a member of the Society of Friends I could not conscientiously fulfil these.' He continued his civic work, nevertheless, retaining his seat on the council and becoming an active member of the citizens' committee which co-ordinated relief work in Birmingham. He also paid frequent visits to France as part of the Society of Friends' work for soldiers' families.

Barrow was also active in a more political sense – in the pacifist anti-war movement. He became a member of the general council of the UDC and was an important financial supporter of its work. It was through the Society of Friends, however, that Barrow found himself in direct conflict with the Government, resulting in his imprisonment in 1918. The Friends Service Committee published a pamphlet, *A Challenge to Militarism*, which it refused to submit to official censorship. Barrow, who was acting chairman of the committee, was charged under the Defence of the Realm Act. He was found guilty and sentenced to six months' imprisonment. He served five months in all, in Pentonville. Following his conviction he was stripped of all his offices on the city council and his name was removed from the Commission of the Peace. While waiting for the result of his appeal against his conviction, Barrow was informed that he had been awarded the OBE in recognition of his services to war-hit families. Barrow refused the honour and also resigned his seat on the council.

As the war ended Barrow joined many Liberals in abandoning the Party for the ILP. Asked subsequently to explain his decision, he said he felt that the Liberal Party was 'too much imbued with Imperialist ideas and had refused to advocate any attempts at real reconstruction on the lines of the nationalisation of the great monopolies of the country'. From 1918 to his retirement from active public life in 1949 Barrow was to work for these two beliefs in his political philosophy through the ILP and the Labour Party.

During these thirty years Barrow played an 'elder statesman' role within the Birmingham Labour movement. He regained his seat on the city council in 1922 and became an alderman in 1930. He again took a leading part in the administration of Birmingham's transport system. As chairman of the traffic committee in the 1930s, a position which kept him in the forefront of public life, he was responsible for the adoption of a one-way system for the city centre. His other special civic interest was education. Apart from his committee work, Barrow was a generous patron of various educational concerns in the city, including the King Edward's Foundation of

Grammar Schools. Although not always agreeing with the policies of the Labour group, Barrow's forthright debating qualities made him one of Labour's most effective councillors. A quality of sturdy independence also ensured him the respect of the majority of his political opponents. His commitment to principle is perhaps best illustrated by his advocacy in 1925 of a 6d increase in the rates to pay for educational developments. His defeat at the subsequent council elections was attributed to this unique proposal.

Outside his council work, Barrow was most active in international causes. Throughout his years in the Labour Party he was in the forefront of support for progressive international policies, from the 'Hands Off Russia' campaign to independence for India and anti-colonialism. In the mid-1930s Barrow was an active member of the Birmingham Council for Peace and Liberty, a left-wing pressure group which led the Birmingham campaign of support for the Spanish Republicans.

Though he only briefly held office in the Birmingham Borough Labour Party, Barrow was a major contributor to its finances. He was particularly instrumental in keeping alive the weekly newspaper, the *Town Crier*. Unlike other wealthy patrons of the Party, particularly those with pacifist views, he usually remained on good terms with the city's trade union leaders. One incident which, in the climate of the 1930s, made a deep impression on the movement was that at the height of the economic depression, he and his wife voluntarily lived on a sum equal to public assistance for a month to show their sympathy for the unemployed.

Throughout his subsequent political career Barrow's prison sentence was used against him. It surfaced most dramatically in 1930 when he was proposed by the Labour Government for a seat on the Public Works Loan Board. In the Commons, Churchill launched a bitter attack on the appointment 'of a man who has to his record a criminal conviction for malicious injury to this country in time of war'. Even nineteen years later his election as a freeman of Birmingham was opposed by some Conservative councillors, who objected to his pacifism. In both instances the opposition was unsuccessful.

After his retirement from public work Barrow led a quiet life. In his younger days he had been an enthusiastic foreign traveller and mountaineer, but his last few years were severely taxed by arthritis. He died at his Selly Oak home on 15 February 1953. He had outlived his wife, the former Mary Kenway from Neath, by six years. They had had no children. A memorial service was held at the Friends Meeting House, Bull Street, Birmingham. He left an estate valued at £34,766.

Writings: (with W. Wellock and Lella Florence), *A Birmingham Peace Plan* (Leicester, 1936) 23 pp.

Sources: *Birmingham Faces and Places: an illustrated local magazine 1* (Birmingham, 1889) 121-3 [profile of R.C. Barrow]; W.A. Cadbury, *Pedigree of the Barrow Family of Allithwaite, Cartmel and Lancaster* (Birmingham, 1906); *Birmingham Mail*, 1 July 1914; *Town Crier*, 10 Dec 1920; *Hansard*, 23 July 1930, cols 2335-46; *Birmingham Post* and *Birmingham Gazette*, 18 Jan 1949; *Sunday Mercury*, 6 Feb 1949; *Birmingham Gazette*, 13 Apr 1949; Barrow's Stores, *A Store Record 1824-1949* (Birmingham, 1949); M.H. Bailey, 'The Contribution of Quakers to some Aspects of Local Government in Birmingham 1828-1902' (Birmingham MA, 1952); biographical information: Mrs B. Smith, Birmingham. OBIT. *Birmingham Gazette, Birmingham Post* and *Times*, 16 Feb 1953; *Birmingham Mail*, 19 Feb 1953; *Birmingham J.* (Mar 1953); *Birmingham Post Year Book* (1953-4) 900-1.

PETER DRAKE

BASTON, Richard Charles (1880-1951)
TRADE UNION LEADER AND CO-OPERATOR

Richard Baston was born at Leamington, Warwickshire, on 20 February 1880, the son of

Charles Baston, a carpenter, and his wife Elizabeth Ann. He was one of five sons and four daughters. He attended Shrubland Street School in Leamington but left early and was largely self-educated. In 1903 he married Rosa Alice Farley, a widow with two young daughters. Their only child, a son, was born in the following year. The wedding took place in Spencer Street Congregational Church, Leamington, and Baston maintained an active connection with Congregationalism as a Sunday School teacher until 1918, when he abandoned all religious observance following the death of his elder stepdaughter after a long and agonisingly painful illness.

Little is known of Baston's early working life except that he eventually became a sheet metal worker at the Parkside works of the Siddeley-Deasy Motor Manufacturing Company in Coventry. He joined the Birmingham and Midland Sheet Metal Workers' Society and after a spell as a shop steward was appointed part-time secretary of the Coventry branch. In 1919 he became full-time secretary of the branch and held this office until 1939. He was then elected general secretary of the union and retained this post until his death.

Baston brought to the position of general secretary 'a wealth of experience' which enabled him to guide the union successfully through an eventful period in its history [Birmingham and Midland Sheet Metal Workers' Society (1959) 5]. During the Second World War he took a leading part in organising the stand which the Birmingham Society made, together with the National Union of Sheet Metal Workers and Braziers, against the dilution of labour in sheet metal working. The successful co-operation between the two unions on this issue encouraged hopes of an amalgamation and during the early years of the war a series of exploratory meetings was held, in which he again played a major role. Agreement was reached on a number of substantive questions but difficulties arose over the financial arrangements and the proposal lapsed. In the immediate post-war years, as changes in the motor car industry began to erode the craft basis of sheet metal working, Baston's negotiating ability was an important factor in protecting the wages and conditions of the Birmingham Society's members. The foundations of his success as a negotiator were thorough preparation, methodical presentation and his 'fighting qualities', although he always regarded strike action as a weapon to be used only in the last resort.

In addition to his trade union work Baston was actively involved in the wider Labour movement in Coventry. At the municipal elections of 1920 he unsuccessfully contested Hearsall ward on behalf of the Labour Party. From 1923 until 1944 he served on the management committee of Coventry and District Co-operative Society. He also played an important part in public life; at various times during the inter-war years he was a member of the Birmingham and District Joint Bakery Board, the Coventry and Nuneaton War Pensions Committee, the Coventry Employment Committee and Court of Referees.

Baston was a man of wide interests; his hobbies included football, cricket, dancing, art and bridge. He was floridly handsome in appearance, with a waxed moustache, and in later life he became rather portly. In personal qualities he was a man of great compassion. He died on 20 March 1951 at his home, 323 Allesley Old Road, Coventry, and was cremated at Canley Crematorium two days later. He left effects valued at £531. His wife and son survived him. At the time of Baston's death his son, Richard Denis Baston, was an executive with a firm of car distributors in Newcastle upon Tyne. The amalgamation of the two sheet metal workers' unions was finally achieved in 1973 when the Birmingham and Midland Society merged with the National Union of Sheet Metal Workers, Coppersmiths, Heating and Domestic Engineers, which had already absorbed the earlier National Union of Sheet Metal Workers and Braziers.

Sources: *Coventry Directory* (1912-13); *Coventry Graphic,* 5 Nov 1920; *Coventry Wheatsheaf* (Feb 1934); A.T. Kidd, *History of the Tin-Plate Workers and Sheet Metal Workers and Braziers Societies* (1949); Birmingham and Midland Sheet Metal Workers' Society, *Centenary Souvenir* (1959) 14 pp.; K. Richardson, *Twentieth-Century Coventry* (Coventry, 1972);

biographical information: Miss V. Gilbert, Coventry Reference Library; F. Warrington, Coventry and District Co-operative Society; personal information: L. Brown, Solihull, nephew; Mrs H. Dowling, Virginia Water, granddaughter; A.G. Smart, National Union of Sheet Metal Workers, Coppersmiths, Heating and Domestic Engineers, Coventry. OBIT. *Birmingham Mail* and *Coventry Evening Telegraph*, 20 Mar 1951; *Birmingham Daily Post*, 21 Mar 1951; *Birmingham Post Year Book and Who's Who* (1951-2).

ERIC TAYLOR

See also: †John Valentine STEVENS

BENNISON, Thomas Mason (1882-1960)
TEACHER, LABOUR COUNCILLOR AND CO-OPERATOR

Thomas Bennison was born at Guisborough, North Yorkshire, on 26 September 1882, the third child of George Bennison, an ironstone miner, and Mary Elizabeth Bennison (née Mason). He was educated first at the local primary school, from which he won the only scholarship to Guisborough Grammar School, and returned to his primary school at fifteen years of age as a pupil teacher. Later he moved to a Stockton-on-Tees primary school, as an uncertificated teacher. But he was clearly a perfectionist as regards his professional qualifications. He had sat for the Queen's Scholarship examination and won a first class. Having next passed the London Matriculation examination, he was a student at the University College (as it was then) of Nottingham, 1905-7. There he passed the London Intermediate examination and got his teaching certificate. He then, after study at the Borough Polytechnic, graduated as BSc. in Geology and Chemistry from King's College, London. This was in 1909. To complete the tale of his education, a quarter of a century later, in 1933, he sat for a London External BSc. and was placed in the second class, with Honours in Geography.

Bennison taught in London from 1909 to 1912. He then had a severe heart attack, which in the First World War caused him to be classified medically as C3, unfit for military service; and he was not called up.

On 27 July 1912 he married Annie Mills, whom he had met at University College, Nottingham, where she too was training to be a teacher. From 1912 to 1920 Bennison taught in a variety of schools, ranging from St Edmund's College, Ware, to country schools in Yorkshire and Lincolnshire. In these last, both he and his wife were oppressed and angered by the plight of the farm workers. They were both outspoken Socialists – Bennison joined the ILP in 1913 or even earlier – but there was little they could do to improve the agricultural workers' lot.

In 1920 Bennison took a post as senior geography master in Clay Cross, Derbyshire, Secondary School. (The school was later transferred as a grammar school to Tupton Hall; it is now (1977) Tupton Hall Comprehensive School.) He became active in local Labour politics, and in 1925 was elected an urban district councillor. He was chairman five times, and continued to hold a seat until 1958. During this time he sat on almost every committee of the council; but his special interests were housing, and the provision of a public library. He persuaded the council to improve water supplies and sewerage, and to build a library (which he opened two months before his death). But housing was probably his central concern. There was much squalor in Clay Cross when the family first moved there – 70 per cent of the houses had no indoor sanitation or indoor water supply. The contract for pulling down Long Row, the last of the slum 'rows', was sealed at the last meeting he attended, and demolition began during the month he died.

In 1949 he was elected to the Derbyshire County Council where he continued as a member for eleven years. He took great pleasure in his appointment as county council representative on the Nottingham University Court. In 1955 he was made an alderman. He was known as 'the father' of the Clay Cross Council. A street is named after him, and a memorial plaque was placed in the Public Library in March 1961.

Bennison was also active in the Chesterfield District Co-operative Society: he was on the district board for twenty-six years, nor was all this the sum of his activities. For many years he was chairman of the Clay Cross Divisional Labour Party. He was asked to stand for Parliament in 1933; but he preferred to support the nomination of Arthur Henderson. In the by-elections of 1936 and 1943 he was shortlisted as a Labour candidate but was not selected. In the latter year he suffered another heart attack and it caused him to retire early from teaching.

Bennison was a devout Methodist and throughout his political life his Socialism was integrally related to his Christianity. He became a local preacher in 1904 and preached for the last time on Christmas Day 1959. He was tough-minded and principled and, within the spectrum of Labour politics, a moderate. As the *Derbyshire Times* (not noted for its Socialist sympathies) wrote of him in 1936: '. . . his Socialism is of the constitutional rather than the "smash and grab" type.' It is an interesting commentary on the political attitudes of the 1930s that Bennison seriously considered volunteering for service on the Republican side in the Spanish Civil War. In the end it was family obligations that decided him against. It was assumed that he would find difficulty in retaining his job when he returned; and his wife was an ardent pacifist and member of the Peace Pledge Union. Bennison himself, until the coming of the Nazis to power, had been pro-German. He had visited Germany in 1920 and was much affected by what he saw as the consequences of the continuation of the allied blockade. He became fluent in German (as well as having some knowledge of French and Russian). He visited Germany after Hitler's accession to power – in company with Alfred Holland, MP for Clay Cross – and was appalled by the Fascist regime. No doubt, as with so many in these years, it was his hatred of international Fascism that encouraged his passionate commitment to the Spanish cause. It certainly was responsible for his support in 1939 for the war against Germany.

Bennison was a smallish man, of slight build, fair hair (although baldness set in at an early age) and with very blue eyes. He played cricket and football into his forties. He died in Walton Hospital, Chesterfield, on 22 February 1960. The funeral was at the Market Street Methodist Chapel in Clay Cross, and he was buried in the Clay Cross Cemetery. He left an estate valued at £3641.

The Bennisons had two children: the elder, Dorothy Elizabeth, now Mrs Lawes, is at present (1977) a senior lecturer at Westminster College, Oxford (a Methodist training college). Her brother, George Mills Bennison, is senior lecturer in Geology in Birmingham University.

Mrs Annie Bennison, like her husband, was an active Party worker throughout most of her life. She was also an urban district councillor (chairman for at least two periods), chairman of the women's section of the Labour Party, and a school governor. She was a committed pacifist, a life-long Methodist (her father was a local preacher), a total abstainer and an ardent republican. She deserted the Labour Party for a brief period during the Second World War when she supported the candidature of William Douglas-Home, the playwright and author, who stood unsuccessfully as an 'Atlantic Charter' Independent Progressive candidate for the Clay Cross division in April 1944. Mrs Bennison took the chair at his eve of the poll meeting, while her husband performed the same function, on the other side of the street, for the official Labour candidate. Mrs Bennison remained active and mentally alert till her death at the age of eighty-two on 27 May 1969.

Sources: *Derbyshire Times*, 2 Oct 1936; ibid., 24 Mar 1961; biographical information: Chesterfield and District Co-operative Society Ltd; personal information: Dr G.M. Bennison, Birmingham, son. OBIT. *Derbyshire Times*, 26 Feb 1960; *Home Mag.* [Chesterfield Edition] (Apr 1960).

MARGARET 'ESPINASSE

BLAND, Hubert (1855-1914)
FABIAN AND JOURNALIST

Hubert Bland was one of the less typical of British Socialists. Born on 3 January 1855, he was not a North countryman born in 1856, as is often stated, but the son of Henry Bland, a Woolwich plumber and painter who subsequently became a clerk and still later a director of shipping companies and a local government councillor. At the time of Hubert's birth his father was described as 'gentleman', a status which the son also claimed for himself. Hubert was educated at schools in Woolwich and Blackheath and subsequently by a private tutor; he was destined for the army. His father's death in 1866 brought about a deterioration in the family finances, however, and at his mother's insistence Bland was forced to enter a bank. Later he set up in business as a brush manufacturer, and he was so described when he was married.

It was probably in 1877 that Bland met Edith Nesbit, the talented daughter of a lecturer in agricultural science. They were married before the registrar of the City of London on 22 April 1880. Edith was pregnant at the time of the marriage and Bland was almost immediately afflicted by both smallpox and financial disaster. It was as a result of the threat of poverty that Edith turned to writing, soon becoming a prolific author of short fiction and verse, and later of the famous children's stories which are still widely read.

The irregularity of the Bland's domestic life is well known. One of Hubert's mistresses, Alice Hoatson, lived in the Bland home with her children and there were a number of other liaisons. (Bland's book *The Happy Moralist* [1907] was dedicated to Alice Hoatson 'in token of a long and an unbreakable friendship'.) The unusual degree to which Bland engaged in this kind of relationship may have owed something to personal insecurity. Married to a woman more accomplished and more successful than himself, he retaliated with a series of love affairs which, as H.G. Wells in the course of a derogatory account of Bland pointed out, Edith 'not only detested and mitigated and tolerated, but presided over.' Bland in turn expressed strong disapproval of Wells's advocacy of 'free love'. Despite his infidelities, however, which began long before Edith became a well-known writer, the marriage seems to have been a stormy but successful one. Bland managed to retain not only Edith's loyalty, but her love and wholehearted participation in his political work. She was in the eighteen eighties one of the most active of Fabian women.

Insecurity arising from his origins in a family of uncertain social status may also help to explain Bland's ultra-correctness in outward appearance, his faultless clothes and monocle, as also his pride in physical fitness and his skill as a pugilist, his continued interest in military matters and membership of the Volunteers, and, probably in his thirties, his conversion or re-conversion to Roman Catholicism. As Edith Nesbit's biographer commented, he was 'Conservative in everything but politics' [Moore (1967) 133]. Yet, whatever Bland's behaviour may have owed to insecurity, both his private and political life were more eccentric than were the lives of his friends and contemporaries of similarly ambiguous social background.

Bland became interested in literature and ideas, and in the autumn of 1883, he was among the early members of the Fellowship of the New Life. But he was also among a number of members who were dissatisfied with its rather vague objectives, and it was he who took the chair at a meeting of the Fellowship on 4 January 1884 which resolved to establish a new and more specifically political organisation, called the Fabian Society. Elected one of the three members of the first Fabian executive committee, Bland immediately became its treasurer, a post which he retained until 1911, three years before his death. One of his early acts, in May 1884, was to recruit Bernard Shaw to the Society. Shortly before, he had helped to revise the first Fabian Tract, *Why are the Many Poor?*

Bland's occupations in the early 1880s remain shadowy, although he seems to have continued to follow commercial and financial pursuits, being at one point the manager of a foreign bank in London. In the middle years of the decade he turned to journalism, a field which he was to make his vocation. It seems to have been Shaw who found him his first journalistic work, and in 1886

Bland and his wife, who had already written a novel in collaboration, became joint editors of the Socialist journal *To-day*, Bland continued as sole editor from 1887 until the paper's demise in 1889. Later he wrote for the London *Daily Chronicle* and, as 'Hubert', for the Manchester-based *Sunday Chronicle*, the paper which Robert Blatchford and his friends left to found the *Clarion*. Bland wrote regularly for about twenty-five years for the *Sunday Chronicle*, his articles gradually becoming more prominent until he came to lead the front page with two columns of moralising and discursive comment on political and social subjects, literature and the arts, relations between the sexes and contemporary manners. His writing was characterised by a kind of metropolitan sophistication which must have seemed titillatingly remote from the life-styles of his northern readers. During the last year of his life Bland also wrote for the *New Statesman* a long weekly review of novels, among them D.H. Lawrence's *Sons and Lovers* [5 July 1913, 408]. A number of his journalistic pieces were reprinted in books published between 1905 and 1914 and were widely praised by reviewers. After his death his friend Cecil Chesterton wrote that his *Sunday Chronicle* articles reached 'almost the high-water mark of English journalism' [Bland (1914) viii].

Bland's importance to a later age, however, lies not in his journalism but in his politics. He was the only leading early Fabian who reached Socialism from a Conservative background, Henry George and H.M. Hyndman being the most influential figures in his conversion. Although Bland never abandoned certain conservative views, it would be a mistake to exaggerate this aspect of his thought. His conservatism in practice was limited to questions of defence and the Empire, fields in which other leading Fabians shared his outlook. He believed in Britain's civilising mission and was a strong defender of the Empire. He belonged to the majority in the Fabian Society which refused to condemn British involvement in the South African war and in fact supported it strongly [*Labour Leader*, 10 Dec 1898, 407; *Clarion*, 7 Apr 1900, 105-6]. Like Shaw and others he was unenthusiastic about free trade, a scepticism which divided the Fabian majority from the mainstream of the labour movement. Bland was also an advocate of a strong army and navy. Cecil Chesterton wrote: 'I think the root of his Socialism was his intense Nationalism. He once said to me that there were two things without which you could not have a democratic State, – Protection and Conscription' [Bland (1914) xi]. Bland also placed himself among the more conservative of Socialists by his intolerably patronising and frivolous attitude towards women's rights – as in his *Letters to a Daughter* (1906) and *Olivia's Latchkey* (1913) – an attitude which probably did not surprise those who were acquainted with his private life.

Bland's distinctive contribution to British Socialism lies principally in his belief in an independent Labour movement. It was this feature of his thought which distinguished him from others among the early Fabian leaders. Like a number of other Fabians he and his wife were briefly but enthusiastically members of the Marxist Social Democratic Federation in 1885, Edith writing in *Justice*: Let us lose no opportunity of preaching our glorious gospel' [12 Sep 1885, 3]. Although the Blands left the Federation about the end of 1885, Hubert's early experience of British Marxism combined with his anti-Liberalism to make him a strong advocate of a Labour party distinct from the Liberals. This was apparent in the lecture delivered in December 1888 which formed the basis of his contribution to *Fabian Essays* (1889) and which remains his most important political statement. Entitled 'The Outlook', it was a remarkably perceptive analysis of political trends, diverging sharply from the position taken by Webb and his friends. Bland was highly sceptical of municipal Socialism and the 'irresistible glide into collectivist Socialism' which Webb acclaimed in his own essay. Bland further expressed marked dissatisfaction with the policy of 'permeation' of the Liberal Party with Socialist doctrines and programmes which was closely associated with the Fabian majority who followed the lead of Sidney Webb, and which was to be, with some doubts and contradictions, Fabian orthodoxy over the next twenty years. (It is an odd fact that Bland, an opponent of 'permeation,' was the first Fabian to use the word in print.) To those Fabians like Webb who believed that the transition to Socialism would be so gradual as hardly to be noticed, Bland replied that Socialism would only arrive when 'no man or group of men holds, over the means of production, property rights by which the labour of the producers can be subjected to exploitation.' He looked forward to the formation of a Socialist political party and to a time when radicals of the type whom Webb hoped to 'permeate' would have to choose between the 'definitely pro-private capital party on the one side, and the definitely anti-private capital party on the other.'

While Bland advocated the creation of a Socialist party with a programme of specific policies as early as 1886, he was not a kind of quasi-Marxist, as is sometimes suggested, despite his early membership of the SDF, the brief but clear analysis of historical materialism in his Fabian essay, and his verbal flirtation with the idea of ultimate social revolution. His belief in a Socialist political party was in specific opposition to 'the idle chatter about violence on the part of many active spirits in the movement.' To him the difference between evolutionary and revolutionary Socialists was 'fundamental'. He was even able on at least one occasion to say a kind word for 'permeation', as a commonsensical method of persuading the Liberals 'that they are much nearer to Socialism than they think.' [*Sunday Chronicle*, 4 Aug 1895, 2].

In short, Bland should not be seen as a kind of Marxist infiltrator among the Fabian ranks but rather as a 'left-wing Fabian,' opposed both to Webb's gradualist ideas and to violent revolution. His belief in independent labour action, however, remained a permanent feature of his thought. It was Bland and Annie Besant who in the autumn of 1886 were responsible for the creation of the Fabian Parliamentary League, the first and short-lived attempt to bring the Fabians actively into Socialist politics. Again in the early 1890s Bland among others strongly supported Fabian involvement in an independent Labour movement. He was originally intended to be a Fabian delegate to the foundation conference of the ILP in 1893 (but dropped out to be replaced by Shaw at the last minute), and was a delegate to Labour Party conferences in 1908 and 1910. In his last Fabian lecture, on 5 July 1912, Bland complained that the Society had still not shaken itself free of Liberalism, asserting that social reform merely made a worker more efficient and profitable to his employer. If the whole of the Minority Report on the Poor Law were adopted, he added, 'Society would still be divided into two classes.'

Bland's personal idiosyncrasies and his unorthodox political views helped to make him less influential a leader than Shaw or Sidney Webb, or, in the early period, Sydney Olivier and Graham Wallas, the other leading Fabians. Bland, as Edward Pease, the Fabian secretary, wrote many years after his death, was 'a little difficult, and a little of an outsider.' Against the four principal Fabian leaders Shaw noted, Bland was 'hopelessly outmatched'. Moreover, Bland, although forceful and energetic, was less hard-working and persistent within the Society than other leading Fabians. He undertook his share of lecturing and attendance at committee meetings; in February 1892, for example, he was reported to be lecturing in Bradford, Darlington, Consett, Dundee, Edinburgh and Nottingham, and later in the year in a number of Lancashire and West Riding towns. By 1909 he claimed to have lectured on Socialism in almost every city in England [*Reformers' Year Book* (1909) 217]. He also played an important part in revising draft pamphlets, but by 1900 according to Shaw he was more notable for 'impromptu criticisms' than for any serious attempt to reconstruct Fabian policy, either by tract or meeting. His duties as treasurer also lay lightly on his shoulders.

Shaw pointed out in a letter in 1900 that Bland had 'a household of nine persons to keep going' [Shaw (1972) 155]. Perhaps this helps to explain why most of his literary output went into well-paid journalism and little into writing Fabian publications. He was one of a Fabian team of five which in 1886 produced a report (not published as a tract) entitled *The Government Organisation of Unemployed Labour.* Apart from this early and tentative foray, Bland's name is associated with only two Fabian tracts, which he edited and largely wrote. These were *After Bread, Education: a plan for the State feeding of school children* (Tract no. 120: 1905), and *Socialism and Labor Policy* (Tract no. 127: 1906), both produced over twenty years after the Fabian Society was founded.

The tracts were pungently written, and it is easy to see Bland's hand in a style far more propagandist and forthright than the usual Fabian approach. Referring to the 'ladder' of educational scholarships associated prominently with Sidney Webb, the first tract stated: 'Our children ask for bread, and we give them a "ladder." ' Arguing strongly for school meals, even at the expense of meals in the home ('Domesticity does not centre around the pudding.'), it concluded: 'It is true that the hungry scholar is a crime; but it is the worst of national blunders too.'

Socialism and Labor Policy is even more direct, though in its assertion that the Labour Party was a Socialist party, more characterised by optimism than by realism. The tract demanded the right to work, a legal minimum wage, universal pensions and the abolition of the Poor Law. It also demanded a graduated income tax and heavier death duties. Its statement on public expenditure was couched in terms that may still be thought relevant: 'The degree of civilization which a state has reached may almost be measured by the proportion of the national income which is spent collectively instead of individually. To the Socialist the best of governments is that which spends the most.'

Bland was only once a candidate for elective office. This was in 1888 when seven Fabians and members of the SDF stood for election to the London School Board, Annie Besant and Stewart Headlam winning their contests with Liberal-Radical support. Bland stood in Finsbury, appealing to the electorate on a number of favourite radical, secularist and Socialist themes, including the ending of religious teaching in Board schools, the abolition of school fees, the provision of school meals and the encouragement of technical education and evening classes. He held several enthusiastic meetings, addressed by other candidates and by such Socialists as Shaw, Hyndman and John Burns; but his 3876 votes were only enough for him to finish second among the unsuccessful candidates, over five thousand votes below the lowest of the victors. Bland seems to have felt his defeat keenly, and this may help to explain his failure to stand again.

Bland was a second rank figure among Socialists of his day. His temperament was more suited to journalism and essays than to more sustained intellectual effort, and the book on 'English Socialism of To-day' on which the *Sunday Chronicle* reported him to be working [30 Nov 1890, 2] seems never to have been completed. (He did, however, write a valuable series of seven articles, which merits reprinting, entitled 'Memories and Impressions of Persons connected with the Socialist Movement during the Last Fifteen Years' for the *Sunday Chronicle* between April and August 1895.) Only his Fabian essay published in 1889 outlived his time, but in his day he was a well-known, colourful and, in some respects, influential figure. Towards the end of his life he lost his sight and suffered increasingly from heart disease. He died suddenly of heart failure on 14 April 1914 at the age of 59, leaving a gross estate of £898. He was buried in Woolwich Cemetery, not far from his birthplace, and was survived by Edith Nesbit, who remarried in 1917 and died in 1924 in her sixty-sixth year. Four of his children also survived him, one of whom, Rosamund, his daughter by Alice Hoatson, married Clifford Sharp, first editor of the *New Statesman*.

Writings: *The Prophet's Mantle* (1889) [a novel published jointly with Edith Bland under pseud. 'Fabian Bland']; 'The Outlook' in *Fabian Essays in Socialism* ed. G.B. Shaw (1889, 6th ed. with an Introduction by A. Briggs, 1962) 237-55; *With the Eyes of a Man* (1905); *Letters to a Daughter* [1906]; *The Happy Moralist* [1907]; *Socialism and the Catholic Faith* (Glasgow, [1910?]) 23 pp.; *Olivia's Latchkey* [1913]; *Essays by Hubert Bland* (1914).

Sources: *Sunday Chronicle*, 30 Nov 1890, 2; *Fabian News* (June 1892) 16 and (Oct 1892) 32; G.B. Shaw, *The Fabian Society: its early history* (1892) 30 pp.; *Workman's Times*, 13 Feb 1892, 7 and 20 Feb 1892, 6; *Labour Annual* (1896) 196-7; *Reformers' Year Book* (1909) 217; *Fabian News*, *23*, no. 9 (Aug 1912); 'The Faith I hold', in *Essays by Hubert Bland* (1914) 212-33; E.R. Pease, *The History of the Fabian Society* (1916, rev. ed. 1925, repr. 1963 with an Introduction by M. Cole); D.L. Moore, *E. Nesbit: a biography* (1933; rev. ed. 1967); H.G. Wells, *Experiment in Autobiography* vol. 2 (1934); A.E. Chesterton, *The Chestertons* (1941); *The Webbs and their Work* ed. M. Cole (1949; 2nd ed. with new Introduction, Brighton, 1974); H. Pelling, *The Origins of the Labour Party 1880-1900* (1954, 2nd ed. 1965); A. Freemantle,

This Little Band of Prophets: the British Fabians (NY, 1960); M. Cole, *The Story of Fabian Socialism* (1961); A.M. McBriar, *Fabian Socialism and English Politics 1884-1918* (Cambridge, 1962); *Collected Letters of Bernard Shaw*, ed. Dan H. Laurence, vol. *1 1874-1897* (1965) and vol. *2 1898-1910* (1972); P. Thompson, *Socialists, Liberals and Labour: the struggle for London 1885-1914* (1967); E.J. Hobsbawm, 'The Lesser Fabians', *Our History* pamphlet no. 28 (Winter 1962) 14 pp. repr. in *The Luddites and Other Essays* ed. L.M. Munby (1971) 231-44; N. and J. MacKenzie, *The Time Traveller: the life of H.G. Wells* (1973); S. Pierson, *Marxism and the Origins of British Socialism* (1973); B. Sewell, *Cecil Chesterton* (Faversham, 1975); W. Wolfe, *From Radicalism to Socialism: men and ideas in the formation of Fabian Socialist doctrines, 1881-1889* (Yale Univ. Press, 1975); N. and J. MacKenzie, *The First Fabians* (1977); biographical information: J. Watson, Local History Librarian, London Borough of Greenwich. OBIT. *Manchester Evening Chronicle*, 15 Apr 1914; *Times*, 16 Apr 1914; *Sunday Chronicle*, 19 Apr 1914; *Kentish Independent* and *Pioneer* [Woolwich], 24 Apr 1914; *Fabian News* (May 1914); Fabian Society, *31st Annual Report* (1914).

DAVID RUBINSTEIN

See also: †William CLARKE; †Edward Reynolds PEASE; Graham WALLAS.

BOWERMAN, Charles William (1851-1947)
TRADE UNIONIST AND LABOUR MP

Charles Bowerman was probably born on 22 January 1851 at Honiton in Devon. It has not been possible to confirm this date from official records and little is known about his family except that his father was a tinplate worker who, having gone to London for the Great Exhibition of 1851, decided to settle there. He worked as a journeyman tinplater in the Clerkenwell Road, and must have had moderately good earnings, since Bowerman recalled his boyhood as having been happy and financially secure.

After five years' education at Barnsbury National School he got a job, on his own initiative, with a watchmaker and jeweller in Clerkenwell at a weekly wage of 8s. Soon afterwards, however, he was persuaded by one of his uncles who was a compositor to enter the printing trade. In 1865 he became apprenticed to this uncle and learned the elements of his trade on the *Watchman* and the *Methodist Recorder*. During this time he supplemented his formal education by reading the works of Dickens, Scott and Disraeli, among others, and by subscribing to Cassell's monthly educational and scientific publications.

When his apprenticeship came to an end in 1872 he became a journeyman compositor on a daily paper called the *Hour*. Later in the same year he joined the *Daily Telegraph*, where he continued to work for nineteen years, and in due course became father of the chapel.

Bowerman had joined the London Society of Compositors in 1873 and became secretary of the news department of the LSC from 1886. In the 1890s he was the beneficiary of a reform movement within the union, one of the most exclusive and conservative of all the craft unions. In 1891 a group of younger members established the London Society of Compositors' Reform League to develop 'honest and legitimate opposition' to the existing leadership, and their agitation was directed particularly against the secretary C.J. Drummond. The Reform League won three seats on the executive in 1892, and both the chairman of the Society and Drummond resigned, Bowerman being elected in the latter's place in the following year [Clegg et al. (1964) 143-4; Howe and Waite (1948) 204]. Bowerman joined the Fabian Society in 1893 although he never became a Socialist but remained always an advanced working-class radical, like so many skilled trade unionists in the closing decades of the nineteenth century. He attended his first TUC in 1893 and was elected to its Parliamentary Committee in 1897, becoming successively treasurer in 1899 and chairman in 1901. In this latter year he presided over the Swansea TUC when the main issue before the Congress was the Taff Vale decision.

In his presidential address Bowerman advised Congress to 'make haste slowly', as the Parliamentary Committee had no immediate proposals to make. It did, however, believe that with 'a judicious amendment of the rules . . . it will be possible to avert many of the difficulties created by the decision of the House of Lords, especially in the direction of protecting the funds of the unions'. The Committee also urged a particularly cautious approach to the question of picketing, 'the most vital question'. Summing up, Bowerman, who was a very strong supporter of Labour representation, insisted that the best course of action was 'the imperative and absolute necessity of securing increased representation in the House of Commons'. He became a member of the NEC of the Labour Representation Committee in 1902.

Bowerman was always passionately concerned with educational matters. The Parliamentary Committee of the TUC was wholeheartedly opposed to Balfour's Education Act of 1902, and Bowerman played an active part in the general opposition of the working-class movement to the destruction of the School Boards and to the continuation of clerical control over educational policies. With the single exception of the Fabian Society, all organisations of the labour movement came out against the Bill. Bowerman was also active in the more specific field of working-class education. He was on the platform at the 1899 inaugural meeting of what was to become Ruskin College and he represented the Parliamentary Committee of the TUC in various capacities on Ruskin College committees. He was opposed to the famous strike of March 1909 and to the establishment of the Central Labour College.

In 1903 in a union ballot for a parliamentary candidate Bowerman defeated the SDF nominee by the narrow margin of 3966 votes to 3205 [Thompson (1967) 204-5] and he was adopted by labour organisations in Deptford. The initiative for an independent Labour representative had come from the Deptford and Greenwich Trades Council. Bowerman received LRC recognition but despite the strenuous efforts of B.T. Hall, chairman of the Deptford Labour Association (and better known as national secretary of the Working Men's Club and Institute Union), the Liberal Party insisted on their own candidate. In the general election of 1906 Bowerman had an easy victory with the Liberal at the bottom of the poll. In later elections he was to have the full support of the Liberal Party, and he retained his seat in January 1910 and in five subsequent elections. His policy in 1910 was an extension of the aims he had long supported as a London 'Progressive' – he was an LCC alderman from 1901 to 1907. The main planks in his 1910 platform were the abolition of the House of Lords and resistance to Tariff Reform. For the rest, he summed up as follows: (1) Popular control of education, no tests for teachers, secondary schools and unsectarian colleges; (2) R.C. on Poor Laws Minority Report proposals; (3) the late Government's Licensing Bill; (4) 'Right to Work' Bill; (5) removal of poor-law disqualification on old-age pensions; (6) appointment of Minister for Labour; (7) minimum wage of 30s weekly for government workers in London; (8) adult suffrage, Home Rule for Scotland, Ireland and Wales; (9) nationalisation of railways, canals, and land; (10) London Elections Bill. In the interview which provided the occasion for this summary of his views [*Christian Commonwealth*, 26 Jan 1910] he insisted he was in Parliament as a trade unionist, that he would 'extract all the practical part of the Socialist programme', and that he and his fellow trade unionist MPs worked in harmony with 'what are known as the more extreme men'.

Bowerman resigned from the general secretaryship of the Compositors on his election to the Commons in 1906, and became parliamentary secretary of the LSC. He was by this time a national figure and in 1911 he was elected secretary of the TUC. He led the trade union side in the departmental committee that recommended a State printing department, and he became a member of George Askwith's Industrial Council in 1911. He found himself in a rather unusual position during the early days of the *Herald*. The proposal to establish a daily Labour paper had been raised at the TUC since 1903, and in 1906 the Joint Board (of the TUC, LRC and GFTU) appointed a sub-committee to report on the idea. The discussion which followed lasted until 1909 when the matter was dropped [Roberts (1958) 229-30]. In 1911, however, the London Society of Compositors – which had been in the forefront of the agitation for a daily paper – was engaged in strike action against the Master Printers' Association for the forty-eight hour week; and to explain their case the LSC published a four-page strike sheet which appeared for four months until their claims were accepted. The attempts made to gain wider support for the transformation of the strike sheet into a daily paper were finally successful when the first issue of the *Daily Herald* appeared on 15 April 1912. Among those most responsible for the establishment of the *Daily Herald* were H.W. Hobart and T.E. Naylor, both near-syndicalist members of the London Society of Compositors. Naylor addressed the 1911 TUC but so did G.H. Roberts, on behalf of the Labour Party, who were promoting their own Labour paper, which eventually appeared in 1912 as the *Daily Citizen*. In the complicated and often acrimonious discussions which followed the launching of the *Herald*, Bowerman and a majority of the Parliamentary Committee first encouraged it, then adopted a position of neutrality, and finally abandoned support for the paper in 1913.

Early in August 1914, when the outbreak of war seemed imminent, a special TUC conference was convened by Arthur Henderson and Bowerman. The intention was to frame a policy which they hoped might prevent an acceleration of events. When the conference finally met, the war had already begun and its terms of reference were consequently amended. It established the War Emergency Workers' National Committee. Like the majority of the Parliamentary Committee, Bowerman was prepared to put the maximum of organised trade union support behind the war effort in the hope of achieving as swift a settlement as possible. When the Joint Labour Recruiting Committee was formed in September 1915 (for which see below) Bowerman became one of its two secretaries. In 1916 he supported conscription; was appointed a Labour Party junior whip, and also made a PC.

Throughout the years of the war Bowerman worked to maintain links with the European trade union movement, particularly with the Belgians, and 'invented means whereby help was periodically conveyed secretly to the workers of that country through German lines' [*The British Labour Party 3* (1948) 277]. In August 1918 he and Arthur Henderson were chosen to lead a joint TUC and Labour Party delegation to a meeting in Switzerland, which had been convened by the International Socialist Bureau to discuss the Allied Labour Memorandum on war aims. In the event the Government refused to issue passports and the party was unable to go. But in the following year, after the conclusion of hostilities, TUC representatives joined those from ten other countries at the Amsterdam Conference which set up the International Federation of Trade Unions. Bowerman included the details of this new body in his report to the Glasgow TUC where it was approved. The other major international organisation to emerge from the wartime and post-war discussions on the future of labour, the International Labour Organisation, was also put before and accepted by that Congress. Bowerman had been closely involved in the consultations which had led to the ILO's initiation and he attended its first conference in Washington in October 1919. There he was instrumental in shaping the Hours Convention which sought to introduce a forty-eight hour working week in all countries. Like G.N. Barnes, Bowerman was much disappointed by Parliament's slowness in endorsing these decisions. He resigned the general secretaryship of the TUC at the Plymouth Congress of 1923 under the new age-retirement limit of seventy years. (In fact he was two years older than this.)

In the House of Commons Bowerman always solidly supported middle-of-the-road Labour Party policies and was a conscientious constituency member, spending a great deal of time on matters concerning the docks and victualling yards around Deptford and on problems of merchant shipping in general. During the war years he was painstaking in putting a large variety of questions on the day-to-day organisation of the war effort at home, and later, questions on the details of demobilisation procedure and the remuneration of ex-servicemen. In each election after 1906 he achieved a steady increase of votes, but in the general election of 1931, standing as 'loyal Labour', he lost to the Conservative D.A. Hanley by 22,244 votes to 26,558, the narrowness of the margin being a marked indication of the esteem in which he was held by many in the constituency.

In later life Bowerman maintained his interest in London municipal affairs (he was made a JP for the Finsbury division in 1919) and in the welfare of the printing fraternity. He represented the

LCC on the Board of Governors of St Bride Institute of Fine Printing and served as treasurer of the Caxton Convalescent Home, Limpsfield, from its foundation in 1894. For a period he was a member of the Arbitration Court of the Board of Trade and was for many years president of the Printing and Kindred Trades Federation. Despite his great age, until shortly before his death he was still chairman of the directors of the Co-operative Printing Society, and a member of the executive committee of Ruskin College. In 1935 he was a member of Harold Macmillan's Next Five Years Group. Only a year before his death he had attended the fortieth anniversary of the foundation of the Parliamentary Labour Party at the House of Commons.

Charles Bowerman died on 11 June 1947 at his home in Battledean Road, Highbury. He had married a Miss Louisa Peach in 1876, and his wife predeceased him. He was survived by several of his five sons and seven daughters. After a funeral service at Christ Church, Highbury, he was buried in Islington Cemetery, East Finchley. He left an estate valued at £3668 which included a legacy of £525 to the Printers' Pension Corporation.

Writings: *Jubilee of the London Society of Compositors . . .* (1898); *Some Industrial Problems* (1919) 11 pp.; 'New Labour Charter', *Reynolds's Newspaper*, 9 Mar 1919; Editor of *Report of proceedings at the [46-47, 54-55] Annual Trades Union Congress* (1913, 1915, 1922 and 1923); *Report of the Committee appointed to select the Best Faces of Type and Modes of Display for Government Printing* (1922); (with W.M. Citrine), *A Short History of the London Trades Council* [1935].

Sources: 'How I got on', *Pearson's Weekly*, 8 Feb 1906; *Hansard* (1906-31); *Reformers' Year Book* (1906); *Christian Commonwealth*, 26 Jan 1910; *Times Guide to House of Commons* (1910); *Daily Citizen*, 18 Aug 1913; S.V. Bracher, *The Herald Book of Labour Members* (1923); *Dod* (1924); *Labour Who's Who* (1927); E. Howe and H.E. Waite, *The London Society of Compositors* (1948); *The British Labour Party 3* ed. H. Tracey (1948) 276-8; F. Bealey and H. Pelling, *Labour and Politics 1900-1906* (1958); B.C. Roberts, *The Trades Union Congress 1868-1921* (1958); H.A. Clegg et al., *A History of British Trade Unions since 1889*, vol. 1:1889-1910 (Oxford, 1964); W.W. Craik, *The Central Labour College 1909-29* (1964); B. Simon, *Education and the Labour Movement, 1870-1920* (1965); P. Thompson, *Socialists, Liberals and Labour* (1967); R. McKibbin, *The Evolution of the Labour Party 1910-1924* (Oxford, 1974); biographical information: the late T.A.K. Elliot, CMG. OBIT. *Times*, 12 June 1947; *Islington Gazette*, 13 and 17 June 1947; *North London Press*, 13 and 20 June 1947; *TUC Report* (1947); *Labour Party Report* (1948).

BARBARA NIELD

See also: †George Nicoll BARNES; †George LANSBURY, for British Labour Party, 1900-13; †George Henry ROBERTS; and below for The Parliamentary Recruiting Committee and the Joint Labour Recruiting Committee.

The Parliamentary Recruiting Committee and the Joint Labour Recruiting Committee in the First World War

Soon after the declaration of war on 4 August 1914 a Parliamentary Recruiting Committee was established. The first preliminary meeting was held on 27 August. It was, in the words of the *Times Recruiting Supplement* of 3 November 1915 'a sort of annex to the War Office'. The main purpose of the Parliamentary Committee was to allow members to take the platform at recruiting meetings, not in support of their own particular party policy, but in the broad interests of the nation, as these were understood at the time by majority opinion in each of the three main parties. The presidents of the Parliamentary Committee were Asquith, the Prime Minister, and Bonar Law and Arthur Henderson, representing the political leaders of the opposition parties.

The joint chairmen of the Committee were the Parliamentary Secretaries to the Treasury and the Chief Whips; and the Labour Party was represented in the General Purposes Committee by G.H. Roberts. The Parliamentary Committee issued leaflets and posters, organised many meetings and quickly built up a staff of expert voluntary workers. The extent of its activities, especially through its many local committees, was considerable. The only significant political groups not represented on the Committee were the anti-war factions of the Labour Party and the ILP. The Parliamentary Recruiting Committee restricted its national and local activities to England and Wales but similar work was carried out in Scotland by the Central Recruiting Committee and in Ireland by the Irish Committee.

During 1915 the issue of conscription became increasingly important. It was a matter of the greatest concern to the Labour movement which in most of its sections was vehemently opposed to the principle of compulsion. In September 1915 the TUC unanimously passed the following resolution:

> That we, the delegates to the Congress, representing nearly three million organised workers, record our hearty appreciation of the magnificent response made to the call for volunteers to fight against the tyranny of militarism.

> We emphatically protest against the sinister efforts of a section of the reactionary Press in formulating newspaper policies for party purposes and attempting to foist on this country conscription, which always proves a burden to the workers, and will divide the nation at a time when absolute unanimity is essential.

> No reliable evidence has been produced to show that the voluntary system of enlistment is not adequate to meet all the Empire's requirements.

> We believe that all the men necessary can, and will, be obtained through a voluntary system properly organised, and we heartily support and will give every aid to the Government in their present efforts to secure the men necessary to prosecute the war to a successful issue.

After the September meeting of the TUC was concluded the EC of the Labour Party took the initiative in calling a Conference of the national committees of the TUC, the General Federation of Trade Unions, and the Labour Party together with members of the Parliamentary Party. The Conference met at the offices of the Board of Education under the presidency of Arthur Henderson. Both the Prime Minister (H.H. Asquith) and the Minister for War (Lord Kitchener) addressed the Conference. Two days later it re-assembled again and agreed to launch a Labour Recruiting campaign, the main purpose of which was to encourage the continuation of the voluntary system and thereby avoid the threatened policy of national conscription. The list of members appointed to what became known as the Joint Labour Recruiting Committee was as follows: H. Gosling, LCC and C.W. Bowerman MP (Trades Union Congress); W.S. Sanders and G.J. Wardle MP (Labour Party); J. O'Grady MP and W.A. Appleton (General Federation of Trade Unions); Arthur Henderson MP (Consultative Member). C.W. Bowerman and A. Peters, JP were appointed Joint Secretaries.

In October 1915 the Earl of Derby was appointed Director-General of Recruiting. He put his proposals at a very early stage to both the Parliamentary Recruiting Committee and the Joint Labour Recruiting Committee and secured their assent; henceforth the names of the two committees were often bracketed together on posters and recruiting material. Events, however, moved very quickly to render the aims and purposes of the two Committees out of date. The failure of the Derby scheme of attestation under which all men were called upon to 'attest' for military service, whether or not they were engaged on essential work, led the Government to introduce the bill for Military Service in January 1916. The confused reactions of the Labour Party are set out in Cole, *History of the Labour Party from 1914* pp. 26 ff. The January Act was followed by the conscription of married men in May 1916; and the original purpose of the Labour Recruiting Committee was now no longer tenable.

Sources: *Times Recruiting Supplement,* 3 Nov 1915; *Labour Year Book* (1916) 70-1; Earl of Derby, *Report on Recruiting* 1914-16 XXXIX Cd 8149; *The Parliamentary History of Conscription in Great Britain being a summary of the Parliamentary Debates etc.,* with a Preface by R.C. Lambert MP (1917); *General Annual Reports on the Army,* 1 Oct 1913-30 Sep 1919, 1921 XX Cmd 1193; M.I. Thomis, 'The Labour Movement in Great Britain and Compulsory Military Service, 1914-16' (London [King's College] MA, 1959); R. Douglas, 'Voluntary Enlistment in the First World War and the Work of the Parliamentary Recruiting Committee', *J. Mod. Hist.* 42, no. 4 (1970) 564-85. The editors wish to acknowledge the information supplied on the Committee by Dr W.J. Reader, London, D.B. Nash, Imperial War Museum and Mrs J. Fiddick, House of Commons Library.

JOHN SAVILLE

BRAUNTHAL, Julius (1891-1972)
JOURNALIST, SECRETARY OF THE SOCIALIST INTERNATIONAL AND LABOUR HISTORIAN

Julius Braunthal was born in Vienna on 5 May 1891 into a lower middle-class Jewish family. His father, Mayer, who was born at Odessa in 1836, emigrated as a young man to Galicia and afterwards to Vienna; he was a book-keeper. Julius attended the elementary and secondary school, and at the age of fourteen was apprenticed as a bookbinder. He grew up in the deeply religious and unworldly atmosphere which surrounded his father; but in 1905, inspired with Socialist ideas by an older friend, Robert Danneberg, he joined the Socialist youth movement, became chairman of one of its district branches in Vienna (Alsergrund) a year later and wrote his first article (on alcoholism, in *Der jugendliche Arbeiter*) in the same year. He soon came under the spell of Otto Bauer, then already a renowned figure in the Socialist movement, who took a personal interest in his education and was to become his mentor. Under his guidance Julius Braunthal attended evening classes of the educational organisation of the Social Democratic Party and started studying Socialist literature systematically. In 1912 he met Karl Kautsky and Rosa Luxemburg in Berlin, and was greatly influenced by the ideas of the latter.

Bauer was also instrumental in turning Braunthal from bookbinding to journalism. On his recommendation Braunthal was invited in 1912 to join the editorial staff of the Socialist paper *Volksstimme* in Warnsdorf, a small town in Bohemia, which was then a province of the Habsburg empire. There he worked until the outbreak of the First World War. He was against the social-patriotic line on the war, but he was called up, and served in an artillery regiment of the Austro-Hungarian Army. He took part in its Russian and Italian campaigns, in the course of which he was awarded the Medal of Bravery and promoted to Lieutenant. Stationed with his off-shore battery at the Bocche di Cattaro, a naval base of the Austrian fleet in Dalmatia (now Boka Kotorska in Yugoslavia), he witnessed the sailors' mutiny, in February 1918, and succeeded in conveying the news about the event, which was kept strictly secret by the authorities, to the Socialist party leaders. On the basis of his report about the execution of four sailors and the threat to the lives of others they intervened immediately with the Government and succeeded in preventing further executions.

At the end of the war, in October 1918, when the Habsburg monarchy disintegrated and its German provinces constituted themselves as the Austrian Republic, the Social Democratic Party formed a coalition government, headed by Karl Renner (1870-1950), with Otto Bauer as its Foreign Secretary; Julius Braunthal was appointed adjutant to the Secretary of Defence, Julius Deutsch (1884-1968), who was faced with the task of constructing a republican army in place of the Habsburg Army which had been dissolved. Braunthal joined the national executive committee of the revolutionary Soldiers' Councils and founded and edited a Socialist weekly for the forces, *Der Freie Soldat*. When the Social Democratic Party resigned from the Government in November 1920, he became a political editor of the leading Socialist daily, *Arbeiter-Zeitung*, and in 1923, acting editor of the theoretical monthly *Der Kampf*. A year earlier, he was sent by the International Federation of Trade Unions on a goodwill mission to Georgia in the Soviet Union, then afflicted by famine and epidemics, to present its Government with a shipload of medical supplies which had been purchased with money subscribed by members of the European trade unions and Socialist parties.

In 1927 he launched a popular Socialist daily with a mass circulation, *Das Kleine Blatt*, and became consequently an *ex officio* member of the national executive committee of the Social Democratic Party and a joint director of its publishing house. He founded and edited three Socialist weeklies: *Der Kuckuck, Die bunte Woche* and *Der Rundfunk* and was a member of the executive committee of the para-military organisation Der Republikanische Schutzbund, founded by the Social Democratic Party as a counter to the rising Fascist threat in Austria. When Dollfuss assumed dictatorial powers in 1933, Braunthal published an underground paper on behalf of the Social-Democrats; and on the very day of the Fascist *coup d'état* by Chancellor Dollfuss (12 Feb 1934), he was arrested, together with other leading Socialists, and kept in prison and the concentration camp of Woellersdorf for a year. He was not ill-treated, however.

After he was released – on condition that he left Austria – he first emigrated to Belgium where his brother, also a political refugee, had settled. Braunthal, however, felt himself 'nearer to English civilisation and the British Labour movement than to the Belgian or French' – although at this time he could speak neither English nor French. After a year in Belgium he emigrated to England. At the end of 1936 Braunthal was invited by Sir Stafford Cripps to join the editorial staff of *Tribune,* which was about to be launched. On *Tribune* Braunthal worked under the editorial direction of William Mellor, 'and in close fellowship with my most generous friend Michael Foot' (*In Search of the Millennium*, 321-2). At the weekly editorial meetings Braunthal met Harold Laski, Aneurin Bevan and George Strauss. He also began lecturing for the National Council of Labour Colleges, and became a friend of Frank Horrabin and J.P.M. Millar. Braunthal wrote a number of articles for *Plebs*, the journal of the NCLC. His first was published in March 1938 and the one that probably received most attention (apart from articles on the German question) was entitled 'Socialism and Morality' (July 1941). Its publication led to a vigorous controversy in the columns of *Plebs* including contributions from T.A. Jackson, W.T. Colyer, G.A. White and Frank Horrabin.

In midsummer 1938 he was invited to join Friedrich Adler, secretary of the Labour and Socialist International, as his assistant and editor of *International Information.* The headquarters of the LSI was in Brussels, and Braunthal worked there until the outbreak of war, when it had been agreed he would return to England. During the war years he had various journalistic jobs – for the Foreign Office, the BBC and the U.S. Office of War Information. His most important post in political journalism was his editorship of the *International Socialist Forum*, a supplement of *Left News*, the monthly journal of the Left Book Club. The first issue of the *Forum* was published in *Left News* in June 1941. The original advisory committee to the editor was made up of Harold Laski (chairman); Louis de Brouckère (Belgium); Lydia Ciolkosz (Poland); Louis Lévy (France); Richard Löwenthal (Germany); Oscar Pollak (Austria); Hans Vogel (Germany). The *Forum* became an important outlet for many of the emigré Socialist groups and parties who found a home in London during the war years. Braunthal himself was especially concerned with two major political problems: the first was the question of German 'guilt' and the opposition to Vansittartism, and the second was the political basis upon which the Socialist International could be re-created after the war.

In an early number of the *ISF* (1 July 1941) he attacked the opinions of James Walker, whose presidential address to the annual conference of the Labour Party had argued that it was not possible to separate the German people from the German Government; that 'The German people are just as responsible for the acts of their Government as that Government itself.' Braunthal noted that these sentiments were contrary to the Labour Party's statement of peace aims laid down in the policy declaration, *Labour, the War and the Peace*, decided upon by the executive on 9 February 1940 and endorsed by the annual conference which met in Bournemouth at Whitsuntide, 1940. James Walker replied to Braunthal with a long letter published in the

September 1941 issue of the *Forum*; and these two statements were the beginning of a vigorous debate on the question of German 'guilt'. H.N. Brailsford followed Walker in October 1941, and in November the whole issue was given over to a symposium on 'the German problem', with further contributions in subsequent numbers. The German question and the re-creation of the Socialist International became inextricably linked, and the arguments were further elaborated in a symposium on 'The Need for International Labour Unity' introduced by Harold Laski in the January 1943 number of the *Forum*, and continued in the following months. At its conclusion in May 1943 Braunthal wrote a vigorous article which first attacked the executive of the former Labour and Socialist International for their failure to maintain the International as a viable organisation during the early months of war and then bitterly criticised the substitution of nationalistic ideas in place of the principles of international Socialism. 'There are prominent Socialists of some countries,' he wrote, 'who seem to have extinguished even the last vestige of the international concept of Socialism.' And he continued:

> If Socialists turn into nationalists and compete in imperialist ambitions and national hatred, how can there be an object common to the international working-class movement? In fact, beyond the desire to defeat the Axis Powers, there is no common object between, say, the Polish and Ukrainian Socialists, the Czech and Sudeten-Germans, the Polish and the Czech, the Lithuanian and the Polish Socialists. And how can one find an object common to German Socialists and to those Socialists who regard this war not as a war against Germany's ruling class alone, but against Germany's working class as well, aiming at its destruction by means of the dismemberment and the de-industrialisation of Germany? If such is the spiritual constitution of a number of responsible Socialists, then the revival of the Socialist International appears indeed inconceivable.

Braunthal developed his ideas more thoroughly in his book *Need Germany survive?*, published as a Left Book Club edition in 1943, with a preface by Harold Laski. Braunthal was primarily concerned to answer the arguments of Vansittart and R.D'O. Butler (*The Roots of National Socialism, 1783-1933* (1941)); but the concluding part of his book argued the case for the re-establishment of the Socialist International. He continued writing on these themes until the end of the war and into the post-war period, with the question of German collective 'guilt' remaining an explosive issue, which sharply divided social-democratic groups and parties. In 1945 Braunthal published his memoirs, *In Search of the Millennium*. This, too, was a Left Book Club choice, with a preface by H.N. Brailsford. It is an interesting book, which in its closing pages has much to say about the lack of international understanding on the part of many of the Socialist parties in the years immediately preceding the outbreak of war in 1939; and he is notably critical of William Gillies, secretary of the British Labour Party's foreign department. German Socialists were excluded from the International Consultative Committee established in London by the British Labour Party soon after the outbreak of war, and a conference of European Socialist parties in March 1945, which adopted a *Statement on the German Problem*, excluded German, Austrian and Sudeten-German Socialists from their deliberations. Braunthal vigorously attacked both this exclusion and the *Statement* itself for its lack of international principles.

With the victory over European Fascism in May 1945 there was a slow coming together of Socialist parties on a world scale. The Committee of the International Socialist Conference (Comisco) prepared the way for the formation of a new International. At the end of 1949 Braunthal, from a shortlist of four, was appointed administrative secretary to Comisco, and in 1951 the name was changed to Socialist International. Braunthal became its first general secretary. He was particularly concerned with the development of Socialist parties in Asia, and he worked closely with the Asian Socialist Conference, attending its Bureau meeting in Tokyo in 1954, and its Congress in Bombay in 1956. He retired from the International in 1956 at the age of sixty-five; and soon after spent about six months on a lecture tour through south-east Asia and Israel.

Braunthal began his career as a labour historian in his own right only after his retirement, although he had already been acting as adviser and critic to G.D.H. Cole's seven volume *History of Socialist Thought*, and wrote the preface to the last (posthumous) volume. He was, in Dame Margaret Cole's words, 'a most careful and friendly critic'. In his farewell speech to the fourth Congress of the Second International in 1955, Braunthal pledged himself to write a history of the International in his retirement. He accomplished the work in three massive volumes, the last published in 1971. During his retirement he also wrote a dual biography of Victor Adler (1852-1918) and Friedrich Adler (1879-1960), and a biographical essay on Otto Bauer (1881-1938) as an introduction to a selection of his writings. In 1952 he had become a member of the Board of the International Institute of Social History in Amsterdam; and the work of the Institute remained very close to his heart for the rest of his life.

For the greater part of his active life, Braunthal was a militant journalist, speaker and writer of the Austro-Marxist school of thought, much involved in the dispute between the ideologies of democratic Socialism and Communism; he was indeed an unrelenting critic of the Communist regime of the U.S.S.R. Yet he shared Otto Bauer's belief in the feasibility of transforming the autocratic structure of the Soviet Union into a Socialist democracy, and he regarded Socialist criticism of the prevailing system of the Soviet Union as an indispensable factor in the process of its evolution towards a freer and more human form of Socialism. He contributed to newspapers and periodicals in many countries, also to the *Encyclopaedia Britannica*, and wrote a number of pamphlets and books. He attended all conferences of the Austrian Social Democratic Party from 1907 until it was suppressed in 1934, and all congresses of the Socialist International from 1921 until 1955.

At the age of eighty, Braunthal concluded his history of the International with a declaration of faith. He wrote:

Socialism is an optimistic belief, a belief in man's capacity for regeneration, in his development to ever higher stages of civilisation. This belief had its theoretical foundations in Marx.

But the vision of Socialism is no utopia. It arose from social and economic necessities. And it has been for half a century in process of realisation: in a third of the world in the form of the communist system of domination, and in a further third under systems of social democracy. It is the predominant tendency in the development of a new age for humanity [Braunthal's own translation from the German edition published in 1971].

On his seventy-fifth birthday in 1966, Braunthal received from the national executive of the Austrian Social Democratic Party the Victor-Adler Tablet, and on his eightieth birthday he was awarded the honorary title of professor by the Austrian Federal President and invested with the Order of the Cross of Merit First Class by the German Federal President. He also received the Prize of the City of Vienna for Literature and the Silver Medal of the Knesset.

In 1917 he married Ernestine Gernreich, also born in Vienna (on 26 August 1889). They had two sons, who for the most part received their education in England and who joined the British armed forces during the Second World War. The elder son, Frederick Gustav, remained in the British Army and concluded his military career as a Lt-Colonel in the Royal Corps of Signals. The younger son, Thomas Otto, served during the war as a district officer in Eritrea, afterwards obtained a degree in Arabic at London University, and entered the Colonial Service as an Assistant District Commissioner in Sierra Leone. He later turned to journalism and became Press Officer of the International Confederation of Free Trade Unions.

Braunthal, who became a British subject in 1948, died at his home in Teddington, Middlesex, on 28 April 1972, and was cremated at South Middlesex Crematorium on 3 May. He left an estate valued at £1058 and was survived by his wife and sons.

Writings: *Die Sozialpolitik der Republik* (Vienna, 1919) 49 pp.; *Die Arbeiterräte in Deutschösterreich* (Vienna, 1919) 55 pp.; *Kommunisten und Sozialdemokraten* (Vienna, 1920) 52 pp.; *Von Kommunismus zum Imperialismus. Bilder aus dem bolschewistischen Georgien*

(Vienna, 1922); 'The Bolshevist Conquest of Georgia', *Soc. Rev. 20*, no. 10 (Nov 1922) 209-13; 'War Resistance in Austria and Germany' in *We did not fight*, ed. J. Bell (1935) 63-94; 'The Hard Facts about Austria', *Plebs 30* (Mar 1938) 55-7; 'Germany and European Security', ibid. *32* (Apr 1940) 94-6; 'War and the Collapse of the Labour and Socialist International', ibid. *32* (Oct 1940) 216-18; 'Socialists and the War', ibid. *32* (Dec 1940) 257-9; 'Revolutionary Defeatism and Disaster', ibid. *33* (Apr 1941) 70-1; 'Nazi Economy and Productivity', ibid. *33* (May 1941) 95-6; 'Guilt and Tragedy of the Germans', *Int. Soc. Forum* (supplement to *Left News*) (July 1941) 1806-8; 'Socialism and Morality', *Plebs 33* (July 1941) 126-8; 'Russia – the Great Opportunity', ibid. *33* (Sep 1941) 167-9; 'The Other Germany – is it a Myth?', ibid. *34* (Feb 1942) 19-20; 'International Labour Unity', *Int. Soc. Forum* (May 1943) 2481-2; *The Future of Austria: a plea for the United States of Europe* [1943] 20 pp.; *Need Germany survive?*, with an Introduction by H. J. Laski (1943); *In Search of the Millennium*, with an Introduction by H.N. Brailsford (1945; repr. in two vols 1948-9); 'Germany and Liberty', *Plebs 38* (Dec 1946) 182; *The Paradox of Nationalism. An epilogue to Nuremberg Trials*, with an Introduction by L. Woolf (1946); Introduction to *Stimme aus dem Chaos* (Eine Auswahl der Schriften von Victor Gollancz) (Nuremberg, 1948); *The Tragedy of Austria*, with an Introduction by M. Foot and an appendix: 'Mussolini and Dollfus. An Episode in Fascist Diplomacy' by P.R. Sweet (1948; Florence, 1955); *Der gegenwärtige Stand der sozialistischen Literatur* (Bielefeld, 1955) 16 pp.; *L'Antitesi Ideologica fra Socialismo e Comunismo*, with an Introduction by A. Schiavi (Rome, 1956); *Ideological Aspects of Socialist-Communist Co-operation*, repr. from *Social Studies* (Patna Univ., [1957]) 31 pp.; 'Socialist Forces in Asia: I, II and III', *Plebs 49* (Nov 1957) 254-5 and (Dec 1957) 283-4; and *50* (Jan 1958) 11-12; *Il Socialismo in Israele*, with an Introduction by A. Schiavi (Rome, [1958]); Editor of *Sozialistische Weltstimmen* (Berlin, [1958]); *The Significance of Israeli Socialism and the Arab-Israeli Dispute*, with an Introduction by J.B. Kripalani (1958); *International Socialism and Israel* (1959); *Il Socialismo in Asia*, with an Introduction by A. Schiavi (Rome, 1959); 'Trotsky – the Symbol of Tragedy', *Plebs 51* (Dec 1959) 247-8; 'Socialism in Asia' ibid. *52* (May 1960) 106-7; 'China, Russia and International Communism', ibid. *53* (May 1961) 402; *Geschichte der Internationale*, 3 vols (Hanover, 1961, 1963 and 1971 with English translation of vol. *1* (1966) and vol. *2* (1967); *Otto Bauer. Einè Auswahl aus seinem Lebenswerk mit einem Lebensbild Otto Bauers* (Vienna, 1961); 'Why the World Labour Movement split', *Plebs 56* (June 1964) 122-5; 'A Hundred Years of International Socialism', ibid. *56* (Sep 1964) 204-6; *Victor und Friedrich Adler. Zwei Generationen Arbeiterbewegung* (Vienna, [1965]).

Sources: (1) MSS: Julius Braunthal Archives, and Archives of the Socialist International: International Institute of Social History, Amsterdam. (2) Other: R.D'O. Butler, *The Roots of National Socialism 1783-1933* (1941); *Socialist International Information*, vol. *16* (1966) 100; *TLS*, 25 May 1967; 1 Feb 1968; 13 Aug 1971; [A list of Professor Braunthal's published works and of the works he has edited etc. was printed in *Archiv. Mitteilungsblatt des Vereins für Geschichte der Arbeiterbewegung 9*, no. 2 (1969) 48-51]; *Geschichte der Internationale*, vol. *3* (1971) [ms. English translation by J. Braunthal]; *Die Zukunft* (May 1971); *Socialist Affairs* (May 1971); *Dictionnaire Biographique du Mouvement Ouvrier International* vol. *1* : *L'Autriche* (Paris, 1971) 56-7; personal information: Mrs E. Braunthal, Teddington, widow; T.O. Barry-Braunthal, Belgium, son; Dame Margaret Cole, London; Drs J.R. van der Leeuw, International Institute of Social History, Amsterdam. OBIT. *Times*, 1 May 1972; *Tribune*, 5 May 1972 [by A.J. Day].

NOTE. A few months before his death, the editors prevailed upon Julius Braunthal to set down the details of his life and the short memoir he produced has been used mainly for his career before he left Austria in 1935.

JOHN SAVILLE

See also: *Harold Joseph LASKI; †William MELLOR.

BURNS, John Elliott (1858-1943)
LABOUR LEADER AND LIBERAL MINISTER

John Burns was born in Lambeth on 20 October 1858, the son of Alexander Burns, an engineer from Scotland who had moved south during the 1850s to search for work, and his wife Barbara (née Smith). The large Burns family – he was one of eighteen children, nine of whom survived infancy – soon moved to a basement dwelling in Battersea and were compelled to live in what Burns himself later called 'the adverse conditions peculiar to children of artisans who have a precarious existence'. Assiduous attendance at night school together with an abstemious style of life enabled him to save enough to become an apprentice engineer, even though he left school at the age of ten or eleven. By his teens he had already developed the love of books that remained with him for the rest of his life, and he avidly devoured advanced political literature and works on the history of London. This reading together with his straitened domestic circumstances combined to produce a critical attitude towards the existing social system and an unwillingness to accept authority without question; his first two employers both cancelled his indentures. He was able to complete his time, however, at Mowlems, then one of the biggest contractors in the South. It was there that he met Victor Delahaye, a refugee from the Paris Commune, member of the London based Comité Revolutionnaire du Prolétariat, and one of the formative influences in the development of Burns's political outlook. Among other things, Delahaye impressed on Burns his belief that the working class, lacking effective physical force and organisation, could only throw off capitalism by means of the ballot box.

In 1878 Burns had his first direct brush with authority when he was arrested for defying a ban on public speaking on Clapham Common. Among the audience who protested against his arrest was Martha Charlotte Gale, who in 1882 became his wife. By then Burns had spent two years in Africa working for the United African Company, an experience that served to confirm Delahaye's expositions about the predatory nature of capitalism. It was in Africa, he said later, that he finally became a Socialist, and when he returned home in 1881 he threw himself vigorously into London's political life.

The upsurge of Socialist activity which took place in Britain in the 1880s focused largely on the issues of free speech and unemployment and it was in the course of his continuing struggle for free speech that Burns first came into contact with the SDF. The Federation's predominantly middle-class leadership welcomed the new recruit eagerly, partly because of his working-class background, but mainly because of his brilliance as a street orator. Even H.M. Hyndman, who later had barely one good word to say for Burns, had to admit that he was 'the best stump orator I ever heard' [Hyndman (1911) 342]. By 1884 Burns had been elected to the Federation executive and in the split which produced the Socialist League at the beginning of 1885 he sided firmly with Hyndman in his advocacy both of a programme of palliative reforms and of parliamentary action.

Later in 1885 Burns, standing as a Socialist, contested Nottingham West in the general election and, although he was soundly beaten, his 598 votes compared very favourably with the derisory totals raised by other Federation candidates at Hampstead and Kennington. Burns was never an advocate of violent revolution. He was more interested in social change than in the means by which it was to be secured, and most of his actions and speeches indicate that he favoured peaceful parliamentary change. Yet there was an ambivalence in his thinking and briefly in the middle years of the 1880s he was tempted by the possibilities of force, as heavy unemployment and repressive police action combined to produce serious disturbances in London. For his part in West End riots following an SDF unemployment march to Trafalgar Square in 1886 Burns was arrested on a charge of riot but acquitted. He was not so fortunate in the following year, however. In November 1887 the Metropolitan Police Commissioner, Sir Charles Warren, imposed a ban on all public meetings in Trafalgar Square in order to appease the numerous local traders and residents who had protested about repeated SDF rallies in the area. The ban offended Irish Home Rulers who had been planning a protest demonstration against the arrest of one of their MPs. It also offended the advocates of free speech, and thus the Metropolitan Radical Federation, an umbrella organisation for advanced radicals in the capital, decided to contest this ruling. On 13 November fighting broke out in several parts of London as demonstrators tried to get to the square, and order was only restored when troops were called in. Burns and the radical MP, R.B. Cunninghame Graham, who together led an assault on the police cordon round the square, were both arrested and received six-week prison sentences. It was in this period that Burns made most of the militant speeches which have so often been cited as proof of his early revolutionary fervour. Yet there is evidence to suggest that many of his remarks were taken out of context, and that he was often tempted into oratorical excesses because he loved the adulation this evoked among his hearers. At most, therefore, Burns may have believed – briefly – that violence could work. But it was never more than a passing phase in his thinking. He openly voiced disgust at the way in which so many of the rioters had apparently been more interested in pillage and theft than in social change, and almost as soon as he left Pentonville he began to decry the political apathy of the masses, turning instead towards the trade union movement as a more promising vehicle of social change.

Even before the riots of 1886 and 1887 he had been coming to the conclusion that the SDF was too dogmatic and narrow in its approach ever to win the wider support that was in his view necessary to secure change. His fears were confirmed when at the meeting arranged to celebrate his release from prison Hyndman launched into a violent harangue against the radicals with whom he was sharing the platform. After the party conference in 1888 Burns noted that 'the SDF as a national body must be remodelled not to say merged with other bodies 'ere it does good work' [Burns Diary, quoted Brown (1977) 36]. Any hope of this, however, was destroyed by the constant bickering within the Federation's ranks and by Hyndman's refusal to countenance any such co-operation. He made determined efforts to drive out H.H. Champion, who was openly espousing the cause of the Labour Electoral Association and its programme of backing independent working-class candidacies for Parliament. Hyndman wanted any successful candidates to wage unceasing class warfare in the House of Commons. Burns supported Champion's view that they should co-operate with everybody in the effort to secure reform.

Notwithstanding his rupture with the national leadership of the SDF, Burns continued to receive the backing of the Battersea branch which he had founded and in which he commanded a strong personal loyalty. It was this branch that took the initiative in putting him up for election to the newly-created London County Council at the beginning of 1889. Burns was returned at the top of poll, a victory which was not so surprising as many contemporaries made out. In a predominantly working-class constituency which by the standards of the late nineteenth century was quite highly unionised, Burns was a well-known champion of working-class interests whose credentials included a six-week prison sentence, and membership of several friendly societies, of the local parliamentary debating society, and of the Amalgamated Society of Engineers.

Barely had the LCC begun its work, however, when Burns was drawn into the great dock strike which threatened to paralyse London. He had long been a strident critic of the old trade unionism as exemplified by Henry Broadhurst and George Shipton and had welcomed the progress made at recent TUC conferences by Socialist ideas and also the signs that hitherto unorganised groups of workers were at last showing signs of restlessness. This was certainly true of the docks, which for years had been among his favourite recruiting-grounds. Indeed, he had himself worked there briefly in 1887, and in 1889 he had helped to inaugurate a union in the Victoria and Albert Dock. Not surprisingly, therefore, he joined in the struggle with considerable enthusiasm, knowing that he was free of the financial worries which had always dogged him before. As his reputation as a trouble-maker had grown so he had found it increasingly difficult to keep a job, but after his success in the LCC elections he was now paid from a specially-created local wages fund, administered by what ultimately became the Battersea Labour League. Although he performed an administrative role in the dock dispute as a member of the United Strike Committee, and also acted as one of the men's chief negotiators, Burns's main contribution lay in his golden voice and his flair for publicity. Almost daily he gave press conferences and led the strikers into the West End. By the time the strike ended, with the men gaining what Burns in one of his most famous speeches had called 'the full round orb of the dockers' tanner', he had become something of a folk hero and in 1890 he was elected to the Parliamentary Committee of the TUC. His relative moderation during the strike had also considerably improved his image with the middle classes who had regarded him as the villain of 1886 and 1887. This cleared the way for the Battersea Liberal and Radical Association to support his candidature for the parliamentary constituency in place of the retiring Liberal member. Mindful of his LCC success and his enormous popularity with working-class voters the Association had in fact approached Burns even before the strike, but in the face of his insistence on standing as a Socialist had tentatively selected an outside candidate. When Burns was nominated almost by public acclaim at the Battersea Town Hall in October 1889 the outsider withdrew and most local Association members ultimately backed Burns, who was further strengthening his claims by his energetic display in the affairs of the LCC.

The seventy Progressives who formed the majority on the first LCC were a heterogeneous mixture of manufacturers, gentlemen, and retired servicemen, but even in this assorted and highly-motivated company Burns soon surged to a position of prominence. The few personal references contained in the various Council committee minute books confirm the judgement of one official that Burns was 'very vocal' and that 'his voice influenced more votes in the Council than that of any other member'. In general terms Burns devoted his time to furthering the interests of London's working people and in 1892 the *South Western Star* commented with some justice that he had 'made himself a kind of inspector-general of London's labourers, and he and others have gone down sewers, investigated pumping stations, looked into personal and staff grievances.' In particular, however, he indulged in a relentless pursuit of those contractors employed on Council works who refused to pay adequate wages or who went in for sub-contracting, a practice widely opposed by Progressives on the grounds that it fostered bad workmanship, long hours, and sweating. Burns pushed hard both for a direct works department and for trade union wages to be imposed on contractors, but at this stage could get nothing more than a recommendation that contractors should be required to pay *fair* wages.

In the LCC elections of 1892 the Progressives once more swept the board and this time their majority included several more Labour councillors. With their support Burns was able to renew his campaign for union rates to be made mandatory on contractors, and the Council finally approved his resolution to this effect in May 1892. Even though this stipulation had run into opposition from Progressives fearful that Burns was trying to foist some sort of trade union tyranny on to London he was not content to rest there. The campaign to establish a works department was excellently co-ordinated by its supporters with Burns once more figuring prominently. It was his colleague, John Benn, who finally moved the resolution calling on the general purposes committee to draw up a plan to establish a new works department; and it was indicative of the amount of preparation that had gone into this campaign that a scheme was produced and discussed as early as November 1892. Burns had been the moving spirit behind the whole campaign and there was much truth in his comment that the establishment of the works department represented the 'biggest thing yet done for Collectivism and into which I have put as much time, energy and ability for four years as for any piece of work I have yet undertaken' [Burns Diary, quoted Brown (1977) 67].

Although Burns continued to serve on the LCC until 1907 and figured prominently in the Progressive campaign to establish a municipal steamboat service on the Thames, his influence waned after about 1894. He was increasingly content to be a devoted committee man, serving variously on the contracts, main drainage, bridges, rivers, technical education, fire brigade, historical monuments, parliamentary and general purposes committees. In part, his relative loss of influence sprang from the growing hold of party politics in Council affairs which made it difficult for an individual, even one as forceful as Burns, to make his weight felt. Moreover, new issues were coming to the fore in London politics, notably the control of water supplies and transport. Burns was a firm believer in the municipalisation of both utilities but was not really very interested. He preferred to continue his own battles against contractors on behalf of public employees, in the new arena of the House of Commons to which he had been elected, with the aid of the Labour League, in 1892. Burns's successes in the LCC had convinced him of the effectiveness of his policy of co-operating 'with everyone with a grievance. This policy has done more for socialism than all the preaching about the class war' [Burns papers, BL Add. MSS 46305 ff. 96-7]. Once in Parliament, therefore, he was drawn almost inevitably towards Liberals of the sort with whom he had co-operated in the Council, a process reinforced by the fact that he found it virtually impossible to work harmoniously with the other leading labour member in the 1892-5 Parliament, Keir Hardie. Having been reared on the secular Socialism of London, Burns was more than suspicious of Hardie's northern Socialism couched in terms of the New Testament. His experience of the LCC had persuaded him that it was worth while to learn the rules and work within the system; hence his irritation with what he saw as Hardie's preference for histrionics and lack of interest in correct parliamentary procedure. But at bottom the clash was basically about the meaning of Labour independence. Hardie had come to believe that within a broad progressive alliance a Labour party had to exist as a recognisably separate and independent entity. Burns, on the other hand, wanted to preserve his freedom to act with anyone who could be helpful on particular issues, irrespective of whether they agreed on all other matters. Nor did he relish the prospect of having his actions determined by a party whip; and this explains why he was so opposed to the ILP, which Hardie launched in 1893, fearing that its stress on party allegiance and orthodoxy would alienate and mislead the working class in the same way that the sectarianism of the SDF had done. This was why he supported – though he did not, as has often been claimed, initiate – moves to emasculate ILP influence within the TUC in 1894 by means of changes in the Standing Orders.

Burns attended the founding conference of the LRC in 1900 but once more argued that it was unrealistic to demand allegiance to a party programme and pointed out with some justification that as leader of the unofficial group of 'Lib-Lab' MPs since 1895 he had been able to make labour's voice quite effectively heard on matters such as workmen's compensation. Even their common opposition to the Boer War did no more than produce a temporary papering over of differences, for Burns remained oddly aloof from the organised anti-war movement, conducting a private opposition in his own constituency. In the years after the war Hardie made further attempts to capture him, but while Burns did sterling work in leading the 'Lib-Lab' MPs, especially in debates on the Trade Disputes Bill in 1904 and 1905, he ignored Hardie's approaches.

All the while his connections with the Liberals had been growing stronger. Despite the superficially Marxist ring about his opposition to the Boer War he really opposed it on the orthodox radical grounds of its imperialist origins and its cost, both human and financial. Work on the Trade Disputes Bills strengthened his links with the Liberal lawyers. When Chamberlain launched his tariff campaign in 1903 Burns's violent reaction caused the Liberal leaders to turn to him as an authentic voice of working-class protest and by the end of 1904 they were regarding him as a likely member of the next Cabinet. Certainly at a time when organised labour was planning its first major intervention in an election it made sense to draw some of its fire by including in the Government a man of Burns's background and experience. This at least was the argument used by John Morley in putting Burns's claims to Campbell-Bannerman. Ultimately Burns was given the Presidency of the Local Government Board, which he held until 1914. For most historians, however, the length of his tenure was in inverse proportion to its fruitfulness. It was Mrs Webb's explanation that has been generally accepted – that Burns's egotism made him so susceptible to praise that the highly conservative officials of the Board were able to flatter him into incompetence and reaction. But Beatrice Webb was hardly a disinterested observer, for Burns was the main obstacle on which her own ambitious plans for restructuring the Poor Law foundered. Her interpretation ignores the nature of the views Burns held by 1906, the institutional difficulties with which he had to contend, and aspects of his character more significant than his egotism.

Burns was not flattered into reaction by his civil servants. By 1906 his views on poverty, for instance, were not markedly dissimilar from those already prevailing in the corridors of the LGB. He believed that pauperism was caused partly by bad environmental conditions and partly by personal failings such as drunkenness and thriftlessness. His policies at the Board were therefore designed to remedy some of the environmental problems. Thus the Housing and Town Planning Act of 1909 introduced for the first time the principle of municipal home ownership and conferred wide permissive planning powers on local authorities, allowing them to ensure that considerations of amenity, health and welfare were duly weighed in local building development. The occurrence of tuberculosis in poor law institutions was made notifiable; a crusade against infant mortality was launched; and the trend within poor law administration to develop specialist institutions to deal with specific categories of pauper was continued. Burns's total conviction that this programme was successful in improving the environment led him naturally to the conclusion that most surviving poverty was due solely to character defects and thus required a punitive rather than a therapeutic approach. Behind his suspicion of labour colonies and insurance, for example, lay the fear that the Government was subsidising malingerers. His censoriousness was reinforced by the strong puritanical streak that made him a lifelong opponent of drinking and gambling, and also by a very parsimonious approach towards government expenditure. He was not, of course, nearly as successful as he imagined – but he did achieve more at the LGB than he is usually credited with.

The real reasons for his relative lack of success lie not so much in his egotism, which was considerable, as in a combination of institutional difficulties and his administrative and executive qualities. The LGB did not possess the necessary statistical expertise that would have facilitated positive approaches to questions of unemployment and infant mortality. A further obstacle was the poor quality of the staff with whom Burns had to work. Clerks in the LGB were generally regarded as being inferior to their equivalents in other departments and the standard was low. The first Oxbridge graduate had not been recruited until the 1880s. Nor were the senior officials much better. The permanent head of the LGB, Sir Samuel Provis, was old and nearing the end of an official career that he had devoted to upholding the principles of the 1834 Poor Law Amendment Act. Almost to a man the poor law inspectorate, shared the reactionary disposition of their chief, J.S. Davy. The Board's legal adviser, Alfred Adrian, was totally incompetent and several of Burns's bills, particularly the 1908 version of the Housing Bill had to be withdrawn and re-submitted because they had been so poorly drafted. When Robert Morant was discussing the possibilities of himself replacing Provis as head of the LGB he made it clear that he would not work with Adrian, who would have to go. Finally, the whole Board was enmeshed in procedural red tape of the most cloying kind, and there is plenty of evidence in Burns's diaries for 1906 and 1907 that he found this highly frustrating.

In the end, however, Burns seems to have given up the effort to invigorate his department and it is to this essential lack of will and other aspects of his character that the historian must also look in seeking to understand his ministerial performance. For one thing, he insisted on being personally involved in all aspects of departmental work. His repeated excursions to visit projects and institutions for which the LGB was responsible were laudable enough but they tended to obscure a wider vision and often on the strength of one such visit he would override the opinions of his technical advisers. Frequently he himself dealt with minor correspondence that might more properly have been left to his subordinates, and generally he lost sight of the wood for the trees. His diary, for instance, reveals a disproportionately childish delight in the passage of the Burials Bill in 1906, although it was nothing more than a measure designed to remove an ambiguity in earlier legislation. Again, Burns's intellectual ability was limited. He lacked the mental equipment necessary to develop an unemployment policy which was anything more than an attack on the character of the unemployed. Nor could he cope with the complexities of rate reform, a matter crucial to the financing of the Liberals' welfare programme. He could do no more than be guided by his officials, who took three years to produce a measure so cautious that it was swiftly overtaken by the alternative proposals contained in Lloyd George's famous budget of 1909. Burns's intellectual dullness also manifested itself in his difficulties in steering bills through Parliament, prompting the remark of a colleague that he 'flunks his bills'. W.H. Beveridge observed that Burns was not 'very good at explaining the complicated provisions of a Bill in Committee'; and one reason why Burns did not implement more of the Poor Law Commission reports was that he could not bring himself to tackle legislation of the magnitude that would have been entailed.

At the beginning of 1914 Asquith offered Burns the Presidency of the Board of Trade. After the legislative achievements there of Lloyd George and Churchill, this department's chief requirement was for an administrator, and that Asquith gave Burns the job confirms that he at least had been impressed with Burns's administrative record at the LGB, where he had kept him for six years. Burns leapt at the chance of a move. For three or four years previously he had been expressing in his diary his dissatisfaction with the monotony of LGB work and in moments of real depression he even longed for a return to back-bench politics or considered a return to the Labour fold. That he even could think in these latter terms, after the way in which his policies, especially on unemployment, had outraged the Labour Party, was evidence of his growing capacity for self-delusion. So, too, was his oft-repeated claim that only a sense of loyalty to his colleagues and his call to be the champion of the working class was preventing his resignation. Despite the impression given in his diaries, Burns played a very minor part in general Cabinet affairs.

When the First World War broke out in August 1914 he resigned, feeling that here was an issue close to the heart of his political faith and one worthy of resignation. It is clear that he felt unable to support a war which in his view was being fought mainly for the territorial aggrandisement of France and Russia. He had always been an advocate of British isolation and the discovery of Grey's secret commitment to aid the French came as a terrible shock. Both financial and human costs would, he believed, fall most heavily on the working classes, of whom he considered himself the special representative, and he therefore refused to have anything to do with the war. But Burns never spelled out publicly the reasons for his resignation, and myth inevitably accumulated around it and also round his subsequent silence. The latter is explicable once more in terms of his self-delusion. He genuinely believed, and this occurred in several diary entries, that any pronouncement from him against the war would seriously damage the Government. Thus he refused several requests to speak out against it and held aloof from formal anti-war bodies like the Union of Democratic Control, with most of whose radical members he would have been quite out of sympathy.

For a time Burns was a member of the government committee established to deal with distress arising from the war. He also served as chairman of the London Relief Committee where he renewed his antagonism with Mrs Webb, mainly over the scales of relief to be paid. Burns feared that too much generosity would encourage malingering. Burns resigned from both committees during the summer of 1915, by which time the war effort had mopped up most employable labour. Thereafter he devoted his time to fighting the commercial interests which, he believed, were threatening the amenities of London under cover of the war. Most importantly he led the campaign to prevent the South Eastern Railway Company from strengthening its ugly iron bridge across the Thames at Charing Cross.

With the ending of war in 1918 Burns found himself in a political void. The Liberal Party had formally disowned him in 1915 for his anti-war attitude and it was in any case divided. Burns had been a long-standing admirer of Asquith, but his faith in his old leader had collapsed when he allowed himself to be outmanoeuvred by Lloyd George, for whom Burns had no time at all. Although in earlier days they had lived close to each other and been involved in many radical causes, Burns had long since grown to distrust the Welshman. In 1912 he had received a severe dressing-down from Asquith for spreading stories about Lloyd George's designs on the premiership. Lloyd George's lax morals and his involvement in the Marconi scandal both outraged Burns, who was a pillar of financial and personal respectability. With a Lloyd George-coalition candidate already in the field for North Battersea, Burns tentatively accepted nomination by the Labour League. During the war, however, the League had affiliated to the Labour Party and Burns was faced once more with the prospect of having to subscribe to the Party programme and of having to act at the dictates of a Party whip. Both requirements were contrary to his convictions and his experience, and in November he withdraw his nomination and ended his public career.

For a few years he tantalised both himself and the public with speculation about his imminent return to politics but, even had he been sure where his political niche lay, the truth was that he had had enough. He had only clung to office before the war out of an ill-conceived sense of calling and the war had been long enough to permit him to indulge his hobbies – he had found great satisfaction, for instance, in conducting parties of visitors round the historic places connected with Westminster – and to break down the disciplines of a lifetime. Diary entries, which had been faithfully made for thirty years, grew sparser and finally dried up altogether in 1920. Several opportunities presented themselves for him to return to public life, either at municipal or parliamentary level, but he refused them all. After 1922, when the son on whom he had doted with a fierce possessive love since his birth in 1895 suddenly died, Burns retreated even more into his private shell. Martha died in 1936 and thereafter Burns made few public appearances, though still attending diligently to his one remaining public duty as a life trustee of the Strathcona Leper Colony. He reviewed many books about the history of London, on which he was an expert, pursued his lifelong interest in cricket and browsed for hours in the bookshops, adding to his unique collection of works on Thomas More. For the last thirty years or so of his life, Burns lived on a Carnegie pension of £1000 a year [*News Chronicle*, 25 Jan 1943]. He died on 24 January 1943. Although the only will found dated from 1911 he left an estate worth £15,137, to which must be added the amount raised by the sale of his books, over £25,000.

Writings: *The Man with the Red Flag* [speech at Old Bailey Trial 5-10 Apr 1886] (1886) 15 pp.; *Trafalgar Square: Speech for the Defence* [when tried himself at the Old Bailey, 16 Jan 1888] (1888) 16 pp.; 'The Great Strike', *New Rev. 1* (1889) 412-22; *Trade Unionism, past, present and future* (Rotherham, 1890) 9 pp.; *Speech on the Liverpool* [TUC] *Congress* (1890) 31 pp.; *LCC Election Address* (1892); 'The London County Council no.1: towards a Commune', *19th C. 31* (Mar 1892) 496-514; 'Let London live!', ibid. (Apr 1892) 673-85; *The Unemployed* (Fabian Tract no. 47: 1893) 18 pp. [repr., with additions, from *19th C.* (Dec 1892)]; *Parliamentary Election Address* (1895); 'The Massacres in Turkey', *19th C. 40* (Oct 1896) 665-70; *The Eight Hour Day* (1897); 'Risks and Casualties of Labour', *CWS Annual* (Manchester, 1899) 383-408 [repr. as *Labour's Death Roll: the tragedy of toil* (Clarion Pamphlet no. 29: 1899) 24 pp.; *South African War: the trail of the financial serpent* [report of House of Commons speech, 6 Feb 1900] (Stop the War Committee, 1900) 7 pp.; *War against the Two Republics: a speech in Battersea Park* (Stop the War Committee, 1900) 7 pp.; *Brains better than Bets or Beer. The Straight Tip to the Workers* [speech, 4 Jan 1902] (Clarion Pamphlet no. 36: 1902) 16 pp.; *Municipal Socialism* [a reply to *The Times*] (Clarion Pamphlet no. 37: 1902) 15 pp.; 'The Political Dangers of Protection' in H.W. Massingham, *Labour and Protection* (1903) 1-37; *Labour and Free Trade* (1903); *Bondage for Black, Slavery for Yellow* (1904) 20 pp.; *Labour and Drink: a lecture delivered in the Free Trade Hall, Manchester, 31 Oct 1904* (1904, 2nd ed. 1904) 32 pp. (further revised ed., 1914) 46 pp.; *John Burns and Unemployment* [1906] 16 pp.; *Judas Iscariot! John Burns's Verdict on himself* [1908] 16 pp.; *The House of the People is the Homestead of the Nation* [foreword to Housing and Town Planning Act 1909] (1909) 4 pp.; *The Liberal Government and the Condition of the People* [speech at Bradford, 11 Nov 1912] (1912) 11 pp.; (with Aston Webb and R. Blomfield), *The Charing Cross Improvement Scheme* (1916) 21 pp. [repr. from the *Observer*, 8, 15, 22 Oct 1916]; 'London, past and present', *Nation and Athenaeum*, 22 Mar 1930, 854-5.

Sources: (1) MSS: Asquith and Harcourt papers, Bodleian Library, Oxford; Beveridge, Lansbury and Passfield papers, BLPES; Blatchford papers, Manchester Central Reference

Library; John Burns papers (including his Diary), Campbell-Bannerman, Gladstone, and Ripon papers, BL; other papers of John Burns are located at Battersea PL and the Greater London Council Record Office; Elibank papers, NLS; McKenna papers, Churchill College Library, Cambridge; Newman Diary, Ministry of Health and Social Security Library; Newman papers, Wellcome History of Medicine Library, London; Runciman and C.P. Trevelyan papers, Newcastle Univ. Library; Samuel papers, House of Lords Record Office. (2) Newspapers: *Battersea Labour Gazette; Justice; Labour Elector; Poor Law Officers' J.; South Western Star.* (3) Theses: J.A.M. Caldwell, 'Social Policy and Public Administration, 1909-1911 (with special reference to the labour activities of the Board of Trade)' (Nottingham PhD, 1956); J.M. Stevens, 'The London County Council under the Progressives, 1889-1907' (Sussex MA, 1966). (4) Other: W. Saunders, *History of the First London County Council* (1892); Nunquam, 'John Burns and the Labour Party: a protest', *Clarion*, 9 June 1894; G.H. Knott, *Mr John Burns, MP* (1901); J. McCarthy, *British Political Portraits: V. John Burns* (1903); R. Donald, 'Mr John Burns the Workman-Minister' *19th C. and after 59* (Feb 1906) 191-204; 'Mr Burns and the Independent Labour Party', *Spec.*, 6 Apr 1907, 522-3; 'Mr John Burns', ibid., 24 Aug 1907, 249-50; 'Mr Burns', ibid., 31 Oct 1908, 662-3; A.G. Gardiner, *Prophets, Priests and Kings* (1908); A.P. Grubb, *From Candle Factory to British Cabinet: the life story of the Right Hon. John Burns, PC, MP* (1908); 'Mr Burns on the Defensive', *Spec.*, 6 Mar 1909, 368-9; 'Mr Burns and the Housing Bill', ibid., 25 Sep 1909, 447-8; J. Bardoux, 'Un Ministre Ouvrier: le très honorable John Burns' in *Silhouettes D'Outre Manche* (Paris, 1909) 1-31; J. Burgess, *John Burns: the rise and progress of a Right Honourable* (Glasgow, 1911); H.M. Hyndman, *The Record of an Adventurous Life* (1911); idem, *Further Reminiscences* (1912); J. Bardoux, *L'Angleterre radicale: essai de psychologie sociale (1906-1913)* (Paris, 1913); S. and B. Webb, *History of Trade Unionism* (1920 ed.); T. Mann, *Memoirs* (1923); A.G. Gardiner, *John Benn and the Progressive Movement* (1925); W. Sanders, *Early Socialist Days* (1927); B. Tillett, *Memories and Reflections* (1931); H. Haward, *The London County Council from within: forty years' official recollections* (1932); G.F. McCleary, *The Early History of the Infant Welfare Movement* (1933); A. Newsholme, *The Last Thirty Years in Public Health* (1936); L. Masterman, *C.F.G. Masterman: a biography* (1939); G. Newman, *The Building of a Nation's Health* (1939); *DNB* (1941-50) [by G.D.H. Cole]; G.D.H. Cole, *John Burns* (Fabian Biographical Series, no. 14: 1943) 36 pp.; B. Webb, *Our Partnership* (1948); W. Kent, *John Burns. Labour's Lost Leader: a biography* (1950); *Beatrice Webb's Diaries 1912-1924* ed. M.I. Cole (1952); W.H. Beveridge, *Power and Influence* [an autobiography] (1953); W.A. Ross, 'Local Government Board and after: retrospect', *Public Administration 34* (1956) 17-25; F. Bealey, 'Keir Hardie and the Labour Group', *Parliamentary Affairs 10* (1956-7) 81-93, 220-33; W.J. Braithwaite, *Lloyd George's Ambulance Wagon* [Memoirs] (1957); J.A.M. Caldwell, 'The Genesis of the Ministry of Labour', *Public Administration 37* (1959) 367-91; A.E.P. Duffy, 'Differing Policies and Personal Rivalries in the Origins of the Independent Labour Party' *Victorian Studies 6*, no. 1 (1962) 43-65; H. Pelling, *The Origins of the Labour Party 1880-1900* (2nd ed. Oxford, 1965); R. Adam and K. Muggeridge, *Beatrice Webb: a life 1858-1943* (1967); P. Thompson, *Socialists, Liberals and Labour: the struggle for London 1885-1914* (1967); R.M. MacLeod, *Treasury Control and Social Administration: a study of establishment growth at the Local Government Board 1871-1905* (Occasional Papers on Social Administration, no. 23: 1968); J. Lovell, *Stevedores and Dockers: a study of trade unionism in the Port of London, 1870-1914* (1969); F. Honigsbaum, *The Struggle for the Ministry of Health 1914-1919* (Occasional Papers on Social Administration, no. 37: 1970); J. Harris, *Unemployment and Politics: a study in English Social Policy 1886-1914* (Oxford, 1972); S. Pierson, *Marxism and the Origins of British Socialism: the struggle for a new consciousness* (Ithaca, 1973); J. Wilson, *A Life of Sir Henry Campbell-Bannerman* (1973); J. Minett, 'The Housing, Town Planning etc. Act of 1909', *Planner 60* (1974) 676-80; C.J. Wrigley, 'Liberals and the Desire for Working Class Representatives in Battersea, 1886-1922', in *Essays in Anti-Labour History* ed. K.D. Brown (1974) 126-58; K.O. Morgan, *Keir Hardie: radical and socialist* (1975); K.G. Young,

Local Politics and the Rise of Party: the London Municipal Society and the Conservative intervention in local elections, 1894-1963 (Leicester Univ. Press, 1975); K.D. Brown, 'London and the Historical Reputation of John Burns', *London J. 2*, no. 2 (Nov 1976) 226-38; idem, 'John Burns at the Local Government Board: a reassessment', *J. of Social Policy 6*, no. 2 (1977) 157-70; idem, *John Burns* (Royal Historical Society, 1977). OBIT. *Birmingham Post, News Chronicle* and *Times*, 25 Jan 1943; *South Western Star* and *Wandsworth Borough News*, 29 Jan 1943; *Dunfermline Press* and *New Statesman and Nation*, 30 Jan 1943.

KENNETH D. BROWN

See also: †Henry BROADHURST; †Allen Clement EDWARDS; †Harry GOSLING; †Amelia (Amie) Jane HICKS; †Benjamin (Ben) TILLETT, and for New Unionism, 1889-93; †John WARD; †Beatrice WEBB; †Sidney James WEBB.

BUXTON, Charles Roden (1875-1942)
RADICAL AND LIBERAL (later LABOUR) MP

Charles Roden Buxton was born on 27 November 1875, at 14 Grosvenor Crescent, London. He was the third son of Sir Thomas Fowell Buxton, third baronet, and Lady Victoria Noel, daughter of the Earl of Gainsborough and a connection of the Byrons. Roden Buxton's family was wealthy – owning estates in Norfolk and at Warlies, Essex, and a family brewery in Spitalfields (Truman, Hanbury and Buxton) – but he chose to live in a very simple style. The family was distinguished for public service: Charles's great-grandfather, the first Sir Thomas Fowell Buxton, was prominent in the anti-slavery movement, and was nominated by Wilberforce to succeed him as leader of the anti-slavery group in the Commons. At Wilberforce's request he brought forward the motion for abolition.

Charles was educated at Harrow and Trinity College, Cambridge, where he took a first class in the classical tripos in 1897. He had already begun to interest himself in social questions: in the early 1890s he and his elder brother Noel (later Lord Noel-Buxton, below) made a private investigation into the conditions of the London poor. But for some years after coming down from Cambridge he had other occupations: he acted in 1897-8, as private secretary to his father when he was Governor of South Australia, he had a period of ranching in Texas, he was reading for the Bar, and he travelled widely in Europe, generally with Noel. Arising from a visit Noel paid to the Balkans in 1899, where he was shocked by the Turkish treatment of the Macedonian minorities, he and Charles assisted in the formation in 1902 of the Balkan Committee along with H.N. Brailsford and James Bryce. In the same year Charles Buxton was called to the Bar of the Inner Temple but he did not take up a legal career [de Bunsen (1948) 176]. Instead he became Principal of Morley College for Working Men and Women, where he remained until 1910; and in this period he was also the first president of the South London branch of the WEA.

In the general election of 1906 he contested East Hertfordshire as a Liberal but was defeated. He continued his interest in working-class conditions by assisting Noel, who was at that time helping George Edwards, the agricultural labourers' leader. He supported schemes for smallholdings and old age pensions and from 1906 to 1908 edited the *Albany Review* (formerly the *Independent Review*). In January 1908 he tried again to enter Parliament by contesting Ashburton (Mid Devon) as a Liberal but was defeated. In January 1910 he won the seat but lost it at the December election of that year. He had now become an admirer of Ramsay MacDonald and was suspected by some fellow-Liberals of having left-wing leanings. This did not, however, prevent his adoption as Liberal candidate for Central Hackney in 1912. From 1912 to 1914 Buxton was honorary secretary to the Land Enquiry Committee, an unofficial body under government auspices which collected evidence for reform of land tenure and local taxation laws.

In 1914 Buxton joined Graham Wallas's British Neutrality Committee whose aims were to prevent British intervention in a European war and, when their efforts failed, he soon became a member of the Union of Democratic Control, founded shortly after the outbreak of war by Norman Angell, Ramsay MacDonald, E.D. Morel, Arthur Ponsonby and Charles Trevelyan. The UDC's aims were a negotiated peace and general post-war disarmament. After Morel, Charles Buxton was one of its most active members, and one of its financial props, a member of its executive and finance committees and a contributor to its literature.

In spite of his opposition to the war he agreed to accompany his brother Noel on a mission to the Balkans in September 1914 at the request of 'Lloyd George and Winston Churchill to recruit for the Entente' [Evans (1960) 151]. In Bucharest a Turk attempted to assassinate the brothers; Charles was wounded in one lung and Noel had a facial injury. Their mission failed but they received a hero's welcome when they returned to Bulgaria and subsequently a street in Sofia was named 'The Brothers Buxton Street'. In 1915 they published *The War and the Balkans* in which they advocated a federation of Balkan states and denied Italian territorial claims to the area. These ideas were later incorporated in the UDC's publication, *Memorandum on War Aims* (1917).

Dissatisfied with the treatment of enemy nationals interned in England, Buxton in 1915 helped to set up the Emergency Committee for the Relief of Germans, Austrians and Hungarians in our Midst. In an article in *Forward* he attacked the rejection of German peace overtures and asserted that the policy of demanding unconditional surrender would lead to another war. In August 1915, along with Clifford Allen and others, he drew up a 'Peace Mandate', calling for a negotiated peace with neutral countries acting as mediators. It was reported in January 1917 that Buxton and Arthur Ponsonby had smuggled letters to the American Neutral Conference Committee, setting out their views on the falsity of the published war aims of the Allies [*New York Times*, 6 Jan 1917 quoted in *Potted Biographies* (1930) 26]. Buxton became treasurer of the Peace Negotiations Committee, of which Mrs H.M. Swanwick was chairman. In 1917 he supported both the Committee's parliamentary candidate, Albert Taylor, in the Rossendale by-election of February and Fred Pethick-Lawrence, who stood as a Peace candidate in the South Aberdeen by-election in April of that year.

Buxton was one of the early members of the famous 1917 Club (for which see M.A. Hamilton). At the Leeds Convention of 3 June 1917 to welcome the Russian Revolution, he voted against W.C. Anderson's resolution that local workmen's and soldiers' councils should be established to work for peace; but like G.D.H. Cole and Leonard Woolf he supported Brailsford's claim that the Revolution was a gain for democracy. He called for British participation in the peace negotiations of Brest Litovsk, for a change of government in Britain, and for an immediate peace without territorial annexations.

In February 1916 the Central Hackney Liberal and Radical Association had rejected Buxton as their prospective candidate on account of his anti-war activities and in 1917 he joined the ILP, whose policies on peace and foreign affairs generally were like his own. At the 1918 'Coupon' election he stood, unsuccessfully, as ILP candidate for Accrington. He opposed the Versailles Treaty as violating the terms of the armistice and sowing the seeds of future war; and he attacked the Government for its intervention in Russia.

Buxton had married, in 1904, Dorothy Frances Jebb, daughter of the late Arthur Trevor Jebb and niece of the distinguished classical scholar Professor Sir Richard Jebb. His wife shared his devotion to public affairs and along with her and his sister-in-law, Eglantyne Jebb, Lord Parmoor and Pethick-Lawrence, founded the Fight the Famine Council, whose first public meeting was held at the Central Hall, Westminster, on 1 January 1919. The Council was created in an attempt to alleviate some of the distress caused by the continuing blockade of the Central Powers – which Buxton stigmatised as barbaric – and it was a forerunner of the Save the Children Fund. Mrs Buxton was actively associated with her sister Eglantyne in founding the Save the Children Fund in 1920 [Freeman (1965) 19-20]. She also collaborated with her husband in several books.

An advocate of the League of Nations – to which he was a delegate in 1924 and 1930 – Buxton supported President Wilson's fourteen points for peace. He believed in the 'open door' policy for Africa and worked actively for the Mandate Commission of the League. Fluent in a number of languages, he served as interpreter to the British delegation at the meetings of the Second International at Berne and Lucerne in 1919 and Geneva in 1920. In the latter year also he was joint secretary of the Labour Party-Trade Union delegation to Russia. Buxton stayed for a time after the delegation left and lived in a peasant's house, an experience he described in his book, *In a Russian Village* (1922).

Although a member of the ILP delegation in 1922 to the meeting in Vienna of the 'Two and a Half International' – which reunited with the Second International in 1923 – Buxton rejected it as merely an anti-Bolshevik body. He also rejected the Third International because of its domination by Moscow but hoped for a change of heart in the latter organisation. In the ILP he worked along with Clifford Allen and H.N. Brailsford and others to produce dynamic programmes which would convert the electorate to Socialism, and in 1923 he attended the inaugural meeting of the Labour and Socialist International at Hamburg. From 1924 to 1927 he was ILP treasurer.

Buxton strongly opposed the exaction of reparations, and in 1922, after visiting France along with his brother Noel, he warned the Government about the French annexation of the Ruhr (where he had lived in a miner's cottage in order to learn about post-war conditions), and made a series of radical proposals including remission of the French debt, revision of the Treaty of Versailles, and withdrawal from the Rhine.

His wide experience and understanding of international questions had led to his appointment in 1920 as adviser to the LP on international and imperial affairs, with a room in the House of Commons whether or not he was an MP. He won Accrington in November 1922, lost the seat in 1923 and failed again in 1924. He re-entered Parliament as Labour member for Elland in 1929 but was defeated in 1931. He left the ILP in 1930 on the grounds that it had become a self-righteous sect. He believed it should no longer try to remain a party within a party, but concentrate on educational and propagandist work. Buxton maintained his political interests after his defeat and even hoped for the readmission of MacDonald into the Labour Party. He contested Elland again in 1935 but without success.

But between the two world wars Buxton devoted the greater part of his time and thought to colonial, especially African, affairs; he visited Kenya and Uganda in 1932, and parts of West Africa, including Liberia, in 1934. This was a period when few Labour politicians (apart from the small group of intellectuals to which Buxton and his brother belonged) showed much interest in the subject. He held strong opinions, reinforced by much travel and study and by his friendship with many leading Africans, on native rights and on the political advancement of colonial peoples. The views which he pioneered in the 1920s and 1930s – such as the paramountcy of native interests and the moral obligation of a colonial power to prepare the indigenous peoples for eventual self-government – later found wide acceptance. Buxton was acting chairman of the Labour Party's Advisory Committee on International Questions in 1924-5 which had an *ad hoc* sub-committee on Imperial Questions. In 1924 the latter became a full committee entitled to send memoranda direct to the NEC. From 1926 to 1937 Buxton was chairman of both committees, with Leonard Woolf as secretary. In the latter year Philip Noel-Baker took over the international committee with Buxton continuing as chairman of the imperial committee until May 1940 when ill-health compelled him to resign.

With many other intellectuals he had joined the Next Five Years Group in 1934 – an all-party organisation devoted to a planned reconstruction of the economy. Though the Group was rejected by the Labour Party, Buxton remained in it. In 1936 he published *The Alternative to War*. At this time he and Noel were members of a private group of about twenty people, including Lord Allen of Hurtwood, 'who shared a common view about the necessity of revising parts of the Versailles treaty, and hoped that by conferring together, and with Germans through Fritz Berber [who was head of the Institut für Aussenpolitische Forschung], they might help to clear the way to peace and counteract the Nazi influence on the German people' [Hughes (1956)

117-18]. Corder Catchpool, a Quaker, became secretary of the group and Berber was able to inform the German Foreign Minister of their views. Buxton's main concern in the years before the outbreak of war in 1939 was to impress upon his countrymen the views about Germany that he had held consistently since the Versailles Treaty was signed, viz., that if the punitive policy towards Germany was not dramatically changed, the whole of Europe would be engulfed in a new war. He understood Hitlerism as the response of the German people to their humiliation by the victors of the First World War. Buxton supported the foreign policy of Neville Chamberlain in general, but considered that the way the Prime Minister yielded concessions piecemeal was trivial and could not be expected to be taken seriously by Germany or Italy. In the months before September 1939 Buxton continued to argue strongly for a policy that would give Germany what he considered her just demands by offering definite and well-thought-out proposals. He wrote to the English press in March 1939:

> I contend that Britain should take the initiative in laying before the world – *urbi et orbi* – a reasonable scheme of collective control, combined with a redistribution of territory, which would give Germany colonies on equal terms. The effect on world opinion would be great. It would be evidence that Britain was reasonable; recognising that the 'exclusive' Empire was out of date, and that a beginning should be made with collective responsibility and trusteeship. The effect on the opinion of the German people would not be less marked . . . [quoted de Bunsen (1948) 156].

Like other upper-class Englishmen of similar views (Clifford Allen for instance) he was convinced of the importance of personal, face-to-face contacts, and he travelled constantly to Germany during the 1930s; in 1939 three times, the last in August just before war was declared. At the end of September he resigned from his position as parliamentary adviser to the LP; argued in the *Manchester Guardian* in October and November 1939 for a positive response to Hitler's speech of 6 October – which he thought offered a basis for bargaining; and strongly supported Lloyd George's proposals for an immediate conference to discuss the reinstatement of a free Poland and a free Czechoslovakia [de Bunsen (1948) 163-4].

Both Buxton and his wife had poor health, and in the spring of 1940 he had a severe illness of an influenzal type, from which it was difficult to recuperate in London during the blitz. The Buxtons therefore left London and went to stay with their daughter Eglantyne in her home at Peaslake in Surrey. Here Buxton spent the last two years of his life. He kept himself informed about the course of the war and political affairs, and in 1941 attended a conference at Oxford of the National Peace Council.

Buxton died at his daughter's home in Peaslake on 16 December 1942, at the age of sixty-seven. His burial in Peaslake Cemetery was preceded by a combined Anglican service and Friends' Meeting in the parish church. He was survived by his wife and his two children. Although the value of his estate was £20,150 (net) only a small sum was left in trust for his family and the remainder was in a public trust for charitable purposes. His son, David, inherited his father's interest in Africa – where he spent many years – and in Eastern Europe.

Writings: Buxton wrote articles in *Foreign Affairs, Labour Leader, Socialist Rev.* and the *U.D.C.* among others. His other publications include: (with others), *Towards a Social Policy* (n.d.); *Electioneering Up-to-Date* (1906); *Companies and Conscience: justice and dividends* (SPCK, 1908) 4 pp.; *Turkey in Revolution* (1909); Editor of *The ABC Home Rule Handbook* (1912); (with others), *Home Rule Problems* (n.d.); (with N.E. Buxton), *The War and the Balkans* (1915); Editor of *Towards a Lasting Settlement* (1915); *Peace this Winter: a reply to Mr Lloyd George* [NLP, 1916]; *Shouted down: lectures on the settlement of the war* (1916) 22 pp.; 'Peace Suggestions: a survey', *Soc. Rev.* 14, no. 80 (Jan-Mar 1917) 7-16; Preface to *The Secret Agreements (concluded during the war between the Allied Governments)* [1918] 22 pp.; *Memorandum on Territorial Claims and Self-determination* (UDC Pamphlet no. 29a: 1919) 7 pp.; (with D.F. Buxton), *The World after the War* (1920) and *In a German Miner's Home*

(1920); 'France and her Ruins' *Soc. Rev. 20*, no. 107 (Aug 1922) 82-91; *In a Russian Village* (1922); *Labour's Work for Peace at Geneva* (1925) 16 pp.; 'Russia 1920-1927: a comparison', *Labour Mag. 6* (Nov 1927) 307-8; 'A Family Holiday in Russia', *Soc. Rev.* n.s. *2*, no. 22 (Nov 1927) 24-31; 'Was Dr. Johnson a Great Man?', ibid. *3*, no. 35 (Dec 1928) 32-41; *A Politician plays truant: essays on English literature* (1929); 'The Government's East African Policy', *Labour Mag. 9* (July 1930) 98-101; 'How Shop Assistants work: report of the Select Committee', ibid. *10* (Dec 1931) 373-7; *The Race Problem in Africa* (1931) 59 pp.; 'Inter-Continental Peace', in *The Intelligent Man's Way to prevent War* (1933) 199-255; *The Alternative to War: a programme for statesmen* (1936); 'The Empire – what next?', *Labour 4* (July 1937) 267-8; *The Case for an Early Peace* (Friends' Peace Cttee, [1940]) 7 pp.; *Prophets of Heaven and Hell: Virgil, Dante, Milton, Goethe* (published posthumously, Cambridge, 1945; reissued in the U.S.A., 1969).

Sources: (1) MSS: C.R. Buxton papers: Rhodes House, Oxford, and with his son, David Buxton, Grantchester; UDC Coll.: Brynmor Jones Library, Hull Univ. (2) Other: S.V. Bracher, *The Herald Book of Labour Members* (1923); LP, *Reports*, 1924-6, 1939-41; *Dod* (1923); H.M. Swanwick, *Builders of Peace* (1924); *Times*, 14 Nov 1924; *Labour Who's Who* (1927); *Potted Biographies* (1930); *Dod* (1931); H.M. Swanwick, *I have been young* (1935); M.A. Hamilton, *Arthur Henderson* (1938); C.F. Brand, *British Labour's Rise to Power* (Stanford, 1941); F. Brockway, *Inside the Left* (1942); *WWW* (1941-50); V.A. de Bunsen, *Charles Roden Buxton: a memoir* (1948); M. Anderson, *Noel Buxton: a life* (1952); *Beatrice Webb's Diaries 1912-1924*, ed. M.I. Cole (1952); J.C. Greaves, *Corder Catchpool* (1953); *Beatrice Webb's Diaries 1924-1932*, ed. and with an Introduction by M. Cole (1956); S.R. Graubard, *British Labour and the Russian Revolution 1917-1924* (Cambridge, Mass., 1956); W.R. Hughes, *Indomitable Friend: the life of Corder Catchpool 1883-1952* (1956); A.J.P. Taylor, *The Trouble Makers* (1957); S.G. Evans, *A Short History of Bulgaria* (1960); J. Braunthal, *History of the International 1914-1943* (1963, English ed. 1967); V. Brittain, *Pethick-Lawrence: a portrait* (1963); C.A. Cline, *Recruits to Labour* (Syracuse (NY) Univ. Press, 1963); M. Gilbert and R. Gott, *The Appeasers* (1963); A. Marwick, *Clifford Allen: the open conspirator* (1964); K. Freeman, *If any Man build: the history of the Save the Children Fund* (1965); M. Swartz, *The Union of Democratic Control in British Politics during the First World War* (Oxford, 1971); biographical information: Dr C. Baier, Hull Univ.; the late T.A.K. Elliott, CMG; S.C. Tongue, London Borough of Hackney Archives Department; J. Trimmer, Save the Children Fund, London; personal information: D.R. Buxton, Grantchester, son; Miss E. Buxton, daughter and Sir B. de Bunsen, nephew, both of London. OBIT. *Manchester Guardian*, 17 and 18 Dec 1942; *Times*, 17 and 21 Dec 1942; *Yorkshire Post*, 18 Dec 1942; *Accrington Observer*, 26 Dec 1942; *Friend*, 1 Jan 1943; *New Statesman and Nation*, 2 Jan 1943; *Labour Party Report* (1943). The editors are indebted to Mr B.H. Sadler, Warwick Univ. for an earlier draft of this biography.

JOYCE BELLAMY
MARGARET 'ESPINASSE

See also: †Reginald Clifford ALLEN; Noel Edward BUXTON; Mary Agnes HAMILTON; †James Ramsay MACDONALD; †Helena Maria Lucy SWANWICK; Leonard Sidney WOOLF.

BUXTON, Noel Edward (1st Baron Noel-Buxton of Aylsham) (1869-1948)
LIBERAL (later LABOUR) MP AND GOVERNMENT MINISTER

Noel Buxton was born in London on 9 January 1869. He was the great-grandson of the anti-slavery leader Thomas Fowell Buxton. His father was Sir Thomas Fowell Buxton and his mother, Lady Victoria Noel, was the daughter of the 1st Earl of Gainsborough, whose family was connected with Byron's. Noel Buxton changed his name to Noel-Buxton on his elevation to the peerage in 1930. His brothers included Charles Roden Buxton and Harold, bishop of Gibraltar (who survived until 1976).

Noel Buxton was educated at Harrow and Trinity College, Cambridge. He was placed in the third class in the history tripos in 1889. In the same year he joined the family brewery in Spitalfields, later becoming a director. In 1892 he made an educational tour of the Far East by which his outlook was much affected, particularly by his contact with Buddhism. In 1896 he acted as aide-de-camp to his father when the latter was Governor of South Australia.

While working at the brewery, Noel, along with his brother Charles and some other Cambridge contemporaries, investigated and attempted to relieve poverty in the East End of London. He met and worked with Canon Barnett of Toynbee Hall, who led his philanthropy into the more practical form of trying to improve wages, working conditions and housing by political means. He was on the Whitechapel Board of Guardians (1897) and stood – unsuccessfully – for the LCC. Buxton then became a member of the Central (Unemployed) Body and worked with the Webbs. In 1900 he stood as parliamentary Liberal candidate for Ipswich, but was defeated. In the following year he collaborated with C.F.G. Masterman and others to produce *The Heart of Empire*, a radical symposium on social problems. Buxton's contribution was on temperance reform, an interest which stemmed from his experience of the London poor, and one which he continued to pursue, but without fanaticism.

In 1899 he travelled in the Balkans and was appalled by the Turkish treatment of minorities. With Lord Bryce, H.N. Brailsford and his brother Charles he formed the Balkan Committee in 1902, and was elected chairman. He made a careful investigation of the Turkish Empire in Europe, and his report led to the formation of the Macedonian Relief Committee in 1903, and to Noel Buxton's personal identification with the Bulgarian cause and his belief – shared by his brother Charles – that Macedonia should be part of Bulgaria.

He resigned his directorship of the family brewery in 1904. In the following year, supported by the Balkan Committee and the influential Christian Social Union, he fought and won a by-election at Whitby – a traditional Tory seat – but was defeated by 71 votes at the general election of 1906. His experience at Whitby strengthened the desire he already had to help agricultural workers. During 1907 he worked with George Edwards, the leader of the Eastern Counties Agricultural Labourers' and Small Holders' Union; he helped the Rev. Rollo Meyer to form farmers' co-operatives in Bedfordshire; and he induced his father to convert his Norfolk estate into smallholdings. In the same year he became president of the Balkans Committee in succession to Lord Bryce, and gained industrial experience through membership of a departmental committee on lead poisoning, appointed in 1908.

He frequently visited Balkan and Turkish leaders in his attempt to solve Balkan problems. The Young Turk revolt of 1908 appeared to bring his work to fruition: in 1909 a public dinner was held in his honour, and he was much eulogised. In January 1910 he was elected Liberal MP for North Norfolk, initial Liberal opposition having been overcome by the Agricultural Labourers' Union statement that they would support Buxton with or without his nomination by the Liberals. He advocated an Agricultural Wages Board and was parliamentary champion of the agricultural workers.

The Agadir crisis of 1911, and renewed Turkish atrocities in the Balkans turned his attention again to foreign affairs. He joined the Anglo-German Friendship Committee and nominated E.D. Morel for membership. The committee's aim was to reduce tension between the two nations – a tension which Noel Buxton asserted was due to British imperialism. In the Bulgarian-Turkish war of 1912 Buxton and his brother Harold went out on relief work, and Buxton was invited to join the Bulgarian general staff. Two books resulted from these events, *Europe and the Turks* (1912) and *With the Bulgarian Staff* (1913). After his visit in 1913 Noel Buxton took up the Armenian cause and became a member of the House of Commons Armenian Committee. Continued dissatisfaction with the policy of Grey, then Foreign Secretary, towards Germany and the Balkans led him to work with Ponsonby and others on the formation of a seventy-strong Liberal Foreign Affairs Committee.

After the outbreak of war in 1914 Noel Buxton and his brother Charles undertook an unofficial mission to Bulgaria, encouraged by Winston Churchill and Lloyd George. Their object was to offer readjustment of the Balkan frontiers in return for Bulgaria's support for the allied cause, or at least for her neutrality. In Bucharest a Turk attempted to assassinate the brothers. Charles was wounded in one lung, and Noel had a facial injury; but they continued with their mission. They returned to Bulgaria and later a street in Sofia was named after them. In spite of their efforts, the mission was not successful, through lack of support in the British Cabinet.

Noel Buxton gave considerable financial support to the Union of Democratic Control, founded in 1914 by Charles Trevelyan, E.D. Morel and Arthur Ponsonby. He became a member, but unlike his brother Charles he took little active part, being in agreement with most of their aims but not with their methods – Buxton preferred to work through the existing traditional diplomatic system in his efforts to obtain peace. In 1915 he was employed in the diplomatic department of the Admiralty, concentrating on his Balkan policy.

In 1916 he visited the U.S.A. to set up an Armenian relief fund after the Turkish massacre. He met President Wilson and he discussed the possibility of American mediation with Wilson's adviser, Colonel House. His efforts were again rendered fruitless by the Coalition Government's policy of 'a fight to the finish'. Buxton then took a more active part in parliamentary affairs, frequently dividing the House, along with other dissenters, on the basic policy of a negotiated peace based on a return to the 1914 *status quo*. He proposed a post-war federation of Balkan states, and he condemned French claims to Alsace-Lorraine as a device to obtain access to minerals. He opposed the breaking up of the Austro-Hungarian Empire, since he believed not in total ethnic nationalism but in workable states with adequate protection for minorities.

In 1917 he welcomed the first Russian Revolution as expressing the highest ideals of the Russian people, and thought peace had become possible now that Russian imperialism was no longer an issue. But hope for a negotiated peace was dashed by American entry into the war. Buxton, however, continued to press for the acceptance of Wilson's fourteen points for peace, in the hope that American influence would prevent a vindictive settlement.

By this time disillusioned with the Liberal Party and its leaders, Buxton had come to think, with his brother Charles, that the place for radicals was in the Labour Party; but he hesitated to take the final step of joining. He stood for North Norfolk as a Lib-Lab candidate in 1918; the Coalition nominee defeated him by a narrow margin of 200 votes. In 1919 Buxton finally joined the Labour Party and became a member of its Advisory Committee on International Questions. He opposed the Versailles and the Balkan Treaties as unjust and vindictive; supported the original principle of a League of Nations, but thought the actual form it assumed would perpetuate division in Europe. Like his brother Charles he attacked the continuation of the Allied blockade of the Central Powers, and became treasurer of the Fight the Famine Council (the president was Lord Parmoor), which later developed its policy to include the economic rehabilitation of Germany. In the same year (1919) he founded the Noel Buxton Trust, giving a large part of his personal fortune for educational, political and religious work. He became a close friend of Ramsay MacDonald; he visited Berlin and attended the meeting of the Second International with him in 1920 and holidayed with him in North Africa.

In 1922 he went to France with his brother Charles. On their return they advocated the remission of the French debt to Britain, the setting-up of an International Reconstruction Bureau, and a revision of the reparations and economic clauses of the Treaty of Versailles in order to forestall the French invasion of the Ruhr. Also in 1922, he resumed his parliamentary career: he was elected Labour MP for North Norfolk. In the Commons he concerned himself with international affairs, attacking the Government for their mishandling of Near Eastern affairs, particularly for the exclusion of Russia and Bulgaria from the peace conference on the Graeco-Turkish war, and for their pro-Turkish policy in general. He also took up again his championship of the agricultural workers: he became Minister of Agriculture in the first Labour Government (Jan-Nov 1924). He secured the passage of the Agricultural Wages Act, in spite of Liberal opposition, by dropping the minimum wage clause to win Tory support. He was again

Minister of Agriculture (1929-30) in the second Labour Government, when he set up the marketing division of the Ministry, appointed inspectors to enforce the 1924 Wages Act, and started schemes for including agricultural workers in unemployment benefit proposals and for the abolition of tied cottages.

Ill-health forced his retirement in June 1930. Although he was opposed to hereditary political power, he accepted a peerage as Lord Noel-Buxton of Aylsham, Norfolk, in order to continue his work. He was succeeded as MP for North Norfolk by his wife, who pressed his policies from the back benches. They were often blocked by the Minister of Labour, Margaret Bondfield, but the Marketing Boards scheme was carried through by the new Minister of Agriculture, Christopher Addison.

Buxton broke with Ramsay MacDonald after the formation of the National Government, and turned his attention chiefly to social matters. He was president of the Save the Children Fund from 1930 to 1948 and chairman of the Miners' Welfare Committee from 1931 to 1934. As joint chairman of the Anti-Slavery and Aborigines Protection Society he was invited to Abyssinia by the Emperor to prepare a twenty-year plan for the abolition of slavery. (He opposed the use of sanctions against Italian aggression in Abyssinia partly because of the existence of slavery there.) He was also a member of the Minorities Committee of the League of Nations.

During the 1930s he continued to argue against the iniquities of the Versailles settlement and became a vigorous advocate of the appeasement of Germany. In general he supported Chamberlain's efforts to avoid war; accepting the German claims on Sudetenland and on Poland and believing that access to colonial territories would greatly lessen the tensions inside Germany. In all these matters he was at one with his brother Charles. His political attitudes inevitably came into conflict with majority views in the Labour Party – although from the outset he had believed that the Labour policy of opposing Fascism abroad and voting against rearmament proposals at home was inconsistent. With his brother he joined a private group in the late 1930s which included Clifford Allen and Corder Catchpool, a Quaker. Their aims were to maintain contact with 'responsible' Germans and to influence policy towards understanding and negotiation.

With the outbreak of war in 1939 Buxton came to fear that a prolonged conflict would drive Germany into Bolshevism. To avert this he circulated among members of the House of Lords a Memorandum on War Aims, urging a negotiated peace based on the formation of genuine Polish and Czech states, disarmament, and the inclusion of Germany in a European system of order. In 1943 he opposed the call for unconditional surrender, and advocated the formation of a fifth column in Germany; he was for offering a negotiated peace in return for the overthrow of Nazism. Appalled by the post-war annexations of German territory and the expulsion of the inhabitants, he supported the 'Save Europe Now' movement, helped to organise relief for German refugees, and agitated for the rapid release of German prisoners of war. As president of the Balkan Committee he worked for the formation of a Balkan Federation, encouraged by President Tito of Yugoslavia's support for the proposal. But his hope was dashed by Russian policies. Buxton resigned the presidency of the Committee in 1945, to make way for a younger man; but failure to find a successor led to its collapse.

Buxton was also president of the National Gardeners' Guild and of the National Laymen's Missionary Movement. During his lifetime he gave much of his private fortune to philanthropic works, and restored and presented to the nation his sixteenth-century family home, Paycocks House, Coggeshall, Essex. In 1914 he had married Lucy Edith, daughter of Major Henry Pelham Burn; there were three sons and three daughters of the marriage. One son died in an accident while on active service in 1940. The other children, together with his wife, survived him. Noel-Buxton died on 12 September 1948. He was buried at Upshire, Waltham Abbey, Essex. He left an estate of £232,828.

Writings: (with C.R. Buxton), 'Labour Homes', *Econ. Rev. 8* (July 1898) 326-48; 'Public-Houses', *Cont. Rev. 77* (Apr 1900) 556-63; (with W. Hoare), 'Temperance Reform' in *The Heart of Empire*, Ch. 4 (1901) 165-210; 'Freedom and Servitude in the Balkan States',

West. Rev. 159 (May 1903) 481-90; (with C.R. Buxton), 'Public Opinion and Macedonia', *Monthly Rev. 13,* no. 39 (Dec 1903) 95-110; (with V. de Bunsen), *Macedonian Massacres* [1907] 15 pp.; *Europe and the Turks* (1907, rev. ed. 1912); *England and Germany* [1911] 15 pp.; *With the Bulgarian Staff* (1913); (with Rev. H. Buxton), *Travels and Politics in Armenia* (1914); (with C.R. Buxton), *The War and the Balkans* (1915); 'The Liberation of Bohemia', *New Statesman 8,* 3 Feb 1917, 419-20; (with C. Phillipson), *The Question of the Bosphorus and Dardanelles* (1917); 'Christian Principles and the War Settlement', *Hibbert J. 16,* no. 2 (Jan 1918) 283-94; (with C.L. Leese), *Balkan Problems and European Peace* (1919); 'The Psychology of Germany', *Nation and Athenaeum 28,* 23 Oct 1920, 131-2; 'Allied Policy towards Germany' [letter], *New Statesman 16,* 6 Nov 1920, 132-3; 'Russia and Armenia' [letter], ibid. 25 Dec 1920, 364; 'The Bright Side of the Succession States' [letter], *Nation and Athenaeum 30,* 17 Dec 1921, 469; (with T.P. Conwell-Evans), *Oppressed Peoples and the League of Nations* (1922); 'Need for the Restoration of the Agricultural Wages Boards', *Labour Mag. 2,* no. 2 (June 1923) 57-8; *Labour looking after Agriculture* (LP, 1924) 11 pp.; 'Agriculture: a survey', in *The Book of the Labour Party 2* ed. H. Tracey [1925] 31-46; 'Developing Agriculture', *Labour Mag. 3,* no. 12 (Apr 1925) 535-7; 'Agricultural Co-operation in Germany' ibid. *4,* no. 9 (Jan 1926) 413-14; 'Labour and the Land', ibid. *5* (Aug 1926) 147-9; *Travels and Reflections* (1929); 'National Minorities Today', *Cont. Rev. 140* (Aug 1931) 161-8; 'Slavery in Abyssinia', *Int. Affairs 11* (July 1932) 512-20; Introduction to T.P. Conwell-Evans, *Foreign Policy from a Back Bench* [based on the papers of Lord Noel-Buxton] (Oxford, 1932); 'A Century of Emancipation', *Int. Rev. of Missions 22* (July 1933) 323-30; 'Policy towards Germany' [letter], *Spec. 151,* 25 Aug 1933, 250; 'Conditions in Vienna' [letter], ibid. *152,* 6 Apr 1934, 543; *Poland: a speech by the Rt. Hon. Lord Noel-Buxton* [extract from House of Lords official report] (1939) 7 pp.

Sources: E.A. Pratt, *Small Holders: what they must do to succeed* (1909); F.S. Cocks, *E.D. Morel: the man and his work* (1920); *Dod* (1923); H.M. Swanwick, *Builders of Peace* (1924); C.F. Brand, *British Labour's Rise to Power* (Stanford, 1941); *DNB* (1941-50) [by M. Anderson]; F.W. Pethick-Lawrence, *Fate has been kind* [1943]; M.A. Hamilton, *Remembering my Good Friends* (1944); G.D.H. Cole, *A History of the Labour Party from 1914* (1948); R. Groves, *Sharpen the Sickle!: the history of the Farm Workers' Union* (1949); M. Anderson, *Noel Buxton: a life* (1952); *Beatrice Webb's Diaries 1912-1924,* ed. M.I. Cole (1952); E. Windrich, *British Labour's Foreign Policy* (Stanford, 1952); H. Dalton, *Memoirs: 1887-1931* (1953); C.L. Mowat, *Britain between the Wars* (1955); *Beatrice Webb's Diaries 1924-1932,* ed. and with an Introduction by M. Cole (1956); S.R. Graubard, *British Labour and the Russian Revolution* (Harvard, 1956); W.R. Hughes, *Indomitable Friend: the life of Corder Catchpool 1883-1952* (1956); R.W. Lyman, *The First Labour Government 1924* [1957]; A.J.P. Taylor, *The Trouble Makers: dissent over foreign policy, 1792-1939* (1957); G.P. Gooch, *Under Six Reigns* (1958); C.A. Cline, *Recruits to Labour* (NY, 1963); A. Marwick, *Clifford Allen: the open conspirator* (1964); personal information: D.R. Buxton, Grantchester, nephew. OBIT. *Times,* 14 and 17 Sep 1948; *London Illustrated News,* 25 Sep 1948.

MARGARET 'ESPINASSE
BRYAN SADLER

See also: Charles Roden BUXTON; Lucy Edith Pelham NOEL-BUXTON.

CHALLENER, John Ernest Stopford (1875-1906)
TRADE UNIONIST

Little is known of Challener's early life. He was born on 11 August 1875 in Islington, London, the son of Edward Challener, a commercial clerk. His mother, Sarah, was illiterate. She had been married before under the name of Stopford. At an early age Challener was orphaned and cared for by a Great Northern Railway employee, who, upon moving from London to Doncaster, the northern centre of the GNR, took the boy with him. He became a probationary junior clerk with the GNR at Doncaster, and rose to the position of correspondence clerk in the GNR works manager's office: a position of some trust. He became interested in trade unionism very early in his career. The National Association of General Railway Clerks had been formed in May 1897, and in November 1897 Challener became one of the foundation members of a newly established branch of the union, which became the Railway Clerks' Association in May 1898.

He attended the RCA's first delegate conference as a visitor and the second RCA conference as the Doncaster delegate. Doncaster quickly established itself as a growth area for the RCA, and in November 1898 was made a District Organising Centre. When, in early 1899, in a revision of organising centres, Doncaster became the focal point for the whole of the North of England, Challener, 'a very able and active member of the Doncaster branch' [*Railway Herald,* 18 Mar 1899], was appointed northern divisional secretary. In May 1899 he led the first RCA concerted salary campaign for GNR clerks; and in June 1899, at the fourth RCA conference, following the resignation of the general secretary through ill-health, he was elected general secretary unopposed. As a result of an EC decision in February 1900 Challener also became treasurer of the RCA; and in October 1902 he became its first full-time official, after having suggested at an EC meeting in January 1902 that the Association would benefit from such a move.

Under Challener's leadership the RCA from 1 January 1900 registered as a trade union, and in 1903 it affiliated to the TUC. Challener was always in favour of industrial conciliation and in 1901 and 1902 he supported the unsuccessful attempts to persuade the TUC to accept a policy of compulsory arbitration.

Challener had taken the initiative in helping to establish the Doncaster LRC, of which he became secretary; and he was a personal advocate of increased labour representation on elected bodies; but he was cautious where his own struggling union was concerned. In a letter to J. Ramsay MacDonald on 21 March 1901 Challener explored the possibility of RCA affiliating to the national LRC, but later he argued that since the RCA had only 3500 members out of a national total of 48,000 railway clerks, the matter should be deferred.

He stood unsuccessfully for the local council on three occasions in 1903 and 1904. His election programme included pleas for more factories in Doncaster in order to break the employment stranglehold exercised by the GNR: a fair wage clause, payment for Sunday labour, technical education, and a public park. Challener was, however, elected to the Doncaster Board of Guardians and was responsible for many minor reforms in the administration. He was also a leading member of the Doncaster Trades Council and in 1903 persuaded the Council to affiliate to the national LRC, and the local branch of the RCA to join the Council. He was, moreover, instrumental in persuading his local RCA to affiliate to the Doncaster LRC, a move which few RCA branches in the country were prepared to follow. Challener was active also in establishing a local Trades Union Club for Doncaster trade unionists and he helped to found a local branch of the Hearts of Oak Benefit Society, of which for a time he became secretary.

At the RCA annual delegate conference of May 1905, in a 'special item' Challener was reproved for financial mismanagement; and although he received a substantial vote of confidence, on further investigation it was found that discrepancies in the finances had occurred. Concern was also expressed at the amount of the general secretary's expenses for 1905. During the later part of 1905 Challener was 'repeatedly absent' from EC meetings.

Early in March 1906 he travelled to London and then to Paris where, on 12 March, he committed suicide by shooting himself. He was in his thirty-first year. For some time he had been in ill-health and the strains of his financial defalcations no doubt contributed largely to his final breakdown. He was found to have misappropriated £380 4s 9d from union funds, of which only £140 was recovered. After what the annual report of 1906 described as 'the deplorable action of the late General Secretary', the union lost membership and its organisation was quite severely tested. From May 1906 the offices of general secretary and treasurer were separated, and A.G. Walkden took office as general secretary in succession to Challener.

During the period of Challener's leadership of the union, membership increased from 537 to about 4500, and he was undoubtedly a young man of great energy, organising ability and imagination. He had married Annie Robinson of Levitt Hagg (near Doncaster) in September 1900 and there were three children of the marriage. His funeral took place in Paris and he left effects valued at £213.

Writings: 'Trade Unionism and the House of Lords' Decision', *Railway Herald*, 3 Aug 1901. Challener contributed regularly to the RCA column in the *Railway Herald*.

Sources: (1) MSS: RCA, EC minutes, 18 Feb 1900, 17 June, 15 July and 10 Dec 1905; Labour Party archives: LRC. (2) Other: RCA, *Minutes of Annual Delegate Conferences*, May and June 1898, June 1899, May 1905, May 1906; RCA, *Annual Report and Balance Sheet* (1906); *Railway Herald*, 18 Mar 1899, 8 Sep 1900, 11 May and 3 Aug 1901, 13 Sep 1902, 7 Feb, 18 and 21 Mar, 18 Apr and 16 May 1903; *Daily Express*, 15 May 1901; *Doncaster Gazette*, 23 Oct, 6, 20 and 27 Nov 1903, 25 Mar, 1 Apr, 28 Oct and 4 Nov 1904; 'Highlights of R.C.A. History 2: the first ten years', *Transport Salaried Staff J.* (June 1951) 231-3; biographical information: R.D. Steward, archivist, Doncaster Metropolitan Borough; P. White, senior research officer, TSSA. Obit. *Doncaster Gazette*, 16 Mar 1906.

ADRIAN TRANTER

See also: Alexander George WALKDEN.

CHELMSFORD, 3rd Baron and 1st Viscount Chelmsford,
see **THESIGER, Frederic John Napier**

CHEW, Ada Nield (1870-1945)
WOMEN'S LABOUR, TRADE UNION AND SUFFRAGE WORKER

Ada Nield was born at Butt Lane, Talke, on the edge of the Potteries, on 28 January 1870. Her parents were Jane Nield (née Hammond) and William Nield, who was a farmer for most of his life. The Nields were a family of Cheshire yeomen from Bunbury. Ada's grandfather, also William Nield, had bought the White Hall Farm, not far from Butt Lane where he also owned houses. His son William worked for him on the farm and took it over when his father retired to one of the houses in Butt Lane.

Ada Nield lived at the White Hall Farm until she was about eleven years old. She was the second child and the eldest daughter in a family of thirteen. Two boys and two girls having died in infancy, Ada grew up with seven brothers and one sister, May, who was an epileptic. May's condition worsened as she grew older, and before 1900 she had to be removed to the Cheshire County Asylum where she died in the 1920s. In effect, therefore, Ada was the only daughter, and from an early age she had to help her mother with the domestic work. She was taken from school for this purpose when she was eleven.

About this time the family moved to the Common Farm near Malvern in Worcestershire, where Ada lived until she was seventeen. For some reason, this was the happiest period of her early life. She used to take her little brothers to a dame school at Hanley Swan, the nearest village – a duty which gave her at least a respite from domestic drudgery – and she had a milk round, with a mare, Polly, drawing the milk float; this gave her a real taste of personal freedom.

But as its name suggests, the Common Farm had poor land, and William Nield lacked capital. So he could not make a success of farming there, and about 1887 the family went back to the Cheshire-Staffordshire border, this time to Crewe. At one time (in fact when Ada was born)

William Nield had a job at a brickworks, but what he did for the rest of his later life is not known; he did not engage in farming again. Ada herself worked first in a shop in Nantwich, then briefly, and she said unsuccessfully, at a Church school somewhere in Lincolnshire. In 1894 she was a tailoress in a Crewe clothing factory. Twenty years later she herself described how, desperate to earn, she started work as a learner in this factory, Compton Brothers, which made uniforms on contract for soldiers, policemen and railwaymen. She had already tried another factory, where she was told she would be paid no wage for the first three months. At Compton Brothers, helped by an older woman, she learned the trade in one week, and after that she was able to earn 8s in each succeeding week. There were men also employed in the factory, as tailors, and Ada noticed that when the government inspectors came round these men were given the job of sewing the sleeves into the tunics, work usually done by the women. When she asked the reason, she was told that the men were paid 1s 5d an hour for this but the women only 5d; and so the men – whose work it was supposed to be – did it only when the inspectors were in the factory.

One of Ada Nield's most prominent characteristics was a burning desire to protest against injustice, whether to workers as a whole or to her own sex in particular. It is not surprising, therefore, to find that on 5 May 1894 a letter appeared in the *Crewe Chronicle*, describing the kind of life the girls in the factory were obliged to lead and the wages they were paid. This letter was the first of a series published under the pseudonym of 'A Crewe Factory Girl'. The factory was not named, but before the series ended it was identified as Compton Brothers. The letters, which continued to appear through June and July, ending in August, gave a vivid account of the daily life, the work, and the just grievances of the factory tailoresses, and immediately exhibited Ada Nield's gift for writing. The tone is courteous but assured – and rightly assured, for her knowledge of her facts and her case is as thorough as her selection and presentation are effective. Her quality may be seen in the very first letter, of 5 May 1894, where she wrote:

> To take what may be considered a good week's wage the work has to be so close and unremitting that we cannot be said to 'live' – we merely exist. We eat, we sleep, we work, endlessly, ceaselessly work, from Monday morning till Saturday night, without remission. Cultivation of the mind! How is it possible? Reading? Those of us who are determined to live like human beings and require food for mind as well as body are obliged to take time which is necessary for sleep to gratify this desire. As for recreation and enjoying the beauties of nature, the seasons come and go, and we have barely time to notice whether it is spring or summer.

And near the end of the letter she observed:

> I have just read the report of the Royal Commission on Labour. Very good; but while Royal Commissions are enquiring and reporting and making suggestions, some of the workers are being hurried to their graves.

This controlled variety in tone and this incisiveness are quite out of the common.

The writer's conclusion was that the root cause of the evils from which she and her workmates suffered was the firm's failure to pay them a living wage – ' "A living wage!" Ours is a lingering, dying wage.' She stated firmly her opinion that the remedy was for the factory girls to join some already existing union.

The second letter, of 19 May, was headed 'A Living Wage for Factory Girls at Crewe'. It gave details of the rates paid: 3d an hour for some kinds of work, $1\frac{1}{2}d$ for others, for some only 1d; very occasionally as much as $4\frac{1}{2}d$. The average weekly wage for a working day of nine to ten hours – at busy times more, and with four hours' work to take home in addition – was 8s.

The letters attracted the attention of a number of people, among them the secretary of the Crewe branch of the ILP, who after the first was published wrote to the *Chronicle* (19 May) asking the writer to get in touch with him. She refused, but added that if her identity were ever discovered she would gladly accept the invitation and work with the ILP to the best of her ability, 'in the effort to improve the conditions not only of the factory girls, but of all other workers'. An offer came from the Gasworkers' and General Labourers' Union (the precursor of the National Union of General and Municipal Workers) to accept the factory girls as members. This was after the Tailors' Union had refused to admit them, on the ground that women had no business in tailoring at all.

The series also led to a direct confrontation between one of the London directors of Compton Brothers and Ada Nield, who at a factory meeting which he called felt morally bound to reveal her identity as the writer of the letters, and who afterwards wrote a moving account of what the editor of the *Chronicle* described as a hurricane in a Crewe factory. A dozen girls who had given overt support to Ada Nield were dismissed (all good workers, and some with over ten years' service). Hoping – though vainly – to prevent this kind of victimisation, Ada herself had given in her notice a day earlier. The coda to this long-drawn-out affair was that she was invited to speak at a Labour meeting in Crewe, called in August under the auspices of the gasworkers' union, at which the other speaker was Eleanor Aveling, the daughter of Karl Marx. The *Chronicle* for 25 August reported that Miss Nield 'delivered an interesting address'. Ada Nield had found her métier as organiser, public speaker and writer.

It is not known whether she did any paid work in the months immediately following these events, but as a direct consequence of her experiences and of the sympathy shown her by the Crewe branch of the ILP, she joined it, and in December 1894 was one of three women, and the first ILP member, to be elected to the Nantwich Board of Guardians, which embraced Crewe [Chaloner (1950) 216]. In the spring of 1895 she moved a resolution that the Board should acquire fifty acres of land to provide work for the unemployed. The resolution was lost.

In June 1896 she became one of another trio of women, pioneer Clarion Vanners, who set out on a tour of fifteen weeks chiefly in the coalfields of Northumberland and Durham. The Van was the brainchild of Julia Dawson, editor of the 'Woman's Letter' in the *Clarion*, and its purpose was to introduce Socialism into country districts. Ada Nield's reports to the *Clarion* show that in spite of fairly constant rain, this was a successful venture: they addressed large and enthusiastic audiences at open-air meetings in a number of places including Newcastle, Jarrow and South Shields. Ada Nield spoke at all these meetings. By this time she had become an eloquent and racy speaker, who never in her life made use of notes. By the end of the tour she was being strongly advised by all to devote more and more time to the Socialist platform. Besides her very clear head and firm grasp of facts, her hold over her audiences resided in her gift for the telling phrase, her eagerness and animation, and her sincerity; also, according to several witnesses, in her appearance – her colouring, and the mobility of her expression, to which no photograph could do justice. She was very pretty, with grey-blue eyes, a fair complexion, and beautiful curling auburn hair – which she herself regarded as ugly because her brothers had told her it was and had called her Carrots; she was completely without personal vanity.

On the Clarion Van tour the three women had been escorted by two male colleagues, who slept in a tent and 'did' for themselves. One of them was George Chew, who had met Ada Nield in the ILP. He was a Lancastrian, born in Clayton-le-Moors, who had begun as a half-timer in a cotton mill, but had educated himself by attending evening classes in Blackburn, and had become an ILP organiser. It was when he was helping to set up ILP branches in Crewe that he and Ada had met. They were married on 13 April 1897 in a registry office. George Chew had gone to live in Rochdale because, according to his daughter, he intensely admired John Bright and the Rochdale Pioneers; and at some date after June 1897 he and Ada settled in Shawclough, a village near Rochdale.

By this time Ada Nield had apparently become a regular travelling speaker for the ILP. In the *Labour Leader* for 3 July 1897 she described a tour she had just made in Scotland, Lancashire (she recommended those of her readers who had never seen Oldham to pray that they never might) and the Midlands, ending with a week in Shropshire, where she met the girls of Madeley who walked two or three miles each way to the pit banks, where they worked from 6 a.m. to 3.30 or 4 p.m. for a daily wage of 8*d* to 1*s*. In the *Labour Leader* for 31 July she gave an account of another tour, this time in East Staffordshire – the Black Country. In June 1898, however, her travels had to end for the time being, when her only child, Doris Nield Chew, was born.

For the next two years Ada Chew left the breadwinning entirely to her husband, who worked for a while as a weaver again, and then as an organiser for the trade union movement or the ILP or both – it is not certain. During the next eighteen months the family lived in Preston and Dunfermline; by 1900 they were back in Rochdale, keeping, and living behind a 'fent' shop near the Pioneers' Toad Lane Stores ('fent' is a northern word for a remnant of cloth). About three years later George Chew gave up this shop and started a retailing business in drapery and footwear which he continued for the rest of his life. He had market stalls in a number of towns and a shop first in Rochdale and then in Manchester.

His wife resumed her career as speaker and organiser when Doris was two years old. (The only way in which a devoted mother, as she was, could manage this was by taking the child with her on her travels, up to the time when Doris went to school at the age of seven.) She became one of the organisers for the Women's Trade Union League (WTUL) in the latter part of 1900, and by 1903 was sole organiser, a position which she held until 1908.

In the course of these eight years from 1900 to 1908 she visited many towns in England and Scotland, and helped many women to organise themselves in trade unions. She acquired insight into a number of varied trades. In 1901 she wrote an article for the *Women's Trade Union Review* on 'Fish Curing in Aberdeen'; and later, one on 'Egg-sorting and other trades in Hartlepool'. She worked for the Weavers' Association in Lancashire, for felt hat makers in Cheshire, for hosiery workers in Derbyshire. It was nearly always uphill work. In October 1902, for example, a hard week of canvassing for the weavers' union had discouraging results; in December she found 'apathy and indifference' among the women in Leicester; while in December 1903 a meeting in Skipton had to be abandoned because 'Friday night is cleaning night'.

In spite of the difficulties, however, she had a good deal of solid success, as can be seen from the reports of Mary Macarthur, organising secretary of the WTUL. In Dunfermline in the autumn of 1901 the union was strengthened even though several meetings were ruined by heavy rain; in October 1904 Hyde Labour Church was packed with women who came to hear her; many were standing, and two hundred and fifty were turned away. One success which must have given particular satisfaction to Mrs Chew was her formation, in 1905, of a strong women's branch of the Amalgamated Society of Tailors in Crewe.

It is not known why Mrs Chew gave up her post of organiser to the WTUL in 1908. But from at least 1903 she had also held another post. In 1898 Gertrude Tuckwell, then honorary secretary of the League, had started the Potteries Fund Committee, whose object was to find and help the victims of lead poisoning in the Potteries. Mrs Chew was employed to find them, visit them and send details to the Committee. The League's Annual Reports show how appallingly numerous they were: in 1903 Mrs Chew found thirty-seven new cases, in 1904 fifty. Besides her detailed reports she also wrote two moving stories about individual victims for the *Common Cause* (4 Jan 1912 and 11 Apr 1913); the first was subtitled 'A True Story' and the second 'Glimpses of Real Life'. In 1915, as a result of the war, the Committee thought they might have to wind up the fund; 'but it was felt that at all costs Mrs Chew's visits were too valuable to lose.' She was then paying something like forty visits a month, and her work in this field continued until the early 1920s.

In 1903, when they gave up the fent shop, the Chews had gone to live in a hamlet on the north side of Rochdale – a move partly due to Ada Chew's feeling that every child ought to grow up in the country. Both husband and wife continued to be active in the local ILP, and Mrs Chew also did a good deal of public speaking, addressing ILP branches, Socialist Sunday Schools and Labour Churches on such subjects as 'Should Women have a Vote?', 'Should Women support Trade Unionism?', 'My Work among Women'. It was natural that she should find the report of the Royal Commission on the Poor Laws (1905-9) of absorbing interest. Both as a Socialist and an ex-Guardian she was passionately in favour of the Minority Report drawn up by Sidney and

Beatrice Webb and supported by Lansbury. The *Rochdale Observer*, on the other hand, approved the Majority Report, and over a period of several months in 1908-9 Mrs Chew conducted a forthright argument with the editor in his correspondence columns.

In January 1908 the famous pioneering WEA University Tutorial class on the economic history of England started at Rochdale with R.H. Tawney as its tutor. Both the Chews eagerly joined. In 1908 also, the Rochdale Corporation opened their first municipal secondary school for boys and girls; in this school Doris Chew was educated, from 1910. Neither of her parents had had any formal education after the age of eleven, but all their lives they read avidly in every spare moment. They likewise seized every opportunity to enjoy such plays, operas and concerts as came their way – and at that time many provincial towns were visited by touring companies, including opera companies.

Many of the early Socialists were personal friends or acquaintances of the Chews, for instance the MacDonalds, the Snowdens, J.R. Clynes, Robert Smillie (of whom Ada Chew had a particularly good opinion), Julia Dawson, Mary Macarthur, and the brilliant young speaker Enid Stacy, whose early death she always regretted; Fenner Brockway and, naturally, R.H. Tawney.

Mrs Chew's pen was kept busy during these years. She wrote articles on women's suffrage for various local papers, and also a number of more general articles and sketches, which she contributed mainly to the *Common Cause*, but occasionally to other periodicals as well. In these she not only drew on her own past experiences as a factory worker but also used to good effect both her direct knowledge and her observation of the lives of married working women – in the Potteries, on a farm situated on the Cheshire-Staffordshire border, and in a Lancashire cotton town. In July 1911 the *Englishwoman* published a sketch entitled 'All in the Day's Work'. This is a blow-by-blow account of the actions and thoughts of a working-class wife and mother during a typical day of her life. So it is difficult to separate out a passage for quotation, in the close weave of detailed action and stream of consciousness. But the sort of minute successive and sequential calculations which fill Mrs Turpin's day are tellingly exhibited in such a passage as this:

> She had meant to do one of the three bedrooms today. Too late now. But she *must* get it in tomorrow, somehow. Must think of a dinner which won't be so much trouble as broth. A good big hot-pot, perhaps. But that doesn't half take a time to prepare, too, though it's no trouble when once you've got it into the oven. And she had meant to have a suet pudding because it fills them so, and 'sticks' so long. And she mustn't have a big fire to boil, and one under the oven as well. Well, she'll have to bake the suet pudding. They like it baked better than boiled (only it doesn't go so far baked as boiled), and with some treacle on the pudding and a bit of bacon to the hot-pot . . . they'll have a good dinner, and if she can only get time to chop the suet to-night it will give her a good 'leg up'.

And her relation with her youngest, her baby, is indirectly and economically indicated in several separate passages; for instance:

> How *could* she have slept so long! A glance at the sleeping baby in the orange-box beside the bed. How cross he has been all night, bless him! It's his teeth, of course.

And again:

> It's dull for him left at home with only a busy mother who hasn't time to look at him, bless him! Quite a quarter of an hour passes in persuading him to forget his woes in the examination of a miscellaneous collection of articles brought out for his benefit. At last he becomes absorbed in a cardboard box which has a fascinating way of opening and shutting, and his mother is at liberty to place the clothes-horse round the fire once more . . .

The part played in Mrs Turpin's life by the lady visitor on her rounds is hit off in half-a-dozen words: 'Miss Seaton, who came hindering yesterday, . . .'

In other sketches Mrs Chew made effective use of her considerable talent for writing (and speaking when this was appropriate) in the dialect of the particular areas in which they were set. Another sketch entitled 'A Woman's Work is never done', gives a brisk interchange of views and experiences between two working-class wives, effective from the opening exclamation 'If only we could live without eatin' ' to the final comment, 'I sometimes wonder whether us women *are* women – or donkeys!' She invented a number of characters, notably Mrs Stubbs, a Cheshire farmer's wife, whose views (published in the *Common Cause* 16 May, 27 June, 29 Aug 1913) on married life, bringing up children, and women's suffrage exude a calm and refreshing common sense.

At some time during these years Ada Chew joined the National Union of Women's Suffrage Societies, the body of constitutional suffragists led by Mrs Millicent Fawcett, distinct from the later body of militant suffragettes who formed Mrs Pankhurst's Women's Social and Political Union (WSPU). Mrs Chew had always been a 'feminist', believing that the mental abilities of women were largely wasted in unnecessary household drudgery and low-paid work. It might have been expected that her forthright and even aggressive resistance to injustice and oppression would lead her to militancy; but she was a convinced opponent of the use of physical force and violence in any form, and was therefore against the methods of the WSPU. One of the people whose ideas she most respected was Charlotte Perkins Gilman, the American writer and lecturer on labour and feminist subjects, whom she heard speak in Rochdale, and who believed that women could only be freed from domestic slavery by co-operative effort.

In a letter to the *Common Cause* (18 Apr 1912) on the need for an effective plan of campaign in order to win the vote, Mrs Chew said that working women distrusted the suffrage societies because they were run by 'fine ladies'; and she argued that there was a need to attract and convert working women, who would then 'look after the working men'. Up to this time the NUWSS had been neutral as far as the political parties were concerned. But when the Labour Party decided to oppose any franchise bill in which women were not included, the Council of the NUWSS resolved, on 23 May 1912, to support Labour candidates in by-elections, especially where the record of the Liberal candidates was unsatisfactory in regard to women's suffrage. There was a crop of by-elections in the next two years, and in consequence of the new policy suffragist speakers who were also Labour women were in great demand. Mrs Chew spoke and worked in support of the Labour candidate in eight constituencies. At the Holmfirth by-election on 20 June she had an audience of eight hundred; on 25 July she arrived at her old stamping ground of Crewe, where some of her relatives were still living, as well as a number of friends. A fellow-worker in the suffrage cause, Wilma Meikle, was also there for the by-election, and five years later she wrote to Mrs Chew:

> I remember well that Crewe election when though I admired and respected your reserve, I often wished that you would come out of it and let me know you better. Especially after I had spent most of polling day in a Labour committee room and heard your praises sung by a little group of Labour men who looked at me distastefully and told me that Mrs Chew was the only one of us who really knew what she was talking about! One of them, I remember, had known you before you were married and was very proud of his old acquaintance with you. [Letter of 11 Jan 1917].

After Crewe came Midlothian. In a report on this by-election Mrs Chew was described as an immensely popular speaker in the Labour as well as the Suffrage cause, and later, as being always eagerly sought after by the organisers of Labour meetings. In the *Labour Leader* for 5 September 1912 Mrs Chew herself wrote: '. . . last night I heard of a Liberal indoor meeting having an audience of fifteen, while we had an outdoor crowd numbering hundreds.'

Ada Chew fiercely resented the legal limitations on the independence of married women; for instance, that a married woman's income and tax were lumped in with her husband's; that she was not acknowledged as one of the legal guardians of her child, but that every document relating to that child had to be signed by the father and by him alone. She had no illusions about the mother's right to keep children in the event of divorce; she once said passionately, 'I'd live with the Devil to keep my child!' These and other legal injustices under which women suffered, especially married women, were illustrated in three sketches she wrote for the *Common Cause* (11 April, 2 May, 12 September 1913) in a series called 'Work-a-day Women'.

From 1912 to 1914 (and possibly earlier and later than these dates) Mrs Chew was NUWSS organiser for Rossendale Valley, the parliamentary constituency next to Rochdale. She wrote articles for the local press, tried to persuade local trade unions and labour bodies to pass resolutions in favour of women's suffrage, and arranged meetings addressed by prominent people such as Philip Snowden, Miss Margaret Ashton, the first woman councillor in Manchester, Miss Margaret Robertson, the chief organiser of the National Union, and Mrs H.M. Swanwick, the suffragist and pacifist, first editor of the *Common Cause*. From the reports in both the *Common Cause* and the *Bacup Chronicle* her efforts would seem to have been steadily successful.

The First World War put an abrupt end to the campaign for women's suffrage. As a pacifist, Mrs Chew was not prepared to do war work, but her public work continued for a time, if only in a minor key. On 2 October 1914 she represented the National Federation of Women Workers and the Women's Labour League on a deputation to the Rochdale Health Committee, to urge that a scheme should be set up for feeding mothers and babies on the lines of the plan initiated in Manchester by Miss Ashton. Largely by the efforts of Mrs Chew the deputation was able to persuade the Committee to follow the Manchester example and put such a scheme into operation.

Ada Chew had been for some time in charge of the drapery side of her husband's retail business, but she now wanted to earn money independently as well. At some point during the war she started a mail-order wholesale drapery business which did so well that by 1922 she had to rent a small warehouse. This was in Chapel Street, Salford. George Chew had already opened a shop in Manchester and closed the one in Rochdale, and the family now moved to Manchester. The political activities of Ada and George Chew had by this time almost come to an end. But they went to the Fabian Summer Schools held at Barrow House, Derwentwater, in 1915 and 1916; and Ada Chew joined the Manchester branch of the Women's International League for Peace and Freedom. She worked extremely hard at her business until she retired in 1930 at the age of sixty. She and her husband then moved to Burnley, where their daughter Doris was working. George Chew carried on his shop in Manchester and his market stalls from there. He died suddenly in 1940.

From her twenties Mrs Chew was a hardened traveller over Britain, from Shropshire to Angus; but she had never been abroad until in 1927 she took a holiday with her daughter in the south of France. In 1932 she and her husband went to South Africa on a visit to her brother Justin – her favourite brother, who like her had been active in trade union affairs. In 1935 she made a voyage round the world, and in each of the next three years she took motoring holidays, the last two in France and Switzerland. She loved foreign travel, but the Second World War put a stop to all that. Moreover, she began to suffer from arthritis.

Ada Nield Chew died suddenly, though not entirely without warning, on 27 December 1945. She was cremated at Rochdale on 31 December. She was survived by her daughter, a school teacher, and left an estate valued at £4914.

Ada Chew was clearly a born public speaker; there is plenty of testimony to that. But she was just as clearly a born writer, in the genre to which she chose to limit herself. Her sharp observation, her warm and sensitive feeling, and her rationality and judgement are communicated with directness, lucidity and economy. She had a natural understanding of the art of expression, an individual and distinguished voice.

Writings: Articles and letters on 'Life in a Crewe Factory' in *Crewe Chronicle*, 5, 19 May, 9, 23, 30 June, 14, 28 July, 4, 25 Aug 1894; 'From Scotland to Salop', *Labour Leader*, 10 July 1897; 'In the Black Country', ibid., 31 July 1897; 'In and out and round about', ibid., 14 Aug 1897; articles in the *Women's Trade Union Rev.* including 'Fish-Curing at Aberdeen', (Apr 1901) 5-6, 'Egg-Sorting and Other Trades at Hartlepool', (July 1901) 15-17 and 'The Case for the Factory Acts', (Oct 1901) 14-16; articles published in the *Common Cause* included: 'The Married Working Woman', 21 Sep, 5 and 12 Oct 1911, 'A Married Working Woman: a true story', 4 Jan 1912; 'The Economic Position of Married Women', 25 Jan 1912, 'An Effective Campaign', 18 Apr 1912, 'Work-a-day Women:glimpses of real life', 11 Apr and 2 May 1913, 'Mrs Stubbs on Woman's Sphere', 16 May 1913, 'Mrs Stubbs on Anti-Suffragists', 27 June 1913, 'Mrs Stubbs on Militancy', 29 Aug 1913, 'Work-a-day Women', 12 Sep and 17 Oct 1913, 'Motherhood', 13 Feb 1914, 'The Problem of the Married Working Woman', 27 Feb, 6 Mar and 3 Apr 1914, 'Work-a-day Women', 9 Apr 1914, 'A Woman's Work is never done', 24 Apr 1914, 'The War and Lancashire Factory Towns', 9 Oct 1914, ' "Womanly" Work and Life Saving in Manchester', 19 Feb 1915; 'All in the Day's Work 1: Mrs Turpin', *Englishwoman* (July 1911) 39-48 and '2: Mrs Bolt' (July 1912) 35-45; 'Women in Midlothian', *Labour Leader*, 5 Sep 1912, 577; 'Woman's Suffrage – from a Working Woman's Point of View', *Burnley News*, 1 Jan 1913; 'Should Working Men be Woman Suffragists? The Woman's Burden', *Labour Leader* [supplement on Women's Suffrage], 9 Jan 1913.

Sources: *Crewe Chronicle*, 25 Aug 1894; *Clarion*, 1895-7, for reports of 'Van' meetings; Women's Trade Union League, *Annual Reports*, 1900, 1904-8, 1911, 1912; *Women's Trade Union Rev.*, 1900-8; *Reformers' Year Book* (1906) 151; Women's Labour League, *Annual Report* (1911); *Rochdale Observer*, 5, 12 Feb, 2, 9 Apr 1910, 22 Apr and 9 Dec 1911; *Bacup Chronicle*, 15 Mar 1913; T.W. Price, *The Story of the Workers' Educational Association 1903-1924* (1924); W.H. Chaloner, *The Social and Economic Development of Crewe, 1780-1923* (Manchester, 1950); personal information: Doris N. Chew, Burnley, daughter.

DORIS N. CHEW
MARGARET 'ESPINASSE

See also: †Mary Reid MACARTHUR; †Robert SMILLIE; *Gertrude TUCKWELL.

CLARKE, (Charles) Allen (1863-1935)
LABOUR JOURNALIST, NOVELIST AND DIALECT WRITER

Charles Allen Clarke was born in Bolton, Lancashire, on 27 February 1863, the eldest of the nine children of two textile workers, Joseph Clarke and Martha Clarke (née Marsh). This was the period of the Lancashire cotton famine caused by the American Civil War. Allen's father was thrown temporarily out of work, and so, like many millgirls, his mother went on working almost up to the time of Allen's birth, and returned to the factory very soon after it. His maternal grandmother looked after him during the day, but his mother used to run home to give him the breast during the short dinner-hour the hands were allowed, and then run back to the factory. In spite of her exhausting life Martha Clarke lived to be well over eighty, and seven of her nine children were alive in 1920.

On his father's side also Allen's family included some not quite ordinary characters. The Clarkes were of Irish descent, and both his great-uncle Peter and his grandfather Thomas had gifts of song and story-telling, and both wrote verses. Thomas, a cobbler by trade, was 'wonderful' as a narrator: 'I used to listen to him spell-bound, for hours', his grandson recorded. His great uncle, also a cobbler and a good workman, preferred to roam the country 'getting his living as best he could', often by dashing off some rhyming advertisement or slogan for a shopkeeper to print on handbills. Allen's father was 'a great reader' and an able speaker, who took an active part in trade union politics. Allen remembered seeing and hearing him address a large meeting of strikers in 1877. And there was an aunt who not only flaunted her party colours, which were radical, at election times, but also 'had read politics, and knew what she was talking about'.

Allen began his education at the early age of three, at a dame school kept by a Mrs English; and he continued full-time schooling until he was thirteen, first at St Matthew's School under the 'well-loved' John Harding, and then at a school which was called Mount Street, and which he remembered chiefly for 'a little MS. magazine' which he and a school-fellow started there. When his parents moved to Mirfield in Yorkshire Allen began work in a mill as a half-timer. But the family soon returned to Bolton, where Allen worked first as an errand-boy and then as a piecer at Cross's Mill, attending part-time at Hulton School. The teacher, J.T. Simpson, must have thought well of him, for when Allen was fourteen he urged the Clarkes to remove the boy from the mill and make him a pupil-teacher. A Mr Hughes, who succeeded Simpson, had a Swiss wife, from whom Allen Clarke and two other pupil-teachers took weekly lessons in French. Altogether, his education was far better than might have been expected for the eldest of nine children of mill-workers, and he profited by it: he was a well-read man in political and social history as well as poetry and fiction. He continued to teach in various schools until he was twenty-one, but he felt himself born to write, and developed a steady resolution to become a journalist. He was equally determined to write for and on behalf of the working class to which he belonged and with which he identified himself.

His introduction to the newspaper world might be regarded as uninspiring: in 1884 he was employed by the owner of the *Bolton Evening News*, Tillotson, to work on compiling the *Bolton Post Office Directory*, and then on copying old parish registers, at a salary of £1 a week. He seems, however, to have greatly enjoyed exploring the moors, roads and villages round Bolton (as he had to do in the course of his directory work) and consorting with some interesting colleagues.

1887 was the year of the strike of the Bolton engineers, Allen Clarke's uncle among them, for the restoration of a wage cut. Special constables were enrolled and soldiers brought into the town for the protection of the 'knobsticks' or blacklegs. They charged the crowd on at least one occasion, severely injuring a number of people. The strike lasted from May to October and was marked by great bitterness. One of its results, according to Allen Clarke, was the return of three Labour members to Bolton Town Council, among them Robert Tootill, who became MP for Bolton in 1914. Another result was Clarke's novel, *The Knobstick* [1893]; first published as a serial in the *Bolton Trotter* for 1892.

The book is characteristic of Clarke as a novelist. His themes as a rule are events in the social and political history of England, which he presents from the workers' point of view. Since he is writing novels, his accounts of these events have necessarily a fictional element: there is a mixture of real and imaginary personages, and dialogue is invented for those who actually existed. The theme of *The Knobstick* is the strike of 1887; there is also a love affair and a murder, both of minor interest. The story is unified by the characters – working-class people – who are concerned in all the events.

There is a good deal of Allen Clarke in the hero, an engineer who becomes a prominent trade unionist, later also a journalist; and in the other important personage, the generous and capable secretary of the engineers' union, who is a Lancashire humorist – as Clarke was then showing himself to be, under the name of Teddy Ashton. The book is staunchly pro-working class and anti-capitalist: the blacklegs are described by the narrator as 'miscreants' 'who would desert the camp of the strikers and come over to the capitalists'; and yet the hero, although a leader in the strike, understands the forces which impel at least some of these deserters, namely unemployment and starvation. In short, while *The Knobstick* is less a novel than a defence of the working-class ethos and of trade unions, it is an interesting and vivid book, and perceptibly a creation of the same mind as only a few years later was to produce the important and wholly non-fictional *Effects of the Factory System*.

In 1888 Tom Mann was invited to organise the Bolton Social Democratic Federation, of which Allen Clarke was an early member. Mann lived in Bolton for two years and exercised a great influence. Clarke had by now declared himself a Socialist; later, he joined the ILP. In the late 1880s he married Lavinia Pilling, of Bolton, who died with shocking suddenness after only a few months of marriage. His second wife was Eliza (Lila), daughter of John Taylor of Chorley. In 1890 Clarke left the *Bolton Evening News*, where Tillotson's successor had refused him a rise in salary (from 25s a week to 30s), and in March began producing a weekly paper of his own, the *Labour Light*, the first Labour journal to appear in Lancashire. He found a job on the *Light* for James Haslam, with whom he and J.R. Clynes had been trying unsuccessfully, to form a Lancashire Cotton Piecers' Association. Indeed, it would seem to have been Allen Clarke who enabled Haslam to become a journalist, and they were colleagues on various papers for the next half dozen years.

The *Labour Light* contained comic dialect sketches and the serialisation of Clarke's story of the Civil War in Lancashire in 1644, *The Lass at the Man and Scythe* (later revised, and renamed *John o' God's Sending*). Nevertheless, the paper did not sell. Clarke opined that mill operatives had the capacity for serious reading and thinking ground out of them by their hard and monotonous lives; they wanted light entertainment only. In 1891 Clarke supplied this in the form of the *Bolton Trotter*, a halfpenny weekly. ('Trotter', as he explained, 'is the nickname of the Bolton folk, and means a practical joker, a jester.') The *Trotter* was a great success: in three months its sales rose to over 25,000. It was almost all written by Clarke, under various names – 'Teddy Ashton', 'Ben Adhem'; and his comic creations Bill Spriggs – 't' biggest foo i' Tum Fowt, or anny other plannet' – and his termagant wife Bet became familiar figures all over Lancashire.

In 1892, however, Clarke discontinued the *Trotter* and joined the staff of the *Cotton Factory Times*, a newspaper written for the cotton operatives. Or perhaps one should rather say that the *Trotter* was partly incorporated into the *Times*, for its features of serial stories and dialect sketches were transferred.

In 1892 also, the Clarkes moved from Bolton to Blackpool, where they shared a house with Alex Thompson – 'Dangle' of the *Clarion* – and his wife. Robert Blatchford, who was a frequent visitor, became a friend, and it was the *Clarion* which published Clarke's volume of poems, *Voices and other Verses*, in 1896. In the same year Clarke left the *Cotton Factory Times*, became editor of the *Blackpool Echo*, and started *Teddy Ashton's Journal*, an immensely popular paper which continued until 1908, with a circulation of over 30,000. (*Teddy Ashton's Christmas Annual* continued until 1940, five years after Clarke's death.) Most important of all, 1897 saw the publication of Clarke's *Effects of the Factory System* as a series of articles in the *Clarion* (Dec 1897-Feb 1898); it was published in book form in 1899.

It is an account of the cotton industry in which the author supports the expression of his 'rage and pity' with copious and telling detail of the operatives' daily life in the factory and in the home (all of which Clarke knew at first hand and from bitter experience), and with clinching statistics; for instance, comparative figures of the death rate and infant mortality rate in Lancashire factory towns and in its rural districts; figures of the increases in productivity per operative between 1819 and 1882 compared with the increases in wage rates. His attack on the half-time system of schooling, which he knew both as pupil and as teacher, is said to have helped to bring the system to an end.

Nor was the book known only in England or only in English. Tolstoy read it, and was so much impressed that he arranged to have it translated into Russian and issued by Posrednik (the publishing house organised and largely financed by himself). The two men never met, but Clarke wrote to Tolstoy on 20 April 1904, describing his plan for 'colonies for people returning to agricultural work'; and Tolstoy's reply, written in English, was published by Clarke in his *Northern Weekly* for 28 May 1904.

  1904, April 30th/May 13th   Yasnaya Polyana
  Dear Friend Allen Clarke,
  I was glad to have news from you. I wish success to your scheme. It is the beginning of a great and very important work which will be done sooner or later. Your book translated in Russian [as Allen Klark, Fabrichnaya zhizn' v Anglii, Posrednik, Moscow, 1904] is very

much apreciated [sic]. Now I will try to translate one of your novels. I have not yet read them, but judging the opinions of the press and my own based on the book what [sic] I know – they must have the same merits as the "Factory System".

Your friend Leo Tolstoy

13th May 1904.

[In his Northern Weekly print, Clarke altered Tolstoy's letter in one or two trifling respects (he added 'have to be done' in brackets after 'will be done', inserted the title after 'Your book', and altered 'in' to 'into' and 'book what' to 'book which'). The original text was kindly located and transcribed by Mr Peter Henry, Professor of Slavonic Languages and Literature, Glasgow University, who gave the following reference for it: L.N. Tolstoy, Polnoe sobranie sochinenii (yubileynoe izdanie 1828-1928) 75 (Moscow, 1956) 90-1].

The plan referred to is the Daisy Colony Scheme (see Clarke's paragraphs in his Northern Weekly for 30 Jan and 13 Feb 1904 and his retrospective article in the Liverpool Weekly Post for 23 Mar 1935). It was 'a "back to the land" experiment', a co-operative farming colony such as many reformers had attempted before him. A company was formed to establish it, with half-crown shares. By Easter 1905 so much support had been given that a farm was rented near Bispham, three miles from Blackpool, and the community was started. The crops did well, and a profit was made from catering for the numerous visitors who came in summer to view the colony. 'But ah! the human nature,' as Clarke lamented: two or three dishonest participants ruined the enterprise – apparently in 1906.

In 1900 Clarke was invited to be the ILP-SDF parliamentary candidate for Rochdale in the imminent election. He made some amusing and spirited speeches during his campaign. He held advanced views, and expressed them with energy and boldness. 'He thought that . . . there was plenty for the Government to do at home without going out to South Africa to civilise people and bring them up to our standard of righteousness with sword, fire, and lyddite. . . . Among the many measures the Government might pass at home was one for the provision of old age pensions, the housing of the working classes, the nationalisation of railways, and the nationalisation of the mines. He held, too, that members of parliament should be paid out of the coffers of the country, and that election expenses ought also to come from that source' [Rochdale Times, 12 Sep 1900]. And further, 'if the electors of Rochdale sent him to Westminster he would go as a delegate of the class to which he belonged – the working class. He was prepared to act as a delegate on all great questions – if not, he would give in his resignation' [Rochdale Observer, 12 Sep 1900]. But money and time were both in short supply during his campaign. On election day he polled 901 votes; the other candidates were A.G.C. Harvey, Liberal – 5185 votes – and Colonel C.M. Royds, Conservative, who was elected with 5204 votes.

In the year before this, the Clarkes's elder child, a boy, was drowned while fishing in one of the many clay-pits in the neighbourhood. His father describes this death very emotionally in a book which he published (serially in 1901) and in book form as The Eternal Question: shall a man live again? (1902). In his youth Clarke had been agnostic, even militantly so, but the early deaths of two of his children and his second wife's psychical experiences combined to convert him to a belief in personal immortality and in communication with the spirit world. This belief was shared by his wife; nevertheless, her boy's death left her so much distressed that her husband determined to move away from the neighbourhood. In 1900 he took her back to his native Bolton, where he became editor of the Northern Weekly – in which he advocated 'labour programmes and the co-operative commonwealth'. But in 1906 the family returned to Blackpool, where they remained.

Besides producing Teddy Ashton's Journal and the Northern Weekly, Clarke was a regular contributor from 1909 to the Liverpool Weekly Post and the Blackpool Gazette, and he continued to write novels and dramatic tales which, like The Knobstick, had a political or a social theme. The last of this kind was The Men who fought for us in the "Hungry Forties" (Co-operative Press, Manchester, 1914), a story of the beginnings of Rochdale co-operation about 1842. The story also involves the Lancashire Plug-drawing Riots of 1842 and the 'Holy Weekers' (general strikers); and Clarke includes a fair amount of comic relief, generally in Lancashire dialect. The historical background is convincing: the local cobbler, of course a radical, is also a practitioner of the 'new science' of phrenology; he reads the hero's head and predicts, 'You'll be sympathetic towards the poor; your heart is with the people – if you're not already a Socialist or a Chartist you will be – though I fancy you'll take the Christian Socialist track.' The fifth chapter is devoted to a survey of the national situation in the 1830s and 1840s. Description of the evils of the period ranges from Glasgow and Dublin to London and Tolpuddle, and includes lists of capital offences (there were over one hundred) and of industries employing children. Against all these evils are pitted the radical movements of the day, such as AACAN (The Association of All Classes of All Nations, 1815) with its paper, the *New Moral World*; Chartism, with the *Northern Star*; co-operation with its numerous journals, the *Co-operative Magazine*, the *British Co-operator*, the *United Trades and Co-operative Journal* – in Clarke's opinion one of the best of the progressive newspapers.

In a later chapter Clarke returns to the subject of the state of Britain in the generation of 'The Twenty-eight Pioneers', and admits some ameliorations – the Reform Act of 1832 and the Health Act of 1848; the repeal of the Combination Laws in 1824; the work of Shaftesbury on behalf of factory children and of John Bright for the Anti-Corn Law movement.

All this sounds like tedious historical detail. But Tolstoy's remark that Clarke's novels 'must have the same merits as the "Factory System" ' is apt: such descriptions in all his social novels are not mere catalogues but are infused with feeling; they interest the reader as they interested the author. Two of the final chapters in *The Men who fought for us* deal with the establishment and the opening on 21 December 1844 of the very modest Rochdale Co-operative Store – the famous Toad Lane Store. They are written with touching earnestness and charming comedy.

Besides these novels with a social theme, Clarke's massive literary output consisted mostly of writings about Lancashire, for which he had a profound affection, and which he knew widely and intimately. He wrote accounts of Lancashire places, characters and folklore; dialect sketches and dialect verses, non-narrative poems of a simple and sentimental kind. His great success was with his comic dialect sketches, which were so much a part of life to thousands of Lancashire people that Clarke was once introduced to the 'real' Bill and Bet Spriggs. Before Clarke died he had the pleasure of finding the Spriggs sketches successful in a new medium, when in September and October 1935 four of them were read by Jim Fleetwood of Bolton on North Regional radio. Allen Clarke also had musical ability, and although self-taught, composed a number of songs, including a Socialist march, the *Song of the Dawn* (Manchester, 1897).

Although his writing appears to belong to so many different kinds, in a deeper sense it is all of a piece. It springs from his idealistic and compassionate Socialism and from his identification with the working class of Lancashire into which he was born and which he constantly celebrated in a variety of genres. He was a fluent and discursive, but seldom a vulgar writer; a serious student of social and political history; a good comedian, and a warm-hearted and likeable man.

He seems to have had no ambition to take part in local government or to stand again for Parliament – he may have thought that he did better service to the working classes with his pen. As an author he reflected that ethical form of Socialism, with its emphasis on humanitarian values, which was then flourishing in the working-class communities of the north of England. He kept a small shop in Blackpool, chiefly for the sale of his own writings. His tastes were always simple, and he accumulated no money; in fact, he was more than once in financial difficulty, even in later life. His wide knowledge of Lancashire was acquired from bicycling excursions, on which his wife was his constant companion. They were both members of the Blackpool Cycling Club and the Clarion Cycle Fellowship. Clarke founded cycling and rambling clubs and attended their meetings as often as possible. It was also he who suggested the foundation of the Lancashire Authors' Association. In yet another sphere he originated and tirelessly publicised the *Liverpool Weekly Post's* 'Babsie Fund', which provided assistance to poor mothers and babies in an age before maternity benefits existed. Many prominent people, both authors and politicians, were among his friends: besides Blatchford, Tom Mann and Clynes, one might mention W.T. Stead, Keir Hardie, J.F. Mills, Conan Doyle, Hall Caine, Lady Warwick and Annie Besant.

His youngest brother was Tom Clarke (1884-1957), the well-known journalist and broadcaster, news editor of Northcliffe's *Daily Mail* from 1919 to 1923, editor of the *Daily News* and then the *News Chronicle* from 1926 to 1933, and author of a number of books. Tom was trained in journalism by his brother Allen (see *Liverpool Weekly Post*, 2 Mar 1935): he began his career by working for Allen's *Northern Weekly*, and in his book *Journalism* he speaks gratefully of his brother's generosity. But there were twenty-one years between them; Tom soon left Bolton, and their lives diverged widely, both literally and ideologically.

Allen Clarke died on 12 December 1935, at the age of seventy-two, and was buried in Marton Cemetery, Blackpool. His wife had died in 1928. He was survived by three sons and a daughter: Franklin Clarke of Bramhall, Cheshire, journalist; Charles Harvey Clarke of Cleveleys; Edward Clarke, and Mrs Dewhurst, both of Blackpool. The gross value of his estate was £553, with net personalty nil.

A few months after his death a fund was set up to renovate as a memorial to him one of the Fylde windmills (the old mill at Marton) which he had written of so affectionately in *Windmill Land* (1916) and *More Windmill Land* (1918) [See *Manchester Evening Chronicle*, 11 Mar 1936, *Manchester City News*, 13 Mar 1936, *Bolton Evening Chronicle*, 6 and 25 May 1936]. But information from the Chief Librarian of Blackpool strongly suggests that not enough money was subscribed to carry out the project.

Writings: It is only possible to include here a selection of Clarke's extensive writings but further details may be found in the BL *Catalogue, WWW* (1929-40) and especially in A. Sparke, *Bibliographia Boltoniensis* (Manchester, 1913) 44-9. He was a prolific contributor to journals and newspapers: he edited and wrote most of *Labour Light* (1890-1); *Bolton Trotter* (1891-4); *Teddy Ashton's Journal* (1896-9), which became *Teddy Ashton's Northern Weekly* (1899-1907) and he contributed weekly to the *Liverpool Weekly Post* from 1908 to 1935. *This Workaday World* (n.d.); *Tum Fowt Sketches* (by Teddy Ashton) (Bolton, 1891 and later editions); *The Knobstick: a story of love and labour* (Manchester, [1893]); *Tales of a Deserted Village* [Barrow Bridge] (Manchester, [1894]); *Voices and Other Verses* (Manchester, 1896); *The Effects of the Factory System* (1899, 3rd ed. rev., 1913); *The Object of Life: being letters to a young man on religion, education, literature, love and business* (Bolton, 1902); *The Eternal Question: shall a man live again?* (Bolton, 1902, new ed. rev. 1919); *Can we get back to the Land? (The Daisy Colony Scheme)* (Manchester, 1904) 16 pp.; *Science and the Soul: some observations on Haeckel's "Riddle of the Universe"* (Daisy Series, no. 1, 1904); *Starved into Surrender* (1904); *What is Man? (a sequel to "Science and the Soul"): an attempt to explain man's place and purpose in the universe* (Daisy Series, no. 2, 1904); articles in *Teddy Ashton's Northern Weekly*, 30 Jan – 28 May 1904; *Lancashire Lads and Lasses* (Manchester, 1906); *Unemployed: a dramatic tale in four scenes; and an out-of-work's reply* (1906); *The Red Flag: a tale of the people's woe* (1908); *The Men who fought for us in the "Hungry Forties": a tale of pioneers and beginnings* (Manchester, 1914); *Windmill Land* (1916, rev. ed. 1933); *When the Hurly-Burly's done* (1919); *Moorlands and Memories* (Bolton, 1920; 3rd ed., 1924); *The Story of Blackpool* (1923); *What do we live for?* (Labour Press Society, Manchester, n.d.) 15 pp.; weekly autobiographical articles, *Liverpool Weekly Post*, 24 Feb – 29 Dec 1934 and 5 Jan – 14 Dec 1935.

Sources: *Labour Prophet 5*, no. 60 (Dec 1896) 185-7 [photograph]; *Labour Annual* (1898); *Rochdale Observer*, 12, 22, 26 and 29 Sep 1900; *Rochdale Times*, 12 Sep 1900 and 3 Oct 1900; A. Sparke, *Bibliographia Boltoniensis* (Manchester, 1913); M. Yates, *A Lancashire Anthology* (Liverpool, 1923); J.R. Swann, *Lancashire Authors* (St Anne's on Sea, 1924); *WWW* (1929-40); A. Maude, *Tolstoy and his Problems* (1931); autobiographical articles, *Liverpool*

Weekly Post, Feb-Dec 1934, Jan-Dec 1935; ibid., 2 and 23 Mar 1935; *Manchester Evening Chronicle*, 16 Sep 1935 and 11 Mar 1936; *Manchester City News*, 13 Mar 1936; *Bolton Evening News*, 25 Apr 1936; *Manchester Evening Chronicle*, 6 and 25 May 1936; T. Clarke, *Journalism* (1945); R. and E. Frow, 'C. Allen Clarke, Lancashire Author', *Eccles and District History Society* (1971-2); biographical information: Blackpool PL; Miss M. Hodgson, BBC Written Archives Centre, Caversham. OBIT. *Bolton Evening News, Daily Dispatch* and *Manchester Evening Chronicle*, 12 Dec 1935; *Blackpool Gazette* and *Liverpool Weekly Post*, 14 Dec 1935; *Labour Party Report* (1936).

The editors are indebted to Mr and Mrs E. Frow for their earlier work on Allen Clarke.

MARGARET 'ESPINASSE

See also: †James HASLAM (1869-1937).

CLARKE, John Smith (1885-1959)
SOCIALIST, LABOUR MP, CIRCUS TRAINER, ART SPECIALIST AND ANTIQUARY

John S. Clarke was one of the most remarkable and unusual personalities ever to become a Labour MP. He was born on 4 February 1885 at 66 Albert Road, Jarrow, County Durham, the thirteenth child of John Smith Clarke and his wife, Sally Ann (née Chiswell). There were to be fourteen children born to Mrs Clarke, of whom only seven lived to adult life. The father was a draper's assistant, and the family travelled around the country as Mr Clarke moved from one job to another. The young Clarke lived for some time in Pentonville Road, Islington, London, and he was later at an elementary school in Castleford, Yorkshire. His education was inevitably peripatetic and his boyhood experiences unusual:

> I could ride without saddle or bridle when I was ten years old – that is, I could stick on a horse at trot, canter, or gallop. Both my grandfathers were superb riders, and an uncle was reputed to be the best horse breaker in Britain fifty years ago. In Yorkshire and Hexham in Northumberland I spent an early youth among horses, and a considerable knowledge of them I picked up from the Grays and Smiths – Romany folk of those districts whose caravans I haunted then and whom I often visited later in life [*Sunday Mail*, 17 Jan 1932].

In his teens Clarke joined a circus and menagerie, learned to break horses and train them for public performance, and then began to work with more dangerous animals, including wolves, pythons and lions. He was always passionately fond of animals, and in later life he used to spend some of his holidays with circuses. He claimed to be Britain's youngest and oldest lion-tamer, starting at the age of seventeen and making his last appearance at sixty-five.

When he was in his early twenties he went to sea, and on a second trip in 1909 visited South and East Africa, and spent some time in Zululand, greatly enjoying himself: 'but one thing I could never get accustomed to – the rancid smell of a Kraal. Every Zulu rubs fat on his body, and the smell of it is sometimes overpowering.'

Exactly when Clarke became a Socialist is not known but it was probably around the turn of the century. Here is his own account of the process:

> I very early saw there was something wrong with the economic system, and nothing I heard from preachers and friends satisfied me. The efforts of religiously-minded people to keep me to the straight and narrow path resulted in sending me the other way. I devoured all the books they condemned, and began to hate the names of respectability, orthodoxy, and conventionality. I eventually joined the Social Democratic Federation, and for some years studied the writings of Marx, Engels, Hyndman and Bax [*Sunday Mail*, 7 Feb 1932].

Clarke first achieved minor notoriety by his involvement with the supply of arms to Russian revolutionaries during 1905-6. The outline of the story of this gun-running has been known for many years [Lee and Archbold (1935) Ch. 18; Hobson (1938) 125-7] and it is clear that the SDF was the organisation mostly involved in the establishment of supply centres at the ports, and boats to take the guns and ammunition to the Baltic ports of Russia. Clarke worked in Newcastle, and was jailed for five days for his part in the operations. It should be added that the sentences passed upon those who were prosecuted for smuggling arms were remarkably lenient.

In 1910 Clarke moved to Edinburgh, where Arthur Woodburn [*Plebs*, Jan 1928] remembered him as a rationalist lecturer on 'The Mound', Edinburgh's debating forum. Clarke used to speak on Sunday evenings to large audiences. He also edited for a time the *Reform Journal*, a rationalist monthly, and began writing for both *Forward* and the organ of the Socialist Labour Party, the *Socialist*. When he joined the SLP is not known, but it must have been soon after he settled in Edinburgh, and by 1914 he had been appointed editor of their journal. During these years before the First World War he met a number of the leading personalities of the Socialist movement, and he later wrote about them in his usual frank and blunt way. He had one encounter only with Victor Grayson, and 'disliked him as a swollen-headed puppy'; H.M. Hyndman 'was one of the most conceited old men I ever met'; but Clarke was enchanted with Cunninghame Graham, and the only critical comment he made on Graham was that 'his calligraphy is the most atrocious on earth'.

The SLP maintained an anti-war position during the First World War. Clarke spent at least the early years in Edinburgh, and in March 1916 when David Kirkwood and other engineering shop stewards were deported from Glasgow to Edinburgh, he was able to help with their accommodation. Clarke himself seems successfully to have avoided military service – by going on the run – and most of the latter part of the war he spent secretly at a Mr Turner's farm at Arleston, near Derby. From there Clarke continued writing for the *Socialist*, and together with Tom Bell and William Paul, was largely responsible for its regular appearance. In 1919, when the war was over, the Clyde Workers' Committee decided to resume publication of the *Worker*, which had been banned in 1916. Clarke accepted an invitation to become editor, and for a while the paper flourished. He was adopted as Labour candidate for Perth in 1918; but he did not contest the seat at the general election of that year.

In July – August 1920 the Second Congress of the Communist International was held in Moscow. Clarke and William Gallacher went as representatives of the Scottish Workers' Committee; other delegates were Sylvia Pankhurst, representing the Communist Party (British Section of the Third International); Dave Ramsay, Jack Tanner and J.T. Murphy from the national shop stewards' committee; Helen Crawfurd and Margery Newbold from the left wing of the ILP. The Congress lasted three weeks, but Clarke stayed on after the Congress was over, and for a time worked in the Kremlin translating Lenin's speeches into English. He became friendly with a number of revolutionary leaders, both Russian and foreign, among them Angelica Balabanova and the Americans John Reed and his wife. Clarke gave a good account of his life during his Russian visit in the *Pen Pictures . . .* (1921). When he returned to Britain he certainly considered himself a Bolshevist, but he never joined the British Communist Party, and was critical of the Comintern's general tactics as they applied to different national situations. He resigned from the editorship of the *Worker* in 1922, and was succeeded by J.R. Campbell. From this time Clarke attached himself to the ILP, and much of his political activity was concentrated upon work for the Plebs League and the Labour College movement. He had already become well known as a Labour College lecturer before the war; and he was an extremely lively and vivid speaker. At the height of his popularity he could fill a cinema for an evening's lecture. Throughout the 1920s he wrote regularly for *Plebs*, the *Socialist* and the Glasgow *Forward*; and he seems to have been on the regular staff of *Forward* from 1925 to 1929. In 1928 he produced the first shilling booklet published by the NCLC, *Marxism and History*, a clear, simple exposition of historical materialism.

In the general election of 1929 Clarke stood successfully as ILP candidate for the Maryhill division of Glasgow. His two years in Parliament were not a particularly enriching experience for anyone concerned. Clarke never acclimatised himself to the atmosphere of Westminster, finding its formalised procedures and ancient traditions tedious and tiresome. On the other hand, it would seem that he really did not try very hard, for his interventions in debate or questions were very few; although he was appointed a member of the Ullswater Conference on Electoral Reform. The bizarre side of his character demonstrated itself by his practice of keeping a couple of live snakes in his locker at the House of Commons, which he would on occasion surreptitiously drop into a colleague's pocket. More acceptable, but no doubt irritating to the victims, was his habit of writing epitaphs for certain of his fellow MPs. There is an amusing example, referring to Ramsay MacDonald at the time of the latter's defection from the Labour Party in August 1931, in *Bull. Soc. Lab. Hist.*, no. 27 (1973) 35. But Clarke was perfectly capable of civilised relationships with those he did not care for. With MacDonald, for instance, he seems to have remained on terms of civility after 1931, partly because of their common friendship with Jane Clapperton, one of the notable Edinburgh literary figures of the last decades of the nineteenth century. But Clarke was certainly not of the stuff that makes MPs; he contested Maryhill in the 1931 election, but was defeated. In the following year he left the ILP when that organisation disaffiliated from the Labour Party. From this time on, he was politically active only at the local level. He had been a Labour representative on the Glasgow City Council from 1926 to 1929, and he was elected again from 1941 to 1951. He also served as a magistrate for six years, was a member of the Clyde Navigation Trust, and was on the board of government of the Glasgow School of Art.

The activities, however, which increasingly occupied his time as he got older were connected with the Arts and Humanities. He was a Fellow of the Society of Antiquaries of Scotland before 1925; a member of the Royal Commission of the Fine Arts for Scotland; and a trustee of the Scottish National Portrait Gallery from 1930 to 1933. He became well known as a specialist on the Primitive and Renaissance periods, and had much to do with the purchase by the Glasgow Corporation of the famous Morton portrait of Mary, Queen of Scots. Clarke also had an expert knowledge of old weapons and armour, and he was frequently consulted by museums on these subjects.

Clarke wrote for newspapers and journals throughout his life. His range was very wide, and he could write verse as well as prose. Besides his mock epitaphs, he published a volume entitled *Satires, Lyrics and Poems* which included serious as well as satiric verse. He wrote on 'Mankind and Civilisation' and on 'The Fallacies of Sir Arthur Keith'; much on politics and economics, particularly on recent and contemporary Scottish economic and political affairs, and several essays on the political ideas of Burns. He always claimed to have been the first Englishman to become president of the Robert Burns Federation. In the last period of his life he gained much personal satisfaction from the many friendships he made with children through editing the Uncle John column and Satchel Club in the *Scottish Daily Express*.

Clarke married Sarah Millicent Balkind – exactly when has so far not been discovered but it was certainly before 1911. They had one son, Dr John H.C. Clarke, who at the time of his parents' deaths was Medical Officer of Health for Cyprus. Clarke's wife predeceased him by three months. At the end of his life Clarke lived in a small rented house in the Ibrox district of Glasgow. Among the antiques and possessions he left were a snuff-box of Marie Antoinette's, comedian Harry Lauder's walking stick, and a signed photograph of Lenin, which Lenin gave to 'Comrade Clarke' for curing his dog of an ailment. Clarke died on 30 January 1959 in Southern General Hospital, Glasgow, and his personal estate was valued at just over £4000.

Writings: *Potted Sociology* (SLP, Glasgow, 1918); *Satires, Lyrics and Poems* (SLP, Glasgow, 1919); *Bombs or Brains? Dynamite or Organisation?* (NWC, Glasgow, [1921]) 32 pp.; *Pen Pictures of Russia under the 'Red Terror'* (NWC, Glasgow, 1921); *Robert Burns and his Politics* (NWC, Glasgow, 1921, another ed. 1925; repr. from *Forward*) 32 pp.; *An Epic of Municipalisation: the story of Glasgow's Loch Katrine water supply* (Forward, Glasgow, 1928) 48 pp.; *Marxism and History* (NCLC, [1928]); 'The Reign of Terror', *Plebs 20*, no. 7 (July-Aug 1928) 150-1; 'Fighting Toryism a Century ago' ibid., *20*, no. 4 (Apr 1929) 81-2; 'Now you've done it', ibid., *21*, no. 7 (July 1929) 152; 'Mankind and Civilisation', ibid., *22*, no. 1 (Jan 1930)

8-9; 'The Fallacies of Sir Arthur Keith', ibid., *23*, no. 7 (July 1931) 159-60; 'Roughing it round the World', *Sunday Mail*, 3 Jan – 14 Feb 1932; *Circus Parade* (1936). He also wrote articles in the *Socialist* (1910-22), *Forward* (1923-8) and in the *Glasgow Evening News* (1935-6). The last three items comprising 300 articles pasted into one scrapbook, have been deposited in the Mitchell Library, Glasgow under the title *Encyclopedia of Glasgow*.

Sources: A. Woodburn, 'John S. Clarke: the man and his book', *Plebs 20*, no. 1 (Jan 1928) 8-9; J.S. Clarke's life story in the *Sunday Mail* (see writings); H.W. Lee and E. Archbold, *Social-Democracy in Britain* (1935); W. Gallacher, *Revolt on the Clyde: an autobiography* (1936); S.G. Hobson, *Pilgrim to the Left: memoirs of a modern revolutionist* (1938); T. Bell, *Pioneering Days* (1941); S.R. Graubard, *British Labour and the Russian Revolution 1917-1924* (Cambridge, Mass., 1956); W. Gallacher, *The Last Memoirs of William Gallacher* (1966); R. Challinor, 'Gun-running from the North East Coast', *North East Group for the Study of Labour History, Bull.*, no. 6 (Oct 1972) 14-16; idem, 'Ramsay MacDonald – John S. Clarke correspondence', *Bull. Soc. Lab. Hist.*, no. 27 (autumn 1973) 34-5, R. Challinor, *John S. Clarke: parliamentarian, poet and lion-tamer* (1977); biographical information: the late T.A.K. Elliott, CMG; personal information: D. Clarke, Huddersfield, nephew; Dr J.H.C. Clarke, Worcester, Cape Province, South Africa, son; L. Hutchinson, Lichfield; J.P.M. Millar, Dartmouth; Mrs S. Sisterson, Gravesend, niece. OBIT. *Scotsman, Scottish Daily Express*, and *Times*, 31 Jan 1959.

RAYMOND CHALLINOR
JOHN SAVILLE

See also: *William GALLACHER.

CREMER, Sir William Randal (1828-1908)
TRADE UNIONIST AND RADICAL MP

Randal Cremer was born on 18 March 1828 at Fareham, Hants, the son of George Morris Cremer, a coach-painter, and Harriet Tutte, the daughter of a local builder. He was brought up in great poverty, his father having deserted the family when his son was little more than an infant. To support herself and her children his mother kept a dame school. Cremer was sent to a church school, but at twelve he had to leave it, to begin earning. He was first employed in a shipyard as a pitch boy – to heat the pitch and do odd jobs. After three years his employer failed in business, and at fifteen Cremer was then apprenticed as a carpenter for six years to an uncle who was in the building trade and who took him without a premium. At some point during this period he became a radical. After his apprenticeship was ended he was for a time employed by a coach-building firm in Fareham, but he soon migrated to Brighton, where he joined the Working-Man's Institute associated with the well-known preacher and social reformer the Rev. Frederick Robertson. It was in Brighton during an election that Cremer made his first political speech and discovered that he was a good speaker.

In 1852, when he was twenty-four, he moved to London, where he found work in the West End and began taking an active part in politics and trade unionism. Between 1858 and 1860 he was involved in the Nine Hours dispute of the London building workers: he was a delegate from his shop to the council of the Nine Hours Movement (for which his employer dismissed him), and ultimately became a member of the 'Conference', which consisted of seven men from each branch of the building trade. The master builders locked out 70,000 men. Cremer made many speeches during the campaign in defence of the right to combine. The result was a drawn battle: the workers failed to win the Nine Hour Day but the hated Document was withdrawn [Webb (1920) 228-9] and the struggle ranks as a leading event in the history of mid-Victorian trade unionism. It not only encouraged general feelings of solidarity between different trades, but it led directly to the establishment of the London Trades Council and to the formation of the

Amalgamated Society of Carpenters and Joiners. Cremer was a foundation member of both, and this strike of the building workers marks his emergence as a leading figure in London radical politics. Cremer, Howell and Odger failed to convert the LTC to the idea of political involvement, and they and others, including Applegarth, promoted the trade unionists' Manhood Suffrage and Vote by Ballot Association in October 1862. T.G. Facey was secretary. The presence of Cremer and his colleagues gave hope that the Association would become the political counterpart of the Trades Council. Certainly this new initiative carried one stage further the revival of interest in political reform which was to develop so vigorously in this decade.

When the American Civil War broke out Cremer, like most (but not all) advanced working-class radicals of his day, supported the North; and early in 1863 he was one of the organisers of the famous meeting of London working men, largely the initiative of E.S. Beesly and presided over by John Bright, about which Marx has left a vivid description in a letter to Engels [9 Apr 1863]. Cremer was also deeply involved in support for Italian unification; he was a friend of Mazzini and met Garibaldi on the latter's extraordinary visit to England in 1864 which so troubled the British Government. When the International Working Men's Association was established following the inaugural meeting, chaired by E.S. Beesly, on 28 September 1864, the first council meeting on 5 October elected Odger as chairman and Cremer as secretary. As Marx explained to Engels [letter dated 4 Nov 1864] he and Cremer were members of the sub-committee charged with producing a statement of principles, and this was the opportunity which led to the Inaugural Address. Cremer remained secretary until the first Congress of the International at Geneva in September 1866; and when it voted for the abolition of standing armies and the general arming of the people, he dissented. To his surprise, evidently, he was not re-elected secretary. He resigned from the council, was not re-elected at the 1867 Congress, and thus ended his connection with the International – with which in any case he must have been increasingly out of sympathy.

At home Cremer continued the part of advanced radical. He was involved, along with Howell, in the foundation of the Reform League in 1865. Edmond Beales was president, Howell secretary and Cremer a full-time organiser. His closest working colleague was George Howell with whom, however, he had many differences. Cremer was quick to take offence and often made accusations that could not be substantiated, characteristics which continued throughout his working life. Howell, on his side, was neurotically sensitive to criticism. The complicated history of the Reform League, the winning of the Reform Bill of 1867 and the general election of 1868 – events in which Cremer played important roles – have been told exhaustively in a number of places [Harrison (1965); Smith (1966); Cowling (1967); Leventhal (1971); Fraser (1974)]. Cremer was party with Howell to the largely secret agreement with the managers of the Liberal Party whereby an independent stance of the Reform League in the general election was sacrificed to the interests of the Liberal Party. Both Howell and Cremer received payment for their services [Harrison (1965) Chs 3 and 4].

Cremer stood for Warwick as a Radical in the 1868 election – a hopeless constituency for him to contest – and the only matter worth noting is the reference in his election address to the importance of international arbitration of disputes between nations: the central concern which was to occupy him for the last thirty years of his life. After the election he continued to be involved as prominently as ever in the industrial and political developments of the period. On 1 March 1867, John Stuart Mill wrote to Cremer giving his views on the Reform League [Mineka and Lindley (1972) 3, 1247-8]; and in December of the same year [ibid., 1341-2] and again in May 1870 [ibid., 4, 1724-5] he wrote letters (to Thomas Hare and to Edwin Chadwick respectively) expressing his high opinion of the abilities and usefulness of Odger, Cremer and Howell. Cremer helped to establish the Labour Representation League in 1869; and he was active in the early years of the Trades Union Congress, being elected to the first Parliamentary Committee which he had himself suggested at the second Congress in 1869. On the outbreak of the Franco-Prussian war of 1870, Cremer formed a Workmen's Peace Committee of about fifty men, most of whom had been his colleagues in the Reform League; and an appeal was made to the working classes to support the neutrality of Britain. The appeal referred to 'arbitration as a substitute for war', and from this committee arose the International Arbitration League. An outline plan was drawn up: 'for the establishment of a High Court of Nations'. The League was supported by – among others – Samuel Morley and George W. Palmer, later by Richard and George Cadbury and Andrew Carnegie. The first president of the League was Edmond Beales; after his death, the Rt Hon. Thomas Burt MP. In 1877 Cremer's close friend (and later biographer) Howard Evans was elected to the chair. In these years Cremer found his real vocation.

But he was still, in the early 1870s, an active working-class politician; a land nationaliser and member of the Land and Labour League; an unsuccessful candidate for the London School Board in 1870 and 1872; a choleric opponent of Applegarth within the Carpenter's Union over the latter's membership of the R.C. on Contagious Diseases [Postgate [1923] 290]; a calumniator of Alexander Macdonald at the 1875 TUC (an attack which he was forced to retract). Cremer retained certain progressive industrial attitudes in later life: he seconded a fair wages resolution in 1891 and during the 1890s he supported the claim of the postal workers for a parliamentary inquiry.

But radical politics were now submerged beneath his total dedication to the cause of the peaceful settlement of international disputes between nation states. He was finally elected to the House of Commons in 1885 as Liberal MP for the Haggerston division of Shoreditch (having stood for a second time at Warwick in 1874) and he used his parliamentary position to extend and develop his work for peaceful solutions to external conflicts. He was in Parliament till 1895, and again from 1900 to his death. The last thirty years of his life, for which he was best known to contemporaries, lie outside the scope of this *Dictionary*; the details have been fully set out in the biography by Howard Evans and the many articles (including obituaries) written about Cremer and his work. The decorations of many countries were bestowed upon him; and in 1904 he was awarded the Nobel Peace Prize. In 1906 Campbell-Bannerman offered Cremer a knighthood, which he refused; to be accepted, however, a year later when he was asked to reconsider his decision.

Randal Cremer was a pugnacious pacifist who aroused the hostility of many against whom he sharpened his differences. In 1871, in connection with the Applegarth affair, Beesly had described him as 'one of the dirtiest scoundrels that the working class has turned up lately' [quoted Harrison (1965) 263 n. 1]. In his last years, after the death of his second wife, he lived in his office in Lincoln's Inn Fields, with a turn-up bed and a small gas stove. On the landing he had put up an iron gate, which he kept locked, and a peephole which enabled him to decide whether to unlock or not. He was noted also in these years for a ferocious opposition to the women's suffrage movement, and spoke at least twice in the House against it, referring on one occasion to 'female hooligans'. His mother had been a strict Methodist; he himself was not altogether an agnostic, but rather a very broad-minded Christian.

He died from pneumonia on 22 July 1908. The funeral service was held at Whitefield's Tabernacle in Tottenham Court Road and he was cremated at Golders Green, his ashes being buried in the grave of his second wife Lucy in Hampstead Cemetery. He married his first wife in 1860 and she died in 1876. Cremer left an estate of £9656. Except for a small legacy to a nephew, his property was to be handed over to trustees for the Arbitration League; but he asked his executors to spend £900 in the completion and upkeep of almshouses which he had planned to erect at Fareham in memory of his mother, and this was done.

Writings: *Shall Men or Women rule the World?* (n.d.) P; *Some of the Legal Privileges of Women* n.d. P; *The Progress and Advantages of International Arbitration: address at Christiania on January 15th 1905* (Stockholm, 1905) 8 pp.; 'Parliamentary and Interparliamentary Experiences', *Independent* (NY) *61*, no. 3013, 30 Aug 1906, 508-13.

Sources: *Times*, 25 Nov 1885; E. Brown, 'Working-Men in the British Parliament', *Harper's New Monthly Mag.* 73, no. 436 (1886) 511 [portrait]; *Dod* (1886), (1894), (1901) and (1905); *Hansard* (1886-95), (1901-08); G.W.T., 'Is the War Sentiment declining?: an interview with Mr William Randall [*sic*] Cremer, M.P.', *Woman's Signal*, 3, no. 72, 16 May 1895, 305-7; *WWW* (1897-1915); *Reformers' Year Book* (1900) 150; *DNB* (1901-11) [by J.R. MacDonald]; H. Evans, *Sir Randal Cremer: his life and work* (1909); F. Chandler, *A History of the Amalgamated Society of Carpenters and Joiners* (1910); A.W. Humphrey, *A History of Labour Representation* (1912); J. Bardoux, *L'Angleterre radicale: essai de psychologie sociale (1906-1913)* (Paris, 1913); H. Evans, *Radical Fights of Forty Years* [1913?]; S. and B. Webb, *The History of Trade Unionism* (rev. ed. 1920); R.W. Postgate, *The Builders' History* [1923]; F.E. Gillespie, *Labor and Politics in England 1850-1867* (Duke Univ. Press, 1927); *Encyclopaedia Britannica* (1929) and (1969) eds.; E.S. Pankhurst, *The Suffrage Movement: an intimate account of persons and ideals* (1931); K. Marx and F. Engels, *Correspondence 1846-1895* (1934); G.D.H. Cole, *British Working Class Politics, 1832-1914* (1941); B.C. Roberts, *The Trades Union Congress 1868-1921* (1958); H.A. Clegg et al., *A History of British Trade Unions since 1889* vol. 1: *1889-1910* (Oxford, 1964); H. Collins and C. Abramsky, *Karl Marx and the British Labour Movement* (1965); R. Harrison, *Before the Socialists: studies in labour and politics* (1965); F.B. Smith, *The Making of the Second Reform Bill* (1966); M. Cowling, *1867: Disraeli, Gladstone and Revolution: the passing of the second Reform Bill* (Cambridge, 1967); H. Pelling, *Social Geography of British Elections 1885-1910* (1967); F.M. Leventhal, *Respectable Radical: George Howell and Victorian working class politics* (1971); *The Later Letters of John Stuart Mill 1849-1873* ed. F.E. Mineka and D.N. Lindley vols 3 and 4 (Toronto, 1972); W.H. Fraser, *Trade Unions and Society: the struggle for acceptance 1850-1880* (1974). OBIT. *Portsmouth Evening News*, 22 July 1908; *Times*, 23 and 27 July 1908; *Holborn and Finsbury Guardian*, 31 July 1908; *Hampstead and Highgate Express*, 1 Aug 1908; *American J. of International Law 2* (1908) 858-62; *Times*, 20 Oct 1908 [will].

MARGARET 'ESPINASSE
JOHN SAVILLE

See also: †Robert APPLEGARTH; *Edward Spencer BEESLY; †Fred MADDISON.

CRUMP, James (1873-1960)
TRADE UNIONIST AND LABOUR ALDERMAN

James Crump was born at Bromsgrove, Worcestershire, on 25 August 1873, the son of Elijah Crump, a nailmaker, and his wife, Mary Ann. He was educated at Bromsgrove Church of England School, working during the evenings and on Saturdays to help pay the school fees of 3 d per week. After leaving school he appears to have worked in and around Bromsgrove until he was in his early twenties, when he moved to Birmingham and found a job as a tram conductor. He subsequently became a tram driver and followed this occupation until he was appointed a trade union officer.

Crump's union activities began when he joined the Amalgamated Association of Tramway and Hackney Carriage Employees, founded in 1889, shortly after starting work in Birmingham. He quickly emerged as a leading figure in the local affairs of the union, which was renamed the Amalgamated Association of Tramway and Vehicle Workers in 1902, and he succeeded A.G. Jones as full-time secretary of the Birmingham branch in 1908. He was one of the union's representatives on Birmingham Trades Council in 1909 and 1910, and served on the executive committee from 1911 until 1918. When the Tramway and Vehicle Workers merged with the London and Provincial Union of Licensed Vehicle Workers to become the United Vehicle Workers in 1920, Crump was appointed secretary of the Birmingham No. 1 branch of the enlarged union. Two years later the United Vehicle Workers amalgamated with thirteen other unions to form the Transport and General Workers' Union and Crump was elected Midlands area secretary of the new organisation, retaining this post until his retirement in 1938.

As the senior TGWU officer in Birmingham Crump 'played an heroic part in the conduct of the General Strike of 1926' in the city [TGWU, *Record* (Feb 1961)]. He represented the TGWU on the Birmingham Trade Unions' Emergency Committee, which was responsible for the overall direction of the strike and whose members were eventually arrested *en masse*. The pretext for the arrests was a report in the *Birmingham Strike Bulletin* of 11 May, to the effect that the Government had been defeated in the House of Commons on a motion to delete from the Emergency Powers Act of 1920 the regulations providing for arrest without warrant for certain acts. The account had first appeared in a London strike bulletin, the *Cricklewood Workers' Gazette*, and was based on a simple error of transposition in the voting figures for the Government and for the Opposition. It was published in the *Strike Bulletin* in good faith but after consultation with the Home Office police searched the offices of the Trade Unions' Emergency Committee and confiscated printing machinery, typewriters and duplicators as well as the remaining copies of the newspaper. Later in the day all the members of the emergency committee were arrested, together with John Strachey, the editor of the *Strike Bulletin*, and Leslie Plummer, manager of the ILP paper, *New Leader*, who had been assisting with production.

The committee members appeared before the Birmingham Stipendiary, Lord Ilkeston, on 14 May. Two of the committee members were discharged because they had known nothing of the report until after it had been published but the remaining sixteen, together with Strachey and Plummer, were found guilty. Sentencing the eighteen, Lord Ilkeston stated that with the General Strike being called off he could take a more lenient view of the offences. Accordingly, eight were bound over for six months and ten, including Crump, were fined £10 each with the alternative of thirty-one days' imprisonment.

The failure of the General Strike badly weakened trade unionism in Birmingham and the surrounding district but Crump did much to revive the TGWU in the Midlands, which was one of the first areas of the union to recover. In Birmingham itself during the ten years following the General Strike the number of TGWU branches affiliated to the Trades Council increased by fourteen while the total number of affiliations rose by only eleven.

In addition to his trade union work Crump was an important figure in the civic and political life of Birmingham for almost half a century. His long involvement in public affairs began in 1911 when he was appointed a member of the Old Age Pensions Committee. During the First World War he served on the Citizens' Committee, which was responsible for directing and co-ordinating relief work. At the municipal elections of 1920 he successfully contested Saltley ward on behalf of the Labour Party. He lost his seat in 1923 but was re-elected two years later and then served continuously as a councillor until July 1937, when he was elected to fill the aldermanic vacancy caused by the death of Henry Simpson. He also became a magistrate in 1937. During his years as a councillor he was a member of many committees, including tramways and omnibus, traffic control, and the watch committee, of which he was appointed chairman in 1936.

Crump rose to prominence on the City Council against a background of dissension within Birmingham Borough Labour Party. During the winter of 1927-28 this culminated in an open split and the expulsion of some leading left-wing members, including Crump's son, J.W. Crump, the chairman of the Edgbaston Divisional Party [Hastings (1959) 99-105; Redman [1957]]. Crump was on the right of the Borough Party and on the crucial motion voted for his son's expulsion. J.W. Crump later became the leader of the Communist Party in Birmingham and an organiser for the AEU.

The effect of these internal differences was intensified by the extreme weakness of the Labour Party in Birmingham during the inter-war years. In this period only three Labour Lord Mayors were elected, all of them from the right wing of the Party. The third of these was Crump, who became Lord Mayor in November 1938. By this time there were indications of some weakening in the tradition of Chamberlainism. Among the first signs was the successful rent strike staged by Birmingham council house tenants during the late spring and early summer of 1939, with the support of all sections of the left. As a Labour Lord Mayor Crump was able to act as a mediator between the Municipal Tenants' Association and the estates committee, and his influence was an important factor in the outcome of the dispute. The final months of his mayoral year were overshadowed by the beginning of the Second World War and one of his last acts was to launch the Lord Mayor's War Relief Fund.

During the war Crump and his wife, Ellen Elizabeth, were bombed out of their home and went to live with their daughter at Drayton, near Belbroughton, Worcestershire. Mrs Crump was the daughter of John Rose, of Little Wolford, Warwickshire. She shared her husband's beliefs and gave him devoted support in his trade union and political work. She died suddenly at her daughter's home on 31 May 1943 and was cremated at Lodge Hill Crematorium, Birmingham, three days later.

After the war Crump became one of Birmingham's elder statesmen. He remained on the City Council as an alderman until 1958 and in spite of advancing years made a valuable contribution to its work. In terms of political attitudes he moved further to the right during these years, to a point where he became almost non-partisan. His main interest outside his work was association football and he always followed the fortunes of Aston Villa FC with keen interest. Photographs of him taken when he was Lord Mayor show a plain, open face reflecting the 'simple dignity' of the man [*Picture Post*, 21 Jan 1939].

Crump died on 5 December 1960 in Selly Oak Hospital, Birmingham, and was cremated at Lodge Hill Crematorium on 9 December. He was survived by one son, James W. Crump, but his daughter and another son had predeceased him. He left effects valued at £258.

Sources: (1) MSS: Minute Books of Birmingham Trades Council, 1909-18. (2) Other: *Annual Reports* of the Amalgamated Association of Tramway and Hackney Carriage Employees, Amalgamated Association of Tramway and Vehicle Workers, United Vehicle Workers, and TGWU, TGWU papers, MRC, Warwick Univ.; Birmingham Trades Council, *Annual Reports*, 1909-18; R.H. Brazier and E. Sandford, *Birmingham and the Great War 1914-1919* (Birmingham, 1921); *Cornish's Birmingham Year Book*, 1927-40; *Birmingham Post*, 30 Jan 1937, 26 and 27 July and 10 Nov 1938, 4 Oct 1958; *Birmingham Gazette*, 30 Jan and 28 Oct 1937, 9 and 10 Nov 1938; *Evening Despatch* [Birmingham], 30 Jan and 24 July 1937, 7 Apr, 7 and 26 July 1938, 9 Nov 1938; *Birmingham Mail*, 28 July 1937, 6 Jan, 7 and 27 July, and 9 Nov 1938, in Birmingham Biography Newscuttings, Birmingham Central Library; *Town Crier*, 29 July 1938; TGWU, *Record* (Dec 1938); *Picture Post*, 21 Jan 1939; *Birmingham Post Year Book and Who's Who*, 1949-62; A. Briggs, *History of Birmingham* vol. *2: 1865-1938* (1952); 'J. Redman' [pseud. of Brian Pearce], *The Communist Party and the Labour Left 1925-1929* with an Introduction by J. Saville (Hull, [1957]) 32 pp.; R.P. Hastings, 'The Labour Movement in Birmingham 1927-1945' (Birmingham MA, 1959); J. Corbett, *The Birmingham Trades Council 1866-1966* (1966); R.A. Leeson, *Strike: a live history 1887-1971* (1973); R.P. Hastings, 'Aspects of the General Strike in Birmingham 1926', *Midland History 2*, no. 4 (autumn 1974) 250-73; A. Sutcliffe and R. Smith, *History of Birmingham*, vol. *3: 1939-1970* (1974); Birmingham PL Social Sciences Department and WEA West Midlands District, *The Nine Days in Birmingham* (Birmingham, 1976) 43 pp.; *The General Strike* ed. J. Skelley (1976); P.D. Drake, 'Labour and Spain: British Labour's response to the Spanish Civil War with particular reference to the Labour Movement in Birmingham' (Birmingham MLitt., 1978); biographical information: P.D. Drake, Birmingham Central Library; Mrs B. Smith, Birmingham. OBIT. *Birmingham Mail* and *Evening Despatch* [Birmingham], 6 Dec 1960; *Birmingham Post*, 7 Dec 1960; *Journal* (Jan 1961); TGWU, *Record* (Feb 1961) [by J.L. Jones]; [obit. for Mrs Crump] *Birmingham Mail*, 31 May 1943, *Birmingham Gazette* and *Birmingham Post*, 1 June 1943.

ERIC TAYLOR

See also: Harrison BARROW; *James (Jim) Walter CRUMP; †Henry SIMPSON; Joseph Edward SOUTHALL; Julia VARLEY.

EDWARDS, Ebenezer (Ebby) (1884-1961)
MINERS' LEADER AND LABOUR MP

Ebenezer Edwards was born on 30 July 1884, at Chevington, Northumberland, one of a family of eleven children of William Edwards, a miner and his wife Esther (née Fish). His father was a freethinker, a disciple of Bradlaugh, and president of the local miners' union. Ebby had an elementary school education, began work at Barrington Colliery just before his twelfth birthday; left there to work at Choppington, and at twenty moved to Ashington. He joined the ILP in 1906 and carried on a vigorous Socialist propaganda, which included long letters to the *Morpeth Herald*. He was greatly influenced by Marxist teaching and became a close associate of 'the famous Jack Williams' as Jim Middleton described Williams to Robin Page Arnot at the 1915 TUC. Williams' affiliation to the SDF went back to its earliest years, and he must have been either living in the North East or making propaganda visits to the district, for Edwards helped Williams on many occasions to sell *Justice* among the pitmen; and for this, as well as his spoken and written criticisms of MacDonald and Snowden, he was asked to resign from the ILP. This was in 1909, and in the same year the MFGB formally affiliated to the Labour Party; after this time Edwards had no other political affiliation [Arnot (1961) 83 n.1].

In 1908 he won a Northumberland Miners' Scholarship to Ruskin College. He found the milieu and the teaching uncongenial and he stayed only ten months – the main reason for his return to the pits however being the need for him to maintain the family after his father had suffered a stroke. Edwards left Ruskin before the strike, but he was in sympathy with those who broke away and founded the marxist Central Labour College and Plebs League. Edwards welcomed these developments of 1909 with enthusiasm. As soon as he returned to Ashington he had begun to be energetic in the organisation of classes among the miners on the lines of the later NCLC. Starting at his own lodge, Ashington, this educational movement gradually spread over the Northumberland coalfield. Edwards was an active member of the Plebs League and a member of the first executive council of the North East Labour College. It was chiefly his advocacy and influence which led the Northumberland Miners' Union to recognise the NCLC, and after the First World War to send students to the Central Labour College.

Edwards was elected delegate of Ashington miners' lodge in 1910 and president in 1912. By 1914 he was on the executive committee of the Northumberland miners' union; and in the same year he was a candidate for the presidency. In 1916 he was a delegate to the LP conference, and to the TUC in 1917. In May 1918, while still working at the coal face, he fought a by-election at Wansbeck as a Labour and anti-war candidate. As such, he was facing fearful odds, yet he came within a few hundred votes of winning. He did less well in the 'Coupon' general election of December 1918, and he did not contest a parliamentary seat again until 1929. In the general election of that ·year Robert Smillie's seat at Morpeth was held for Labour by Edwards; but he lost it in the 1931 landslide. He did not try to enter Parliament again. During his period as an MP his sole concern was with the mining industry. His maiden speech related to the Government's plans to reorganise and nationalise the industry and although he supported the Coal Mines Bill in 1929 he did not regard it as a fundamental solution to the coal industry's problems since it did not extend to public ownership of the mines. In 1931 he was a member of the executive committee of the PLP.

His energies throughout his life were concentrated on mining and miners' trade unionism. In 1919 he was elected assistant financial secretary of the Northumberland Miners' Association, and in the next year permanent financial agent and secretary. In 1926 he was elected to represent the NMA on the MFGB executive. Two years later when A.J. Cook, the MFGB general secretary, was fiercely attacked for his actions during the General Strike, and after, the Federation set up a committee of inquiry to censure him. S.O. Davies and Arthur Horner rejected this action as an insult and refused to serve, but Edwards decided to do so in order 'to frustrate Cook's enemies' [*Coal News* (Aug 1961)]. Horner, in a memorial tribute, suggested that it was probably Edwards who was right and that he had shown shrewdness and cunning in a complicated and difficult situation [ibid.]. Henry Hicken accepted nomination on the sub-committee but refused to look at the papers submitted, and did not sign the committee's report which was published in the MFGB *Annual Report* for 1929, 17 ff.

Edwards was made vice-president of the MFGB in 1930 and president in 1931, in which year he also became a member of the TUC General Council. The annual salary of the miners' president at this time was £104 and after his defeat in the parliamentary election of 1931 he returned to work in the mines. This period coincided with the final illness of A.J. Cook and Edwards was more and more responsible for the direction of the Federation. After Cook's death in November 1932 Edwards succeeded him as general secretary. Joseph Jones of Yorkshire was the runner-up, with W.H. Mainwaring of South Wales and P. Pemberton of Lancashire trailing a long way behind. Edwards held the post of secretary as long as the MFGB existed, that is till 1944.

The Miners' Federation, when Edwards became general secretary in 1932, was at its lowest ebb of any time during the twentieth century. Unemployment was rising; money wages were dropping; after 1926 district agreements had taken the place of a national bargaining structure; and company unionism had struck some roots in certain coalfields. 'The Miners' Federation had indeed fallen upon evil days', wrote the official historian of the MFGB [Arnot (1961) 36]. The Federation could no longer speak with one voice, and its effective power was minimal. Edwards believed that a patient rebuilding of numbers and morale was the only practicable way forward, and he insisted on negotiation and conciliation at a time when the Government was unhelpful and the mineowners consistently hostile.

During the decade of the 1930s the miners slowly but steadily regained their strength; and Edwards was inevitably at the centre of the many developments, and conflicts, of these years. In the middle of the decade the Federation put forward its first national wage claim since 1926; company unionism was ended; during the same years the split in Scottish mining unionism was healed [Arnot (1955) 235-7]; and the miners played a full part against Fascism abroad and its Mosley-ite manifestations at home.

Edwards took a lively interest in international affairs. He was already treasurer of the Miners' International Federation, and at the Lille Conference of August 1934 he took on the position of international secretary. In April 1935 he reported to the national sections of the Miners' International: 'With deep feelings of grief and sorrow and bitter and intense anger against his enemies, I write to inform you that our German comrade, Fritz Husemann, has been brutally murdered.' And Edwards went on to describe the circumstances. Fritz Husemann was a Socialist deputy and at the time of his arrest in 1933 president of the Miners' International; and it was events of this kind, and the publicity given by the trade union movement in all the non-Fascist countries, that helped to produce the hatred of Fascism that reverberated around the world. During the years of the Spanish Civil War Edwards was a strong supporter of the Republican Government and was vigorously opposed to the policy of non-intervention. In his capacities as secretary of both the MFGB and the Miners' International, Edwards was resolute in his advocacy of the Spanish cause. He was a left-wing Socialist with the typical ideas of this period: pro-Soviet, anti-Fascist and against the appeasers.

He was a member of the R.C. on Safety in Coal Mines appointed in 1935 after the Gresford disaster of 1934. The final Report was published in December 1938 with a short reservation from Edwards relating to piecework, age of entry into mines and general working hours [Arnot (1961) 141-3].

When the Second World War began in September 1939 Edwards actively supported the campaigns for raising coal production. He was a member of the Coal Production Council set up by the Secretary of Mines in April 1940. Throughout the war years Edwards was always a member of the negotiating committees authorised by the executive committee. During the war years also the Federation was preparing a new trade union structure for the industry, whereby the federation of district associations of miners – the MFGB – was converted into the more integrated, unified organisation which became the National Union of Miners on 1 January 1945. Edwards was its first general secretary. He regarded these changes as a necessary preliminary to the nationalisation of the mines, and when nationalisation was carried through by the new Labour Government which came to power after the victory in Europe, Edwards joined the National Coal Board as its first chief labour relations officer. He remained with the Board until his retirement in 1953. There was a great deal of rank and file criticism of Edwards at the time he joined the NCB, but Arthur Horner, who had been offered the job but refused it, said in a memorial tribute to Edwards that 'Ebby was perhaps more logical than I was. He argued that we fought for nationalisation so it was our duty to take responsibility and work for its success. How could we do this unless we were inside the new NCB organisation?' [*Coal News* (Aug 1961)].

Edwards had been president of the TUC in 1944, and was again in 1945, when he deputised for George Isaacs, who had just been appointed Minister of Labour in the Attlee Government. In 1946 Edwards was presented with the TUC gold medal. In 1944 he attended the conference of the United Mineworkers of America, and in the following year the UN conference in San Francisco, where he campaigned for trade union representation. He also attended meetings of the ILO in Geneva, first as representative of the miners and then on behalf of the NCB.

After he retired in 1953, Edwards and his wife settled in Gosforth where their daughter, Mrs Irene Kennedy, was already living. He died on 6 July 1961, one month after his wife Alice, whom he had married in 1911. He was survived by his daughter and by his son Dennis who is now (1978) general secretary of the Miners' International Federation. Ebby Edwards left an estate valued at £5521 net.

He was always known as Ebby, with which name he signed himself. Physically he was quite a small man, but of stocky build, with light blue eyes. He always lived simply and used to enjoy playing the concertina; he was also at one time a competent performer on the organ. He became somewhat less intransigent in his ideas and attitudes as he got older, but he never lost his deeply held political beliefs, and it was as an internationalist and a Socialist that he was remembered by his contemporaries.

Writings: *A Plea for Real Working-Class Education* (Newcastle upon Tyne, [1917?])P; 'The Miners' Tragedy', *Plebs 18* (July 1926) 243-4; '1917-1937: Anniversary Greetings', *Lab. Mon.* (Nov 1937) 671; R.C. on Safety in Coal Mines 1938-9 XIII *M of E* (non-parl) [memorandum of reservations by E. Edwards]; 'Tasks of Trade Unions in War and Peace', *Labour 7* (n.s.) (Nov 1944) 76-9.

Sources: *Times*, 30 May 1918; *Dod* (1919) and (1931); *Western Mail*, 19 July 1926; *Labour Who's Who* (1927); *Miner*, 3 Nov 1928; MFGB, *Annual Report* (1929); *Blyth News*, 22 Apr 1929; *Hansard* (1929-31); S. Rees, 'Ebby Edwards', *Plebs 23* (Sep 1931) 204; *Daily Herald* and *Manchester Guardian*, 11 Mar 1932; J. Lawson, 'Ebby Edwards', *Labour Mag. 10* (Apr 1932) 530-3; H. Laski, 'The Man behind a Great Fight', *Daily Herald*, 7 Oct 1933; *Daily Worker*, 23 Aug 1936; *Labour* (Nov 1944); *Kelly* (1952); R. Page Arnot, *The Miners 2* (1953); C.L. Mowat, *Britain between the Wars* (1955); R. Page Arnot, *A History of the Scottish Miners* (1955); idem, *The Miners 3* (1961); *WWW* (1961-70); A.R. Griffin, *The Miners of Nottinghamshire 1914-1944* (1962); W.W. Craik, *The Central Labour College 1909-29* (1964); biographical information: the late T.A.K. Elliott, CMG; Dr P.E.H. Hair, Liverpool Univ.; personal information: Dr R. Page Arnot, London; D. Edwards, London, son. OBIT. *Newcastle Evening Chronicle*, 7 July 1961; *Daily Worker, Journal* [Newcastle], *Manchester Guardian* and *Times*, 8 July 1961; *Coal News* (Aug 1961); *TUC Mag.* (Aug 1961); *TUC Report* (1961).

JOHN SAVILLE

See also: †Arthur James COOK, and for Mining Trade Unionism 1915-26; †Peter LEE, for Mining Trade Unionism 1927-44.

FARMERY, George Edward (1883-1942)
TRADE UNIONIST AND LABOUR ALDERMAN

George Edward Farmery was born on 1 July 1883 at Kingerby, Lincolnshire, the son of William Farmery, a waggoner, and his wife Eliza (née Brown). His first acquaintance with Hull was when, as a young man, he joined the Hull Police Force. He disliked the work, however, and left after eleven months. The facts of his early working life are not known except that he became Boston district secretary of the Dock, Wharf and Riverside Union, probably some time after 1914. From 1919 to 1922 he was a member of Boston Borough Council and when his union amalgamated with the Transport and General Workers' Union in the latter year, he moved to Hull as the TGWU's first area secretary. By the time of his death the Humber and East Coast area, which extended from north of Bridlington to south of Peterborough and west to Goole and Selby, had more than doubled its membership.

During the General Strike, Farmery was a member of the Hull Council of Action and in its aftermath was much involved in getting his members back to their jobs. As TGWU representative he attended a meeting between local employers and trade union representatives, arranged under the auspices of the Lord Mayor, on 13 May 1926 and after hard negotiation was able to report that: 'Work has been resumed at all the Hull docks this morning, and generally speaking, *bona fide* dockers are being employed' [*Hull Daily Mail*, 18 May 1926]. However, the union on the whole was poorly organised and other workers, the seed crushers, for example, were not so fortunate.

His other major confrontation as a local union leader was the fishermen's strike of 1935. In that year the trawler owners reduced the amount of 'oil-money' – a traditional payment for fish livers made to the men – and fishermen reaching port refused to sign on for further trips. The degree to which this was a spontaneous action was a matter of dispute at the time, and Farmery, at the Court of Inquiry which followed, was eager to suggest that the fishermen had received advice only, not instructions, from the TGWU [*Hull Daily Mail*, 18 Apr 1935]. Certainly the union was not in a strong position, for when the strike started it represented only 500 fishermen. Membership rose to 1500 in the first few days, but this was still only about half the total number of fishermen at the port [Tunstall (1962) 39]. The union initially asked the owners to receive a deputation, but they received no answer, and the strike broadened into one over the fishermen's right to union representation. At the Inquiry Farmery was at pains to present himself as a moderate man, in contrast to the image some people had of him: 'he had been regarded as an agitator and one who indulged in fighting speeches for no purpose. He had been regarded as a Bolshevik by certain employers' [*Hull Daily Mail*, 18 Apr 1935]. The strike eventually ended after a month, when a Conciliation Board cut by half the amount by which the oil money was to be reduced.

Apart from his trade union activities, Farmery also involved himself in the political side of the local Labour movement. He helped form the North West Hull branch of the Independent Labour Party; was well known for taking part in street-corner meetings and propaganda work; and was a frequent attender of Labour functions. He first entered Hull City Council on 24 November 1926, representing Myton ward, and was made an alderman (for Botanic ward) in 1930. At the general election in the following year he contested Grimsby for Labour. Although unsuccessful, he polled almost a third of the votes; but he never stood again. During the following decade he was an active member of the Hull City Council and served on several committees, including the watch committee (1930-1 and 1935-7) and works committee (1928-35), and he had a particular interest in the work of the markets and abattoirs committee, of which he was a member from 1928 until his death, and chairman 1930-1 and 1935-8. He was also for a time president of the Northern Markets Authorities' Association. The committee also brought him into contact with Hull Fair, at the official opening of which he often spoke; and he took a personal interest in the welfare of showmen and their families.

With his special knowledge of Hull as a port and his interest in the welfare of seamen, he was an obvious choice as a member of the North Sea Fisheries Committee (1930-1), the Committee for the Training of British Seamen (1930-1) and the Seamen's (Tuberculosis) Advisory Committee (1930-42). He was also a Humber Conservancy Commissioner from 1935 until his death, and an enthusiastic supporter of the idea of a Humber Bridge.

He died on 10 September 1942 after a car crash on 1 September. His wife, Betsy May, also sustained serious injuries, but survived, and lived till 1973. There were no children of the marriage.

Farmery was a big man and is remembered as forceful and quick-tempered; in public a powerful rather than a good speaker, but in private a very generous and thoughtful friend with a sense of fun. He was an effective leader of his union, with a personality ideally suited to the dockers and fishermen who made up the bulk of his membership: he 'spoke their language'. He was a loyal supporter of the TGWU leadership and in general political terms was on the right wing of the Labour Party. His funeral, at Holy Trinity Church, was attended by representatives of Hull City Council, the Port, the Conservancy Board, his own and many other unions. Ernest Bevin and Arthur Deakin were both personally represented. The funeral service was followed by a private burial at Sutton. He left an estate of £4062, and his name is perpetuated in Farmery Hall, a large room used for meetings and social functions at Bevin House, the local Hull office of the TGWU.

Writings: 'We will be Free', *Farm, Forestry and Nursery Workers' Special*, repr. *Hull Sentinel* (June 1937).

Sources: *Hull Daily Mail*, 5, 17 and 18 May 1926; *Kingston upon Hull Year Books* (1927-41); *Times House of Commons* (1931); *Hull Daily Mail*, 28 Mar-4 May 1935; *Hull Sentinel* (Apr 1935); TGWU, *Souvenir* (1939); J. Tunstall, *The Fishermen* (1962); G.A. Lee, 'The Tramways of Kingston upon Hull' (Sheffield PhD, 1968); P.J. Edwards and J. Marshall, 'Sources of Conflict and Community in the Trawling Industries of Hull and Grimsby between the Wars', *Oral History 5*, no. 1 (1977) 97-121; personal information: S. Clayton, Ald. F. Holmes, J.W. Smith, J. Webster, all of Hull. OBIT. *Hull Sentinel* (Sep 1942); *Hull Daily Mail*, 11 Sep 1942; *Hull Times*, 12 Sep 1942; TGWU, *Record* (Oct 1942).

ANN HOLT

See also: John (Jack) HENSON.

FOX, Thomas (Tom) Samuel (1905-56)
MINEWORKERS' LEADER

Tom Fox was born on 26 April 1905 at Ashington, Northumberland, the second son in a family of three sons and one daughter of Thomas Samuel Fox, of Penrith and his wife Ann (née Ferrell). Tom's father had moved to Northumberland as a young man to work as a hewer in the coalmines and at the time of his son's birth was employed as a deputy at Woodhorn Colliery.

Tom Fox was educated at the Hirst North Elementary School, Ashington, and left school at the age of fourteen. He worked for a few months at the Ashington Co-operative Bakeries before starting work as a shaft landing lad at Woodhorn Colliery; he then joined a team working on the electric coal-cutting machines. After working hours Fox travelled sixteen miles to attend evening classes in general subjects held at Dame Allan's School, Newcastle upon Tyne, and between

1922 and 1925 he attended the Ashington Coal Company's day continuation school for two days a week, where he passed his school certificate examinations.

His ambition at this time was to follow his father into mining management, but the General Strike and the long coal lock-out which followed ended these hopes and he emigrated to Australia, under the Ministry of Labour's scheme, in November 1926. For the next five years he worked at a number of jobs in Western Australia, including wheat-and sheep-farming and laying railway track. When the world depression hit Australia Fox decided to return home. He found temporary employment in the rating office of Ashington Urban District Council, and after this worked for a time as a brush salesman. Fox then took a job as bellman, servicing the telephone and signals at Woodhorn Colliery.

He joined the Northumberland Colliery Mechanics' Association, but his interest in trade unionism did not develop until he moved from Woodhorn to Ashington Colliery in 1940. He became secretary of the Ashington branch of the NCMA, served on the county executive committee 1946-48, and was president of the Northumberland Mechanics' section of the NUM from 1948 to 1955. In February 1956 he succeeded Walter Lockey as general secretary of the Northumberland Mechanics, becoming the first man to hold this office who had not served an apprenticeship as a craftsman. In the same year he was elected president of the Northumberland Mineworkers' Federation, having served on its executive committee since 1954.

Fox played a major role in the affairs of Ashington. In 1953 he was elected secretary of the Ashington Mineworkers' Federation, which represented 12,000 mineworkers in the Ashington district and constituted a powerful pressure group in the affairs of the colliery town. It was his initiative and energy which pushed through a free coal scheme for Ashington's retired mineworkers. Under this scheme Ashington's mineworkers gave up one load of their annual free coal allowance to form a pool to supply retired mineworkers or their widows with seven free loads of coal every year. Fox was also secretary of the Ashington Mineworkers' Joint Welfare Committee and played a leading part in the committee's successful campaign to improve the local hospital emergency services. Always keenly interested in sport, Fox played a big part in implementing the welfare committee's £60,000 scheme to modernise local sports facilities.

Fox's term of office as general secretary of the Northumberland Mechanics was tragically short. He took up his duties on 8 February 1956 and died in Newcastle General Hospital on 16 May 1956, after receiving head injuries in a car crash. He was cremated at Cowpen, near Blyth, on 19 May. By religion Tom Fox was a Presbyterian, although he was not a regular churchgoer in his adult years. He was an avid reader and often attended summer schools during his annual holiday. In his politics he was a Labour Party supporter and was a union delegate to several Labour Party committees and conferences, but his main interest lay in the industrial side of the labour movement. He may never, in fact, have been an individual member of the LP and he was known to dislike the jobbery to be found in local Labour politics. He had never married and lived with his unmarried sister and a younger brother at St Andrews Terrace, Ashington. He left effects valued at £528.

Sources: (1) MSS: Minutes of the Northumberland Colliery Mechanics' Association and the NUM (Northumberland Mechanics), 1940-56: Northumberland CRO, Gosforth. (2) Other: *Annual Reports* of the Northumberland Colliery Mechanics' Association and the NUM (Northumberland Mechanics), 1946-56: Northumberland Mechanics' Office, Blyth; Files of *Ashington Post, Evening Chronicle* [Newcastle upon Tyne] and *Newcastle J.*, 1948-56; *Ashington Colliery Mag.*; A. Potts and E. Wade, *Stand True* (Blyth, 1975) 36 pp.; personal information: George Fox, Morpeth, brother; Margaret Fox, Ashington, sister. OBIT. *Evening Chronicle* and *Newcastle J.*, 17 May 1956; *Ashington Post*, 22 May 1956.

ARCHIE POTTS

See also: Walter Daglish LOCKEY.

FOX, William (1890-1968)
LABOUR ALDERMAN

It has not been possible to verify the facts of William Fox's birth from official records. According to a press report he was born in Hull, although there is a family account that his birthplace was Leeds and he was brought to Hull by his mother after his father's death. It is, however, known that Mrs Fox kept a lodging house in Hull and subsequently married an Irishman, Maurice O'Malley. After attending St Charles's Roman Catholic School, Fox went to work on the docks, and remained a docker for thirty-five years, interrupted only by military service during the First World War. He joined the Army in 1914, shortly after his marriage, and served with the 13th Battalion, East Yorkshire Regiment, was seriously wounded at La Bassée and was for two years deaf and dumb in a military hospital. During this period he learned sign language and in later life was able to utilise this skill when, as Lord Mayor, he gave a 'speech' in sign language at the East Yorkshire Institute for the Deaf and Dumb. He remained proud of his association with his wartime regiment and was a member of the British Legion; in 1956 as Lord Mayor he led a civic visit to the Hull memorial at Oppy Wood where his regiment had suffered heavy casualties.

His entry into public life was in 1925 when he attended his first meeting as a member of the Sculcoates Board of Guardians, and he remained a member until the Board went out of existence in 1930. In 1929 he was elected to Hull City Council as a Labour member for Drypool ward and held the same seat until 1952 when he was made an alderman and sat for Stoneferry ward. He served as Lord Mayor in 1955-6, and then as Sheriff in 1962. On the council a major interest was the markets and abattoirs committee and the Hull Fair sub-committee. In connection with the latter, his concern for the activities and welfare of showmen was recognised in 1955 when he was elected an honorary member of the Amusement Rides Association. He also served on the health and public assistance committee for many years – 1930-9, 1954-60 and 1962-8 – and was deputy chairman in 1934; he was particularly interested in the work of the aftercare committee. From 1954-60 and 1962-8 he was a member of the watch committee.

Alderman Fox remained a docker until 1939 when, dock work being scarce, he joined a Hull firm of boilermakers and shiprepairers as a general labourer with duties which included the supervision of the central heating plant. During the Second World War the family were bombed three times and lost everything. Among the lost treasures were the Royal Humane Society's certificate on vellum and the *Daily Herald* Industrial Order of Merit awarded to him when he rescued two boys and a dog from drowning in a dock in 1929. He was a lifelong member of the Labour Party and the Transport and General Workers' Union, which he joined in 1912. A devout Roman Catholic with strong anti-Communist views, he was politically on the right of the Labour Party and a loyal supporter of Ernest Bevin and his successor Arthur Deakin, the leaders of his own union.

In private life he was a keen and knowledgeable spectator of swimming and boxing, and did a great deal of charitable work for the St Vincent's Children's Home. A quiet man with strong features, a broad forehead and a cheerful countenance, he was of medium height and rather stout; he was a well-informed and interesting talker in private conversation. In 1914 he married Ethel Mary Larkin, of Hull. There were three children of the marriage: the elder son William was an electrician, and the younger son, Bernard, who worked as an electrician's labourer and as a painter and decorator, was at one time a member of Hull City Council but he was killed in a road accident in 1962. The daughter, Mrs Patricia Hall, was a tailoress until her marriage and then kept a public house. Alderman Fox was awarded the CBE in June 1967. He died on 21 April of the following year at the age of seventy-eight and was buried at the Eastern Cemetery, Hull, after a Requiem Mass at St Charles' Church. He left effects valued at £2972.

Sources: (1) MSS: Sculcoates Board of Guardians, Minutes (1925-30): Record Office, Guildhall, Hull; (2) Other: *Kingston upon Hull Year Books* (1929-68); *Hull Daily Mail*, 1 Feb and 23 Mar 1955, 7 Jan and 10 June 1967; *Hull Times*, 20 Aug 1955; personal information: S.

Clayton, Mrs E.M. Fox, widow, Mrs P. Hall, daughter, Ald. F. Holmes, J.W. Smith, J. Webster, all of Hull. OBIT. *Hull Daily Mail*, 22 Apr 1968.

ANN HOLT

GOLDSTONE, Sir Frank Walter (1870-1955)
TRADE UNIONIST AND LABOUR MP

Frank Goldstone was born on 7 December 1870 in Sunderland, the third son of Thomas Frederick Goldstone, a stained glass artist, and his wife Sarah Trigg (née Blott). He was educated at Diamond Hall Council School in Sunderland; became a pupil teacher at Simpson Street, and later spent a year in further training at the Borough Road Training College in Isleworth, Middlesex.

In October 1891 Goldstone was appointed assistant master at the Bow Street Council School under the authority of the Sheffield School Board and he continued to teach in the city until 1910. During these years he became actively involved with the local branch of the National Union of Teachers and also with the National Federation of Class Teachers. This latter body was one of the several sectional associations which crystallised in the 1890s out of informal pressure groups within the NUT. Although it concerned itself chiefly with matters affecting assistant teachers' salaries and promotion, its trade union perspectives made it an influential group in the formulation of NUT policy. Goldstone served three terms of office as president of the Sheffield Class Teachers' Association. He was elected president of the Federation in 1902 and was founder and first editor of its journal, the *Class Teacher*.

In 1904 he was elected to the executive of the NUT and two years later to the chairmanship of its law committee, and he became a spokesman for the union at meetings with the Board of Education and at the National Association of Education Committees. He was a member of the Joint Committee on the Teachers' Register and for a time a director of the *Schoolmaster*. In 1910 he was appointed to the full-time position of organisation secretary of the NUT.

Exactly when, or why, Goldstone became a Socialist is not known, but in December 1910 he stood as a Labour candidate for the two-member constituency of Sunderland. Thomas Summerbell had been the previous Labour member, but he had lost his seat in the January 1910 election to a Unionist. Goldstone's campaign was inevitably much concerned with the question of the House of Lords as an obstructive force in British politics, but he also called for a greatly improved system of technical education, particularly in connection with the engineering and shipbuilding industries. Goldstone was a good platform speaker, and he was returned at the head of the poll with the Liberal candidate. At this time his general educational programme, summed up in a publicity leaflet, was for 'a national system of education with a free teaching profession; one register of teachers; increased salaries for rural and class teachers; an improved system of superannuation applied to all teachers working under Local Education Authorities; a code of professional honour; a "forward" policy generally.'

In the House of Commons Goldstone inevitably was most concerned with matters of education; and he proved himself a hard-working back-bench MP. He asked many questions of ministers and his general educational views were well summarised in an article he wrote for the *Socialist Review* in May 1911. It began with a vigorous attack on the permanent secretary of the Board of Education, Sir Robert Morant – 'this clever and masterful gentleman [who has] . . . absorbed more and more the powers of an educational dictator'. Goldstone was especially critical of the Morant policy towards state-aided secondary schools. He concluded his article:

> The way [forward] lies in throwing off the shackles imposed on our educational system by interested supporters of privilege; in opening wide the doors of our Secondary Schools and Universities freely to all who have the ability to profit by further education. England will only attain its highest power when every child has access to the fullest education for which it

is adapted; and when capacity and not social position shall be the basis of selection for the responsible positions in the State service. Poverty must be no barrier; Privilege must give way or go under; and Oxford and Cambridge, and all they connote, fulfil the mission it is the part of Universities to fill in every Progressive State.

Among the issues he raised in the Commons before 1914 were improved medical inspection for children, the need for special provision for the handicapped, the problem of large classes and the need for a clearly defined school-leaving age. He was one of the sponsors of the 1914 Bill to abolish the half-time system.

From 1914 to 1916 Goldstone was the Labour Party's Chief Whip in the Commons. He was not an opponent of conscription although he argued for its sympathetic application to 'difficult' cases. In 1916 he served on the Departmental Committee on Juvenile Education and Employment, the main recommendations of which were the establishment of a uniform school-leaving age of fourteen, with no exemptions (and this meant the abolition of the half-time system). There was a further recommendation that children from fourteen to eighteen should attend day continuation classes.

In the last year of the war Goldstone was commissioned in the RASC and became a Captain on the General Staff with a seat on the newly-created Army Education Board. When he returned to the Commons for the debates on Fisher's Education Bill, Goldstone acted effectively as the spokesman for the NUT. He took up again his pre-war campaign for the widest possible opportunities to be created whereby all children might qualify for secondary education. Both he and Ramsay MacDonald preferred the educational structure that had been developing before the Cockerton judgment and the 1902 Act [Barker (1972) 30 ff.]. He was able to take the argument further when he was appointed in 1919 to serve on the Departmental Committee on Scholarships and Free Places. The Committee established that a large number of potential entrants to the secondary schools were being excluded for lack of space. Further, the Committee concluded that 'practically all children, except the subnormal' were 'capable of profiting by full-time education up to 16 or beyond.' The Committee was agreed that all secondary education should be free, and on the transfer of children taking place at the age of eleven, but was divided as to the means. The majority recommended a formal test of 'capacity and promise rather than attainment' while the minority of four, of whom Goldstone was one, argued for a competitive test based upon normal school work [Simon (1974) 21 ff.].

Goldstone had been appointed to the Departmental Committee by virtue of his chairmanship of the Labour Party's newly established Advisory Committee on Education, the most dynamic member of which was R.H. Tawney. The latter warmly welcomed the Report of the Departmental Committee, and it provided an important element in the development of opinion which produced the Advisory Committee's famous policy statement of 1922, *Secondary Education for All*.

Goldstone had lost his parliamentary seat at the 'Coupon' election of 1918. In 1924 he was elected general secretary of the NUT, succeeding Sir James Yoxall, having served for the previous four years as assistant secretary. The decade was one of considerable ferment in the educational world with the Labour Party elaborating a programme of advance and progress that was to influence thinking and practice well into the years after the Second World War. More immediately the NUT and other bodies were faced with threats and the actuality of financial retrenchment. Goldstone was a member of the Consultative Committee to the Board of Education for a period up to 1923. The well-known report, *The Education of the Adolescent*, was published on 16 December 1926 and Goldstone was prominent in the national discussions which followed. In particular the NUT statement of the autumn of 1928, *The Hadow Report and After*, was a realistic appraisal of the strengths and weaknesses of the original report and of the attempts by the Board of Education to smother certain crucial recommendations [Simon (1974) 137 ff.].

During his period as general secretary of the NUT Goldstone was much in demand for other public services. He was for a time a member of the Speaker's Conference on the Franchise, and he was inevitably involved with the Burnham Standing Joint Committee. Together with Mary Agnes Hamilton and Barbara Ayrton Gould he was a member of the Tomlin Commission on the Civil Service, which reported in 1931.

He retired from the secretaryship of the NUT in July 1931 and in the same year received a knighthood. And then for three years he was principal of the University Tutorial College which was originally established in conjunction with a correspondence college.

Goldstone had married Elizabeth Alice Henderson, of Whittingham, Northumberland, in 1895 and there were one son and one daughter of the marriage. He died on Christmas Day 1955 at his home in Ipswich, and the funeral took place at Ipswich Crematorium. His wife had predeceased him in 1942. Tributes to Goldstone allude to his mild and cheerful nature, and to his careful attention to matters of personal relationships. He can certainly be accounted a successful general secretary of the main teachers' organisation, and the toughness and dedication to the cause of education for all children, which had been central to his political purpose in the years before 1914, remained when he moved into the educational establishment in the 1920s. He left an estate of £21,379 (net) of which £500 was made over to the benevolent and orphan fund of the NUT.

Writings: 'The Spirit of the ''Holmes''' Circular', *Soc. Rev.* 7 (May 1911) 233-40; articles in the educational press.

Sources: *Sunderland Daily Echo,* 30 Nov and 2 Dec 1910; *Hansard* (1911-18); *Pall Mall Gazette 'extra'* (1911) [with portrait]; *Times House of Commons* (1911); *Dod* (1912) and (1918); *Schoolmaster,* 15 Feb 1924 and 9 July 1931; D.F. Thompson, *Professional Solidarity among the Teachers of England* (Columbia Univ. Press, 1927); NUT, *The Hadow Report and After* (1928); H.A.L. Fisher, *An Unfinished Autobiography* (1940); J.H. Bingham, *The Period of the Sheffield School Board 1870-1903* (Sheffield, 1949); *WWW* (1951-60); *Kelly* (1952); H.A. Clegg et al., *A History of British Trade Unions since 1889* vol. 1: *1889-1910* (Oxford, 1964); A. Tropp, *The School Teachers: the growth of the teaching profession in England and Wales from 1800 to the present day* (1957); B. Simon, *Education and the Labour Movement 1870-1920* (1965); W. Roy, *The Teachers' Union* (1968); R. Barker, *Education and Politics 1900-1951: a study of the Labour Party* (Oxford, 1972); P.H.J.H. Gosden, *The Evolution of a Profession* (1972); B. Simon, *The Politics of Educational Reform 1920-1940* (1974); biographical information: Central Library, Ipswich; Central Library, Sunderland; Professor B. Simon, Leicester Univ.; Mrs V.A. Brinkley-Willsher, Librarian, NUT. OBIT. *East Anglian Daily Times,* 28 Dec 1955; *Times,* 29 Dec 1955; *Schoolmaster,* 6 Jan 1956.

BARBARA NIELD
JOHN SAVILLE

GOODALL, William Kenneth (1877-1963)
CO-OPERATOR AND LABOUR PARTY WORKER

William Kenneth Goodall was born on 23 February 1877 at Reading, the fourth of the seven children of Thomas Goodale and his wife Eliza Ann Wheeler (née Wilkins). The first three children were registered as Goodale, the last four as Goodall. Thomas Goodale was a soldier for ten years in the Cape Mounted Rifles, after which he returned to Reading where he worked first in a brewery, then in a biscuit factory until his retirement. His son William was educated at Katesgrove Board School, Reading, and later at Aldworth Hospital, Reading, the so-called Reading Blue Coat School, where he became head boy, gained his certificate of the College of Preceptors and passed the South Kensington Mathematical Examination, the thirteenth out of 26,000 candidates. He left school with a £20 premium awarded by the governors and was apprenticed to Newbury's Ltd as an upholsterer. He moved to Hereford in 1905 as a craftsman upholsterer with Searle and Son and finally set up his own small business as an upholsterer and house furnisher after the First World War.

His father was a staunch Conservative, but William was attracted early to Socialism; an intelligent and omnivorous reader, particularly of Ibsen, Shaw and Wells, he was also an emotional man deeply moved by injustice. Keir Hardie was his hero. Before the First World War he became involved in Hereford Labour politics and was active in the Hereford City Parliament. This had been instituted in 1908 by the Hereford YMCA and a committee of local residents. It took the form of a debating society organised as a mock parliament by a committee representing three parties: Conservative, Liberal and ILP. It was a great success and membership increased until the meeting had to remove from the YMCA to the assembly room of the Town Hall, at which point – March 1909 – it had 443 members. No record of the parliament's existence has been found after 1913, but it had provided a lively focus of local discussion on political matters and current affairs. There is no evidence that William Goodall held office in the parliament, but he spoke in debate in the Labour interest. Through his membership of the Hereford Labour movement he knew many Labour politicians, including George Lansbury, who stayed with him on visits to the area and became godfather to his daughter Marjorie Edna.

William Goodall was an active co-operator and served on the Board of the Hereford Co-operative and Industrial Society, but his primary interest was a co-operative housing scheme, Hereford Co-operative Housing Ltd, known locally as 'the Garden City'. This had been pioneered by Hereford Town Council under powers granted by the Housing of the Working Classes Acts of 1890 and 1903. The Council bought the land and provided essential services. The land was then leased to the housing co-operative at a ground rent which would pay off the debt to the Council in fifty years. Its organisers were keen to deny that it was a philanthropic venture and stressed the business principles on which it was founded; but they clearly had high hopes of its influence on both residents and the city: 'It is one step higher in that stage of evolution for which our fathers prayed, and which we are helping to actualize' [Collins (1911) 194]. Goodall moved into the Garden City soon after its completion and was from 1914 until 1954 a member of the committee of tenants which ran it and allocated houses. During the First World War he served in the Hereford Red Cross VAD and nursed wounded soldiers in local hospitals and country houses.

In 1934 he became a JP, the duties of which he took seriously. Another interest was Hereford Cathedral. He had a considerable knowledge of its history and architecture and acted as a voluntary guide. He loved the Cathedral services and music, but this taste seems to have been more aesthetic than religious. Although brought up in the Church of England his attitudes were those of a freethinker and humanist. He was also a keen gardener and angler, an early radio enthusiast and a member of Woolhope Naturalists' Field Club, Hereford. He maintained his interest in Labour politics in the 1930s and was a member of the Left Book Club. His political attitudes seem however always to have been moderate.

Of slim build, William Goodall was of medium height, with blue eyes and a moustache. He had brown hair which turned grey as he grew older and after his fifties he went partly bald. He married Florence Ada Bate in 1904 and there were two children of the marriage: Kenneth Leslie Goodall OBE, a physicist who served for thirty-eight years in H.M. Factory Inspectorate and retired as H.M. Senior Chemical Inspector; and Marjorie Edna, who trained as an orthopaedic nurse, physiotherapist and masseuse.

William Goodall died on 11 January 1963, aged eighty-five, at St Mary's Hospital, Burghill, and after cremation at Breinton his ashes were scattered on Dinmore Hill, Hereford, and in a Reading churchyard. His wife had predeceased him in 1953 but he was survived by his son and daughter and he left effects valued at £8272.

Sources: J.S. Nettlefold, *A Housing Policy* (Birmingham, 1905); *Hereford Times*, 13 Feb 1909; W. Collins, 'The History of our Local Parliament', *An Echo from the City of Hereford*, no. 1 (Mar 1909) 2-15; *Hereford Times*, 12 Mar 1910; W. Collins, *Modern Hereford* pt 2 (1911);

idem, *A Short History of Hereford* (Hereford [1913]); *Rules of the Hereford Co-operative Housing Ltd* (repr. 1919) 38 pp.; W. Collins, *Records of Organised Labour in the City of Hereford* (1920); biographical information: Hereford Library; Hereford and Worcester Record Office; Messrs Whatley, Weston and Fox, solicitors, Hereford; personal information: K.L. Goodall, OBE, Watford, son. OBIT. *Hereford Times*, 18 Jan 1963.

KENNETH GOODALL
ANN HOLT

GOSSLING, Archibald (Archie) George (1878-1950)
TRADE UNIONIST AND LABOUR MP

Gossling was born in East London on 10 May 1878, the son of Harry Turner Gossling, a builder, and his wife Lucy (née Barlow). Young Gossling went to Westbourne Park School, Paddington, and was apprenticed to his uncle, a joiner, in Wimborne, Dorset. It was at this time that he met Joseph Arch, whom he used to drive to general meetings in the countryside around. Gossling returned to London as an 'improver' and at the time of his marriage in 1903 he was living in Willesden. He had become a member of the Amalgamated Society of Carpenters and Joiners in 1901 and helped to found the Paddington branch of the union, in which he served in various positions – money steward, branch auditor and branch president; one of his contemporaries was to become another prominent union member, S.P. Viant, who was also later to be elected as a Labour MP.

Gossling played an active part in most of the industrial issues affecting London members. When the London district of the union came out against their district delegates, Gossling became a member of the south-western organising committee in opposition to the district committee. He was involved in the exposé of the exploitative working conditions in the joinery works of the Salvation Army [ASW, *Monthly Reports* (1929) 170] and he was active on behalf of the children's fund at the time of the London building lock-out in the early months of 1914. At the outbreak of the First World War Gossling found work in an aircraft factory and, as secretary of the aircraft shop committee, he led the fight against payment by results. Subsequently he was successful in opposing attempts by the Ministry of Labour to introduce a piecework system. By this time he was an experienced union official and in 1917 he was elected to the general council of the ASCJ. He served on its compiling committee for the rules revision of 1919.

In 1918 the ASCJ amalgamated with the National Amalgamated Furnishing Trades Association, and at the time Gossling voted with a majority of the general and executive councils of his own union against the continuation of piecework in the furnishing trades. Gossling resigned from the executive committee of the ASCJ in 1919 but he was elected to the EC of the new Amalgamated Society of Woodworkers which was formed in 1921. He continued to serve on the society's executive until 1929 when he entered Parliament. During these years he was also a member of the EC of the National Housing and Town Planning Council and an honorary auditor for the general purposes committee of the NJC of the Building Industry. In 1926 he represented the ASW at a meeting of the League of Nations in Geneva on industrial questions.

His interest in politics developed early in his career. He joined the ILP in 1903 and served on the EC of the West London Federation of the Party. He was a delegate to the annual conference in 1914. In 1918 he was nominated to the parliamentary panel of the ASCJ, and he contested unsuccessfully the Yardley division of Birmingham in 1922, 1923 and 1924, gradually eroding the Conservative majority. In 1929 he was elected for the same constituency, his parliamentary contributions being mostly limited to housing and building matters. A member of his family remembers him at this time as ' . . . so very dedicated to the cause – with lots of all night sittings. . . and walking home in the early hours of the morning many miles to Kensal Rise, very tired and off again later in the day to another meeting' [letter dated 10 Aug 1975]. He lost his seat in the landslide election of 1931, and he never contested a parliamentary constituency again.

Gossling had a special interest in education for trade unionists. He lectured in his early days in

London to trade union branches, and took advantage of Ruskin College's correspondence courses, although for financial reasons he was never able to take up a residential place at Oxford. He was for a time treasurer of the Workers' Educational Trade Union Committee (founded in October 1919) and was on the EC of the WEA before 1926. He was also on the EC of the Labour Research Department in 1922 and 1923, but did not stand for re-election in 1924: facts which tell us something of his general politics. Many at the centre or left-centre of the Labour Party did not continue their association with the LRD after it came under Communist Party control during 1924 [see Postgate (1934) 178-81; M. Cole (1949) 95-7 and (1971) 126-8], despite the concentration of the work of the LRD upon economic and industrial affairs to the exclusion of any extended discussion of politics as such.

Gossling had resigned from the EC of the ASW when he was elected to Westminster in 1929, and after his political defeat in 1931 he and his wife retired to the Norfolk coast where they kept a guest house until the Second World War when they had charge of the East Anglian Trustee Savings Bank at Wymondham. Gossling also did war work as an auxiliary coastguard and as a site officer for essential works. He was still an EC member of the NFBTO in 1933 and remained president of the Wymondham branch of the ASW until his death, but during the 1930s he ceased to play an active part in trade union affairs.

In 1903 he married Anne Elizabeth Tweed, of Wimborne, Dorset, who was a draper's assistant. His wife involved herself in his career, but was also one of the founders of the North Kensington Baby Hospital, to which she gave much of her time. Gossling died on 19 May 1950, leaving effects to the value of £1041.

Sources: LRD, *Monthly Circular* (Nov 1922) 175-6; *Labour Who's Who* (1924) and (1927); *Times House of Commons Guide* (1929) and (1931); *Hansard* (1929-31); 'Notable Members of our Society 13', ASW, *Monthly Reports* (1929) 170; *Dod* (1931); *Kelly* (1932); R. Postgate, *How to make a Revolution* (1934); S. Higenbottam, *Our Society's History* [Amalgamated Society of Woodworkers] (Manchester, 1939); *WWW* (1941-50); M. Cole, *Growing up into Revolution* (1949); idem, *The Life of G.D.H. Cole* (1971); biographical information: Mrs N. Branson, LRD, London; Ms J. Druker, MRC, Warwick Univ.; the late T.A.K. Elliott, CMG; Mrs B. Smith, Birmingham; personal information: Mrs B. Barlow, Exmouth, niece. OBIT. *Woodworkers' J.* (July 1950) 399; *Labour Party Report* (1950).

ANN HOLT
JOHN SAVILLE

GROVES, Thomas Edward (1882-1958)
TRADE UNIONIST AND LABOUR MP

Thomas Edward Groves was born at Newtown, Stratford, East London, on 23 July 1882. He was the son of George Everett Groves, a railway engine driver working for the Great Eastern Railway and a prominent member of the Amalgamated Society of Railway Servants, and his wife Emma (née Stares). Educated at the Maryland Point Elementary School, the Carpenters' Company Technical Institute and the Great Eastern Mechanics' Institute, Tom Groves was apprenticed from 1898 to 1905 in coachbuilding with the GER at Stratford, and subsequently worked as a coachbuilder with the London General Omnibus Co., the Underground Railway, and LCC Tramways. In 1907 he went to Ruskin College, Oxford, on a scholarship provided by his union, the United Kingdom Society of Coachmakers (later the National Union of Vehicle Builders, which in 1972 amalgamated with the TGWU). When he left in 1910 he returned to LCC Tramways as a cost clerk and remained there until 1922, when he became MP for the Stratford division of West Ham.

During the First World War he was unfit for war service, but in any case apparently had pacifist views. In his union branch's minutes for July 1916 he is mentioned as having been elected to attend 'Peace meetings' which were being held in various districts. In December 1917 he was invited to visit the British front with members of the union executive; he refused and put forward a resolution criticising them for associating themselves with an anti-labour government in this way. Later, as an MP, he voted in 1924 against provision for five cruisers in the Navy in Estimates; while in 1927 he voted for the reduction of the RAF, in 1931 against the Air Estimates. Interestingly, he was in 1939 a member of the Labour Party Peace Aims Group which advocated an early peace with Germany, and in 1940 he voted (as many Chamberlainite and few Labour MPs did) against Churchill's request for a secret session.

By the time he became an MP Tom Groves was already a man of considerable experience in the labour movement. Originally a member of the ILP, he later joined the Labour Party – he was a delegate to the ILP conference from North West Ham in 1910 and to the Labour Party conference from West Ham Trades Council in 1918. He joined the United Kingdom Society of Coachmakers at the age of twenty, and served for several years as branch delegate on West Ham Trades Council and the London District Committee of the union. After he was elected to the House of Commons his relations with the branch became difficult, and after a long wrangle over contributions by the branch to his election expenses, his membership was finally transferred to the head office of the union in 1931. His own branch firmly believed that they had treated him generously.

In 1913 he was a delegate to the TUC, representing the United Kingdom Society of Coachmakers. In 1914 he was involved with the setting up of a Trades and Labour Council for Leyton and Leytonstone (the meeting place in Leyton High Road still retains the name 'Groves House'). He was elected to West Ham Borough Council in 1919, and remained a member until 1945. During this time he was on many committees – education, finance, legal and general, tramways, and special schools and welfare. Deputy mayor in 1929, he was mayor in 1934, in which year he also became an alderman. He was JP for West Ham from 1928. His impulse to try to relieve distress meant that he was a member of many local committees and voluntary bodies. He was particularly interested in the welfare of the blind, in anti-vivisection, prison reform and pensions. In 1918 he is reported as having been secretary of the West Ham branch of the National League of the Blind.

As MP for the Stratford Division of West Ham from 1922 to 1945 he survived the National Government landslide of 1931, retaining his seat with a majority of 203. He was a junior Labour Whip from 1931 to 1943. While in the House he showed great interest in welfare and education, particularly of the handicapped; in pensions, and in opposing compulsory vaccination. The latter, he felt, often caused more harm than good and he waged a personal campaign against it. In 1931 he voted with the left of the Labour Party against the Unemployment Insurance Bill and the Anomalies Bill. Later, however, he supported right-wing attitudes on a number of issues, voting for the Silver Jubilee expenses in 1935 and for a pension for the King's widow in 1936.

His attitudes in general seem to have been far from revolutionary – statements recorded in *Hansard* show him to have believed that one of the reasons for alleviating social conditions was to avoid social upheaval: in December 1925 he said:

> When West Ham, like other necessitous areas shouldered the burden of unemployment it stood between this country and revolution. There is no doubt about that. These men in the East End of London would not stand starvation after so many of them had been through the War . . . if the Government want to put off the revolutionary spirit I hope they will learn that one way to keep it back is, first of all, to feed the people.

Ten years later his constituency suffered from the meetings and demonstrations of Sir Oswald Mosley's Fascists, and Tom Groves spoke out in Parliament of the Fascist brutality which occurred on these occasions, and the apparent condoning of it by the police authorities. His parliamentary record also shows that he devoted an enormous amount of time and effort to his constituents' individual problems. This is corroborated by the recollection of his son, who remembers that 'no-one was ever turned away from our house – we literally all lived with our constituents' problems.' Yet in 1945 he was not readopted by the constituency, being replaced as candidate by Councillor H.R. Nicholls, JP. Groves did not accept this decision and stood as an

Independent, but was soundly defeated. In his last years in the House of Commons he had diversified his private activities, holding some chairmanships of companies and becoming a nurseryman and fruit farmer; on his defeat he retired to South Benfleet to become a mushroom farmer.

He had all his life a great interest in the provision of education for other people and a love of learning for himself: after leaving Ruskin he continued to study, and he became a lecturer on such topics as local government, sociology and astronomy, among others. In 1925 he was admitted as a student at Gray's Inn, but was never called to the bar.

In 1915 he married Esther Louise Dow, and in 1923 they won the Dunmow Flitch competition for having satisfied a jury of spinsters and bachelors that they had lived together for a year and a day without a quarrel. There were three children of the marriage, two sons – Thomas Edward, who is a systems analyst with the Ford Motor Co., and Dennis, a supermarket manager – and one daughter, Mary. Groves died on 29 May 1958, survived by his widow and children. An obituary in the *Stratford Express* recalled him as having been 'a jaunty figure, always immaculately dressed and seldom without a big cigar!' The funeral took place at Southend Crematorium, and he left effects to the value of £4657.

Sources: T.W. Walding, *Who's Who in the New Parliament* (1922); S.V. Bracher, *The Herald Book of Labour Members* (1923); E.G. Yates, *Labour Personalities in the House of Commons, 1922-3* (Watford, n.d.); *Labour Who's Who* (1924); *Railway Rev.*, 1 Dec 1927; *Stratford Express*, 20 Apr 1929; *Kelly* (1932) and (1949); *Mayors and Alderman of Great Britain* (1935); *Dod* (1939-44); *WWW* (1951-60); biographical information: the late T.A.K. Elliott, CMG; Gray's Inn Library, London; W.S. Stirrup, TGWU, London; personal information: T.E. Groves, Benfleet, Essex, son. OBIT. *Times, East Anglian Daily Times, Manchester Guardian*, 30 May 1958; *Stratford Express*, 6 June 1958.

MARGARET 'ESPINASSE
ANN HOLT

GURNEY, Joseph (1814-93)
SECULARIST AND RADICAL

Joseph Gurney was born at Watford, near Daventry, Northamptonshire, on 15 April 1814. His father was at various times a tailor, draper and grocer. Gurney was apprenticed to tailoring, and lived and worked for a long time at Long Buckby, Yelvertoft and Braunston before settling in Northampton, where he spent the rest of his life. In Northampton he started as a journeyman tailor and then opened a shop in partnership with his brother. A radical from early youth, he was a member of the Northampton Political Reform Union in the 1830s. In 1840 he was secretary of the Northampton branch of the Universal Community Society of Rational Religionists and was a leading Owenite organiser in the town in the early 1840s. Later in that decade he became one of its leading Chartists. He was a founder member of the Freehold Land Society formed there in December 1848, and was secretary of the Society from 1856 until 1889 when failing eyesight forced him to relinquish the post for that of president, which he retained till his death in 1893.

Gurney was a member of the Northampton Secular Society, founded in 1854 by John Bates, who was a local retailer of newspapers and radical literature and who became election agent for Charles Bradlaugh when the latter contested Northampton borough in the general election of 1868. The Secular Society had a sporadic existence. It was an active body from 1854 to 1856 and appears to have lapsed from then until 1860. It was active again from 1860 to 1864 and lapsed again from then till 1866. But in the latter year it was one of the first six secular societies to affiliate to Charles Bradlaugh's National Secular Society. Gurney was one of the two secularists who invited Bradlaugh to lecture in the town, which he did for the first time in January 1859. It was the beginning of Bradlaugh's long association with both Northampton and Gurney.

Gurney first entered Northampton municipal politics in 1849 when he was nominated as a Chartist candidate for the West ward and polled eighty of the 880 votes cast. He contested the election for the West ward again in 1850 and 1855 without success, but he was returned in the municipal elections of 1858. He was a successful candidate again in 1861, 1864, 1867, 1870 and 1873, in which year he topped the poll for the first time. He became an alderman in 1874, was elected mayor in 1875 and was re-elected to that office in 1879. He was retiring alderman in October 1880, was defeated in the elections of 1881, and also in by-elections in April and November 1882, but was returned to the council in a West ward by-election in October 1883. He finally retired from municipal politics in October 1889.

Local progressive politics in Northampton in the 1850s were dominated by Whig-Liberals who effectively controlled nominations in municipal as well as parliamentary elections. In October 1855 Gurney led the more advanced progressive elements in the town into the New Reform Association, with the aim of giving an independent expression in town politics to those of more advanced views. In particular the members of the New Reform Association wanted an extension of the suffrage and the introduction of secret voting. Gurney became chairman of this short-lived body. It appears that the New Reform Association joined with other Liberals in the town in 1855 to form the United Liberal Association, the first formal Liberal organisation in Northampton. In spite of this, discontent with the continued failure of the Liberals to wrest control of the town council from the Conservatives led Gurney to try to set up a more radical organisation, but without success. The continuing inertia of the Liberals in the early 1860s led Gurney to attempt to get independent Radical candidates elected, but in this too he was not successful. In 1864 he returned to the United Liberal Association.

It was not until the year 1866, when Gladstone introduced an electoral Reform Bill in Parliament, that the reform question won much attention or reform politics much support in Northampton. The Northampton branch of the Reform League was founded on 16 July 1866 and Gurney was active in it from the outset. He was at the head of the Reform League demonstration in Northampton on 22 October 1867, along with Edmond Beales and Charles Bradlaugh. From this time Gurney's association with Bradlaugh became close, and in 1868 together with John Bates he encouraged Bradlaugh to contest the parliamentary election there. From that time until the latter's death in 1891 he was the most prominent and loyal of Bradlaugh's Northampton supporters. Indeed, during Bradlaugh's exclusion from Parliament over the Oath question Gurney became involved in the legal struggle it created. Bradlaugh administered the Oath to himself on 21 February 1882 and took his seat. A vote for his exclusion and the vacation of his seat was carried next day and a new writ issued. Bradlaugh was again returned for Northampton, and on 6 March the House refused him the Oath. Gurney, as president of the Liberal and Radical Union, thereupon began a friendly action against Bradlaugh for failing to take the Oath, in order to test Bradlaugh's action of 21 February and the Commons' action of 6 March; but a court ruling of 15 May refused to hear Gurney's action on the ground that it was collusive. Four years passed before Bradlaugh was finally permitted to take his seat. As for the general election of 1868, it was not the first time that Gurney had been engaged in promoting the cause of a radical parliamentary candidate in Northampton; he had been involved, along with Bates, in the return of Charles Gilpin for the first time as early as the general election of 1857.

It was Bradlaugh's candidature which led to the foundation of the first self-styled Radical organisation in the town, namely, the Northampton Radical Association, which was set up in September 1868. Between that date and September 1877 the organisation of Radicals in Northampton appeared under several names, as the Radical Union from 1869 to 1871, the Northampton Radical Society from 1872 to 1874, the Radical Political Guardians' Association from 1875 to 1877, and simply as the Northampton Radical Association from then until 1880 when it merged into the Northampton Liberal and Radical Union after the acceptance by the local Liberals of Bradlaugh as an official Liberal candidate. How effective Radical organisation was from its foundation in 1868 it is difficult to say. Three years passed before the local Liberals were prepared to recognise the Radicals as a force to be reckoned with and before they were prepared to share any nominations with them in municipal elections. It was not until 1871 that the Radicals succeeded in electing a colleague to sit with Gurney, who had been the town's sole Radical councillor for the previous thirteen years. From 1871, however, the fortunes of Northampton Radicals in municipal politics improved. Following sweeping Conservative successes in the municipal contests of 1872, gained against a background of deep division between the Liberals and Radicals, a pact to share the nominations was arranged between them in the next year. The result was success in four of the six seats, the Liberals winning the two in the East ward and the Radicals winning the two in the West ward, where Gurney headed the poll.

Although the Radicals led by Gurney were beginning to emerge as a political force that could no longer be ignored in town politics in the early 1870s, in parliamentary politics they were still too weak to carry Bradlaugh to success without Liberal support. Gurney tried to get this support in 1873, but he found the Liberals adamantly opposed to Bradlaugh. They were prepared to unite with the Radicals in nominating an agreed second candidate only if Bradlaugh stood down. After the loss of both parliamentary seats to the Conservatives in 1874, one in the general election that spring, the other in the by-election that autumn, when a vacancy was created by the death of Charles Gilpin, it was clear that the Liberals could not confidently hope to win in future without the backing of Bradlaugh's Radicals, nor could the latter expect to win without Liberal support. This support the Liberals as a whole were not prepared to give. Following the first loss in the spring, it was they who now approached Gurney to see if Bradlaugh could be induced to relinquish his parliamentary ambitions in Northampton, but Gurney refused to abandon Bradlaugh. After the second loss, in the by-election that autumn, a leading moderate Liberal, J.M. Vernon, met Gurney to discuss the impasse. The result of this meeting was an election compact relating to both municipal and parliamentary elections. In regard to municipal elections, both sides were to have one candidate each to contest the East and West wards in all future elections, all four candidates to be supported fully by Liberals and Radicals alike. The Radicals benefited greatly from this aspect of the arrangement worked out on the initiative of Vernon and Gurney. As a result of it, Radical strength on the town council rose to four in 1875, with Gurney in addition becoming the town's first Radical mayor. In November 1876 they gained control of all six seats in the West ward, although, like the Liberals, they suffered losses over the next two years. Nevertheless, they had made a breakthrough few could have predicted six years earlier.

In regard to parliamentary elections, the compact simply declared the right of the Radicals to nominate one of the two candidates, without stating who that candidate was to be, and without stating explicitly that future elections were to be fought on a joint campaign, each side supporting the candidate of the other. Initially winning the acceptance of Liberals in the town, the compact led to a division among them by 1876. At the beginning of December 1876 the smaller group of Liberals most hostile to Bradlaugh, led by Jonathan Robinson and the Nonconformist minister, Thomas Arnold, set themselves up as the New Liberal Association. The larger group of more moderate Liberals, whose basic position at that stage was that they wanted neutrality on the Radical candidature of Bradlaugh, and who were led by Philip Manfield, J.M. Vernon and P. Perry, later that month converted the original United Liberal Association into the Old Liberal Association. In December 1876 the Birmingham Liberal Association intervened in an attempt to secure unity on the model of their own party organisation. The result was the formation of the Northampton Liberal Association in the next year, but the anti-Bradlaugh New Liberal Association rejected the scheme because it did not provide explicitly for the exclusion of Bradlaugh from the Radical half of a joint future candidature. At the same time Gurney and the Northampton Radicals rejected it because it did not provide explicitly for Bradlaugh's inclusion. By the middle of 1877 the parliamentary aspect of the 1874 compact had become meaningless, but for municipal elections it survived until 1879. In that year, when the adopted parliamentary candidate of the moderate Northampton Liberal Association, A.S. Ayrton, pointed out to Gurney that the compact of 1874 said nothing about a joint campaign but merely pledged both sides to neutrality, Gurney responded by declaring that as far as the Radicals were concerned this meant an end to the municipal alliance. This, however, did not lead to a civil war between Radicals and Liberals in the local elections of that year: the Northampton Liberal Association simply decided that as a body it would abstain from the contest. In the event only two Liberals fought those elections, one in the East and one in the West ward, and both were defeated. The Radicals fared better, running two candidates for the West, both being successful, and one for the East, who failed.

Despite the grave disunity which existed as late as February 1880 and which seriously threatened the chances of victory for Bradlaugh or the Liberal candidate, Gurney's persistence in maintaining the right of the Radicals to promote Bradlaugh and to refuse to support a Liberal candidate without reciprocal arrangements finally bore fruit. Ayrton had to withdraw after a riding accident and his replacement, Balfour, found it pointless to continue in his candidature for the Liberal Association while disunity prevailed. It was finally the insistence of the next replacement, Labouchere, that there must be fusion with the Bradlaugh Radicals if there was to be a chance of victory, that led to a crumbling of Liberal opposition. In consequence of this, after two decades of disunity, Liberals and Radicals came together in the summer of 1880 and formed the Northampton Liberal and Radical Union, with Gurney as president and the Liberal shoe manufacturer, Philip Manfield, a future member for the borough, as vice-president. Despite some tension between the Manfield Liberals and the Gurney Radicals over the former's view that Bradlaugh was not paying his fair share of Union registration expenses, the new organisation lasted during Bradlaugh's lifetime.

With this union of forces the Northampton Radicals could have expected a long period of increasing power. Instead, within a few years of their acceptance by the Liberals, the Radicals found themselves challenged by the development of labour consciousness and by the rise of Socialism in the town. The recognition that they had interests separate from their employers was slow to develop among Northampton working men, and any early signs of it were quickly scotched by the Radical Gurney. In 1876 for instance, when a working man, W.C. France, objected to the nomination of two employers as Radical candidates in the municipal elections, Gurney dismissed the objection, declaring he 'disliked anything in the shape of class distinction. He did not like the idea of any working men setting up as a class in opposition to another class because one was the employer and the other the employed.' Again, in 1886, when W.L. Roberts was chosen as the first 'Labour' candidate to stand in a Northampton municipal election, it was greatly resented by the Liberal and Radical Union. Gurney commented: 'Did a man cease to be a working man when he ceased to be a journeyman? He had been a working man all his life.'

The fortunes of Radicalism received a further setback after Bradlaugh's death in 1891. Manfield was elected MP in Bradlaugh's place, on the understanding that he would serve only one term. When in February 1892 the executive of the Liberal and Radical Union nominated him to be a candidate for the second time in the next election, which took place in July 1892, Gurney felt that the electoral agreement of 1880, embodied in the very name Liberal and Radical Union, had been broken. He therefore joined with several other Radicals who had set up the Bradlaugh Radical Association in February, and Gurney became president of the new body in March 1892. They attempted without success to put forward Bradlaugh's disciple, John M. Robertson, as a candidate in rivalry to Manfield. This split was carried over to municipal contests, and in the local elections of October-November 1892 the Radical party was fragmented and suffered a rout. Gurney, who for over half a century personified in his attitudes and activities the spirit of Northampton radicalism, did not long survive this débâcle. He died on 10 December 1893 at the age of seventy-nine. He was survived by no immediate relatives, and bequeathed the bulk of his estate, valued at £2935, to grand-nephews and nieces and to his housekeeper, Martha Waters.

Sources: (1) MSS: Bradlaugh Coll.: National Secular Society and Northampton PL. (2) Other: *Reasoner*, 26 Aug 1846, 19 Apr 1857; *London Investigator 1*, no. 7 (Oct 1854); *Northampton Mercury*, 27 Oct, 3 Nov 1855, 6 Nov 1858, 7 Nov 1863, 29 Oct 1864, 1 Dec 1866, 11 Jan, 17 Aug, 8 Nov 1873, 30 May, 31 Oct 1874, 24 Apr, 4, 11 Nov 1875, 5 Jan, 7 Oct 1876, 19 Jan 1878, 15 Nov 1879, 13 Nov 1880, 5 Nov 1881, 22 Apr, 4 Nov 1882, 6 Oct 1883, 31 Oct 1885, 7

Aug 1886, 12 Oct 1889, 15 Feb 1890, 5, 19 Feb 1892; *Reasoner Gazette*, 9 Sep 1860; *National Reformer*, 27 Sep 1868, 17 Aug 1873; *Northamptonshire Guardian*, 17 Feb, 3, 24 Mar, 7 July, 25 Aug, 8 Sep, 15 Dec 1877, 13, 20, 27 Mar, 10 Apr, 21 Aug, 9 Oct, 6 Nov 1880; H.B. Bonner, *Charles Bradlaugh* 2 vols (1894); W.L. Arnstein, *The Bradlaugh Case* (Oxford, 1965); D. Tribe, *President Charles Bradlaugh, M.P.* (1971); E. Royle, *Victorian Infidels* (Manchester, 1974). OBIT. *Northampton Mercury*, 15 Dec 1893.

NOTE: The author and the editors are much obliged to Dr E. Royle, York University, for his comments on an earlier draft of this biography.

FERGUS D'ARCY

See also: *Charles BRADLAUGH.

HAMILTON, Mary Agnes (1882-1966)
AUTHOR, JOURNALIST, AND LABOUR MP

Mary Agnes Hamilton was born Mary Adamson on 8 July 1882, in Withington, Manchester, the eldest child of Professor Robert Adamson, professor of logic in Manchester at the time of her birth, and later in the universities of Aberdeen and Glasgow. Her mother was Margaret, daughter of David Duncan, a Manchester linen merchant; she had been on the teaching staff of Manchester High School. Molly, as she was called, went to Glasgow High School and then spent nine months perfecting her German in the family of a professor at Kiel, before taking up a scholarship to Newnham College, Cambridge. At Newnham she gained a first class in the Modern History Tripos, and subsequently in economics, at a time when few women studied that subject. She did not, however, pursue it further, as while still at college she had become keenly interested in home and foreign affairs. She was a lively debater and played an eager part in college political discussion – university politics being still closed to women at that date. In a volume of autobiography, published in 1944 under the title *Remembering my Good Friends*, she gave a vivid description of Cambridge University life before the wars as it appeared to an intelligent young woman with leanings to radicalism. Even at that early age she was a determined controversialist with a loud commanding voice, a trait shared with others of her family; later on, when they were living in the Hertfordshire countryside, neighbours amusedly commented that the sound of the Misses Adamson having a friendly argument carried well across the adjoining valley. After completing her college career she took a post as assistant to the professor of history in the University College of South Wales in Cardiff; but resigned after less than a year to marry Charles J. Hamilton, a lecturer in political science in the same university. The marriage was not a success, and in after years she preferred not to refer to it.

Her political ideas developed rapidly, as did her writing. In the period before the First World War she had already published several books and translations, and written articles for various journals; and in 1913 she took a job on *The Economist*, then edited by the well-known Liberal journalist F.W. Hirst. Her main interest was in women's suffrage and the reform of the poor laws, and in the latter field, after some hesitation, she accepted the proposals of the Minority Report and advocated them on public platforms. In 1913 she worked for a year in Lloyd George's Land Commission, whose report made a considerable sensation at the time; but she was rapidly moving towards moderate Socialism, encouraged by those of her friends who knew more than the mass of the public about what was brewing on the European continent. In July 1914 she joined the ILP, and in August the Union of Democratic Control, according to herself as 'a founder member'. Her third and in many ways her best novel, *Dead Yesterday*, though not published until 1916, presented an unforgettable picture – which is still interesting today – of the dilemma of the British intellectual before and after the fateful fourth of August. By 1916, also, she had become strongly opposed to the war, and followed Hirst in resigning from *The*

Economist in order to write for the weekly *Common Sense* and for Norman Angell's monthly *War and Peace*. She took a lively part in political discussion within the ILP, serving on several of its committees, including the Policy and Programme Committees.

She joined the 1917 Club in Gerrard Street – see special note on the Club below – which was founded just after the March revolution in Russia, partly under the inspiration of Ramsay MacDonald, for whom at that time she had a regard almost amounting to hero-worship: using the pseudonym 'Iconoclast' she wrote just before and immediately after the first Labour Government two eulogistic brief studies of him, which were reprinted, in a revised edition of one volume, in 1929. Holding such views, she was naturally a strong opponent of Communism or anything which savoured of the Bolshevik revolution of October 1917, and eagerly absorbed any derogatory reports on the Soviet Union brought back by visitors like Clifford Allen. So it was hardly surprising that in the mid-twenties, when Allen's fund-raising powers had put the ILP on its financial feet and Brailsford's brilliant editorial gifts were making the *New Leader* a weekly of merit and power far surpassing the *Labour Leader* which it replaced – when, nevertheless, the sharp quarrel between MacDonald and the bulk of the ILP was reaching a critical stage – that Mrs Hamilton was appointed assistant editor of the *New Leader* in order to act as a check on Brailsford's leftward leanings – a decision which Brailsford took as a personal and deliberate insult.

Mary Hamilton did not succeed in getting into Parliament until 1929, though she stood, unsuccessfully, for Chatham in 1923 and for the two-member constituency of Blackburn in the Red Letter election of 1924. Before and after that failure she worked hard on the Balfour Committee on Industry and Trade (1924-9), to which MacDonald had appointed her. She signed the final report of that Committee, but added, with six other signatories, a memorandum declaring that the proposals of the main report were inadequate and needed further strengthening – e.g. by nationalising the Bank of England. During these years she was becoming better known and more highly regarded, with the result that in the summer of 1929 she topped the poll in Blackburn, and after a successful maiden speech was made parliamentary private secretary to Clement Attlee. She was appointed a member of the Royal Commission on the Civil Service which sat from 1929 to 1931; and was British delegate to the 1929 and 1930 assemblies of the League of Nations. It was through the League and its discussions on disarmament and other aspects of international co-operation that she came into contact with Arthur Henderson, for whom she developed a very high regard; and after his death made him the subject of the best of her biographical books, *Arthur Henderson* (1938). She served on the Refugee Committee of the League and also on the Committee for Intellectual Co-operation, on which she collaborated with, among others, Professor Gilbert Murray.

Partly owing to this occupation with these problems of world peace, but more because of her growing realisation of the social conditions of her Blackburn electorate as the world depression began and intensified, Mrs Hamilton's political outlook underwent a thorough change. By the beginning of 1931 she had become a violent critic of what she felt to be the complete failure of the Labour Government to produce any remedy for the growing unemployment; and the political manoeuvres of the summer which resulted in MacDonald's emerging as head of a National Government completed her disillusion with her one-time idol. In August of 1931 she was elected to the executive committee of the Parliamentary Labour Party, and from that position led a fierce attack on Philip Snowden's financial policies, demanding instead redistributive taxation, a planned economy, and the nationalisation of the basic industries. Her revulsion led her to the extent of standing as an ILP candidate in the October general election, in which she was heavily defeated; she never returned to Parliament.

During the remainder of the thirties she shared the depressing uncertainties of many intellectuals of the time: she had joined, in 1931, G.D.H. Cole's New Fabian Research Bureau, but played little part in its efforts to work out new forward policies in practical detail; in 1934, reversing engines, she joined the multi-party body of the centre known as the Next Five Years Group and associated in the public mind particularly with Harold Macmillan and Clifford Allen, but soon gave it up until the Labour Party's attempted ban induced her to rejoin as a gesture; later she became a vigorous opponent of the British acquiescence in Mussolini's conquest of Abyssinia and of the appeasement attitudes which culminated at Munich. [See *Remembering my Good Friends*, pp. 288 ff., for her detailed description of the frustrations of those years.]

Her main activity during the thirties, however, was not in politics direct, but in lecturing and broadcasting. She went on several lecturing tours to America, where she was very popular; and was regularly heard over the radio – from the beginning of 1932 to the end of 1936 she was a governor of the BBC, and one of her best-known efforts was a regular series of talks on new books. From 1937 to 1940 she served as co-opted alderman on the Labour-controlled LCC.

All this, however, came to an end soon after 'appeasement' ended, and all-out war followed in 1940, greatly to her relief. In that year she became a wartime civil servant, working first with the Ministry of Information and, after a year, with the Ministry of Reconstruction, which sent her on an official tour to expound the Beveridge proposals in the United States. In 1944 she returned to the former Ministry, and when two years later its overseas department was transferred to the Foreign Office she continued there as head of the American section until her retirement in 1952, having been rewarded in 1949 with the CBE. For the remainder of her life, though she continued to publish, her main interest lay in the English-Speaking Union, for which she did a great deal of work, including many articles written for its journal.

Mary Agnes Hamilton died on 10 February 1966; she was cremated at Golders Green and left an estate valued at £6723. She was a humanist by upbringing, deeply interested in literature and in music, and a natural extrovert, with a wide circle of friends. In her second volume of autobiography, *Up-hill all the Way* (1953) she expressed her philosophy of life and politics, including her own partial and individual acceptance of Christianity.

MARGARET COLE

Writings: Books on Greek and Roman history, some novels and a number of translations are included among Mary Hamilton's publications. She also contributed to such journals as *Common Sense, The Economist, Foreign Affairs*, the *New Leader*, the *Rev. of Revs, Time and Tide* and *War and Peace*. Only her main political and trade union works together with her biographical and autobiographical works are listed here: 'Nietzsche: the laughing philosopher', *Soc. Rev. 17* (Jan-Mar 1920) 33-40; 'William Morris and Bruce Glasier', ibid. *18* (July-Sep 1921) 245-9; *Socialism and Liberty* [ILP, 1921?]; 'The Twilight of the Entente', *Soc. Rev. 19*, no. 103 (Apr 1922) 200-3; *The Principles of Socialism* [ILP Study Courses no. 2: 1922] 28 pp.; 'The Cenotaph of Liberalism', *Soc. Rev. 21*, no. 115 (Apr 1923) 166-71; 'Individualism and Individuality', ibid., *22*, no. 120 (Sep 1923) 109-16; under the pseud. 'Iconoclast' she wrote: *The Man of Tomorrow, J.R. MacDonald* (1923, 3rd imp. 1924, rev. ed. 1929), *Fit to Govern* [short biographies] (1924) and *J. Ramsay MacDonald (1923-1925)* (1925, rev. ed. 1929); *Margaret Bondfield* (1924); 'Rt Hon. J. Ramsay MacDonald MP: Labour's First Prime Minister', in *The Book of the Labour Party 3* ed. H. Tracey [1925] 118-141; *Mary Macarthur: a biographical sketch* (1925); *Thomas Carlyle* (1926, 2nd ed. 1930); 'First Impressions', *Labour Mag. 8* (July 1929) 107-9; *J. Ramsay MacDonald* [revised from *The Man of Tomorrow* and *J. Ramsay MacDonald (1923-1925)*] (1929); 'My Impressions of the Tenth Assembly', *Labour Mag.* (Oct 1929) 254-5; 'The Labour Party and Protection', *Spec. 144*, 28 June 1930, 1039-40; 'Labour Members and the Government' [letter], *New Statesman and Nation*, 19 Sep 1931, 333; *In America Today* (1932); *Sidney and Beatrice Webb: a study in contemporary biography* (1933); *John Stuart Mill* (1933); 'No Peace apart from International Security: an answer to extreme pacifists', in P.L. Baker et al., *Challenge to Death* (1934) 261-74; 'Changes in Social Life' in *Our Freedom and its Results*, ed. R. Strachey (1936) 233-85; *Newnham: an informal biography* (1936); 'Ramsay MacDonald', *Spec. 159*, 12 Nov 1937, 835; 'The World and the Jew', *Spec. 161*, 25 Nov 1938, 898-9; *Arthur Henderson: a biography* (1938); *The Labour Party Today: what it is and how it works* (1939); *Women at Work: a brief introduction to trade unionism for women* (1941); *British Trade Unions* (1943) 31 pp.; 'Beatrice Webb', *Spec. 170*, 7

May 1943, 423-4; *Remembering my Good Friends* (1944); 'Miss Wilkinson', *Spec. 175*, 24 Aug 1945, 169-70; *The Place of the United States of America in World Affairs* (Nottingham, 1947) 21 pp.; *Up-hill all the Way: a third cheer for democracy* (1953).

Sources: Most Labour biographies and histories written after 1938 refer to Mary Hamilton's political writings but few mention her own career. Her autobiographical works, *Remembering my Good Friends* (1944) and *Up-hill all the Way* (1953) are, therefore, the principal published sources. All her papers were destroyed after her death in accordance with instructions in her will, see: C. Cook et al., *Sources in British Political History 1900-1951 3* (1977). Other sources are: H.M. Swanwick, *Builders of Peace* (1924); Balfour Committee on Trade and Industry, *Final Report* 1928-9 VII Cmd 3282; *Hansard* (1929-31); J. Johnston, *A Hundred Commoners* (1931) 283-5; H.M. Swanwick, *I have been young* (1935); L. Abercrombie et al., *The Next Five Years: an essay in political agreement* (1935); G.D.H. Cole, *A History of the Labour Party from 1914* (1948); C.L. Mowat, *Britain between the Wars* (1955); M. Cole, *The Story of Fabian Socialism* (1961); C.A. Cline, *Recruits to Labour: the British Labour Party, 1914-1931* (Syracuse, 1963); A. Marwick, *Clifford Allen: the open conspirator* (1964); R.E. Dowse, *Left in the Centre: the Independent Labour Party 1893-1940* (1966); P. Brookes, *Women at Westminster: an account of women in the British Parliament 1918-1966* (1967); M. Swartz, *The Union of Democratic Control in British Politics during the First World War* (Oxford, 1971); biographical information: the late T.A.K. Elliott, CMG; personal information: Miss M.R. Adamson, Welwyn Garden City, sister; personal knowledge, Dame Margaret Cole. OBIT. *Times*, 11 Feb 1966; *Guardian*, 12 Feb 1966; *Blackburn Times*, 18 Feb 1966. The editors are indebted to B.H. Sadler, Warwick Univ., for an earlier draft of this biography.

See also: †Henry Noel BRAILSFORD; †Arthur HENDERSON; †James Ramsay MACDONALD; *Edmund Dene MOREL; †Helena Maria Lucy SWANWICK; and below: The 1917 Club.

The 1917 Club

A surprising number of labour and Socialist personalities were members of the 1917 Club during the inter-war years. The name has a revolutionary sound about it and indeed the Club's establishment was in part a response to the overthrow of Tsarism in 1917, always the main external enemy of British radicals. But the 1917 Club was not, in any way, a sectarian venture and its membership included radically-minded Liberals of the Union of Democratic Control variety and labour people of all shades of opinion. In other words, despite its title, the 1917 Club was not a by-product of the Bolshevik revolution. Ramsay MacDonald was the Club's first president.

Its origins have been written about by a number of people and there is a confusion of personalities in different accounts. One usually reliable witness, Leonard Woolf, gave the following details in the third volume of his autobiography:

> I do not remember in whose brain the idea of a left wing club originated in 1917. I rather think it started in a conversation between Oliver Strachey, Lytton's brother, and me. At any rate in April we were sounding all kinds of people about the idea and found everywhere enthusiastic support for it. We got together a kind of informal committee which met for the first time on April 23 and continued to direct affairs until the first general meeting of the Club on December 19. I have forgotten who all the people were who worked with us, but the following certainly were concerned in it with us: Ramsay Macdonald, J.A. Hobson, Mary Macarthur, a prominent woman trade unionist; and her husband, W.C. Anderson; H.N. Brailsford; Molly Hamilton (Mrs M.A. Hamilton), who became a Labour MP and wrote the life of Macdonald; Emile Burns who became a communist. By July we were looking at houses in Long Acre and elsewhere and eventually we took the lease of a house [No. 4] in

Gerrard Street, in those days the rather melancholy haunt of prostitutes daily from 2.30 p.m. onwards. On December 19, as I said, we held the first general meeting; I was elected to the committee and remained a member of it for a good many years.

The membership of the club during its first years was a curious mixture. It was mainly political and the politicals were mainly Labour Party, from Ramsay downwards. But there was also an element of unadulterated culture, literary and artistic, and during the first two or three years of its existence it was much used by culture, particularly at tea time, so that if one dropped in about 4 o'clock and looked round its rooms, one would hardly have guessed that it was political. Virginia was often there and there was a strong contingent of Stracheys, including Lytton and a retinue of young women and young men who often accompanied him. Years later the stage must have invaded and captured the club, for, when I had long ceased to use it, I was asked, as a founder of it, to come to a dinner to celebrate its foundation. Ramsay Macdonald presided and I sat at the high table, as it were, with him and some other ageing politicians, while the active members seemed to be mainly actors and actresses and musicians. In its beginnings the stage gave us, I think, only one member, Elsa Lanchester, and music only Cyril Scott [*Beginning again* (1964) 216-17].

Mary Hamilton [*Remembering my Good Friends* (1944) 78-9] wrote that Henry Nevinson, and J.A. Hobson were 'its original moving spirits' and that the Club 'was planned to be a point of rapprochement for Liberal and Labour people who felt the same about the war. Its actual birthday coincided with the first Russian Revolution'. Francis Meynell [*My Lives* (1971) 236] wrote that the 1917 Club:

was founded by people who today would be called the 'Labour Left', and its name was a tribute to the first (Menshevik) Russian Revolution. Most of its members were anti-war, but, that apart, they were almost Irish in their divisions of opinion. After the Bolshevik Revolution a pro-Communist group monopolised the 'long table' and made almost a club within a club, a conscious huddle within the muddle. Alfred Bacharach was its leader and Miles Malleson his lieutenant.

Ramsay MacDonald, a founder member and the club's best-known politician, was not welcome at 'the table'. Interesting characters were Henry Nevinson, Charles Laughton, H.N. Brailsford, Raymond Postgate . . . The club, tiny and rather unkempt, died before the last war. Its premises now house strip-teasers.

In her biography of F.W. Pethick-Lawrence (1963) Vera Brittain stated that he and E.D. Morel and Roden Buxton founded the 1917 Club. The longest account of the Club is to be found in Douglas Goldring's *The Nineteen Twenties* (1945) 145-52. Of the personalities who used the Club he wrote: 'Among the more prominent figures who used the club in its heyday were H.W. Nevinson, H.N. Brailsford, F.W. Pethick-Lawrence, Sir Charles Trevelyan, Joseph King, H.G. Wells, E.D. Morel, Clement Attlee, C.G. Ammon, Noel and Charles Buxton, Mary Agnes Hamilton, Stanley Unwin, Leonard Woolf, Evelyn Sharp, Rose Macaulay, Sir Osbert Sitwell, Francis Birrell, Aldous Huxley, and Lord Ponsonby . . . Of the younger members, so many of whom have since achieved fame, Dr C.E.M. Joad, Harold Scott and Elsa Lanchester stand out in my memory.'

There are further references to the 1917 Club in A. Marwick's book on Clifford Allen, *The Open Conspirator* (1964) and C. Cross's *Philip Snowden* (1966). The entries in *Labour Who's Who* for 1924 and 1927 usually included membership of the 1917 Club as a biographical fact worth noting. The range and variety of membership seems to have continued throughout the 1920s; in 1924 members included G.D.H. Cole, Hugh Dalton, Isabella Ford, J.L. Hammond, Herbert Morrison, Evelyn Sharp and Helena Swanwick; in 1927 E.M. Forster, J.A. Hobson, Miles Malleson, Oswald Mosley, Eva Reckitt, Shapurji Saklatvala and Ben Turner were among the names listed. Finally, two comments from contemporaries who used the Club. The first is from Dame Margaret Cole [letter dated 1 Dec 1977]:

The 1917 Club (in a dingy house in Gerrard Street, with some pretty poor food in the basement) was really a sort of fringe affair, a place of meeting and gossip for those on the Left who couldn't afford to join established Clubs. Also, where those who couldn't afford even its own modest subscription would hang around, hoping that a member might turn up who would stand them a meal, or at least a drink. There were, besides, speakers from time to time whom it was interesting to hear – and you never knew who you might meet there. But it had very little influence . . .

The second comment comes from Katherine B.M. Cope (née Wattie) in a letter dated 28 Nov 1977. Mrs Cope joined the 1917 Club in 1923 at the age of twenty-seven. She had recently come to London to work. She stated that the Club was closed down in 1932 and she further commented:

I should say that after 1924 the general atmosphere was one of benevolent bohemianism, enlivened by regular and well-organised parties and moderated by some character-assassination on the part of the wittier and more articulate members. We had also some interesting addresses from (amongst others) J.B.S. Haldane, Herbert Samuel, Compton Mackenzie, John Galsworthy, and, of course, J.R. Macdonald.

Later on, with the influx of new members, of whom many were jobless and impecunious, the standards slowly declined, and what would now be reckoned as a very mild form of gang-warfare began to supersede the benevolence. One of the gangs insisted that the "high table" be reserved for its relatives and friends and for those whom it chose to invite to join them: the other gang deeply resented this attempt at apartheid. When the time arrived for the appointment of new club officers, the feuding of the two groups resulted in mutual charges of election-rigging. At this point the patience of the guarantors became exhausted and the club was wound up.

JOHN SAVILLE

HAMSON, Harry Tom (1868-1951)
JOURNALIST AND SOCIALIST

Harry Hamson was born on 21 June 1868 at Great Creaton, Northamptonshire, the son of George Best Hamson, a journeyman carpenter, and his wife Faith (née Everard), who came from a Naseby farming family. Harry Hamson attended the village school at Thornby, where he spent his early years, but then the family moved to Leicester. Details of his youth are obscure but he is known to have attended weekly Sunday lectures organised by local radicals in Northampton, where he was apprenticed, and these seem to have been the beginning of his political education. At a meeting of the College Street Mutual Improvement Society in the late 1880s, Hamson opened a discussion on the celebration of the Queen's Jubilee by moving a motion for the abolition of all hereditary government. He also gave lectures on Darwinian theory.

His first job was in the composing room and then as a junior reporter for the Bedford weekly *Times and Independent*. He then moved to Hitchin and later to Taunton where he was chief reporter on the *Somerset Express*. It was at the Unitarian Chapel there that he married Bessie Sealy Chown, a dressmaker, in April 1897. By this time, however, he had changed jobs once again and had become assistant editor of the *Merthyr Express*, a strongly Liberal paper, owned and edited by H.W. Southey. He was already a committed Socialist and indeed there is some evidence that his Socialist leaning had hindered promotion in his earlier positions. In Merthyr he was the foremost member of a small group which established the Ruskin Institute and started Oxford University extension lectures. He gave classes in shorthand and among his students were the Berry brothers, later to become Lord Kemsley and Lord Camrose. Their father was J.M. Berry, election agent for the Liberal coalowner and MP, D.A. Thomas. Hamson was also active in Merthyr's debating life and he was among the founding members of the town's Ethical Society.

The Merthyr ILP was not founded until 1896 and its early growth was slow. Hamson, together with Oliver Jenkins, N.W. Scholefield, George McKay, Richard M. Martin and Edmond Stonelake, was among its most committed members. During the strike of 1898 the ILP brought Keir Hardie into the coalfield on two occasions, and it was the Merthyr group together with the militants on the Aberdare Trades Council who were largely responsible for Hardie's nomination in 1900 for the Merthyr Tydfil constituency. The story has been told in detail in Fox (1964), Morgan (1966) and Pelling (1967). Hamson's position on the *Merthyr Express* was obviously of considerable assistance in this as in other campaigns of the local labour movement.

Hamson remained in close touch with Keir Hardie between 1900 and 1906 but after Hardie's re-election in 1906 and the emergence of the Parliamentary Labour Party, a considerable anti-Socialist current welled up in the Merthyr district; and prominent advertisers in the *Express* threatened to withdraw their support. Hamson was obliged to resign, although his personal relationships with the Southey family always remained amicable. At a farewell smoking-concert Hamson was presented with fifty sovereigns and an illuminated address to record his association with the paper.

After leaving Merthyr he edited a newspaper in Bromley but after a few weeks he became editor of the *Middlesex Advertiser and Gazette*, a position he held until his retirement forty years later in December 1946.

Hamson had been a member of the Institute of Journalists since the early 1890s but he became dissatisfied with its record; and in 1909 he joined the National Union of Journalists, established two years earlier in Manchester. He was a founder member of the West London branch and for the rest of his long professional life he remained active in the union. Between 1924 and 1929 he was the London suburban representative on the NEC. He was always especially interested in training and education for journalists and he emphasised the importance of 'a complete training and educational system' in his evidence to the R.C. on the Press in 1948.

Hamson put down roots in his adopted district. He was a strong advocate of town planning, a supporter of the garden city movement, an early conservationist, and an enthusiastic local historian. He was a member of the Uxbridge Youth Committee and a founder of the public library, of which he was chairman for twenty-five years. The museum section of the library was named after him. In 1937 he was a founder member of the first editors' organisation – the London Suburban and Home Counties Editors' Association – of which he was chairman for nine years until July 1946 when it was merged in the Guild of Newspaper Editors, an organisation he had helped to inaugurate. He was elected a vice-president of this as the representative of the weekly papers. In the 1940s Hamson was a member of the Advisory Press Committee to the London Region of the Ministry of Information.

Hamson was slim-featured and in profile resembled Ramsay MacDonald. His wife had predeceased him in 1949 and Hamson died on 16 September 1951 in Hillingdon Hospital. He was buried at Hillingdon Cemetery and left effects valued at £813. He was survived by his daughter Sybil, a lifelong supporter of the Labour Party, who had married John F. Maclean of Glasgow in 1939, and by their two sons, Kenneth and Ian. The former is an active Labour Party worker and trade unionist and now (1977) represents the NUGMW on the GMC of the Southampton Labour Party.

Writings: Articles in *Middlesex Advertiser and Gazette*; 'The County of Middlesex', *London Calling: the overseas journal of the British Broadcasting Corporation*, no. 276 (Jan 1945) 8-9; *Memorandum on the Reform and Improvement of the Press* and evidence before the R.C. on the Press 1947-8 XV Cmd 7508 Qs 12883-926.

Sources: (1) MSS: Labour Party archives: LRD; letters from J.K. Hardie to H.T. Hamson dated 24 Nov 1900, 7 Mar and 10 Dec 1901, 4 Sep 1902, 17 Feb and 4 May 1903, 26 Dec 1905, 28 and 29 Jan 1906 and letter from H.T. Hamson to Vincent Hamson, his nephew, 18 Apr 1949: photocopies in *DLB* Coll. (2) Other: *Merthyr Express*, 17 Mar 1906; ILP, *Souvenir 20th Annual Conference* [Merthyr, 1912]; *Glasgow Herald*, 5 Apr 1926; *Hertfordshire Mercury*, 3 June 1938; F.J. Mansfield, *"Gentlemen, The Press!" Chronicles of a Crusade (official history of the National Union of Journalists)* (1943); *Middlesex Advertiser and County Gazette*, 5 July and 13 Dec 1946; F. Bealey and H. Pelling, *Labour and Politics 1900-1906* (1958); K.O. Morgan, *Wales in British Politics 1868-1922* (Cardiff, 1963, 2nd ed. 1970); K.O. Fox, 'Labour and Merthyr's Khaki Election of 1900', *Welsh History Rev. 2* (1964-5) 351-66; K.O. Morgan, 'The Merthyr of Keir Hardie', in *Merthyr Politics: the making of a working-class tradition*, ed. G. Williams (Cardiff, 1966) 58-81; H. Pelling, *Social Geography of British Elections 1885-1910* (1967); K.O. Morgan, 'Labour's Early Struggles in South Wales: some new evidence, 1900-8', *National Library of Wales J. 17*, no. 4 (winter, 1972) 364-70; *South Wales Echo*, 20 Feb 1973; biographical information: J. Perfect, NUJ, London; Central Library, Cardiff; Miss M. Pearce, Hillingdon Borough Libraries, Uxbridge; Editor, *Middlesex Advertiser and Gazette*, Uxbridge; *South Wales Echo*, Cardiff; Dr K.O. Morgan, Oxford; personal information: K.J.H. Maclean, Southampton, grandson. OBIT. *Middlesex Advertiser and Gazette*, 21 Sep 1951; *Journalist* (Nov 1951).

JOYCE BELLAMY
BARBARA NIELD

HARFORD, Edward (1837/8-98)
RAILWAYMEN'S LEADER

Edward Harford was probably born in Bristol on 21 March 1837 or 1838; but neither place nor date can be confirmed. His father, also Edward, was in the police force. Edward Harford senior resigned his post in June 1838 on his appointment to the New Gaol at Bedminster, but when his son was five the family moved to Tiverton in Devon, where he was head constable. Young Edward was educated at Tiverton Factory School until he was fourteen and then apprenticed to the confectionery trade. Disliking this, he joined the Devon county constabulary on the establishment of this force, living in Hatherleigh. He married Fanny Ann Reed Sanders, a domestic servant, on 26 October 1857.

The date when he commenced his railway career is not known but his first job was as a porter for the Bristol and Exeter Railway Company. He then transferred to the Midland Railway Company, where he worked in various capacities, including general shunting. By the mid 1860s he had joined the Manchester, Sheffield and Lincolnshire Railway Company, where he served as a goods guard for five years and a passenger guard for nearly two and a half years. An enthusiastic trade unionist, he was present at the first Great Delegate Meeting of the Amalgamated Society of Railway Servants held in London on 24 June 1872, when the Society's rules were formulated. Harford's experience of most grades of railway service coupled with an ability to organise made him a popular choice as a union leader; and in June 1873 his fellow railway workers persuaded him, by a 1000-signature petition, to leave the service and become organising secretary for the Sheffield district of the ASRS. He had just been promoted to inspector, so it was to his disadvantage to accept the union post, and he took on a very difficult task. G.W. Alcock in his *Fifty Years of Railway Trade Unionism* quotes Harford as having written at this time: 'I cannot get the branches to send their share for this district. It is starvation work, and I heartily wish myself back again on the M.S. & L.' [Alcock (1922) 105].

Trade unionism on the railways had its special problems. At best some companies operated a very strict paternalism; but all were vehemently opposed to unionisation. For many years after the first significant union growth of the early 1870s companies refused to negotiate with union officials, and the term 'railway servants' is an indication of the attitudes that prevailed. As Sir George Findlay, the general manager of the LNWR, said to the R.C. on Labour in 1892: 'you might as well expect to have Trades Unionism in Her Majesty's army as to have it in the railway service. The thing is totally incompatible' [Vol. XXXIII, Q. 25949]. The accident rate on the railways was appalling. As late as 1906 the rate of mortality in that year among goods guards, brakesmen and shunters was twice as high as that for coalminers. Harford gave evidence before the R.C. on Railway Accidents in 1875, and financial compensation for injury or death was always one of his central concerns.

Harford represented the Sheffield district on the national executive in 1875, but shortly afterwards the districts were enlarged, and he lost his job. He found work in an iron foundry, but retained his union membership, and by 1878 he was again representing the Sheffield district on the ASRS executive. From 1879 he was reinstated as organising secretary, and in 1882 he was promoted to national assistant secretary. By this time the union was at its lowest ebb in its history. At the end of 1872 there were 17,247 members; by September 1882 there were under 6000. Frederick Evans, general secretary since the autumn of 1874, was overworked and disheartened, and he suffered a nervous breakdown towards the end of 1882. Harford was the only applicant for the now vacant post of general secretary. 'Though he lacked the brilliance of his predecessor and was a man of stolid rather than mercurial temperament, Harford was a conscientious and hardworking organiser' [Bagwell (1963) 89].

By the date Harford took office a number of important changes in union structure, organisation and membership had already occurred or were in progress. The AGM of 1879 and of 1880 had altered certain parts of the constitutional structure of the union – a protection fund had been established (which gave victimisation grants and provided for strike pay under certain conditions), and the superannuation fund was wound up – and the weekly subscription had been increased to 5d per member. There had also been a breakaway of engine drivers and firemen to form ASLEF in 1880, and these and other factors had largely contributed to the decline in membership which so troubled Evans. But membership was already recovering by the end of 1882 and it reached over 10,000 by 1887 – mainly because of a growth in numbers in Northumberland and Durham – while the funds of the union had more than doubled in the same period. The emergence of the workers on the North Eastern Railway as a militant grouping was to have important consequences for the internal development of the ASRS. The Darlington programme of 1888 encouraged the formulation of a national programme, which was to be much assisted by the general upsurge of unionism in 1889 and 1890. It must be emphasised, however, that these developments inside the ASRS were well under way before the autumn of 1889 and owed nothing to the Socialist revival or the organisation of the unskilled. Indeed, Harford was against recruiting casual staff and labourers, and the 1889 AGM turned down a suggestion that the lowest-paid grades should be offered special terms to encourage their recruitment. The consequence of this decision was the establishment of the General Railway Workers' Union, in the organisation of which H.H. Champion and the Fabian, De Mattos, played important parts [Gupta (1966) 132 ff.].

By the early 1890s the ASRS had changed its character from its early friendly society type to that of a more normal union. Harford underlined the change in a report to the 1890 AGM:

> We have now, while still adhering to our old principles, adopted methods which are associated with robust and even aggressive trade unionism . . . We are a trade union with benefit funds, not a friendly society with a few mutual protection benefits, and this cannot be made too clear to members of the railway service [quoted Bagwell (1963) 149].

Excessive hours of work were endemic among railway companies. At the end of the 1880s Harford and the ASRS leadership had achieved some successes in selected areas in their campaign to reduce hours; and this inspired the Scottish ASRS (an independent organisation) to organise a major strike on the hours question. The six-week struggle ended in failure at the end of January 1891, and the Scottish society, which had already been having merger talks with the English ASRS, amalgamated in 1892. One important consequence of the Scottish strike was the first major debate on railway labour in the House of Commons on 23 January 1891, and the setting up of a S.C. on Railway Servants (Hours of Labour) which began to hear evidence early in March. The leadership of the ASRS decided to play a full part in the S.C.'s deliberations, and Harford presented a well-documented statement in evidence. The weight of information on constant overwork was overwhelming, but unfortunately the union leaders who presented evidence were not agreed as to what should be done to improve the situation. Harford, who had seconded a resolution at the 1883 TUC which asked for a legal limitation of hours for certain groups of workers, was no longer in favour of statutory regulation of railwaymen's hours. He preferred the Board of Trade to be given powers to fix hours, where necessary, by order; and he looked mainly to industrial pressure and collective bargaining to achieve the ten-hour day. In this, as in other matters, he ranged himself against the New Unionists. Harford also devoted much time to workmen's compensation, an issue of the greatest importance for railwaymen in view of the high incidence of injury and death among them. Harford was a member of the TUC Parliamentary Committee from 1887 to 1892 (Chairman in 1890) and from 1894 to 1897, and, as he frequently moved the resolutions on workmen's compensation at meetings of Congress, he became known as 'The Father of Employers' Liability'. He lived to see the Workmen's Compensation Bill of 1897 become law.

The liberal-minded trade unionists who led the ASRS were well aware of the importance of parliamentary lobbying and parliamentary representation. As early as 1873 F.W. Evans campaigned actively in a by-election at Exeter on behalf of a Liberal railway director, Sir Edward Watkin. After the passing of the third Reform Act of 1884 and the Re-distribution Bill of 1885, Harford took an active part in the establishment of the Labour Electoral Committee in 1886. Its officers were all Lib-Labs, Harford himself being treasurer. As a nominee of the Committee, he addressed the council of the East Hull Liberals in an attempt to win the local nomination. His platform was typical for the time: Home Rule for Ireland, manhood suffrage and triennial parliaments, state-paid secular elementary education, reform of the land laws and establishment of peasant proprietors, disestablishment of the Church, and a large measure of local government in the counties, with local control over water supplies, lighting, sanitation, working-class housing, and public house licences. Harford was also against hereditary legislators and perpetual pensions. But he failed to win the nomination, and Fred Maddison, president of the Hull branch of the LEA, was criticised for not encouraging Harford to stand as an Independent Labour candidate. Harford was accepted as a Liberal candidate for Blackburn in 1891, but withdrew before the election. By this time the principle of parliamentary representation was being increasingly debated within the union [Bagwell (1963) 201 ff.]. In 1892 the AGM accepted Harford as an official ASRS candidate, and he was adopted by the Northampton Liberals to run with Henry Labouchere in the July 1895 general election. Labouchere was elected but Harford lost the second seat to a Conservative by 117 votes out of a total poll of 18,148. The working-class vote was split three ways: between Harford, J.M. Robertson, who represented the Bradlaugh interest in the town, and F.G. Jones of the SDF. The latter two candidates between them received 2347 votes.

Harford represented the railway servants on the Artisans' Official Visit to the International Exhibition in Paris in 1889, as one of seventy-five trade delegates sponsored by the Lord Mayor of London and the Mansion House Committee; and he reported on the locomotives and carriages shown in the Exhibition for the report which was published on their return. He was also a governor of the Imperial Institute, later the Commonwealth Institute, and vice-president of the London Conciliation and Arbitration Board. In 1896 he was TUC delegate to the annual congress of the Co-operative Union.

Although a deeply committed trade unionist who served his Society well over a twenty-five-year period, he did not always appreciate the changing attitudes of his own members in the later years of his career. This was evident during the Cardiff railway strike of 1890 (Taff Vale, Rhymney and Barry Docks Companies), when the terms he had negotiated were rejected by a mass meeting of the strikers. It was also in evidence during the controversy which raged in the union before his final dismissal. This occurred at the AGM in October 1897, when his actions during negotiations following a strike in the North East earlier in the year were severely criticised. He was accused of having acted against the men's interests, having compromised with the railway company before fully consulting the local committee, and finally arriving in an intoxicated condition when settlement terms were to be negotiated. By this time, Harford, like his predecessor Evans, was a sick man. He was not without supporters but had made sufficient enemies to bring about his downfall, and he was replaced by Richard Bell. He was paid a month's salary in lieu of notice and was awarded a pension of one hundred guineas a year for life; but he had little time to enjoy his retirement.

Harford died on 4 January 1898, on board the *St Paul*, a day before it was due at Southampton, on his return from attending the American Labor Federation's annual convention as one of the two British representatives elected by the TUC. At first a private funeral was planned, but pressure for a public funeral was strong, and his burial at Abney Park Cemetery was attended by large numbers of railway workers walking beneath their banners, and by many other trade union representatives. He was survived by his wife, five sons and two daughters and left effects valued at £227. Two of the sons and two grandsons made their careers in the railway service.

Writings: Evidence before R.C. on Railway Accidents 1877 XLVIII Qs 18032-364; *Railway Coupling Competition* (1886) P; *Suggestions for Safe Railway Working made in Reply to Numerous Inquiries* [1886] 7 pp.; 'Railway Servants', in *Reports of Artisans selected by the Mansion House Committee to visit the Paris Universal Exhibition, 1889* (1889) 559-65; Evidence before S.C. on Railway Servants 1890-1 XVI Qs 2004-3122; speech by Harford at a dinner on 23 May 1894 to the Labour Representatives, published in 'Eighty Club', *Labour Questions* [1894?] 19-25 [copy in *DLB* Coll.].

Sources: (1) Primary: Printed reports and proceedings of the ASRS which are included in the phased deposit of the pre-1945 records of the NUR: MRC, Warwick Univ.; (2) Other: *The Mail Train: Commercial Travellers' Advocate, and Post Office and Railway Services' Guardian* (1884-7) [edited by Harford]; *Eastern Morning News*, 28 Apr and 4 May 1887; *Times*, 9 Aug 1890; *Trade Unionist*, 18 Apr 1891; R.C. on Labour 1893-4 XXXIII Group B vol. III; *Northampton Mercury*, 12 July 1895; *Labour Annual* (1897) 226; G.W. Alcock, *Fifty Years of Railway Trade Unionism* (1922); *TUC Report* (1932); G.C. Halverson, 'The Development of Labour Relations in British Railways since 1860' (London PhD, 1952); H. Pelling, *The Origins of the Labour Party 1880-1900* (1954; 2nd ed. Oxford, 1965); P.S. Gupta, 'History of the Amalgamated Society of Railway Servants 1871-1913' (Oxford DPhil., 1960); P.S. Bagwell, *The Railwaymen: the history of the National Union of Railwaymen* (1963); H.A. Clegg et al., *A History of British Trade Unions 1: 1889-1910* (1964); P.S. Gupta, 'Railway Trade Unionism in Britain, c. 1880-1900', *Econ. Hist. Rev.* 2nd ser. *19* (1966) 124-53; personal information: Mrs B.N. Sealey, Northampton, great-granddaughter. OBIT. *Times*, 6 Jan 1898; *Northampton Mercury*, 7 Jan 1898; *Railway Rev.*, 14 Jan 1898. NOTE. The editors wish to thank Mrs Brenda Sealey for an earlier draft of this biography.

JOYCE BELLAMY
ANN HOLT

See also: †Richard BELL; Joseph GURNEY; †Fred MADDISON.

HEATH, David William (1827/8?-80)
CHARTIST AND RADICAL

David William Heath was born at Nantwich in 1827 or 1828. Nothing is known of his parentage or childhood. In 1844 he became a solicitor's clerk, and in 1851 he moved to Nottingham to become clerk in the office of Michael Browne, the Borough Coroner. Heath completed his articles in the Trinity Term of 1861, and entered into partnership with John Buttery of Wheeler Gate, Nottingham, solicitor and Tory agent. He subsequently built up a flourishing independent practice in the Nottingham area, acting as solicitor to a variety of companies and trade societies. In 1867 he was elected County Coroner for Nottinghamshire, and also held the office of clerk to the Local Board of Sutton-in-Ashfield. His elder son, Samuel Edward Heath, became a partner in the firm in 1876 and took over the practice on his father's death in 1880. Heath was succeeded as County Coroner by his nephew, David Whittingham.

Heath's successful professional career was based upon his considerable natural talents which he excercised in a wide variety of social and political activities in the community. He was a member of the Nottingham Christian Temperance Society from its inauguration in May 1851, although he opposed the society's discrimination against secularists: only members of Christian churches being acceptable as office holders. Heath was a founder of the Nottingham auxiliary of the United Kingdom Alliance, and during 1856-8 he campaigned in surrounding villages on behalf of the UKA. In 1860 the newly-formed Nottingham Band of Hope Union presented him with a gold watch as a testimony to his devotion in the temperance cause. Heath's debating and oratorical skills had been fostered by membership of the discussion class of the Nottingham Mechanics' Institute, which flourished from 1845 to 1864 and numbered among its members many of the rising young men of the town, among them William Ward, lace merchant and mayor in 1871 and 1878.

David Heath emerged as a Chartist leader during the movement's last years of activity in Nottingham. In 1857 and 1859 he helped organise support for the election campaigns of Ernest Jones, attracted both by Jones's radicalism and his endorsement of a Permissive Bill. Heath joined James Sweet and other 'advanced Liberals' in opposing 'Number 30', the Whig clique controlling the Nottingham Town Council, and in the by-election of 1861 he was one of the backers of the Tory-Radical Sir Robert Clifton. In November 1863, Heath himself stood for the town council in St Ann's ward, intervening as an Independent Liberal to break an election pact effected by Whig and Tory parties two years previously. After a rowdy campaign Heath, who enjoyed strong popular support, defeated the Tory candidate by 109 votes. Heath held the seat until November 1875, when ill-health compelled him to retire.

Heath campaigned for parliamentary reform during the years 1865-7 – he was a member of the Reform League – and won the office of County Coroner with radical support, being nominated by the ex-Chartists E.P. Cox and George Harrison. His support for radical causes continued undiminished into the 1870s. He was a supporter of the Nine Hours Movement and of the agricultural labourers; and in the *International Herald* of 23 November 1872 there was advertised a course of seven lectures by John De Morgan at Nottingham with Heath in the chair for the first meeting. (The lecture titles were: Trades Unions, and how to make them a Success; Ireland, Past, Present and Future; The Grand Idea of the Nineteenth Century; Republic v. Monarchy; Hereditary Government opposed to Progress and Common Sense; The Age of Shams; The Rights of Man.). Heath also supported the campaign against the truck system. There is no evidence one way or the other about his attitude towards the Paris Commune, a rather crucial test of radical opinion at this time, although it is reasonable to infer that Heath was a Republican.

On 17 June 1873 a mass meeting of Nottingham trade unionists – including representatives of the Lace Trades Association, ironfounders, tailors and the newly-established Building Trades Council – was convened in the Exchange Hall under the chairmanship of W.H. Leatherland of the Operative Lace Makers, who had presided over the 1872 Trades Union Congress in Nottingham. After some discussion the meeting invited Heath to contest the next election as a trade union candidate. The main plank of Heath's platform was opposition to the Criminal Law Amendment Act and the modified but still unsatisfactory Master and Servant legislation; he also declared his enduring commitment to the Chartist programme and to unsectarian public education, religious equality, and the abolition of sinecures. Despite his early prohibitionist ardour he now, controversially, opposed both the Permissive Bill and Sunday closing. Heath's intervention produced a bitter internecine struggle within Nottingham Liberalism and finally split the Liberal vote: in the general election of February 1874, the Tories, Denison and Isaac, totalled 5268 and 4790 votes respectively, against the 4732 and 3545 votes of the Liberals, Laycock and Labouchere. Heath polled 2752 votes.

After a prolonged illness, David Heath died from cancer of the throat at his home, Grove House, Newstead Grove, Nottingham, on 24 September 1880. He was buried at the Church Cemetery on 29 September, his funeral being conducted by the Rev. William Felton, of St Mark's Church, where Heath had worshipped. He was survived by his widow, Mary Ann Heath, two sons and two daughters. He left an estate valued at under £7000.

Sources: *Nottingham Rev.*, 1851-65; *People's Paper*, 1853-8; *Alliance*, 1855; *Alliance Weekly News*, 1855-60; *Nottingham Daily Express*, 1861-74; *Nottingham J.*, 1867-74; *International Herald*, 23 Nov 1872, 8; E. Button, 'Trades Councils: past and present Nottingham Trades Council', *Industrial Rev.* (Sep-Oct 1931) 330-2, 341-3; C. Holmes, 'Chartism in Nottingham, 1837-1861' (Nottingham Univ. BA dissertation, 1960); R.A. Church, *Economic and Social Change in a Midland Town: Victorian Nottingham, 1815-1900* (1966); P. Wyncoll, 'The First International and Working Class Activity in Nottingham 1871-73', *Marxism Today* (Dec 1968) 372-9; J.J. Rowley, 'Drink and Temperance in Nottingham, 1830-1860' (Leicester MA, 1974); biographical information: P. Wyncoll, Coalville. OBIT. *Nottingham Daily Express, Nottingham Daily Guardian, Nottingham J.*, and *Times*, 25 Sep 1880.

JOHN ROWLEY

See also: †James SWEET.

HENSON, John (Jack) (1879-1969)
TRADE UNIONIST AND LABOUR ALDERMAN

John Henson was born at Humbleton Grange, Holderness, East Yorkshire, on 3 April 1879, the son of George Tom Henson, a farm labourer, and his wife Hannah (née Sprowson). After working at Willerby for the Hull and Barnsley Railway, which he left after a dispute about hours, he was employed on a farm near Hornsea; he then went to London, where he worked for a time with a wholesale drapery firm. A spell as an insurance agent introduced him to urban poverty and aroused his interest in politics and social welfare. He returned to the Hull area in 1903, and became a tram conductor.

He was not opposed to the First World War and volunteered in spite of being thirty-five. He served with the 10th East Yorkshire Regiment in Egypt and France. On his return to Hull he became a tram driver, and an active trade unionist. His abilities as a negotiator were recognised when in 1921 he became full-time secretary of the Hull branch (Passenger and Commercial) of the United Vehicle Workers. He had been a member of the union, and its predecessor, the Amalgamated Association of Tramway and Vehicle Workers, since 1903. In 1922, on the merging of the Vehicle Workers into the Transport and General Workers' Union, he became full-time trade group secretary of the Passenger and Commercial Section. He held this position until his retirement in 1944. George Farmery was the TGWU's area secretary, and they were never easy colleagues.

Henson was for a time general secretary of Hull Trades and Labour Council; Humber district secretary of the National Transport Workers' Federation; and a member of several Joint Industrial Wages Boards. He was minute secretary of the Trade Union Congress held in Hull in 1924, and in 1926 was closely involved with the local organisation of the General Strike and the return to work – a matter which was very difficult for groups such as the tramwaymen.

In politics he began on the Left. Before the First World War he was a member of the Social

Democratic Federation and when the British Socialist Party was formed he became secretary of the Hull branch. After the War he was an orthodox member of the Labour Party, developing an anti-Communist attitude in later years. His career on Hull City Council began in 1929, when he was elected for Coltman ward (he had unsuccessfully contested Paragon ward three years earlier). Other political and semi-political activities included membership of the Hull Clarion Cycle Club; secretaryship of the local branch of the Labour League of Ex-servicemen, after 1918; and representative of the Hull branch of the League of Nations Union at Geneva on two occasions.

Election addresses for 1926 and 1929 show his main concerns to have been housing, education and unemployment. He wished to see this last alleviated by 'the Council initiating bold schemes of Work of Public Utility' (1929). In 1945 he was made an alderman for St Andrews ward and in 1949 was elected Lord Mayor. At that time he stated that his main interests were housing and the rehabilitation of industry – both very necessary in view of the devastation of the city by air raids earlier in the war. He was also greatly concerned with the dilapidated condition of Hull's waterfront and old town. On trips abroad he had seen what could be done with such areas, and he longed to see the same imaginative approach in his own city. It was a hope, however, which attracted little support from the rest of the Labour group on the Council.

He naturally took a keen interest in transport. He was chairman of the transport committee from 1946 until 1965, and at the time of his death it was calculated that he had been associated with the Transport Department in one capacity or another for sixty-three years. He was also deputy chairman of the property and bridges committee from 1946 to 1964.

As noted already, his politics moved to the right in later life. He was considerably embittered by a dispute over his pension from his union. He had arranged for most of his pension to go to his wife, but she predeceased him, which meant that his own pension was very small. He felt that he had worked hard in labour politics and that a little more flexibility could have been shown towards him at the end of his life. His personal experience made him feel that old age pensioners were not treated well enough – he made a speech to that effect while he was Lord Mayor – and may also have led him to believe in his last years that the unions had become too powerful and that the Labour Party had disappointed his hopes. However, for most of his life he was a cheerful, optimistic, rather flamboyant personality, and something of a dandy. His whole life was taken up with union and local government matters, but he did find some time for reading, particularly Blatchford's books, Shakespeare and books about Russia.

He died on 12 December 1969, at the age of ninety. His wife, Mary Ellen (née Bridgeman) whom he had married in 1907, died in 1944. He was survived by two daughters, one of whom, Winifred, who was a librarian at Boots, was his Lady Mayoress; she died a few years ago. His other daughter, Vera, was a dressmaker before her marriage. The funeral took place at Chanterlands Crematorium, Hull. He left no will.

Sources: *Election Addresses*, (1926) and (1929); *Labour Who's Who* (1927); *Kingston upon Hull Year Books* (1929-69); *Hull Daily Mail*, 31 Jan and 17 Aug 1949, 24 May 1950; personal information: Mrs R.V. Stevens, Ferriby, daughter. OBIT. *Hull Daily Mail*, 13 Dec 1969.

ANN HOLT

See also: George Edward FARMERY.

HOLWELL, Walter Charles (1885-1965)
LABOUR ALDERMAN AND TRADE UNIONIST

Walter Charles Holwell was born in Hull on 18 February 1885, the son of Walter Charles Holwell, a painter's labourer, and his wife Susan (née Garbutt). After attending Charterhouse Lane School and Craven Street Secondary School he took a job in a solicitor's office at the age of thirteen. Later he gave this up to become an apprentice bricklayer. He was, however, a studious boy who attended evening classes in technical subjects at the Hull Young People's Institute and Hull Technical College, and later also became a corresponding student of Ruskin College and the Central Labour College.

An interest in the labour movement was part of Holwell's family background as his uncle, Matt Emmerson, was one of its pioneers in Hull. Holwell's active political career began in 1906 when he joined the Social Democratic Party. When this merged in 1911 with other Socialist organisations to form the British Socialist Party he became the Hull branch's first president. He had been elected to the management committee of his own union, then the Operative Bricklayers' Society, in 1910 and in June 1916 became president. For three years before serving with the Army in the First World War he was a member of the executive committee of Hull Trades Council. In 1922 he succeeded Matt Emmerson as Hull organiser of the Amalgamated Union of Building Trade Workers. He is recalled as a 'sane' union negotiator; effective but not one to fight hopeless cases.

He was first elected to Hull City Council in 1925, representing East Central ward (Emmerson's old ward) where he was born. He became an alderman in 1929 for Paragon ward, then represented Southcoates ward from 1931 to 1934, when he went back to East Central ward. He was made a JP in 1933 and was a member of the Ministry of Labour's Juvenile Advisory Committee, and of the Court of Referees – which heard appeals from people disallowed unemployment benefit by the Insurance Officer. He was a member of many council committees, including finance (1930-65), watch (1939-43, 1952-4, 1955-7), works (1927-8, 1930-44 – chairman 1930-8), health (1929 and 1945-65). He was also a member of the housing and town planning committee from 1930 to 1965 and its deputy chairman, 1929-32 and 1934-7. He was therefore involved in the hearings of the Ministry of Health Public Inquiry (held in 1932 at the request of the City Council) into a scandal over the chairman of the committee profiting from Corporation land deals. In this connection Alderman Holwell was completely exonerated by the Recorder, who added 'I was much impressed by his demeanour and obvious honesty of purpose' [Special Inquiry Committee, *Report* (1932) 26].

In 1942 he was elected Lord Mayor, but ill-health prevented him from accepting the office. When he recovered, however, he continued his public life in Hull. After the formation of the National Health Service in 1948 he was made chairman of the Kingston General Hospital House Committee and later took over the chairmanship of Hull A Group Management Committee.

He began politically on the Left. An early interest in Socialism was fostered by reading Robert Blatchford's *Merrie England* and he was always a student of William Morris and of the medieval guilds, in which he took a great interest. Later he became a middle-of-the-road Labour Party member and anti-Communist. He was much impressed with the achievements of the 1945-50 Labour Government, particularly the National Health Service to which he was strongly committed. He admired Herbert Morrison for his ability to get things done, and in local affairs Holwell strongly supported a direct labour department as one way of achieving this end.

He was a slightly-built man of medium height with a thin, sensitive face; of a quiet disposition, never heated in debate and able to defeat arguments without being discourteous. He had a great interest in young people, and was always prepared to help them and willing to encourage them to serve on committees when no longer able to do the job himself. He was very unassuming: he was offered the mayoralty several times, but only accepted once (in 1942); and also declined an OBE. After his death a tribute was paid to him when a road in Hull was named after him – a thing he would never have allowed in his lifetime.

In May 1964 he collapsed during the speeches after the mayor-making lunch at Hull Guildhall. He died on 27 February 1965, aged eighty. His wife, Lily, whom he married fifty-eight years earlier, had died in 1963, and his eldest son, Walter, a bricklayer who became a clerk of works, had died in 1951. His middle son, Arthur, a joiner, died in 1968, but the youngest, Alan, an architect, is still alive (1977). The funeral, at Chanterlands Crematorium, was attended by the Lord Mayor and many councillors. No will has been found.

Sources: (1) MSS: Minute books of Operative Bricklayers' Society, 1913-18: Humberside Libraries; Local History Library, Hull. (2) Other: *Kingston upon Hull Year Books* (1925-65); *Hull Daily Mail*, 22 Mar 1932, 27 July and 29 Oct 1942; *Report* of City of Kingston upon Hull Public Local Special Inquiry Committee of Council (bound with Council Minutes for 29 Apr 1932); *Hull Times*, 1 Aug and 31 Oct 1942; personal information: Cllr V. Mitchell, JP and Miss L. Mitchell, nieces; Ald. F. Holmes, all of Hull. OBIT. *Hull Daily Mail*, 27 Feb 1965.

ANN HOLT

HORNER, Arthur Lewis (1894-1968)
COMMUNIST AND MINERS' LEADER

Born on 5 April 1894 at Merthyr Tydfil, Arthur Horner was the son of a Northumbrian father, James Horner, and a Welsh mother, Emily (née Lewis). He was the eldest son of a family of seventeen, eleven of whom died at birth or in early childhood. Horner's mother looked after the local co-operative store and his father, who was a railwayman, did the book-keeping in the evenings for the shop and was the first chairman of the Dowlais Co-operative Society. He was also secretary of the Rechabites, the temperance society, and both parents were ardent Baptists. The young Horner was a regular attender at Sunday school, and at the age of fifteen had become known as 'the Welsh boy preacher'. His education was at elementary schools in Merthyr, but at the age of eight he was already working part-time at a barber's, and later as a grocer's delivery boy. When he was twelve he began full-time work in the local railway office but at seventeen he was awarded a two-year scholarship at the Baptist College in Birmingham. By this time he was not only a local preacher but also a very active sportsman – in boxing, football and athletics – and this helped to develop a physical toughness and stamina that were to prove very useful in later life. He stayed at the theological college for only six months and then left, having decided that it was politics rather than preaching that really interested him; and he started work at the Standard Collieries at Ynyshir in the Rhondda.

Horner's early political education was greatly influenced by Keir Hardie, one of the MPs for Merthyr and Aberdare; but it was Noah Ablett who made the greatest impact upon him in these first years. Ablett was one of the authors of *The Miners' Next Step* (1912) and a leading figure in the Unofficial Reform Movement. From this influence there always remained a strain of near-syndicalism in Horner's ideas and activities. He joined the ILP and studied Marxism in the classes organised by the Plebs League. Like so many of his generation he was much impressed with H.N. Brailsford's *War of Steel and Gold* (1914), and when the war broke out in August 1914 Horner took up a revolutionary position, opposing the war as a clash of economic interests between rival imperialisms. He was still a practising Baptist and preached a few sermons on the text 'Thou shalt not kill'; but his activities became increasingly political and his religious beliefs steadily waned. He engaged in active anti-war politics as a member of the Rhondda Socialist Society and the South Wales Socialist Society. In 1917 he was victimised at his own pit, and through the Reform Committee he then moved to Maerdy, where he worked under an assumed name. Early in 1918, by which time he was chairman of the Reform Committee, he went to Ireland to avoid military service, enlisted in the Citizen Army, joined the Irish Transport Union and worked on a variety of jobs under the name of Jack O'Brien. He was never, he wrote in his autobiography, 'in a pitched battle, but was concerned in a number of minor incidents like the release of prisoners' [p. 29]. He returned to Wales in August 1918, was immediately arrested at Holyhead and was sentenced to six months' hard labour, which he served at Wormwood Scrubs. On being released after a few months, he was turned over to the military and court-martialled at Llannion Barracks, Pembroke Dock, for refusing to serve in the armed forces. He was at the same time discharged from the Army for 'incorrigible misconduct' (hence the title of his autobiography) and sentenced to two years' hard labour in Carmarthen Gaol. In April 1919 he got news that, largely through the influence of Noah Ablett, he had been elected checkweighman for Maerdy, and to force the issue Horner went on hunger strike. He was released on 19 May

1919 under the Cat and Mouse Act (introduced before the war to deal with hunger-striking suffragettes) and immediately took up his position at Maerdy. He was, in fact, never re-arrested. When he arrived at the pit the colliery agent said to him: 'These top pits have always elected their checkweighmen from the scum of the coalfield and this time they have chosen the worst b—— of all' [Horner (1960) 37].

Maerdy was a strategic centre for the young Horner, and the militant traditions of the pit much assisted his rapid rise within the South Wales Miners' Federation. Maerdy was a large mine in the Rhondda No. 1 district, itself the biggest district in the coalfield; and Horner, with his co-checkweigher, the ebullient Dai Lloyd Davies, was able to win many concessions not obtained elsewhere. The Maerdy group of the Rhondda Socialist Society sent a delegate to the inaugural conference of the British Communist Party in 1920, and both Horner and his wife Ethel became foundation members. By 1923 Horner, and Wal Hannington, had become part-time members of the Political Bureau, and in the same year Horner, along with A.J. Cook, Noah Ablett and S.O. Davies, took a leading part in establishing the Miners' Minority Movement (MMM) in South Wales. He also made the first of many visits to the Soviet Union: on this occasion to a conference of the Red International of Labour Unions (RILU) in Moscow. It was Horner at the now famous Cardiff meeting of the Unofficial Reform Committee who gave his casting vote in favour of Cook against Ablett in the nomination for the post of general secretary of the MFGB. This vote, which was not, of course, official, nevertheless settled the issue in South Wales, and on a national vote Cook was elected. In his autobiography [pp. 43-4] Horner tells only part of the story of his rejection of Ablett, the most important influence on him in his early years as a militant, and a man for whom he had great respect and affection. Horner had, of course, known Cook from the days when he himself was a crusading Baptist and Cook an active member of the Salvation Army.

When Cook was elected as general secretary of the MFGB he vacated his position as miners' agent for the Rhondda district; and Horner was urged to stand for election. He refused, in order to devote his energies to the MMM in South Wales; and before the General Strike he had considerable success. The arrest and imprisonment of the twelve Communist Party leaders in October 1925 led to a rearrangement of posts at Party headquarters. Bob Stewart acted as general secretary and Horner was put in charge of the industrial department. He was always close to A.J. Cook and never more than in the months before the General Strike and in the Miners' Lock-out which followed. Horner wrote of their collaboration in his autobiography:

> In the later phases of the long Miners' Lock-out which followed the General Strike, Cook and I parted company on a number of vital matters, but I never lost my admiration for him. In the months before the 1926 strike, and during the strike, we spoke together at meetings all over the country. We had audiences, mostly of miners, running into many thousands. Usually I was put on first. I would make a good, logical speech, and the audience would listen quietly, but without any wild enthusiasm.
>
> Then Cook would take the platform. Often he was tired, hoarse and sometimes almost inarticulate. But he would electrify the meeting. They would applaud and nod their heads in agreement when he said the most obvious things. For a long time I was puzzled, and then one night I realised why it was. I was speaking *to* the meeting. Cook was speaking *for* the meeting. He was expressing the thoughts of his audience, I was trying to persuade them. He was the burning expression of their anger at the iniquities which they were suffering. It was the sort of demagogic appeal which in unscrupulous hands would be dangerous, the sort of appeal that a dictator might have, but Cook was utterly honest and selfless [p. 72].

Horner added that during the months of 1926 he was probably the closest confidant of A.J. Cook. After the defeat of the miners, and their return to work, Horner moved into a more intransigent political and industrial position. He had become a member of the executive committee of the MFGB in 1926, but was removed a year later. He was now wholly convinced that the MFGB was not capable of recovering its former place in British trade unionism unless it reformed its existing federal structure. He argued for 'One Mineworkers' Union' – the title of a pamphlet he wrote in 1927 – and he intensified his attacks on the miners' leaders. At the same time he was finding himself at odds with the political and industrial policies being adopted by the Comintern, which found fullest expression in the resolutions and decisions of the Sixth World Congress of the Communist International, 17 July to 1 September 1928. Horner was centrally involved in the bitter debates and controversies that engulfed the British Communist Party between 1928 and 1931. In general Horner accepted the approach of the majority of the Central Committee (notably Albert Inkpin, J.R. Campbell and Andrew Rothstein) and he was particularly opposed to the application of the 'social-fascist' line to trade unions. What became characterised as 'Hornerism' – which included an opposition to the establishment of revolutionary unions regardless of the particular situation prevailing in the industry – was passionately and bitterly denounced by the new leadership of the Communist Party which emerged from the factional and fractional struggles of 1929. The detailed story of this period of British Communist history has not yet been written, but it was a time when Horner was being systematically criticised for his alleged reformist views. He refused to accept the vote of censure passed on him by the Political Bureau; he appealed to the Central Committee, and was turned down; and finally he went before the 11th Party Conference at Leeds which opened on 30 November 1929, and was again defeated. Horner tells a confused story in his autobiography, but the event which finally caused him to consider seriously his resignation from the British Communist Party was his removal from the leadership of the Minority Movement. During the South Wales miners' strike of January 1931, Horner refused to follow the official party line of establishing independent strike committees and also of continuing the strike after the SWMF had called it off. For this opposition he was disciplined by being taken off the national secretariat of the Minority Movement [Daily Worker, 28 Feb 1931]. Then, at some point, Gresha Slutsky, the secretary of the Miners' International, came to see Horner in Maerdy to try to persuade him not to leave the CP; and after long discussions Horner agreed to make a final appeal to the Communist International; and he went to Moscow to appear before an international committee of five members, with Otto Kuusinen as chairman. Robin Page Arnot, at the time the British representative on the CI, 'put the case against me in a very kindly and objective way' [Horner (1960) 111]. The appeal went on for three months, and the committee's decision was that Horner was wrong in not observing the discipline of the Party, but that to suggest his mistakes were 'a philosophy' was unjustified, and that there was no such thing as 'Hornerism' – the differences were arguments about tactics. In private Horner always considered himself vindicated by this appeal committee, but the bitterness of the public debate was not easily overcome. Will Paynter, who became general secretary of the NUM in 1959 on Horner's retirement, has noted in his own memoirs how much the whole episode was resented by militants like himself [Paynter (1972) 82].

The late 1920s were exceptionally difficult years in South Wales. Horner took a prominent part in the Welsh hunger march of 1927, and in the general elections of 1929 and 1931 he stood unsuccessfully as Communist candidate on the Rhondda constituency in opposition to Colonel D. Watts-Morgan, the official Labour nominee. Horner's own lodge at Maerdy was expelled from the SWMF in February 1930 for supporting him as well as for their general attacks on the industrial and political policies of the SWMF. Horner was in Russia at the time. After 1926 Maerdy was a ghost area; there was almost no employment in the pits after 1927, and only a partial recovery in the 1930s. But Maerdy continued its traditions of uncompromising opposition to authority, and was consistently hostile to the policies of the SWMF and the MFGB. In the late autumn of 1931, soon after the general election, Horner was involved in an eviction case in Maerdy which was settled before the police arrived. The same night Horner travelled to London on his way to a RILU meeting in Moscow. He was away for about four months and on his return was arrested for his part in the eviction incident, much of the evidence for which, according to Horner, was fabricated. Horner was given fifteen months, five members of the committee had nine months each, and the remainder of the thirty-two charged received lighter sentences. Horner served his time in Cardiff Gaol, and in the early days of his sentence discovered once again that the Bible 'was a source of beautiful literature'. Later he was allowed to have a correspondence course from Marx House in London, and he went through the first volume of *Capital* in a systematic way. He became librarian, and was greatly influenced by Clausewitz, who taught him, Horner records in his autobiography, 'that if you enter into active struggle you can succeed only if you adopt the principle of inflicting the greatest possible degree of damage on your opponents, with the least possible hurt to your own forces' [p. 125]. Horner was clearly much impressed.

Soon after he was released he stood again as Communist candidate in the Rhondda, Watts-Morgan having died in March 1933. The Labour candidate was W.H. Mainwaring, who also received the official support of the SWMF. It was a bitterly fought election in which Horner obtained 11,228 votes against Mainwaring's 14,127. Within six months, however, Horner's fortunes had changed. He was elected agent, on the third ballot, for the Anthracite district. It removed him from the depressed east of the coalfield to the more prosperous west; and it was from this new position of strength that he began a campaign against the company unionism that had established itself in the coalfield after 1926. Just before his election as agent he had begun publishing a fortnightly paper, the *South Wales Miner*, and he used his journalism very effectively. In the course of this struggle the Welsh miners pioneered the technique of the stay-down strike, and it was during this growing campaign that Horner was elected the first Communist president of the SWMF, in May 1936. He continued to retain the nominal position of agent for the Anthracite area until 1944, with Gomer Evans standing in for him.

Horner was to prove an excellent administrator and an outstanding negotiator. He carried through the final agreement in 1938 which brought all the remaining members of the Industrial Union into the SWMF. The terms of the agreement were attacked by left-wing members of the Federation, but as a matter of general principle, throughout his long years as a miners' official, Horner always insisted that agreements must be strictly honoured. On the political side of the Labour movement, his election to the presidency coincided with the growing threat of the Fascist countries and the outbreak of the Civil War in Spain. The executive committee of the SWMF sent Horner to Spain in 1937 as an expression of their solidarity with the Spanish Republicans, and on his return he took a most active part in encouraging political sympathy and practical help for the Republican side. He accepted completely the orthodox Communist position on POUM. In 1938 he went a second time, on this occasion with Jim Bowman, Will Lawther, and Walter Schevenels of the International Federation of Trade Unions; and this visit followed soon after he had visited the Soviet Union on the first official MFGB delegation to that country. The delegation was so divided politically that no official report of the visit was ever issued.

At the outbreak of war in September 1939 the official Communist argument that it was an imperialist war (adopted after a few weeks' hesitation) was not accepted by Horner, and in this he was in agreement with Harry Pollitt, the general secretary. In spite of his personal convictions, Horner nevertheless gave public support to the CPGB position and to the Peoples' Convention, but it is doubtful whether his pro-war assessment altered in any significant way. Indeed, he revealed in his autobiography that after the fall of France in 1940 he was nominated by the TUC to serve on the Invasion Trade Union Committee for South Wales which was responsible for measures of resistance in the event of a German invasion. Neither his colleagues in the SWMF nor his comrades in the CPGB knew of the committee's existence or of Horner's membership of it. 'We drew up plans', Horner wrote in his autobiography, 'for miners to get hold of the powder which was to be kept in every pit, in order to blow up the mines if the Germans got there. We were ready to form guerilla bands in our mountains, and to fight against Nazi tanks with picks and shovels. I used to lecture them about my experiences in Ireland' [p. 163]. With Russia's entry into the war, the personal and public conflict ended, and Horner worked unremittingly both for the continued improvement in the miner's economic position and general welfare, and for the war effort. Sometimes this dual stance was difficult to maintain so that Horner found himself damping down the militant resentment that led to unofficial strike action in South Wales, especially in the wake of the Porter Award of 1944. In November 1944 he was nominated by the TUC to attend as delegate the annual conference of the American Federation of Labor, the only Communist ever to be sent as an official delegate to the United States. In the following year, after the victory of the Labour Party in the general election of 1945, he was appointed National Coal Production Officer by the MFGB, in response to a request from Emanuel Shinwell, the new Minister of Fuel and Power; and it was in this post that he drafted a new Miners' Charter. In 1946 he was elected general secretary of the National Union of Mineworkers (established in 1944), and he was to remain in this position until his retirement in 1959.

Throughout the post-war years Horner was at the centre of mining politics, and his history is in large measure the post-war history of the miners. Throughout his period as general secretary the miners' executive had a right-wing majority, as did the TUC. The greater part of his really serious differences with his mining colleagues were political differences. The issues concerning the international trade union movement were one, and German rearmament, for which the MFGB as a whole voted, was another. For many years Horner was a member of the executive committee of the Communist Party, and his Communist politics naturally coloured his attitude towards industrial problems. At the same time Horner accepted his position as an elected general secretary, and he always carried out decisions democratically arrived at. There was always some vigorous criticism from the left of the Communist Party of his industrial attitudes and policies during the period of the secretaryship of the NUM, and it is still too early for a considered judgement to be offered, since much basic research has yet to be done. It must, of course, be appreciated that there was always a right-wing majority on the executive committee during his period of office, and that there was an enormous amount of work involved in the consolidation of the NUM as an effective national body.

Horner travelled abroad on many occasions in the post-war period – to West Germany, Czechoslovakia, Yugoslavia, Russia and China. He was deeply shocked at the revelations of the 20th Congress of the Russian Communist Party in 1956, and his own analysis is discussed at some length in his autobiography. He was equally shocked at the events in Hungary in the same year, and on the execution of Imre Nagy he issued a press statement deploring the action of the Hungarian Government. But he never resigned from the British Communist Party, and to the end of his life he continued to express his belief in the future of Communism and of the Soviet Union.

He retired in 1959 and was succeeded as general secretary of the NUM by Will Paynter. Horner was quite exceptional in his abilities as a trade union leader. An outstanding orator with an utter dedication to the cause of miners, he combined these qualities with warm human sympathies and a sincerity which disarmed many who on political grounds were strongly opposed to him. He had married Ethel Mary Merrick in 1916, and his wife, who shared to the full his ideas and outlook, was a constant source of strength and sympathy throughout his turbulent career. There were three daughters of the marriage: Voltairine (called after the famous American anarchist Voltairine de Cleyre), Rosa (after Rosa Luxemburg) and Joan (after Joan of Arc). He died on 4 September 1968 at his Wembley Park home and left an estate valued at £1169.

Writings: 'The Coal Report and after', *Lab. Mon. 8* (May 1926) 272-83; 'Another Stage in the Miners' Struggle', ibid. (Sep 1926) 534-43; 'Forward to Victory', ibid. (Nov 1926) 657-64; *Coal: the next round* [1926] 17 pp.; 'The Need for One Mineworkers' Union', *Lab. Mon. 9* (Mar 1927) 146-54; 'The Miners' Fight continues', ibid. (Aug 1927) 474-82; *One Mineworkers' Union – Why?* [1927] 14 pp.; *British Mineworkers' Union: a constitution* (National Miners' Minority Movement, 1927); 'The Significance of the Miners' March', *Lab. Mon. 10* (Jan 1928) 23-30; 'The T.U.C. and the Future of Trade Unionism', ibid. (Oct 1928) 594-605; *The Bureaucracy in the Miners' Federation* (Minority Movement [1928]) 22 pp.; Foreword to A.J. Cook, *Mond's Manacles – The Destruction of Trade Unionism* [1928] 15pp.; 'The Miners and their Struggle' pt 2 of *Communism and Coal* (CPGB, 1928) 149-308; 'The Minority Conference and the T.U.C', *Lab. Mon. 11* (Oct 1929) 603-10; *Towards a Popular Front* (CPGB, 1936) n.p.; 'The Miners' Two Bob', *Lab. Mon. 18* (Feb 1936) 120-3; 'Problems of Trade Unionism in 1936', ibid. (Oct 1936) 277-81; 'The Results of the Plymouth Congress', ibid. 605-13; *Trade Unions and Unity* (CPGB, 1937) 14 pp.; 'British Labour and the World', *Lab. Mon. 20* (Jan 1938) 18-21; (with others). 'World Trade Union Unity', ibid. (Feb 1938) 95-9; 'International Trade Union Unity', ibid. (Sep 1938) 537-47; 'The Supreme Issue at Southport', ibid. *21* (June 1939) 342-6; 'The War on the Home Front', ibid. (Nov 1939) 655-65; 'Coal and the Nation's War Effort', ibid. *24* (June 1942) 180-4; 'T.U.C. 1924', ibid. (Sep 1942) 274-7; Editor of *The Soviet Trade Unions* (1942) 26 pp.; 'How Trade Unions aid the War Effort', *Labour* n.s. *6* (Sep 1943) 6-8; 'T.U.C.', *Lab. Mon. 25* (Oct 1943) 301-6; *Coal and the Nation: a square deal for miners* (1943) 24 pp.; Foreword to I. Cox, *Forward to a New Life for South Wales* [S. Wales Cttee of CP, 1944] 16 pp.; 'The World Trade Union Conference', *Lab. Mon. 27* (Feb 1945) 41-6; 'Coal Situation in Great Britain', ibid. (Oct 1945) 293-9; *The Communist Party and the Coal Crisis* (CPGB [1945]) 8 pp.; 'Nationalisation of the Coal Industry', *Lab. Mon. 28* (Feb 1946) 41-6; 'Unity, then and now', ibid. (Mar 1946); 'Coal and the Miners', ibid. *29* (Jan 1947) 14-17; 'What to do', ibid. (Sep 1947) 265-9; *Trade Unions and Communism* [repr. with additions from *Lab. Mon. 30* (Feb 1948) 41-8, (1948)] 11 pp.; 'How Communists hoodwinked the Dockers', *Labour* n.s. *12* (Jan 1950) 586-7; 'The Struggle for Peace', *Lab. Mon. 32* (May 1950) 202-9; 'The Right to Strike', ibid., *37* (Aug 1955) 352-4; Foreword to G. Hardy, *Those Stormy Years* (1956); 'I remember', BBC Sound Archives (1959); 'Coal: what future' *Lab. Mon. 42* (Sep 1960) 397-400; *Incorrigible Rebel* (1960). Horner also wrote articles in the Communist press including the *Workers' Life* and *Daily Worker*.

Sources: (1) MSS: Arthur Horner Coll., Univ. College of Swansea Library. (2) Other: *Communist Policy in Great Britain* [British Commission at the Ninth Plenum of ECCI, 1928]; *Daily Worker*, 16 and 28 Feb 1931; 'Political Bureau Statement re Arthur Horner', *Communist Rev. 3*, no. 4 (Apr 1931) 145-57; T. Clifford, 'Horner v. the Political Bureau', ibid. no. 5 (May 1931) 183-8 and 'Our Reply' ibid. 188-93; CPGB, *Central Committee Resolutions* (Dec 1931) 21 pp.; T. Bell, *British Communist Party: a short history* (1937); A. Hutt, *The Post-War History of the British Working Class* (1937, repr. Wakefield, 1972); Anon., 'Welsh Profile, 5: Arthur Horner', *Welsh Rev. 6*, no. 1 (Spring 1947) 21-6; G. Romilly, 'Gentle Revolutionary: a portrait of Arthur Horner' in *The Changing Nation* ed. A.G. Weidenfeld (1947) 36-41; G.D.H. Cole, *A Short History of the British Working Class Movement* (1948); 'Mr Horner's Dilemma', *New Statesman and Nation*, 23 Oct 1948, 337; R. Page Arnot, *The Miners: years of struggle* (1953); H. Pelling, *The British Communist Party: a historical profile* (1958); A.L. Horner, *Incorrigible Rebel* (1960); R. Jenkins, 'Not really a Rebel', *Observer*, 18 Dec 1960; R. Page Arnot, *The Miners in Crisis and War* (1961); *WWW* (1961-70); M. Foot, *Aneurin Bevan 1: 1897-1945* (1962); L.J. Macfarlane, *The British Communist Party* (1966); J. Klugmann, *History of the Communist Party of Great Britain 1: 1919-24* (1968), *2: 1925-7* (1969); W. Kendall, *The Revolutionary Movement in Britain 1900-21: the origins of British Communism* (1969); R. Martin, *Communism and the British Trade Unions 1924-1933* (Oxford, 1969); W. Paynter, *My Generation* (1972); D. Smith, 'The Struggle against Company Unionism in the South Wales Coalfield, 1926-1939', *Welsh History Rev. 6*, no. 3 (1973) 354-78; R. Page Arnot, *History of the South Wales Miners 2* (Cardiff, 1975); D. Egan, 'The Swansea Conference of the British Council of Soldiers' and Workers' Delegates, July, 1917: reactions to the Russian Revolution of February, 1917, and the anti-war movement in South Wales', *Llafur 1*, no. 4 (1975) 12-37; D. Smith, 'Leaders and Led', in *Rhondda Past and Future* ed. K.S. Hopkins (Rhondda Borough Council, 1975) 37-65; idem, 'The Future of Coalfield History', *Morgannwg 19* (1975) 57-70; M. Woodhouse and B. Pearce, *Essays on the History of Communism in Britain* (1975); H. Dewar, *Communist Politics in Britain: the CPGB from its origins to the Second World War* (1976); D.B. Smith, 'The Rebuilding of the South Wales Miners' Federation: a trade union in its society' (Univ. of Wales, PhD, 1976); personal information: Dr R. Page Arnot, London; A.L. Horner in letters dated 12 Sep and 6 Oct 1966; W. Paynter, Edgware, Middlesex. OBIT. *South Wales Echo*, 4 Sep 1968; *Times, Western Mail* and *Yorkshire Post*, 5 Sep 1968; W. Paynter, 'Tribute to Arthur Horner 1894-1968', *Lab. Mon. 50* (Oct 1968) 469-70.

NOTE: The editors are much obliged to Dr D.B. Smith, Department of History of Wales, University College, Cardiff, for his comments on an earlier draft of this biography.

JOHN SAVILLE

See also: †Noah ABLETT; †William ABRAHAM (Mabon), and for Welsh Mining Trade Unionism; †Arthur James COOK, and for Mining Trade Unionism, 1915-26; Ebenezer (Ebby) EDWARDS; *Wal HANNINGTON; †Peter LEE, and for Mining Trade Unionism, 1927-44; *Harry POLLITT.

HUGHES, Will (1873-1938)
SOCIALIST AND TRADE UNION ORGANISER

Will Hughes was born at Claughton, Birkenhead, in December 1873, the son of William Hughes, baker, and his wife Elizabeth (née Powell). He attended Palm Grove Methodist School, Claughton, and remained a lifelong Methodist. He was apprenticed to an organ builder and proved an apt pupil, for he was earning the full adult wage rate by the age of nineteen; although in 1893, when he was out of his time, he was unemployed for several months. It was during this period of unemployment that with his elder brother Alfred he joined the Bebington and Birkenhead branch of the ILP. He was, however, forced to leave the district in order to find work and he obtained a job as a carpenter in Salford. He was always a good tradesman, studying at evening classes, and eventually he became a foreman and manager in the building trade.

His trade union and political career really began after his move to the Salford area. He joined the Eccles branch of the Amalgamated Society of Carpenters and Joiners and in 1895 the Eccles branch of the SDF. He was much influenced at this time by Tom Mann, a frequent visitor to the Hughes household. In 1896 Hughes was among the delegates attending the formation of the Eccles Trades Council and three years later he took over the secretaryship of the Council. During this period of office he was always active in the encouragement of union organisation in many different trades. After the formation of the Workers' Union in 1898, in which Tom Mann was actively involved, Hughes was for a short period a delegate to the Lancashire District Council of the Union.

In 1905 Hughes became secretary of the Eccles Labour Representation Committee. The Committee adopted Ben Tillett as their candidate; and in the 1906 general election, Hughes acted as election agent. Tillett was away on a Caribbean cruise for health reasons, but despite his absence the Labour vote was a very creditable one: 3985 for Tillett, 5246 for the Conservative, and 5841 for the successful Liberal candidate, Dr G.H. Pollard. During the years 1905-7 Hughes was also responsible for the publication of the *Eccles Pioneer*, the organ of the Eccles Divisional LRC. In the latter year, 1907, he also became secretary of the Eccles branch of the SDF. He was an active co-operator but was unsuccessful on the several occasions when he was a candidate for the Board of Management.

In the turbulent years which preceded the First World War Hughes supported the policies of industrial syndicalism, and in 1911 he worked with Sam Harlow and Tom Mann in the dock strike of that year, and for these months acted as one of the organisers around the Manchester and Salford docks and the smaller quays at Eccles, Irlam and Partington. In the next year he founded a branch of the Municipal Employees' Association and between 1913 and 1919 he became a part-time organiser for the Association in Lancashire, Cheshire, Yorkshire and Durham. For a time he himself worked as a sanitary inspector with the Manchester Corporation, but in 1919 he became the full-time organiser for the north-west district of the Municipal Employees'

Association. When the Association merged into the National Union of General and Municipal Workers, Hughes continued as a full-time organiser, retiring in January 1938.

After the First World War he became a member of the Labour Party, and in 1922 was elected for the Barton ward of the Eccles Borough Council. In the same year he was elected Lancashire county councillor for the Patricroft division and he held both the local and county positions until his death.

He died of cancer on 7 December 1938 in Christie Hospital, Manchester, after a long period of indifferent health. He was survived by his wife, three daughters and a son. He was cremated at Manchester Crematorium, the funeral oration being given by Alderman George Hall, and he left effects valued at £376.

Writings: *Housing Conditions of the Working Class in Manchester* (1917).

Sources: *Eccles and Patricroft J.*, 10 Dec 1897, 17 June 1898; *Eccles Pioneer*, (Dec 1905), (Jan 1906), (Mar and Apr 1907); LRC, *Report* (1906) 75; *Labour Who's Who* (1927); Eccles Trades Council, *Reports* (1931) and (1945); J.B. Smethurst, 'History of the Eccles Trades Council and Labour Party' [unpublished ms.]; personal information: Mrs W. Bradley, Eccles, daughter; Tom Shorrocks, Bishop's Stortford, son-in-law. OBIT. *Eccles and Patricroft J.*, 9 and 16 Dec 1938.

JOHN B. SMETHURST

JEWSON, Dorothea (Dorothy) (1884-1964)
FEMINIST AND LABOUR MP

Dorothea Jewson (always known as Dorothy) was born on 17 August 1884 at Thorpe Hamlet, Norwich. Her family were Liberals and well known in East Anglia. Dorothy's father, Alderman George Jewson, JP, was a wealthy coal and timber merchant and her mother was Mary Jane (née Jarrold). The family firm (Jewson & Sons) was established in 1836 and had built sawmills at Norwich, Yarmouth, Lowestoft and Lincoln. Dorothy Jewson was educated at Norwich High School and Cheltenham Ladies' College and finished her academic career at Girton College, Cambridge, where she took the Classical Tripos in 1907. She became a BA of Trinity College, Dublin, in the same year. It was while she was at Girton that she became attracted to Socialist ideas and joined the University Fabian Society. She went to the Cambridge Training College after leaving Girton, obtained her teacher's certificate in 1908 and was an assistant mistress at West Heath, Ham Common, Richmond, from 1908 to 1911.

She then returned to Norwich where she at once involved herself in social questions. She became a militant suffragette and at some point joined the local ILP, in which she was soon prominent. She became joint secretary, with her brother, of an inquiry into poverty in Norwich; there were fifty-nine investigators and their work was organised along the lines made famous by Seebohm Rowntree in his study of York. *The Destitute of Norwich and how they live: a report into the administration of out-relief* was a booklet of sixty-two pages, first published in March 1912 and with an introduction by Seebohm Rowntree. A second edition appeared in the same year and a third in 1913.

For some years Dorothy Jewson was a teacher in one of the local schools and when the war of 1914 broke out she took charge of a workroom for girls under seventeen established by the Norwich Distress Committee to relieve unemployment. Her Christian Socialism within the context of her ILP politics meant that she was a confirmed pacifist (as she was to be in the Second World War). In 1916, at the invitation of Mary Macarthur, she left Norwich for London to become an organiser for the National Federation of Women Workers. She worked closely with Margaret Bondfield, who was assistant secretary of the NFWW from 1915 to 1921; and when the NFWW merged with the Women Workers' Section of the NUGMW in 1921 Miss Bondfield became Chief Women's Officer and Dorothy Jewson head of organisation. She left in 1922.

In the general election of 1923 Dorothy Jewson was elected as one of the two Labour members for the two-member constituency of Norwich. Her successful colleague was W.R. Smith, organiser for the National Union of Boot and Shoe Operatives. Both were defeated in the 'Zinoviev letter' election of 1924 and contested the seat again in 1929 and 1931. On the four occasions she ran in double harness with W.R. Smith, who got 2600 more votes than she did in 1929 (and unlike her, was elected); in 1931 when she was an ILP candidate Smith got 1700 more votes than her but they were both defeated.

The 1920s and early 1930s were Dorothy Jewson's most active period in Labour politics. She was one of the two ILP delegates on the Standing Joint Committee of Women's Industrial Organisations. She was, on occasion, ILP delegate to the Labour and Socialist International and to the Socialist Women's International. In August 1925 she was a member of the British delegation to the International Conference on Labour and Socialist Women in Marseilles. She served on many internal committees of the ILP, was a member of the National Women's Advisory Council, edited its *Monthly Bulletin* for the women's groups, and from 1925 to 1935 was on the National Administrative Council, representing the Eastern division. She remained with the ILP after the decision to disaffiliate from the Labour Party in 1932; and Norwich continued as one of the few ILP strongholds in England. Fenner Brockway fought the seat for the ILP in the general election of 1935.

Her strong feminist attitudes were much in evidence both during her short parliamentary career and as part of her general political approach within the labour movement. Her maiden speech was seconding a resolution to bring down the voting age for women to twenty-one. Her feminist position was made clear in a debate in the Commons in April 1924 on the guardianship of infants: 'Modern opinion recognises husband and wife to be equal partners . . . The whole tendency of recent legislation has been to put a woman on equal terms, as regards property and civil rights, with a man, and this is only another phase of the application of the principle that a woman is an equal citizen with a man.' Moreover, as a Socialist, she understood the ways in which working-class women were especially deprived. As she said in the same debate:

> I feel that the present position, where the husband neglects to maintain the children, is very hard on the poor woman. The rich woman can pledge her husband's credit if he does not support the children, but what is the position of the working woman? She has to apply for a maintenance order and break up her home. The man may be ordered to support his wife and children, but if he goes to prison – and we all know of cases where that has been done as a last resort – a month or few weeks in prison are held to wipe out the whole of his debt in regard to the wife and children. That is grossly unfair, and I think we ought to take the provision made in this Bill for the maintenance of the wife and children from the income of the man [*Hansard*, 4 Apr 1924].

After she left Parliament she was a member of the House of Lords committee, appointed in 1925, which dealt with legal aid for the poor.

She advocated easy availability of birth control information for working-class women. She had become converted to the birth control movement by Stella Browne [Rowbotham (1977) 52] and was president of the Workers' Birth Control Group, which was formed in 1924 with Dora Russell as secretary. Dorothy Jewson's public advocacy of birth control was particularly courageous for a single woman at this time, and she faced vigorous opposition both within and outside the labour movement. But she was in no doubt about the support working-class women were giving the movement. As she wrote about the 1925 Labour Party conference, where the Labour women's resolution had been narrowly defeated:

> Even at the Conference, if there had been as good a representation of mothers as there was of fathers, there is no doubt what the verdict would have been, for there is no subject on which the women feel with such passionate earnestness at the present time [*New Generation* (Nov 1925) 127, quoted Rowbotham (1977) 35].

Another considerable intervention within the Labour Party by Miss Jewson was on the matter of children's allowances: an issue that feminists were debating vigorously in the 1920s. At the 1928

LP conference, on behalf of the ILP she moved the reference back on children's allowances in the Executive's Report, although the motion was later withdrawn; and at the following year's conference she introduced a resolution on the subject. The debate which followed illustrated the strong hostility of certain trade union leaders to the principle involved. No vote was taken after the debate since the previous question was moved and carried [*LP Report* (1929) 170].

Dorothy Jewson, after her brief stay in Parliament and her failure again in 1924 and 1929 at the general elections of those years, continued to be active in local politics in Norwich. She served on the City Council from 1929 to 1936 and was active in a number of social causes. She was twice married: first, in 1936, to R. Tanner Smith and at this point in her life she seems to have given up active political work. Her husband died in 1939 and in 1945 she married again; this time it was to Campbell Stephen, a very well known personality in the ILP. He was MP for Camlachie, and died in 1947.

Of middle stature, she had lively brown eyes, a shock of brown (later grey) hair and, as a relative recalls, 'never lost her youthful enthusiasm' [letters from C.B. Jewson, 2 and 31 Dec 1976]. Miss Jewson had been brought up as a Baptist, but her pacifism in both wars had attracted her to the Society of Friends and during the Second World War she attended Ilford Meeting. When she moved to Orpington after her second husband's death she attended Petts Wood Meeting, and was formally admitted as a member of Croydon and Southwark Monthly Meeting on 12 November 1958. She returned to Norwich in 1963 to live in a cottage in the grounds of her brother's home at Hellesdon. She died on 29 February 1964, leaving an estate valued at £15,430. Her funeral service took place at the Friends' Meeting House, Norwich, and was followed by cremation at St Faith's Crematorium, near Norwich.

Writings: [with W.H. Jewson], *The Destitute of Norwich and how they live: a report into the administration of out-relief*, with an Introduction by B. Seebohm Rowntree (1912, rev. eds 1912 and 1913); 'The Labour Party Conference and Birth Control', *New Generation* (Nov 1925) 127; *Socialists and the Family: a plea for Family Endowment* [1926] 7 pp.

Sources: *Girton College Register* (1904); Evidence with Miss M. Symons to Committee of Inquiry into the Scheme of Out-of-Work Donation, 1919 Cmd 407 Qs 2404-573; S.V. Bracher, *The Herald Book of Labour Members (supplement)* (1924); *Dod* (1924); *Labour Who's Who* (1924); *Hansard* (1924); *ILP Reports*, 1926-33; *LP Reports*, 1925 and 1928-9; *WWW* (1961-70); *Eastern Daily Press*, 17 Aug 1964; *Eastern Evening News*, 27 Aug 1964; P. Brookes, *Women at Westminster* (1967); S. Rowbotham, *A New World for Women: Stella Browne – Socialist Feminist* (1977); D. Russell, *The Tamarisk Tree* (1977); *Women in the Labour Movement: the British experience*, ed. L. Middleton (1977); biographical information: Central Library, Norwich; the late T.A.K. Elliott, CMG; Library of the Society of Friends, London; Mrs J. Woods, archivist, Labour Party Library, London; personal information: C.B. Jewson, Norwich, first cousin once removed. Obit. *Eastern Daily Press*, 2 Mar 1964; *Times*, 3 Mar 1964.

ANN HOLT
JOHN SAVILLE

JOHNSTON, James (1846-1928)
CO-OPERATOR AND SOCIALIST

James Johnston was apparently born in Jarrow in 1846, although no record of his birth has been located. His father was a coal trimmer and the family were poor, so James began work at the age of eleven after only four years of schooling. But as soon as was possible he enrolled in evening classes and continued to educate himself with zeal and determination. For two years he worked as an office boy in the shipbuilding and engineering firm of Palmer Brothers in Jarrow, served an apprenticeship there for six years, and then, after spending a few months at sea as an engineer, entered the drawing office of the firm. He was already a competent draughtsman, since he had been attending technical classes during the winter months of his apprenticeship. He had also joined a literary and debating society and begun to interest himself in political and social questions. His political interest was translated into action in 1866 when he joined the struggle to secure a charter of incorporation for Jarrow. At this time he had long been an abstainer and a strict vegetarian. From the age of sixteen until he left Jarrow six years later he was a very successful Sunday School superintendent for the Church of England in a populous district of the city.

In 1868 he moved to a post with a marine engineering company in Sunderland. Later, he was chief engineer at a Glasgow ironworks, while at the same time he studied engineering in evening classes, for three years at Anderson's College in Glasgow and for two years at the University. In 1871 he took a post in London, and then one in Rotherham, before he moved to Manchester in 1880 to practise successfully as a consultant mechanical and civil engineer. In Manchester he soon found scope for his energetic interest in new ideas and progressive schemes. He supported with enthusiasm the project for a Manchester Ship Canal. In 1882 he was a member of the provisional committee which was promoting this; and according to one account it was he who intervened at a critical moment to 'stave off the abandonment of the scheme' [*Co-op. Congress Report* (1929)]. On the parliamentary committee which was later set up he gave invaluable help in drafting the bill which in 1885 became an Act of Parliament authorising the construction of the canal. Two years after this Johnston joined in promoting the Royal Jubilee Exhibition: he became a member of the Council of Guarantors and of a local committee.

His own struggles in early life made Johnston sympathetic with young people and an active supporter of working-class education. He founded, and for some time conducted, a boys' club in Manchester, and in the 1890s he started a series of seaside camps to give poor girls from the slums a holiday by the sea. He was active in the Manchester Working Men's Association, of which he was chairman for several years in the late 1890s.

One of the many concerns of Johnston which illustrates his farsightedness was 'clean air'. In 1900 he was a member of a committee conducting an inquiry into smoke pollution in Manchester; and when the Smoke Abatement League of Great Britain was formed (or re-formed) in 1911, Johnston represented Manchester on its executive committee from that year until the time when the League temporarily ceased to be active, during the First World War. Indeed, Johnston had been prominent in a much earlier league, national or local, which petered out sometime before 1911; for in *Labour Who's Who* (1927) he is described as 'president of the Smoke Abatement League from 1884 to 1890'.

It is not surprising that before he was forty this brilliant and energetic man should have been drawn into parliamentary politics. In 1885 he stood as Labour candidate for his native town of Jarrow. This was a characteristically courageous entry into a hopeless contest – hopeless for two reasons: his party was short of funds and his opponent was the wealthy shipbuilder Charles Palmer, a member of the important firm for which Johnston had worked in his youth and which employed thousands of men in Jarrow. Nevertheless Johnston polled 1731 votes; Palmer had 5702.

It is not surprising either that so staunch a supporter of radical and labour ideals as Johnston should have joined the ILP as soon as it was founded. In 1894 he helped to set up a branch in Macclesfield, where he was then living, and was its first chairman (1894-1903). In the general election of July 1895 he stood as ILP candidate for the North-East division of Manchester. The circumstances again throw light on Johnston's character. The invitation to stand (which was unanimous) came from an ILP meeting hurriedly convened to replace Leonard Hall, who had withdrawn his candidature just over a fortnight before polling day. So that want of campaigning time was added to the perpetual want of funds – the reason Hall had given for withdrawing. Struggling with these difficulties, Johnston naturally polled few votes – only 546.

In the later 1890s he became active in the Clarion Socialist movement: he was president of the

Macclesfield Clarion Cycling Club, and he was a Vanner – that is, he travelled about the country with the Clarion Van, speaking and lecturing for Socialism. His last attempt to enter Parliament was in 1900, when he stood as a Socialist in a three-cornered contest at Ashton-under-Lyne. Again, Johnston was replacing at short notice a candidate who had withdrawn (this time through ill health); again he was undaunted by his difficulties and made spirited fighting speeches. His poll was 737, the winning Conservative's 3548.

Johnston was not a man to neglect local for parliamentary affairs. He had been appointed a JP for Manchester in 1892. Four years later he stood – unsuccessfully – for Manchester City Council as ILP candidate for Medlock Street ward. In 1898 he was returned for St George's ward. He was a council member till 1901 and again in 1902; in 1916 he became an alderman. The particular value of his municipal work lay both in the technical knowledge he brought to such committees as electricity, waterworks and town planning, and likewise in his unwearied support for progressive schemes: for example, he advocated the establishment of municipal banks.

Johnston also carried out prolonged and valuable work for the co-operative movement, both locally and nationally. He joined the Manchester and Salford Equitable Co-operative Society soon after arriving in Manchester, was elected honorary secretary in January 1884, and remained in office until July 1885; he was then president for three years from January 1886. In 1899 he was a delegate to the Co-operative Congress at Liverpool, where he proposed on behalf of his Society the appointment of a special committee to investigate and report on the extent of overlapping in the co-operative movement. This committee presented its report to the Cardiff Congress of 1900. In 1906 Johnston delivered an address to Congress on the subject, and in the same year he served on a CWS special Committee of Inquiry set up to investigate the constitution of the executive committee, the remuneration of directors on the committee, and various other organisational matters. In his local Society he continued to serve as a committee member or as president until January 1910, when he retired from office-holding. In 1884 the Co-operative Union United Board set up an educational sub-committee entitled the General Education Committee of the Board. Johnston was elected to this as one of the two representatives from the North-Western section. Education committees were also set up in each of the three sections – Southern, Northern and North-Western – and Johnston was elected to the committee for his section, the North-Western. He was chairman or president (the title changed) of the general education committee of the United Board in 1888, 1889 and 1890. In 1891 he was not on the United (now the Central) Board; but he was re-elected in 1901, and then annually till 1923, when he retired and was made an honorary member. The *Report* already mentioned describes him as having had 'a range of interests that would have confounded many men much his junior in years', and adds: 'Frequently, his plans did not command the support of his colleagues, for his impatient idealism often soared above practical politics. Yet the passion for innovation was not wasted. Some of the soundest and most useful institutions in the co-operative framework owe their inception largely or wholly to his vigorous championship.' An example of this is the establishment of co-operative convalescent homes, on which Johnston read a paper to Congress as early as 1900. He became chairman of the provisional committee which paved the way for the formation of the North-Western Convalescent Homes Association; later, he was chairman of the Homes Committee. Homes were set up in Yorkshire and Lancashire. When the Blackpool Home was opened in 1906 Johnston became its chairman, a position he held until his death.

Johnston was an enthusiastic climber, both in this country and in Switzerland, and an even more enthusiastic traveller. He made two voyages round the world, and numerous visits to Canada, the USA and Western Europe. Travel is listed among his recreations in *Labour Who's Who* (1927), but many of his journeys were not made merely for pleasure; in the late 1890s, for example, he toured Germany, Denmark and Sweden in order to study methods of milk supply. And the numerous articles he contributed to Manchester newspapers on a variety of subjects show how much he was a keen observer in any country he visited; an article on land settlement in Western Australia appeared in the *Manchester Guardian* on the very day of his death.

Johnston would have been remarkable in any society for the range of his progressive ideas together with the practical ability and the immense energy which he devoted to them. The *Report* already quoted pays him an enthusiastic tribute: 'A man of dauntless enterprise and courage that years could not dull, an idealist who never spared himself in attempts to translate ideals into practice, he won the regard even of his opponents by his transparent selflessness, his innate sincerity and sweet personality.' Johnston was also a 'character'. Not long before his death, when he attended the Lord Mayor's reception in the Manchester Town Hall, he showed 'deference to the conventions by wearing a dress suit; but, as usual even on such occasions, he upheld his old Socialist ardour by wearing a red bow tie' [*Co-op. News*, 5 May 1928].

In his later years Johnston suffered from failing eyesight and deafness, although his mental and his other physical faculties were unimpaired. He died in his eighty-third year, on Friday 27 April 1928, at his house in Oak Bank Avenue, Moston. He was a widower, and was survived by two daughters – Mrs Rosalind Everett and Mrs Adeliza Green – to whom he left an estate of £6442. He bequeathed his body to the College of Anatomy of the University of Manchester – a final characteristic gesture. There was therefore no funeral, but a memorial service was held on Tuesday 1 May. It was attended not only by 'an array of civic dignitaries', but also by 'a large number of poor women. The poor know their friends' [*Co-op. News*, 5 May 1928].

Writings: *Trades Unionism and Co-operation* (Manchester, [1897?]) 12 pp.; 'Overlapping: its evils and remedies', *Co-op. Congress Report* (1906) 365-78; 'Belgium and the Methods of the Belgians in applying Co-operative Principles and Practice', *CWS Annual* (1908) 295-311; *How best to secure the Solidarity and Permanent Security of Societies in the Movement* (Co-op. Union, N.W. Section, 1913) 11 pp.

Sources: *Jarrow Express*, 23 Oct 1885, 6, 20 and 26 Nov 1885; *Manchester Evening News*, 8 July 1895; *Manchester Weekly Times*, 12 July 1895; *Labour Annual* (1897); *Labour Chronicle* (Feb 1897), *Co-op. Congress Report* (1899); *Reporter* [Ashton], 29 Sep 1900; *Labour Who's Who* (1927); biographical information: Co-op. Union Library, Manchester; W.E. Pollitt, secretary, N.W. Division National Society for Clean Air, Swinton. OBIT. *Manchester Guardian*, 28 Apr 1928; *Co-op. News*, 5 May 1928; *Manchester and Salford Co-op. Herald*, 40, no. 475 (June 1928); *Co-op. Congress Report* (1929).

MARGARET 'ESPINASSE
JUDITH FINCHER LAIRD

See also: †Robert BLATCHFORD; †Fred HALL, for Co-operative Education: *(William) Leonard HALL; †Fred HAYWARD, for Co-operative Union; †William Robert RAE.

JONES, Joseph (Joe) (1891-1948)
MINERS' LEADER

Joseph Jones was born on 22 August 1891 at St Helens, Lancashire, the son of Benjamin and Joanna Jones. He was educated at the Parr National School, St Helens, until he was about nine years of age, when he moved with his family to South Yorkshire and attended the Sir David Gamble Technical School, Sheffield. Under the 'Glen Scholarship' scheme he took courses in mining science, with considerable success. His parents wanted him to become a mining surveyor, and in 1906 placed him with a qualified surveyor at Ashton's Green Colliery. A year later his father was victimised, and for financial reasons Jones was unable to continue his training. He found work at the Wharncliffe Woodmoor Colliery, remained there until 1913, and then moved to the newly-opened pit at Thurcroft, near Rotherham. Jones continued his education by studying at evening classes at Sheffield University, where he obtained certificates in mining science and related subjects.

At Thurcroft he enthusiastically entered into political, trade union and local government activities. He became the delegate of the Thurcroft branch of the Yorkshire Miners' Association in 1914, and in 1918 was elected a member of the Association's executive committee. A year later he joined the South Yorkshire Joint Board, and when the Miners' Welfare Committees were established in 1921 he was chosen to represent the Rotherham area. As a local official Jones was active and outspoken; his controversial speeches brought him much publicity. During the 1921 lockout, for example, he delivered a speech at Thorpe Hesley in which he opposed the National Wage Pool – for which the Miners' Federation of Great Britain was fighting – and advocated a settlement by which wages would be regulated by the cost of living. Jones quickly became respected in the Rotherham area as an assertive miners' leader. In 1922 he was appointed treasurer of the YMA, and after the death of Samuel Roebuck in April 1924 he became general secretary of the Association. In the same year, when Frank Hodges became an MP, Jones was nominated as a candidate for the vacant post of secretary of the MFGB – to which A.J. Cook was finally elected; Jones, however, was elected to the executive committee of the MFGB, and retained this position until 1931. During the 1926 lockout, he was secretary to a delegation which was sent to the U.S.A. to raise money for the starving miners and their families. The delegation, which included Ellen Wilkinson, representing the Women's Committee, and Ben Tillett, representing the TUC, received widespread publicity as the result of a telegram that Stanley Baldwin despatched to the U.S.A., in which he declared there was no hardship among the British mining population. The telegram aroused a storm of protest in trade union circles.

In 1932 Jones came second to Ebby Edwards in the ballot for a new secretary to the MFGB; but in the same year he was elected vice-president. In 1934 he became president of the MFGB and a member of the council of the TUC. In these early years of the 1930s the Miners' Federation was at a low ebb, and their relations with the TUC were seriously strained. Jones was an industrious and hardworking president. His political moderation was matched by his approach to industrial relations, and he firmly believed that the strike was a weapon of the very last resort. In the autumn of 1934 occurred the Gresford Colliery disaster, when 256 men and boys were killed. Jones was appointed one of two assessors to the Court of Inquiry, the other being John Brass, a Yorkshire coalowner. Peter Lee and J.A. Hall represented the MFGB, and Sir Stafford Cripps, Geoffrey Wilson and Arthur Henderson, Jr were the legal representatives on the workers' side. Hartley Shawcross, later Attorney-General in the 1945 Attlee Government, was Counsel for the colliery company. The Inquiry lasted more than two years, and produced three Reports: one from Sir Henry Walker, the Commissioner who was also Chief Inspector of Mines; a second from John Brass, and a third from Joseph Jones. Jones described the Mines Inspectorate as 'both inadequate and ineffective', listed over a dozen serious breaches of the law on the part of the colliery management, disagreed vigorously with the official explanation of the explosion, and criticised the appointment of the Chief Inspector of Mines as the Commissioner responsible for the inquiry into the disaster. The Reports were issued early in February 1937, and on 23 February a six-hour debate on the Gresford explosion was opened in the Commons by David Grenfell [Arnot (1961) 131ff.].

The miners' annual conference of July 1935 heard a speech from Jones which marked the beginning of a revival within the MFGB. The executive committee put forward a demand for a flat increase of two shillings a day, and thus began the campaign for the 'Miner's Two Bob'. While the demands were not to be fully met, and there were many inequalities in the offers made between different districts, there was a feeling that the campaign in general had achieved more than was expected at the outset, and – just as important – had induced a more militant mood and a greater sense of common purpose throughout the Federation.

Jones was closely involved in the famous dispute of 1936-7 at Harworth Colliery, Nottinghamshire where the establishment of the Spencer Industrial Union, supported by the colliery owners, was the cause of victimisation and a negation of the trade union rights of the Nottinghamshire Miners' Association. Together with Ebby Edwards and Will Lawther, Joseph Jones obtained overwhelming support from MFGB members throughout the country for a national strike. Eventually this was averted by a fusion of the Nottinghamshire Miners' Association and the Industrial Union 'substantially on Spencer's terms' [Griffin (1962) 274].

The British miners had a record of vigorous support for Republican Spain after the Fascist rising of July 1936. The attitude of the leaders of the MFGB became increasingly critical of the foreign policy of the British Government. There were many visits to the battlefields of Spain by British miners, and Joseph Jones went early in 1938 with J. Little (Amalgamated Engineering Union) and W. Squance (Locomotive Engineers and Firemen). Jones reported fully to the executive committee in May 1938, and then went to the 33rd Miners' International Congress in Luxembourg where again he spoke passionately in support of Republican Spain. At the annual conference of the MFGB later in 1938 Jones moved a resolution, approved unanimously, urging maximum assistance to the Spanish people and calling upon the TUC to organise a national campaign. The resolution was seconded by Arthur Horner.

As a recognised expert on industrial matters in general, and on the economics of the coal industry and mine safety in particular, Jones gave evidence before the Samuel Commission in 1925, and four years later was a member of a Commission which examined conditions in the cotton industry. He was also one of the members of a delegation to the Mining Association of Great Britain which considered action in connection with the expiry of the Coal Mines Act of 1931. In 1931 he became a member of the Coal Mines Reorganisation Commission, which had, in theory, extensive powers concerning colliery amalgamation. In 1936 he published a book, *The Coal Scuttle*, which examined the case for the nationalisation and rationalisation of the industry, and for the development of coal by-products. He gave lectures throughout the country on the financial reorganisation of the coal industry. At one lecture, at Oxford University, he delighted his audience by cataloguing a long list of products which could be extracted from coal and concluding with the words 'In fact you can get anything from coal except a decent wage for the miner' [*Sheffield Telegraph*, 2 Apr 1948].

In politics, Jones was a fervent supporter of the Labour Party. He was agent of the Rother Valley Divisional Labour Party from 1918 to 1924, and secretary from 1920, and a member of the NEC of the Labour Party from 1926 to 1931. In addition he was one of the founders of the *Rother Valley Labour Journal* which he edited for several years. He also edited the *Yorkshire Mine-Workers' Quarterly Journal* from 1924 to 1926. As a lifelong opponent of those on the extreme left of the political spectrum, he was during the whole of the inter-war period a bitter opponent of the Communist Party of Great Britain. Jones led the campaign against the Communists in Yorkshire, claiming that he wished to dispel Communism from the coalfields as a surgeon would cut a cancer from the human body. Accordingly, he was a common subject for scathing attacks in the *Askern Turn Plate*, the *Thorne Butty Squasher* and other Communist pit newspapers.

Long before his election to positions of leadership on the Miners' Federation, Jones had become active in local government affairs. He was a member of Thurcroft Parish Council and in 1919 became a member of the Rotherham RDC, the Rotherham Board of Guardians and the West Riding CC; in the years that followed he served on many County Council Committees. For over twenty years he was a member of Barnsley Town Council; from 1935 to 1937 he was mayor, and during his term of office received the King and Queen on their official visit to Barnsley. He was the first chairman of the Barnsley Public Assistance Committee and one-time chairman of Barnsley Borough Finance Committee, chairman of the Education Committee, chairman of the governors of the Barnsley High School for Girls and chairman of the licensing justices. He was also a JP for Barnsley and the county of York.

He was brought up in the Nonconformist tradition, frequently occupied Wesleyan Methodist pulpits in his earlier days, and did much to establish the Wesleyan Chapel at Thurcroft. He was on the plan of the Barnsley Wesleyan Circuit, but after he became secretary of the YMA he was unable to devote much of his time to preaching. In addition he was a prominent temperance worker and was the first chairman of the Workers' Temperance League.

Joe Jones, as he was popularly called, reached the climax of his career in 1938. The decade that followed brought him disappointments, and isolation from the miners' organisations. In 1938 he accepted a relatively well-paid position on the new Coal Commission, which had greater powers than the Coal Mines Reorganisation Commission which it superseded. The Coal Commission was charged with the duty of suggesting and encouraging colliery amalgamations in order to concentrate production at the most economic pits. It was a job for which he had obvious abilities, but the YMA insisted that he could not simultaneously be a district official of the Association and a Commissioner. As a result Jones was forced to resign the presidency of the MFGB and the secretaryship of the YMA. Soon afterwards rumours began to circulate alleging that he had betrayed the miners in order to obtain a large salary as a member of the Coal Commission. He was also compared with Frank Hodges, who had previously abandoned the miners to become an affluent company director. Supporters of Jones argued that this was not the case, and that he had only accepted the position of Commissioner because he considered it consistent with his desire to serve the miners.

During the early years of the Second World War his career began to fall apart. The district auditor's report for the year ending March 1940 made some rather damaging allegations against the Borough Treasurer of Barnsley, and against Alderman Joseph Jones in his capacity as chairman of the finance committee. The auditor's report was published in full in the *Sheffield Telegraph* for 28 August 1941, and an editorial comment promised to publish any further statement; but no comment seems to have been made by the parties concerned. In 1943 the Coal Commission ceased to function, and Jones found himself temporarily unemployed. Eventually he was appointed to minor positions as technical officer for the Ministry of Works, honorary fuel overseer for Barnsley, chairman of the Civil Defence War Emergency Committee and chairman of the War Savings Committee. When the war ended, a number of attempts were made by influential friends to find him employment, and in 1947 he accepted a position in the Manpower and Welfare Department of the newly formed National Coal Board as an adviser on questions of social insurance and workmen's compensation.

Joseph Jones was a man of considerable ability, an eloquent and convincing speaker, and a good administrator. He could certainly have had a parliamentary career. The decision to leave the trade union movement was his own. 'Why then', wrote Harold Bunting in an obituary notice, 'did this man of many talents fall short in his achievements? My view is that after lean years of poverty and struggle, opportunities came to him too thickly and too quickly. He was offered a seat on the Coal Commission . . . [and] he accepted' [*Sheffield Telegraph*, 2 Apr 1948].

Jones married Edith Hannah, daughter of John and Emma Morritt, in 1912, and they had one son (Joseph Jones, one-time Town Clerk of Ilkley) and five daughters. He was awarded the CBE in 1932, was made an honorary DLitt. of the University of Leeds in 1937, and became a freeman of the Borough of Barnsley in October 1943. Jones died on 1 April 1948 in St Helen's Hospital, Barnsley. He was survived by his wife, and family and left an estate valued at £4062.

Writings: *Organise for Victory* (n.d.) P; *Why I am in the Labour Party* (n.d.) P; *The Case for Labour* (n.d.) P; *Issues involved in the Miners' Epic Struggle* (Nov 1927) 36 pp.; *The Coal Scuttle* [on the State of the Coal-mining Industry] (1936); Foreword to George Ridley, *Labour's Policy for Coal and Power* (Labour Party [1937]) 12 pp.

Sources: *Yorkshire Mine-Workers' Q.J.* (Sep 1925) and (Sep 1926); *Labour Who's Who* (1927); *Edlington Lamp*, 26 Dec 1930; *WWW* (1941-50); *Barnsley Chronicle*, 23 Aug 1941; *Sheffield Telegraph and Independent*, 28 Aug 1941; R. Page Arnot, *The Miners: years of struggle* (1953); *Sheffield Telegraph*, 11 May 1955; R. Page Arnot, *The Miners in Crisis and War* (1961); A.R. Griffin, *The Miners of Nottinghamshire* (1962); R.G. Neville, 'The Yorkshire Miners 1881-1926: a study in labour and social history' (Leeds PhD, 1974); personal information, Mrs E. Jones, Barnsley, widow. OBIT. *Sheffield Telegraph*, 1 and 2 Apr 1948,

Times and *Yorkshire Post*, 2 Apr 1948, *Barnsley Chronicle*, 3 Apr 1948; *Labour Party Report* (1948).

ROBERT G. NEVILLE
JOHN SAVILLE

See also: †Arthur James COOK, for Mining Trade Unionism, 1915-26; Ebenezer (Ebby) EDWARDS; †Joseph Arthur (Joe) HALL; †Peter LEE, for Mining Trade Unionism. 1927-44;†George Alfred SPENCER.

KNEE, Fred (1868-1914)
SOCIALIST, LONDON LABOUR PARTY PIONEER AND HOUSING REFORMER

In 1883, at the age of fifteen, Fred Knee believed that God intended him to become a missionary; and although he lost his religious faith in adult life, the sense of vocation remained: his 'duty and privilege' to work in the mission field was transformed into a duty and privilege to work, strenuously and with unswerving conviction, for the cause of labour.

He was the second child in a family of four. The eldest, Willie, was a mental defective; Fred's younger brother Arthur died in 1881 at the age of eight, and the last child was a daughter, Amelia Rose (Millie). Fred was thus the only breadwinner in the younger generation. He was born on 16 June 1868 at Frome in Somerset. His father, James Knee, was a woollen weaver and his mother, Elizabeth (née Poynter) was engaged in silk weaving, a trade which she continued to practise after her marriage. Fred was a frail little boy who from the age of three was liable to severe attacks of pulmonary trouble – bronchitis, asthma, pneumonia, pleurisy; and it was this – combined with prolonged and incessant over-work – that finally killed him. With his weak physique and small stature (even as an adult he was barely five feet tall) he combined an exceptional intelligence, quick, clear and penetrating; a driving desire to know; and dynamic energy. When he left the British School in Frome at the age of thirteen, he was employed by a large printing and publishing firm, Butler & Tanner Ltd, and while working there was apprenticed as a compositor (1882-9).

His life in Frome during these years is mirrored in the diaries he kept from 1884, when he was fifteen, until pressure of work made 'diarizing', as he called it, impossible, in 1896. He joined his parents' Congregational Church (on 3 January 1884), and spent anything from thirty to fifty hours a month in attending services, Sunday School, prayer meetings and other meetings connected with the Church. In 1884 he took a marathon series of examinations in Scripture and in March 1887 he passed an examination in Congregational Principles; this qualified him to preach, which he did regularly in the chapels of the villages round about Frome. During this period he also taught himself shorthand and – since he had a good powerful voice, enjoyed singing, and belonged to a singing class or choir – the tonic sol-fa notation.

All this devotion and zeal for improvement suggest a rather earnest and priggish character; but he could amuse his numerous friends, and in spite of his physical handicaps he enjoyed life enormously. His chief recreations were long walks; cricket, where he considered himself 'second to none in bad playing' [Diary, 28 May 1885]; bathing – he taught himself to swim; and very mild flirtations.

In December 1888 his employers took over the *Somerset and Wiltshire Journal*, and seeing a chance of getting about and enlarging his experience, Fred applied successfully for a job on the paper. He combined part-time reporting with part-time work in the composing room until late in 1890. He had become interested in politics in his teens, and like his forebears, he was a radical. He was attending political meetings by 1884, and at the general election of 1886 he worked hard for the Liberals, whose candidate at Frome, however, was defeated by the Conservative.

By the end of 1890 Knee felt Frome to be too constricting, and in December he left for London. The printing trade was not at this time in a very thriving state, and Fred had some difficult weeks before he found a steady job (though at 2*s* less than the agreed rate) with Harrison's of St Martin's Lane. He had already joined the London Society of Compositors, and wrote a paper for them on 'Practical Politics for the Worker' shortly after his arrival in London [Nash (1969) 13]. In 1896 he was father of the chapel at Harrison's.

The year 1891 opened a new life for Fred Knee. His diaries reflect the novelty of it all and his absorption in it. In January he joined the Regent Street Polytechnic, where keen and intelligent young men conducted the 'Poly Parliament', with its bills, debates and voting divisions. This institution was of great use to Knee. There, as 'Radical member for Frome' he had scope for learning the arts of debating (in which his wide reading and familiarity with the Bible were useful assets) and of committee work, and in particular the art of drafting parliamentary bills – for instance, he drafted an eight hours' bill in September 1891. By July of that year he and his friends had formed a Social Democratic Party in the 'Poly Parliament'. On 5 May Knee went to a Fabian Society meeting (where he heard Shaw and Sidney Webb speak in the discussion), and joined the South West Group of the Society. On 20 May he went to the Eleusis Club, described by Sir Charles Dilke [quoted Gwynn and Tuckwell *1* (1917) 144] as 'the centre for the Radical working men in Chelsea', where 'I was catechised as to my political creed and antecedents and received' [Diary, 20 May]. From the Eleusis Club he went on to a meeting of the Social Democratic Federation, 'where I was welcomed, and whom I joined'. His membership immediately involved him in numerous branch and committee meetings. His diary for 1891 records an extraordinary number of these; sometimes he hurried to as many as three on the same day (e.g. 12, 26 July). On 28 June the SDF sent him as delegate to the Early Shopping League, where on 3 July he seconded a motion for forming a shop assistant's union.

In June he applied for the secretaryship of the Chelsea Labour Bureau, with Hyndman's support; but unsuccessfully. He also has an interesting account of one of the clashes between the police and the SDF in the struggle for free public speech. When John Webb and Hyndman were summoned for causing obstruction in Sloane Square (one of the open-air forums) on 5 July 1891, Knee gave evidence, at Hyndman's request, on behalf of Webb. The endemic friction between the SDF, the ILP and the Fabians is also reflected in the diaries. Knee's attitude was consistent – a steady adherence to his principles combined with a steady effort to promote tolerance [see entries for 6 Jan, 5 Feb and 23 Mar 1892, for example].

In the midst of all this political and trade union activity, Knee found time to court and marry Annie Francis, in April 1892. He had had a savage attack of illness in the preceding weeks. The Knees lived in Wandsworth until 1894, when they moved to Wimbledon (Knee was immediately put on the local co-operative education committee and the cheap trains committee). In 1898 they were in Sugden Road, Lavender Hill, where they moved in order to be near their friend, Robert Phillimore. Their last home, from November 1901, was in Radlett, Herts, where Knee became a parish councillor.

Fred Knee stood as SDF candidate in several local government elections, and although one might have expected his special interests – housing, unemployment and education – to appeal to urban voters, he was not successful and did not join in London local government until 1900, when the Vestries were replaced by Borough Councils. He was chosen as alderman for Battersea Council, where he served until 1906; he was a member of the health, housing and finance committees. Fred Knee was never afraid to voice his convictions, and by this time he was an experienced and formidable debater. At the Battersea Council meeting of 25 January 1901, amid cheering, hissing, personal abuse and a good deal of general disruption, he moved a resolution condemning the British military conduct of the South African War and demanding the restoration of Boer independence and an immediate cessation of hostilities. It was not accepted. Knee resigned from the Council in 1906 because of political disagreements with John Burns, then MP for Battersea. On 1 June 1907, as a member of the London Trades Council, Knee was on the platform at the meeting held in Holborn Town Hall to welcome a delegation of Russian Social Democrats led by Trotsky.

The year before, he had applied for the general secretaryship of his union, the Compositors, which he failed to get. But his candidature may have been half-hearted: his work for *Justice* and the Twentieth Century Press may have suited him: he was first reader, then sub-editor of *Justice* under Quelch, and from 1909 was a full-time employee of the paper and the Press [Lee and Archbold (1935) 229]; he was thinking of standing for Parliament; and he was secretary of the Workmen's National Housing Council – perhaps his most important function at this period.

His native town of Frome was in an area which was not only agricultural but also had coalmines, so that in his youth Fred Knee must have known different kinds of workers' houses, including cottages tied to farms or mines. When he came to London and encountered its slums, he began to study the subject of workers' housing and to familiarise himself with council schemes, by-laws, national legislation, political forces. During the summer of 1898, Fred Knee and two of his colleagues in the SDF composing room formed themselves into an *ad hoc* body which they called the London Workmen's Committee on Housing. They took soundings of opinion to ascertain what support they might expect for a housing campaign. The results were so encouraging that in September 1898 Knee and his colleagues arranged a meeting of representatives from labour organisations such as trade unions, co-operative societies and the London Trades Council. Two LCC councillors came, both representing Deptford. One was Sidney Webb, the other a friend of Knee's, Robert Phillimore, who took the chair at the meeting (Phillimore was already interested in housing; and in 1900 he built some blocks of workmen's flats at Radlett, Herts, where he owned land). This September meeting brought into being the Workmen's National Housing Council (WNHC). Its programme included pressure on municipalities to build large numbers of workers' houses and to let them at low, even unprofitable rents, by means of government loans to be made to the town councils. Other ideas advocated by Knee included government purchase of land to be given to the councils for housing.

The WNHC was able to divert the LCC from a policy of slum clearance preceded by evictions and followed by reconstruction on the site, to a new policy of building houses on the outskirts of urban development where land was cheaper, and rehousing people there before demolishing their old homes – a policy which spread to most other town councils. Knee had early grasped the interrelationships of housing with other social problems. Hence his connection with the demand for cheaper transport for workers: he was secretary of the Cheaper Trains and Trams Committee in 1895.

By the end of the century the WNHC had decided to introduce a bill of its own into Parliament. W.C. Steadman brought it to the House in 1900, and thereafter a bill sponsored by the WNHC was brought before Parliament almost every year up to 1914 [Englander (1977) 17; List of Housing Bills in *General Index to Parliamentary Papers 1900-1949*, HMSO (1960) 334]. It seems likely that Knee had a major part in their drafting. His early experience in the 'Poly Parliament' proved very useful to him in the special and intricate business of parliamentary drafting, an art which he seems to have mastered with his usual ability, indeed with an ease which astonished his colleague the architect Robert Williams [*Housing J.* no. 99 (Feb 1915)]. Williams was a Socialist and LCC member for N. Lambeth in 1901. He and Fred Knee collaborated in a practical book on housing, *The Labourer and his Cottage* (1905).

The Council saw some of their proposals adopted in the Housing Acts of 1900 and 1903, while the Liberal Government's bill of 1909 contained 'several of our minor proposals' [*Trades and Labour Gazette* (Apr 1909)]. The most important point in the bills introduced by the Conservative opposition in 1912 was the proposal of state aid for local authority housing. This was a principle which the Council had been urging for years, and which was adopted, subject to certain conditions, in the Housing Act of August 1914.

Knee wrote most of the WNHC's *Housing Journal* from 1900, when it was started, until his death in 1914. He also bore the chief brunt of public speaking on behalf of the Housing Council and its programme. He himself estimated casually that he had spoken in more than a hundred provincial towns. His ability to persuade enlisted Keir Hardie as a speaker and Ramsay MacDonald as a member of the executive. A lively potted account of the WNHC up to that date – and also of the current situation in Labour politics – was given by Knee in an interview published in the issue of the *Trades and Labour Gazette* (Apr 1909) referred to above. The Housing

Council was an outstanding example of successful co-operation among Labour and trade union groups of different political complexions and this success was widely attributed to Fred Knee's personal qualities.

These qualities were exhibited again in the great achievement of his last years, the formation of the London Labour Party. Like others Knee had come to believe that the immediately important task was the welding together of the scattered Labour bodies in London in order to capture the LCC. In the years before the First World War, while the Conservative and Liberal Parties each had a central organisation in the capital, Labour had no such thing. There were many local Labour Parties, but they were small, scattered and working independently. The ILP, while it had a Metropolitan District Council, was never very powerful in London. The SDF, which also had a London District Council, had withdrawn from the Labour Representation Committee in 1901. Attempts were repeatedly made on the executive to have this decision reversed; but it was not until 1913, with the death of Harry Quelch, the most obdurate defender of separatism, that re-affiliation could be effected. The London Trades Council's efforts at unification were persistently impeded by Quelch as chairman and by the equally separatist secretary James Macdonald. Fred Knee had been a member of the LTC since 1905, and had urged the necessity for unification, as he had on the SDF executive. Ben Cooper, in 1914 the eldest delegate to the Trades Council, 'said that throughout his whole experience he knew no one who had left a greater mark on the policy and disposition of the Council than had Fred Knee' [*Justice*, 17 Dec 1914]. In 1913 Knee's efforts began to bear fruit; when Quelch died in that year and James Macdonald resigned, and when their places were taken by John Stokes and Fred Knee, the formation of the London Labour Party was at last under way. In March 1914 the London Trades Council proposed a conference 'of those eligible for affiliation to the national Labour Party for the purpose of establishing a united working-class party on the LCC at the 1916 elections.' There was criticism; Stokes and Knee were accused of betraying the class war in allying themselves with ILP members and Fabians. Knee defended the Trades Council position with spirit. 'If we accept and believe in the class war,' he wrote, 'we must take our place in the van of the organised working class movement. Socialism implies a state of society – a movement of society rather than an absolutely fixed condition. It is all nonsense to suppose that to achieve anything like a Socialist community everybody or even a majority must consciously hold and intellectually understand the tenets of the B.S.P. . . . with the working class we are invincible, if we leave that ground we are not only lost but cease to be Socialist workers through and with society and become mere sectaries' [*Justice*, 14 May 1914, quoted Nash, 39].

The remarks he made at the inaugural conference on 23 May, equally characteristic, were on the level of everyday practical advice. The object of those present, he said, was to combine in order to win a considerable number of seats at the LCC elections, and to have a London Labour Party controlling the LCC. To start this process of winning control by forming such a party was what Knee and his friends had been working for, especially in the last eighteen months of preliminary negotiations and arrangements in which Knee played a large part.

It is Herbert Morrison's name which is generally linked with the early London Labour Party, and in his autobiography Morrison passed rapidly over the parts played in the Party's formation by Knee and Stokes. The latest biography of Morrison, however, gives a more accurate version and accorded full and proper emphasis to the efforts of Knee, Stokes and their colleagues [Donoughue and Jones (1973) 38]. Knee was elected secretary of the provisional committee of the London Labour Party on 23 May 1914, and confirmed in the position at the first annual conference on 28 November. At the latter he was elected in his absence, for he was already ill. If he had lived, he might have had a parliamentary career before him. He had been adopted as candidate by Clapham ILP in 1903 and as SDF candidate for Leeds West in 1907, but he did not contest either seat. In July 1911 he was adopted as BSP candidate for Aberdeen North, which was a Liberal seat until 1918, but after that went to Labour.

Knee's support for international labour became stronger as the First World War came nearer. In May 1913, at the invitation of the London Trades Council and with arrangements made by

Knee, a group of German trade unionists visited London, and in August, together with Ben Tillett, John Stokes, George Isaacs, and others, Knee headed a delegation on a return visit. Knee was, besides, on the advisory council of the European Unity League. When the war actually began, Knee was instrumental in the formation of a London Labour Emergency Committee, to protect the interest of the workers [*Herts. Advertiser and St Albans Times,* 19 Dec 1914]. He was also a member of the War Emergency Workers' National Committee.

Knee died of asthma, pleurisy and physical exhaustion on 8 December 1914, and after a service in the Wesleyan Chapel was buried in Radlett parish churchyard on 12 December. There is no doubt, as the many tributes paid to him made clear, that he was an uncommon man. He was survived by his wife and six of their seven children – one daughter, Maggie, died in hospital a week before her father, although he was not told of her death. The elder son, Arthur William, was a civil servant, and the second son, Harold James, who served as a lieutenant in the First World War, and was wounded and gassed, was a businessman until his retirement.

Writings: Knee wrote many articles in *Justice* between 1896 and 1914: see list of selected writings in *The Diary of Fred Knee,* edited with an Introduction by D. Englander (Society for the Study of Labour History, Aids to Research, no. 3: 1977) 120-2. He also contributed to the *Somerset and Wiltshire J.,* 21 Mar. 1891, *Wimbledon Rev.* and *Wimbledon News* (Nov 1896) and the *Housing J.* (1900-14). Other writings included: (with R. Williams), *The Labourer and his Cottage* (1905); Evidence before S.C. on the Housing of the Working Classes Acts Amendment Bill 1906 IX Qs 3166-459 and 'The Revolt of Labour', *Social Democrat* (Nov 1910) repr. in *Lab. Mon.* (June 1950) 275-9 and in *Industrial Democracy in Great Britain: a book of readings and witnesses for workers' control* ed. K. Coates and A. Topham, 1968, rev. ed. entitled *Workers' Control,* 1970, 24-7].

Sources: (1) MSS: Letters and personal papers and diaries of Fred Knee in the possession of Harold J. Knee, Woking, Surrey, son, including a typescript biography, 'Fred Knee 1868-1914' (July 1969) by Barbara Nash, niece. (2) Other: London Society of Compositors, *Reports* (1906-14), TUC Library; 'Mr Fred Knee', *Trades and Labour Gazette* (Apr 1909) 9; *Times,* 20 Aug 1914; S. Gwynn and G.M. Tuckwell, *The Life of the Rt Hon. Sir Charles Dilke 1* (1917); H.W. Lee and E. Archbold, *Social-Democracy in Britain* (1935); E. Howe and H.E. Waite, *Centenary History of the London Society of Compositors* (1948); G. Tate, *London Trades Council 1860-1950* (1950); H. Morrison, *Herbert Morrison: an autobiography* (1960); P. Thompson, *Socialists, Liberals and Labour: the struggle for London 1885-1914* (1967); B. Donoughue and G.W. Jones, *Herbert Morrison: portrait of a politician* (1973); G. Page, 'The Mighty Atom: London Labour Party's first secretary', *Labour London,* no. 4 (1975) 3; biographical information: D. Englander, Corpus Christi College, Oxford; personal information: H.J. Knee, Woking, son. OBIT. *Aberdeen Daily J.,* 10 Dec 1914; *Justice,* 10, 17 and 24 Dec 1914; *Herald,* 12 Dec 1914; *Clarion,* 18 Dec 1914; *Herts Advertiser and St Albans Times,* 19 Dec 1914; *British and Colonial Printer and Stationer,* 14 Jan 1915; *London Typographical J. 10,* no. 100 (Jan 1915); *Housing J.* no. 99 (Feb 1915).

MARGARET 'ESPINASSE

See also: *James MACDONALD; *Harry QUELCH; William (Will) Charles STEADMAN.

KUMARAMANGALAM, Surendra Mohan (1916-73)
INDIAN COMMUNIST AND LATER CONGRESS SOCIALIST

Mohan Kumaramangalam was born on 1 November 1916, in Westminster, London, and his childhood and youth was spent in England. His parents' name was Subbarayan, the name he was registered in at birth, when his father was described as a law student: Kumaramangalam was the name of the family estate. Mohan's father came of a wealthy landowning family from Tiruchengode, Salem, in Madras province. He was prominent in politics during the inter-war years and after independence, and he was appointed Governor of Maharashtra in the year that he died. He was also for many years president of the Indian Cricket Board [*DNB* [Indian] 4 (1974) 267-9]. Mohan's mother, Radhabai (née Kudumal) was a woman of outstanding personality. She represented Indian Women at the London Round Table Conference in the early 1930s and, as an elected member of the Congress Party, was the first woman member of the Central Legislative Assembly in 1938. On grounds of nationalism she refused the award of the Kaiser-i-Hind gold medal (for social work). Mohan's father, unlike his mother, was not a Brahmin, and for its day their marriage was a radical break with tradition, especially on his mother's part. Both parents studied at Oxford and became friends of Arthur Gillett and his wife Margaret Clark, members of two well-known Quaker families. The Kumaramangalam children were all sent to school in England and many of their holidays were spent with the Gillett family. Mohan was at Eton, and left a year early because, as he told a friend, Victor Kiernan, he was not made a prefect, and he believed this to be due to his being an Indian [Kiernan, *Socialist India*, 23 Feb 1974, 6].

He entered King's College, Cambridge, in October 1935. He had intended to read for an engineering degree, but the growing importance of left-wing politics in his life turned his attention to the humanities, and he finally decided to read history. Among his closest friends at Cambridge were Victor Kiernan, James Klugmann, John Cornford and Reginald Trim. A later, and very close friend, was Ram Nahum. There was a considerable number of Indian students in Cambridge during the 1930s, and many were later to become leading figures in an independent India. Most of the Indian students belonged to the Majlis Society, and already before Mohan's arrival there was a large group, which had set itself the aim of transforming the Majlis into an educational and political organisation. Mohan was soon elected to its committee.

The Communist Party was illegal in India, and in Britain there was a constant surveillance of Indian radicals by the authorities. There was a close relationship between Indian Communists and the British Communist Party whose leading theoretician, Rajani Palme Dutt, was especially interested in Indian affairs. Exactly when Mohan joined the CP is not known, but it was early in his career at Cambridge. In his case he made no secret of his Marxist politics although never formally acknowledging his Party membership.

The radicalisation of a significant minority of British students was a notable feature of the nineteen thirties, and the three main centres of the student Left were Oxford, Cambridge and the LSE. All had large student Communist groups, and the movement was sufficiently vigorous and promising for a full-time Communist organiser to be appointed. This was Jack Cohen, much liked by his student members. During his years at Cambridge Mohan took an active part in general student politics in addition to his special commitment to the cause of Indian freedom. He represented Indian students at the first Congress of the World Youth Movement in Geneva in the summer of 1936, and was in the chair for one of its sessions; and towards the end of 1936 he was much involved in the establishment of a Federation of Indian Students in Britain. Agreement was first reached between the Cambridge and Oxford Majlis and then with the London University Society. Early in 1937 a London conference (8-10 Jan 1937) formally brought the new organisation into existence. In May 1937, together with all the left-wing students in Cambridge, he helped with the local busmen's strike, and in the following month, June, he stood for the secretaryship of the Cambridge Union, which led automatically to the presidency. He lost by five votes. The summer vacation of this year was spent in India and on his return he showed a growing dissatisfaction with student politics, finding them rather narrow and cramping. But he stood again for the Union secretaryship and on 30 November 1937 he was elected by a comfortable majority. He stayed up an extra term in the autumn of 1938 to take his place as President of the Union, the first Indian to hold that office. He was called to the Bar in the following year, but his mind was turning more and more towards India and its struggles. He left England some time in 1939, was imprisoned in the early years of the war and was released in 1942 when, after the change of political attitude towards the war, many Communist *détenus* were set free. He was soon elected to the Central Committee of the Party and was attached to the Party headquarters in Bombay.

The subsequent life of Mohan Kumaramangalam belongs to the history of Indian politics. He took an active part in the bitter sectarian disputes within the CPI at the end of the 1940s, but in March 1952 he went back to Madras to practise – very successfully – at the Bar. He was still a prominent figure in Indian Communism, and he formally resigned from the CPI only when he was appointed Advocate General of Madras in 1966. In the late 1960s he was chairman of Indian Airlines, a post which he resigned when he stood for election as a Congress candidate in 1971. It was this election which gave Indira Gandhi a massive majority and Mohan was invited to join her Cabinet. He was soon accepted in Delhi as one of her closest advisers. At the time of his death he was Minister of Steel and Mines, a position which he greatly welcomed since he was deeply committed to the extension of the public sector in the Indian economy. He was killed in an air crash at New Delhi on 31 May 1973.

Henry Ferns, now (1977) Professor of Political Science at the University of Birmingham, first met Mohan Kumaramangalam in October 1936, soon after coming from Canada to read history at Cambridge. They became close friends. 'I was at once attracted', Ferns wrote to Kiernan, 'by the beauty of his English speech and the charm of his manner rendered somehow extraordinary by his large eyes and mobile hands. It has always been my wife's opinion that Mohan spoke English more beautifully than anyone she has encountered, and likewise that he was one of the most attractive human beings she has ever met. Like me she holds this opinion after the passage of almost a third of a century' [quoted Kiernan, *Socialist India*, 2 Mar 1974, 14].

Mohan had two brothers and a sister. The eldest brother, General P.P. Kumaramangalam, is a former Chief of Staff of the Indian Army; the second, Gopal, was a government servant, first in the Ministry of Supply and then as head of the nationalised sector in coal. He was one of the architects of coal nationalisation carried out when Mohan was Minister, and was its first chairman, retiring in 1975. Parvathi, Mohan's sister and the youngest child of the family (now Mrs Krishnan) is still involved in left-wing politics, and is (1977) a Communist member of the Indian Parliament. The indispensable source for Mohan's life in Britain is Victor Kiernan's two articles in *Socialist India*.

Writings: Articles in the Indian English language journal *People's War* during the Second World War.

Sources: G.D. Overstreet and M. Windmiller, *Communism in India* (Univ. of California Press, 1959); *Times of India Directory and Yearbook* (1960-1); V.G. Kiernan, 'Mohan Kumaramangalam in England', *Socialist India*, 23 Feb and 2 Mar 1974; Institute of Historical Studies, *Dictionary of National Biography* [Indian] vol. 4, ed. S.P. Sen (Calcutta, 1974); J.A. Ellis, 'The Structure of Politics in South India 1918-39: conflict and adjustment in Madras City' (London PhD, 1975); biographical information: P. Strong, Eton College; Miss N. Travis, Librarian, India House, London; personal information: J. Cohen, London; Professor H.S. Ferns, Birmingham Univ.; Professor V.G. Kiernan, Edinburgh Univ.; Mrs P. Krishnan, New Delhi, sister. Obit. *Times*, 2 June 1973.

JOHN SAVILLE

LAW, Harriet Teresa (1831-97)
FEMINIST, SECULARIST AND RADICAL

Harriet Law (née Frost) was born on 5 November 1831 at Ongar in Essex. Her father was a farmer and refreshment contractor who, on selling his business and investing the money unwisely, fell on hard times. He brought his large family to live in London where Harriet took a house of her own, ran a school and helped to support her parents. By religion she was a Strict

Baptist, being baptised at about the age of twenty by Dr Angus at College Chapel, Bethnal Green. Her views were rigidly sabbatarian and she taught in the Sunday school.

In East London she came into contact with militant freethought lecturers, first in the open air in the Mile End Road where she attempted to answer these critics of her faith, and then in the Philpott Street Secular Hall where she heard and opposed G.J. Holyoake, Charles Southwell, Charles Bradlaugh and other leading secularists and freethinkers. Gradually her views began to moderate, her first doubts were characteristically about St Paul's injunction to women to be silent in church. It was at the Philpott Street Hall that she met her future husband, Edward Law, who also was a Christian undergoing a religious crisis of faith. He was the son of William Law of Newton Abbot, and they were married on 11 January 1855.

Both Harriet and her husband shortly afterwards became secularists, and in 1859 Harriet began as a public lecturer on freethought and radical topics. She appeared for the first time at the City Road Hall of Science on 24 June 1860, and in the autumn of the following year she made her first provincial lecture tour of freethought societies in Lancashire and Yorkshire. She was hailed immediately as the best female advocate of the popular cause since Emma Martin and her reputation was quickly established in the English provinces and in Scotland. Thereafter she made regular tours outside London, leaving her husband to care for their children aided by a nurse.

As a young woman she was remembered as having a low, pleasant voice, but her later efforts in large halls and out-of-doors gave her a harsher tone. She was a small, stout woman, whose physical courage in the face of hostile mobs was renowned (she once escaped a furious rabble by wearing a man's top hat and coat, while on another occasion she threw pennies to divert a crowd hotly in pursuit of the cart from which she had been speaking). She was also noted for her wit and sarcasm in debate with the clergy and others hostile to her views. Her character was sturdily independent, an embodiment of her unfashionable opinion that women were the equals of men – 'a plain, blunt, honest woman, utterly free from all suspicion of humbug' [Ross in *Agnostic J.*, 11 Sep 1897]. Among her idiosyncrasies was a hostility towards the medical profession not uncommon among women of her age and outlook. Her frequent comment was 'that there was little to choose between the mystery men of Æsculapius and the mystery-men of Christ' [Wheeler in *Freethinker*, 1 Aug 1897].

She was not an intellectual: her early reading, apart from *Pilgrim's Progress* and Young's *Night Thoughts*, had been largely in the Bible of which she had a profound knowledge. As a popular lecturer she identified herself with no particular party, and, although her principal audiences were among those radicals and freethinkers who followed Charles Bradlaugh, she refused to join his National Secular Society or to accept his leadership. He later recalled her as being 'brusquely honest' and he could not conceal his delight when, after 1874, Annie Besant joined his camp and displaced the resolute Mrs Law as chief female advocate. In 1869 she accepted the presidency of the short-lived, non-Bradlaughite Freethought League.

During the 1860s and 1870s she appeared on Reform League, Secularist and Republican platforms, advocating universal suffrage, women's rights and the destruction of all religious influence. On 23 July 1866, when a Reform League crowd broke down the railings of Hyde Park, she was one of the first to address the crowd in a two-hour speech in defiance of the Commissioner of Police; and on 18 June 1867 she was elected a member of the general council of the First International. Politically she remained on the Left and in 1878 when Karl Marx could find no publisher for a reply to George Howell's criticism of him she published it in her *Secular Chronicle* [4 Aug]. In the same periodical she wrote a short biographical article on Marx [7 July 1878].

The *Secular Chronicle* was her principal venture in publishing and it contains nearly all she wrote. Begun in 1872 by George Reddalls of Birmingham, it was taken over by Mrs Law in 1876 as a penny weekly 'established to promote free inquiry into social, political and theological questions', her policy being liberty, equality and fraternity, atheism, republicanism, women's rights and Owenite co-operation. She kept the paper going for three years during which time she lost £1000 on it. The most unusual feature of the paper was a Ladies' Page devoted to 'the advocacy of those political, social and domestic matters that especially affect women'.

After the rise of Annie Besant and the failure of the *Secular Chronicle* in 1879, Mrs Law, who was suffering from bronchitis, retired from public life to her home at 38 Boyson Road, Walworth; she later moved to 7 Victoria Road, Peckham. She died on 19 July 1897 from a heart attack and was buried at Forest Hill Cemetery on 23 July 1897. She was survived by her husband, son and three daughters, and left effects valued at £238.

Her forte was as a public speaker rather than as a writer or editor. She had little business ability, her life's work being financed by her husband who made his living out of property dealing.

Sources: Scattered references to Mrs Law's weekly activities are to be found in the freethought press: *National Reformer*, 1860-93, *Secular Rev.*, 1876-88, *Freethinker* (from 1881), *Agnostic J.* (from 1889), as well as in the *Secular Chronicle*, 1872-9 which Mrs Law edited, 1876-8. See, especially, *National Reformer*, 22 June 1873, *Secular Chronicle*, 31 Mar 1878, *Freethinker*, 6 June 1915 [by A.B. Moss, based on recollections of Alice Law, a daughter] and ibid., 4 July 1915 [by G.W. Foote]. She is also mentioned in the *Marx-Engels Correspondence*: see especially vol. *31* p. 553, Marx-Kugelmann, 13 July 1867, but also vol. *32* p. 97, Marx-Engels, 20 June 1868, and vol. *35* p. 147, Marx-Longuet, 4 Jan 1881. Other sources: M. Quin, *Memoirs of a Positivist* (1924); H. Collins and C. Abramsky, *Karl Marx and the British Labour Movement* (1965); W.S. Smith, *The London Heretics, 1870-1914* (1967); D. Tribe, *100 Years of Freethought* (1967); E. Royle, *Radical Politics 1790-1900* (1971); D. Tribe, *President Charles Bradlaugh MP* (1971); E. Royle, *Victorian Infidels* (1974); S. Budd, *Varieties of Unbelief* (1976). OBIT. *Freethinker*, 1 Aug 1897 [by J.M. Wheeler] and 8 Aug 1897 [by G.W. Foote]; *Agnostic J.*, 11 Sep 1897 [by W.S. Ross] and 16 Oct 1897 [by G.J. Holyoake].

EDWARD ROYLE

See also: †Annie BESANT; *Charles BRADLAUGH; †George Jacob HOLYOAKE; *Emma MARTIN.

LOCKEY, Walter Daglish (1891-1956)
MINEWORKERS' LEADER

Walter Lockey was born on 7 February 1891 at Holywell village, Northumberland, the eldest son (in a family of three sons and one daughter) of Samuel Lockey, a coalminer, and Mary Nelson Lockey (née Atkinson). He was educated at elementary schools in Holywell and Blyth and left school at the age of fourteen. He served an apprenticeship as a blacksmith with Thompsons Ltd, a firm of agricultural engineers at Backworth village; and completed a four year evening course in mechanical engineering at the Rutherford Technical College, Newcastle upon Tyne. After serving his time he got the job of shoeing pit ponies at East Holywell Colliery, where his father worked as a deputy.

Lockey joined the Northumberland Colliery Mechanics' Association; he became secretary of the East Holywell branch and a branch delegate to county delegate meetings and he served on the NCMA's executive committee from 1922 to 1924. He was elected president of the NCMA in 1924 and held this post until 1935, when he was elected to the full-time post of general secretary after the death of J.M. Gillians. In the same year he became president of the Northumberland Mineworkers' Board and retained this post until his retirement in 1956. He was also for many years a governor of the Northumberland Aged Mineworkers' Homes Association.

Once established in the Northumberland mineworkers' organisations he became well known among colliery craftsmen in other coalfields. He served on the executive council of the National Federation of Colliery Mechanics from 1925 to 1935, represented the colliery craftsmen of Group No. 1 on the national executive committee of the MFGB from 1936 to 1937 and 1940 to

1941, and served on the national executive of the NUM from 1951 to 1953. In 1938 he attended the Miners' International Conference at Luxembourg as a member of the MFGB's delegation.

The war years were very busy ones for Lockey: he served on a wide range of joint consultative, safety, health, training and production committees, and continued to serve on a number of similar committees after the nationalisation of the coal industry in 1947. He was widely acknowledged to have a flair for committee work.

On 1 January 1945 the NCMA ceased to exist when it became part of the NUM, and Walter Lockey played a major part in securing for the Northumberland Mechanics' section a large measure of autonomy inside the new industrial union. As T.S. Fox, Lockey's successor, wrote in the Northumberland Mechanics' 1955 Annual Report:

> There has been a great fear that the NUM would absorb small organisations like our own. Mr Lockey came to office at a time when our position was anything but healthy and he has slowly built it up to the present position by using great economy and diligence . . . the Committee feel that the integrity and financial acumen of Mr Lockey was [sic] the main factor in us being allowed to conduct our affairs as in the past.

During his period of residence in Seaton Delaval Lockey was very active in local affairs. R.F. Wearmouth described him as 'tall, robust, confident, courageous, sociable, and kindly, prominence in public service came to him naturally' [Wearmouth (1957) 100]. He served on the Seaton Delaval Urban District Council from 1927 to 1935 and was its chairman in 1929; he was a member of the Seaton Burn Valley Sewerage Board from 1932 to 1936; the Earsdon Joint Hospital Board from 1928 to 1929 and he was appointed a Justice of the Peace in 1932. He was treasurer of the Seaton Delaval Labour Party for over fifteen years. Lockey also taught mathematics to evening class students at Seaton Delaval for thirteen years.

In 1935 he moved to Newcastle upon Tyne to take up his full-time appointment as general secretary of the NCMA. This move ended Lockey's work in local government, but he developed a special interest in the work of Newcastle's hospitals. He was for many years a governor of the Fleming Memorial Hospital for Children, and at the time of his retirement was vice-chairman of the Newcastle Hospital Management Committee. After several years of service on this body, he represented the teaching hospitals on the council of the King's College section of the University of Durham for three years in the middle 1950s.

In his politics Lockey stood on the right wing of the Labour Party and he adopted a firm anti-Communist position in all his trade union activities. He was a member of the Primitive Methodist Church and a local preacher on the Seaton Delaval Primitive Methodist Circuit from 1919 to 1936, and when he took up residence in Newcastle upon Tyne became a member and official of the Central Methodist Church and Circuit. Lockey's recreations were listed as 'public work, preaching, gardening and mathematical problems'.

Lockey retired from the secretaryship of the Northumberland Mechanics in February 1956 and moved to Amble on the Northumberland coast. However, the death of his successor, T.S. Fox, in May of the same year brought him out of retirement to assist in the union office until a new secretary could be elected. But Lockey himself fell ill and died of pernicious anaemia in Newcastle General Hospital on 2 September 1956, and was cremated three days later at Newcastle's West Road Crematorium after a service held at the Central Methodist Church. Lockey's union erected a plaque to his memory in the Fleming Memorial Hospital for Children.

In 1923 Walter Lockey had married Eva, daughter of Samuel Jones, and they had one daughter, Margaret. Mrs Lockey played an active part in her husband's trade union work. The general secretary of the NCMA was provided with living accommodation in the same building as the union's offices at 34 Falconer Street, Newcastle upon Tyne, and during her husband's absences Mrs Lockey manned the office and became conversant with the union's affairs. Walter Lockey was survived by his wife and daughter and left effects valued at £1891.

Sources: (1) MSS: Minutes of the Northumberland Colliery Mechanics' Association and the NUM (Northumberland Mechanics), 1921-56 and the National Federation of Colliery Mechanics, 1925-35: Northumberland CRO, Gosforth. (2) Other: *Annual Reports* of the NCMA and the NUM (Northumberland Mechanics) 1921-56: Northumberland Mechanics' Office, Blyth; *Who's Who in Northumberland* (Worcester, 1936); *The Northumberland Aged Mineworkers' Homes Association Jubilee Souvenir Brochure 1900-1950* (Newcastle upon Tyne, [1950]) [37] pp.; R.F. Wearmouth, *The Social and Political Influence of Methodism in the Twentieth Century* (1957); R.P. Arnot, *The Miners in Crisis and War* (1961); A. Potts and E. Wade, *Stand True* (Blyth, 1975) 36 pp.; personal information: J.E. Leathem, Wideopen, Northumberland. OBIT. *Newcastle J.,* 3 Sep 1956.

ARCHIE POTTS

See also: Thomas (Tom) Samuel Fox.

McADAM, John (1806-83)
RADICAL

John McAdam was born at Port Dundas, Glasgow, on 5 August 1806, the son of James McAdam and Helen Baxter. His father, formerly a farmer in Stirlingshire, was then a carter and vintner. McAdam's early working years were spent as apprentice to a shoemaker. In his spare time he joined a book club, and educated himself with the help of the other members, mainly Calton weavers and warpers. When his apprenticeship expired in 1828 he went into business for himself.

Shortly afterwards, he began to agitate for political reform. As the Glasgow United Committee of Trades' delegate for the North West Quarter, he led, according to his own account, 25,000 demonstrators to Glasgow Green in 1832. He took part also in the preparation of the Committee's petition to the House of Commons for repeal of the newspaper stamp duty. In the Committee's journal, the *Herald to the Trades' Advocate*, he argued in favour of the establishment of a general trade union open to individual membership rather than one formed by amalgamation of existing unions. The proposed union under discussion was probably the Glasgow and West of Scotland Association for the Protection of Labour, afterwards known as the General Union of Glasgow, established in 1831 by Alexander Campbell.

In July 1833 McAdam emigrated to Upper Canada and a few years later to the United States. His main occupation in North America appears to have been horse-trading. His autobiography and his letters home tell of his disapproval of the corruption and mismanagement of the Government of Upper Canada and of the condition of the native Indians in both countries. It was during his American stay that he first gave public expression to his sympathy for the oppressed peoples of Europe. At a public meeting in Vicksburg, Mississippi, and in letters to the newspapers, he defended Mazzini and Young Italy against the attacks of the 'Native American' press.

On his return to Glasgow in 1847 McAdam took employment with his brother William, a successful master potter and a member of Glasgow City Council for many years. Soon he was again active in the cause of reform. He found the Glasgow Chartists divided into two groups, those who would limit their activities to moral persuasion and those who preferred more forceful means. He called a meeting of both groups and tried to persuade them of the need for united action, but his efforts were misconstrued as an attempt to create a third party. However, under stress of the European revolutions of 1848, according to McAdam, the extremists of both groups were quietly set aside and a harmonious working unit formed from the remainder. The election of John Moir to the City Council was seen as a triumph for this central group of Chartists.

During the 1850s McAdam's efforts for reform at home merged with his work for European freedom. He and his friends had begun working for Italian and Hungarian independence as early as 1849. The two causes were, in his view, inextricably linked, for only by a wholesome dread of revolution on the Continental pattern could any substantial measure of parliamentary reform be attained at home; and, conversely, the Europeans required the constant support of British public opinion to ensure that their inevitable revolutions were as bloodless and as complete as possible. Kossuth's visit to Glasgow in 1854 encouraged the establishment of a working men's organisation which, under a variety of names and sometimes in loose association with other organisations, existed continuously in Glasgow until the achievement of Italian unification.

Shortly after Kossuth's visit, Jessie Meriton White lectured in Glasgow on behalf of Mazzini. After her lecture a branch of the Italian Emancipation Committee was formed, on which McAdam served actively throughout its existence. Money raised by this Committee was used to finance the unsuccessful expedition by Carlo Pisacane to instigate revolt in Naples in 1857. When two British engineers went on trial at Naples for suspected involvement in this affair, McAdam induced the working engineers of Glasgow to send a petition for their release to the Neapolitan Government.

After the failure of Pisacane's mission and the abortive uprising in Genoa of the same year, Mazzini was much criticised in Britain. McAdam defended him in a pamphlet, *Mazzini vindicated by a Sketch of his Eventful Life and the Struggle for Italian Liberty* (1857). This was addressed to the working classes and was intended not only to persuade them to support Mazzini but also to arouse them out of their 'listless apathy' concerning their own political rights. The one hopeful sign McAdam saw in the political doldrums of 1857 was that a common sympathy for the Italians had held together a nucleus of really active men ready to rally to the cause of manhood suffrage when the time came.

From 1857 McAdam was constantly engaged in collecting funds for European revolutionaries, especially the Italians. Some of the meetings he spoke at were convened by the Glasgow Parliamentary Reform Association to support the various reform proposals being put forward by John Bright. When Garibaldi appealed for 'a million muskets' in 1859, several subscriptions were raised, mostly through McAdam's efforts; and on 1 May 1860, this 'Garibaldi Rifle Fund' was transformed into the Glasgow Garibaldi Italian Fund. By the time the subscription list closed in November 1860 just over £2668 had been raised. Earlier McAdam had decided to start a parallel organisation among working men. Matthew Cullen, a former Chartist, was chairman of the inaugural meeting and McAdam was appointed secretary. He also helped, although somewhat doubtful about its usefulness, to raise money to send Scottish volunteers to enlist in Garibaldi's army; and it was at his suggestion also that the Glasgow Ladies' Garibaldi Benevolent Association for the Relief of the Sick and Wounded was established.

McAdam visited Italy in 1860. He took with him money subscribed by the Glasgow ladies for the sick and wounded and toured the hospitals on their behalf. He went to Salerno, where the Scottish volunteers were by this time attached to the 53rd Regiment of the Sardinian army while awaiting discharge. From the money allocated for this purpose by the Glasgow Garibaldi Fund Committee, he supplied the men returning home with clothing and gave 'handsome uniform tunics' to the twelve who elected to enrol for a further term of service with the Sardinians. Then he visited Garibaldi at Caprera and extended to him the Garibaldi Fund Committee's invitation for a tour of Britain.

After the establishment of the Kingdom of Italy in 1861, McAdam continued to support Mazzini in his plans for the liberation of Rome and Venice, and he served on the Garibaldi Italian Unity Committee. Along with Mazzini, he took up the cause of the Polish revolutionaries in 1863. During the later years of his life, McAdam continued to correspond with Mazzini, Garibaldi, Kossuth, Louis Blanc, Karl Blind, and other protagonists of European liberty, advising them and smoothing out differences between them. His work did not go unappreciated. Kossuth referred to him in his *Memories of my Exile* as holding 'the first place amongst my Glasgow friends', and Mazzini and Garibaldi were lavish in their praise. In token of their gratitude for his services to their country, some anonymous Italians left £220 and a bottle of Italian wine at his house when he died.

McAdam's advocacy of a further extension of the suffrage led him to support those parliamentary candidates or members who shared his beliefs. Both before and after the passing of the second Reform Act he was a leading member of many Liberal parliamentary election committees in Glasgow, especially those of Robert Dalglish and George Anderson. Municipal affairs also occupied a generous share of McAdam's time and energies. He served on the twelfth ward committee, and was its chairman for many years.

McAdam belonged to the Church of Scotland and attended the old Barony Church, Cathedral Square, Glasgow. He had married Mary McIntyre, the daughter of William McIntyre, a well-known market gardener, on 12 December 1851. They had ten children, Jane (1852-1909), James (1854-1921), Mary (1856-7), William (1858-1916), Robert (1859-1931), Alex Whyte (1861-1902), Joseph Mazzini (1863-5), Walter (1866-1935), and the twins, Menotti Garibaldi (1869-1936) and John Chambers (1869-1937). James had business interests associated with the Forth and Clyde Canal. Robert was editor of *Titbits*, Walter an artist of some note, and Menotti Garibaldi a chartered accountant.

Owing to the failure of his brother's pottery business, McAdam was during his last years in reduced circumstances. He died on 18 November 1883, and was buried in the Old Burial Ground of Glasgow Cathedral. Special permission had to be obtained since by that date the Ground was officially closed. No will has been located.

Writings: 'On a Unity of Trades', *Herald to the Trades' Advocate*, *29*, 9 Apr 1831, 457; *Mazzini vindicated by a Sketch of his Eventful Life, and the Struggle for Italian Liberty* (Glasgow, 1857) 16 pp.

Sources: (1) MSS: McAdam MSS (including unpublished autobiography), Bedlay Castle, Chryston, Glasgow; Mazzini Coll., Glasgow Univ. Library; occasional references in Cowen Coll., Tyne and Wear CRO, Newcastle upon Tyne; occasional references in Curatulo MSS, Museo del Risorgimento, Milan, Italy. (2) Other: L. Kossuth, *Memories of my Exile* (NY, 1880); D.F. Mackay, 'The Influence of the Italian Risorgimento on British Public Opinion' (Oxford DPhil., 1959); D.F. Mackay, 'Joseph Cowen e il Risorgimento', *Rassegna Storica del Risorgimento 51* (1964) 5-26; E. Terra, 'Le Patate Scozzesi di Giuseppe Garibaldi', *Gazzettino* [Venezia], 7 febbraio 1965; E. Terra, 'Preziosi Documenti inediti. Lettere di Giuseppe Garibaldi a uno Scozzese amico dell'Italia', *Gazzettino* [Venezia], 19 marzo 1965, also published under the pseudonym of 'Diplomaticus' as 'Ad un Amico Scozzese Garibaldi chiedeva i Fucili per la Causa Italiana', *Voce Republicana*, 25 marzo 1965; E. Morelli, *L'Inghilterra di Mazzini* (Rome, 1965); J. Fyfe, 'Scotland and the Risorgimento' (Guelph PhD, 1976); biographical information: Dr A. Wilson, Manchester Univ.; personal information: Captain Alex McAdam, grandson, Chryston, Glasgow. OBIT. *Evening Times* [Glasgow], 19 Nov 1883; *Glasgow Herald* and *North British Daily Mail*, 20 Nov 1883.

JANET FYFE

McBAIN, John McKenzie (1882-1941)
TRADE UNIONIST AND COMMUNIST

John McBain was born in Edinburgh on 27 August 1882, the son of Margaret McBain, a domestic servant. Of his father no details are known. McBain spent his young life in Elgin where he began his apprenticeship but soon moved to western Glasgow, and then, when he had served his time, to the eastern end of the city.

Jock McBain, as he was always called, was a large, powerful man, and in his youth a keen wrestler. An injury forced him to abandon the sport and his energies were turned towards the trade union and labour movement. On 5 February 1906 he became a member of the Glasgow Eastern branch of the Associated Iron Moulders of Scotland. He lived in Parkhead, then a lively centre of working-class politics. He was at first a member of the ILP but later, under the influence of Tom Bell, joined the Socialist Labour Party. Bell recounts how Jock McBain attended his study classes in an old hand-loom weaver's outhouse in Dalmarnock Street, Parkhead [Bell (1941) 134]. McBain, like so many Glasgow militants in the SLP, became an active worker/tutor, developed a powerful platform style, and gained valuable organising experience within his union. He lectured regularly under the auspices of the Scottish Labour College.

Prior to the amalgamation of the foundry unions, McBain was elected to the executive committee of the AIMS. He campaigned consistently for amalgamation, which was realised in 1920 with the formation of the National Union of Foundry Workers. But before this, McBain had played an active part in the industrial movement on Clydeside during the war years. After the deportations of many of the leading militants of the Clyde Workers' Committee in 1916, McBain was among those who kept the Committee alive, mainly as a fund-raising organisation for the deportees [Hinton (1973) 248]. During 1917, together with Tom Bell, Jim Gardner and others, McBain led a movement for workshop organisation in the Scottish foundries. In August 1917 an emergency committee was established and on 13 September Scottish foundry workers came out on a three weeks' unofficial strike. When the workers went back, in good order, the emergency committee remained in being, and for the next two years, working closely with the Clyde Workers' Committee, it led all the rank-and-file activities among the Scottish foundry workers [ibid., 251]. McBain was also involved in the political actions of these years, and was injured in the famous 'Battle of George Square' at the end of January 1919.

He became a founder member of the Communist Party in 1920. He seems to have been out of work at this period and organised mainly among the unemployed, but in September 1922 he was appointed by the NUFW as temporary organiser for Scotland and Northern Ireland – on the occasion of the death of J. Whyte – and early in November he was confirmed in the position. At the beginning of the General Strike in 1926 he was chairman of the Glasgow Central Strike Co-ordination Committee, being succeeded after a few days by Peter Kerrigan in order to devote himself more fully to his own union activity [Kerrigan (1976) 321]. He was a member of the Minority Movement from its foundation in 1924, the Glasgow members of which met in the back room of a newsagents and bookshop in Shuttle Street, owned by an old Socialist called McGill.

As the years went by, McBain took an increasingly prominent part in the national affairs of the Foundry Workers' Union. In 1928, against strong opposition from the union's Rules Revision Committee, McBain, together with the two Scottish delegates to that Committee, established a district committee for Scotland. This operated on a voluntary basis, but none the less succeeded in drawing in representatives from a wide range of branches. McBain was elected secretary of the new committee, and despite a rather slow start, its influence expanded throughout the thirties. It played a leading role in a number of major disputes – for example in the Cathcart dispute, 1932, against the 'open shop' and in Blackness Shop, Dundee, on the same issue. Moreover the Scottish district committee provided a model which was emulated in other areas, strengthening the position of rank-and-file members within the union.

The NUFW was burdened with debt for almost the whole of the inter-war period. The Scottish District Committee, of which McBain was secretary, led a vigorous campaign for financial reconstruction, and produced a pamphlet, *Stability or Drift – Which?*, arguing the case for unified grading and reduced superannuation payments in order to keep the union solvent. Criticisms that his scheme was unworkable provoked McBain to bring out another pamphlet on the subject and the conflict between himself and the three assistant secretaries of the NUFW became so acute that McBain was threatened with legal action for libel – a threat which was not fulfilled and which in any case had no effect on McBain, who continued to publicise his case. His ideas on financial matters were to provide the basis for reorganisation at a later date.

The rise of Nazi Germany and the growing threat of war found McBain arguing strongly the Communist line during the second half of the 1930s. In his New Year message for 1937, McBain told his Scottish members that 'against the solid front of his enemies the only weapon which the worker can effectively wield is the "United Front" and it is to this end we should concentrate' [Fyrth and Collins (1959) 226].

After a short illness he died on 28 January 1941. At the time of his death Jock McBain had become one of the best loved and most respected Scottish trade unionists. He was a militant and skilled negotiator; somewhat dour-looking but a kindly man and utterly dependable. The funeral took place at Maryhill Crematorium on 31 January and was attended by many foundry workers, including the general secretary and many of his other union and political friends and colleagues. Mr Andrew Fleming conducted the farewell service. Jock McBain was survived by a wife and son.

Writings: *Stability or Drift – Which? Proposed Financial Scheme* (NUFW District Committee, District no. 1, 1930-1) 8 pp.; *Stability or Drift – Which? Reply of District Committee no. 1 to the observations of your three assistant secretaries* (NUFW District Committee, District no. 1, 1931) 6 pp.

Sources: (1) MSS: AUEW (Foundry section) MSS 41: MRC, Warwick Univ. [This includes McBain's reports as organiser]. (2) Other: W. Gallacher, *Revolt on the Clyde* (1936); T. Bell, *Pioneering Days* (1941); H. Fyrth and H. Collins, *The Foundry Workers* (Manchester, 1959); J. Hinton, *The First Shop Stewards' Movement* (1973); P. Kerrigan, 'From Glasgow' in *The General Strike, 1926* ed. J. Skelley (1976); personal information: the late Peter Kerrigan, London. OBIT. NUFW, *Journal and Report* (Jan 1941); *Glasgow Eastern Standard*, 8 Feb 1941; *World News and Views*, 21, no. 7, 15 Feb 1941; T. Bell, *Biographical Appreciation of Bro. John McBain* (NUFW, 1941).

JANET DRUKER
JOHN SAVILLE

McELWEE, Andrew (1882-1968)
TRADE UNIONIST AND LABOUR MP

Andrew McElwee was born on 24 December 1882 at Gortaway, Rametton, Donegal, the son of Andrew McElwee, a farmer and carpenter and his wife Margaret (née Lockhart). Little is known about his early life. He became a woodworker, the same occupation as his father, grandfather and great-grandfather. He is reported to have been a joiner in Belfast in 1909 but he was certainly in Clydeside for some time for he was admitted to the first Clydebank branch of the Amalgamated Society of Woodworkers in 1907. In his early twenties he went to America, where he worked for two years in the eastern states before going on to South Africa for eighteen months. After a short spell again on Clydeside he returned to the U.S.A.; but was back in Scotland by 1919. While in America he had become an active trade unionist and on his return he was elected to the Clyde District Committee of the ASW.

In 1919, when he was living in Dalmuir, Dunbartonshire, he was co-opted to the Dunbartonshire Education Authority and became chairman of one of its standing committees. He held several other positions connected with educational administration; and he retained an abiding concern with educational affairs. McElwee was also involved in local politics; he was secretary of Dumbarton and Clydebank Divisional Labour Party in 1919 and by 1929 its chairman.

For some time before the 1923 general election he was full-time political agent for David Kirkwood but then gave it up to fight the Hulme division of Manchester, sponsored by the ASW. He entered the contest very late and came bottom of the poll, but there was general agreement that he had made a great impression on the electorate. He had clearly done so within the union, as in the following May he was unanimously elected chairman of the general council, a position he retained for two years. He fought the Hulme seat again in 1924, greatly increasing the vote and finishing above the Liberal candidate, but did not win it until 1929 when he had a majority of two-and-a-half thousand. He was by this time an official of the union's Scottish section.

In the House he spoke on a wide range of subjects including colonial affairs and stag hunting as well as topics connected with his interests in education, his union and his constituency. He made his maiden speech on 22 January 1930 proposing that a Select Committee be set up to consider ways of rationalising the sittings of the Commons. He had been successful in the ballot for Notices of Motion and chose this topic arguing that on grounds of good legislation, the health of members and improved working conditions for all, sittings should begin and end earlier. The motion was seconded by G.D. Hardie, MP for Glasgow Springburn, and after a lively debate was carried by a majority of thirty. A Select Committee was set up and reported but its main recommendations were not implemented.

During his period of office as an MP (1929 to 1931), McElwee's relations with his union became very difficult. On 20 September 1930 he wrote a letter to the *Daily Herald* attacking a campaign about to be launched by the NFBTO on grounds of its excessive expense compared with the return which could be anticipated. This public attack violated union rules and he was suspended in November 1930. In April 1931 he made a hostile reference to the NFBTO in the House of Commons and in November 1931 the ASW *Journal* reported that he had been making 'grotesque and defamatory allegations against the Executive Council'. The article explained that the ASW's income from the political levy had been much reduced from 1929 and that financial support to the union's six sponsored MPs had to be reduced. The article continued: 'Brother McElwee's hostility to control was, and has continued to be, most marked. He has resented every decision and inquiry regarding his position and his political expenditure which the Council in its executive capacity was entitled to make . . . he resorted to charges against the E.C. which he was unable to substantiate though given full opportunity. When called upon to prove his allegations, and on being informed that he would be dealt with in default, he wrote a letter of complete withdrawal and apology. He has now renewed his campaign . . .' [pp. 684-5].

McElwee lost his seat in the landslide general election of 1931, and he continued his defamatory campaign. In early May 1932, at the Manchester Assizes, McElwee pleaded guilty to five charges of criminal libel, and he was bound over for two years in his own recognisances. The charges were brought by Frank Wolstencroft and T.O. Williams, general secretary and assistant secretary respectively of the ASW, and five members of the executive council. The whole episode from 1929 to 1932 is detailed in full in successive issues of the relevant trade journals.

Little is known about his life after 1932. As far as can be discovered he returned to his trade, and the family seems to have lived in Streatham Hill in South London at least from the early 1940s. A neighbour remembered a son, who was killed in Normandy in 1944, living with his parents. This was Captain Andrew McElwee of the Argyll and Sutherland Highlanders. When McElwee was visited just before his death on 18 June 1968 he was living in an old people's home in Streatham, reading Boswell's *Johnson* and full of speculation about the American presidential election of that year. His wife, whom he had married in 1909, died in 1970. There were four children (three daughters and one son) of the marriage. No will has been located.

Sources: (1) MSS: Correspondence and other papers, including copies of the ASW *Monthly Journals*, 1924-6, Nov 1931 and 6 June 1932: MRC, Warwick Univ., Ref. 78/ASW 34 and UCATT 78 (2). Other: *Hansard* (1929-31); *Daily Herald*, 20 Sep 1930; *WW* (1930); *Dod* (1931); *Manchester Guardian*, 3 May 1932; S. Higenbottam, *Our Society's History* [ASW] (Manchester, 1939); biographical information: Ms J. Druker and R. Storey, MRC, Warwick Univ.; the late T.A.K. Elliott, CMG; personal information: B. McHenry, London. The editors wish to acknowledge their indebtedness to Mr McHenry for permission to use his undergraduate essay on McElwee's parliamentary career.

ANN HOLT
JOHN SAVILLE

McGURK, John (1874-1944)
MINERS' LEADER

John McGurk was born at Hoyle Mill, Barnsley, on 17 September 1874, the eldest of the fifteen children of John McGurk, a coalminer, and his wife Hannah (née Lord). Six months later, the family moved to Pendlebury near Manchester, where his father worked in a local colliery and where McGurk went himself at the age of twelve after an elementary education. Later, he attended night school and technical classes. He soon began to be interested in trade union affairs, becoming in time secretary to the Pendlebury branch of the Lancashire and Cheshire Miners' Federation, the delegate to the monthly Federation conference, and an elected member of the Federation executive. In this work he found Pendlebury a useful base since it covered no fewer than thirteen pits.

On 22 February 1908, McGurk became a full-time official of the Federation when he was elected to one of two vacant agencies from a field of seventeen candidates. He was placed in charge of the Federation's North-East Lancashire area, at a salary in the early days of £12 a month; and as a matter of geographical convenience he established his home and office at Bury, where he remained for the rest of his career. His responsibilities covered a wide area extending from Oldham to Burnley, Great Harwood and Accrington. This region was, perhaps, the most moderate and traditional part of the Lancashire coalfield: independent Labour politics developed sluggishly there in contrast with their early and rapid growth in the southern part of the coalfield. McGurk was a diligent and effective worker, and he continued to rise in the Lancashire Federation. As agent, he was now an *ex officio* member of the Lancashire executive; and in 1912 he was elected as the Lancashire representative on the MFGB executive. He held this post on five subsequent occasions, since it was the Lancashire tradition that the position should rotate among the officials.

During the First World War McGurk was a firm supporter of the Allied cause. In January 1916 he was prepared to advocate conscription if the Prime Minister could guarantee that it was essential. The war period also increased McGurk's involvement in Labour Party affairs. In January 1917 he was elected as a miners' representative on the Party's executive committee. He became vice-chairman at this time and chairman in June 1918, presiding over the Party's Southport conference a year later. During his first year on the executive committee he was present at many meetings held to discuss Labour's strategy in the post-war years, although it appears that his role was generally passive. At the beginning of 1918 he was forced to defend the Party's new draft constitution against criticisms from members of the Lancashire Federation, who feared the erosion of trade union control over the Party. McGurk reassured them with his view that, under the new arrangements for electing the executive committee, trade unionists could still dominate:

> The strength of the trade union vote can put twenty trade unionists on. Anyone who has attended the conferences is aware of the wire pulling that goes on [LCMF, special conference, 5 Jan 1918].

With his increased involvement in Labour Party affairs, it is not surprising that McGurk had begun to show interest in the possibility of a political career. His experiences in this regard shed some light on the labyrinthine processes by which affiliated organisations attempted to increase their parliamentary representation in a period of Labour Party growth. In January 1918, the Lancashire Federation reconsidered the future of sponsorship in the light of MFGB's allocation to them of five sponsored candidates. Attempts were made to find a suitable seat for McGurk. Initially these concerned the Clitheroe seat, but here the Federation met the entrenched position of the cotton workers who formed the most significant section of the electorate, had spent considerable money there, and had already decided to nominate a candidate. The Federation prudently shifted its interest to Rossendale as a possible constituency for McGurk, and by April 1918 he had been selected as the prospective Labour candidate. A complication arose, however, although one very different from that in Clitheroe. At a recent by-election a British Socialist Party member, A. Taylor, had stood, (on a 'Peace by Negotiation' platform), and the BSP still maintained an interest in the constituency. In a letter to the national executive, the BSP spokesmen objected to the selection of McGurk on the ground that they had not been invited to the selection conference, while Taylor claimed that he had been adopted by the BSP and intended to fight the seat. This incensed the Lancashire Federation, but after further discussions between the national executive and those involved, the Federation decided to withdraw McGurk from Rossendale in order to avoid a split vote. Later on, in October, McGurk was adopted by the Darwen Labour Party and Trades Council, standing there as a sponsored candidate in both 1918 and 1922. Darwen was a curious constituency for a miners' candidate to fight, being far-flung and partly rural, with a history of close clashes between Liberal and Conservative. It is not surprising, therefore, that in both elections McGurk finished third – polling 23.4 per cent. of the vote in 1918 and only 15.8 per cent. four years later – or that in December 1922 a Federation executive sub-committee recommended withdrawal from the Darwen constituency. Although McGurk was a candidate for the Federation nominations at Farnworth in 1926 and at Ince in 1929, he was not selected. The only elected public office that he ever held as a Labour Party representative was as a Bury councillor for just one three-year period.

During this period of involvement in party affairs, obviously the most publicity attached itself to McGurk's Address from the Chair at the 1919 conference. The most significant feature of this was his attack on 'direct action' – 'an innovation in this country which few responsible leaders would welcome' – and his presentation of parliamentarianism and the Labour Party as the way forward. His support for constitutionalism could be seen also in his actions within his own union: at the MFGB Special Conference in September 1919, he opposed attempts to cast the miners' vote for direct action at the subsequent conference of the Triple Alliance.

In the critical year of 1921, McGurk was one of the Lancashire representatives on the MFGB executive. At first, during the dispute, he advocated the two demands of a National Wages Board and a National Profits Pool as crucial to the future of Lancashire, one of the poorer coalfields. But, he voted with the minority on 'Black Friday' – in favour of going to meet Lloyd George and the coal-owners – although he claimed that his motivation was tactical, to continue the negotiations so as to leave no time for the Triple Alliance to crumble. What was more important, however, was that McGurk had strong reservations about the feasibility of the demand for a National Profits Pool. As early as the second week of the lockout, he told a delegate conference of Lancashire miners, 'if you strike until next Christmas Day, we shall not get a National Pool' [LCMF minutes, 18 Apr 1921] – but the meeting unanimously resolved that both demands should be adhered to. On 16 May 1921, however, the *Manchester Evening News* carried this assertion by McGurk:

> The strike will surely continue unless some consideration is given to the idea of dropping the National Pool. As soon as the Miners' Federation realise this fact, the better it will be for the whole industry.

This public disavowal of a central plank of MFGB and Lancashire policy produced a storm. A motion of protest was moved at a delegate conference on 28 May, but was amended to a motion of censure by seventy-nine votes to seventy-six. The target was not only McGurk but also the veteran Thomas Ashton, who had made a similar statement. One month later, with the stoppage drawing to a close, an attempt was made – unsuccessfully – to rescind the censure motion. Subsequently, McGurk read out his resignation, which was not accepted, although a second attempt at rescindment of the censure failed at the end of July. Only at the Lancashire Federation's annual conference in January 1922 was the censure annulled. McGurk's public position had produced a serious rift between himself and the rank and file. At this period Lancashire was one of the more militant coalfields, being the only large one to vote for rejection, of the MFGB executive's terms at the end of June 1921. On this issue McGurk kept in step with the rank and file, strenuously opposing the majority position in the MFGB executive.

In spite of the friction created by his disavowal of the National Pool, McGurk's stature grew inside the Lancashire Federation after 1921. The Lancashire attitude to the 1921 settlement led to his appearing at the national level as an advocate of a more forward policy. In Lancashire, he was elected vice-president in January 1924, in succession to Stephen Walsh; and although he did not get the post, he was the Lancashire nominee for the MFGB secretaryship when Frank Hodges resigned.

McGurk's moderately radical position was suggested early in the 1926 dispute, at the MFGB conference of 9 April, when he appeared to desire some strengthening of the executive resolution. At first, Lancashire refrained from voting on the MFGB executive resolution, but it subsequently voted in order to produce unanimity [Arnot (1953) 408]. McGurk's most notable appearance in the stoppage was at the TUC in September 1926, where he played the leading part in the attempt by some of the miners' delegation to shout down John Bromley of the locomotive men when the latter rose to second the resolution on the coal stoppage. Bromley had been publicly critical of the miners' leaders, and the choice of him as seconder was seen by several miners' delegates as an insult. Eventually McGurk was alleged to have shouted that the General Council were 'cowards and traitors', and he was ordered by the chairman, Arthur Pugh, to leave the Congress. This decision was withdrawn, however, after a break in the proceedings during which McGurk and W.P. Richardson met Pugh and Citrine, and Bromley was allowed to speak [LCMF conference, *Minutes*, 11 Sep 1926].

After this emotional scene McGurk played a major part in attempting to salvage something from the wreckage in Lancashire: he strongly advocated a settlement for the whole district as the only alternative to a slow drift back to work with settlements at individual collieries. Yet a tendency in him to stand out against the moderate wave which followed the collapse of the stoppage appeared in the autumn of 1927, when he opposed the MFGB acceptance of the 'contracting in' proposals within the Trades Disputes Bill.

In April 1929, McGurk was elected president of the Lancashire and Cheshire Miners, a position that he was to hold for almost fifteen years. In 1932-3 he was on the General Council of the TUC. During the early 1930s, though aware of the difficult situation of his own members, he nevertheless continued to be something of a thorn in the flesh of some of the miners' national leaders: for example, he complained about the timidity in their conduct of the 1935 National Wages Campaign. Three years earlier he had been an unsuccessful candidate for the MFGB presidency, coming third in the vote behind Peter Lee and Herbert Smith. Although firmly at the top of the Lancashire organisation, he never acquired the same prominence nationally.

Perhaps his adoption of a comparatively militant industrial line at this time was encouraged by a feeling that he was an outsider, although his specifically political statements were rooted firmly in a loyalty to the Labour Party. He refused vehemently to have anything to do with proposals for Popular or United Fronts. To some extent this reflected a distaste for 'Communism'. At the 1936 MFGB conference, he came into bitter conflict with Arthur Horner on the question of Communist affiliation to the Labour Party. His most vehement comments however, were reserved for Sir Stafford Cripps as an electoral handicap, someone likely to travel in the same direction as Sir Oswald Mosley. These views became the subject of a protest from the MFGB executive after a speech by McGurk at the 1937 Labour conference. It is clear that he objected to Cripps and Laski, not merely because of their political views, but also because of the type of people that they were:

> Sir Stafford Cripps is a rich man with rich pals around him, and they are the biggest danger to the Labour Party in this country [*Labour Party Report* (1937) 160].

Although politically on the moderate wing of the Labour Party, he had a highly developed class consciousness. While, especially in later life, he spoke the rhetoric of Socialism, his attachment to the Labour Party owed almost everything to that organisation's role as the guardian of working-class and more particularly of trade union interests.

Although he remained Lancashire president until January 1944, McGurk's health began to fail soon after the outbreak of war and he gradually relinquished his dominance in Lancashire. However, his closing years witnessed another personal crisis paralleling that of June 1921. This originated in the proposed introduction of compulsion into the mining industry in the shape of an

Essential Work Order. Although McGurk opposed this on the MFGB executive, when the issue came before the Lancashire delegates in June 1941, he refused to accept a resolution that Pit Production Committees do not co-operate and collaborate in the functioning of the Essential Work Order. Once again, as twenty years earlier, the coalfield erupted. Ten resolutions attacking his conduct of the meeting were tabled for the next delegate conference, with only four motions in support. On 28 June 1941, a Lancashire delegates' conference carried by 429 votes to 301 a vote of censure on McGurk and asked for his resignation. McGurk did not stand and fight the issue through as he had done in 1921. Instead he apologised and asked to be allowed an appeal to the next delegate conference. This was permitted, and the vote of censure was rescinded. After this McGurk played a diminishing role in Lancashire affairs although he was a Bury County magistrate. He was plagued by ill health and also distressed by the death of his wife Eliza. She was a keen Labour Party worker in Bury, and a devout Anglican. There were two daughters of the marriage. Mrs McGurk died in July 1943. Not long after, McGurk resigned his presidency as from 8 January 1944. In September 1944 he retired from his agent's post on reaching the age limit of seventy. He died in Bury on 22 November 1944 leaving effects valued at £1255.

McGurk's methods were often unorthodox and his reactions sometimes owed much more to emotion than to conscious strategic considerations. In his handling of delegate meetings he was often accused of authoritarianism, but usually his behaviour showed considerable sensitivity to the feelings of the rank and file. He had a reputation for being quick-tempered, and the records of the Lancashire Federation contain several references to what one critic delicately described as 'language not becoming to a person of his standing'. In some ways, he was a characteristic trade union leader of his generation. He had a reputation as a hard but flexible negotiator and appears to have learnt much under the tutelage of Thomas Ashton. Politically, he was a moderate Labour Party member, committed to the advancement of the interests of organised labour rather than the pursuit of any abstract principles; a patriot and a dedicated opponent of 'Bolshevism'.

Sources: LCMF, *Minutes:* NUM, Bolton; LP executive cttee, *Minutes* (1917-19): Labour Party archives; LP, *Conference Reports* (1919), (1937); *Manchester Evening News*, 16 May 1921; *Labour Who's Who* (1924); R. Page Arnot, *The Miners: years of struggle* (1953); idem, *The Miners in Crisis and War* (1961). OBIT. *Manchester Guardian*, 23 Nov 1944; *Bury Times*, 25 Nov 1944; *TUC Report* (1945).

DAVID HOWELL

See also: †Thomas ASHTON, for Mining Trade Unionism, 1900-14; †Arthur James COOK, for Mining Trade Unionism, 1915-26; †Peter LEE, for Mining Trade Unionism, 1927-44; †Stephen WALSH.

McKEE, George William (1865-1949)
TRADE UNION LEADER

George William McKee was born on 6 January 1865 at 9 Adelaide Street, West Hull, the son of William McKee, a master shoemaker and his wife Ann (née Brown). Chapel was an important influence on his early life as his father was also a lay preacher and his mother remained a devout chapelgoer until her death in her nineties. McKee first went to sea in 1886 and by 1900 was working as a donkeyman on the east coast routes. In 1891 he married Clara Sampson and they had two sons, George and Edmund.

In 1902 he became a full-time official of the Hull Seamen's and Marine Firemen's Amalgamated Association, working as assistant to the general secretary, J.B. Butcher. The local union had remained more or less intact after the strike of 1893 and its consistently moderate policies had continued to earn it the co-operation of local shipowners. Membership was mainly confined to those employed on short regular voyages and weekly boats and this also reduced the difficult problems always associated with the organisation of seamen. For a decade after 1893 relations with Havelock Wilson's National Sailors' and Firemen's Union were unfriendly and uncooperative, but in the strikes of 1911 the two unions began to work together, and this, according to McKee's later statements, was always one of his objectives when he became a union official.

He succeeded J.B. Butcher in 1912, and his insistence that no union could stand alone began to find organisational expression. The Hull union became a member of the National Transport Workers' Federation, and McKee was especially enthusiastic about the steps being taken in the spring of 1914 that were to lead to the establishment of the Triple Industrial Alliance. His advocacy of trade unity was always, however, moderate in intention. He told his own union in the summer of 1914: 'There is one fact which members must not lose sight of: Our aim is **Defence** not Defiance' [*Report* of Hull Seamen's Union, 30 June 1914]. McKee also made tentative approaches to Havelock Wilson in the early part of 1914 about the possibility of amalgamation with the national union, and this was a subject discussed regularly at the time at branch meetings. Nothing came of these initiatives and McKee's union changed its name to Hull Seamen's Union in the summer of 1914, having much increased its membership among the fishermen sailing from the port.

The outbreak of war shelved amalgamation plans. McKee, and the Hull union in general, do not seem to have been as enthusiastic about the war as were Havelock Wilson and the NSFU. Hull seamen supported the local Labour paper, the *Dawn*, run by Sydney Smith and other left-wing members of the movement; and McKee was also against his own sons volunteering for active service. They disregarded his advice: George was killed in 1915, and Edmund was seriously wounded on the Somme in 1917.

The war brought many problems to the seafaring unions, among them the widespread employment of semi-skilled or Asiatic labour. It also brought great suffering and hardship to seamen. Submarine warfare aroused great bitterness, and McKee himself was deeply affected by what he described as 'murder on the high seas'. One political consequence was that he became opposed to the idea of an early peace, especially one without compensation for seamen. He and his union fully supported Havelock Wilson's refusal to allow Ramsay MacDonald and others to visit Petrograd in 1917. McKee was made a JP during these war years.

McKee became a member of the new national tripartite board – the National Maritime Board – representative of the shipowners, unions and government, which was established in 1917; under the 1919 constitution of the Board the Hull Seamen's Union was a full constituent. In the same year McKee was a member of the executive committee of the NTWF and Triple Alliance, the Seafarers' Joint Council, the Standing Joint Committee of the Pension Fund for Seamen and the secretariat of the International Seafarers' Federation. At this time the rank and file of his own union appear to have been well satisfied with his work on their behalf, for a monthly meeting in June 1920 passed a resolution expressing gratitude and appreciation for his efforts and he was presented with the sum of £25 from union funds.

During 1920 the question of amalgamation was pushed strongly by McKee. He encountered opposition from his more militant members who were critical of both Havelock Wilson's national union and their own. In late December 1920 their spokesman, W. Ridley, wrote a vigorously-worded open letter to McKee, and this precipitated a bitter quarrel between the militants, who formed themselves into a Vigilance Committee, and the Hull Seamen's Union executive. Two militants were expelled, and a ballot of the Hull membership on the amalgamation issue in April 1921 voted 986 to 150 in favour. The two unions amalgamated at the end of March 1922, and McKee took over as Humber District secretary of the NSFU.

There was still some local opposition to him, and this was investigated in April 1923 by the national executive. A sub-committee reported that there was no proof that McKee had been negligent in his duties, although Havelock Wilson added his comment in the discussion that he had been to Hull and felt that McKee should get out among his members more.

It was at the end of November 1925 that G.W. McKee decided to retire at the age of sixty-one and on his retirement he was presented with a chiming clock by members of the Trawler Section. He remained in his union-owned house in Withernsea until 1929 and his widowed daughter-in-law became his housekeeper after his wife's death in 1926. In 1929, after winning a large amount of money in a national crossword competition, he bought a house in Seahouses, Northumberland, his daughter-in-law's home village, and registered it in her name, retaining only a £5 investment. He continued to be active, though his health was not good, and took an interest in the local co-operative society. He remained a trustee of the Hull Widows' and Orphans' Fund and used to travel to Hull twice a year for meetings, until he resigned in September 1936. He is also remembered for help he gave fishermen in Northumberland in various ways and as a widely read man able to talk on a variety of subjects. In his later years he appears to have had a particular interest in spiritualism and held seances.

McKee visited Hull regularly until the early 1940s when a heart attack prevented him travelling and he died on 5 February 1949 and left £92 gross to his daughter-in-law Nellie McKee. He was cremated in Newcastle, and there was no mention of his death in the Hull newspapers. His son Edmund was a clerk for the Hull Seamen's Union and later for the National Union of Seamen, and died in January 1977.

Sources: (1) MSS: Minutes of the NSFU executive meetings, 1920-6: NUS. (2) Other: Hull Seamen's Union, *Half-yearly Reports*, 30 June 1914 and Dec 1920: NUS; *Hansard*, 14 July 1915; *Minutes of National Maritime Board*, meetings 1917-22: Brynmor Jones Library, Hull Univ.; *Dawn* (July 1915); *Eastern Morning News*, 7 and 11 June 1917; *Hull News*, 7 and 21 Feb 1920; B. Mogridge, 'Militancy and Inter-Union Rivalries in British Shipping, 1911-1929', *Int. Rev. Social Hist. 6*, pt 3 (1961) 375-412; P.S. Bagwell, 'The Triple Industrial Alliance, 1913-1922', in *Essays in Labour History* vol. *2: 1886-1923*, ed. A. Briggs and J. Saville (1971) 96-128; personal information: E. McKee, Hull, son; N.W. Robinson, great-grandson.

NORMAN W. ROBINSON

See also: †James Benjamin BUTCHER.

MACPHERSON, John Thomas (1872-1921)
TRADE UNIONIST AND LABOUR MP

John Macpherson was born at 4 Spring Gardens, Poplar, on 10 October 1872, the elder son of Hugh Macpherson, iron and steel worker, and his wife Rebecca (née Luke). In the following year the Phoenix Ironworks in Millwall, at which Hugh Macpherson was employed, closed down, and Hugh migrated northwards, first to Sheffield, then to Workington, and finally to Middlesbrough, where the family settled. After an elementary education in several different schools, John started work at the age of twelve in the North-Eastern Steel Works, Middlesbrough. Three years later he moved to join his father at the works of Dorman, Long & Co., where he remained until he was eighteen. John Macpherson had been brought up in a home where (to use his own words) 'the whole of the talk was of steel, iron, and Trade Unionism' [*Pearson's Weekly*, 1 Mar 1906]. He was soon involved in trade union actitivies at Dorman, Long's, for which he was dismissed and blacked among local employers. Finding himself unable to practise his trade in Middlesbrough, he went to sea as a fireman. In the course of the next two years he visited India, Burma, the U.S.A., and a number of European ports. It may have been his observations during this period which led him, when the Boer War broke out, to oppose it, although his younger brother fought in the British forces. A few years later John Macpherson asserted that the war was fought so that the capitalists might introduce Chinese labour into the mines. Macpherson was never anything of a pacifist, however, but supported the policy of keeping up a strong army and navy.

On returning to Middlesbrough he found work as a steel smelter at his old firm of Dorman,

Long. In 1899 he married Catherine Ann MacArthur, whose father had been a master mariner, but had left the sea to settle down as a steel smelter in Middlesbrough. The MacArthur family were people of some education; Catherine and her mother were a constant help to John Macpherson in his intellectual progress. Indeed, John spoke of his mother-in-law as 'probably the greatest friend that ever entered my life. Well-educated herself, she was never too weary or tired to help me and she opened up many avenues, along which I trod and continue to tread today' [Pearson's Weekly, 1 March 1906]. As a basis for his progress, his union was to send him for a year's study at Ruskin College (then Ruskin Hall) in January 1903.

When Macpherson came back to work at Dorman, Long's, he had resumed his trade union activities. He became president of the Middlesbrough branch of the British Steel Smelters' Association, and a delegate to the Middlesbrough Trades Council, and in January 1899 he was appointed as the union's first organising secretary. He took up his duties in February. Macpherson was an energetic worker, as his reports to the Association show. In the business of establishing new branches and enrolling new members he was particularly successful in South Wales, where the Association had just undertaken to organise the tinplate workers, who had no union of their own. By the end of July 1899 the membership of BSSA had increased by over two thousand. The burden of organising workers in a number of different sections of the iron and steel trade over an area stretching from South Wales to South Scotland was too much for one man, and over the following years more organisers were appointed: the first to join Macpherson was Thomas Suffill.

In the autumn of 1899 Macpherson was busy organising an industrial struggle at Mossend works in Lanarkshire, mills owned by the Neilsons, 'the most vindictive anti-trade union employer in the Scottish iron and steel industry' [Pugh (1951) 217]. A branch of the Steel Smelters had been formed at Mossend in August and a not unexpected train of events followed: dismissals, a strike, evictions, the introduction of blacklegs from Graeme Hunter's Free Labour Association; arrests, fines, and gaol sentences; also, on the other hand, widespread moral and financial support for the strikers in the West of Scotland. The strike dragged on to a virtual stalemate in 1901, when the union called it off. It cost Neilsons a great deal in low output, wasted material, damaged machinery and products returned as sub-standard. It cost the union £30,000 [Pugh (1951) 117]. About this time Macpherson seems to have been appointed assistant secretary of the union – in the monthly reports for 1900 he has this title, but from January 1902 (perhaps earlier), he had reverted to being 'organising secretary'. The general secretary, John Hodge, had been an enthusiastic supporter of the LRC since its foundation in 1900, and had (unsuccessfully) contested Gower as LRC candidate in that year. In February 1902 Preston LRC invited John Macpherson to be its parliamentary candidate, and his union agreed. Four years later, Hodge and he were conducting election campaigns in Gorton and Preston respectively. From the election reports in the local press, it would seem that Macpherson campaigned mainly on the issue of Free Trade; there was hardly any other political or industrial issue mentioned in his speeches. Preston, a two-member seat and a Tory stronghold for the preceding forty-one years, was won by a Labour and a Liberal candidate, Macpherson topping the poll with 10,181 votes and the Liberal Harold Cox following with 8538; the two Unionists were defeated.

Macpherson spoke in the House several times during the session of 1906-7, but he made no great impression. One of his actions during this period is worth noting. In 1909 the strike at Ruskin College led to the establishment of the breakaway Central Labour College. A smallish group of Labour MPs strongly encouraged and supported the CLC; they included George Barker, Joseph Pointer, and John Macpherson.

Macpherson failed to hold his Preston seat in the January 1910 election. He was attacked during the election for his passive record at Westminster, although the sectarian issue of schooling played a major part in his defeat, a large section of the Irish Catholic population voting against him. When the union executive decided that their funds could not support more than one candidate in the next few months, Macpherson seems to have put away parliamentary ambitions.

In February 1916 the executive council of BSSA decided to rearrange their organising work.

Macpherson was asked to move from the North East and to become responsible for the Northern district (Workington, Cumberland and as far east as Barrow). Relations between Macpherson and his executive were apparently unhappy, at this time and probably much earlier, for Macpherson seems to have had his share of vanity and self-assertion. The decision to move him from the North East, where he had lived and worked for a great part of his life, may have acted on Macpherson as a final goad. At all events he declined to leave the North East, and resigned his office: 'an unfortunate ending to seventeen years' service', as the official history put it. The author was Arthur Pugh, and he continued:

> Yet, it had for some time been evident that 'Mac's' service was deteriorating and the proposal to remove him to the West coast was not unassociated with reports that had come from his district. Moreover, he had not succeeded as assistant secretary in the early years of his appointment, nor later as a member of the House of Commons. He did not seem able to get down to 'the daily toil, the common task'. Bohemian in temperament his character tended to instability, yet he had some desirable qualities. He had a charming personality, a fine voice, and on the platform he was capable of moving eloquence. Had he chosen to apply himself to that line of activity he could, no doubt, have made his mark [*Men of Steel* (1951) 195].

After this, Macpherson seems to have taken no interest in the trade union and labour movement. He had not made a success of his career in it, and he may have felt both tired and embittered. During the First World War, after his departure from the union, he worked for Armstrong Whitworth, as a foreman in the shell shed.

Macpherson was by religion a Free Methodist. Although he had read economics at Ruskin College, the books he listed as having had the greatest influence on him are not books on economics. They are Ruskin's *Unto this Last*, Carlyle's *Heroes and Hero Worship* and the *French Revolution*; the works of Herbert Spencer and Charles Darwin, and of poets: Keats and Byron, Tennyson and Browning, Omar Khayyam, and Lowell. His novel reading reached below Dickens, Hardy and Meredith to Hall Caine and Edna Lyall.

Macpherson died on 2 July 1921 at the home of his sister, Mrs Elizabeth Ann Mays, at Carlin House, Saltburn-on-Sea. He was buried in Brotton Cemetery. No will has been located.

Writings: 'How I got on', *Pearson's Weekly,* 1 Mar 1906.

Sources: *Monthly Reports* of British Steel Smelters' Amalgamated Association, 31 Oct 1898 – Feb 1916 *passim*; *Rev. of Revs 33,* no. 6 (1906); *Preston Guardian,* 13 Jan 1906 [with portrait]; *Hansard,* 25 June 1907; *Dod* (1909); *Preston Herald,* 1, 8, 15, 22 Jan 1910 and 3 Dec 1910; British Steel Smelters' Mill, Iron and Tinplate Workers' Association, *Macpherson v. Beadle. The Truth about the Controversy* (Middlesbrough, 1912); [A. Pugh], *Men of Steel* (1951); W.W. Craik, *The Central Labour College 1909-29* (1964); biographical information: R.H. Clayton, ISTC, London; personal information: C. Featherstone, Skelton, great nephew; C. May, Skelton, nephew. Obit. *J. of ISTC* (Aug 1921).

MARGARET 'ESPINASSE

See also: †John HODGE.

MELL, Robert (1872?-1941)
TRADE UNIONIST AND LABOUR ALDERMAN

No details of Robert Mell's early life have been found, although there is a record of the birth of a Robert Mell on 26 June 1872 at Kilpinpike, near Howden, East Yorkshire, the son of Thomas Mell, a labourer, and his wife, Sarah Ann (née Wilby). Mell is known to have come to Hull in

1887 and secured employment on the railway, eventually becoming an engine driver. He joined the ASRS, was a delegate to the AGMs at Glasgow in 1908 and Barry in 1910, and he served on a number of deputations, national as well as local. He was much influenced by the ideas of the Plebs League, and became an advocate of industrial unionism. He was an enthusiastic supporter of the National Union of Railwaymen, officially inaugurated on 29 March 1913; and he became corresponding secretary of Hull No. 2 branch.

The Labour Party in Hull dates its beginnings from 1911, when the decision was taken that all working-class representatives should vote as a single group on the City Council. Some of the older Trades Council stalwarts – Francis Askew, T.G. Hall, Watson Boyes, Herbert Dean and R.H. Farrah – refused to accept the ruling, and for some time the Hull newspapers referred to them as the 'Labour representation', to distinguish them from the 'Socialists' of the new Labour Party. In the name of the Labour Party, committees were formed in every ward, and in 1912 it was decided that Dr Webster should contest North Newington in the local elections, and that Mell should stand for South Newington, where Webster had been several times unsuccessful. Mell's election programme was similar to that of other Labour candidates: fair wages, improved housing and sanitation, and schools – including the need for playgrounds. Mell's opponent was T.G. Hall, a staunch trade unionist and ex-president of the Trades Council who, by this time, was a Conservative in politics. Mell lost by only 101 votes. In the following year he stood again and this time was successful. His campaign was very lively: a copy of the *Dawn* (the new Labour Party monthly which began in April 1913) was placed in every house in South Newington, and Mell especially concentrated his attention upon the attitudes and policies of the local Poor Law Guardians. The result was a considerable victory, and while Mell became the sixth Labour member on the Council, he was the first to be elected since the formation of the new Labour Party in 1911.

He remained a councillor until 1929, when he was elected an alderman. He was never leader of the Hull Labour Party, although by the end of the 1920s he was its senior member on the Council, and in 1930-1 became the first Labour Lord Mayor of the town. It was Mell who first suggested the name 'Ferensway' for one of Hull's new thoroughfares, in memory of the former High Steward of Hull, T.R. Ferens, who died in 1930. Mell was chairman of the mental hospital committee and of a special inquiry committee into land purchases; he was also deputy chairman of the Queen's Dock committee. Although one of his favourite phrases from his pre-war days was 'I am a class-conscious man', he was never very far, throughout his political career, from an orthodox Labour position. He continued working on the LNER, where eventually he became locomotive superintendent, and he remained active in the NUR.

The local elections of 1938 gave the Independents (*sc.* Conservatives) a majority on the council, and Mell and Alderman Dr Webster were deposed. In the subsequent by-election Mell was defeated, and neither he nor Webster ever tried for office again. For his remaining few years Mell relaxed in the pubs and clubs he knew so well. He died in his council house on 11 November 1941, aged sixty-nine. His funeral service was at the Church of the Ascension, Priory Road, and he was buried in the Western Cemetery. He was survived by two sons and two daughters and left effects worth £728.

Sources: *Election Address* (1912); *Dawn* (Oct 1913) and (Mar 1914); *Hull Times,* 7 May 1932. OBIT. *Hull Daily Mail,* 11 and 15 Nov 1941; *Hull Times,* 15 Nov 1941.

RAYMOND BROWN

MILLIGAN, George Jardine (1868-1925)
DOCK LABOURER AND TRADE UNIONIST

George Milligan was born on 11 December 1868, the son of Samuel Milligan, a compositor and his wife Mary (née Jardine). Samuel Milligan worked for the *Liverpool Mercury* (which amalgamated with the *Liverpool Daily Post* in 1904) for over forty years. Little is known of George Milligan's early life except that he won a scholarship to the Liverpool Collegiate High School in Shaw Street. By 1890 he was working as a barman, but about that time he applied for work at the Liverpool docks and for the next twenty-one years was employed first as a quay porter and then as a specialised checker. Like all dock labourers he was employed daily on a casual basis; but he rapidly became a 'preferred' man or 'blue-eye' for the White Star Line at the north end of the docks. For twenty years he worked on a regular basis for that company.

The National Union of Dock Labourers (NUDL) was formed in Glasgow in February 1889 and branches were established in Liverpool and Bootle by June of that year. Membership soared in the following months. The two seamen's strikes of December 1888-February 1889 and June-July 1889, although largely unsuccessful, encouraged the dock labourers to look for redress of their own grievances, and sporadic strikes broke out in September 1889, developing into a major conflict in March 1890, involving up to 40,000 men, and lasting a month. Although the men won marginal improvements in conditions, by 1891 the union had been virtually stamped out at the north end of the docks where the large steamship companies, operating on the North Atlantic run, berthed. Milligan became a dock labourer, therefore, at a time when trade union organisation had disappeared from that part of the docks where the White Star Line operated. In his later life he commented graphically on this period from 1891 to 1911:

> The twelve thousand and odd men working for the great companies were in the industrial wilderness. No voice in their pay or conditions . . . the thronged hiring stands open to all and sundry, encouraged the foremen to tyranny and bullying. It was a sad and bad time, that twenty one years, and many of us, for the writer was one, felt bitterness of soul and longed for the restoration of that manhood which had been beaten down in the great strike of '90. But there, still plastered up on the walls of the sheds, was the ominous notice, 'Men wearing Union buttons (badges) will be immediately discharged'! [*Record 2* (June 1923) 6].

It was not until 1908 that Milligan, with a handful of colleagues, planned and formed a small organisation of some two hundred dockers, and this became a branch of the NUDL in 1909. It operated in clandestine fashion; any man discovered to be a union member being instantly discharged. Nevertheless they paid their contributions and hoped for better times. The one tangible short-term result was the publication of the *Mersey Magazine* founded, edited, and largely written by Milligan. It was published for seventeen months (the exact dates of publication are unknown as no copies appear to have survived) and consisted of articles, poems and 'letters' of interest to dock labourers. It collapsed finally through lack of support. Much of the blame for this rests with James Sexton, the general secretary of the NUDL. Although from time to time Sexton spoke of the need for a union journal, this never came about. There is little doubt that Sexton could have supported Milligan's enterprise and transformed the magazine into a union journal. That this did not happen was probably due to Sexton's apprehension that Milligan might emerge as a rival to his position and authority. It might also have offended his own literary pretensions. It is clear that at this time Milligan was a frequent visitor to the headquarters of the union in Hanover Street, where he often wrote copy for his magazine and asked for comments from the office staff.

By 1911, therefore, Milligan had established a position of minor importance within the union as a leader of a 'secret' branch in the hostile north end of the docks, and he enjoyed a reputation among a growing number of dock labourers as a man of courage, integrity, and intelligence. The great transport strike of 1911 translated him into a major figure along the Liverpool waterfront. This strike – the most important in Liverpool's labour history – involved virtually all the transport workers of the city: seamen; ships' stewards, cooks, butchers and bakers; dock labourers, carters, coalheavers, tugboatmen, railwaymen, and tramwaymen. The strike committee, led by Tom Mann, dominated the movement of all goods within Liverpool. The city authorities, buttressed by the import of policemen from other areas, troops, and a gunboat in the Mersey, were powerless as the strike wave swept all before it in July and August. Although pay and conditions were important factors, the major issue was recognition of the unions by the employers. Perhaps the most surprising and unexpected feature of the prolonged dispute was the co-operation among hitherto disparate work groups, who struck work in sympathy for their colleagues at the waterfront. The initial impetus came from the seamen's strike, rapidly followed by the ships' stewards, cooks, butchers, and bakers, organised into a union by Joe Cotter in 1909. Thus dock labourers were not directly involved, but to the astonishment of union officials, the unorganised dockers of the north end came out in sympathy, flocked into the union, and demanded union recognition from the employers. Much later, Milligan claimed he was instrumental in bringing the men out by distributing 'a carefully drawn up handbill, which, while not definitely advising the men to cease work immediately, in general terms said the strike was imminent' [*Record 2* (June 1923) 6]. On the first day of the strike four thousand men enrolled in the branch that hitherto had contained two hundred men. Within a week virtually all the men were in the union. Branch No. 12, of which Milligan was secretary, became the biggest branch in the Mersey district. He was looked upon as the hero of the north end dockers. Milligan was co-opted on to the strike committee, and with Mann and Sexton toured the docks with hectic activity, negotiating with one employer after another, and announcing victory to large, exultant meetings of dockers. In this highly charged emotional atmosphere of 'industrial solidarity' Milligan's future was assured as a major figure in the NUDL hierarchy.

The strike was an immense victory for the union: it was now recognised throughout the port, and in Birkenhead; union rules of pay and conditions were implemented after negotiation; and no man could secure work unless he was a union member. Success, however, created as well as solved problems. Indiscipline among members and unofficial strikes persisted, in spite of the pleas of Milligan and Sexton to use official union machinery. In August 1911 a joint committee of employers and union officials was set up to hammer out a final agreement and create a procedure for the resolution of any future disputes without the need for strike or lock-out. Although the joint committee, of which Milligan was a member, encountered serious problems at the outset, it survived and grew in importance as the institution to which all labour problems of the waterfront were referred.

In the following year a further step was taken to overcome some of the more obvious iniquities and inefficiencies of the casual labour system: the Liverpool Clearing House scheme was brought into existence. The scheme involved the registration of dockers, and efforts to overcome the maldistribution of labour at the various docks by the creation of surplus stands. It introduced a system whereby dockers were paid their wages from one point on a Saturday irrespective of the number of firms a man had worked for during the week. Thus while the scheme did not seek to end the casual system it did reduce some of its more debilitating features. Its introduction was not initially supported by the labour force, and unofficial strikes took place against the NUDL leadership who supported the system. A strike developed in Birkenhead in July 1912. This extended into August and the men were only cajoled to return to work under the threat of the expulsion of the branch. In the bitter conflict that surrounded this dispute Milligan consistently supported Sexton, the main target of the dissidents, in what was clearly an unpopular cause. The system was imposed upon the dockers and Milligan was made a member of the joint board set up to administer the scheme. It must be added that after the initial problems the scheme proved to be advantageous to the genuine docker, although the high hopes of the initiators of ending the gross inefficiency of the casual system were not realised. Nevertheless the triumph of the 1911 strike made Liverpool by 1913 the best-organised port in the country. Milligan had played a considerable role in support of all these developments and was an important member of the various boards and committees set up. He remained secretary of No. 12 branch but was also made secretary of the Mersey District of the union, which, in effect, meant that he was the chief union official of the major branches of the NUDL.

The adoption of Sexton as prospective Labour candidate for the St Helens constituency in 1913 and the outbreak of the First World War further enhanced Milligan's position. Any difficulties that existed between the two men had been resolved. Sexton no longer saw Milligan as a threat to his position, and Milligan in turn proved to be a loyal supporter of Sexton, content in his position as a senior trade union official at local level.

The war brought new problems to the port and to the union. Congestion of goods to be cleared proved to be an intractable problem – many dockers enlisted and new men had to be found, often of inferior quality. Full employment was assured for those who wished to work. The soaring cost of living led to claims for higher wages and frequent unofficial strikes. The union executive and officials were strongly in support of the war effort, and an industrial truce had been declared by the NUDL executive within a few days of the outbreak of war. Sexton increasingly became a national figure, vying with Tillett in jingoistic speeches and declarations. Sexton was also anxious to make a favourable impression in the St Helens constituency; and an increasing burden of union work fell upon Milligan. He emerged as the chief negotiator of the NUDL, with Sexton tending to get involved only in the more serious issues. In the general election of 1918 Sexton became MP for St Helens and Milligan was appointed to the new post of assistant secretary of the union, a position he had held *de facto* for some years. In 1917 he had been awarded the OBE for his contribution to the war effort and by 1919 was vice-president of the Mersey District of the National Transport Workers' Federation (NTWF).

The immediate post-war period from 1919 to 1922 was dominated by the two issues of a national dockers' wage claim presented by the NTWF, and the amalgamation of inland transport unions that led to the creation of the Transport and General Workers' Union (TGWU) in 1922. Negotiations with employers on a national level over the wage claim took place in November and December 1919, but finally broke down, the employers suggesting that the problem should be referred to the newly created Industrial Court. The NTWF and the Government were prepared to accept a Court of Inquiry and it began proceedings in January 1920. The Shaw Inquiry and Report were dominated by Ernest Bevin, and publicly Milligan played no role. Nevertheless at local level Milligan provided information that Sexton and others used for the factual and statistical data presented by Bevin in his speeches to the Court and published as appendixes to the Report. The Inquiry proved to be a triumph for Bevin and his colleagues. The Report recommended: a national basic wage rate for dockers of 16s per day for a 44-hour week; registration of dock labour in all ports; the acceptance of the principle of maintenance of unemployed casual labour; the weekly payment of wages; and the establishment of a national joint council with local joint bodies. The Report was accepted, the basic wage implemented, and negotiations started within the newly formed national joint council for dealing with the other provisions of the Report.

On the issue of amalgamation preliminary talks began in 1920, involving the two biggest unions of dock workers, the NUDL and the Dock, Wharf, Riverside and General Labourers' Union (DWRGLU). A joint sub-committee was formed that began discussions in July 1920. Milligan was one of the six representatives of the NUDL. He was a strong supporter of amalgamation, and used his prestige and authority in Liverpool to persuade the membership to vote in favour. The TGWU was formally created on 1 January 1922, although the NUDL did not enter until 1 April 1922, owing to balloting problems. Milligan was well known to Bevin, and apparently Bevin wanted to make him a national officer for the docks group. Apart from Milligan's known experience and popularity, Bevin no doubt wished to ensure that the Liverpool men would see that their most respected official held high office. Sexton, very much less popular on Merseyside, was by then sixty-six years of age and an MP; he was appointed national supervisor to the docks group, a sinecure, in recognition of the services he had given over the years to the cause of trade unionism among waterfront workers. Milligan, however, rejected Bevin's offer, his wife not wishing to leave the Liverpool area. He became secretary of the Mersey Area (Area No. 12), a position he held until his death in 1925. In 1924 he was made a JP.

Although Milligan spent most of his working life as a docker and trade union official, it was typical of the man that he did not forget his early days before 1890, when he had worked as a barman with average wages of 3d an hour for some seventy to eighty hours per week. In 1908

J.S. Healy formed the Bar Assistants' Union, and Milligan accepted the honorary presidency of the union until it amalgamated with the Warehouse Workers' Union in 1920.

It is mainly from Milligan's writings in the *Mersey Magazine* that his views on politics and religion can be discovered. No copies of the magazine have been found but in 1911 Milligan published extracts from it in *Life through Labour's Eyes.* The book contains twenty-four essays, twenty-one poems and twelve letters, the letters being in simple satirical style, addressed to such characters as I. Knowall, Tom Lightfinger, and Jim Careless. The poems are doggerel, full of simple humour, although many show genuine emotion and are expressed in telling phrases. The most immediate and striking feature of the essays is the deep religious motivation. Milligan was a devout Catholic all his life, and in the essays he exhorted his fellow-dockers to adopt the principles of Christianity. The following extract from the essay 'Manual Labour' illustrates this commitment:

> Christianity has always been the friend of the worker. She has stood by him fearlessly at all times, protecting the weak and defenceless from oppression by the strong. Her sympathies have ever been on the side of the helpless, and, fighting for justice, she has ever fought in her favour . . . She teaches that . . . if the King or Government has authority to suppress all disorder, and to exact obedience from subjects, they have also the sacred duty of protecting the toiling millions from oppression at the hands of the powerful few . . . for Christianity ever has held the balance of justice evenly between master and servant, owner and labourer, rich and poor [Milligan (1911) 39-40].

Milligan was active in Catholic circles: he joined a local group that studied the encyclicals of Pope Leo XIII – a group which ultimately developed into the Catholic Social League; and while too much emphasis should not be put on sectarianism, the point must be made that the majority of dockers at the north end of the docks were also Catholics. Milligan was a strong supporter of the Labour Party; but he was never a Socialist, and he was equally opposed to the syndicalist elements that were present in the great transport strike of 1911. His passionate belief in industrial trade unionism derived from deep moral conviction, and although he deprecated strikes and favoured conciliation, he was a tough negotiator who won respect from both employers and his union membership. His ambitions did not go beyond service to his fellow-workers in Liverpool. In 1917 he was approached by the British Empire Workers' League [this was probably the BWL] to stand as a party candidate. He replied that his 'chief interests are with the dockers and transport workers of Liverpool and not with any particular political body . . . I am a servant of the dockers and others and it is for them to say how I shall be employed' [*Liverpool Daily Post and Mercury*, 25 Oct and 2 Nov 1917, 3]. In 1920 he was offered the Labour candidature at Warrington but again refused.

The early unskilled unions always experienced great difficulty in finding officials who possessed the qualities and skills required to build and develop both local and national organisations. Certainly on the waterfront in the early years of this century such skills were rare; and the NUDL in all its history possessed no more than a handful of men with these qualities. George Milligan was one of these exceptional personalities. He died on 30 May 1925 at the age of fifty-six years. He had become ill a few days before; and died of pneumonia at his home in Makin Street, Walton, where he had lived for many years. Requiem Mass was held at St Francis de Sales Church, Walton, on 3 June and he was buried in Anfield Cemetery. The route to the cemetery was lined by a large number of union members and of the public. He left a widow, and the list of chief mourners suggests that he had at least one brother and two children. No will has been located.

Writings: *Life through Labour's Eyes: essays, letters and lyrics from the workers' point of view* (1911) [extracts from the *Mersey Mag.*]. The *Mersey Mag.*, published in Liverpool for seventeen months between 1908 and 1910 (exact dates unknown), was edited and largely written by Milligan. He contributed a number of short articles for the *Transport Worker 1*, nos. 1, 2 and

3 (1911) and the *Record* [TGWU journal] *2*, nos. 23 and 24 (1923). He also wrote religious articles for Catholic journals.

Sources: *Liverpool Daily Courier, Liverpool Daily Post and Mercury*, and their weekly editions; TGWU, *Annual Reports* and *Record*; Inquiry into the Wages and Conditions of Employment of Dock and Waterside Labourers *Report* 1920 XXIV Cmd 936 and 937 [Shaw Inquiry]; A. Bullock, *The Life and Times of Ernest Bevin*, vol. *1: 1881-1940* (1960); H.R. Hikins, 'The Liverpool General Transport Strike, 1911', *Trans Historic Soc. of Lancashire and Cheshire 113*(1961) 169-95; R.J. Holton, 'Syndicalism and Labour on Merseyside', in *Building the Union: studies on the growth of the workers' movement: Merseyside, 1756-1967* ed. H.R. Hikins (Liverpool, 1973) 121-50; E.L. Taplin, *Liverpool Dockers and Seamen 1870-1890* (Univ. of Hull, 1974); personal information: J.L. Jones, TGWU; A.J. Langshaw, formerly of the NUDL and TGWU. OBIT. *Liverpool Daily Courier* and *Liverpool Daily Post and Mercury*, 1 June 1925; *Record 4*, no. 47 (June 1925) [with an appreciation by James Sexton].
                                                                                              ERIC TAPLIN

See also: *James O'Connor KESSACK; *James SEXTON.

MOSLEY, Cynthia Blanche, Lady (1898-1933)
LABOUR MP

Cynthia Mosley was the second daughter of the 1st Marquess Curzon of Kedleston and his first wife Mary Leiter, and was born at Reigate on 23 August 1898. Her grandfather was Levi Ziegler Leiter, originally a dry goods merchant and then a real estate speculator in Chicago, who left a fortune of between $25 and $30 million. The *Dictionary of American Biography* states that Levi Leiter was a descendant of James Van Leiter, a Dutch Calvinist who came from Australia in 1760. According to the *Western Mail*, 17 May 1933, Cynthia inherited an income of approximately £30,000 a year from her grandfather. Another source indicates that she had a trust fund of $1 million and a marriage settlement of $700,000. There was to be considerable family litigation over the Leiter inheritance. Oswald Mosley went to some pains in his autobiography to refute the story (often heard in the 1930s) that Cynthia's mother was Jewish.

'Cimmie' (or 'Cimmy'), as she was called in her circle, showed early signs of independence by setting up house in a Mayfair maisonette with her elder sister, Irene, and during the First World War worked at the War Office at a salary of 30s per week. This was regarded as somewhat daring, but at the same time she was firmly embedded in London Society, a very rich, well-born woman who looked the part: tall, with strong, regular features, an attractive speaking voice and great charm of manner which, those who knew her agreed, came from a genuinely sincere and lovable personality.

Her wedding to Oswald Mosley (then Mr, and Conservative MP for Harrow) on 11 May 1920 was very much a Society occasion: it took place at the Chapel Royal, attended by the King and Queen, the King and Queen of the Belgians, and many members of the diplomatic corps and both Houses of Parliament. (Her father was, at the time, Foreign Secretary.) The marriage was a political partnership from the beginning; both joined the Labour Party together in 1924, and she worked hard on her husband's behalf in his unsuccessful campaign at Birmingham, Ladywood, in 1924 and in his successful by-election at Smethwick in 1926. She herself was adopted as candidate for Stoke in 1925 and won the seat in 1929 with a majority of 7850, defeating Colonel John Ward. Her political career in the Labour movement necessarily appears largely as an adjunct of that of her husband, but, in spite of her loyalty to him, her personality emerges from the record as one of considerable strength of character.

Within the Labour Party Cynthia Mosley seems in general to have been well liked, and more trusted than her husband. Her record in the House shows her to have been mainly interested in social problems, and she was also concerned with preserving the rural environment. She made a memorable maiden speech in support of the Widows', Orphans', and Old Age Pensions Bill in which she demolished, with great gusto, Neville Chamberlain's argument that people were demoralised by being given 'something for nothing':

I have noticed a word that has been greatly in use since this Measure was brought in, and that is the word 'demoralisation,' demoralisation of giving something for nothing. That is ground on which I am very much at home. All my life I have got something for nothing. Why? Have I earned it? Have I deserved it? Not a bit. I have just got it through luck. Of course, some people might say I showed great intelligence in the choice of my parents, but I put it down to luck. And not only I, but, if I may be allowed to say so, a great many other people on the opposite side of the House are also in that same position. They also have always got something for nothing. Now the question is: Are we demoralised? . . . I stoutly deny that I am demoralised. I think that I am as good a citizen as I would have been if I had been born in much less fortunate circumstances [*Hansard*, 31 Oct 1929].

As Beatrice Webb wrote in her Diary on 2 November 1929 she 'charmed the House' [Cole (1956) 225].

In the opposition which her husband was developing against the leaders of the Labour Government, and their apparently total incapacity to offer any practical policies towards mounting unemployment, Cynthia supported him constantly. Mosley resigned from his Government post (Chancellor of the Duchy of Lancaster) on 21 May 1930, and he issued his famous Manifesto on 1 December 1930. It was signed by seventeen Labour MPs (including Cynthia) and the miners' leader, A.J. Cook. Before this Cynthia had been on a visit to Russia with John Strachey in September 1930; on the way she met Trotsky in Istanbul. Trotsky wrote that the meeting 'proved banal in the extreme' [*Trotsky's Diary . . .* Zarundnaya (1976) 88-9]. Cynthia's letter to Trotsky [dated 4 September 1930] offers an interesting statement of her political attitudes at the time:

Dear Comrade Trotsky,

I would like above all things to see you for a few moments. There is no good reason why you should see me as (1) I belong to the Labour Party in England who were so ridiculous and refused to allow you in, but also I belong to the ILP and we did our very best to make them change their minds, and (2) I am daughter of Lord Curzon who was Minister for Foreign Affairs in London when you were in Russia.

On the other hand I am an ardent Socialist. I am a member of the House of Commons. I think less than nothing of the present Government. I have just finished reading your life which inspired me as no other book has done for ages. I am a great admirer of yours. These days when great men seem so very few and far between it would be a great privilege to meet one of the enduring figures of our age and I do hope with all my heart you will grant me that privilege. I need hardly say I come as a private person, not a journalist or *anything* but myself – I am on my way to Russia, I leave for Batoum – Tiflis – Rostov – Kharkov and Moscow by boat Monday. I have come to Prinkipo this afternoon especially to try to see you, but if it were not convenient I could come out again any day till Monday. I do hope however you could allow me a few moments *this* afternoon.

Yours fraternally,
Cynthia Mosley

When Oswald Mosley, his wife and four colleagues were expelled or resigned from the Labour Party in February or March 1931, Cynthia took an active part in the launching of the New Party. Mosley was ill at the time, and she travelled round the country speaking for the new organisation. In the industrial north especially she met with hostile receptions from angry Labour supporters. She attended the House of Commons only very occasionally but went back to speak in the debate on the Unemployment Insurance (No. 3) Bill – an effective, and bitter, intervention. 'If I had shut my eyes in this Debate', she said, 'I might well have believed that it was the Conservative Government bringing in a Conservative measure' [*Hansard*, 15 July 1931].

In the general election of 1931 Oswald Mosley was the New Party candidate for Stoke, Cynthia's constituency. He was defeated in a three-cornered contest; and his ideas shifted rapidly towards Fascism. Cynthia Mosley became increasingly distressed about the political direction of her husband. Harold Nicolson's comments about her were at times odd, but he noted on 24 November 1931 how violently anti-Tory she still was, and how much she detested the growing *rapprochement* between her husband and Lord Rothermere. Cynthia was recorded by Nicolson as saying that she wanted to put a notice in *The Times* dissociating herself from her husband's 'fascist tendencies' [Nicolson (1966) 98]. Nevertheless, she did not break away from either Mosley or his Party. Her health had been causing much concern since 1929 when she suffered a miscarriage just after the general election. When Mosley became seriously ill at the time of the formation of the New Party, Cynthia had born much of the strain. She became pregnant again in July 1931 and experienced an exceedingly difficult period until the birth of her third child, and second son, in late April 1932. She had a long convalescence in Italy.

After her health recovered she appears to have become increasingly reconciled to Fascism. Undoubtedly her continued love for her husband greatly influenced her political attitudes. She accompanied him on a visit to Rome in April 1933 when they both took the Fascist salute, along with Mussolini, on the balcony of the Palazzo Venezia at a huge parade [Skidelsky (1975) 297]. This, Mosley's biographer states, was one of the very rare occasions when she showed public sympathy with the Fascist movement.

In May 1933 she was operated on for appendicitis. Peritonitis set in and she died on 16 May at the age of thirty-four. She was buried at Mosley's Denham estate just outside London.

Cynthia Mosley was undoubtedly a pleasanter and certainly less complicated personality than her husband, and as far as the evidence goes, she was probably more reliable in her political sympathies with the Labour movement. As Mrs Hamilton wrote twenty years later: 'We all liked her; most of us were desperately sorry for her. We kept our sympathy to ourselves; she would have fiercely resented anything of the kind' [Hamilton (1953) 54].

Her estate in England was valued at £20,951. After her death a public appeal was launched and the money raised resulted, with help from the LCC and Lambeth Borough Council, in the Cynthia Mosley Day Nursery being opened in Kennington. It is now (1977) administered by Lambeth Borough Council, and caters for some seventy children under school age.

Sources: *New York Times*, 23 May 1913; *Western Mail*, 17 May 1923; *Scotsman*, 10 Nov 1925; *Daily Express*, 7 Dec 1926; *Labour Woman*, 1 July 1927; *Daily Herald*, 10 July 1928; *Daily Telegraph*, 15 Aug 1928; *Hansard* (1929-31); *WWW* (1929-40); *Dod* (1931); J. Johnston, *A Hundred Commoners* (1931) 289-91; *Times*, 5 Mar 1931; *London News* (Apr 1933); J. Drennan, *B.U.F.: Oswald Mosley and British Fascism* (1934); M.A. Hamilton, *Up-hill all the Way* (1953); *Beatrice Webb's Diaries 1924-1932*, ed. M. Cole (1956); H. Nicolson, *Diaries and Letters 1930-1939* ed. N. Nicolson (1966); P. Brookes, *Women at Westminster* (1967); R. Skidelsky, *Politicians and the Slump* (1967); O. Mosley, *My Life* (1968); *The Diaries of Sir Robert Bruce Lockhart 1:1915-1938* (1973); H. Thomas, *John Strachey* (1973); *Trotsky's Diary in Exile 1935*, trans. E. Zarudnaya (Harvard Univ. Press, 1976); R. Skidelsky, *Oswald Mosley* (1975); D. Mosley, *A Life of Contrasts: the autobiography of Diana Mosley* (1977); biographical information: the late T.A.K. Elliott, CMG; Labour Party Library; A. Wilson, Chief Public Relations Officer, London Borough of Lambeth. Obit. *Manchester Guardian*, *Morning Post* and *Times*, 17 May 1933.

John Saville

MUGGERIDGE, Henry Thomas Benjamin (1864-1942)
SOCIALIST AND LABOUR MP

Henry Muggeridge was born in Croydon on 26 June 1864, the eldest of a large family (probably nine). His father, Henry Ambrose Muggeridge, who had an undertaker's business in Penge, abandoned the family when the boy was twelve years old and his mother supported them by running a second-hand furniture shop in Penge High Street. Henry attended St John's School, Penge, and later the City of London College, leaving at the age of thirteen-and-a-half to enter a lawyer's office in London. When it became clear that his prospects of becoming anything more than a lawyer's clerk were slight, he left, and in 1880 joined a company of shirt manufacturers with whom he was to remain until his retirement. He was head of the counting house in 1893. In 1907 he was appointed secretary to the company, the offices of which were in New Basinghall Street. At some later point in his career the opportunity arose of his joining the board of directors but his political affiliations were against him.

Muggeridge's first political commitment was to the Liberal Party. As a young man he joined the Penge Liberal Association and played an active part in the pressure for a free library in the borough (this was subsequently achieved) and for public baths. No doubt for financial reasons he used to travel to London Bridge Station by the early workmen's train, at seven o'clock each morning, and he used the hours before he was due at the office in reading. The keeper of a coffee shop became a friend, and young Muggeridge read widely in social and political subjects: Carlyle, Ruskin, Morris, Whitman, Kropotkin, Edward Bellamy and the Webbs. By the early 1890s he had become a Socialist: he joined the Fabian Society in 1892 and later the ILP. Like many others he was active in both. He was also a member of the SDF for a few years and was secretary of the Croydon Socialist Society in 1895.

He married Annie Booler in 1893 and moved first to Sanderstead near Croydon and then to South Croydon itself. It was a borough with which he was already familiar, having unsuccessfully contested local council elections at South Norwood in 1896 and Upper Norwood in the year following. On both occasions he stood as an SDF candidate. Croydon in these years was an interesting centre of progressive ideas. W.J. Jupp, John Page Hopps and J. Bruce Wallace (the founder of the Brotherhood Church) all settled in Croydon during the 1890s [Armytage (1961) 335]. J.C. Kenworthy became a member of the committee of the Fellowship of the New Life in 1894, and by the middle of the decade Croydon was the main centre of the Fellowship's English following. The Croydon Brotherhood Church was opened in June 1894. There were to be Croydon Socialists, anarchists and freethinkers in a number of the communities that established themselves in these decades before 1914: Purleigh and Whiteway among them. He became close friends with Will Straughan – 'a most agreeable and kindly character' as Muggeridge's son, Malcolm, described him [letter, 22 Dec 1976] – and this maintained Henry Muggeridge's interest in the affairs of the Whiteway Community.

He gave much of his time to his Socialist activities and travelled a great deal around the country to fulfil lecturing engagements. He seems to have been particularly successful in the Leicester area. By the end of the 1890s he was prominent in the affairs of the Fabian Society – he took the pro-Boer side in the great debate within the Society over the war [Cole (1961) 95 ff.] and from 1901 to 1904 he served on the executive. He was at the same time active in the ILP, and in 1903 he was a delegate to the annual conference from the City of London branch.

Henry Pelling has noted that the Borough of Croydon was in his 'Category A' at the turn of the century, i.e. a prosperous, predominantly middle-class or upper-class electorate, although by 1911 there had been an influx of a considerable artisan population [Pelling (1967) 29, 64-5]. The early strength of the Labour movement is therefore remarkable. In 1890 a Croydon Federation of Trades and Labour Council was established; and in 1891 Labour obtained a seat on the School Board and in 1892 one on the Borough Council. In the opening years of the new century progress was more rapid and by 1903 the Labour movement had five out of the thirty-six seats on the Council and three members on the Board of Guardians. In 1904 it began to publish weekly the *Croydon Citizen* and in August 1905 a branch of the ILP was formed, followed a few months later by a further branch at Thornton Heath. In the 1906 general election there was an LRC candidate; but after 1906 the local movement declined and only revived again in the years immediately preceding 1914 [Tichelar (1975) *passim*].

In November 1911 Muggeridge was elected to the Croydon Council as a member for the West ward. His platform was the need for increased and vigorous municipal enterprise; he urged that municipal powers should be extended to cover, among other local services, the trams, housing, health and the welfare and safety of school children. Several years before when *The Times* had attacked municipal enterprise, Muggeridge had replied with a pamphlet, *The Anti-Municipal Controversy exposed*, which had attracted considerable attention. He wanted local taxation to be more equitably based and, above all, that trade union rates of pay and working conditions should be the right of all municipal employees. In 1914 he was returned unopposed but after the war, when the wards were reorganised, he represented Whitehorse Manor ward. He continued to serve on the borough council until 1930, when he did not stand again following his election to Parliament. In 1913 he became a JP for Croydon.

During these years Muggeridge was the recognised leader of the Labour Party (of which he was for many years chairman) on the Croydon Council. He had a reputation as a forceful and entertaining debater, with a particular love of the apt quotation. Debate was one of his greatest pleasures and his house in Birdhurst Gardens was a regular meeting place for Socialist discussion groups. Ramsay MacDonald, Philip Snowden, J.R. Clynes and many Fabian notables were among those who came to address Labour meetings in the borough. As a councillor, Muggeridge's principal interests were municipal housing (he was instrumental in getting the first block of council houses built at Woodside) and education. From 1912 until his election to the Commons he served on the education committee. For a time he was chairman of the school managers and at the request of the Labour Party's Advisory Committee on Education, of which he became a member in February 1921, he wrote a memorandum on educational administration in the spring of 1922. He also wrote a note on social welfare and after-care committees in February 1922. He took an active part in plans for municipal management of electricity supplies and from 1927 to 1930 chaired the borough's electricity committee. He helped in the formation of the Croydon Foreign Languages Club; he had taught himself French many years previously. From 1925 he was a member of the management committee of the Workers' Travel Association. He was a lifelong supporter of the co-operative movement and of the WEA.

Muggeridge contested parliamentary elections on four occasions in South Croydon – in December 1918, November 1922, December 1923 and October 1924: he was each time defeated by the Conservative candidate. His programme in 1922 included support for the League of Nations and international labour agreements, the cancellation of international indebtedness, the conversion of the British Empire into a Federation of Free States and a massive reduction in the Government's spending on the Services and in the ambitiousness of its foreign policy. At home he wanted to see the introduction of a wealth tax, government help for local programmes of housing reform, a better system of pensions and nationalisation of the mines and railways. In 1924 he defended substantially the same points of view but also made a lengthy defence of the Labour Government's recently-negotiated treaty with Russia.

In the general election of 1929 Muggeridge contested Romford, where he was returned with a large majority in a three-cornered fight. As an MP he was interested in a wide cross-section of subjects but in the main he continued to work for the causes to which he had already devoted so many years as a borough councillor. On education, he stressed the need for many more free places to be made available in secondary schools and for the leaving age to be raised. He supported Commonwealth preference in trade and wanted to see a greater measure of central control and planning through the setting up of a 'purchasing board' [*Hansard*, 29 Oct 1930]. He envisaged such a board giving special encouragement to home agricultural production to help unemployment and with the same object in view he also, in 1930 and 1931, strongly supported greater commercial contacts with the Soviet Union. He was one of ten signatories, in December 1930, of the Mosley Manifesto which called for a planned economy to stimulate exports, control imports and plan home consumption.

In 1931 Muggeridge was defeated in Romford, losing to the Conservative candidate. He returned to Croydon Council as a member for Broad Green ward and served until January 1940, when recurrent periods of ill-health caused him to offer his resignation. During these years he was a member of the finance and education committees and he was chairman of the libraries committee, 1938-9. In 1933 he was chairman of the London and Home Counties Electricity Authority.

Henry Muggeridge died at Sedlescombe, Sussex, on 25 March 1942 in his seventy-seventh year. The funeral took place at Whatlington Church near Battle on 27 March and he left an estate valued at £1695. He and his wife had been recently made homeless by the bombing raids on London. His wife and four of his five children – all sons – survived him. She came from Sheffield, where her father and brothers worked in the cutlery trade and they met on holiday on the Isle of Man. In early adulthood in Penge Muggeridge had attended the Baptist Church but later in life he accepted a more agnostic position towards religious belief. His earliest cultural and political activities were all connected with the chapel he attended. He remained committed to a pacifist position, although his two elder sons served in France in the First World War; one was a subaltern and the other, Stanley, was in the Royal Flying Corps. Both survived but Stanley later died from injuries received in a cycle accident. Another son, Malcolm, is the well-known man of letters.

Writings: *The Housing Question in Croydon. Some Facts and a Remedy* (Croydon [1901]) 10 pp.; *The Anti-Municipal Conspiracy exposed* (ILP [1903?]) 24 pp.; 'Municipal Trading in Croydon', *Annual Report of the Croydon and District Trades and Labour Council* (1904); 'Why the Labour Party is Independent', ibid. (1905) [in TUC Library]; *The Labour Pilgrim's Progress* (ILP [1916?]) 38 pp.; 'Note on Social Welfare and After-Care Committees' (Feb 1922) [typescript]; 'Educational Administration: draft suggestions' [typescript] (spring 1922); 'Seek ye first – a Suggested New Approach to Unemployment', *Soc. Rev.* n.s. *4*, no. 44 (Sep 1929) 5-9; 'The Gateway to Progress', No. 7 in a series 'As I see Croydon', *Croydon Times*, 20 Oct 1934.

Sources: (1) MSS: Labour Party archives. (2) Other: *Croydon Advertiser*, 26 Dec 1891; *Justice*, 1 Aug 1896; *Ward's Commercial and General Croydon Directory* (1902); *Labour Who's Who* (1924) and (1927); *Croydon Labour Outlook 2*, no. 3 (June 1925) [with portrait]; Debrett, *House of Commons* (1929); *Hansard* (1929-31); *Croydon Advertiser*, 30 Aug 1930; *Dod* (1931); N. Shaw, *Whiteway: a Colony on the Cotswolds* (1935); *WWW* (1941-50); H. Pearson, *Bernard Shaw* (1942); M.M.P. McCarran, *Fabianism in the Political Life of Britain 1919-1931* (1954); Anon., 'Father and Son' [H.T. and M. Muggeridge], *New Statesman and Nation*, 27 Aug 1955, 238-9; W.H.G. Armytage, *Heavens Below* (1961); M. Cole, *The Story of Fabian Socialism* (1961); H. Pelling, *Social Geography of British Elections 1885-1910* (1967); M. Muggeridge, *Chronicles of Wasted Time 1: The Green Stick* (1972); Bernard Shaw, *Collected Letters 1898-1910*, ed. D.H. Laurence (1972); H. Thomas, *John Strachey* (1973); R. Skidelsky, *Oswald Mosley* (1975); M. Tichelar, 'Labour Politics in Croydon 1880-1914' (CNAA BA dissertation, 1975); biographical information: Croydon Central Library; the late T.A.K. Elliott, CMG; Dr D.E. Martin, Sheffield Univ.; M. Tichelar, Sheffield Univ., to whom the editors are indebted for permission to use his dissertation, and for other information; personal information: Malcolm Muggeridge, Robertsbridge, son. OBIT. *Croydon Advertiser*, 27 Mar 1942; *Croydon Times*, 28 Mar 1942 [photograph].

BARBARA NIELD
JOHN SAVILLE

See also: †Arthur Daniel WHITE.

MURDOCH, Mary Charlotte (1864-1916)
SOCIAL REFORMER

Mary Murdoch was born on 26 September 1864, the youngest of seven children of William Murdoch of Elgin, a solicitor and his wife Jane (née Connell). Mary used a legacy left to her by her mother to become a doctor, and after various appointments in London she accepted the post of house-surgeon in the Victoria Hospital for Sick Children in Hull in 1893; and most of the rest of her life was spent working and living in that city.

Mary Murdoch, Hull's first woman doctor, was always intensely interested in political and social questions. Before 1900 she actively supported the Liberal Party but in the last decade and a half of her life her energies were devoted to specific campaigns and causes. She was president of the Hull Suffrage Society and remained always an ardent suffragist. In 1905, largely on her initiative, a branch of the National Union of Women Workers was established in Hull, and she became president. The NUWW had been founded in 1891, not as another propagandist body, but to provide women working in different fields with the opportunity to exchange information and expertise. It was directed by a general committee composed of representatives of a large number of women's organisations, including its own local branches, which were largely autonomous. The NUWW was not an exclusively labour organisation although a number of labour and social groups and personalities were associated with its work. Margaret MacDonald, for example, was secretary and later chairman of its Industrial Committee from 1896 until her death; Beatrice Webb was for some years on its EC; and in the 1890s Amie Hicks represented the Women's Industrial Council. Mary Murdoch was elected to the London EC of the NUWW in 1908 and became a vice-president in 1910.

As far as can be ascertained Mary Murdoch had no institutional links with the labour movement. At the Glasgow conference of the NUWW in 1911 she spoke in vigorous criticism of the housing conditions in Hull, using the statistics of a local Fabian pamphlet on which to base her case. Her speech caused an immense furore in Hull, a fact which she greatly enjoyed and she did all in her power to keep the controversy going.

She was small, pretty and vivacious, a good public speaker and lecturer who made and kept many friends in spite of a hot temper and controversial habits. She never married. She died on 20 March 1916 and was cremated. She left effects valued at £2117. Following a Requiem at St Francis's Church, Sculcoates, a second service was held at All Saints' Church at which the Bishop of Hull officiated. Many tributes were paid to her work among the women and children of Hull and for the NUWW; her biography was written by Hope Malleson in 1919.

Writings: 'Pressing Reforms to be accomplished in the Health of the Nation', in *Women Workers: papers read at the Conference held in Glasgow 9-13 Oct 1911*, 16-25.

Sources: *Report of the Annual Meeting of the General Committee of the National Union of Women Workers* (1895); *Reports* of the NCWW, 1910-14; *How the People of Hull are housed* (Hull, 1910); *Eastern Morning News* (Oct-Nov 1911); J.R. MacDonald, *Margaret Ethel MacDonald* (1912); *Labour Year Book* (1916); H. Malleson, *A Woman Doctor: Mary Murdoch of Hull* (1919); *Hull Times*, 24 May 1941; H.P. Adam, *Women in Council: the jubilee book of the National Council of Women of Great Britain* (1945). OBIT. *Hull Daily Mail* and *Hull Daily News*, 20 Mar 1916; *Eastern Morning News*, 21 Mar 1916; *Common Cause*, 24 Mar 1916; *Lancet*, 1 Apr 1916; NCWW, *21st Annual Report* (1915-16).

ANN HOLT

NICHOLLS, George (1864-1943)
LIB-LAB MP AND TRADE UNIONIST

George Nicholls was born at Whittlesea, Cambridgeshire, on 25 June 1864. He attended a dame school for a few years, and at the age of eight or nine started earning. He had various labouring jobs throughout his younger days. From a boy he was full of a deep religious faith, nourished on the texts of English Protestantism – the Bible, Foxe's *Book of Martyrs* and Bunyan's *Pilgrim's Progress* – and he later became a well-known lay preacher. At evening classes he attended in Whittlesea he met his future wife and they were married in 1888.

A year or two later, Nicholls, who was then working in the Whittlesea gravel pits, began to be drawn into the wider world of Liberal politics. He was elected as a *bona fide* labourer to the Gladstone conference of 1891, and he began to be politically associated with Richard Winfrey (later Sir Richard and a well-known MP) who at this time was agent for the Hon. Arthur Brand, Liberal candidate for Wisbech. Nicholls took to making propaganda caravanning trips for the Liberal Party, and he had considerable success. He was by this time becoming known as a spokesman for the agricultural labourers and he also became a smallholder. From 1894 till 1902 he was lay pastor of Chatteris Congregational Church – a church which he revitalised by his eloquent preaching and devoted work: as would be expected of a man of Nicholls's religious persuasion, he was active in the temperance movement. He also served on the Chatteris Urban District Council.

In 1902 or 1903 he left Cambridgeshire for Staffordshire to become lay pastor of the Congregational Churches at Silverdale and Chesterton; and in 1904 he was adopted Liberal candidate for North Northamptonshire, a seat which he won in the Liberal landslide of 1906 by a majority of 685. On this occasion he claimed to represent the Labour interest. He was not really a Lib-Lab in the sense normally accepted, but at the time his Labour sympathies were recognised by contemporaries. Some of his admirers and supporters bought him a house in Peterborough, in which he continued to live for the rest of his life.

It was also in 1906 that Nicholls, Winfrey and Herbert Day, who was the owner of a boot and shoe business in Norwich, joined with George Edwards in the revival or re-creation of a farm workers' union. It was called the Eastern Counties Agricultural Labourers' and Small Holders' Union. Day and the two MPs (Nicholls and Winfrey) provided finance; Nicholls became president, Winfrey treasurer, and Day was on the executive [Madden (1956) 2]. For Nicholls and Winfrey the union was a political instrument rather than a genuine industrial union; one method of organising rural support for the Liberal Party. But the vision of the farmworkers' leaders was different. George Edwards from the first saw that wages would inevitably be an issue, and the founding meeting of the new union emphasised the need to improve housing, to guarantee protection from political victimisation – a central concern for Edwards – and abolition of the tied cottage. The union was not a failure, although it quickly ran into problems. The success of the strike at Trunch was followed by the defeat in 1910 at St Faiths and this led directly to the split in the union after the general council meeting of February 1911. Nicholls and Winfrey resigned; and the new committee was both more proletarian and Labour-oriented.

In the House of Commons Nicholls naturally did all he could to support the Small Holdings and Allotments Bill of 1907. He spoke most frequently on agricultural affairs, as well as on matters such as old age pensions. In the first 1910 election he contested the Northern division of Northamptonshire officially as a Liberal (but still a Lib-Lab according to Craig (1974) 359), without success; and he was defeated also in six later general elections and two by-elections. His divagation to Labour and back again to Liberal was probably not helpful. It was about 1918 that he joined the Labour Party and in the 'Coupon' election of that year he contested Camborne, Cornwall. His opponent was the distinguished Liberal, Sir Francis Acland, and Nicholls was defeated by 532 votes. By 1922 Nicholls had returned to the Liberal fold but he lost the elections of 1922 (Peterborough), 1923 and 1924 (Warwick and Leamington) and 1929 (Harborough, Leicestershire).

From 1912, when he was elected to Peterborough Town Council, to 1920, when he retired from it, Nicholls took a considerable part in local affairs. He succeeded Winfrey as mayor in

1915, and was re-elected twice. He was made a JP in 1913 or 1914, and was for many years chairman of the juvenile court.

Nicholls served for a year – 1917 to 1918 – on the Agricultural Wages Board. He was at this time head of the small holdings section of the Agricultural Organisation Society. In July 1919 he was invited to serve on the R.C. on Agriculture. Nicholls signed the Majority Report, along with all the farming representatives. The Minority Report was signed by the representatives of the NUAW, the Workers' Union, the Scottish Farm Servants' Union and Professor A.W. Ashby.

George Nicholls was married three times. He had no children. He died at Peterborough on 30 November 1943, after an operation, and the funeral service was held in Millfield Congregational Church, of which he had been for several years in pastoral charge. He left an estate valued at £6418.

Sources: *Northampton Herald*, 5, 12, 19 and 26 Jan 1906; *Northampton Mercury*, 5, 12, 17 Jan 1906; *Rev. of Revs 33* (1906) 577-8; *Hansard* (1908-9); *Dod* (1909); *Northampton Herald*, 7, 14, 21 Jan 1910; G. Edwards, *From Crow-Scaring to Westminster: an autobiography* (1922); *100 Years of Congregationalism* [booklet on hundredth anniversary of Chatteris Congregational Church] (1938); *WWW* (1941-50); R. Winfrey, *Great Men and Others I have met* (Kettering, 1943); R. Groves, *Sharpen the Sickle!: the history of the Farm Workers' Union* (1949); M. Madden, 'The National Union of Agricultural Workers 1906-1956' (Oxford BLitt., 1956); H.A. Clegg et al., *A History of British Trade Unions since 1889* vol. *1: 1889-1910* (Oxford, 1964); F.W.S. Craig, *British Parliamentary Election Results 1885-1918* (1974); biographical information: Cambridgeshire Libraries, Peterborough; Rev. D.A. Cox, Chatteris; A. Howkins, Univ. of Sussex; D. Newton, East Midland Allied Press Archives, Stamford; Northamptonshire County Library, Corby; N. Scotland, Univ. of Aberdeen; Rev. L. Wide, Kettering; personal information: Mrs K.E. Boyd, March, niece; A.G. Larkinson, Rushden. OBIT. *Peterborough Advertiser*, 3 Dec 1943; *Peterborough Citizen*, 7 Dec 1943.

MARGARET 'ESPINASSE
JOHN SAVILLE

See also: *George EDWARDS.

NOEL-BUXTON, Lucy Edith Pelham, Lady (1888-1960)
LABOUR MP

Lucy Edith Pelham, Lady Noel-Buxton, was born on 14 December 1888 at Winchester, the eldest daughter of Henry Pelham Burn, of Lockerbie, Dumfriesshire, a captain in the Rifle Brigade, and his wife, Janet Edith (née Orr-Ewing). She was educated at St James's, West Malvern, and Westfield College, London University. She first met her future husband, Noel Edward Buxton, who was twenty years her senior, when she was organiser of the Conservative 'No Noel for North Norfolk League' against his candidature as a Liberal for the constituency in 1910. Buxton was elected, however, and their relationship developed to the point that they were married on 30 April 1914. Noel and Charles Buxton became members of the UDC at the outbreak of war although Noel, unlike his brother, did not play an active role. By the end of the war Noel's sympathies were leaning towards the Labour Party. He still contested North Norfolk as a Liberal at the 1918 'Coupon' election but was defeated. In 1919 he joined the Labour Party and at the 1922 general election regained his former constituency in the Labour interest. His wife was among those Labour Party politicians' wives whom Beatrice Webb, in the early 1920s, had drawn into the Half-Circle Club – a group of Labour women from various professional and working-class backgrounds [Webb (1952) 209]. In 1924 Mrs Webb noted in her diary that 'to Mrs. Noel Buxton belongs the credit of finding fit premises and furnishing them with distinction and charm' [Webb (1956) 26-7].

Lucy Buxton entered Parliament herself as Labour MP for North Norfolk at a by-election in 1930 when her husband was elevated to the House of Lords as the 1st Baron Noel-Buxton. She won the seat by 179 votes in a memorable campaign in which Lord Beaverbrook supported her Unionist opponent, T.R.A.M. Cook, as part of his Empire Free Trade movement. Her first parliamentary period lasted only until the 1931 general election. Her maiden speech was made during her own parliamentary motion that unemployment insurance should be extended to agricultural labourers. It was a speech which showed great understanding of the plight of her poorer constituents, and for the remainder of the parliamentary session she spoke exclusively on agricultural matters. She lost her seat in 1931, fought it again without success in 1935 and withdrew from the candidature in 1936.

In 1945 she was returned top of the poll for the two-member constituency of Norwich. Her speaking record has shown her to have been particularly interested in colonial affairs in Africa, but she was also a member of Parliamentary Labour Party groups on arts and amenities, housing and town planning, defence and agriculture. However, she had poor health at this period and was less active in the House towards the end of the 1945-50 Parliament. Her husband had died in 1948 and she did not stand again in 1950.

Lady Noel-Buxton was one of the quietest and most reticent of the women MPs of the post-war years. She was tall and slim with a somewhat patrician appearance, dark hair, and bright expressive eyes. Her manner was friendly, but more than any of her women colleagues in the Commons she seemed always to avoid contact with members of the other side of the House. When asked about this on one occasion she replied: 'You see, I knew too many of them in earlier days. Now I find companionship among those who understand the things I'm working for' [letter of Lucy Middleton, 16 Feb 1977].

The mother of six children, two of whom predeceased her, she had a lifelong interest in child welfare and was on the committee of the Mothercraft Training Society. In the House of Commons she had been concerned with the welfare of service personnel, and stated, 9 May 1946, that she had worked for SSAFA for three and a half years. She was also interested in gardening, was a Fellow of the Royal Horticultural Society and was at one time president of the London Gardens Guild, a body seeking to promote a love of gardening among Londoners. She was also the author of a volume of poetry.

She died at the age of seventy-one at Frinton, Essex, on 9 December 1960, and the funeral took place at St Thomas's Church, Upshire, Essex. She left an estate valued at £56,919 (net).

Writings: *Hay Harvest, and other poems* (1918) 47 pp.

Sources: (1) MSS: Noel-Buxton papers: Mrs J.G. Hogg, Tonbridge. (2) *Hansard* (1930-1) and (1945-50); *Times House of Commons Guide* (1931) and (1945); *Dod* (1931) and (1949); *Eastern Daily Press*, 24 Feb 1936; C. Bunker, *Who's Who in Parliament* (1946); *Kelly* (1949); *WWW* (1951-60); M. Anderson, *Noel Buxton: a life* (1952); *Beatrice Webb's Diaries 1912-1924*, ed. M. Cole (1952); *Beatrice Webb's Diaries 1924-1932*, ed. M. Cole (1956); P. Brookes, *Women at Westminster* (1967); personal information: Mrs Lucy Middleton, London. OBIT. *Eastern Daily Press* and *Times*, 12 Dec 1960; *Labour Party Report* (1961).

ANN HOLT

See also: Charles Roden BUXTON; Noel Edward BUXTON.

NOEL-BUXTON, 1st Baron Noel-Buxton of Aylsham,
see **BUXTON, Noel Edward**

PATERSON, Emma Anne (1848-86)
TRADE UNIONIST AND FEMINIST

Emma Anne Paterson was born on 5 April 1848 at St Peter's National School House, Belgrave Street, London, the daughter of Henry Smith, headmaster of the St George's Hanover Square parish school, and his wife Emma (née Dockerill). Emma was devoted to her father, who encouraged her to study. Among her young friends and relations she was known as 'the book-worm'. On leaving school she served a short apprenticeship with a bookbinder, but on her father's death in 1864 she and her mother had to seek employment. Twice her mother tried to establish a school, at the second of which Emma taught for a time; but she disliked this, and about 1866 became secretary to a lady clerk employed by the Working Men's Club and Institute Union; in July 1867 she was promoted to be assistant secretary of the Union. The three honorary secretaries who held office with her were the Hon. Auberon Herbert, Thomas Paterson, a cabinet-maker (whom she later married), and Hodgson Pratt, social reformer and co-operator.

On her own admission she was not at this time 'an agitator', so her resignation from the Working Men's Club in February 1872 to become secretary of the Women's Suffrage Association was surprising. Her stay with the Association was, however, short. While most accounts of her life report that she left the WSA on her marriage to Thomas Paterson in July 1873, Lady Dilke, a close friend, quoted Emma Smith as saying:

> The ladies have complimented me on my zeal but they say that my bodily presence is weak and my speech contemptible; so I must make room for someone who can represent them better. I've saved a little money, and I'm going to America to see for myself how the women's friendly societies work there. You know, I don't think the vote the only panacea for all the sufferings of the weaker sex. I am a working woman myself (she was a printer by trade) and my work for this society has brought me into contact with large bodies of women in other trades, so when I have picked up some hints on the other side of the Atlantic, I hope to induce Englishwomen to try whether they cannot help themselves, as men have done, by combination [*Fortn. Rev., 51* (May 1889) 852].

Emma Smith married Thomas Paterson on 24 July 1873 at Holborn Register Office soon after she left the Suffrage Association; and she and her husband went off to America on a working honeymoon. They found working conditions for women no better than in Britain; but the examples of the Parasol and Umbrella Makers' Union and the Women's Typographical Union – both successful and both wholly managed by working women – provided Emma Paterson with some of the arguments she was looking for. When she returned from America she expounded her views in a seminal letter dated April 1874 and printed in the *Labour News* in June 1874 [repr. in Goldman (1974) 117 ff.]. After emphasising the wretched conditions of women workers she went on to outline a plan for a National Protective and Benefit Union of Working Women: a general union embracing all women workers, in order that those tolerably well paid could help those badly paid; and she set out in the article draft rules for its organisation.

On 8 July 1874, in the Quebec Institute in Lower Seymour Street, near Marble Arch, with Hodgson Pratt in the chair, the inaugural meeting was held of what was first to be called the Women's Protective and Provident Committee. An executive committee was elected, with Emma Paterson as secretary, although three people not on the original committee – Edith Simcox, Emilia Pattison (later Lady Dilke) and George Shipton, secretary of the London Trades Council – were to prove her most helpful allies. The Committee changed its name to 'League' after a few months, the words 'trade union' being deliberately avoided in order not to cause alarm.

In September 1874 Mrs Paterson read a paper – 'The Position of Women engaged in Handicrafts and other Industrial Pursuits' – at the Glasgow meeting of the Association for the Promotion of Social Science; and she began organising working women in a number of trades. Before the end of 1874 a Society of Women Employed in Bookbinding had been formed with three branches in London and two in the provinces [Boone (1968) 23]; and during 1875 the Dressmakers', Milliners' and Mantlemakers' Society, the Hat Trimmers' Society, the Society of

Women employed in the Upholstery Trade, and the Shirt, Collar and Underlinen Makers' Society were instituted by the League. Mrs Paterson had from the first given up the idea of a general union and from the beginning of the League it was, as she reported to the R.C. on the Factory and Workshop Acts in May 1875, 'a society for assisting working women to form trades unions'. Her evidence before this R.C. is instructive. While she was wholly in favour of the Factory Inspectorate enforcing adequate public health facilities and general conditions for women workers she was firmly against state regulation of women's hours of work. This was a common argument of many early feminists: that any special regulation of women's conditions would prejudice their chances of employment and could be understood as manoeuvres by the men to drive women out of industry. The Women's Suffrage movement, led by prominent Liberal women such as Mrs Fawcett, warmly supported these arguments on individualist grounds.

In October 1875 Emma Paterson and Edith Simcox (representing a women's union of shirt and collar makers) attended the Glasgow TUC. The year before, the Bristol National Union of Working Women – which Mrs Paterson had helped to establish – had sent a man to represent them at the TUC; and he had been admitted only after discussion, and some opposition, on the grounds that if a man was allowed to come as representative of the women the next thing would be that the women would want one of their own sex as a delegate. This was indeed what happened in 1875, but there was in fact no opposition, and Emma Paterson attended every TUC between 1875 and 1886 (except for 1882 when her husband died); and she was nominated several times for the Parliamentary Committee – on the last occasion, at the Hull Congress of 1886, she received forty-two votes, only seven below the lowest elected. She became a much respected delegate whose advocacy of women factory inspectors was one of the features of every Congress she attended. It was, too, one of her main campaigns outside the TUC. In 1881, for example, she organised a national conference on the issue, presided over by Lord Shaftesbury.

The leadership of the Women's Protective and Provident League had some obvious mid-Victorian attitudes. The first annual report disclaimed 'any views of antagonism towards the employers of female labour as a class' and deprecated a strike as 'rash and mistaken action'.

The object of the League [the first annual report stated] is to provide an *entente cordiale* between the labourer, the employer and the consumer: a revision of the contract between the labourer and employer is only recommended in those cases in which its terms appear unreasonable and unjust to the dispassionate third party, who pays the final price for the manufactured goods and is certainly not interested in adding artificially to their cost.

Fine words achieved little in the harsh world of Victorian industrial relations, and Emma Paterson and the League soon came to appreciate the realities involved in attempts to unionise working women. During the period of Mrs Paterson's leadership, the League had established between thirty and forty unions in Britain, but their membership was always small and few enjoyed a long life. Only the women's membership of the cotton unions increased steadily, but their unions were in a quite different world. Six months before she died, Mrs Paterson reported in July 1886 on the League's history during the first twelve years of its life:

In London ten societies have been formed, among women employed in bookbinding, dressmaking, upholstery work, hat-sewing, shirtmaking, sewing machine work, tailoring, laundry work (at Hampstead) and one of the women engaged as clerks and bookkeepers; four of these ten societies have failed and been dissolved, two of the tailoresses' branches are still very small, but the five other societies are thriving. . . . Since the first year of their establishment the league has given them no other help, and they are entirely managed by the committees and the quarterly meetings of their members. In the Provinces the league has formed, or helped to form, twenty-one societies viz., in Bristol, Dewsbury, Leicester, Manchester (2), Glasgow (2), Brighton, Dublin (2), Liverpool (3), Birkenhead, Oxford (2), Portsmouth, Nottingham, Aberdeen, Leeds, Dundee; of these only *nine* are still in existence.

Women were also admitted last year to the National Union of Operative Boot Rivetters and Finishers in Leicester, and more than 300 have joined. Wherever it is practical, and the men will agree to it, the league is strongly in favour of mixed societies, consisting of men and women working in the same trade. . . . what was desired was the establishment of 50 or 100 societies in the large centres of industry, so that women may no longer be mere blind ignorant tools in the hands of unscrupulous guides, but may have a voice and status in the industrial world [*Englishwoman's Rev.*, 14 Aug 1886, 372-3].

Throughout these years Emma Paterson was the driving force behind the League's work. She was its secretary, principal organiser and editor of its journal, the *Women's Union Journal*, established in February 1876. In this same year she founded the Women's Printing Society at Westminster. She had begun her working life as a bookbinder (and Henry King, secretary of the London Consolidated Society of Journeymen Bookbinders was always a close ally); but even in her women's suffrage days Emma Paterson had been interested in the printing side of the industry. A close friend, Emily Faithfull, worked at the Victoria Press, whose composing room was staffed entirely by women. Emma Paterson joined the business, learned the necessary printing skills, and in 1876 established her own Women's Printing Society, which she kept going with a fair degree of success to the end of her life.

Emma Paterson was above all other things a trade union organiser of working women; but she was a public figure too, and involved in many of the reform issues of her day: women's suffrage, parliamentary and school board elections, the formation of clubs for women and the establishment of productive co-operative societies. She was a determined feminist in the strict meaning of that term. The *Women's Union Journal*, most of which she wrote herself, was always, for instance, encouraging readers to learn to swim and there was an interesting advocacy of a 'reformed, rational and national' dress for women.

In physical appearance she was small-featured with an oval face and dark hair parted in the middle, pulled back from her forehead. She suffered much from what the second half of the twentieth century has called 'middle-class do-gooders' – those with a belief, as a contemporary of Emma Paterson's put it, that all social evils can be cured with 'half a crown and a bunch of grapes' [*Women's Union J.* (Dec 1886) 117]. She was a proud woman who often found it easier to do things herself than delegate, and she could be brusque and impatient with those she considered incompetent and unhelpful. But she was warmly respected by most and loved by many. Her mother and her husband provided her with a stable and affectionate domestic life and the death of both was a grievous loss to which she never fully adjusted. She herself was diagnosed during 1885 by Mrs Garrett Anderson, MD, as suffering from diabetes, and although she accepted medical advice to rest from her work her condition deteriorated and she died on 1 December 1886 at her Westminster home. Her funeral service at Paddington Cemetery was conducted by the Rev. Stewart Headlam, a close friend and associate for many years.

In memory of her and also of Miss Jeannette Wilkinson, a suffragist who assisted Mrs Paterson with work for the League and who had died earlier in 1886, a fund was set up and the money used to provide new accommodation in 1893 for the League's offices in the same building as the Working Men's Club and Institute Union in Clerkenwell Road. Immediately after Mrs Paterson's death, Lady Dilke took over her work for the League, assisted by Edith Simcox, but in 1887 Clementina Black was appointed secretary. In the following year the League's title was changed to Women's Trades Union Provident League and in 1890 to the Women's Trade Union League – a title which Emma Paterson had preferred when the organisation was originally founded.

Among the tributes to her work was one from W.J. Davis (secretary of the Brass Workers' Union and an opponent of the League's policies). In his *History* of the TUC he wrote: 'Mrs Paterson's views on restrictions of women's work were always unpopular, but she expressed them fearlessly, and no lady delegate was ever more respected.' From the members of the Women Bookbinders an inscription on vellum was hung in the League's office and concluded with the words: 'So long as these Associations shall continue to exist, women will owe to Emma Paterson an infinite debt of gratitude, which can best be manifested by following her rule of life, which was "To be unwearied in well-doing" ' [*Women's Union J.* (Feb 1887) 13]. On 20 April 1969, Audrey Prime, a member of the TUC General Council, unveiled a plaque on Emma Paterson's grave at Paddington Cemetery, and her role in the early history of women's trade unionism is being increasingly recognised by labour historians.

Writings: 'The Position of Working Women, and how to improve it', *Labour News* (Apr 1874) [repr. in Goldman (1974)]; 'The Position of Women engaged in Handicrafts and other Industrial Pursuits' in NAPSS, *Trans* (1874) [repr. in *Englishwoman's Rev.* (Jan 1875) and as a pamphlet by the WPPL, n.d.]; Evidence (with others) before R.C. on Factory and Workshop Acts 1876 XXX Qs 2704-814; 'Continuity of Employment and Rates of Wages', *Industrial Remuneration Conference* ([1885] repr. with an Introduction by John Saville, NY, 1968) 199-207; Preface to T. Paterson, *A New Method of Mental Science, with Applications to Political Economy* (1886) [this includes a memoir of T. Paterson repr. in Hall (1912)]. Mrs Paterson edited the *Women's Union J.* (1876-86) and wrote much of it herself.

Sources: WPPL, *Annual Reports*, nos 1-13 (1875-87); *Women's Union J.*, 1876-86; 'Women's Trade Unions, and their Founder', *Pall Mall Gazette*, 10 Apr 1884, 4; E.F.S. Dilke, 'Benefit Societies and Trades Unions for Women', *Fortn. Rev. 51* (1889) 852-6; idem and F. Routledge, *Trades Unionism among Women* [1893, repr. from *Fortn. Rev.* (May 1891)] 12 pp.; A.A. Bulley and M. Whitley, *Women's Work* (1894); *Fifth Report* of R.C. on Labour 1894 XXXV pt II App. III B; S. and B. Webb, *The History of Trade Unionism* (1894, later eds); *DNB 15* (1895-6); *Women in the Printing Trade* ed. J.R. MacDonald (1904); W.J. Davis, *The British Trades Union Congress: history and recollections* (1910); B.L. Hutchins and A. Harrison, *A History of Factory Legislation* (1911); B.T. Hall, *Our Fifty Years: the story of the Working Men's Club and Institute Union* (1912); B.L. Hutchins, *Women in Modern Industry* (1915); B. Drake, *Women in Trade Unions* [1920]; A.M. Anderson, *Women in the Factory* (NY, 1922); J. Blainey, *The Woman Worker and Restrictive Legislation* (1928); M.A. Hamilton, *Women at Work* (1941); G. Boone, *The Women's Trade Union Leagues in Great Britain and the United States of America* (NY, 1942; repr. 1968); B.C. Roberts, *The Trades Union Congress, 1868-1921* (1958); C.J. Bundock, *The Story of the National Union of Printing, Bookbinding and Paper Workers* (Oxford, 1959); K.A. McKenzie, *Edith Simcox and George Eliot* (Oxford, 1961); TUC, *Women in the Trade Union Movement* (1965) P; *Tribune*, 18 Apr 1969; H. Goldman, *Emma Paterson* (1974); T. Olcott, 'Dead Centre: the women's trade union movement in London, 1874-1914', *London J. 2*, no. 1 (May 1976) 33-50; S. Lewenhak, *Women and Trade Unions: an outline history of women in the British trade union movement* (1977). OBIT. *Women's Union J.* (Nov 1886), (Dec 1886) and (Feb 1887); *Pall Mall Gazette* and *Times*, 6 Dec 1886; *Englishwoman's Rev.*, 15 Dec 1886; *Club and Institute Union J.*, 18 Dec 1886.

JOYCE BELLAMY
JAMES A. SCHMIECHEN

See also: †Emily (Emilia) Francis Strong, Lady DILKE; †Mary MACARTHUR.

PEET, George (1883-1967)
TRADE UNIONIST

George Peet was born at Derby on 24 August 1883, the son of Thomas Peet, an engineering fitter, and his wife Elizabeth (née Brath). After leaving school, he served his time as an apprentice fitter in the railway workshops in Derby and joined the Derby branch of the ASE on 26 September 1904. He later moved to Manchester to work in the Gorton Railway Works, known as the 'Gorton Tank'; and transferred his union membership to Gorton 4th branch. He soon became active and was elected first a branch officer and then secretary. He represented Gorton 4th at the first conference on industrial syndicalism held under the leadership of Tom Mann at the Manchester Corn Exchange on 26 November 1910.

Exactly when and why Peet became a Socialist is not known; but some years before 1914 he was a member of the Openshaw Socialist Society [for which see Mahon (1976) 23-6 and App. 2] where he was influenced by Jim Crossley and Gilbert Roberts, and where he also became friends with Jack Munro (who later succeeded A.A. (Alf) Purcell as secretary of the Manchester and Salford Trades Council) and Harry Pollitt. Pollitt worked for a time in the boiler shop at Gorton Tank and they both became members of the Openshaw BSP.

Early in 1915 Peet was elected a shop steward at Gorton Tank, and a year later, in February 1916, he stood for assistant general secretary of the ASE. On the first ballot, after which he was eliminated, he came eighth out of twenty-two candidates.

George Peet and William McLaine, both members of the BSP, were the prime movers in the establishment of the Manchester Workers' Committee in early April 1916. This was within a week of the Clyde deportations, but the Committee did not become active in an effective way until the autumn. Then, in September 1916, the award of three shillings for time-workers only in engineering shops infuriated the pieceworkers to whom the award did not apply and on 2 December 2000 workers came out. They were persuaded to return by the EC of the ASE but it was a further three months before the dispute was settled. The strike committee remained in being, and in the meantime, at the end of 1916, Peet and McLaine brought together the original Workers' Committee and the Strike Committee into a Joint Engineering Shop Stewards' Committee. George Peet was secretary. There were two issues confronting the engineers at this time. One was the threat to abolish the trade card scheme, whereby all members of craft unions on munitions work were guaranteed exemption from military service; and the second was the attempt to introduce dilution to private work, i.e. work other than munitions. It was this latter issue that precipitated a strike at Tweedales and Smalley, near Rochdale. In March 1917 the firm had sought to transfer women dilutees to commercial work, and when the craftsmen refused to accept them, the firm locked them out. From the beginning of April the Rochdale district committee of the ASE supported their locked-out members and the national executive took up their case with the Government. Meanwhile the Joint Engineering Shop Stewards' Committee decided to arrange a workshop ballot on sympathetic strike action with the Rochdale engineers. The ballot went in favour of strike action and on the 29 April the Shop Stewards' Committee called the men out. By 5 May the issue of the threatened withdrawal of the trade card scheme had become part of the demands of the strikers.

This was the beginning of the largest strike of the war, involving 200,000 engineering workers for more than three weeks. The complicated history of the strikes – which spread irregularly throughout the country – has been told in detail in Hinton (1973) Ch. 5. On 18 May George Peet was arrested in London along with a number of other rank-and-file militants (including Arthur MacManus) but when they were tried at Bow Street on 23 May they were offered their freedom on condition that they signed the agreement which had been negotiated between the ASE and the Ministry of Munitions. They all signed.

The first representative national conference of shop stewards' organisations was held at Manchester on 18 and 19 August 1917. It elected a National Administrative Council with MacManus as chairman, George Peet as secretary, and J.T. Murphy assistant secretary. Peet was also an active member of the amalgamation committee movement which had been established in some centres immediately prior to the war, and had linked together in a national committee in 1915. Peet's friend, Percy Keeley, was a vice-president. On 13 and 14 October 1917 in Newcastle upon Tyne a national conference of the movement voted for the fusion of the amalgamation movement and the national shop stewards, thereby averting the alternative, which W.F. Watson favoured, of the amalgamation movement attempting to transform itself into a new union for engineering workers. Peet, with Ted Lismer and others, strongly opposed Watson in this matter; and a joint conference of the two organisations was held in the Milton Hall, Manchester, on 5 and 6 January 1918. A new NAC included Watson and Keeley, with Peet again as secretary and J.T. Murphy as his assistant. The conference report in *Solidarity* (Jan 1918) was signed by both Peet and Murphy.

In 1918 Peet stood for the official position of organising district delegate. His election address of 12 June 1918 called for 'the control of policy to be vested in the rank and file of the workshop' and for 'transforming the trade unions into industrial unions'. He came second out of four candidates in the ballot, but managed to secure election as one of the ASE's delegates to the 1918 TUC. In addition to his trade union and shop steward activities, Peet was a prominent member of the Manchester Labour College. He was class secretary and tutor, and reported in *Plebs* (Nov 1917) that there were classes operating in Openshaw, Salford and Stockport for the 1917-18 season.

During 1919 Peet represented the Shop Stewards' Committee on the National Committee of the 'Hands off Russia' movement. In January 1920, in London, he was at the national conference at which major changes were made in the composition of the NAC, William Gallacher and Nat Watkins being among those elected. The NAC decided to apply for affiliation to the Third International, and J.T. Murphy, Dave Ramsay, Gallacher and Jack Tanner went to Moscow in the summer of 1920 for conversations with the Russians on the future of international trade unionism. In September the meeting which heard the report back from Russia accepted the decision that since the shop stewards' movement was not a political party it could not affiliate to the Third International, but agreed to adhere to the provisional International Council of Trade and Industrial Unions (later the Red International of Labour Unions (RILU)). Within a few weeks a British Bureau was established in Manchester, with George Peet and Ted Lismer as joint secretaries. In the meantime in August 1920 George Peet, together with other members of the Openshaw branch of the BSP, became a foundation member of the Communist Party.

The NAC of the shop stewards' movement decided early in 1921 to try to bring together all the rank-and-file movements in the country. A Sheffield conference from 31 March to 2 April 1921 established the National Workers' Committee movement. There were sub-sections for mining and engineering. Peet and his colleagues were immediately involved in the events which led to 'Black Friday' [Bagwell (1971) 117 ff.] and Peet, on behalf of the NWC issued a leaflet *A Call to Action* addressed to railway and transport workers. It was an all-out attack upon the union leaderships and called, unsuccessfully, for a total stoppage on 16 May. Peet was arrested under the Emergency Powers Act, then still in operation, and he was sentenced to one month's imprisonment and a fine of £100.

In June 1922 the National Workers' Committee movement was merged with the British Bureau, with Peet and Lismer remaining as joint secretaries. By this time Peet was a member of the Manchester district committee of the Communist Party, and also of the district Political Bureau. He represented Manchester at the 5th Congress of the CPGB in London on 5 and 6 October 1922, and he and W. Duggan were elected to represent Lancashire and Cheshire on the council formed to advise the executive committee.

George Peet's close connection with revolutionary trade unionism came to an end in the summer of 1923 when, following a directive from the presidium of the Comintern, Gallacher and J.R. Campbell replaced Peet and Lismer as joint secretaries of the British Bureau of the RILU. The rest of Peet's union life seems to have been devoted almost wholly to an active role in his AEU branch. He held many offices and was a Referee for over forty years. He received his superannuation benefit on 17 July 1955 and he was still branch treasurer when he died on 21 November 1967 at the age of eighty-four. He left his body, for research purposes, to Manchester Infirmary.

For ten years George Peet had been at the centre of militant near-revolutionary trade unionism; and the decades of quiet, local service after 1922 offer a rather extraordinary contrast with his earlier career. Apart from his unshakeable belief in trade unionism, what his other attitudes and opinions were in the last forty-five years of his life, no one seems to know. He resigned from the

Communist Party, but when is not known, and he does not seem to have been involved in further political work in his area. He married but there were no children. J.T. Murphy summed him up: 'A quiet, plodding worker with whom it was a pleasure to be associated; a most painstaking, loyal comrade, a good-humoured and tireless worker for Socialism' [*New Horizons* (1941) 60].

Sources: *Industrial Syndicalist 1*, no. 6 (Dec 1910) [repr. Nottingham, 1974]; Minutes of the ASE District Committee [typescript], 1915, 1917; *ASE Monthly J.* (1916-18); *Plebs* (Nov 1917) 232; *Fusion of Forces: report of the Fifth National Rank and File Conference . . . Newcastle-on-Tyne October 13 and 14th, 1917* 22 pp.; *Solidarity* (Jan and May 1918); *ASE Election Address* (1918); J.T. Murphy, *The Workers' Committee: an outline of its principles and structure* (Sheffield Workers' Committee, Sheffield, 1918) 16 pp.; NWC, *A Call to Action* [leaflet] (1921); *Communist*, 14 Oct 1922; J.T. Murphy, *Preparing for Power* (1934); idem, *New Horizons* (1941; repr. 1942); R.P. Arnot, *The Impact of the Russian Revolution in Britain* (1967); J. Hinton, *The First Shop Stewards' Movement* (1973); J. Mahon, *Harry Pollitt: a biography* (1976); personal information: E. Clarke, secretary Gorton 4th AEUW, Manchester; Mrs E Davies, Denton [former member of Openshaw Socialist Society]; private papers and personal information: E. and R. Frow, Manchester.

EDMUND AND RUTH FROW
JOHN SAVILLE

PHILLIPS, Marion (1881-1932)
LABOUR PARTY ORGANISER AND MP

Marion Phillips was born on 29 October 1881 in Melbourne, Victoria, Australia. She was the youngest of seven children, three boys and four girls, born to Phillip David Phillips, a well-to-do Australian-born Jewish lawyer and his New Zealand wife Rose (née Asher). The family lived in Carlisle Street, St Kilda. They formed part of a prosperous, confidently-established Jewish community which contributed leaders such as Isaac Isaacs and John Monash, or like the Goldstein family, whose daughter Vida became the first woman to stand for parliament in Australia. Like Vida, she had part of her education, 1897-8, at the Presbyterian Ladies' College, perhaps Australia's most advanced girls' school at that time. From there she matriculated at Melbourne University, where she studied philosophy and history, graduating BA with honours in 1903.

In 1904 she came to London and won a research scholarship at the London School of Economics. There, under the supervision of Graham Wallas, she prepared a thesis on the role of Governor Macquarie in New South Wales for which she was awarded a DSc (Economics), and won the Hutchinson medal. The thesis was published as *A Colonial Autocracy* in 1909. In December 1906 she began work, under the direction of Beatrice Webb, on an inquiry into the condition of the children of widows in Derby as part of the Commission into the working of the Poor Laws. The next year it was decided to widen the inquiry. Mary Longman began work on Paddington, and the general direction of the research was handed over to Ethel Williams, a prominent feminist with a medical practice in Newcastle upon Tyne. In that year, 1907, Marion Phillips probably laid the real foundations for the rest of her life's work and associations. She became a member of the Fabian Society and the ILP. She also met Ethel Bentham, who had been at the London School of Medicine for Women with Ethel Williams and had gone to practise with her in Newcastle upon Tyne, before returning in 1909 to London and to active politics through the Fabian Society and the Women's Labour League. Both Mary Longman and Marion Phillips were installed in Ethel Bentham's house at 74 Lansdowne Road, Holland Park, working on their report for the Poor Law Commissioners on children in England and Wales, to be followed by another report on children in Scotland. For the next ten years Lansdowne Road, Holland Park, served as an alternate centre of feminist Socialist activity to the MacDonald home in Lincoln's

Inn Fields. It was from Lansdowne Road that the North Kensington branch of the Women's Labour League was established by Marion Phillips in 1910, and various practical projects like the Bonchurch Road Women's Co-operative Store and meeting rooms, and the Middleton-MacDonald Memorial Baby Clinic and Hospital were organised. For a time Susan Lawrence lived close by, as did Aino Malmberg, and at various times both Ethel Bentham and Marion Phillips served as borough councillors for Kensington. When Ethel Bentham moved from 74, Marion Phillips and Mary Longman moved to another house further down the road at 61. Mary Longman's marriage and departure for Stockholm after the end of the war, and Marion Phillips's appointment as chief woman officer of the reconstituted Labour Party, which gave her a regular source of income, brought about the end of Lansdowne Road as a centre of activity, and thenceforth Marion Phillips lived at 14 New Street Square.

The reports for the Poor Law Commissioners were finished by 1910. For a while, Marion Phillips acted as secretary to the National Union of Women's Suffrage Societies, then in June 1911 she became, for six months, organising secretary to the Women's Trade Union League. It was this work which gave her experience of organising and which first brought her into public prominence. It had been intended that she should assist Mary Macarthur in consolidating the gains made recently for women workers under the wages boards; and her expertise proved valuable in negotiations following the introduction of the National Insurance Bill. The strike of women workers that erupted that August in Bermondsey was, however, quite unforeseen, and Marion Phillips spent several weeks organising the strikers, speaking at meetings, leading processions in support, raising funds, and negotiating a settlement. She now became a lecturer in Public Administration at LSE for the session 1911-12, but this obviously did not occupy all her time.

She had been a member of the Women's Labour League since 1908, and in 1909 became an executive member on the nomination of Ethel Bentham, taking particular interest in questions relating to children and to the franchise. In November 1911 she offered to act as temporary secretary of the League while Margaret Bondfield, who had been elected secretary, was on sick leave. Thenceforth Marion Phillips became the effective secretary, being appointed officially when Margaret Bondfield resigned in 1912. At that time she also became editor of the *League Leaflet*; in May 1913 this became the *Labour Woman*, which she continued to edit (and half write) until her death. When Marion Phillips was heavily pressed during the war years, Mary Longman took over the secretaryship of the Women's Labour League in her place. In the years before the war, Phillips was a candidate for the NAC of the ILP in 1912 and 1913, and was elected to it in 1914.

At the outbreak of war, as secretary of the Women's Labour League she became a member of the War Emergency Workers' National Committee; and she was a regular attender. She accepted nomination to the Queen's Work for Women Fund Committee in 1914, thereby helping to transform a potential charity into a major policy-forming body on women's work throughout the war. In 1917 she was present at the formation of the Standing Joint Committee of Industrial Women's Organisations, of which she became secretary. This body represented the three main groups of women within the labour movement; those who were organised into unions or the co-operative movement, and the growing number of women who were in neither movement but who had joined a branch of the Women's Labour League. Gradually the Standing Joint Committee assumed responsibility for all questions relating to women in the working classes. The activities of other *ad hoc* bodies set up for specific purposes, for instance the Central Committee on Women's Employment, or the committee to watch over the implementation of the National Insurance Act (in both of which Phillips was a moving and guiding force) gradually came under the umbrella of the SJC. In her capacity as secretary, Phillips was in a strong position to claim to speak for a very large number of women; and it was probably in this capacity rather than in any other that she was invited to serve on government committees and inquiries during the war and the period of reconstruction; most significant of these committees were undoubtedly the Consumers' Council of the Ministry of Food and the Women's Advisory

Committee of the Ministry of Reconstruction. While the problems of women's employment and unemployment after the war remained one of her most substantial concerns during the immediate post-war years, she also developed a new concern with housing policy; and the questionnaire technique which she had used effectively to produce her report *The School Doctor and the Home*, published in 1913, was employed again. With the help of Averil Sanderson Furniss, *The Working Women's House* was published in 1919 and for a time Dr Phillips was active at conferences on housing policy and a vice-chairman of the Garden Cities Association. She was also a lecturer in Social Science at LSE from 1918 to 1920.

The reorganisation of the Labour Party necessitated restructuring the Women's Labour Leagues, and this was Marion Phillips's major activity towards the end of the war and in the early twenties. It was decided to retain a women's movement within the new branch structure of the Labour Party. The women were to continue to meet as women's sections, and the structure of regional and district conferences was retained in the new Women's Advisory Councils. By these arrangements it was hoped that the real objects for which the Women's Labour League had been formed in the first place might still be achieved, namely that women themselves would be personally active and involved in politics, not leaving to the men attendance at meetings, discussion, and policy-making. In 1914, carrying out one of Margaret MacDonald's unfinished projects, Phillips had produced a small pamphlet called *How to do the Work of the League*. It was a very simple instruction manual for women who were inexperienced in the conduct of public organisations, explaining what officers were needed, what their duties were, how meetings were run, records kept and other details. This admirable manual was up-dated for the new women's sections, renamed *Women's Work in the Labour Party*, and reissued for 6*d*. In 1918 a rather larger volume was compiled by Phillips, called *Women and the Labour Party*, containing essays written by a galaxy of leading Labour women and with a foreword by Arthur Henderson; it outlined and discussed matters of policy which were of particular interest to women. Phillips herself spent a great deal of time going about the branches explaining what their new role might be. Backed by the resources of the whole Labour movement – hitherto funds had come from memberships, donations, a few small bequests, and some traditional fund-raising – it was possible to expand the number of women organisers in the Party who were not restricted to organising women's sections. Phillips was certainly the woman for the job; as Beatrice Webb noted in 1917-18 she was 'shrewd and capable' and also 'redoubtable' [Cole (1952) 85 and 116].

It seems likely that this unusual concern about the place of women in the Party was due to the way in which the franchise was extended after the war. Special techniques were needed to mobilise the votes of working women over thirty. The way in which Marion Phillips as chief woman officer organised and ran the women's section through the twenties certainly showed a fine kind of positive discrimination, recognising and providing for many of the peculiar difficulties which women experience in entering active politics. She attempted to cater not only for shyness and diffidence and total inexperience, but also for the inability to relate a housebound existence to the issues of politics. Often in the *Labour Woman* she took time to explain the simple whys and wherefores, ranging from 'what the League of Nations means to you and your children' to 'why and how do I canvass for the coming election?' Her role was often that of an advocate. She used the *Labour Woman* and her regular visits and addresses up and down the country to create opinion among women, and to inform and educate them about issues which their education and daily life had made remote. In matters connected with food, housing and the position of children it was very easy to produce a well-formed debate. Other areas of potential policy-making were more sensitive. Subjects such as venereal disease, abortion and contraception were treated with great care. She tried to ensure that such difficult matters were treated as educational rather than political questions, and she rejected attempts to debate them at party conferences. She willingly published articles and book reviews when they were available. Whatever her own personal responses to these issues, she was very much aware of the possibility of creating embarrassment, splitting branches, or driving away those women she sought most to include if such problems became matters for policy discussion. All this, and her handling of news relating to the royal family suggests a very interesting readership and group of correspondents and contacts. The births, marriages, and deaths of members of the royal family seem to have occasioned the same kind of interest among readers of the *Labour Woman* as was appreciated and fostered by more conventional women's magazines. Rather than ignore or ridicule this somewhat illogical behaviour, Phillips would respond with firm editorials or articles pointing out the superior advantages which would be available to the latest royal child, or how many working women could be clothed on a royal lady's dress allowance, and how many working families could be kept on a royal marriage grant.

By 1925 the Women's Section was firmly established. Her contacts abroad had also developed. This international aspect of her work had gained considerably in significance since the early days of the British section of the Women's International Council of Socialist and Labour Organisations, of which she had been chairman. Throughout the war she sought to further the cause of peace by maintaining links with women's Socialist organisations throughout Europe, and after the war, she played a prominent role in the formation of the International Federation of Working Women, of which she was international secretary for six years. In 1921 she also represented the Standing Joint Committee on a women's committee which successfully pressed for greater representation and involvement of women in the League of Nations. By 1920 her annual holidays had come to mean another conference or meeting somewhere in Europe. In 1920, for instance, she visited Norway to address a women's conference on housing organised by the Norwegian Garden Cities Association and took the opportunity also of visiting Sweden and Finland; in 1922 it was the International Trades Union Congress in Amsterdam. By the late twenties she had built up a wide connection of friends in Socialist movements throughout Europe and she took advantage of this connection to see for herself the progress of Socialism in post-war Europe and to keep her readers at home interested and informed.

The success of Labour in the general election of 1924 was the signal for accelerated activity on the part of the chief woman officer, but she saw the events of that year mainly as an incentive for increased membership and through this for increasing pressure on the Government to carry women's demands on housing, pensions, and the vote. It is a measure of her own political position, however, that she placed the recognition of Russia ahead of all these in her editorial on the new Government [*Labour Woman* (June 1924)]. And despite the events of the later part of that year and the general election which followed, it seems likely that she had time to think about writing, in collaboration, the only large book she produced after the publication of her thesis. There is no indication of when she began or of how much she actually wrote herself of *English Women in Life and Letters* (1926). Her co-author was William Shirley Tomkinson but the plan of the book, its approach and its style suggest considerable Phillips influence. Its emphasis on working women rather than on significant or achieving women seems unusual even now. And its intention remained admirable – to provide a simply written (and fascinatingly illustrated) account of life through the ages as viewed by women from their kitchens or doorsteps. Unfortunately it was too early for cheap cheerful production, and more unfortunately it stopped abruptly about the beginning of the nineteenth century. It caused little interest, and was even omitted from the list of publications in her entry in *Who's Who*.

She was inevitably deeply involved in the crisis which grew out of the miners' lock-out in 1926. Under her guidance a kind of 'Industrial Red Cross' was formed to support the wives and children of those men who were locked out, and thereby considerable strength was added to the men's determination not to give in. A women's committee was formed in London to raise money to provide milk for mothers with babies, shoes and clothes for children, and ultimately even holidays, and a temporary foster scheme for children who were victims of the shortages caused by the lock-out. In all £313,000 was raised in Britain and abroad by this committee, and when the work was over, Marion Phillips wrote an account of how and why it was done, this time with a foreword by A.J. Cook. *Women and the Miners' Lock-Out* drew together some of her most telling experiences.

At the end of 1926 Marion Phillips was announced as prospective parliamentary candidate for the Labour Party in Sunderland. Her chief sponsors were the Durham Women's Advisory Council, who promised £70 p.a., raised mainly from their annual bazaar, towards the expenses of the constituency. The women's division in County Durham was one of the strongest (and oldest) outside London. Dr Phillips had long-standing links with it, considerably strengthened by the Miners' Lock-out. In 1929 she was able, as their newly-elected MP, to help them to celebrate their 21st birthday; and it seemed appropriate that she should be their candidate at the first election in which all women over twenty-one were entitled to vote.

The Standing Joint Committee produced a report in 1929 on women and the coming general election, pointing out that of 25 million registered voters that year, 14 million were women. Although a great deal of amusement was found by the popular press in the 'flapper vote', in the *Labour Woman* Phillips continued to stress the opportunities now open to working girls to cast their votes for the Labour Party. When the election was over, she wrote to the Durham women thanking them for all their help – which included getting ready a house where she lived during the last month of the campaign – and emphasising the crucial importance of the women's vote in winning the election for Labour.

The auspicious aspects of the 1929 election for Marion Phillips faded rather quickly. Sunderland was still a two-member consituency, and Dr Phillips's fellow-member was Alf Smith. His death on 12 February 1931 necessitated a by-election just six months before the general election in October that year. The local Party's financial resources were put under serious strain but even more important was the steady erosion of confidence in the MacDonald Government. Disillusion was felt first at the municipal level, and political disagreements led to a breakdown in relations between the Labour Party in Sunderland and the members of the ILP. Harry Leedale, Phillips's agent in Sunderland, found he could no longer stand the pressures, and resigned, suffering a series of strokes soon after. The new agent was a Sunderland man (Leedale had come over from Bishop Auckland) and seemed better able to reconcile the factions, but the strain of two strenuous jobs was beginning to tell on Phillips herself. She usually managed to spend one weekend each month in Sunderland, staying most often at the Palatine Hotel, leaving Kings Cross early on Friday afternoon, and often travelling back overnight on Sunday. This weekend was packed with meetings, functions, appointments, and discussions. Indeed she wrote once that she did not 'want to have nothing to do'. The rest of her time when the House was not sitting was still taken up with travelling and organisational work as chief woman officer. She still regarded this as her most important work and felt that the constituency came second.

One of the causes of tension in the Sunderland constituency was a constant shortage of money. Alf Smith had been partly supported by his union – the TGWU. But Marion Phillips could contribute little – £50 p.a. to the agent's salary, and an occasional small donation. It is difficult to discover what her relations with her constituents were like. D.N. Pritt, who was her fellow candidate in 1931 said she was 'idolised' in Sunderland [Pritt (1965) 29]. The women certainly approved of her, and she was respected for her efficiency, organising ability, her fearless and often very sharp wit on public platforms; but in other respects she was probably not really suited to the role of constituency MP. She often appeared autocratic and her failing health must also have been a contributory cause of the strains and tensions that developed. She lost the 1931 election, despite a last-minute appeal to Liberal voters to come out for Phillips and Pritt.

She entered the Empire Nursing Home in Westminster a few days before Christmas 1931 for an exploratory operation which revealed extensive cancer of the stomach. The January number of the *Labour Woman*, which she edited from her hospital bed, was her last. She died on 23 January 1932, and was cremated at Golders Green. The gross value of her will was £267. The Rev. A.D. Belden conducted a memorial service at Whitefield's Tabernacle. In his address he stressed both her Jewishness and her Socialism, but neither he nor any of the other speakers was able to say how much the Jewishness meant to her. She had, as member for Sunderland, been co-operative with the local Zionists, but that is all the evidence there is.

In her capacity as chief woman officer or as secretary to the Standing Joint Committee she was the automatic choice to represent working women on inquiries and committees, and she was able to put their case on a great many occasions simply because she knew how to insist that it would be heard. The range of her interests and involvements was enormous, from national insurance and pensions to housing, from income tax to the double-shift system and night baking, from the League of Nations to the cost and quality of milk. Her guiding principle was always the need to improve the position of working women, especially working men's wives, and working girls destined to become the wives of working men, and the children of these women. The one thing on which all of Marion Phillips's contemporaries were agreed was that she had a magnificent talent for organisation. Even so, they failed to appreciate the size and number of the problems she overcame in bringing the message of the Labour movement and of Socialism to the women who by the nature of their work were furthest removed from its theory and influence.

Marion Phillips was a small, dark woman, with a firm chin and a serious expression which was sometimes made formidable by her rimless spectacles. In middle age she grew heavier and looked very matronly and increasingly Jewish. She was known at Labour Party headquarters affectionately as Maid Marion, in Sunderland as Dr Marion, and when seen in the company of Leah Manning in the bar at Parliament House as 'United Dairies'. In the House of Commons, opposition members sometimes called her 'The Kangaroo'. The most apt description is the one she used herself invariably – Marion Phillips, chief woman officer, with no favours asked and none given.

Writings: *How to raise Money for Public Services without increasing the Burdens of Poverty* [1909?] 14 pp.; *A Colonial Autocracy. New South Wales under Governor Macquarie, 1810-1821* (1909); 'New Names or New Meanings: the reports of the Royal Commission on the Poor Laws', *Englishwoman 1* (Mar 1909) 156-78; 'The Claim of the Illegitimate Child', ibid., *3* (Sep 1909) 147-53; *The School Doctor and the Home: results of an inquiry into medical inspection and treatment of school children* [1913] 32 pp.; 'Suffrage and Militancy', *Soc. Rev. 11* (June 1913) 257-62; *The Green-Sprig Party: a story for young people* (1913) 32 pp.; *How to do the Work of the League* (1914) 12 pp.; (with G.D.H. Cole et al.), *Some Problems of Urban and Rural Industry* (Birmingham, 1917); editor of *Women and the Labour Party* (1918); (with A.S. Lawrence and G. Tuckwell), *Labour Women on International Legislation* (1919) 16 pp.; *Co-operation in House Management* (1920) 3 pp.; (with A.D.S. Furniss), *The Working Woman's House* [1920]; *Organisation of Women within the Labour Party: a handbook for officers and members of women's sections* (1921) 15 pp.; *The Young Industrial Worker: a study of his educational needs* (Oxford, 1922); *Women and Children in the Textile Industry: an international survey of hours of work and age of entry* (Amsterdam, 1922) 29 pp.; (with G. Tavener), *Women's Work in the Labour Party: notes for speakers' and workers' classes* [1923] 19 pp.; (with W.S. Tomkinson), *English Women in Life and Letters* (Oxford, 1926); *Women and the Miners' Lock-Out: the story of the women's committee for the relief of the miners' wives and children* (1927); 'Maternity: a primary problem of Socialist policy', *Labour Mag. 7* (May 1928) 19-20; *Socialism and Women* [1931] 32 pp. Marion Phillips edited and largely wrote the *Labour Woman* (1911-32) and was either a member of, or gave evidence before several Government Commissions and Committees. These included: (with M. Longman and E.M.N. Williams), *Report on the Condition of the Children . . . in receipt . . . of Poor Law Relief in England and Wales*, Cd 5037, and (with M. Longman and C.T. Parsons), *Report on the Condition of the Children . . . in receipt . . . of Poor Law Relief in certain parishes in Scotland*, Cd 5075 in R.C. on the Poor Laws 1910 LII Apps XVIII and XXIII; Evidence before the S.C. on Pensions and Grants (Naval and Military) 1914-16 IV Qs 875-1072, R.C. on Income Tax 1919 XXIII Qs 3497-569, and Departmental Committee on the Employment of Women and Young Persons on the Two-Shift System 1920 XIX Qs 1524-620; Member of Civil War Workers' Committee 1918 XIV Reports Cd 9117, 9192 and 9228, the Ministry of Reconstruction Women's Advisory Committee on the Domestic Service Problem 1919 XXIX and the Ministry of Health Inter-Departmental Committee on the Rent Restriction Acts [Marley Committee] 1930-1 XVII.

Sources: (1) MSS: Labour Party archives especially the Marion Phillips papers and papers relating to the Workers' National Committee, the Consumers' Council, Women's Labour League and Standing Joint Committee; see also C. Cook et al., *Sources in British Political History 1900-1951* 4 (1977) 105-6. (2) Files of *Women's Trade Union Rev.* (1910-21) and *Labour Woman* (1911-21); M.A. Hamilton, *Mary Macarthur: a biographical sketch* (1925); *Labour Who's Who* (1927); *WWW* (1929-40); *Daily Herald*, 11 July 1929; Debrett, *House of Commons* (1930); LSE, *Register* (1934); M.G. Bondfield, *A Life's Work* [1949]; *Beatrice Webb's Diaries 1912-1924*, ed. M.I. Cole (1952); D.N. Pritt, *The Autobiography of D.N. Pritt 1* (1965); P. Brookes, *Women at Westminster: an account of women in the British Parliament 1918-1966* (1967); L. Manning, *A Life for Education: an autobiography* (1970); S. Lewenhak, *Women and Trade Unions: an outline history of women in the British trade union movement* (1977); biographical information; the late T.A.K. Elliott, CMG; personal information: Len Fox, Sydney; A.A. Phillips, Melbourne, nephew. OBIT. *Daily Herald, Manchester Guardian, Morning Post, News Chronicle, Times* and *Western Mail*, 25 Jan 1932; *Arbeiter Zeitung*, 26 Jan 1932; *Labour Mag. 10* (Feb 1932) 460-1; *Railway Service J.* (Feb 1932); *Labour Woman* (Mar 1932).

BEVERLEY KINGSTON

See also: †Margaret Grace BONDFIELD; †Mary MACARTHUR.

PHIPPEN, William George (1889-1968)
TRADE UNIONIST AND LABOUR COLLEGE ORGANISER

George Phippen (he did not use his first given name) was born in Ystrad, Glamorgan, on 22 October 1889, the son of William Phippen, a miner, and his wife Jane (née Collins). He was the oldest of seven children, four sons and three daughters. His father was a strong influence – he was prominent in the South Wales Miners' Federation; was one of the early Socialist candidates in local government elections; a founder member of the Ystrad Rhondda Labour Club, and active in the Ton Pentre Co-operative Society, in the ILP, and later on in the Labour Party.

George went to Bodringallt Infant and Boys' Schools; but at twelve years of age, having taken what was familiarly called 'a labour exam' – to pass it meant permission to leave school – he went into the pits. He remained there until the later part of 1917, when he and his brother Frank and Jack Jones, later an NCLC lecturer [Craik (1964) 177], went to Ireland to avoid being conscripted. When the war ended George returned to the pits of the Rhondda and worked there till September 1919, when he, his brother and Jack Jones each won a South Wales Miners' Scholarship to the Central Labour College in Earls Court, London. The scholarships were for a two-year course; also at the College in Phippen's time, 1919-21, were Aneurin Bevan, Ness Edwards, Jim Griffiths, and Len Williams. While he was still at the college he helped to form the London Council for Independent Working-Class Education, which later became absorbed into the National Council of Labour Colleges.

Even before this, George Phippen had been active in trade union affairs, and he was a member of the Unofficial Reform Committee which was set up to alter the cautious and conservative approach to mining problems associated with the policies of William Abraham (Mabon). Phippen also contributed to local Socialist journals, the *Rhondda Socialist* and the *South Wales Worker*, for example. Later he wrote for the *Plebs*, the journal of the NCLC.

When he had finished his college course, since no work was available in the Rhondda after the 1921 strike, he became the first London and district organiser for the NCLC – a cause to which he devoted the rest of his life. For a long period he was secretary of the NCLC London Council.

NCLC courses were Marxist, and at first dealt almost wholly in economics, industrial history, and philosophy; but later on they became rather wider in scope. Phippen supplied every kind of instruction asked for – courses, single lectures, weekend and day schools, conferences – for trade union branches, Labour Parties, and Co-operative Guilds. He was an excellent teacher, clear, logical, very knowledgeable, with the relevant facts and figures stored in his reliable memory. It was also part of his business to find lecturers and speakers among trade unionists and Labour workers; and he was always ready to urge on beginners, give them information or tell them where to find it, and show them the best techniques for teaching an audience. He spent a lot of time visiting trade union branches and Labour Parties and Co-operative Guilds, and persuaded a majority of these to affiliate to the Labour College. With local help he formed a Labour College in Southall, his own area of London, and he also joined and often visited the Southall Labour Club, and was a life member after his retirement.

During the Second World War, finding that attendance at courses was falling off, Phippen and his colleague Eric Hutchison persuaded Civil Defence and Fire Service sections – which included many trade unionists – to listen to talks from NCLC speakers who came to the various posts. At the time of the flying bombs the Phippens' house was badly damaged, and they themselves shaken, though not hurt.

When George Phippen retired, in 1954, a dinner was held in his honour in the House of Commons. He was then living in Margate, and Margate kept him in touch with old friends and with Labour happenings by its popularity as a conference centre. Moreover, he continued to teach, and to be active as honorary secretary to the London District Council of the NCLC. When this organisation was finally wound up, on being absorbed into the TUC education department in 1964, a meeting was held to pay tribute to George Phippen and his work. In replying, Phippen said, 'the movement has existed firstly to make Socialists and then Activists. We fashioned the tools for others to use.' This was a characteristically modest description of his devoted work. It is worth noting that he always refused to stand for any local government or parliamentary seat, lest he should be distracted from what he regarded as his proper job, the education of the workers. It is also worth noting that Phippen won the respect and affection of individuals on the extreme Left of the movement as well as those who held more orthodox opinions. As far as can be discovered Phippen was not a Stalinist and certainly not a Trotskyist. Jock Haston writes that he had an excellent Marxist library but only three of Trotsky's books – *History of the Russian Revolution, Literature and Revolution* and *In Defence of Terrorism* – and that Phippen was almost certainly unfamiliar with Trotsky's polemical writings [letter dated 18 Nov 1976].

When Labour came into office in 1964, Phippen hoped for great changes; but as time went on he complained that the Government was only patching up capitalism. He even spoke of resigning his membership of the Labour Party, though he does not seem to have carried out this threat. His wife and coadjutor Mary Shaw died on 18 April 1968, and George Phippen himself died only a fortnight later, on 4 May. His death seems to have been hastened by pneumoconiosis contracted while he was a miner. He left an estate valued at £6450. There were no children of the marriage. After his death most of his books were purchased by the ETU and are now in the library of Esher College, the union's educational centre. A small commemorative plaque was put up in the library.

George's three brothers were also Marxists. The youngest, Harry, born in 1908, was an active trade unionist and ILP member. He worked as an agent for the Co-operative Insurance Society until his retirement in 1967 because of ill-health [private information from Harry Phippen, 1976].

Writings: 'Purchasing Power Parity' [letter], *Plebs 17* (Dec 1925) 486; 'Against Family Allowances', ibid., *22* (July 1930) 150-1; 'A British-Made Socialist Classic', ibid., *34* (Nov 1941) 209.

Sources: W.W. Craik, *The Central Labour College 1909-29* (1964); biographical information: J.W. Kenyon, Sherwood, Nottingham; personal information: S. Bidwell, MP; A. Bottomley OBE, MP; Idris Cox, Prague; J. Crispin, Derby; F. Crump, Newbury; D.J. Davies, Ystrad, brother-in-law; G. Evans, Southall; Jock Haston, London; E. Hutchison, Rustington; Harry

Phippen, Barton, Torquay, brother; A. Vandome, Buntingford, Herts. OBIT. *Plebs* (June 1968).
The editors are indebted to Mr D.J. Davies for an earlier draft of this biography.

MARGARET 'ESPINASSE

PLUNKETT, Sir Horace Curzon (1854-1932)
CO-OPERATOR AND POLITICIAN

Horace Plunkett was born on 24 October 1854 at Sherborne House, Gloucester. He was the third
son of the 16th Baron Dunsany and of Anne Constance Dutton, daughter of the 2nd Baron
Sherborne. He was educated at preparatory school, Eton and University College, Oxford. In
1878, on coming down from Oxford, he founded a co-operative store at Dunsany, Co. Meath,
the Irish home of his father's family. The following ten years, however, were spent in the United
States, where Plunkett engaged in ranching. The death of his father in 1889 left him financially
independent and charged with the management of the family's commercial interests, which
included coal, coal-carrying and boat-building concerns. From this time onward Ireland became
the main centre of his activities, as evidenced by an article he had written, 'Co-operative Stores
for Ireland' [*19th C.* (Sep 1888)]. This brought him into contact with J.C. Gray of the
Co-operative Union, who had come to Ireland to assess the progress of co-operation there and to
assist in the formation of Irish societies. It was on Plunkett's initiative that the organisers of an
Irish Exhibition, held in London in July 1888, had invited the southern section of the
Co-operative Union to organise a conference on the prospects of the extension of co-operation to
Ireland; but it would seem that his meeting with Gray initiated Plunkett's formal connection with
the co-operative movement. An Irish section of the Co-operative Union was established, under
the aegis of which co-operation was promoted in the early years. Plunkett became chairman of
the section and R.A. Anderson, a land agent recruited to the movement by Plunkett, was
appointed secretary.

In those days of the 'Plan of Campaign', the radicals of the Irish nationalist movement were
urging tenants to withhold rents from certain landlords, who included Plunkett's sister. The
co-operative gospel evidently came as a welcome enlightenment to one supporter of the landlord
class, as a method whereby 'wealth was not to be taken from one class to enrich another, but
actually to be *created,* by thrift, by honest dealing and by the loyalty of the participants in
partnership one with another' [Anderson (1935) 4].

At the outset Plunkett was unaware of developments in the Irish dairying industry which
would make it the most successful area of co-operative enterprise, and he was also unfamiliar
with the situation in Europe. His knowledge of co-operation, acquired from reading and limited
to the English experience (though he was aware of the early-nineteenth-century Owenite
experiment at Ralahine, Co. Clare), had led him to the conclusion that Irish co-operators must
develop a strong distributive base before co-operative production was attempted. This belief was
fortified by a conventional and simplistic analysis of the Irish situation. Plunkett had to learn
quickly during the following years; but certain features of his thinking were already established:
the importance of co-operation as a character-builder, in inculcating the qualities of industry,
thrift and sobriety; the important role which the 'wealthier and more intelligent classes' must
play in the development of co-operation in Ireland and the function of co-operation in eradicating
hostility between the classes; and his hostility to one particular section of Irish society, the
retailer or 'gombeen man'.

Following the constitution of the Irish section of the Co-operative Union, Plunkett quickly
gathered round him the body of men who pioneered the Irish movement: men like Anderson, the
Rev. T.A. Finlay, Lord Monteagle, and the poet, mystic and painter 'AE' (George W. Russell).
Plunkett was indefatigable in the promotion of the movement, contributing financially,
canvassing the support of anyone who might be useful to the cause, and travelling ceaselessly on
exhausting organising tours.

Co-operation developed quickly in its first decade, in terms of membership and the number and types of society, and also geographically. Creamery societies were the most numerous form, but there were also agricultural societies, credit societies on the German Raiffeisen model, poultry societies, and other miscellaneous types. As the propaganda work progressed, Plunkett obtained valuable assistance from the Irish clergy, who in many areas played an important role in the growth of the movement. It is clear that Irish farmers were prepared to accept the technical assistance and the practical benefits of organisation which Plunkett and his co-workers placed at their disposal, without being influenced (as nationalist politicians like John Dillon feared they would be) by their unionist politics; for the most part, also, they remained uninfluenced by the idealism of the idealogues of the movement – Plunkett, Father Finlay and 'AE'. As the movement grew, new forms of organisation developed. In 1893 the Co-operative Agency Society was founded for the marketing of butter. In 1894 the Irish Agricultural Organisation Society (IAOS) was founded on Plunkett's initiative to carry on the propaganda work begun by the Co-operative Union in the agricultural sector and to provide technical assistance to societies. Plunkett was president of the IAOS until 1899, and again from 1907 until his death; R.A. Anderson was secretary until 1926. Considerable care was taken over the composition of the committee of the new organisation to ensure that it would consist equally of nationalists and unionists. Plunkett was now placing the emphasis quite firmly on producer co-operation and assuring the public that the establishment of co-operative stores in rural districts was 'a project which is no part of our movement' [letter in *Irish Times,* 7 Oct 1895]. In 1895 a dispute between the producer-orientated Irish movement and the consumer-orientated English movement, concerning the promotion of creameries in Ireland by the CWS, came to a head with a resolution moved at the Co-operative Congress by Plunkett criticising the action of the CWS. Although English co-operators such as Thomas Hughes, E.O. Greening and H.W. Wolff spoke in favour of the motion, another delegate of the Irish section, W.L. Stokes, a butter merchant and an agent for the CWS, spoke against it. The motion was lost and Plunkett and his supporters seceded from the English movement by the end of the year, though Plunkett was made an honorary member of the Co-operative Union, a position he held until his death. In 1896 the *Irish Homestead* was founded as the mouthpiece of the Irish co-operative movement, being edited successively by Finlay and 'AE'. It played a central role in the attempt to inculcate the ideals of the movement among its readers. In 1898 the Irish Agricultural Wholesale Society was established to handle the bulk produce of goods for societies.

His philanthropic work brought Plunkett public notice and in 1892 he became a member of the newly constituted Congested Districts Board, a post which he held until ill-health forced him to restrict his activities in 1918. From 1892 to 1900 he represented the Southern division of Dublin County in the Conservative and Unionist interest at Westminster. Plunkett's friends in the co-operative movement generally regretted his incursions into politics, which created complications for the non-political movement. But his involvement increased his public reputation; a result due in no small measure to the eccentric nature of his political stance, based on an often naive idealism. Possibly the greatest of his political achievements was the assembling of the 'Recess Committee' in the aftermath of the general election of 1895 which placed Home Rule outside the realm of practical politics for a number of years. The committee was remarkable in that it brought leading Irishmen of every persuasion together (the elected representatives of the anti-Parnellite nationalists excepted) to press the government for certain reforms without prejudice to long-term objectives. From Plunkett's point of view, his experience in the co-operative movement had persuaded him that voluntary effort must be supplemented by State assistance, and he was fully convinced that Ireland's relative backwardness agriculturally and industrially was in no small degree the result of deficiencies in the educational system. He was particularly concerned at the lack of proper agricultural and technical education. Plunkett was chairman of the committee, which recommended the setting up of a Ministry of Agriculture and Industries for Ireland, to be advised by a consultative council representing the agricultural and industrial interests of the country. Within this framework, the complicated system under which Irish education and agriculture was administered would be rationalised. An important principle laid down in the report (issued in 1896) was that State aid should be strictly supplementary to local initiative – and not a substitute for it.

In 1899 the Irish Department of Agriculture and Technical Instruction (DATI) was established, with a structure and powers which owed much to the *Report of the Recess Committee*. Plunkett became vice-president of the Department, of which the Irish Chief Secretary was president. He began his term of office by antagonising Irish Unionist opinion through the appointment of T.P. Gill, a nationalist who had been an agent of the 'Plan of Campaign' (which had urged the withholding of rents from some landlords), to the important post of secretary of the Department. He lost his parliamentary seat in 1900, failed in a by-election in Galway Town in 1901, and did not stand in any subsequent election.

In 1904 he published his book, *Ireland in the New Century* – a survey of the factors which went into the shaping of the Irish character, of the self-help movement, and of the DATI and its policies. Although the book represented an honest attempt to come to terms with the realities of the Irish situation, it suffered from certain weaknesses in the analysis which arose from Plunkett's basic assumptions. The most important of these was that all progress depended primarily on individual moral development. His view also that Ireland's relative backwardness at that time was largely due to the effect on the Irish character of the nature of Irish politics and to certain aspects of Roman Catholicism was a gross simplification as well as highly controversial. The publication of the book was probably the most disastrous step of Plunkett's career. John Redmond, who had co-operated with him in the 1890s and who was now leader of the reunited Irish Parliamentary Party, broke publicly with Plunkett.

Despite the loss of his seat in Parliament, Plunkett had continued as vice-president of the DATI, but relations between the IAOS and the Department quickly became strained. Plunkett, absorbed in the work of the Department and eager to ensure the success of the new institution, tended to side more with the Departmental officials. With the return of a Liberal Government to office in 1906, his position at the Department became anomalous and hostile nationalists (among whom the leading personality was John Dillon) were encouraged to press for his dismissal. In 1906 a Commission of Inquiry was set up to examine the working of the Department, and this reported favourably (with the exception of a minority report) in 1908. But meanwhile, Plunkett himself had been forced to resign his vice-presidency in 1907 by continuing pressure on the Government from the Irish Parliamentary Party and in this year Plunkett resumed the presidency of the IAOS, which he had vacated in 1899. With the advent of T.W. Russell (whose hatred of landlordism had been a major factor in his conversion from Unionism to support for Home Rule) as Plunkett's successor at the Department, relations between the IAOS and the DATI deteriorated seriously.

In 1908 Plunkett published his pamphlet, *Noblesse Oblige: an Irish rendering,* calling yet again, and for the last time, upon his own class – the Anglo-Irish gentry – to play their part in the economic, social and cultural regeneration of Ireland. He was now becoming more concerned in a systematic way with the 'rural life problem': the unhalting flow of population from country to city, and the effects of this on the whole structure of rural life. In this pamphlet he used the slogan, which he had taken over from Theodore Roosevelt, 'better farming, better business, and better living' [p. 15]. In 1908 he read a paper, 'Science and the Problem of Rural Life', to the British Association for the Advancement of Science, then meeting in Dublin. In 1910 he founded, with the help of his friend, Lady Fingall, and others, the United Irishwomen (the present-day Irish Countrywomen's Association), an organisation which aimed at the promotion of a better quality of rural life in Ireland. In the same year his book, *The Rural Life Problem in the United States,* appeared. Here he stated the problem as he saw it: that the city had been developed to the neglect of the country, and, as a consequence, 'our civilisation has become dangerously onesided' [p. 3]. One of the dangers he saw arising from this was the growth of 'predatory Socialism' in urban areas; the conditions for the emergence of which did not exist in a prosperous farming community. For this reason he believed that 'the orderly and safe progress of democracy demands a strong agricultural population' [p. 51]. The machinery of distribution was controlled by the businessmen in the towns and was worked by them in their own interests (and in Ireland these businessmen were also the political bosses who led the agrarian agitation). In order to achieve a high degree of economic organisation comparable to that in the towns, the farmer must adopt co-operative methods. But this economic organisation was only a means towards 'better living'. By means of organisation and through education they must create an attitude and an environment which would make the country 'morally and mentally satisfying to those who are born to it, or who, but for its social stagnation, would prefer a rural to an urban existence' [p. 125]. He instanced the situation in Ireland, where he believed that co-operative societies exercised a social as well as co-operative function.

Plunkett's health had never been good, and after about 1910 it became worse. But in spite of this, he continued to work unceasingly on his many projects. The Irish Question loomed important during the rest of his life and from about 1907 onwards he was moving to a position of support for Home Rule. In 1911 he informed the Conservative Central Office that he was no longer a Unionist, though, under pressure from his co-operative colleagues – who feared the consequences of further political controversy – he did not make the fact public for the moment. In 1914, however, he spoke out against a partition solution to the Irish question in *A Better Way: an appeal to Ulster not to desert Ireland*. In 1917 he became chairman of the Irish Convention, set up by Lloyd George in response to American pressure in the aftermath of the 1916 Dublin insurrection, with the task (virtually impossible in the light of Lloyd George's guarantees to the Ulster Unionist representatives) of formulating an acceptable solution of the Irish Question. With the failure of the Convention, he threw his efforts into the attempt to secure Home Rule with Dominion status for Ireland – founding the Irish Dominion Party in 1919 and launching the short-lived *Irish Statesman*. During the Anglo-Irish war, the reprisal policy of the 'Black and Tans' was directed against co-operative creameries. It was a policy which drew strong protests from Plunkett and others who did not see eye to eye with the Republicans. It was Plunkett who outlined the situation to the Co-operative Congress at Scarborough in 1921, which adopted a resolution calling for a government investigation and compensation for damage caused by the Crown forces; and which called, as well, for a policy of conciliation in Ireland and the formulation of a measure of self-government which would be generally acceptable to the Irish people. In 1922, with the setting up of the Irish Free State, Plunkett was nominated a member of the Senate by the Irish Government. A consequence of this was the destruction of his home and its contents (including many of his private papers) in 1923 in the course of the Irish civil war, when the Republican forces adopted a policy of destroying the property of supporters of the new regime.

Following the establishment of the Free State, the most important task, as Plunkett saw it, was to establish good relations with the new Government. Throughout his life he had made a point of knowing 'the right people' and of promoting his policies by personal contact where possible. He quickly established a good relationship with Patrick Hogan, the Irish Minister for Agriculture. The latter was sympathetic, and in the report of the Free State's Commission on the Depression in the Agricultural Industry (1924), the value of co-operation was fully recognised; as it has been in subsequent reports commissioned by Irish Governments, especially with regard to the problems of underdeveloped areas. In 1926 Hogan's brother-in-law, Henry Kennedy, became secretary of the IAOS. Kennedy was a technocrat rather than an ideologist of co-operation, and his appointment marked a new phase in the development of the co-operative movement [see Bolger (1977) 114 ff.].

Following the destruction of his Irish home, Plunkett moved to England, where he spent his last years. He continued to interest himself in Ireland, founding a second *Irish Statesman* in 1923 which was published until 1930 under the editorship of 'AE', in the hope of influencing the politics of the new state.

Plunkett's influence abroad on the development of agricultural co-operation and as a social thinker was of no less significance than his work in Ireland. He was one of those who prepared the way for the foundation of the International Co-operative Alliance in 1895. At the beginning of the twentieth century, the less successful English, Welsh and Scottish Agricultural Organisation Societies were founded on the model of the IAOS. In 1905 an IAOS organiser, the future Sir Patrick Hannon, became Superintendent of Agricultural Co-operation in the Cape Province of South Africa, marking the beginning of substantial co-operative organisation there. In this year also Plunkett renewed an acquaintance with President Theodore Roosevelt and met Gifford Pinchot, the chief influence behind the president's conservation policies. From them he took a heightened awareness of the 'rural life problem', and in return he was able to place at their disposal his knowledge of co-operation in Europe; a method of organisation which, as *The Rural Life Problem in the United States* shows, held the key to a solution of the problem in his view.

In 1914 Plunkett secured the foundation of the Co-operative Reference Library, with generous assistance from the Carnegie United Kingdom Trustees. In 1919 he himself endowed the Horace Plunkett Foundation, the object of which was to work for rural, social and economic development; in particular to promote the study of the principles and methods of co-operation. From 1927 onwards the *Year Book of Agricultural Co-operation* was published by the Foundation. In England his influence was felt in the setting up of rural community councils, the first of which was established in 1920 in Oxfordshire.

In 1916 he had been invited to go to India as a member of the Indian Industrial Commission, but had been unable to do so; however, in 1927 he contributed a memorandum on the application of co-operative methods of organisation there to the Royal Commission on Agriculture in India. In 1924 he was responsible for the first Conference of Agricultural Co-operators in the British Empire. One of his distinguished disciples, W.G.S. Adams, has written how, when visiting China in 1931, he was repeatedly asked to address audiences on Plunkett's ideas and work. His influence in the realm of agricultural co-operation was indeed world-wide.

Plunkett was a profoundly conservative thinker, who saw in co-operation the possibility of a peaceful, traditional restructuring of society. In his economic and ethical thinking, he showed a preference for individual effort and a suspicion of the activities of the State – or of any other organisation which would remove the initiative from the individual. He was an idealist in his basic outlook, all human progress was for him a question of individual moral progress, of the development of character; and while, in practice, he recognised the importance of certain structural factors and limited State intervention, these were very much secondary in his scheme of things. Absorbed as he was by his economic work, he was never greatly concerned with the major political questions of the day, except in so far as they might affect his own work; though, of course, he did share the main features of the outlook of his class – both Irish self-government and the land question, even if experience and contemporary developments were to modify these views gradually.

Plunkett has been perceptively depicted in two semi-fictional autobiographies: in George Moore's *Hail and Farewell* (1911-14) – where Plunkett and T.P. Gill are mischievously compared to Flaubert's *Bouvard et Pécuchet* – and more sympathetically in *As I was going down Sackville Street* (1937) by Oliver St John Gogarty. He is affectionately remembered in Lady Fingall's *Seventy Years Young* (1937). A lonely, and sometimes outwardly cold and aloof man, he inspired deep confidence and warm affection in those who worked with him in the co-operative movement. He was unmarried. He died at Weybridge, Surrey, on 26 March 1932. After a funeral service at Byfleet Parish Church he was buried in St Mary's Churchyard, Byfleet. He left an estate valued at £45,033.

Writings: 'Co-operative Stores for Ireland', *19th C. 24* (Sep 1888) 410-18; 'The Working of Woman Suffrage in Wyoming', *Fortn. Rev. 53* o.s. (May 1890) 656-69; 'The Best Means of promoting both Distributive and Productive Co-operation in the Rural Districts of Ireland', *Co-op. Congress Report* (1890) 16-21 [repr. Manchester [1890] 12 pp.]; *Co-operative Dairying: an address* (Co-op. Union, [1890]) 8 pp.; *Co-operation for Ireland* (Co-op. Union, [1890]) 13 pp.; (with C. Tupper), *3rd Report* of R.C. on Crofters, Cottars and Colonization 1892 XXVII C

6693 [on scheme for the colonization in Canada of crofters and cottars from the Western Highlands and Islands of Scotland]; 'Ireland Today and Ireland Tomorrow', *Fortn. Rev. 61* o.s. (Mar 1894) 277-93; 'Agricultural Organisation', *New Ireland Rev.* (June 1894) 197-205; *Irish Times,* 7 Oct 1895 [letter]; *Help for Self-Help in Ireland* (Dublin, 1898) 15 pp.; *The New Movement in Ireland* [Address before the Economic Society of Newcastle upon Tyne, 27 Oct 1898], 2nd ed. (Dublin, 1899) 19 pp.; 'Balfourian Amelioration in Ireland', *19th C. 48* (Dec 1900) 891-904; *L'enseignement technique en Irlande* (Paris, 1900) 3 pp.; *Memorandum on Agricultural Education for Ireland* (DATI, Dublin, 1901); 'The Trend in Co-operation in Great Britain and Ireland' in *Ireland, Industrial and Agricultural* ed. W.P. Coyne (Dublin, 1902) 230-4; *The Progress of Economic Thought and Work in Ireland: four addresses to the first Council of Agriculture (1900-1903)* (DATI, Dublin, 1903) 56 pp.; *Ireland in the New Century* (1904; popular ed., with epilogue in answer to some critics, 1905); *Letter to the Members of the Agricultural Board* (DATI, Dublin, 1906) 3 pp.; *Memorandum on Agricultural Organisation* (DATI, Dublin, 1906) 27 pp.; *Addresses delivered at the Meetings of the Council of Agriculture during the first Vice-Presidency (1900-1907)* (DATI, Dublin, 1907); Evidence before the Departmental Committee of Inquiry into the Provisions of the Agriculture and Technical Instruction (Ireland) Act, 1899, *M of E* 1907 Cd 3574 Qs 104-659 and 17210A – 17452; *Noblesse Oblige: an Irish rendering* (Dublin, 1908) 38 pp.; 'Science and the Problem of Rural Life' [Address before the Agriculture Sub-section], *British Association Report* (Dublin, 1908) 796-804; *The Neglect of Country Life: a plea and a policy* (Plunkett House Series, no. 1: Dublin 1908) 16 pp.; *A Country Life Institute: a suggested Irish American contribution to rural progress* (Plunkett House Series, no. 2: [Dublin, 1909]) 34 pp.; 'Mr Birrell's Irish Land Bill', *19th C. 65* (June 1909) 946-64 [repr. as *The Unsettlement of the Irish Land Question* (Dublin, 1909)] 50 pp.; 'Agricultural Co-operative Awakening in England', *Spec. 103,* 11 Sep 1909, 371-2; *Plain Talks to Irish Farmers* (Dublin, 1910) 46 pp.; *The Rural Life Problem of the United States: notes of an Irish observer* (NY, 1910); Introductory notes to H.L. Pilkington, *Land Settlement for Soldiers* (1911); (with others), *The United Irishwomen: their place, work and ideals* (Dublin, 1911) 50 pp.; Introduction to S.F. Bullock, *Thomas Andrews, Shipbuilder* (1912); *The Crisis in Irish Rural Progress . . . being three letters reprinted from 'The Times' December 1911* [1912] 20 pp.; Introduction to C. Holdenby, *Folk of the Furrow* (1913); *Some Tendencies of Modern Medicine from a Lay Point of View* (2nd impression, Dublin and Belfast, 1913) 31 pp.; 'Brotherhood through Business: T.A. Finlay', *Constructive Q. 1* (Dec 1913) 719-33; Foreword to *The Irish Question* [repr. from the *Round Table, 4* (Dec 1913)] (1914); *A Better Way: an appeal to Ulster not to desert Ireland* (1914) 38 pp.; 'McCarthy of Wisconsin', *19th C. 77* (June 1915) 1335-47; *Memorandum upon American Agricultural Organisation Society* (NY, 1916) 23 pp.; *A Defence of the Convention. . . A Speech delivered at Dundalk, June 25, 1917* (1917) 13 pp.; *The Irish Convention: confidential report to His Majesty the King by the Chairman* (Dublin, 1918); *Home Rule and Conscription* (1918) 31 pp.; *Irish Chaos, the British Cause and the Irish Cure* [repr. of letter published in *The Times,* 2 June 1920] 8 pp.; *The Irish Situation in America, at Westminster and in Ireland, being two speeches Mar 4 1920 and Oct 29 1919* (Irish Dominion League, 1920) 40 pp.; *Oxford and the Rural Problem* (Barrett House Papers, no. 6: 1921) 18 pp.; *Agricultural Co-operation as a Factor in Ireland's Agricultural Policy* (Dublin, 1922) 8 pp.; *Ireland's Own Agricultural Policy* (Dublin, 1922) 23 pp.; *Farmers' Co-operative Organisations* (Washington, 1923); *The I.A.O.S.: the founding of a great movement and the evolution of Ireland's agricultural policy* (1925) 18 pp.; Introduction to *Agricultural Co-operation in its Application to the Industry, the Business, and the Life of the Farmer in the British Empire* (1925) 1-28; 'Ireland's Economic Outlook', *Foreign Affairs 5* (Jan 1927) 205-18; 'Co-operation as a Factor in the Economic, Social and Political Development of Rural India' [Memorandum to the R.C. on Agriculture in India, 1927], *Bombay Co-operative Q.* [supplement] (Sep 1928) 33 pp.; 'The Purpose of Rural Life Organisation' [an address] (Agricultural Economics Society, Oxford, 1928) 55 pp.; 'The Essentials of an Agricultural

Policy', *Spec. 146*, 4 and 18 Apr 1931, 538-9 and 611-13; Foreword to *Agricultural Co-operation in Ireland: a survey by the Horace Plunkett Foundation* (1931).

Sources: (1) MSS: Papers (mainly correspondence) of Sir Horace Plunkett but including personal diaries, and letters to Plunkett from 'AE' (George Russell): Plunkett Foundation for Co-operative Studies, Oxford; the American letters of Plunkett and also his diaries are on microfilm with Introductions by B. Crick. T.P. Gill papers: National Library of Ireland; Irish Convention papers: Trinity College Library, Dublin; see also C. Fielden, 'Plunkett Correspondence' in *Report of the Secretary to the Commissioners 1969-1970* (R.C. on Historical Manuscripts, HMSO, 1970) 35-8, and correspondence between Plunkett and Balfour in the Balfour papers, Handlist of Accessions (1956-60) nos 49828-30: BL. (2) Other: 'The Irish Creameries and the Wholesale Society', *Co-op. Congress Report* (1895) 29-30, 139-43; K. Tynan, 'Sir Horace Plunkett and his Work', *Fortn. Rev. 74* (Sep 1903) 454-65; Rev. M. O'Riordan, *Catholicity and Progress in Ireland* (2nd ed. 1905); 'The Dismissal of Sir Horace Plunkett', *Spec. 98*, 27 Apr 1907, 661-2; 'Sir Horace Plunkett and Mr Birrell', ibid., *102*, 12 June 1909, 924-5; G. Moore, *Hail and Farewell* (1911-14; ed. and with an Introduction by R. Cave, Gerrards Cross, 1976); E.E. Lysaght, *Sir Horace Plunkett and his Place in the Irish Nation* (Dublin, 1916); 'The Plunkett Scheme: its reception and prospects', *New Statesman 13*, 26 July 1919, 412; T. Roosevelt, *An Autobiography* (NY, 1924); R. Metcalf, *England and Sir Horace Plunkett: an essay in agricultural co-operation* (1933); R.A. Anderson, *With Horace Plunkett in Ireland* (1935); Countess of Fingall, *Seventy Years Young* (1937); M. Digby, *Horace Plunkett, an Anglo-American Irishman* (Oxford, 1949); *The Letters of Theodore Roosevelt*, vol. 6 ed. E.E. Morison (Harvard Univ. Press, 1952); W.G.E. Adams, 'Rural Development Abroad', L. Bennett, 'Plunkett Economic Pattern', W.P. Watkins, 'Influence of Horace Plunkett', M. Digby, 'Horace Plunkett Foundation', and D. Flanagan, 'Horace Plunkett in England', all five articles in National Co-operative Council, *Sir Horace Plunkett Centenary Handbook* (Dublin, 1954) 1-4, 9-10, 14-16, 26-30, and 31-6; M.J. Bonn, 'A la Recherche du Temps Perdu' [Reminiscences of AE (including Plunkett)] in *Printed Writings by George W. Russell (AE): a bibliography*, compiled by A. Denson (Northwestern Univ. Press, 1961) 15-21; F.S.L. Lyons, *John Dillon: a biography* (1968); L. Nelson, 'Sir Horace Plunkett: a promoter of rural sociology', *Rural Sociology 34*, no. 1 (Mar 1969) 91-5; M. Campbell, *The Oxfordshire Rural Community Council* (Oxford, 1970); S. Hutton, 'Horace Plunkett agus Fothoghchán na Gaillimhe 1901' ['Horace Plunkett and the Galway by-election of 1901'], *Studia Hibernica*, no. 16 (1976) 158-74; P. Bolger, *The Irish Co-operative Movement: its history and development* (Dublin, 1977). OBIT. *Irish Times, Morning Post* and *Times*, 28 Mar 1932; *Belfast Telegraph*, 29 Mar 1932; *Belfast Weekly News*, 31 Mar 1932; *Spec., Surrey Advertiser and County Times* and *Surrey Comet*, 2 Apr 1932; *Leader* [Dublin], 9 Apr 1932; *Nature 129*, 16 Apr 1932, 568-9. The editors are indebted to Miss J. Elise Bayley, Librarian of the Plunkett Foundation, Oxford for bibliographical assistance and to Dr R. Fanning and Dr C. Ó Gráda of University College. Dublin for comments on an earlier draft of this biography.

SEÁN HUTTON

See also: †Patrick GALLAGHER and for Irish Co-operation; †Jesse Clement GRAY; †Edward Owen GREENING; and below: Agricultural Co-operation in Great Britain and Ireland.

Agricultural Co-operation in Great Britain and Ireland:

(1) **For MSS** see Sir Horace Plunkett's biography above and papers of the Irish Agricultural Organisation Society, The Plunkett House, Merrion Square, Dublin.

(2) **Theses:** A.V. Vickery, 'An Historical Review of the Development of British Agricultural Policies and Programmes since 1900' (Oxford, BLitt., 1959); A.V. Bhuleshkar, 'Economic Characteristics of Agricultural Bargaining Co-operatives' (Nottingham MSc., 1970); W.J. Taggart, 'Some Aspects of Co-operation in Farming, with Special Reference to a Group of Arable Farms in the East of Scotland' (Edinburgh PhD, 1972); W. Kennedy, 'Amalgamation of Co-operatives' (National Univ. of Ireland, Cork, MSc. (Dairying), 1972); D. Carter, 'An Examination of Agricultural Co-operation in Relation to the Benefits claimed to result from Co-operation in Agricultural Marketing' (Oxford, BLitt., 1976).

(3) **Departmental Committees and other Government Reports:** *Report of the Recess Committee on the Establishment of a Department of Agriculture and Industries for Ireland* (1896); Department of Agriculture and Technical Instruction (Ireland) [DATI], *Report* 1907 Cd 3572-4 and *Minority Report* 1907 Cd 3575; DATI, *Report of the Departmental Committee on the Irish Butter Industry* 1910 Cd 5092-3; Board of Trade (Labour Dept), *Directory of Industrial Associations in the U.K. for 1911* 1911 Cd 5619 [see pp. 161-78 for Co-operative Agricultural Societies and pp. 179-80 for Co-operative Agricultural Insurance Societies]; idem, *Report on Industrial and Agricultural Co-operative Societies in the U.K.* 1912-13 LXXXV Cd 6045; DATI, *Report of the Departmental Committee on Agricultural Credit in Ireland* 1914 XIII Cd 7375-6; Agricultural Tribunal of Investigation, *Report* 1924 VII Cmd 2145; Ministry of Agriculture, *Co-operative Marketing of Agricultural Produce in England and Wales* (Economic Series no. 1: 1925); Committee on Agricultural Co-operation in Scotland, *Report* 1929-30 VIII Cmd 3567; Welsh Land Settlement Society, *Co-operative Farms and Smallholdings with Centralised Services in Wales: reviews for the years 1936-50 and accounts for 1949-50,* HMSO (1952) 39 pp., (1954) 36 pp.; Ministry of Agriculture, Fisheries and Food, *Some Problems of Horticultural Co-operative Marketing in England and Wales* (Economic Series, no. 52: 1961); J.G. Knapp, *An Appraisement of Agricultural Co-operation in Ireland* (Dept of Agriculture, Dublin, 1964) Pr 7467; J.R. Parkinson, *Agricultural Co-operation in Northern Ireland: a report on the place of co-operation in the future development of Northern Ireland Agriculture* (1965) Cmd 484; *Report of the Committee of Inquiry on Contract Farming* 1971-2 VI Cmnd 5099; J.S.G. Wilson, *Availability of Capital and Credit to United Kingdom Agriculture* HMSO, 1973 [see Ch. 13 (iii) pp. 182-91].

(4) **Reference works and periodicals:** Irish Agricultural Organisation Society, *Reports,* 1895-1924: National Library of Ireland, Dublin, and Plunkett Foundation for Co-operative Studies, Oxford (incomplete file); *Irish Homestead: organ of Irish agricultural and industrial development 1-30* (1895 – 8 Sep 1923, then merged in *Irish Statesman*); ICA, *Bibliographie Coopérative Internationale* (1906) 103-26; *Better Business 1-6* (1915-21) then *Irish Economist 7-8* (1921-3). The Horace Plunkett Foundation published its first *Year Book* in 1925 under the title of *Agricultural Co-operation in its Application to the Industry, the Business, and the Life of the Farmer in the British Empire* [see 5 **(iii)** below]. The title was changed in 1926 to *Year Book of Agricultural Co-operation in the British Empire* and from 1930 onwards the annual volumes carry the shorter title of *Year Book of Agricultural Co-operation.* Bibliographies were published from 1928 in chronological format but in 1935 a subject listing was adopted and in 1937 H.A. Izant compiled *A Selected Bibliography of Co-operation* [repr. from HPF *Year Book* (1937) 539-80]. In the 1947 *Year Book* a revised selected bibliography was published, followed by supplements for the years 1948-53. In 1954 the HPF produced another *Select Bibliography on Co-operation* followed by supplements until 1958 after which a select bibliography for the years 1955-9 was published, to be used with the 1954 volume to provide a complete list of major works in the library. Thereafter the bibliographies published in the *Year Books* have usually been reproduced in offprint form.

Other sources include: Agricultural Co-operative Association, *Year Book for 1947* (1948 to date); *Farm and Market* [J. of the ACA], 1951-4 [in 1956 the ACA became the Agricultural

Central Co-operative Association Ltd and published a quarterly newsletter, 1957-61]; ACCA, *Statistical Survey of the English Agricultural Co-operative Movement* (1954 to date); Welsh Agricultural Organisation Society, *Rural Wales: a year book of Welsh Agricultural Co-operation* (Aberystwyth, 1964 to date); *Farming Business: co-operation in the United Kingdom* [J. of CCAHC] (1964 to date); PFCS, *Agricultural Co-operation in the U.K., Summary of Statistics* (1968 to date); J.E. Tschiersch, *Co-operation in Agricultural Production: a selective bibliography* (Research Centre for International Agrarian Development, Saarbrücken, 1974); *Agricultural Co-operatives in Europe: an annotated bibliography for 1965-1975* ed. K.P. Broadbent and F.H. Webster (Commonwealth Agricultural Bureaux and PFCS, Oxford, 1976); PFCS, *Directory of Agricultural Co-operatives in the United Kingdom* (Oxford, 1977) [contains details of 600 agricultural co-operatives registered in the U.K.].

(5) Contemporary Works:

(i) Pre-1890
J. Gurdon, 'Co-operative Farms at Assington, Suffolk', *J. of Royal Agricultural Society 24* (1863) 165-73; R. Bewick, *The Advantages and Practicability of applying Co-operation to the Wants of Farmers* (1864) 24 pp.; Anon., 'Co-operative Agricultural Societies', *Chambers J.*, 13 Feb 1869, 97-9; W. Pare, *Co-operative Agriculture: a solution of the Land Question, as exemplified in the History of the Ralahine Co-operative Agriculture Association, County Clare, Ireland* (1870); Rev. A. Church, 'An Irish Utopia' [Co-operative Agriculture at Ralahine], *Cont. Rev. 16* (Dec 1870) 71-83; R. Stapleton, 'Co-operative Agriculture', *Co-op. Congress Report* (1872) 50-2; M.B.E. [M. Bentham-Edwards], 'Three Experiments in Co-operative Agriculture', *Fraser's Mag. 91* o.s. (Apr 1875) 529-39; W. Lawson et al., *Ten Years of Gentleman Farming at Blennerhassett with Co-operative Objects* (Glasgow, 1874, 2nd ed. 1875); W.H. Hall and G. Hines, 'The Spread of Co-operation in Agricultural Villages: its difficulties and how they may be overcome', *Co-op. Congress Report* (1879) 42-6; A. Scratchley, *The Law of Land Societies and Co-operative Farming and Land Societies with Withdrawable and Transferable Shares and the Law of Co-operative Banks and Co-operative Societies generally* (1880, 3rd ed. enlarged, 1881); C.W. Stubbs, *Glebe Allotments and Co-operative Small Farming* (1880) 32 pp.; M.A., *Co-operation in Land Tillage* (1881); 'The Land Question in connection with Co-operation', *Co-op. Congress Report* (1881) 54-6; W.H. Roberts, 'Co-operative Farming', *Fortn. Rev. 36* (Aug 1881) 195-203; E.T. Craig, *The Irish Land and Labour Question illustrated in the History of Ralahine and Co-operative Farming* (Manchester, 1882); Rev. G.W. Kitchin, 'Co-operation and Agriculture', *Co-op. Congress Report* (1882) 54-7; S. Taylor, 'Profit-Sharing in Agriculture', *19th C. 12* (Oct 1882) 583-90; A. Randle, *A District Co-operative Farm* (Manchester, [1883]) 12 pp.; D. Johnson, 'Co-operative Farming', *Co-op. Congress Report* (1884) 46-7; R.J. Kelly, 'A Co-operative Farm in Ireland Fifty Years ago', *Month 52* (1884) 247-59; C.W. Stubbs, *The Land and the Labourers. A Record of Facts and Experiments in Cottage Farming and Co-operative Agriculture* (1884, 5th ed., 1904); Editor of the *Agricultural Economist*, 'Co-operative Agriculture applied to Market Gardening and Fruit Culture', *CWS Annual* (1885) 194-7; B. King, 'Co-operative Agriculture', ibid., 187-94; G. Hines, 'Co-operation in its Application to Agriculture', ibid. (1887) 210-32; W.G. Loveday, *Co-operative Agriculture* (Manchester [1887]) 12 pp.; D. McInnes, *Co-operative Agriculture* (1887) 14 pp.; H.E. Moore, *Co-operative Agriculture* (Chelmsford, [1887]) 27 pp.

(ii) 1890-1923
H.C. Plunkett, 'The Best Means of promoting both Distributive and Productive Co-operation in the Rural Districts of Ireland', *Co-op. Congress Report* (1890) 16-21 and for further writings by Plunkett *see* his biography above; G. Thorpe, *Co-operative Agriculture* (1893) 8 pp.; W. Campbell, *Co-operative Agriculture* (Manchester, 1894) 11 pp.; B. Jones, *Co-operative*

Production (Oxford, 1894) 614-74; E. Mitchell, 'Co-operation and the Agricultural Depression', *West. Rev. 142*, no. 3 (1894) 241-47; D. McInnes, *Co-operation as applied to the Agricultural Population and to Agriculture* (1895) 11 pp.; *Land, Co-operation and the Unemployed*, ed. J.A. Hobson (1895); T.A. Finlay, 'Agricultural Co-operation in Ireland', *Econ. J. 6* (1896) 204-11; E.J. Dyer, 'Co-operation amongst Farmers', *New Century Rev. 4* (1898) 59-67; J.C. Gray, *Co-operation in Agriculture* (1898) 16 pp.; F.L. McVey, 'Co-operation by Farmers', *JPE 6* (June 1898) 401-3; J. Long, 'Co-operation as applied to Agriculture', *CWS Annual* (1899) 409-41; J. Rowbottom, 'The Co-operative Wholesale Society in Ireland', *New Ireland Rev.* (May 1899) 139-49; P.J. Hannon, *Co-operative Production, with Special Reference to Agriculture* (Labour Co-partnership Association, 1900) 8 pp.; IAOS, *Co-operative Agricultural Societies* (Leaflet no. 4: Dublin [1900?]) 4 pp.; W.D. Rowland, *Co-operative Agricultural Organisation* (1900) 11 pp.; G.W. Russell, 'The Application of Co-operation in the Congested Districts', *J. of the Statistical and Social Inquiry Society of Ireland 11*, pt 80 (Aug 1900) 517-27; R.A. Anderson, 'Agricultural Co-operation in Ireland: the work of the Irish Agricultural Organisation Society', in DATI, *Handbook for the Irish Pavilion, Glasgow International Exhibition 1901* (Dublin, 1901) 137-49; A. Dulac, 'Agricultural Co-operation in the United Kingdom', *Econ. Rev. 12* (Apr 1902) 185-98; *The Irish Agricultural Organisation Society: its organisation and what it has accomplished* (1903) 20 pp.; E.A. Pratt, *The Organisation of Agriculture* (1904, 2nd ed., 1905); R. Winfrey, *Small Holdings* (1904) 12 pp.; J. Dorum, 'Co-operation in Irish Agriculture', *West. Rev. 164* (Sep 1905) 267-72; D.A. McCabe, 'The Recent Growth of Co-operation in Ireland', *QJE 20* (Aug 1906) 547-74; E.A. Pratt, *The Transition in Agriculture* (1906, reissued 1909); W.L. Charleton, *Co-operation and the New Small Holdings Act, 1907* (1907) 12 pp.; L. Jebb, *The Working of the Small Holdings Act* (1907); L.P. Byrne, 'Agricultural Co-operation in Ireland', *International* (1909) 236-41; J.N. Harris and J. Mastin, 'Agricultural Co-operation and its Relation to Co-operative Distributive Societies', *Co-op. Congress Report* (1909) 416-41 and 442-56; E.A. Pratt, *Small Holders: what they must do to succeed* (1909); C.R. Fay, 'Small Holdings and Agricultural Co-operation in England', *QJE 24* (May 1910) 499-514; G. Radford, *Agricultural Co-operation* [repr. from *Our Land* [1910]]; A. Aronson, 'A Co-operative Land Society', *Cont. Rev. 99* (Apr 1911) 448-51; E.A. Pratt, *Agricultural Organisation: its rise, principles and practice abroad and at home* (1912); H.W. Wolff, *Co-operation in Agriculture* (1912); W. Adair, 'Small Holdings and Co-operative Trading', *CWS Annual* (1914) 259-79; G. Russell, 'Seeing the Interests of Agricultural, Productive and Distributive Co-operative Societies are necessarily interdependent how best can a means be devised for the advantageous exchange of goods and the adoption of a common policy of propaganda and defence?', *Co-op. Congress Report* (1914) 541-57; D. McInnes, *Farming by Distributive Co-operative Societies* (1917) 8 pp.; L.L. Price, *Co-operation and Co-partnership* [1914]; L. Smith-Gordon and L.C. Staples, *Rural Reconstruction in Ireland: a record of co-operative organization* (1917); 'Co-operation in Agriculture' [Statistics from Ministry of Labour on registered co-operative societies in the U.K.], *People's Year Book* (1918) 211; L. Smith-Gordon, *Co-operation for Farmers* (1918) [bibliography pp. 235-40]; L.R. Byrne, *Twenty-one Years of the Irish Agricultural Wholesale Society, 1897-1918* (Dublin, 1919); T. Williams, *Co-operative Farming* (1920) 12 pp.; W.H. Warman, *Agricultural Co-operation in England and Wales* (1922).

(iii) 1924-39

Agricultural Co-operation in its Application to the Industry, the Business, and the Life of the Farmer in the British Empire with an Introduction by Sir Horace Plunkett, Pt 1, Preliminary Survey and Pt 2, Report of Conference at Wembley, 28-31 July 1924 (1925); W. Meakin, 'Irish Agricultural Co-operation', *People's Year Book* (1926) 228-34; J.M. Jones, *Agricultural Co-operation in South Wales. An Economic and Financial Analysis* (Univ. College of Wales, Agricultural Economics Dept Bull. no. 1: 1927) 40 pp.; HPF, *Producers and Consumers* ed. M. Digby (1928, rev. ed., 1938); J.M. Jones and R.H. Wynne, *Agricultural Co-operation in North*

Wales (Univ. College of Wales, Agricultural Economics Dept Bull. no. 3: 1928); HPF, *Agricultural Co-operation in England. A Survey* (1930); idem, *Agricultural Co-operation in Scotland and Wales* with a Foreword by Sir J. Gilmour (1933); idem, *Co-operation and the New Agricultural Policy* (1935); J.S. Hoyland, *Digging for a new England: the co-operative farm for the unemployed* (1936); A.W. Ashby, 'Agricultural Co-operation and Society', *People's Year Book* (1939) 5-11.

(iv) 1948 to 1977

M. Digby, 'The Prospects for Agricultural Co-operation' in *The Co-operative Movement in Labour Britain*, ed. N. Barou (1948) 51-64; idem, *Agricultural Co-operation in Great Britain* (1949, new ed. with S. Gorst, 1957, rev. ed. 1968); A.W. Ashby et al., 'Agricultural Co-operation and the Modern State' in *Proc. Seventh International Conference of Agricultural Economists held at Stresa, Italy, 21-27 August 1949* (OUP, 1950) 64-129; C.C. Riddall, *Agricultural Co-operation in Ireland: the story of a struggle* (Dublin, 1950) 48 pp.; J. Johnston, *Irish Agriculture in Transition* (Dublin and Oxford, 1951); A.W. Ashby, *Some Principles of Organisation and Operation in Agricultural Co-operative Societies* (Oxford, 1952) 13 pp.; Commonwealth Conference on Agricultural Co-operation, Oxford 1951, *Report of Proceedings* (1952); M. Digby, *Financing of Agricultural Co-operatives* (HPF Occasional Paper no. 4: 1953) 57 pp. [mimeograph]; ACA, *Farmers' Co-operation in England: an outline of the English agricultural co-operative movement* (1954) 28 pp.; M. Digby, *Co-operative Farming* (HPF Occasional Paper no. 6: 1954) 46 pp.; idem, 'Agricultural Co-operation in England and Wales' in *Agriculture 61* (Apr 1954) 26-9; P.G. Gorst, *Review of Agricultural Co-operative Statistics for the United Kingdom* (HPF Occasional Paper no. 7: 1954) 24 pp.; National Co-operative Council, *Sir Horace Plunkett Centenary Handbook: a symposium on co-operation* (Dublin, 1954); M. Digby and R.H. Gratton, *Co-operative Marketing for Agricultural Producers* (FAO, Rome, 1955); M. Digby, *Agricultural Co-operation in the Commonwealth* (Oxford, 1956; repr. 1970); idem, *Co-operatives and Land Use* (FAO Agricultural Development Paper no. 61: Rome, 1957; repr. 1965); F. Brundrett, *Agricultural Co-operation and Technical Progress* [address to the British Association meeting in Dublin, 1957] (ACCA, [1957?] 10 pp.; Southern Counties Agricultural Trading Society, *Fifty Years of Service by the Southern Counties Agricultural Society* (Winchester, 1957) 28 pp.; Pumpsaint and District Agricultural Society, *Progress and Development, 1908-1958* (Llanwrda, 1958) 48 pp.; W. Morgan, *Survey of Capital and Credit in Agricultural Co-operative Societies in Great Britain* (Oxford, 1960); S. Gorst, *Co-operative Credit for Producers and Consumers* (Oxford, 1962); M. Digby, *Co-operative Land Use: the challenge to traditional co-operation* (Oxford, 1963); R.F. Tapsell, *Farmers' Co-operatives in the South-West* (PFCS, 1964) 29 pp.; J. Johnston, *Agricultural Co-operation in Northern Ireland: a history of the Ulster Agricultural Organisation Society Ltd – the first fifty years* (1965); J.G. Knapp, *An Analysis of Agricultural Co-operation in England* (ACCA, 1965); J.G. Maxwell Stamp Associates Ltd, *Financing Agricultural Co-operatives* (1967); G.H. Caramile, *Co-operation in Farm Production* (ACA, 1968); Country Landowner's Association, *Joint Enterprise in Farming: a guide to the formation of farming partnerships and limited companies* (1968) 46 pp.; Dept. of Agricultural Economics, Univ. College of Wales, *Agricultural Co-operative Trading in Wales* (Aberystwyth, [1969]); D.G. Bailey and E.T. Gibbons, *Agricultural Co-operative Activities and Case Histories of Co-operatives* (Newcastle, 1970); CCAHC (Co-operative Planning Unit), *Agricultural Co-operative and Related Organisations in the UK* (1970) 23 pp.; K.J. McCready, *A Study of Multi-purpose and Specialist Organisations in Agricultural Co-operative Marketing* (PFCS, Oxford, 1970); H.R. Piddington, *New Forms of Mutual Assistance among the Farmers in the U.K.* (PFCS [1970]) 24 pp.; CCAHC, *Report of the Working Party on Agricultural Co-operative Law* (1971); M. Brown and R. Scase, *Boards and Management in Farmers' Co-operatives: a pilot study in England and Wales* (CCAHC, 1973) 26 pp.; CCAHC, *Report of the Working Party on Investment Capital in Agricultural Co-operatives* (1974); ICA, *The Role of Agricultural Co-operatives in Economic and Social*

Development [Report of an Open World Conference on 22-26 May 1972] (1974) 48 pp.; ICFC Ltd, *Agricultural and Horticultural Co-operatives: comparison with other organisations* (1974) 13 pp. [typescript]; K.J. McCready, *The Land Settlement Association: its history and present form* (Oxford, 1974); J. Morley, *British Agricultural Co-operatives* (1975); R. Gasson, 'Farmers' Participation in Co-operative Activities', *Sociologia Ruralis 17* (1977) 107-21; H. Kimble, *Effective Membership of Agricultural Co-operatives: report on a pilot study in Oxfordshire* (PFCS, 1977) 24 pp.; C. LeVay and M. Lewis, *Farmer Participation in Co-operatives: a study of the Brecon and Radnor area* (Univ. College of Wales, 1977).

(6) **Other works:** L.P.F. Smith, *The Evolution of Agricultural Co-operation* with an Introduction by M. Digby (Oxford, 1961); ACA, *Agricultural Co-operation in England: beginning and growth* (1966) 15 pp.; D. Hoctor, *The Department's Story: a history of the Department of Agriculture* (Dublin, 1971); WAOS Ltd, *Farmers together: Golden Jubilee volume of the Welsh Agricultural Organisation Society* ed. E.R. Thomas (Aberystwyth, 1972); P. Bolger, *The Irish Co-operative Movement: its history and development* (Institute of Public Administration, Dublin, 1977); C. Ó Gráda, 'The Beginnings of the Irish Creamery System, 1880-1914', *Econ. Hist. Rev.* 2nd ser. *30*, no. 2 (May 1977) 284-305; S. Heiseler, 'The History and Development of Agricultural and Horticultural Co-operatives in East Anglia', *Oxford Agrarian Studies 6* (1977) 71-9.

PRICE, Thomas William (1876-1945)
ADULT EDUCATIONALIST AND WEA ORGANISER

Thomas William Price was born at Kidderminster, Worcestershire, on 5 May 1876, the second of three sons of William Henry Price and his wife Ann (née Hassell). His father had been a shoemaker, but had given up this trade, we do not know why, to become a timekeeper and afterwards a clerk at one of the Kidderminster carpet works.

Little or nothing is known of T.W. Price's schooling; but he had been born into a family of book-lovers – he later said that he first read Gibbon's *Decline and Fall of the Roman Empire* at the age of twelve. In his early teens he went to Rochdale, where a relation of his father's lived, and found work as a warehouseman in the dyeing department at John Bright & Brothers Ltd, Fieldhouse Mills. In 1899 he married Kate, the daughter of Charles Williams of Madeley, Shropshire. He early developed an interest in politics and joined the local branch of the Social Democratic Federation. But he was soon involved in his real vocation, the adult education movement.

Time and place were both fortunate for him. The first few years of the twentieth century were those in which Albert Mansbridge was busy laying the foundations of what was to become the Workers' Educational Association. T.W. (as he was called by all close associates) was much attracted by Mansbridge's ideas and got in touch with him; and so began the close and lifelong connection of the two men. At this time, too, Rochdale was a place which had long been pre-eminent for its keen interest in adult education. University Extension lecturers found enthusiastic audiences in the town, and there were besides, as Price puts it, 'two other educational enterprises which . . . were more definitely working class in their personnel.' One consisted of classes arising (as they did in many towns) from the Ruskin College correspondence courses: two of these classes were formed in Rochdale in 1901. The second enterprise developed out of the first: some members of these classes who belonged to the Clover Street Unitarian Sunday School suggested to the Young Men's Class there that they might form another Ruskin College group. But 'the idea of education by correspondence did not meet with favour; it was therefore decided to form a class independently of the Ruskin College scheme, and under the guidance of a definite leader.' Two such classes were started in January 1902, and the leader of one of them was T.W. Price; it studied sociology and economics.

Two years later the infant WEA began to be known in Rochdale. In November 1904 the local Extension Committee resolved to affiliate to the Association which was soon to be known as the WEA. In March 1905 a Rochdale branch was started, one of the first four WEA branches to be formed; but since the Association's title was felt to be not only cumbrous but patronising as well, the branch called itself 'The Rochdale Education Guild'. Price was a member of its executive. It was started with the greatest enthusiasm, and its achievement in the first year was remarkable. Both Mansbridge and Price give details of this work in their books on the WEA (see pp. 69-72 and pp. 25-6 respectively), because the branch was 'so successful in revealing the possibilities of the Association' (Price).

In 1907 there was a further advance: a University Tutorial Class was suggested. On being consulted about the possibility, Mansbridge was delighted. He promised that if Rochdale could produce thirty working people who would pledge themselves to study in this class for two years and write regular essays, he would provide a tutor. After some months of negotiation with the Board of Education and the Local Education Authority, a class of forty, which included T.W. Price, started a course in economic history in January 1908, with R.H. Tawney as tutor. Tawney also undertook a tutorial class at Longton (Staffs.) which was inspired by Rochdale's example and which agreed to accept the same subject and the same tutor. Later tutorial classes – which were speedily started in large numbers – followed the Rochdale/Longton model.

The years up to 1914 saw the rapid development of district organisations in the WEA. The Midland District was formed as early as 1905, and W.J. Sharkey was appointed as full-time secretary in 1907; T.W. Price succeeded him in 1909. The University of Birmingham had provided an office in Edmund Street, and Price had as secretary a young girl, Gertie Smallwood – who remained with the District till she retired.

While he was Midlands secretary Price played an important part in the organisation and superintendence of the first WEA summer school, held at Oxford University in 1910. The school developed out of the Extension summer meetings, which WEA students were attending in ever increasing numbers. By 1907 the WEA members were becoming conscious of themselves as a group with their own needs and interests – a situation which was recognised by the universities when during the Extension meetings of 1907, 1908 and 1909 they placed rooms at the disposal of the group. For 1910 it was resolved that the WEA should organise a summer school of its own. The school became a regular event, and soon extended to other universities besides Oxford.

In 1913 Mansbridge was invited by the United Universities of the Commonwealth to visit Australia in order to 'explain, propagate, and establish' the WEA movement there. He spent five months in Australia, New Zealand and Canada, and during his absence Price acted as general secretary. Not long after his return Mansbridge fell dangerously ill in June 1914 with cerebro-spinal meningitis. He slowly recovered a good deal of his health, but the illness caused him to resign the general secretaryship, in late 1915, and serve the Association in less strenuous ways. During the very difficult early months of the First World War he was incapacitated. His absence from the central office 'was compensated', as Mrs Stocks justly observes, 'by the unstinted devotion and quiet efficiency of T.W. Price and Dorothy Jones' (of the office staff) [(1953) 67]. These two organised not only traditional classes but also a vast number of classes and lectures in new places (such as training camps) and on new subjects now in demand; for instance, the study handbook compiled at the request of the central executive of the WEA by A.E. Zimmern and T.W. Price (*War and the Workers*) dealing with 'European history, international relations, and various economic, political and philosophical aspects of the war'. Price also took Mansbridge's place as WEA secretary of the Central Joint Advisory Committee, a body set up to encourage the development and safeguard the quality of the Tutorial Classes. This secretaryship, which he continued to hold until the Second World War, involved a great deal of extra work.

In 1919 Price succeeded Mrs Hugh Dalton as assistant general secretary. About the same time, Mr and Mrs H.N. Spalding put at the disposal of the WEA Holybrook House in Castle Street, Reading, which Mr Spalding had bought to live in when he was prospective Liberal candidate for the town. One of the uses to which the house was put was as a residential centre for training tutorial class students to become teachers of one-year classes and leaders of study circles. Price was asked to become Warden and to organise this training. During the early years there were three courses annually, each lasting for a month, in July, August and September. But this proved to be too much of a strain for both T.W. and his wife, and in later years there were two only, in July and August. The teaching was undertaken by Price and by one resident tutor for each course. About fifteen students attended a course; the subjects were in the fields of literature, economics and social studies. Guest speakers were frequently invited; among those who came to Holybrook were Professor R.H. Tawney, Bishop (later Archbishop) Temple, R.H. Crossman, A.E. Zimmern, G.D.H. Cole, and a number of prominent trade unionists. The Prices likewise arranged social events for the students – visits to Windsor, Oxford, London; boating on the river, whist drives and sing-songs.

These summer courses, however, by no means represented the whole of Price's activities in the years following the war. He took two tutorial classes, one at Witney and one at Steeple Claydon, each involving a night away from home. From 1921 to 1942 he was a member of the Reading University Joint Committee for Tutorial Classes. He was also involved in the Adult School Movement and was for many years the leader of the Holybrook School held there on Sunday mornings. In 1924 he published a short work, *The Story of the Workers' Educational Association from 1903 to 1924*. In some ninety concise and lucid pages it gives a useful, interesting and reliable account of the movement. But the book is more than a history; it is a mirror of T.W. Price's personality, of his gentleness, his practical sense, and his remarkable modesty – even self-effacement: one would never gather from the book how valuable a servant he was to his Association for over thirty years.

Although he was so much involved in teaching others Price managed nevertheless to make a start at this time with his ultimate plan for his own formal education – the achievement of a university degree. In 1920 a Cassel Scholarship enabled him to enter St Catherine's College, Oxford (then St Catherine's Society). To read for a degree was to add a formidable burden to an already weighty load, since his WEA work continued as before. But he succeeded in carrying both, and in 1930 he took the degree of BLitt. with a thesis on 'Social Legislation and Theory 1906-1914'.

In 1939 he retired from full-time WEA work, and with the outbreak of the Second World War the summer school had to be abandoned. The central office of the Association was evacuated from London to Holybrook, and for some months Mrs Price catered for and mothered the general secretary, Ernest Green, and his office staff, until they returned to London. Reading Corporation then requisitioned Holybrook House as a day nursery. The Prices continued to live there, and Mrs Price acted as housekeeper for the nursery.

Price did devoted and intelligent work in almost every field of WEA activity. Among other achievements, he created its organisation in the Midlands; he inaugurated the scheme for training tutorial students as teachers; he played an important part in the inception of tutorial classes and in the organisation of the summer schools. Although he would have been the last to agree to the fact, in the course of a long and energetic working life he accomplished a great deal.

T.W. Price was a rather short, round-faced man with a deep dimple in his chin. About 1940 a rodent ulcer developed in the region of this dimple. In spite of treatment it got steadily worse, and eventually caused him to suffer a very painful death on 31 October 1945. After a service at the municipal church of St Lawrence, Reading, he was cremated on 2 November. He left effects valued at £470.

The Prices had three sons: Charles, who went to live with his daughter in British Columbia; Walter, who died in 1969, and Harold, who was killed in action in February 1945. Mrs Price herself died on 11 September 1953.

In a note added to E.S. Cartwright's appreciation of T.W. Price, Albert Mansbridge wrote: 'If any man triumphed over difficulties, he did. His radiant personality, never tired until the last sad year, brightened not only his own path but those of many. His gentle wife cheered him on. We sorrow with her.'

Writings: (with A.E. Zimmern), *War and the Workers* (1915); *The Story of the Workers' Educational Association 1903-1924, with an Introduction by R.H. Tawney* (1924).

Sources: A. Mansbridge, *An Adventure in Working Class Education 1903-1915* (1920); *Oxford Univ. Calendar* (1927) and (1934); *Reading Univ. Calendar* (1935-6); M.D. Stocks, *The Workers' Educational Association* (1953); biographical information: St Catherine's College, Oxford; Reading University; personal information: Dr E. Green, Harrogate, secretary of WEA 1922-50; C. Price, Canada, son; W.J. Price, Reading, grandson; personal knowledge. OBIT. *Berkshire Chronicle*, 9 Nov 1945; E.S. Cartwright, 'T.W. Price: an appreciation' [with a note by A. Mansbridge], *Highway* [J. of the WEA] *37* (Dec 1945).

MARGARET 'ESPINASSE
FREDERICK C. PADLEY

See also: †Fred HALL (1878-1938); †John Ernest JOHNS.

SKEFFINGTON, Arthur Massey (1908-1971)
TEACHER AND LABOUR MP

Arthur Skeffington, who was MP for the Hayes and Harlington division of Greater London when he died, at an early age for a practising politician, was in many ways typical of the normal middle-class men who in 1945, having served the Labour movement faithfully and without much in the way of reward through the years of frustration, first came into their own in the *volte-face* of that year's general election. He was a short, stocky, friendly man who generally wore a home-grown flower in his button-hole. He was an effective speaker, an excellent chairman who was remarkably good at conciliation of 'awkward characters', and he never allowed his political preoccupations to prevent him enjoying ordinary simple pleasures such as walking, gardening, etc. For many years his home was at Meopham in Kent, near a famous cricket ground; but his real cricketing love among the county clubs was not Kent, but Surrey, of which he was a lifelong member. He had played in his youth for Surrey's second eleven; and, even after he was a Member of Parliament, when business there was slack of an afternoon he would often take a friend with him to look in on a match on the Oval ground, where the big clock would warn him in good time to start back to Westminster.

Arthur Massey Skeffington was born on 4 September 1908, the son of Arthur James Williams, a pottery manufacturer's clerk, and his wife Edith (née Massey). He was educated at Streatham Grammar School; thereafter he studied economics as an external student at the University of London and between 1930 and 1941 he taught at Maidstone Commercial School (The Elms). In 1942 he was awarded a BSc. (Econ.) degree.

He became a Socialist at an early age – he joined the Fabian Society in 1933; and in the same year he changed his name by deed poll from Williams to Skeffington – understood to have been an earlier family name. Following the example set by Sidney Webb, he studied law and was called to the Bar in 1951. Like Webb, he took his bar examinations for the purpose of securing a useful qualification rather than for practising – though he did occasionally practise – and the legal knowlege which he acquired by this means stood him in good stead when he returned to Parliament and also helped him in advising his friends and his constituents. He was closely in touch with Labour Parties in South London, and in the general election of 1935 was chosen to contest Streatham – a hopeless constituency for the Labour interest. In 1938 he stood for West Lewisham at a by-election, but was again unsuccessful. Earlier, he had joined the Battersea Parliament originally established by John Burns; it had relapsed into obscurity, but in 1937

Skeffington reorganised it (he was always a good practical organiser), and it took on another lease of life. His other keen interest was in co-operation: he was a member of the Royal Arsenal Co-operative Society, and served on its political purposes committee. This Society is affiliated to the Labour Party, and it was by its nomination that Skeffington first took his seat on the Party's national executive. He also served on the Civil Service Arbitration Tribunal, as nominee of the staff side of the Whitley Council.

He went several times to Europe, visited the Soviet Union in 1938, and in the same year was granted a scholarship to study in Prague; but the war intervened to prevent further travel. Meantime, as a Fabian he had played a considerable part in the revivification of the Fabian Society after its amalgamation with the much younger and livelier New Fabian Research Bureau which had been set up in 1931 by G.D.H. Cole with the blessing of Arthur Henderson and the Webbs. His past experience in the local Labour movement caused him to take particular interest in the rapid growth of the local Fabian societies which effectively began with the Nazi invasion of the U.S.S.R. in the summer of 1941, when people wanted to discuss and to plan for post-war reconstruction, and the political truce had resulted in the practical hamstringing of the pre-war local Labour parties. The Fabian Society established a large Socialist Propaganda and Local Societies Committee to oversee and co-ordinate this activity: its secretary for over thirty years was Mrs Dorothy Fox. In 1944 Skeffington, who had been co-opted to the Fabian executive committee in the previous year, became chairman of the Local Societies Committee, an office which he continued to hold until his death. In 1957 he was chairman of the Fabian Society.

He was able to do this, and to keep lively contact with the local societies, and also with the summer schools, of whose directing committee he was a member, because he was not called up into the fighting services on account of poor eyesight. In 1941 he became a wartime civil servant, working first in the Board of Trade on industrial concentration, and then in the Ministry of Supply, where he became assistant director in charge of the production of medical supplies. When the end of the war was in sight he thought he would take advantage of the Government's offer to pay for suitable civil servants to study at a university and had actually made his application (backed by G.D.H. Cole) to Oxford when it gradually became apparent that the post-war election would probably result in a good many Labour gains. He was still candidate for West Lewisham, and accordingly he withdrew his university application, and in due course fought the election. His opponent was Henry Brooke (later Lord Brooke of Cumnor, and from 1945 to 1952 leader of the Conservative Opposition on the London County Council): he was a fairly formidable opponent, but Skeffington beat him easily. He lost the seat in the 1950 election and was again defeated in 1951 but returned to Parliament at a by-election in 1953 for the Hayes and Harlington division, which seat he retained, notwithstanding some efforts by near-Communists to oust him, through several elections until his death. After his first defeat, he solaced himself by standing for the LCC in Peckham, which he won and held until he resigned in 1958. While on the LCC, he served on its education committee, and was for some years vice-chairman of the sub-committee on further and higher education. He was a member of the executive committee of the London Labour Party as well as of the national executive, for which he was nominated, after 1946, by the Fabian Society as well as by the Royal Arsenal Co-operative Society to represent the Socialist societies. He was on the NEC of the LP from 1953 to 1958 and from 1959 until his death. He was also a member of the LP Sub-Committee on Party Organisation, chaired by Harold Wilson, which reported to the LP annual conference in March 1955.

Once in Parliament, he made his mark quickly, though without much publicity, because, though an effective speaker, he did not specialise in the kind of flamboyance which attracts reporters. He was a middle-of-the-road politician with some leanings to the Left but with no sympathy for the extreme fringe. Skeffington's strong point was quiet efficiency. He was first parliamentary private secretary to the Chancellor of the Duchy of Lancaster (1945-7) and then in 1947 he was made parliamentary private secretary to the Minister of Pensions. In the following year he joined with the Commonwealth Society in a visit to East Africa – a tour which he repeated in 1957. He also visited the United States several times (first in 1949), India, and Australia, thus adding experience of other countries to his English training. Back in Parliament after the Hayes by-election, he took special interest in housing and planning, also in leasehold enfranchisement and regulation of drug manufacture. While still a backbencher he had taken up strongly the question of the right use of the land of this country; and this eventually resulted in his being made chairman of the Committee on Public Participation in Planning. When a Labour Government took office in 1964, Skeffington was clearly ripe to take part in it. He was made joint parliamentary secretary to the Ministry of Land and Natural Resources, and three years later exchanged that post for a similar one in the Ministry of Housing.

Skeffington's political interests are well defined by his record in Parliament, including the fierce, though vain, opposition which as a London MP he put up in 1963 to the Tory-promulgated London Government Act which destroyed the LCC; as joint president of the British section of the Council of European Municipalities, and a member of the Commonwealth Association of Municipalities, he knew what he was talking about. He was a freeman of the City of London. But he had other, less political, occupations. In his entry in *Who's Who* he listed among his recreations 'bee-keeping'; he did not bring his bees to Westminster, but he was president of the Arboricultural Association, a life member of the National Trust, of the Council for Nature, and of the Ramblers' Association; he enjoyed nothing better, in leisure moments, than making little maps for friends who wanted to take uncrowded country walks in the northern parts of Kent. These pursuits made his constituents, and other Labour friends, feel that he was no resident of an ivory tower but a normal man with normal reactions, and so to be trusted. Within the national Labour Party he rose to become its chairman for the year 1969-70; unfortunately, the disease which killed him was already so far advanced that his chairman's address to the 1970 Conference had to be read for him. He died on 18 February 1971 and left an estate valued at £8694.

Skeffington was twice married; first, in his youth, to Sadie Isabel Belvin. As his political work developed, however, they gradually drifted apart, and separated finally soon after the war. In 1952 he married Sheila McKenzie, (daughter of Thomas Clyde McKenzie of Birmingham), who had been a temporary wartime civil servant, and had also done some work within the Fabian Society before becoming his private secretary. She, and their two sons, survived him. After his death there was planted in Israel a Garden of Trees in commemoration of his seven years' chairmanship of the National Council of Labour Friends of Israel. Memorial trees were also planted in Cranford Park in his old constituency, on the Denton Estate in the London Borough of Camden, and in his home village. Two of the Meopham trees are in Camer Park, the first country park to be opened in Kent under the Countryside Act 1968 with which, as Minister, he had been particularly concerned.

MARGARET COLE

Writings: *Leasehold Enfranchisement* (Fabian Research Series, no. 180: 1956) 38 pp.; *Tanganyika in Transition* (Fabian Research Series, no. 212: 1960) 44 pp.

Sources: C. Bunker, *Who's Who in Parliament* (1946); LP, *Annual Reports*, 1953-71; M. Cole, *The Story of Fabian Socialism* (1961); *The Times House of Commons Guide* (1964); Committee on Public Participation in Planning, *People and Planning* [Skeffington Report] HMSO (1969, repr. 1970); *Fabian News 81*, no. 10 (Nov 1970) 2; biographical information: J.P. Sassoon, Secretary for External Students, London Univ.; personal information: Mrs S. Skeffington, Meopham, widow. OBIT. *Financial Times, Guardian* and *Times*, 20 Feb 1971; *Times*, 24 Feb 1971; *Fabian News 83*, no. 3 (Mar 1971) 2-3; no. 4 (Apr 1971) 2, and no. 6 (June 1971) 5; *Labour Party Report* (1971).

SKINNER, (James) Allen (1890-1974)
SOCIALIST, PACIFIST AND TRADE UNIONIST

Allen Skinner was born in Dulwich, South London, on 16 January 1890, the son of a cabinet-maker. After elementary schooling he started work as a telegraph boy; later he became a postman and then a sorter.

He must have been a practising Christian in his youth since there are family reminiscences of the possibility of his entering the Church. It was almost certainly his wife who led him away from religion into free thought. Skinner married young, and his wife Phillis (née Emerson) was many years his senior. It was her second marriage. Her father had been a trade unionist and a 'free thinker', and she herself was a vegetarian, secularist and radical who much influenced her young husband. Skinner was also influenced by Orage's *New Age*. He and his wife were both politically active before 1914 and by this date he may have already joined the ILP.

When war broke out Allen Skinner first opposed it on Socialist grounds and then on absolutist pacifist principles. After being called up for military service in 1916 he refused alternative employment which the Appeal Tribunal offered and began his prison career in Wormwood Scrubs on the last day of 1916. After some weeks he was offered, and refused, the Home Office scheme [for which see Rae (1970) Ch. 8]. Skinner suffered terribly from hunger and cold that winter, among other reasons because no vegetarian diet had yet been granted. He was released at the end of March 1917, refused military service once again and began a second prison sentence on 12 April. He served 141 days and was discharged with a serious condition of tuberculosis of the bone in knee and elbow. He was operated on several times and remained a cripple for the rest of his life. His wife also went to prison for three months under the Defence of the Realm Act (DORA) for distributing anti-war leaflets.

Skinner became employed at the head office of the Union of Post Office Workers in 1919, and with the rest of the staff moved from Manchester to London in 1920. Skinner became assistant to the editor of the UPW journal the *Post*, and in addition to the usual routine work of make-up, proof-reading and so on he wrote book reviews and critiques of plays and films. Some of these were signed. He was also active in the work of the staff committee and joint committee, and took a leading part in negotiating a staff superannuation scheme.

When he came to work and live in London he seems to have immediately associated himself with the ILP. He stood unsuccessfully as parliamentary candidate at Hendon in 1924 and at Wandsworth in 1929, but throughout the 1920s he was a considerable political personality at the regional level of Labour politics. *Labour Who's Who* in 1927 records him as occupying a number of leading positions in the ILP: secretary of the London and Southern Counties division; chairman of the Inner London Federation and chairman of the London central branch; member of the national industrial policy committee. He was a consistent advocate of workers' control, not least in his own organisation of the Post Office. Many of his political attitudes – for instance on workers' control – he shared with Francis Andrews who edited the *Post* between 1931 and 1945.

Skinner remained with the ILP when it disaffiliated from the Labour Party in 1932 and his political views during the 1930s were typical of many of the ILP, including a lively anti-Stalinism. His own independent political stance was well illustrated in a letter he wrote to the *New Statesman* (10 April 1937), in which he deplored the near monopoly of left-wing publication represented by the success of the Left Book Club:

> It can be assumed that it is not the intention of such a Club to publish works expressing an orthodox or right-wing Labour Party point of view; but as instances of 'Left' attitude which are not likely to get a reasonable place the points of view represented by the Independent Labour Party and the Socialist League may be cited, and also the point of view generally described as Trotskyist.
>
> I suggest that if a book club is to cater for the Workers' Movement in the way the Left Book Club purports to do, the selecting committee should be representative of a much wider range of Socialist thought.

During the 1930s he continued to be intensely active in many of the sections of the pacifist movement and he was one of the influential group which ran the Pacifist Research Bureau. It was at this time that he became a very close friend of Reginald Reynolds.

Skinner was a trusted adviser to the Central Board for Conscientious Objectors in the Second World War. After the war ended he became secretary of the No Conscription Council, chairman of the board of *Peace News*, and between 1952 and 1955 – in the depth of the Cold War – he edited the paper. He had already retired from the UPW on reaching the age of sixty in 1950. During the period of his editorial control of *Peace News* he worked closely with A.J. Muste of the United States – with whom he developed strong bonds of affection and political outlook – and he and Muste were part of the 'Third Way Movement' which figured prominently at the time of the Bandung Conference in April 1955. When the campaign against the nuclear bomb began to assume the proportion of a mass movement Skinner was the sponsor in 1957, together with Bertrand Russell, Reginald Reynolds and others, of the Emergency Committee for Direct Action against Nuclear War. Despite certain reservations about civil disobedience he supported fully the activities of the Direct Action Committee and served a two-month prison sentence in Brixton Prison in 1959/60 arising out of the illegal demonstration at the Harrington rocket base. Fenner Brockway sent a telegram to Brixton Prison on Skinner's 70th birthday. During the 1960s Skinner monitored foreign affairs (especially Chinese) for the national council of the Peace Pledge Union, an organisation of which he had been a member since its foundation.

Skinner was not a man given to self-pity. His physical disablement did not prevent him from country walking, in which he took great delight, or in becoming an effective table tennis player. After his retirement he indulged his serious interest in classical music; spent much time in art galleries; practised his considerable skills as a chess player and became keenly interested in ecclesiastical history. During his life he spent many holidays in France and with a good command of the language read widely in French literature.

He felt in close sympathy with Quakers, but never joined the Society of Friends. A Quaker and militant pacifist in whose house Skinner lived for many years wrote the following note about him:

A healthy, open-air complexion, genial warmth and kindliness would be first to strike one on meeting J. Allen Skinner; not until he was seen awkwardly rising from his chair would one know that since the end of World War I he had been handicapped by a crippled arm and leg, and that it would be almost impossible for him to get up un-aided should he fall.
The iron self-discipline which made him take long walks to keep fit (backed by an enthusiasm for vegetarianism which he did not thrust at others) also made him a self-effacing committee man and a much sought after chairman or rapporteur for study groups. Any hint, however, of dishonest political manoeuvring could bring a withering attack, as with eyes flashing he would use a pointed finger to drive home his comments. But such occasions were rare: with genuine opponents there was no less firmness but a much more gentle manner. It was perhaps his patient ability to expound policies and tactics to the politically inexperienced that brought him the lasting friendship and respect of so many young people [personal letter from Hugh Brock, 17 Dec 1976].

Skinner's wife, who, unlike her husband, became in her later years set in her ideas and somewhat intolerant, died soon after his retirement from the UPW, and it greatly affected him. There was a son of the marriage, Jack, who with his wife, Joy, is now (1977) on the stage. Skinner himself died on 20 January 1974 and a memorial meeting was held on 8 February at the Westminster Friends Meeting House. He left an estate valued at £1959.

Writings: 'C.3' [letter], *Nation and Athenaeum 36*, 28 Mar 1925, 883-4; 'The Most Pressing Task', *Soc. Rev. 25*, no. 140 (June 1925) 269-72; 'Workers' Control in the Post Office', ibid., *26*, no. 147 (Jan 1926) 297-302; (with others), *The Organised Worker: problems of trade union structure and policy. A Report* (ILP Industrial Policy Cttee, [1927]) 29 pp.; 'On Heresy and

Schism', ibid., n.s. 3, no. 34 (Nov 1928) 23-8; 'Carlisle and after', ibid., n.s. 4, no. 41 (June 1929) 5-12; 'The Left Book Club' [letter], *New Statesman and Nation*, 10 Apr 1937.

Sources: J.W. Graham, *Conscription and Conscience* (1922); ILP, *Reports*, 1923 and 1926-9; *Labour Who's Who* (1927); J. Rae, *Conscience and Politics* (Oxford, 1970); personal information: P. Arrowsmith, London; H. Brock, Dartford; E.R. Hardcastle, London; J. Skinner, Stanford, Kent, son. OBIT. *Peace News*, 25 Jan 1974; *Peace Pledge Union Newsletter* (Jan 1974); *Friend*, 1 Feb 1974.

JOHN SAVILLE

SOUTHALL, Joseph Edward (1861-1944)
ARTIST AND SOCIALIST

Joseph Southall was born on 23 August 1861 in Portland Road, Nottingham. His father, Joseph Sturge Southall, a wholesale grocer and a nephew of the radical Quaker Joseph Sturge (1793-1859), was married to Eliza Maria Baker, who also came of a Quaker family with reforming sympathies (and who must have been a remarkable woman, to judge from the portrait painted by her son in 1902). Not long after Joseph's birth his father died, and his mother took him to Birmingham to be under the guardianship of her brother, Alderman George Baker, who in 1876 was to succeed Joseph Chamberlain as Mayor of Birmingham. After an education at Quaker schools in Ackworth and Scarborough, Southall returned to Birmingham, where in 1878 he was apprenticed to the architects Martin and Chamberlain. Under the influence of the latter, an enthusiastic disciple of Ruskin and devotee of Venetian architecture, Southall became convinced that, like the medieval craftsman, the architect must also be a sculptor and a painter; he therefore studied drawing and carving. On a visit to Italy in 1883 he fell in love with the Italian primitives. In particular, he was fascinated by the paintings in tempera, and determined to learn the art. By 1884 he had produced 'a very satisfactory panel' in tempera [Hodson (1920) 7]; but he continued for years to experiment with this very difficult technique, until he had mastered it so thoroughly as to be able to teach it to pupils. It was in this medium that he achieved most success, and his paintings were exhibited quite widely, abroad as well as in England. *The Times* obituary of Southall gives some detail:

> In 1884 his work was brought to the notice of Ruskin and was much admired by him. In 1897 Gaskin, to whom Southall had taught the method of tempera, showed some of Southall's tempera-paintings to Burne-Jones, who enthusiastically praised the work, and in 1900 Southall founded the Society of Painters in Tempera, of which both Crane and Holman Hunt were members. He first exhibited at the Royal Academy in 1895, when a watercolour, 'Cinderella', was hung on the line. From then on he exhibited regularly at the New Gallery until it closed in 1909. He was elected a member of the New English Art Club in 1925, and an ARWS in the same year, and was elected a full member of that Society in 1931. He first exhibited in Paris in 1905 at the New Salon, and was made an associate of the Société Nationale des Beaux Arts in 1926.
>
> One of his most notable works is the large panel in true fresco done for the Birmingham Art Gallery; this, technically, is a masterpiece, and an interesting record of local life. His work has been lent by the British Government to international exhibitions in Rome, Turin, St Louis, and Ghent; he lectured on the technique of painting to the Royal College of Art, South Kensington, and to several notable societies. His speciality was always egg tempera and buon fresco, although he was a highly skilled artist in all media of painting; his work is to be seen in the permanent collections at Birmingham, Nottingham, Bury, Oldham and Dudley, and a set of his original engravings on copper is in the print room at the British Museum [9 Nov 1944 (reproduced from *The Times* by permission)].

There was a Southall exhibition at the Leicester Galleries in 1926, and one in Birmingham in 1927; but since then he has been comparatively little known. His reputation has suffered from the general unfashionableness of the art of his time – together with the particular unfashionableness of the Birmingham School. But although Southall was influenced by Ruskin, Burne-Jones and Morris, he is not to be regarded as a mere follower – 'he is nobody's imitator' [Hodson (1920) 7] – nor a mere medievalist. He took the view that the artist has a public function to perform and that he will reflect contemporary life. These views are illustrated by the notable fresco mentioned in *The Times* article above. This fresco was an undertaking in every way congenial. It represents a part of Corporation Street, Birmingham, and embodies middle-class elegance – hobble skirts, top-hats and all – in portraits of his contemporaries. Even in a picture so apparently unmodern in theme as 'New Lamps for Old', the figures are again contemporary portraits (they include Southall himself and his wife) and '. . . his sketch-books are full of the most vital, vivid, and witty notes of people, attitudes and portraits' [Armfield (1945) 146].

His art is all of a piece with his social and political ideas. A direct fusing is seen in a booklet entitled *Fables and Illustrations*, which his hatred of war and warmongers goaded him into publishing in 1918. The text consists of short, keenly-pointed satirical pieces, the illustrations are anti-war cartoons. The book was printed and sold by the National Labour Press, Johnson's Court, Fleet Street.

Southall's politics were as distinctive as his painting: they consisted of a mixture of pacifism, radicalism and, later, left-wing Socialism. Originally, his social conscience seems to have been formed by the reformist Quaker tradition into which he had been born. He was therefore not unexpectedly drawn towards the utopian socialist vision of *News from Nowhere*, especially in view of Morris's reputation as an artist. His political instincts were further aroused by the jingoistic reception in England of the leaders of the Jameson Raid, an episode which he regarded as shameful.

In the early years of the century Southall was a leading supporter of the Birmingham branch of the ILP. In 1913 he became chairman of the Birmingham Auxiliary of the Peace Society, and he opposed the First World War both as a pacifist and on internationalist grounds, speaking on anti-war platforms with a dry humour and keen sense of satire. From 1915 to 1919 he was chairman of the city branch of the ILP, and its vice-chairman after 1919. During the early part of the 1920s members of the Communist Party could also be individual members of the Labour Party, and many were. But at the Liverpool Conference of the Labour Party in 1925 a successful resolution excluded Communists from future membership; and largely to counter what was regarded by some sections of the Labour Left Wing as part of a general move to the Right, the National Left-Wing Movement was inaugurated in December 1925. After preliminary meetings in London and Birmingham a national conference was held under the sponsorship of Councillor Joe Vaughan (member of the London Labour Party executive), Alex Gossip of the furniture workers, Tom Mann of the CPGB, and Joseph Southall. William Paul, Communist editor of the *Sunday Worker* (which had been founded in March 1925) was also present, and the *Sunday Worker* was to become the main organ of the new movement. The story of the National Left Wing Movement has been briefly told in Joseph Redman's pamphlet of 1957.

Its declared aim was not to 'break away from the Labour Party', but 'to take the lead in bringing the Labour Party back to its proper sphere of working-class politics and activity' [*Sunday Worker*, 3 Jan 1926]. About fifty divisional and borough Labour Parties associated themselves with the new movement. Birmingham was always an active centre, with Southall as one of its leading figures. He was chairman of both the local Left Wing Labour Group and the official Edgbaston branch of the Labour Party. The Labour Left Wing soon came into conflict with the official Labour leadership. The centre of the dispute was the action of the Edgbaston and Moseley Divisional Parties in continuing to support the candidature of Dr Dunstan. Dunstan was a Communist who had stood for West Birmingham in 1924 with a great deal of backing, some of it open, from members of the local Labour Parties. In 1926 O.G. Willey was adopted as official

Labour candidate for the division, and this led to two years of bitter wrangling between the local left-wing leadership and the Birmingham Borough Labour Party, on general political grounds as well as on account of the continued support for Dunstan. In December 1927 Southall was expelled from the Borough Labour Party, with a further recommendation that he should leave the Edgbaston Divisional Party, but in January 1928 the latter body reaffirmed their support for him. On 27 March 1928 the organisation sub-committee of the national executive of the Labour Party recorded a letter from the Birmingham Borough Party asking for the disaffiliation of the Edgbaston and Moseley Divisional Labour Parties. A committee of inquiry from the national executive – composed of George Lansbury MP (chairman of the executive), F.O. Roberts MP (ex-chairman), Arthur Henderson (secretary), and G.R. Shepherd (assistant national agent) – proceeded to Birmingham early in May 1928 to undertake an official investigation. The representatives of the two Divisional Parties laid down certain conditions which had to be met before they were prepared to take part in the inquiry; and when these were refused they withdrew, and took no part in the proceedings. The committee made a report to the LP national executive later in the same month: they unanimously recommended the disaffiliation of the Edgbaston and Moseley Divisional Parties. The local newspapers carried full reports in May 1928, and there is a brief reference in the 1928 report of the Labour Party Conference.

Southall made some bitter remarks about the proceedings of the investigating committee, and in particular vigorously attacked George Lansbury's part in the affair. He quoted against Lansbury a damning statement which the latter had made in an interview in 1926 [published in the *Sunday Worker*, 19 Sep 1926], in which Lansbury had protested against the introduction of an official Labour candidate to stand against Dunstan. Lansbury was reported as saying:

The opposition to Dr Dunstan is a disgusting procedure. Dr Dunstan fought the seat at the last election, was supported by the great bulk of the Labour men and women in the division, and received the benevolent assent and definite support of the borough Labour Party. It is disgraceful that a new candidate should be brought from Yorkshire.

I would be glad to support Dr Dunstan's candidature at any time. The Communists are not our enemies, but our friends. I have not changed my attitude on political action, but I want the same thing as the Communists – the replacement of capitalism by Socialism. The movement is bigger than individuals, and, therefore, I cannot take part in or support any division of forces. Dunstan was the first man in the field in West Birmingham, and received, and should continue to receive, the support of the Workers in the district.

It is only fair to Lansbury to point out that the policy of the Communist Party was changing by 1928. By the time of the ninth Plenum of the Communist International (Feb 1928) there had developed a vigorous minority within the Communist Party – led by R. Page Arnot, Harry Pollitt and R. Palme Dutt – which strongly criticised the majority on the central committee for their alleged opportunism and which argued for the acceptance of the theory and practice of class against class, as elaborated in the summer of 1928 by the Sixth Congress of the Communist International. The detailed history of Communist politics, national and international, can be found in many places such as the introduction to Redman (1957); Macfarlane (1966) and Klugmann (1969). The January 1929 Congress of the CPGB passed, by a narrow majority, and against the opposition of the Central Committee, a resolution that all party members should leave the National Left-Wing Movement; and soon after, the national committee of the Movement, on which Communist members were in the majority, decided to dissolve the organisation, with the advice to its members to join the Communist Party. Joseph Southall was among the many who protested against this decision – not least on the grounds that there had been no consultation at all with the ordinary members – and the pages of the *Sunday Worker* from February to May 1929 contained many protests from readers.

Southall continued to work in the ILP against the Labour leadership. At the 1926 ILP Conference he had been in a minority when he sought changes at the head of the Parliamentary Labour Party, but disillusionment with the second Labour Government brought others round to his view. There was an unsuccessful attempt by Southall and Fred Silvester, the secretary of the Birmingham Left Wing Group, to reform the ILP Parliamentary Group. At the 1930 conference Southall moved a motion, seconded by W.J. Brown MP (and warmly supported, among others, by Jennie Lee MP) calling for the reconstruction of the ILP Parliamentary Group on the basis of ILP policy. The motion was carried overwhelmingly, but when the conference decision was forwarded to the 147 members in the Commons who were formally also members of the ILP, only eighteen accepted it. These then became the ILP Parliamentary Group [Brockway (1946) 266-8; the names of the eighteen are given in a footnote on p. 267]. In the following year, Southall moved for the disaffiliation of the ILP from the Labour Party; the motion was defeated by 173 votes to 37, but opinion in the ILP was shifting towards Southall's position, and in 1932 a similar motion was carried.

Earlier in 1926, Southall had keenly supported the General Strike, partly for a rather unusual reason. He described the strike as 'the most magnificent exhibition of Passive Resistance that we have yet seen', and went on to suggest that it could be developed as a method to stop war [*Friend*, 25 June 1926, 596]. Despite advancing years he remained politically active and retained his firm and vigorous views. These are exemplified in a *Labour Monthly* article of October 1932 which also provides a statement of his campaign for the severance of political ties with the Labour Party:

My own personal experience of the Conferences of the Labour Party goes back some six years when I was sent by my own divisional Labour Party as a delegate. There I saw for myself how the rule of the official clique was maintained and fortified by the monstrous institution of the block vote, a machine more anti-Socialist and anti-Democratic than any other political device that I know of in this country. I saw that four or five trade union bosses handling hundreds of thousands of votes, with little or no reference to the opinions of the rank-and-file, could do what they liked with the Conference and crush any opposition that might arise. It was and is government of the officials, by the officials and for the officials, and far from being the champion of the working class, the Labour Party has become its most subtle and dangerous enemy.

The pitiful struggles of the I.L.P. delegation were treated with impatient contempt by the serried ranks of trade union officials for whose personal advantage and advancement the whole institution seemed to exist. Its hatred of the Communists was positively hysterical and its injustice to them was, I have no doubt, dictated by the knowledge that such an element in their midst would bar the way to office, a goal which they would do almost anything to attain. To us in Birmingham the conduct of the second Labour Government caused no surprise; we had accurately gauged the character of the Labour leaders, and unlike some of our I.L.P. fellows, we were not disappointed.

In the later 1930s he appeared occasionally at left-wing proceedings, and remained a dedicated pacifist. He was at a meeting called to support the Peace Council's Petition for a Constructive Peace shortly before his death, which occurred on 6 November 1944. His beliefs were dictated by his conscience, and he could be stubborn in holding fast to them; a friend described him as a man who exemplified the old Puritan virtues, whose watchword might be taken as 'I believed, therefore have I spoken'.

One of his campaigns he sustained for over forty years. In 1900 he had become a 'passive resister' on the question of religious teaching in schools, and withheld a proportion of his rates in protest. On being summoned for non-payment, he would appear in court to explain his objection, and afterwards have ready for distraining two silver teaspoons. These would be seized, and Southall would attend the public auction and buy them back, to be used again on the next occasion. It was characteristic of him that he refused to concede the principle, and up to the time of his death he went before the court twice yearly to state his case. He remained, too, a working artist, and his last painting was a portrait of Fred Jowett which was presented by the Jowett Memorial Committee to the City of Bradford. He had married Anna Elizabeth Baker in 1903, and she survived him. In his will he left effects to the value of £13,707. At the Annual Gathering of the Society of Friends in London in 1945 a short account was read of the life and service of Joseph Southall. It concluded with the following passage:

> His wonderful and unfailing courtesy was remarkable even in a Society that bases itself on friendship. Younger Friends especially will remember his kindness to them, the respect and gentleness with which he received them, and the hope which he always expressed that they might develop qualities in which an older generation had seemed to him to fail. He could identify himself with the forward-looking spirit of men and women of every race and colour. Towards any form of pretence, hypocrisy, shallow or muddled thinking, he was merciless. He had a shattering way of evoking the memory of George Fox at the most inconvenient moment. Many of his comments, and much of himself, will be found in his letters, to the great satisfaction of the reader. Gatherings of Friends were often put upon their mettle by a summing up from Joseph Southall, and many were the sharp encounters which reminded us of simple but vital principles in danger of being smothered by more material concern. And then, the battle over, who has not seen him shaking hands with his late adversary over a cup of tea, beaming through his half-moon spectacles with the world's most celestial twinkle in his eyes, the clear parchment pallor of his face broken into what would have been the smile of a benevolent old gentleman had it not somehow been pointed with the wit of a Joseph Southall.

> The broad hat, the small attentive beard, the flowing coat, the artist's white hands, the courage, the humour, the grace, these we shall not see again. But we can be glad that he was faithful to what he felt was the Christian message on war – and we can be glad to have known a Friend who had so much in him of the qualities which once made Charles Lamb say of the Quakers, 'they show like troops of the shining ones'.

Writings (including illustrations): Drawings in C. Perrault, *The Story of Blue Beard* (1895); 'Grounds suitable for Painting in Tempera: a reply to R.E. Fry's paper on Venetian Tempera', *Society of Painters in Tempera Papers 1* (1901-7) 2nd ed.; *Art and Peace* (League of Peace and Freedom, 1915) 8 pp.; drawings in R.L. Outhwaite, *The Ghosts of the Slain* (Manchester, 1915) 30 pp.; *Fables and Illustrations* [1918] 31 pp.; *Paintings and Drawings by J. Southall* (Alpine Club Gallery Catalogue, [1922]) 13 pp.; 'Margate and the Left Wing', *Lab. Mon. 8* (Oct 1926) 607-12; Satirical Preface to A.J. Cook, *The Mond Moonshine: my case against the "Peace" Surrender* (Workers' Publications Ltd, [1928]) 12 pp.; 'No More War', *Midland Socialist* (May 1928) 4; 'The Work of Arthur J. Gaskin' in *City of Birmingham Museum and Art Gallery Memorial Exhibition* (1929); 'In Memoriam Arthur Joseph Gaskin', *Studio 101* (Jan-June 1931) 253-5; 'Socialism versus the "Labour Government" ', *Lab. Mon. 13* (July 1931) 444-6; 'The Position of the ILP', ibid., *14* (Oct 1932) 623-5; *Life in the Forest* (n.d.) 2 pp.; *Geneva examined* (n.d.) 7 pp.

Sources: A. Finch, 'The Paintings of Joseph Southall', *Studio 71* (1917) 42-53; L.W. Hodson, 'The Birmingham Group: Arthur J. Gaskin and Joseph Southall', ibid., *79* (1920) 2-8; *Sunday Worker*, 3 Jan and 19 Sep 1926; *Labour Party Report* (1926); *Labour Who's Who* (1927); J. Hill and W. Midgley, *The History of the Royal Birmingham Society of Artists* (Birmingham, [1928?]); *Birmingham Post*, 12 and 24 May, 7 and 18 June 1928; *Labour Party Report* (1928); *Town Crier*, 25 May 1928; *Who's Who in Art* (1934); U. Thieme u. F. Becker, *Allgemeines Lexicon der bildenden Künstler 31* (Leipzig, 1937) 312; *WWW* (1941-50); F. Brockway, *Socialism over Sixty Years: the life of Jowett of Bradford* (1946); 'J. Redman' [pseud. Brian Pearce], *The Communist Party and the Labour Left 1925-1929*, with an Introduction by J. Saville (Hull, [1957]) 32 pp.; R.P. Hastings, 'The Labour Movement in Birmingham 1927-1945' (Birmingham MA, 1959); R.E. Dowse, *Left in the Centre: the Independent Labour Party 1893-1940* (1966); L.J. Macfarlane, *The British Communist Party: its origin and development* *until 1929* (1966); J. Klugmann, *History of the Communist Party of Great Britain* vol. *2: 1925-7* (1969); A. Everitt, 'The Minor Masters that Birmingham has forgotten', *Birmingham Post Saturday Magazine*, 30 Sep 1972; biographical information: Birmingham City Library; J. Murdoch, Birmingham City Museum and Art Gallery; D. Rolf, Middlesbrough; personal information: C.A. Barnwell, J.W. Crump and Professor G. Shepherd, all of Birmingham. OBIT. *Birmingham Gazette, Birmingham Mail* and *Birmingham Post*, 7 Nov 1944; *Evening Despatch*, 7 and 11 Nov 1944; *Times*, 9 Nov 1944; *Town Crier*, 11 Nov 1944 [by J. Simmons]; *Sunday Mercury*, 12 Nov 1944; M. Armfield, 'Joseph Southall: introductory notes', *Friends' Quarterly Examiner* (July 1945) 141-9; *A Testimony to the Life of Joseph Edward Southall*, ed. W.A. Cadbury (1946) 8 pp. The editors are indebted to Dr Malcolm Easton, formerly hon. curator, Hull University Art Collection for assistance with this biography.

MARGARET 'ESPINASSE
DAVID E. MARTIN
JOHN SAVILLE

See also: *Frederick William JOWETT; †George LANSBURY; †Percy Lionel Edward SHURMER.

STEADMAN, William (Will) Charles (1851-1911)

TRADE UNIONIST AND LIB-LAB MP

Will Steadman was born on 12 July 1851 in Poplar, the eldest child of William Steadman, a shipwright, and his wife Jane. William Steadman joined the Navy at the end of the Crimean War as a carpenter and the family (there were probably two other children) moved to live in Portsmouth for a time; but young Will was soon sent back to live with relations in Poplar, where he attended the local National School. Later the rest of the family returned to London, where they lived in conditions of poverty and hardship.

At the age of eight Will Steadman started work as an errand boy and between then and his fifteenth birthday did various jobs, including newspaper selling and serving as a barman in a public house. In June 1866, at considerable cost to his family, he was apprenticed to a Poplar shipwright and bargebuilder and he continued to work on the Thames until 1892. During his apprenticeship he attended evening classes in Battersea and also began his political education, being much impressed by William Newton's candidature in Tower Hamlets in 1868. From this time he seems to have been a radical of the kind that Newton had become by the late 1860s, and in his later life Steadman was closely associated with the Liberal Party.

The Barge Builders' Union was established in 1872. It was a small craft union of about 400 members when Steadman joined it in 1873 on completing his apprenticeship. Six years later he became secretary of the union and he steadily established a reputation in London trade union circles as a skilful and tough negotiator. His reputation was especially connected with the conduct of an eighteen-week strike by barge builders in 1890. His evidence to the R.C. on Labour in May 1892 is an excellent statement of the principles and practices of craft unionism by a trade union official who at this date would certainly be classified among the 'old' unionists, although, it should be noted, he was in favour of a legislative limitation on the hours of labour (Q.20325). He represented his union on the London Trades Council from 1882 and soon became one of its more prominent members. He went on to the EC in 1886, became treasurer in 1890, and represented the LTC at various times at the TUC. In 1892 he was a member of the delegation from the Trades Council who met Salisbury and Balfour to discuss the Eight Hours question. In 1893 he was LTC delegate to the Congress of the Second International in Zurich.

Steadman always remained involved with radical politics. He was greatly influenced by Henry George and as late as 1910, in the year before his death, he was still insisting that 'The great curse of this country is the present ownership of the land' [Hammond (1910) 91]. He was active in various radical causes in the 1880s, and in 1890, after three previous unsuccessful attempts, he was elected a vestryman for Mile End. His particular interests were unemployment and the payment of union rates for council contracts. At this time Steadman was critical of both political parties, being quoted in the *Star* of 13 May 1891 as saying that 'as regards labour there is not much to choose between either party' [Thompson (1967) 146, n.1]. But this attitude was to change. In March 1892 he was elected to the LCC on the Progressive ticket as member for Stepney. He was at this time a member of the Fabian Society – although never in political terms more than a collectivist Lib-Lab – and he worked closely with other Fabians, and in particular with Sidney Webb [McBriar (1962) *passim*]. Steadman served continuously on the LCC until 1907 when he resigned because of parliamentary duties. He ceased working at his trade in 1892 on his election to the LCC and, like a number of Labour leaders at this time – Barnes and Crooks for example – was financially supported by a 'wages fund' raised in his case by a Stepney committee, mostly of his own union members. He continued to act as secretary of the Barge Builders.

His first attempt to enter Parliament was in 1892 when he stood for Mid-Kent on behalf of the local Liberal and Radical organisation. He was beaten by a majority of 1900 and attributed his defeat to the 3500 plural votes in the constituency, of which he estimated he received only 10 per cent. He stood again in the general election of 1895, this time for the Hammersmith Liberal and Radical Association, and he was also unsuccessful. At this time an extended biographical account in the *West London Weekly News* [11 Aug 1894] quoted him as being a governor of the People's Palace, as treasurer of Toynbee Hall, on the management committee of the Hearts of Oak Benefit Society, and especially active on various unemployment committees in the East End of London. He was also noted as having lectured to undergraduate audiences at Oxford and Cambridge. Three years later in 1898 he stood as Lib-Lab candidate in a Stepney by-election which followed the death of the Conservative MP and he won the seat by the narrow margin of twenty votes.

In the House of Commons Steadman pursued interests for which he had long campaigned. His general concern was with working conditions and housing, but it was the postal workers who took most of his parliamentary attention. In each session until the general election of 1900 Steadman spoke more than fifty times on matters connected with postmen or the Post Office. It was a long-standing concern, Steadman being described by the historian of the Postal Workers as 'the most persistent and the most pushful' of all their parliamentary advocates [Swift (1929) 298]. Steadman was interested, of course, in other issues; he was sometimes described as the 'Fabian MP' and he took an active part in the debates on the London Government Bill of 1899 which for its enactment *Fabian News* [May 1899] exaggeratedly claimed a victory. Steadman was also closely associated with housing matters in the final months of his last session; and in 1900 one of his Commons speeches was published as a Fabian tract on overcrowding. He lost his seat at Stepney in the 1900 'Khaki' election. His election speeches and addresses strongly criticised those responsible for the war and he attempted, unsuccessfully, to shift the emphasis of the campaign towards social reforms. But he was labelled pro-Boer – he had supported S.G. Hobson's protest against Fabian sympathy for imperialism in South Africa – and his aristocratic Unionist opponent won a clear victory on a straight pro-war platform.

By this time Steadman was one of the outstanding personalities of the trade union and labour worlds. He was a leading figure in the national campaign for old age pensions which had been initiated in 1898 by the establishment of the National Committee of Organised Labour, of which Frederick Rogers became organising secretary; and he was chairman of the founding conference of the Labour Representation Committee at the end of February 1900. Steadman himself was decidedly in favour of independent labour representation in the Commons, but he was equally opposed to any Socialist connection, and he was one of a small group, which included Richard Bell, who fought a vigorous rearguard action against the LRC as led by Hardie and Ramsay MacDonald. It was implicit in his political attitudes that Steadman would join the National Democratic League, of which he became a vice-president, and that he would in due course refuse to sign the LRC constitution. He took Sam Woods's place as secretary of the TUC Parliamentary

Committee in 1904 when the latter retired through illness, and at the next TUC Congress he was confirmed in the office by a narrow victory over Albert Stanley of the MFGB, the voting being 770,000 against 752,000. The position was now made full-time except, Steadman informed the delegates, for parliamentary duties in the event of his being elected to the Commons. The secretaryship was also removed from annual elections: in future the holder of the office would be in permanent tenure 'so long as his work and conduct gave satisfaction to the Parliamentary Committee and the representatives attending Congress'. It was at the 1904 conference of the LRC that Steadman was quoted by MacDonald as among those who had not signed the constitution. By 1905 when the LRC had completed its list of endorsed candidates for the general election which was to follow at the end of the year, only John Ward, Richard Bell and Steadman were excluded. Steadman now contested Central Finsbury as the Progressive and Liberal candidate. He had been adopted for Stepney in 1903 but withdrew for lack of funds. In 1906 he was supported by a fund to which many prominent Liberals subscribed; and he had a majority of 694. Earlier he had been a member of the Mosely Industrial Commission to the U.S.A. [for an account of which see below].

Steadman continued to work for his radical causes in the 1906-10 Parliament. He backed strongly the Education, Licensing and Old Age Pension Bills, and although he does not appear to have accepted the Labour Party whip he normally voted with them and his personal relations with the Labour group were in most cases on a friendly basis. His ambiguous position was discussed at the 1907 TUC when an amendment to standing orders was moved by which any candidate who refused to sign the constitution of the Labour Party was ineligible to hold the post of secretary to the Parliamentary Committee. Steadman assured Congress that he was now a wholehearted supporter of the Labour Party but the president, A.H. Gill, apparently still felt that Steadman's position was equivocal and emphasised that the amendment did not apply to the present secretary but 'only to any future candidate' [Roberts (1958) 207]. Steadman was defeated in the first (January) election of 1910, and he did not contest the December election. He died on 21 July 1911.

Steadman was an exemplar of the Lib-Lab tradition. He was a tough, uncompromising advocate of trade union principles and practices; he believed fervently in the general cause of working-class advance in a parliamentary democracy; and he remained hostile to Socialist ideas, tactics and strategy. Apart from his industrial and political positions, he was for some years a Poor Law Guardian and for many a Justice of the Peace. His favourite authors, so he wrote to the *Review of Reviews* in 1906, were Sidney Webb, Henry George, Robert Blatchford, Thorold Rogers, Kingsley and Ruskin. In religion he seems always to have remained a believer but was critical of the Established Church and its social attitudes. Despite his hostility to the Socialist Left, he judged issues on what he regarded as their merits and in 1903 he not only supported the SDF's unemployment campaign but spoke at a demonstration in Trafalgar Square alongside Harry Quelch.

Steadman was a stocky, thick-set man, with the heavy moustache typical of his time. He always spoke with a marked Cockney accent. He was an opponent of compulsory vaccination. He married Jessie Wall in 1875 and they had four daughters. All his family survived him. He left effects worth £1014 (£622 net). The funeral took place on 26 July at the East London Cemetery, Plaistow, after a service at Barking Parish Church attended by many trade unionists. Among them were the MPs C.W. Bowerman, John Hodge, Will Thorne and Alexander Wilkie.

Writings: Evidence before R.C. on Labour 1892 XXXII Group A vol. III Qs 20271-413; 'Shipbuilding' in *Workers on their Industries* ed. F.W. Galton (1896) 56-66; *Overcrowding in London and its Remedy: a speech . . . reprinted from Hansard . . . with the text of the Housing of the Working Classes Act* (Fabian Tract no. 103: 1900) 15 pp.; 'Report by Mr W.C. Steadman, of the Parliamentary Committee of the Trades Union Congress', in *Mosely Industrial Commission to the United States of America, Oct-Dec, 1902* (1903) 257-63; Evidence before S.C. on Aged Pensioners Bill 1903 V Qs 491-702; *Election Address* (Dec 1909); 'Trade

Unionism and the Law of Christ' in *Labour and Religion by Ten Labour Members of Parliament and Other Bodies* ed. W.A. Hammond (1910) 86-93.

Sources: *Times*, 11, 14, 16 Apr, 14 June and 22 Aug 1890; J.M. Ouseley, *Mr. W.C. Steadman, L.C.C., the Liberal candidate for Hammersmith. An interview re-printed from the "West London Weekly News" August 11th 1894* (1894) 11 pp.; *WWW* (1897-1916); *East End Advertiser*, 5, 12, 19 Mar 1898, 24 Feb, 22, 29 Sep, 2 and 6 Oct 1900; *Hansard* (1898-1900) and (1906-10); *Dod* (1899), (1901) and (1909); *Report of the Old Age Pensions Conference held in Memorial Hall . . . London on . . . 14th and 15th January, 1902* (1902); *Finsbury Weekly News*, 6, 13, 20 Jan 1906 and 14 Jan 1910; 'How I got on', *Pearson's Weekly*, 8 Feb 1906; *Rev. of Revs 33*, no. 6 (1906) 580; R.C. on Poor Laws and Relief of Distress, *M. of E.* 1910 XLVIII App. vol. VIII Evidence of G.N. Barnes, Qs 82764-765 [includes a reference to statement by W.C. Steadman representing views of the Parliamentary Committee of the TUC]; *Pall Mall Gazette 'extra'*, (Jan 1911); H. Gosling, *Up and Down Stream* (1927); H.G. Swift, *A History of the Postal Agitation* (1929); B. Tillett, *Memories and Reflections* (1931); R.V. Sires, 'The Beginnings of British Legislation for Old-Age Pensions', *J. of Econ. Hist. 14* (1954) 229-53; F. Bealey and H. Pelling, *Labour and Politics 1900-1906* (1958); B.C. Roberts, *The Trades Union Congress 1868-1921* (1958); A.M. McBriar, *Fabian Socialism and English Politics 1884-1918* (Cambridge, 1962); H.A. Clegg et al., *A History of British Trade Unions since 1889* vol. 1: *1889-1910* (Oxford, 1964); H. Pelling, *The Origins of the Labour Party 1880-1900* (1954, 2nd ed. Oxford, 1965); P. Thompson, *Socialists, Liberals and Labour: the struggle for London* (1967); H.V. Emy, *Liberals, Radicals and Social Politics 1892-1914* (Cambridge, 1973). OBIT. *Times*, 22 and 27 July 1911; *Islington Daily Gazette and North London Tribune*, 24 July 1911.

BARBARA NIELD
JOHN SAVILLE

See also: †George Nicoll BARNES; †Richard BELL; †William NEWTON; †Frederick ROGERS; and below: The Mosely Industrial Commission.

The Mosely Industrial Commission

Alfred Mosely was born on 18 October 1855 at Bristol. His parents must have been reasonably well-to-do, since in his *Who's Who* entry he listed himself as having been educated privately and at Bristol Grammar School. While still a young man he went to South Africa, where, for many years – his own words – he was engaged in diamond mining operations at Kimberley; he made enough money to be able to retire at what his obituary notice in *The Times* called a comparatively early age. Mosely had been much impressed with the technical abilities and competence of American engineers in South Africa, and a visit to the United States convinced him of the advantages in many fields, above all in education, which that country possessed over Britain. Mosely organised at his own expense two commissions of inquiry into American attitudes and practices; the first was an Industrial Commission which took a party of trade unionists to the United States in 1902, and which is the subject of this Note, and the second, an Educational Commission in 1903. In 1907 he sent 700 English schoolteachers to study educational methods in both the United States and Canada, and he himself also made extended tours in both countries during which he arranged for a return visit of 1000 schoolteachers to Britain. Mosely was converted to Joseph Chamberlain's tariff reform movement and in 1904 became a member of the Tariff Commission. He died on 22 July 1917 at his Hadley Wood, Middlesex home, leaving his wife Florence Louisa (née Roberts), two sons and four daughters. He was a Knight of Grace of the Order of St John of Jerusalem, and during the Boer War he equipped a hospital at the Cape, being awarded the CMG in 1900 in recognition of his services.

The trade union movement in Britain was under severe critical scrutiny in the early years of the twentieth century. The most serious manifestation of its worsening legal position was represented by the Taff Vale decision. Public opinion had been moving against the unions from the time of the 1889 Dock Strike [Saville (1960)] but the more immediate causes of the growing concern at trade union practices, especially restrictive practices, were discussed in the famous articles in *The Times* in 1901 under the heading 'The Crisis in British Industry' (for which see the Special Note under 'Ca-Canny' in Vol. 6 of the *DLB*, appended to the biographical entry of W.J. Davis).

Alfred Mosely's decision to send a representative party of trade unionists to the United States was made against this general background of anxieties and fears about the role and place of trade unions in society; on the trade union side their threatened legal status was a matter of equal concern. There were other reasons, too, why America was chosen, in addition to Mosely's own admiration for much of the American way of life. During the 1890s the United States had become a large-scale exporter of manufactures, a relatively new development which had surprised most Englishmen and one which was widely discussed in the closing years of the decade. 'Made in Germany' was already a popular 'catchword of alarm' [Clapham (1938) 38]. The national debate concerning Britain's manufacturing competitors was linked with analyses of those matters considered inadequate or obstacles to improved performance in British industry itself. The purpose of the visit was summarised in a rhetorical question Mosely included in his preface to the published Report – 'How is it that the American manufacturer can afford to pay wages 50 per cent, 100 per cent, and even more in some instances, above ours, and yet be able to compete successfully in the markets of the world?'. It was with these general and particular considerations in their minds that the British delegation invited by Alfred Mosely set off for the study of industrial conditions and practices – mainly in the United States, although about half of the delegation spent a few days in Canada before going south.

There were twenty-three trade unionists in the party which left England towards the end of October 1902 and returned during December. Only one member – James Macdonald of the London Trades Council – failed to produce a report and answers to the standard questionnaire of forty-one questions which presumably Mosely himself drew up. The individual reports varied a good deal in length as well as in their coverage and usefulness, and some delegates were more helpful in their specific answers to the questionnaire than in their particular reports; and the same is true the other way around. Mosely provided a preface to the published volume, which appropriately was printed by the Co-operative Printing Society Ltd of Manchester.

The members of the Industrial Commission were: Thomas Ashton (Operative Cotton Spinners); G.N. Barnes (ASE); C.W. Bowerman (London Compositors); W. Coffey (London Bookbinders); James Cox (Associated Iron and Steel Workers); H. Crawford (Carpenters and Joiners); D.C. Cummings (Boilermakers); M. Deller (Plasterers); William Dyson (Paper Makers); T.A. Flynn (Tailors); Harry Ham (Furnishing Trades); R. Holmshaw (Sheffield Cutlery Council); W.B. Hornidge (Boot and Shoe Operatives); Thomas Jones (Midland Counties Trades Federation); G.D. Kelley (Lithographic Printers); G.J. Lapping (Leather Workers); James Macdonald (London Trades Council); J. Maddison (Ironfounders); W.C. Steadman (TUC Parliamentary Committee); H.R. Taylor (Bricklayers); P. Walls (Blastfurnace-men); Alexander Wilkie (Shipwrights); and W.H. Wilkinson (Northern Counties Amalgamated Associations of Weavers).

The unskilled workers of Britain were not represented and what we have therefore in these interesting reports is the viewpoint of the (mostly) trade union official or skilled worker who operated within the environment of the skilled craftsmen and labour aristocracy. While it is not the purpose of this Note to provide a detailed summary of the Commission's work, certain general points are worth making. There was, for example, pretty well unanimous agreement that the primary educational system in America was much superior to that in Britain; but this did not apply to technical education, where, although there was less unanimity, many delegates felt the American system to be no better, and some felt it to be worse, than the British. There was also a general agreement about the marked American superiority of conditions inside factories and workshops, although this did not apply to hours of work, which in many cases were longer in America than in Britain. But the emphasis upon labour-saving machinery, the more efficient layout of plants, the more relaxed relationships between employers and employed were widely commented on with approval. What is interesting, however, is the hard-headedness of the delegates in appraising the total situation of the American and British workers. There was no yielding in their belief that the British skilled workman was as good as, and usually better than, his American counterpart; and there was common agreement with Steadman's remarks: 'The English worker has nothing to learn from America, but the employers have a lot. I do not assume for one moment we are the best, but this I say, we cannot be beaten in the world for good, solid, well-finished work that will stand the test of years to come.' Steadman continued in exemplary labourist vein: 'Let our employers realise that labour is as much a partner in the business as his capital, and that the success or failure of that business depends upon both; he has the best material to work upon. . . . .'

This was a theme much emphasised: 'It is not a question of men, but methods', wrote James Cox of the Associated Iron and Steel Workers. The critical appraisal of the delegates came out further when they were asked to consider the general conditions of life of American workers (as against the specific conditions of life in the factory). Here there was fairly common agreement that although wages were higher, drunkenness much less, and education at the general level much superior, the delegates were not especially impressed with the quality of working-class life. 'The English workman', Holmshaw of the Sheffield Cutlery Council reported, 'has more leisure, and consequently more opportunities for enjoyment and recreation, than the American workman'; and it was a point made by a number of others. The representative of the Blastfurnacemen, P. Walls, concluded his report with these words: 'If the Americans have something to teach us in the way of highly specialised machinery and rapidity of production, they might profit by taking a few lessons from us in political and civic life. Public honour may be deteriorating in the old country, but it cannot yet be measured by dollars.' And it was the same delegate who earlier in the account of his visit had denied that American blastfurnace workers were subject to 'speeding-up' processes, but who went on to remark: 'The objectionable features in the life of the American workman are long hours and often a monotonous task. The American mechanic is what Ruskin termed "a segment of a man" '.

There were some exceptions to the majority view that, whatever the undeniable advantages American workmen enjoyed, British life in general was to be preferred. Harry Ham, of the Furnishing Trades, and Dyson, of the Paper Makers, were among those who emphasised the greater opportunities enjoyed by working men in the United States, and Ham was enthusiastic enough to recommend emigration to his fellow-craftsmen. No doubt there would have been even more to support him had the sample of delegates not been restricted to representatives of the skilled unions.

Alfred Mosely himself was particularly interested in the methods and techniques of industrial conciliation in the States; and he was especially impressed with the American National Civic Federation. Its aims were to bring representatives of industry and the workers into closer touch, and it attempted to offer its services for conciliation during industrial disputes. All the British delegates who were in New York to inquire into the workings of the Federation signed a statement urging the establishment of a similar institution in Britain, and most delegates in their individual reports also affirmed their support for the idea. No doubt there were some who signed or affirmed out of courtesy to Alfred Mosely, but these delegates, it must be stressed, were already working within or towards conciliation procedures in their own industries. Their support for conciliation was part of their labourist ethos and while they may well have been sceptical about transplanting a foreign institution like the Civic Federation into British soil, there was no fundamental disagreement about the general principles involved.

The contemporary response in Britain to the Report of the Industrial Commission was muted; the later Educational Commission received wider publicity. *The Times* gave the Industrial Commission's journeyings systematic coverage, and of the trade union papers the *Yorkshire*

Factory Times was among the most sympathetic. When the actual Report was published in the spring of 1903 the *Statist*, in two long articles, summarised fairly and adequately its main findings; but the impact of the Commission's conclusions does not appear to have been very great. Nor has the Mosely Commission been much discussed in the later secondary literature of the labour movement. The Commission's work is not of major significance for the British labour historian, but there is material on working conditions, industrial practices and industrial attitudes on both sides of the Atlantic that might find a more useful place in particular or general studies than has so far been the case.

Sources: *Mosely Industrial Commission to the United States of America Oct-Dec 1902: reports of the delegates* (Co-operative Printing Society, 1903); *Reports of the Mosely Educational Commission to the United States of America Oct-Dec 1903* (Co-operative Printing Society, 1904); *WWW* (1916-28); *Times*, 24 July 1917 [obituary of Alfred Mosely].

Contemporary Works: (1) Industrial Commission: *Times*, 16 Jan 1902; *Engineer*, 17 Oct 1902; *Times* (Oct-Dec 1902; but especially 15 Oct, 18 Nov, 2, 9, 22 and 27 Dec 1902); *Economist*, 22 Nov 1902; *Yorkshire Factory Times*, 5 Sep, 14, 21, 28 Nov, 5, 12, 19, 26 Dec 1902; *Statist*, 2 and 23 May 1903. (2) Educational Commission: *Times* 17 Dec 1901; *Schoolmaster*, 9 and 16 May 1903, 923-4 and 969, 22 Aug and 12 Sep 1903, 309 and 431; from 3 Oct 1903 to 2 Jan 1904 the *Schoolmaster* published weekly articles on the Educational Commission by H. Coward, president of the NUT; C.J. Hamilton, 'Notes on the Mosely Educational Commission', *Econ. J. 14* (Mar 1904) 111-15; 'The Mosely Educational Commission: America's Enthusiasm for Education', *Schoolmaster*, 16 Apr 1904; C. Menmuir, 'The Mosely Educational Commission', *West. Rev. 162* (Nov 1904) 555-62; 'With the Mosely Teachers in America', *Schoolmaster*, 5, 12, 19 Jan 1907.

Other Works: G.N. Barnes, *From Workshop to War Cabinet* [1923]; J. Clapham, *An Economic History of Modern Britain 3* (Cambridge, 1938); H.J. Fyrth and H. Collins, *The Foundry Workers* (Manchester, 1959); J. Saville, 'Trade Unions and Free Labour: the background to the Taff Vale decision', in *Essays in Labour History* ed. A. Briggs and J. Saville (1960) 317-50; J.E. Mortimer, *History of the Boilermakers' Society 1: 1834-1906* (1973).

JOHN SAVILLE

STRINGER, Sidney (1889-1969)
TRADE UNIONIST AND LABOUR ALDERMAN

Sidney Stringer was born in Tower Street, Coventry, on 13 October 1889, the youngest of a family of thirteen. His father, Edwin Stringer, was a master baker who made a comfortable living, although his business was less prosperous by the time his youngest son was born. Edwin was a radical who brought his children up to love books – especially Dickens – and to attend the classes given by the Co-operative Society. Although his father died when Sidney was only nine, he passed on to the boy a deep interest in politics. Sidney's mother, née Emma Bull, had died when he was only two years old. He was educated at the Holy Trinity School and at the age of thirteen began an apprenticeship as a baker, although not in the family business. Disliking the working conditions, he abandoned the post and began training at the Technical College to become an engineer. He worked for a time in Birmingham, but later returned to Coventry to work at the Ordnance factory.

Sidney Stringer became a Socialist and a member of the ILP early in his life. In 1913 he married Gwladys Morris, who was to support his work for the labour movement throughout his life. At the outbreak of war he was a conscientious objector who vigorously defended his principles. There is one story [Mrs E. Mayell (1967)] to the effect that he kept an iron bar by his lathe at work, saying that he was not so much of a CO that he would not defend himself if attacked. He became a member of the ASE and was active as a shop steward, playing his part in the strike of 1922. In the years which followed he worked at the Monk Engineering Company. He also attempted to start up in business with one partner, but the venture was unsuccessful. In 1932 he was made redundant from Monk, and blacklisted by members of the local Engineering Employers' Federation. He was unemployed until 1937.

It was at this time that he began to involve himself in municipal activities. He was elected a member of the City Council in 1928 and in 1932 he became chairman of Coventry Labour Party. Together with other local Socialists he worked to pass measures which would improve conditions in the city, even before the Labour Party achieved a majority on the Council in 1937. Always an enthusiast of the co-operative movement, he became president of the local Coventry Co-operative Society in the same year. From 1937 he took up full-time work with the Society as a mutuality collector, a post which paid only a low wage but which allowed him to vary his hours to fit in with his political activities. In the same year he became an alderman and deputy mayor of the city of Coventry.

From August 1938 Sidney Stringer was acting mayor of the city as a result of the illness of Miss Alice Arnold, then mayor. From this time he showed an awareness of the crisis in Europe and of the need to prepare, in Coventry, for the coming hostilities. In November 1938 he was formally invested as mayor and during his year in office he was to confront the dual problems of defence, and planning for population expansion in a city where industry was increasingly geared to wartime needs. In contrast to his activities in the previous war, Alderman Stringer urged the local AEU to encourage union members to volunteer for National Service, despite the fact that many of them were in reserved occupations. He also suggested an approach to Coventry workers through local employers, since a large proportion of workers were not in unions.

Sidney Stringer became a member of the Wartime Emergency Committee set up to administer the city after the blitz night of 14/15 November 1940. Late in the following year and before Stalingrad had become famous, an *ad hoc* committee organised by Labour alderman Sally Griffiths and Margaret Cohen (wife of the Coventry Communist organiser, Jack Cohen), sent a message of greetings, with 7000 signatures, to the women of Stalingrad. Some months later, when Stalingrad had become a household name, a book was received containing tens of thousands of signatures from the women of Stalingrad; and these exchanges encouraged the establishment of the Coventry Anglo-Soviet Unity Committee. Stringer, with George Briggs and George Hodgkinson, were among the leading supporters of this initiative.

These war years were a period of intense activity for Stringer in local affairs. He became a JP in January 1942; and in the following year he persuaded the Labour Party to set up a Policy Advisory Committee of which he was chairman from 1943 until 1967. He naturally served on nearly all the committees of the City Council, on many as chairman at various times; but throughout his life he showed a particular interest in education. In the post-war years he served on the executive of the Association of Education Committees; he was chairman of the Nursery Schools Association, and in 1951 he was appointed a member of the Burnham Committee. He showed especial concern for the physically handicapped and the educationally sub-normal; and he was to become a pioneer of comprehensive education in the city. Much later a school was named after him. When the University of Warwick was established Stringer was elected to its first Council.

Towards the end of his political career he precipitated a discussion on Civil Defence that for a time received national publicity. In April 1954 the Coventry Civil Defence Committee, of which Stringer was chairman, announced its intention to disband itself. In the same month, at a conference of the Co-operative Party, Stringer argued that 'time and money spent on Civil Defence is wasted in view of the tremendous advances in science'. He was referring to nuclear weapons, their destructive power being such, in his opinion, that any one local authority would be quite incapable of dealing with the problem. Civil Defence could, therefore, only be organised on a national basis. The subsequent public discussion was short-lived although it provided an early forerunner to the great national debate on 'the Bomb' at the end of the decade. The Council resumed their statutory duties in the area of Civil Defence during 1955. Stringer was not directly involved in CND, and indeed it is not quite clear exactly what his position was.

Sidney Stringer retired in 1959 from his work as a mutuality collector and during the same year he resigned from the chairmanship of the Coventry Labour Party. He was now seventy. In November 1962 he was awarded the honorary freedom of the city and in June he received the CBE. He never stood as a parliamentary candidate but more than anyone else in the local Labour movement his administrative abilities (much helped by an excellent memory) and sober political views shaped Labour politics in Coventry in the post-war era.

Labour lost control of the Council in the municipal elections of 1967 and Stringer was removed from the aldermanic list. On 7 May 1969 he died, leaving a widow (now deceased), two sons and a daughter. One son was Chief Inspector of Weights and Measures in Coventry and the other a local school teacher. The funeral service address on 14 May 1969 was given by the Bishop of Coventry; and the service was followed by a private cremation at Canley Crematorium. He left an estate valued at £1480.

Sidney Stringer was a man of medium height, inclined to stoutness in later life, but always active and vigorous. Carefully and soberly dressed, he had a homely appearance and kindly and tolerant manner. Although nominally Church of England, Stringer had no strong religious beliefs. His own moderate, labourist attitude to life was summed up in lines from Tennyson's *Locksley Hall* which he was fond of quoting:

Men, my brothers, men the workers, ever reaping something new:
That which they have done but earnest of the things that they shall do:
For I dipt into the future, far as human eye could see,
Saw the Vision of the world, and all the wonder that would be; . . .

[lines 117-20]

Sources: (1) MSS: Coventry Borough LP papers (MSS. 11) and Sidney Stringer papers, Civil Defence (MSS. 24): MRC, Warwick Univ.; Sidney Stringer papers, misc.: Coventry Record Office; Tape of Mrs E. Mayell, Sidney Stringer's older sister: Lanchester Polytechnic Library (1967). (2) Other: *Coventry Standard*, 1928-67; *Midland Daily Telegraph/Coventry Evening Telegraph*, 1928-67; J. Yates, *Pioneers to Power* (Coventry LP, 1950); *Daily Herald* and *Tribune* (Apr-June 1954); Co-op. Party, *Conference Proceedings* (1954); G. Hodgkinson, *Sent to Coventry* (1970); E.B. Newbold, *Portrait of Coventry* (1972); K. Richardson, *Twentieth-Century Coventry* (Coventry, 1972); personal information: Jack Cohen, London; G. Stringer, Coventry, son; Mrs Trent, Coventry, niece (daughter of Mrs E. Mayell). Obit. *Coventry Evening Telegraph*, 8 and 15 May 1969.

JANET DRUKER

See also: †Alice ARNOLD.

THESIGER, Frederic John Napier, 3rd Baron and 1st Viscount Chelmsford (1868-1933)
ADMINISTRATOR AND POLITICIAN

Viscount Chelmsford secures an entry in this *Dictionary* for events which occurred during rather less than one year in his life. In the first minority Labour Government of 1924, although not a member of the Labour Party, he was appointed First Lord of the Admiralty. The *DNB* (1931-1940) provides details of his political and public career.

He was born in London on 12 August 1868, the eldest of five children. His grandfather, the 1st Baron Chelmsford, twice served as Lord Chancellor in the Conservative Governments of Lord Derby. His father was an Army officer, his mother the daughter of a major-general in the Indian Army. He was educated at Winchester and Magdalen College, Oxford, obtained first class honours and was elected a Fellow of All Souls (1892-99). He was called to the Bar in 1893 but family tradition and personal inclination drew him into public service. From 1900 to 1904 he served on the London School Board and in the latter year he was elected a member of the London County Council, on which one of his fellow councillors was Sidney Webb, a future Cabinet colleague.

In the following year he succeeded to the barony, and at the same time moved into a wider political world when he was appointed to the Governorship of Queensland (1905-9); this was followed by the Governorship of New South Wales (1909-13). It was during this latter period of office that the first Labour Government of New South Wales took office. On his return to Britain, he was re-elected to the London County Council, this time with an aldermanic seat. When war broke out in August 1914, he joined his regiment, the 4th Dorset Territorials, in which he was a captain, and sailed with it to India. He had not taken part in any fighting when, in the spring of 1916, he was appointed Viceroy of India. It was an unexpected and extremely surprising choice, the Indian press viewing his appointment with pessimism, and describing him as a mediocre unknown.

The years of war witnessed significant developments within the Indian nationalist movement, and the initiative of Edwin Montagu, the Secretary of State for India, towards a degree of responsible government, were a direct reaction to nationalist pressures. Chelmsford was a good deal more cautious and hesitating, but in the end signed the Montagu-Chelmsford *Report* of 1918 which inspired the Government of India Act of the following year. It was, however, in this same year of 1919 that the Amritsar massacre took place; and for the long delay in conducting an inquiry into the killing of nearly 400 Indians, and the wounding of many hundred others, 'Chelmsford and his colleagues must bear their share of blame' [Sir R. Coupland in *DNB* (1931-1940)].

Chelmsford returned to England in 1921. He was chairman of the Committee of University College, London, from 1920 to 1932, and was a member of the statutory commission of 1923 appointed to draft revised statutes for the University of Oxford. It was the general election of late 1923 that provided him with another opportunity of public office. The new House of Commons, which first met early in January 1924, contained 259 Conservatives, 191 Labour, 159 Liberals and six others. The Conservatives were defeated on a 'no confidence' amendment to the Address, and the next day, 22 January, Stanley Baldwin resigned, and Ramsay MacDonald became the first Labour Prime Minister. The story of the construction of his Cabinet has been told in many volumes, including Mowat (1955), Lyman (1957), Cowling (1971). Among the surprising appointments was Chelmsford as First Lord of the Admiralty. There are no papers in the MacDonald MSS which offer a direct explanation for the Prime Minister's decision. Chelmsford was apparently Haldane's recommendation, and Sidney Webb, in the memorandum he wrote immediately after the fall of the 1924 Government, commented:

With regard to the Cabinet, the great surprise, to the Labour Party, even its inmost circle; to the other two Parties, and to the world at large, was the appointment of Chelmsford to the Admiralty. It was a most difficult post to fill, as the Sea Lords, with Beatty at their head, might have resigned in disgust if a trade unionist had been made First Lord; and might have been sullen and obstructive if a mere 'socialist agitator' had been put there. . . . Now MacDonald had found unsuspected resources in Haldane and Parmoor . . .; and most surprising of all, an ex-Viceroy of India, who was known only as a mild and pious Conservative. As it happened, we had known the Chelmsfords rather well. He had been made an Alderman of the L.C.C. by the Moderates; and as he was genuinely 'progressive' in sympathy, we had made acquaintance, and had even stayed with him once at his house near Poole about 1906. . . [*Pol. Q.* (1961) 12-13].

The Admiralty was still a major department, perhaps the most important pressure group at the time, and a Conservative ex-Viceroy would allay some fears. It was known that two naval issues of the first importance were awaiting decision; one was the Singapore base and the second was the Cruiser programme. Mr David Marquand comments:

> Given that the Government was facing all this trouble with the Admiralty even when they had a solidly respectable ex-Tory as its political head, they would presumably have faced even more trouble if the First Lord had been a member of the Labour Party. I think it is easy to forget now, looking back, just how weak the political position of the 1924 Government was and I suspect the real answer to the question is that MacDonald felt (probably rightly) that a minority government in as weak a position as it was simply could not survive a major revolt by the Admiralty and that they would be less likely to revolt if the First Lord were 'respectable' than if he were a dangerous Bolshevik. But as I say, this is only speculation [letter, 18 Dec 1973].

In the House of Lords on 12 February 1924 the Earl of Birkenhead made a savage attack upon Lord Parmoor and Viscount Chelmsford (and especially on the former) for joining the Labour Government. In explanation of his decision Chelmsford said:

> When I was approached by the Prime Minister it was made perfectly clear on what conditions I came in. I came in not as one who took the Labour label, but as one detached from politics, who was prepared, as a colleague, to help to carry on the King's Government on a disclosed programme. I was told before I accepted office what the policy of the Government was likely to be in the immediate future. It was distinctly understood between ourselves that, if occasion arose where I was unable to follow the policy of the present Government, it would be regarded as fair on both sides that I should give in my resignation . . . I cannot in any way divorce myself from any Cabinet decision. I accept full responsibility, and of course will be prepared to resign if, at any moment, I find myself in disagreement... [*Hansard*, 12 Feb 1924, 114-16].

- In the Cabinet Chelmsford confined himself mostly to naval affairs, although he spoke occasionally in the Lords on India. The biggest clash within the Cabinet was over the Admiralty demand for eight new cruisers, each to cost one million pounds. Philip Snowden, the Chancellor of the Exchequer, was able to get the number reduced to five, and he was also successful in stopping any further extension to the defence of Singapore. Snowden's biographer characterises Chelmsford as 'a virtual nonentity' [Cross (1966) 203] and Cabinet papers make clear the leading role which Earl Beatty, the First Sea Lord, played in all the negotiations. In the summer of 1924 Chelmsford was firmly against acceptance of the 'Geneva Protocol', but this was an issue upon which the Cabinet was sharply divided. The Labour Government resigned in early October 1924, and the general election, held at the end of that month, gave the Conservatives a large majority.

Chelmsford never again played any part in politics. In 1929 he was elected for the second time to a Fellowship at All Souls, and in 1932 he became Warden. But he suffered a heart attack on 1 April 1933, and died the same day. There is a portrait by David Kelly at All Souls.

He had married in 1894 Frances Charlotte, the eldest daughter of Ivor Bertie Guest, 1st Baron Wimborne, ironmaster, and they had a family of two sons and four daughters. Chelmsford left net personalty of £25,789.

Sources: *Times*, 19 Apr 1919; *Manchester Guardian*, 25 Jan 1924; *Forward* [Glasgow], 8 Mar 1924; *Annual Register* (1924) and (1933); *Hansard*, 12 Feb 1924, 114-18; *WWW* (1929-40); *DNB* (1931-40) [by R. Coupland]; P. Snowden, *An Autobiography*, vol. *2* (1934); G.D.H. Cole, *A History of the Labour Party from 1914* (1948); C.R. Attlee, *As it happened* (1954); C.L. Mowat, *Britain between the Wars* (1955); V.P. Menon, *The Integration of the Indian States* (1956); R.W. Lyman, *The First Labour Government 1924* (1957); R.R. Sethi, 'The Government of India Act, 1935' and 'Transfer of Power' in H.H. Dodwell, *The Cambridge History of India, 6* (New Delhi, 1958); C.H. Philips, H.L. Singh and B.N. Pandey, *The Evolution of India and*

Pakistan, 1858-1947: select documents (1962); V. Brittain, *Pethick-Lawrence: a portrait* (1963); A.H. Nethercot, *The Last Four Lives of Annie Besant* (1963); S.D. Waley, *Edwin Montagu: a memoir and an account of his visits to India* (1964); C. Cross, *Philip Snowden* (1966); *Burke's Peerage* (1970); M. Cowling, *The Impact of Labour 1920-1924* (Cambridge, 1971); S. Roskill, *Hankey: man of secrets, 1919-31* (1972); *Debrett* (1972-3); biographical information: David Marquand; personal information: F.J. Thesiger, 3rd Viscount Chelmsford, London, grandson. OBIT. *Times*, 3 Apr 1933.

STEPHEN GOSLING
JOHN SAVILLE

See also: †Arthur HENDERSON, for British Labour Party, 1914-31; †James Ramsay MACDONALD.

VARLEY, Julia (1871-1952)
TRADE UNION ORGANISER

Julia Varley was born in Horton, Bradford, on 16 March 1871, the eldest child of Richard Varley, an engine feeder in a worsted mill, and Martha Ann Varley (née Alderson). She attended St Andrew's School, Listerhills, Bradford, and the Quakers' Sunday School in Fountain Street, but, owing to family circumstances, left school when she was twelve and became a part-time mill worker. A year or so later she was employed full time as a weaver at 7s 6d a week. She joined the Weavers' and Textile Workers' Union and at fifteen became secretary of the Bradford branch. When her mother died prematurely Julia Varley gave up her full-time mill work in order to care for her younger brothers and sisters but she remained active in trade union affairs. When she was a young child her maternal great-grandfather Joseph Alderson, a master tailor, had told her that when she grew up she 'must work for the people, think for the people and live for the people' [TGWU, *Record* (Mar 1931)]. A veteran of Peterloo, he had later been imprisoned for Chartist activities and died in March 1886, aged ninety.

In the late 1880s few Bradford mill workers were union members and Julia Varley's own account of her first attempt to get recruits for the movement reflects the apathy at that time:

> It was a thankless task . . . I stood on a table in the square and argued the merits of trade unionism to a few children, two cats and an occasional passerby. While I was talking I heard a window being raised, and looking round, I saw a fat old woman leaning out of a bed-room window. She listened to me for a minute, then with a grunt of disgust, she said 'Silly bitch' and slammed down the window! That ended my speech. The collection amounted to twopence halfpenny! [*Evening Despatch* [Birmingham], 7 May 1936].

Ben Turner referred to Miss Varley's work for the union in these terms: 'Her period with us was in the hard days, when it was a moral crime for women to be in Unions, and she and others of us have gone Sunday after Sunday to the Bradford Trades Union Clubs to try to urge men Unionists to do their duty' [Turner (1920) 126]. Towards the end of her life Julia Varley recalled that when she became a trade unionist her own father was not very sympathetic but 'I could feel great-grandfather's hand on my shoulder' [*Bournville Works Mag.* (Sep 1951) 272].

Her first experience of industrial conflict was the famous strike at Manningham Mills (1890-1) and from this time she became increasingly involved in union work. She represented her union branch on the Bradford Trades Council – the first woman member – and served on its executive committee from 1899 to 1906. In 1903, at a time of severe economic depression, she was appointed by Bradford Corporation to inquire into employment conditions and assist in the organisation of school meals. From 1904 to 1907 she served on the Bradford Board of Guardians and this work brought her in touch with tramping women. Determined to investigate their living conditions, she disguised herself and tramped from Leeds to Liverpool in search of an imaginary husband called John Thompson. She slept in casual wards, in one of which a woman advised her how to manage one's husband in a fight: 'Always go for his nose with something sharp, my dear' [Swaffer (May 1935)]. She also investigated life in London common lodging houses by staying in six of them as an ordinary 'ninepenny dosser' [*Evening Despatch* [Birmingham], 8 May 1936].

Concurrently with her work on the Bradford Board of Guardians Miss Varley took part in the fight for women's suffrage, and served two terms of imprisonment: she was released from her first on 27 February 1907 together with other suffragettes, and on the same day they were all fêted at one of the public breakfasts regularly held for newly-released members of the Women's Social and Political Union. The day of her second release from prison, 20 April 1907, was celebrated in a similar manner. After her experiences in lodging houses and casual wards she found the food and accommodation provided in Holloway Gaol comparatively good.

During these years she also worked with Mary Macarthur for both the Women's Trade Union League and the National Federation of Women Workers, and in 1907 they succeeded in establishing a branch of the NFWW among the small chainmakers at Cradley Heath. Subsequently a vigorous agitation by the NFWW and the Anti-Sweating League secured the inclusion of small chainmaking within the provisions of the 1909 Trade Boards Act.

In 1909, at the invitation of Edward Cadbury, Miss Varley moved to Birmingham to organise trade unionism among women there. This involved acting as secretary to the Birmingham Women's Organisation Committee in addition to continuing her work for the NFWW. She quickly established a Card Box Workers' branch of the NFWW at Bournville, which affiliated to Birmingham Trades Council in September 1909. She was appointed the branch's delegate to the Trades Council and in January 1910 was elected to the executive committee, on which she served continuously for the next nine years apart from a break of three months early in 1913. As at Bradford she was the first woman member of both the Trades Council and its executive committee.

As a member of the Trades Council's executive committee Julia Varley was closely involved in three important trade union campaigns in and around Birmingham during 1910 and 1911. The first of these was the fight by the Associated Operative Bakers' and Confectioners' Union to improve wages and conditions in Birmingham bakeries. A public inquiry by the Trades Council revealed that operative bakers in the city frequently worked over ninety hours per week for a wage of little more than 20s and 'a vigorous agitation was entered upon'. Eventually, after a series of conferences between employers and operatives, 'a platform was agreed to of a 54-hour working week, payment for overtime, and a 26/-per week minimum wage' [*Birmingham Trades Council Annual Report* (1910)]. The agreement came into operation early in December 1910, and to make it effective the Trades Council published a 'White List' of employers observing its terms. For 'their services in assisting to bring the agitation to such a successful conclusion' presentations were made to Miss Varley and to Joseph Kesterton, the president of the Trades Council. Miss Varley received a gold watch and Kesterton an umbrella.

The second campaign was organised by her own union, the NFWW, to secure the application of the minimum wage rates established in the small chain trade under the terms of the 1909 Trade Boards Act. When the Act took effect, in January 1910, a number of employers sought to avoid paying the 2½d per hour minimum 'by contracting-out and other subterfuges', and the NFWW accordingly 'advised all the women, whether in the Union or not, not to sign any agreements'. The women were locked out but a fighting fund organised by the Trades Council and the NFWW enabled them to continue their resistance until they achieved 'a glorious victory' [*Birmingham Trades Council Annual Report* (1910)]. John Beard later recalled Julia Varley and Mary Macarthur walking in the processions of women who paraded the streets of Birmingham, carrying chains and singing militant songs.

The third fight was less successful in its immediate outcome, but had important consequences in the longer term. It followed from the establishment of a branch of the Workers' Union in Bilston during the early months of 1911. Towards the end of May the union's steward at the Etruria works was dismissed and other members, who were mainly women, were ordered to leave the union. After a long and bitter lock-out the union's resistance was broken but the industrial and political education of the workers laid the foundations for the subsequent dramatic expansion of the WU in the Black Country.

Miss Varley again played a vigorous and fearless part in the struggle. She was constantly on hand to offer encouragement to the women and on one occasion suffered an attack from an infuriated employer who threw her down an eight-foot bank. Her experiences in Bilston prompted her to remark that 'the only kind of peaceable persuasion she believed in was that done with a brick' [*Birmingham Daily Post*, 9 Oct 1911].

During this period she also contributed substantially to the work done by the Trades Council to implement the provisions of the 1909 Labour Exchanges Act and the 1911 National Insurance Act. In 1910 she served as one of the Trades Council's representatives on the Juvenile Employment Committee for Birmingham; and in 1912 she was one of two Trades Council members among a delegation which went to London to interview the Commissioners concerning the appointment of a Provisional Insurance Committee for Birmingham. By this time she had reached the conclusion that men and women should be organised in the same union. Accordingly, towards the end of 1912 she joined the WU as women's organiser for the Birmingham district, so becoming the first woman member of the union's staff. She also gave up the position of secretary to the Birmingham Women's Organisation Committee.

In 1913 the WU was involved in two major strikes, the first of which was in the Black Country. During the late spring and early summer, strike action spread across the district until up to 50,000 workers in the metal-using trades were involved. Julia Varley was especially successful in drawing the womenfolk of the strikers' families into the struggle. The strike came to a successful conclusion in July with the establishment of a minimum wage of 23s for men and 12s for women, and the WU benefited from a very large increase in membership. By August 1914 Birmingham and the Black Country provided a quarter of the union's members and six full-time organisers were at work in the district.

The second strike took place in Cornwall, where the WU was seeking a minimum wage of 21s for clay miners. Here the union suffered 'a reverse, but not a defeat' [Hyman (1966) 66]. What Miss Varley called 'the three Ps, police, poverty and parsons' prevented the establishment of the minimum wage, but the union preserved its organisation intact despite violence and intimidation by the employers. On one occasion the police made a baton charge against a group of strikers engaged in peaceful picketing, injuring a number of them.

The effect of the First World War on the engineering trades provided the WU with an unexpected opportunity to consolidate its previous achievements. The great growth of the labour force in the munition centres made possible a massive expansion of membership, particularly amongst the women workers who displaced men in many sections of production. During the war years the number of women members in the WU rose from 5000 to over 80,000. This latter figure was nearly a quarter of the union's total membership. Until August 1915 Julia Varley was the union's only women's organiser and despite indifferent health during the later war years – early in 1917 she had a major throat operation which required long convalescence – she was a constant source of inspiration and encouragement to her less experienced colleagues.

In the last year of the war Miss Varley was selected to serve on two important bodies set up by the new Ministry of Labour. At the end of 1917 she was appointed a member of the Labour Advisory Board, which was responsible for investigating the working of Labour Exchanges throughout Britain and making suggestions for improving their future operation. Early in the following year she was one of a commission of five representative women sent to France to inquire into allegations of immoral conduct against members of the Women's Army Auxiliary Corps. The commission visited twenty-nine camps and several hospitals in eight days and Julia Varley reported that 'this magnificent body of women and girls' had been 'grossly libelled' by the charges [*Workers' Union Record* (Apr 1918) 4].

There were also important developments within Birmingham Trades Council during the last year of the war which brought to an end Miss Varley's long association with it. When the war began the Trades Council declared its opposition to 'any attempt to hinder defensive or military measures being taken by those responsible for the safety of this Country'. At the same time it recognised that 'the workers are ever the sufferers from the devastating effects of war' [*Birmingham Trades Council Annual Report* (1914)]. The executive committee accordingly held urgent discussions with the Lord Mayor of Birmingham to consider ways of dealing with the dislocation of civilian life and it was agreed to form a Central Citizens' Committee to direct and co-ordinate relief work in the city.

Julia Varley was among the first members of the Trades Council to serve on this committee (which performed excellent service during the war) and she was also one of the Trades Council's representatives on a sub-committee formed by a second emergency committee, established to deal with the problems of Belgian refugees in Birmingham during the early days of the war. The particular function of the sub-committee was 'to see that British labour was not injured, and that in every case of employment the recognised British rate of wages was paid' [*Birmingham Trades Council Annual Report* (1914)].

The Trades Council's initial support for the war was progressively eroded by what it considered the manifest injustice of the Government's social policies and the introduction of conscription, until by the early months of 1918 a clear majority of members were in favour of immediate peace negotiations. A minority group, which included Julia Varley, John Beard, Joseph Kesterton and W.J. Davis, then broke away to form the Birmingham Trade Union Industrial Council for the purpose, according to a BTUIC leaflet, 'of safeguarding and promoting trade union interests', which they claimed had 'been made secondary to political action'. There were some defections to the new organisation but the great majority of unions in Birmingham remained loyal to the Trades Council, and when an attempt to launch a national movement on similar lines was overwhelmingly defeated at the annual conference of the TUC in September 1918 the Industrial Council collapsed.

Most of the unions which had seceded soon re-affiliated to the Trades Council, but the damage which the breakaway movement caused to personal relationships proved irreparable. Towards the end of 1918, to conform with the new constitution of the Labour Party, the Trades Council was reorganised as Birmingham Trades Council and Central Labour Party and in January 1919 elections were held for industrial and political executive committees. Julia Varley was not nominated for either committee and seems to have had no further connection of any kind with the Trades Council. She gave other evidence of her political attitudes during the First World War when she accepted an invitation to serve on the executive committee of the National Alliance of Employers and Employed. The more radical members of the trade union movement were strongly opposed to the organisation, and the executive committee of the WU gave Miss Varley permission to join only in a personal capacity. After the war she was a member of the Council of the Industrial Welfare Society from 1922 to 1940, and a member of the EC from 1923 to 1928.

Through the 1920s she continued to work as chief women's organiser for the WU and thus established herself as a leading figure in the wider trade union movement. In 1921 she was elected to the newly-established General Council of the TUC as one of two representatives of women workers; she served until 1924 and after re-election in 1926 held the position continuously for nine years. She was also chairman of the TUC Women's Group (from 1930 the National Advisory Committee on Women's Organisation). As a member of the General Council she attended a number of ILO conferences in Geneva, Rome and Vienna.

Her position in the trade union movement led, in turn, to Miss Varley serving on Government committees concerned with the employment of women. In 1920 she was appointed a member of the Departmental Committee on Employment of Women and Young Persons on the Two-Shift System and in the same year was on the Committee on Work of the Employment Exchanges. Three years later she served on the Ministry of Labour Committee on the Supply of Female Domestic Servants. In 1928 she was appointed to serve on the National Advisory Council for Juvenile Employment in England and Wales and in 1934 she sat on another Departmental Committee on Employment of Women and Young Persons on the Two-Shift System.

In addition to her trade union activities Miss Varley played an important part in the work of the Society for the Oversea Settlement of British Women during this period, serving on both the council and the executive committee. In 1925 she went to Canada, with a party of fifty emigrants, to visit some of the women already settled there and report on their circumstances. During her membership of the executive committee of the Industrial Welfare Society she consequently came to know the Duke of York (later King George VI), who was president of the Society. The Duke admired Miss Varley's ability and sense of humour. He wrote several letters to her, including one of sympathy when she had an eye operation in 1928. She, in turn, described the Duke as 'a good sport and a great soul'.

In 1929 the WU, which had been badly weakened by the General Strike, amalgamated with the TGWU and Julia Varley became chief women's officer of the enlarged union. Two years later she was awarded the OBE for her public work. At the annual conference of the TUC shortly after the announcement of the award she was presented with roses on behalf of the Women's Conference. Making the presentation Dr Marion Phillips described Julia as 'a good colleague, a good citizen, a good friend' [*TUC Report* (1931) 58].

Julia's lifetime of dedicated work in the causes of trade unionism and women's welfare was rewarded by two further distinctions in 1935. She was the principal speaker at an international conference on the status of women, held in Geneva before the president of the League of Nations Assembly; and on retiring from the General Council she was presented with the TUC gold badge.

Her official connection with the trade union movement ended in March 1936 when she retired from her position with the TGWU. In retirement she continued to live alone in her cottage in Hay Green Lane, Bournville, in spite of a progressive loss of vision which eventually became total blindness. She maintained her local church connections, and also attended the TUC and its Women's Conference where she was an interested auditor.

Julia Varley was sturdily built, with a rather serious, determined countenance and she wore pince-nez. One interviewer described her as 'formidably alert of mind and direct of speech' but she was capable of both kindness and gentleness to others. Her dedication to the service of her fellows through the trade union movement is obvious from the story of her career, but despite her industrial militancy her political attitudes were never left-wing and she became more moderate as the years went by. She had friends in all social classes, and one of her most prized possessions was an amber necklace given to her by Nancy Astor MP, 'From one rebel to another'.

Julia Varley died on 24 November 1952 at the family home in Bradford where she had come to live with her sisters, Mrs Martha Barrett and Mrs Jessie Wooller. She was buried in Undercliffe Cemetery after a service in All Saints' Church. A memorial service was held in Bournville Parish Church on 30 November when, at her request, the Hallelujah Chorus from Handel's *Messiah* was sung. She left an estate valued at £1419.

Writings: 'Life in the Casual Ward: experiences of a Bradford Guardian' [1907?] [article, source not known, in Varley papers]; 'Cradley and its Chainmakers', *Bournville Works Mag. 8*, no.13 (Nov 1910) 412-13; 'Sweated Needlework', ibid. *9*, no. 5 (May 1911) 150; 'The White Country: remarkable revelations of police brutality in Cornish strike', *Wolverhampton Worker* (Sep 1913); 'Women Organiser's Reports', *Workers' Union Record* (Aug 1915-May 1919 passim*); 'Yesterday and To-day', *Record* [TGWU] (Mar 1931) 234; 'Yesterday, To-day and Tomorrow: 32 years out of 64 at the Congress', *Reynolds's T.U.C. Supplement* (Sep 1932) 3; 'Smile your Way to Freedom', *Reynolds's Illustrated News*, 9 Dec 1932; 'The Joy of Service', *Labour* (Sep 1935); 'Women and Trade Unions', *Bournville Works Mag. 49*, no. 6 (June 1951) 180-1; 'The Happy Warrior', ibid., *49*, no. 9 (Sep 1951) 272-3.

Sources: (1) MSS: Julia Varley papers: Brynmor Jones Library, Hull Univ.; Minute Books of Birmingham Trades Council, 1909-21. (2) Other: 'Burial of "Old Chartist Guard" ', *Bradford Daily Telegraph*, 25 Mar 1886; Anon., 'Holloway from the Inside: a suffragist's fourteen days',

[6 Mar 1907?, newspaper article, source not known: Varley papers]; Birmingham Trades Council, *Annual Reports*, 1909-21; *Birmingham Daily Post* and *Birmingham Gazette*, 1909-18; *To Trades Unionists* [a leaflet about blacklegs from J. Beard and Julia Varley], Birmingham, 1912 in Webb Coll. E Ref: B XXXVII/5, BLPES; *Illustrated Western Weekly News*, 6 Sep 1913; R.H. Tawney, *The Establishment of Minimum Rates in the Chain-making Industry under the Trade Boards Act of 1909* (Studies in the Minimum Wage no. 1: 1914); *Workers' Union Record* (July 1914) 7-8; B. Turner, *Short History of the General Union of Textile Workers* (Heckmondwike, 1920); R.H. Brazier and E. Sandford, *Birmingham and the Great War 1914-1919* (Birmingham, 1921); [Beatrice], 'Domestics and the Dole: the views of Julia Varley', *Evening News* [Glasgow], 21 Dec 1923; *Labour Who's Who* (1927); *Birmingham Despatch*, 6 and 17 Mar 1928; J. Woollcombe, 'Julia Varley: a life-long campaigner', *Gateway*, 3, no. 14 (June 1930) 60-1; *Birmingham Mail*, 3 June 1931; *TUC Report* (1931); H. Swaffer, 'Julia Varley's Swan Song', *Daily Herald*, 23 May 1935; idem, 'You live what you preach: open letter to Julia Varley', *John Bull*, 1 June 1935; Anon., 'Bradford Woman's Life Work for Labour Movement', *Telegraph and Argus* [Bradford], 20 Jan 1935; TGWU, *Record* (Apr 1936); *Evening Despatch* [Birmingham], 7, 8, 9 and 15 May 1936; *Birmingham Mail*, 18 Dec 1936; W. Citrine et al., 'How Women played their Part' [Discussion] in *Seventy Years of Trade Unionism 1868-1938* [TUC, 1938] 65-79; 'A Lifetime of Achievement', TGWU, *Record* (Apr 1951) 286; J.M. Leask and P. Bellars, *"Nor shall the Sword sleep . . ."*: *an account of industrial struggle* [1953?] 32 pp.; *Women in the Trade Union Movement* (TUC, 1955) 96; J. Corbett, *The Birmingham Trades Council 1866-1966* (1966); R. Hyman, *The Workers' Union* (Oxford, 1971); E. Taylor, 'The Working Class Movement in the Black Country 1863-1914' (Keele PhD, 1974); C. Pearce, *The Manningham Mills Strike, Bradford December 1890-April 1891* (Univ. of Hull, 1975); M. Rix, 'I talked to Julia Varley', *Blackcountryman 8*, no. 3 (summer 1975) 37-42; biographical information: Dr R. Hyman, Warwick Univ.; Mrs J. Scott, Bradford; D. Fazakerley, secretary, The Industrial Society, London; Miss M.E. Willmott, Bradford Central Library; personal information: Dame Margaret Cole, London; T. Insull, Cadbury Schweppes Ltd; Mrs M.D. Horwill, Wordsley, Stourbridge; Mrs J. Wooller, Bradford, sister; the editors also wish to acknowledge their indebtedness to the Pro-Vice-Chancellor of Bradford University, Mr R.A. McKinlay, for his assistance with this biography and to Mrs M.D. Horwill, Wordsley, for donating the Julia Varley papers to Hull Univ. Library. OBIT. *Birmingham Despatch* and *Telegraph and Argus* [Bradford], 24 Nov 1952; *Birmingham Gazette*, 25 Nov 1952; *County Express* [Stourbridge], 6 Dec 1952; *Bournville Works Mag. 50*, no. 12 (Dec 1952); TGWU, *Record* (Dec 1952); *Labour Woman* (Jan 1953); *Parish Mag. of St Francis, Bournville* (Jan 1953); *TUC Report* (1953).

JOYCE BELLAMY
MARGARET 'ESPINASSE
ERIC TAYLOR

See also: †Margaret Grace BONDFIELD; †William Henry DREW; *Florence HANCOCK; †Mary MACARTHUR; †George SHANN.

WALKDEN, Alexander George (1st Baron Walkden of Great Bookham) (1873-1951)
TRADE UNIONIST AND LABOUR MP

Walkden was born on 11 May 1873 at Hornsey, Middlesex, the second son of Charles Henry Scrivener Walkden and Harriet Walkden (née Rogers). His father was first a clerk with the GNR at King's Cross, and then an accountant with the company, the family moving to Hertfordshire where Walkden attended the Merchant Taylors' School at Ashwell. His father, a Socialist and interested in smallholdings and agricultural labourers, had contributed articles to William

Morris's *Commonweal*, and this influenced Walkden, who in later life became a keen countryman.

At the age of sixteen Walkden left school and started work as a probationary clerk with the GNR. He proved to be a lad of ability, who rose to become goods traffic representative for the GNR at Nottingham, and in 1905 agent at Fletton, near Peterborough.

He became interested in politics and trade unionism as a young man, being influenced, like so many of his generation, by the writings of Robert Blatchford. In November 1897, he joined the newly founded Nottingham branch of the National Association of General Railway Clerks, acting as an executive member and as its first part-time secretary. He served as branch chairman from 1898 until December 1905, when the railway company moved him to Peterborough, where he was again branch chairman from April to June 1906. In his last year at Nottingham he had served as a councillor of Carlton District Council, a suburb of Nottingham. At the first NAGRC conference, held at Nottingham on 7 November 1897, he was elected a national executive member.

By November 1898, however, the Railway Clerks' Association (as the union was now called) was in a moribund condition; a special conference was convened to discuss the winding-up of the union and amalgamation with the ASRS. Walkden, however, proposed that they should fight on and successfully influenced five of the nine conference delegates to vote for his resolution. A new general secretary, F. Parrish, was appointed, and the union's head office moved to Nottingham, where the local RCA branch had become the leading section of the Association. As branch chairman Walkden became increasingly involved with national issues. In September 1899 the head office of the union, now in a stronger position, was transferred to Doncaster. During the time the Association's lead came from Nottingham, Walkden and Parrish had been responsible for contributions to a new journal, *Nibs and Quills*, aimed at clerks in general and including a special page of interest to railway clerks. The hope was that this might become the 'official organ' of the RCA, but the journal was only published once and official RCA news continued to be included in the *Railway Herald*, and – from January 1904 – its successor, the *Railway Clerk*.

Between 1899 and May 1906 Walkden held various national RCA offices. He served on the executive from 1899 to 1904, and acted frequently as chairman; he was a working committee member of the EC, responsible for routine matters, from March to November 1900, when a smaller, more manageable executive was elected, of which he retained membership; and he also sat on the superannuation sub-committee from September 1900 and the parliamentary sub-committee from January 1902. In September 1904 he attended the annual TUC as a RCA delegate, and was elected to serve on the wages policy committee, at this his first Congress.

Throughout his EC service Walkden particularly concentrated on the Association's educational and political activities. At early conferences he was called upon to give papers on railway problems and advocated reforms in clerical work to the benefit of clerk and employer alike; and he often gave talks to branches on the Association's education policy. In a competition for members endowed by the president, he gained the Sir Fortescue Flannery Gold Medal for an essay entitled 'The Technical Education of Railway Clerks', and this was circulated to all branches. Such activities marked his concern that railway clerks should increase their understanding of their own industry, and at an EC meeting in May 1904, he proposed that members should be encouraged to join Ruskin College's correspondence classes, holding to his adage 'make the clerk a better man and the man a better clerk', which became a popular slogan of the Association. At branch meetings he frequently urged that members should interest themselves in politics and that the RCA should affiliate to the LRC. In October 1903 he successfully proposed W.J. West, an all-out supporter of independent Labour representation, as the union's first parliamentary secretary and as editor of its new journal to commence in January 1904; and at an EC meeting, in December 1905, he influenced the executive to commit itself to endorsing only members who ran independently of the two main political parties in municipal or national elections, although the RCA was not then affiliated to the LRC.

At the May 1906 RCA conference, as a result of the president's resignation, Walkden took the chair until the conference dealt with the election of a new general secretary to fill the vacancy left by the death of J.E.S. Challener in March. Walkden, one of several nominations, easily won in the ballot held after the EC had been requested to give their opinion on the candidates and had strongly recommended him. After seventeen years with the GNR and with excellent prospects of achieving more senior managerial positions, Walkden left the company and became the RCA's general secretary in June 1906. Working to revive his flagging union, he became editor of its journal, the *Railway Clerk*, from January 1908 to March 1909 and then continued to contribute 'From the Secretary's Desk'. He was elected parliamentary secretary at the 1909 conference, and held this post until his retirement from the general secretaryship and the RCA in May 1936.

As general secretary Walkden entered into the wider labour movement. He represented the RCA at conferences of the TUC from 1907 to 1935, and of the Labour Party from 1911 to 1936, and thereafter on occasions up to 1945. On behalf of the RCA he gave evidence before the Departmental Committees on Railway Superannuation and on Railway Agreements and Amalgamations, and to the R.C. on the Railway Conciliation Scheme of 1907. At a meeting with Lloyd George held on 17 August 1911, about the exemption of railway clerks from the National Insurance Bill, he had suggested that a solution to the present railway crisis might be a quick and expeditious Royal Commission to inquire into the dispute and to guarantee a speedy report. Accepting this advice Lloyd George convened an inquiry on 22 August which reported only eight weeks later.

In May 1909 Walkden became treasurer to the National Federation of Shopworkers and Clerks (to which the RCA affiliated in June 1908) and served as its president from 1912 until April 1914, when the Federation broke up. Further recognition of Walkden's abilities came in 1912, when he led TUC delegations at meetings with Asquith to register the labour movement's dislike of the Government's Trade Unions (No. 2) Bill, and the movement's support for the nationalisation of the railways in preference to the Government's Railways (No. 2) Bill. Although not a member of the Parliamentary Committee, he achieved prominence as a result of RCA resolutions passed at the 1911 TUC which urged liberty of political action for trade unionists and a defined government policy for the future of the railway industry. In 1916 he tried, unsuccessfully, to become the Labour Party's treasurer. In 1917 he was a member of the Party's Committee of Inquiry into the Clydeside engineers' deportation.

Within the RCA Walkden's stature also increased, recognition by the railway companies finally being accorded the Association in February 1919. By December 1918 it represented 71,500 of the 77,000 salaried railway staff. At the 1919 conference Walkden, who had led the 'recognition battle' since 1911, was presented by a grateful membership with a gold watch and chain, a bank draft for £700 and £34 of bank notes, together with a gold wristlet watch for his wife.

The drive for industrial recognition, however, did not overshadow the RCA's desire to return one of its members to Parliament. Affiliation to the Labour Party was completed in 1911, after a voluntary political fund had been established at the 1910 conference and Walkden selected as the Association's first (and only) official parliamentary candidate. Although the Labour Party executive considered him for the December 1910 general election for the Wolverhampton West constituency, confusion between the executive and the local party resulted in no Labour candidate running at all for the seat. It was not until February 1912, when the RCA saw itself clearly able to back Walkden financially, that he became the official Labour candidate at Wolverhampton West; the Party only sanctioning candidates with some promise of finance. He had, however, previously been nominated for the Oldham seat by the local RCA branch, but he failed to be accepted by the local Party, being absent through illness from the election meeting. His first election address at Wolverhampton showed that he closely followed the broad Labour Party programme; and it especially emphasised free trade, nationalisation of land, mines and railways, and adult suffrage, irrespective of sex; the latter cause he also fostered through his executive membership of the People's Suffrage Federation.

His parliamentary career was slow in starting: He lost Wolverhampton West in 1918, again at a by-election in 1922, and in the general election of the same year; in 1923 he did not stand, and in 1924 he again failed, this time as a candidate for the Heywood and Radcliffe division of Lancashire. His career in the trade union movement, however, continued unchecked. After the constitutional reorganisation of the TUC in 1921, he was elected to the new General Council and retained his membership until his retirement from the RCA in 1936. His interest in workers' education was shown in 1922 in his role in drafting a scheme between the Workers' Educational Trade Union Committee and the General Council which later resulted in the General Council having representation on the governing bodies of the National Council of Labour Colleges, the Labour College, Ruskin College and the WEA. From 1922 he also served on the new National Council of the Workers' Travel Association (with H. Gosling as president and J.J. Mallon, warden of Toynbee Hall, as secretary) which sought to encourage working people to take holidays abroad.

During 1924 he served on the mediating committee which looked into the ASLEF and National Railway Wages Board dispute and successfully achieved a settlement on 29 January; and, at the TUC, he was selected to chair the committee to report on 'Organisation by Industry' for trade unionism. At the 1927 Congress when this report was presented, Walkden emphasised that because of the difficulties of demarcating an industry in precise terms no general scheme of industrial unionism could be suggested; even the expert witnesses from the unions being unable to define their own industries [Lovell and Roberts (1968) 100]. Other appointments included: membership of the General Council's committees on disputes and on national debt and taxation, the professional workers' joint consultative committee, and the joint committee on civil rights for civil servants. He also chaired the amalgamation talks between the NUC and the Association of Women Clerks and Secretaries (his experience of white-collar trade unions standing him in good stead), led a TUC deputation to the Home Secretary on unhealthy offices (of special interest to the RCA), and served on the Industrial Court for Civil Service arbitration cases.

It was the miners' crisis that confirmed Walkden as a leading personality of the trade union movement. He was a 'moderate' in political terms, who could always be relied upon to pursue a cautious and conciliatory policy. When the Special Industrial Committee of the TUC was established on 10 July 1925 to deal with the coal crisis, Walkden was appointed as one of its nine members [Lovell (1977) 36], and until the ending of the General Strike in May 1926 he was at the centre of negotiations. The letter that he sent to his members after the TUC's instructions to return to work, signed 'Yours in Victory' and insisting that definite guarantees had been obtained in matters such as victimisation can only be characterised as an inaccurate and misleading appraisal of the massive defeat that the movement had just sustained [Farman (1974) 291]. It was in keeping with his general attitude that Walkden warmly supported the industrial initiatives known as 'Mondism' in the years immediately following 1926.

In the general election of 1929 Walkden was elected to the House of Commons for Bristol South. He spoke on only five occasions in the Commons and in general made little impact. He lost his seat in 1931. A year later he was elected chairman of the TUC, an office which also meant chairmanship of the important National Joint Council of Labour (as it was renamed in 1934). This was a tripartite grouping of the General Council of the TUC, the PLP and the EC of the Labour Party. The NJC was the most powerful single body within the labour movement in the 1930s, and Walkden remained a member until 1936.

He regained his old seat in the general election of 1935, and retired in the following year from the general secretaryship of the RCA, after thirty years' service. A testimonial fund collected £1150 (as well as a number of gifts), and it was agreed between the EC of his union and Walkden that the fund should be divided between the Manor House Hospital and a new library at Ruskin College, Oxford. When the latter was opened, in November 1936 – named after Walkden – the RCA agreed to make an annual grant of twenty guineas.

Walkden retired from the Commons in 1945 at the age of seventy-one. His ten years had been a good deal more productive than his first period in Parliament, and he had spoken on many subjects, including agricultural and rural affairs, education, and post-war reconstruction. His central concern, however, remained the issue of railway nationalisation, one which had been a major part of his industrial and political thinking since his early days in the movement. Throughout his whole career he had been a persistent advocate of a co-ordinated, centralised control, and his evidence to the Royal Commission on Transport, presented in January 1929, was an imaginative statement of the new possibilities that nationalisation would make available. The RCA later published his evidence as a pamphlet.

Walkden was given a peerage in the dissolution honours list in June 1945, and became Baron Walkden of Great Bookham (the village where he lived, near Leatherhead). He was the second full-time trade union official to become a peer. Under the Attlee Government Walkden became a Party Whip in the Lords, and took responsibility for all matters relating to health and transport. He also became Captain of the Yeomen of the Guard in H.M. Household. When the Government introduced the Railway Nationalisation Bill Walkden took charge of it in the Lords. The Bill passed into law in early August 1947.

Walkden continued to hold several public offices. He was chairman of the Domestic Poultry Keepers' Council from June 1945, and was chairman of the water softening sub-committee of the Central Advisory Water Committee from July 1946 until 1949. He made his last speech in the Lords on 19 February 1949, and then retired to his country home, where he died on 25 April 1951, aged seventy-seven. His funeral at the Great Bookham Parish Church on 1 May was widely attended by representatives of the many aspects of public life he had been involved with, especially, of course, by the Labour movement.

He had married Jennie Wilson of Market Rasen, Lincolnshire, in 1898, and had had three daughters. His wife died in 1934 while he was visiting America on behalf of the TUC, and his eldest daughter died in May 1951, only a short time after his death. He left effects valued at £346.

Writings: *The Life of a Railway Clerk* (1911) 32 pp.; Evidence before the Departmental Committee on Railway Superannuation Funds 1911 xxix Pt 1 Qs 402-760, 5691-6027, Departmental Committee on Railway Agreements and Amalgamations 1911 xxix Pt 2 Qs 11080-337, and the R.C. on Railway Conciliation and Arbitration Scheme of 1907 1912-13 xlv Qs 6603-868; *The Future of the Railway Service: permanency or dismissal* (1913) 35 pp.; *To a Lady Clerk* (1916) 32 pp.; *The Railways Act 1921: notes and observations mainly for the information of the staff* (1922); *The RCA and its Path of Progress* (1928); Evidence before the R.C. on Transport [non-parl.] 17 Jan 1929 Qs 2214-430 including a memorandum submitted to the R.C. entitled *A Practical Scheme for the Nationalisation and Co-ordination of Public Transport* (RCA, 1929) 48 pp.; Evidence before the R.C. on Unemployment Insurance [non-parl.] 19 June 1931 Qs 8890-976 and Paper No. 74; contributions to the *Railway Clerk* and its successor *Railway Service J.* [official organs of the RCA] including 'From the Secretary's Desk', 1906-36.

Sources: (1) MSS: Labour Party archives: LP/CAN/06/1295, 303, LP NEC Minutes (Apr-Dec 1910) [microfilm]; TSSA papers, MRC, Warwick Univ.: NAGRC Notts Branch Minutes, 21 Nov 1897, 9 Dec 1898, Ref. 55B/1/BR/N/1; RCA EC Minutes, 10 Oct 1903, 28 May 1904, 16 Apr and 10 Dec 1905, Nov 1936, Nov 1941-Mar 1942, Ref. 55B/1/EC/1, 19, 24; RCA, *National Testimonial to 'AGW'* (1936), Ref. 55/3/WA. (2) Other: *Railway Herald*, 13 Nov 1897, 28 Feb 1903; *Nibs and Quills: the official organ of the NAGRC and Other Clerks' Associations* (Dec 1898); *Railway Clerk*, Jan, July, Nov 1904, Sep, Oct 1911, Feb, June 1912, June 1919, Mar 1922; *Railway Service J.*, Aug 1922, Apr 1923, Aug 1924, Feb 1929, Aug 1933, July 1936; RCA, *Annual Conference Minutes*, 1906, 1919; *Co-operative Employee*, Aug 1908, June 1909, May 1914; *Wolverhampton Express and Star*, 13 Feb 1912; RCA, *Annual Report*, 1912, 1916, 1923, 1924, 1927, 1929; *TUC Report*, 1924, 1927, 1951; H.J. Laski, 'Saturday Pen Portrait of A.G. Walkden', *Daily Herald*, 10 Dec 1932; *Labour Party Report*,

1943, 1945, 1946; *Hansard*, 13 Dec 1935, 17 Nov 1937, 18 Oct and 22 Nov 1939; *Times*, 3 Mar 1944, 7 June 1945, 22 Jan 1946, 9 May 1946 (1st ed.); *WWW* (1951-60); B.C. Roberts, *Trade Union Government and Administration* (1956); V.L. Allen, *Trade Union Leadership: based on a study of Arthur Deakin* (1957); D. Lockwood, *The Blackcoated Worker: a study in class consciousness* (1958); P.S. Bagwell, *The Railwaymen* (1963); E.E. Barry, *Nationalisation in British Politics: the historical background* (1965); J. Lovell and B.C. Roberts, *A Short History of the TUC* (1968); C. Farman, *The General Strike* (1974); G.A. Phillips, *The General Strike: the politics of industrial conflict* (1976); J. Lovell, 'The TUC Special Industrial Committee: January-April 1926', in *Essays in Labour History 1918-1939*, ed. A. Briggs and J. Saville (1977) 36-56; biographical information: R.A. Storey, archivist, MRC, Warwick Univ.; P. Wyall, senior research officer, TSSA. OBIT. *Times*, 26 Apr 1951; *Transport Salaried Staffs J.* (June 1951).

ADRIAN TRANTER

See also: John Ernest Stopford CHALLENER.

WALLAS, Graham (1858-1932)
FABIAN SOCIALIST AND POLITICAL PSYCHOLOGIST

Graham Wallas, one of the early leaders of the Fabian Society, was born at Monkwearmouth, Sunderland, on 31 May 1858, the fifth child and eldest son of Gilbert Innes Wallas, curate at Bishopswearmouth, and his wife, Frances Talbot Peacock. In 1861 his father became vicar of Barnstaple, and the family moved to north Devon. Gilbert Wallas was an Evangelical in religion and a Liberal in politics, and though he discarded these paternal convictions, his son was shaped by both. The Evangelical heritage, rejected for Secularism, made itself felt in an intense concern with ethical questions (Beatrice Webb noted his 'extreme moral refinement' in 1893, and Harold Laski was to find him 'a bishop *manqué* in the 1920s). His Socialism was always rather close to an advanced Liberalism, and in his later years was implicitly abandoned for a return to something not unlike his father's political creed.

Wallas was sent, as a matter of course, to public school and university. After six years at Shrewsbury, he won a scholarship in open competition to Corpus Christi College, Oxford. There, between 1877 and 1881, his youthful rebellion began. Readily taking to the utilitarian philosophy that still dominated that college, he lost his faith and pronounced himself a rationalist, with Darwin and John Stuart Mill as his intellectual heroes. At the same time, he formed a close friendship with a fellow-undergraduate at Corpus Christi, Sydney Olivier, like himself a son of an Evangelical cleric. Together, they explored 'advanced thought' at Oxford, and acquired a reputation as 'pretty extreme Radicals'. Wallas was to develop a Socialist image of Aristotle to match the Socialist interpretation of Mill he and his Fabian colleagues were later to set forth. He left Oxford in 1881.

In poor health during his last year at the university, Wallas took only a second-class honours degree. Perhaps with a first he might have gone into the Civil Service, as Olivier did. Instead he became a classics master for three years at a preparatory school near Maidenhead. Wallas continued to correspond with and visit Olivier, who was in the Colonial Office, and was attracted to his friend's new acquaintances, among them another clerk in the Colonial Office, Sidney Webb. Anxious to be in London himself, Wallas obtained a post in late 1884 as an assistant master at Highgate School, and took up residence in that suburb. He immediately joined his friends in their round of activities, including a reading circle of Radicals and Socialists devoted to studying Marx's *Capital*. Marx's economic doctrines did not however convince them, his disparagement of ethics repelled them, and his revolutionary approach seemed unnecessary.

Meanwhile, Wallas's life had reached a crisis: prompted by conscience, he refused to take communion as part of his duties at Highgate, and was forced to resign. With the aid of a small sum of money from his father, he decided to study in Germany and think out his future. While abroad he became acquainted with a far more developed Socialist movement than existed in England, and formed friendships with several young Socialists. Upon his return home in the spring of 1886 he followed Shaw, Webb and Olivier into the Fabian Society. Very quickly these four dominated the Society, settling down to think out, and win others to, their form of practical and evolutionary Socialism. Wallas had found a vocation. Fabian gradualism in these early years was grounded in idealism as much as in pragmatism. In this mental climate Wallas was thoroughly at home. Among his Socialist colleagues in the years just before and after the publication of *Fabian Essays* in 1889, he could exercise fully both his leading propensities: to examine critically the *status quo*, and to deliver ethical exhortations. It was a happy time for Wallas. Socialism for him above all else meant the supplanting of competition by co-operation as the fundamental principle of social organisation. Along with this shift he looked forward to the elimination of great disparities of wealth and towards a sweeping extension of public control over economic life. Both redistribution of wealth and collectivism, however, were essentially only instruments for Wallas; the end was a humane society. Wallas's Socialism was the 'good life' first defined by his beloved Greeks, translated into modern terms. Industrialism, he believed, had changed the possibilities of life; Greek ideals of the realisation of human intellectual and spiritual potential could now be achieved, not just for the few but for the many. This was the message, ethical as much as egalitarian or collectivist, that he propagated through speeches, writings and political efforts in the later eighties and early nineties.

Within Fabian circles, Wallas was perhaps the firmest 'opportunist', urging fellow-Socialists to take part in the existing system of politics. He became chairman of the Fabian Parliamentary League in 1887 [for which see Cole (1961) 19-21], and of its successor, the Political Committee of the Fabian Society. Through this position he worked to establish liaison between Socialists and advanced Liberals, looking towards the 'socialisation' of Liberalism. As the Society's chief representative in the Metropolitan Radical Federation, he struggled there against the propagandists of the Social Democratic Federation. Within the Fabian Society, he took a leading role in the arguments between 1889 and 1894 over whether to support the creation of a separate Socialist party, and helped Sidney Webb to turn back the 'purist' assault. Wallas's support for permeation arose from a deep commitment to Liberal principles that Webb did not fully share, and that remained with Wallas long after Webb himself had altered his views.

Wallas continued to be one of the leaders of the Fabian Society until 1895, coming near or at the top of the poll in the annual elections for the executive committee. After the appearance of *Fabian Essays* to which he contributed 'Property under Socialism', he began moving in new directions. The result was his gradual abandonment of Socialism in favour of an advanced Liberalism, and his evolution into one of the first political and social psychologists. He was led away from Socialism and Labour politics, ironically, by two activities that had begun as by-products of his commitment to the movement: involvement with the London School Board, and the writing of labour history.

Wallas's teaching background and his ethical outlook made him particularly suited to doing battle with the conservative domination of London's educational system. Having rejected class war and dismissed political revolution, he was left with education and the existing political system as the vehicles for social change. In 1894 Wallas was elected to the London School Board, having written in the same year, with Harold Spender as co-author, a 200-page tract for the Progressive Campaign entitled *The Case against Diggleism* (the Rev. J.R. Diggle being the 'Moderate' chairman of the LSB). In this election the Progressives nearly achieved victory over the Moderates. Stewart Headlam – who had been first elected in 1891 – was the other successful Fabian candidate. The campaign, which was a bitter one, was also assisted by the publication of two Fabian Tracts: *Questions for School Board Candidates* (first published in 1891) and *The Workers' School Board Programme* (1894). These events introduced Wallas to democratic politics in action, and started a process of disillusionment that was to culminate in *Human Nature in Politics*. Wallas watched a 'missionary campaign' of high moral tone degenerate into party strife, decided by the manipulation of ignorant and prejudiced voters. He remained on the

Board (and its successor, the LCC Education Committee) until 1907, submitting to ever less palatable electoral ordeals every three years, and attempting to adjust his political philosophy to take account of this reality. Practical politics led him to question his youthful ardent faith in democracy – not his faith in the ultimate rightness of democracy as an end, but in the efficacy of the electoral mechanism for producing good government. These growing doubts led in a direct line to his major contribution to social thought, *Human Nature in Politics*.

His position on the London School Board was important, however, beyond its effect on his philosophical development. This was a period of remarkable vigour and accomplishment in London local government. He was chairman of the school management committee from 1897 to 1904 and worked tirelessly with Sidney Webb on the LCC to expand the scope and raise the quality of state education. In particular, he pushed forward the development in the Board Schools of 'Higher Elementary' education, the precursor of universal secondary education. Yet he also came into conflict with Webb, and these conflicts were crucial in leading to his resignation from the Fabian Society in 1904. The two chief educational issues, which came to a head in the struggle over the Education Act of 1902, were over state aid to the voluntary (Church-run) schools, and the crippling of the developing 'Higher Elementary' curriculum in the Board Schools in favour of a sharp separation between elementary and secondary schools. The Cockerton judgment of 1899 and the violent Conservative opposition to the advanced work of the School Boards led directly to the Education Act of 1902, in the formulation of which Robert Morant played the key role [Eaglesham (1956) *passim*; Simon (1965) Ch. 7]. In May 1899 a special members' meeting of the Fabian Society had been held to discuss 'The Education Muddle and the Way Out'. Discussion on the executive's proposals, strongly opposed by Headlam and Wallas, was adjourned; but dissension continued. Wallas found himself increasingly at odds with Sidney Webb, and Webb's vigorous support of the 1902 Act was a major fact influencing him to leave the Fabian Society. But the issue which formally precipitated him into resigning was his opposition to Tariff Reform. At a meeting in January 1904 Wallas moved that the draft of Shaw's Tract No. 116, *Fabianism and the Fiscal Question*, should not be published. He secured only a handful of supporters and offered his resignation in a letter published in *Fabian News* of February 1904.

Wallas did not consider at the time that this resignation was a renunciation of Socialism, only of the doctrinaire collectivism that he considered the Webbs had imposed on the Society. Wallas had, it should be noted, a strong dislike of professional associations, including trade unions. Socialism for Wallas had always been an extension, not an abandonment of Liberalism; it could not be divorced from moral and spiritual concerns without degenerating into yet another form of élitist manipulation of the masses. He continued to consider himself an independent social radical, taking public positions attacking money-power and supporting a great extension of public services. He kept his friendships with his former Fabian colleagues, and took an active part in Beatrice Webb's national campaign for the break-up of the Poor Laws in 1909-11.

Wallas's career as a pioneer in labour history began with a series of lectures to the Fabian Society in 1888 on Chartism. He wanted to know how earlier social reformers had fared and what lessons could be drawn from their experience. His appointment in November 1890 as a University Extension lecturer enabled him to devote the bulk of his time to this work, and he began to sketch out a full-length history of the Chartist movement. His approach broke with the political orientation of current historical writing; and as a result of his Socialist leanings Wallas wanted to understand the political movements of the early nineteenth century as expressions of the social conditions of the time. Had his research not been diverted into a study of Francis Place, and thereafter into political and social psychology, he might have become one of the recognised founding fathers of labour history. However, while researching for his projected book on Chartism, he discovered in the British Museum an extensive uncatalogued collection of the papers of Francis Place. He put aside his more ambitious plans in order to write a biography of Place, an important figure in early-nineteenth-century radicalism who had been almost entirely forgotten. By 1898, when he published his *Life of Francis Place*, a book that had a great influence on the next generation of historians, Wallas's attention was fixed on present matters, and he never returned to the writing of history. His immersion in Place's career reinforced his growing concern with the fragile psychological underpinnings of representative democracy, and from the completion of the work on Place he moved directly to the writing of *Human Nature in Politics*. Asked many years later by Beatrice Webb why he had launched into psychology when they had stuck to the study of institutions, he replied that by the later nineties he had found himself pondering the question 'did he or did he not believe in the psychological basis of democracy as set out by the Utilitarians?' He found that he did not, and his books were the result.

By the time of this realisation, the new pattern of Wallas's life had taken shape. He was one of the early teachers at the London School of Economics and Political Science, which he had helped to establish. And he had finally ended his bachelor existence by marrying in 1897 Ada Radford, from a Plymouth family well known in local public life. Herself an author, she shared in his work and interests. Her book on early literary women in England, *Before the Bluestockings* (1929), like his work on Francis Place, helped to rescue a significant part of the past from obscurity. They had one daughter, May, born in 1898.

Henceforth Wallas's life followed the pattern of a progressive academic intellectual, not attached to any political party or organisation. This pattern was completed by his defeat in the 1907 LCC elections, ending a decade and a half of involvement in London government. His public influence thereafter was through his books, most notably *Human Nature in Politics*, a foray into the unexplored regions of political behaviour. The thesis that underlies his classic work is that politics is the process of appealing to the springs of human motivation, which are chiefly neither rational nor even conscious. Wallas set out to explore these motivations, not in order to expose democracy as a sham, but in order to protect it from its own tendencies to self-destruction. Only a harshly realistic assessment of human behaviour, he argued, could provide a firm basis for its improvement. *Human Nature in Politics*, appearing in 1908, had a wide and lasting influence upon political thought in Britain and, even more, in America. From it, and from Arthur Bentley's *Process of Government*, which was published in the same year in the United States, sprang the modern study of political behaviour.

Wallas's following two books, *The Great Society* (1914) and *Our Social Heritage* (1921), explored the social psychology of modern society, with its new scale of life. The theme of both was at bottom the tensions between a relatively fixed human nature (seen through Darwinian eyes) within a drastically transformed environment. The sweep was wide, influenced by his close friendship with H.G. Wells between 1902 and 1910. Wallas gave warning of the fragility of modern civilisation, yet, like Wells, remained an optimist. He looked forward to the transformation of the Great Society by reason and social feeling into the Great Community, a re-creation under modern conditions of the Greek *polis*. The weaknesses of these successors to *Human Nature in Politics* were that Wallas never succeeded in answering the questions he had posed in that book; and all his later writing was less satisfactory than his original volume. The approach to social inquiry that underlay his writings, which were pyschological and generalising, found more favour in America than in England. Wallas lectured in the United States on five visits between 1897 and 1928, and found a receptive audience in the Progressive generation of intellectuals. The American political commentator Walter Lippmann was a student of his at Harvard in 1910, and did much thereafter to spread his ideas. Through his editorship of the *New Republic*, starting in 1914, Lippmann introduced Wallas to leading Progressives like Herbert Croly, Walter Weyl, and Justice Brandeis, and helped to draw Wallas closer to Felix Frankfurter, whom he had met in America in 1910. In America he also met and encouraged the young Harold Laski, then an instructor at Harvard. After *Human Nature in Politics*, Wallas happily played the role of intellectual godfather to a generation of American liberal intellectuals. In 1919, at the crest of his influence, he lectured at the New School for Social Research in New York, at Yale, Harvard and the University of Chicago – the focal points of American intellectual life. The University of Chicago, he wrote to a friend in the nineteen-twenties, was 'the most interesting place in the world just now – except, perhaps, New York'.

Wallas's enthusiasm for America did not detach him from English public affairs. After his departure from the Fabian Society he took his stand with the New Liberalism of his friends J.A. Hobson and Leonard Hobhouse. He wrote frequently for the *Nation*, supported the left wing of the Liberal Party, and urged reforms in governmental administration and in education to cope with the problems he was exploring in his more theoretical writings. Between 1912 and 1914 he served on the Royal Commission on the Civil Service, where he was more far-seeing than most of his colleagues. He called for a similar Commission to examine the public schools and the universities, but without success. When war threatened in the summer of 1914 Wallas organised a British Neutrality Committee, in some ways a forerunner to the Union of Democratic Control [Swartz (1971) *passim*]. Wallas's career in certain respects reached its peak during the war years. He was appointed in 1914 to the newly-created chair of political science in the University of London, and became head of the department at the LSE. His book *The Great Society*, published on the eve of war, with its stress on the fragility of modern society, seemed to have proved prescient indeed. A considerable following for him developed among the intellectuals of the Civil Service; when the Institute of Public Administration was founded in 1922, he was created its first Fellow. By then his substantial work was done. Manchester University gave him an honorary degree in that year (Oxford was to do the same, to his great pleasure, in 1931), and he retired from his chair amid congratulatory ceremonies in 1923. During the nineteen-twenties – like many other pre-war New Liberals – he was torn between Liberalism and Labour. The Labour Party, he recognised, had become the chief practical force for reform, yet he could not accept either its dogmatism or its domination by the narrow interests of the trade unions. He was attracted to the intellectually revivified Liberalism of Lloyd George in the later twenties, but its failure in 1929 left him without a political creed.

In his later years Wallas turned ever more completely to psychology, coming to feel that in ideas and feelings, rather than in institutions and movements, lay the key to social change. *The Art of Thought* (1926) sought to show how mental processes could be cultivated so as to provide society with the intelligence it needed to solve its problems. To most of his friends and students it seemed an irrelevant exercise – 'elegant trifling' in Laski's private phrase. Wallas's last, unfinished work, *Social Judgment* (1935), continued this psychological preoccupation.

Wallas's influence on the British Labour movement lay chiefly in his early years, when he helped to create Fabian Socialism, and in the process to reinforce the gradualist and ethical character that sets off English Socialism from its counterparts on the Continent. He stands as a representative of those Socialist converts from the comfortable classes who turned the impulses of Victorian Evangelicalism towards furthering social reform. He saw himself, accurately, as a 'working thinker', immersed in practical problems for social improvement.

Wallas died, still working, at Portloe, Cornwall, on 9 August 1932 and left an estate valued at £3971. He was survived by his wife and his daughter May. The latter was a distinguished scholar who graduated at Newnham College in 1920 and took a London PhD. She lectured for a time at Morley College – where she later served as a member of council and vice-president – and at the LSE. In 1945 she returned to Cambridge, where she specialised in the history of French thought. She died in 1972.

Writings: A comprehensive bibliography of the writings of Graham Wallas is included in M.J. Wiener, *Between Two Worlds: the political thought of Graham Wallas* (Oxford, 1971) 217-21. Only his principal works and some omissions from the published bibliography are therefore listed here: 'Property under Socialism', in *Fabian Essays in Socialism*, ed. G.B. Shaw (1889, 6th ed. with a new Introduction by A. Briggs, 1962) 165-83; 'The Story of Eleven Days: (May 7th-18th, 1832), *Fortn. Rev. 52* n.s. (July-Dec 1892) 767-79; (ed.) English edition of G. von Schulze-Gaevernitz, *Social Peace: a study of the trade union movement in England* (1893); (with H. Spender), *The Case against Diggleism* (1894); *The Life of Francis Place, 1771-1854*

(1898, 4th ed. 1925); *Human Nature in Politics* (1898, and later eds); *The Great Society: a pyschological analysis* (1914, and later eds); *Our Social Heritage* (1921); *The Art of Thought* (1926, reissued 1931, abridged 1945 and 1949); 'Notes on Jeremy Bentham's Attitude to Word-Creation, and Other Notes on Needed Words', in *Needed Words* (SPE Tract no. 31: Oxford, 1928) 333-4; *Social Judgment* (1935); *Men and Ideas*, ed. May Wallas (1940).

Sources: (1) MSS: Archives of the Fabian Society, Nuffield College, Oxford; Lippmann papers, Yale Univ.; Passfield and Wallas papers, BLPES; Shaw papers, BL Ref. 50665-705; H.G. Wells Coll., Illinois Univ., Urbana-Champaign. (2) Theses: G.S. Hopcutt, 'The Political and Social Thought of Graham Wallas: a critical survey' (Oxford BLitt., 1958); M.J. Wiener, 'New and Untried Circumstances: the intellectual career of Graham Wallas (1858-1932)' (Harvard PhD, 1967); E.J. Walters, 'Moral Basis of the Great Society: a study of Graham Wallas' (Chicago PhD, 1968); S. Kang, 'Graham Wallas, Political Thinker: an intellectual portrait' (Columbia PhD, 1972). (3) Other: The major source is M.J. Wiener, *Between Two Worlds: the political thought of Graham Wallas* (Oxford, 1971); see also: *Practical Socialist* (1886-7); *To-day* (1887-9); *Our Corner* (1883-8); *Fabian News* (1891-1914); *Daily Chronicle* (1894-6); *Speaker* (1899-1906); *Nation* (1906-29); *New Statesmen* (1913-31); *New Republic* [U.S.A.] (1915-23); E.R. Pease, *History of the Fabian Society* (1916, 2nd ed. 1925; repr. with a new Introduction by M. Cole, 1963); *DNB* (1931-40) [by A. Zimmern]; H.J. Laski, 'Lowes Dickinson and Graham Wallas', *Pol. Q. 3*, no. 4 (Oct 1932) 461-6; B. Webb, *Our Partnership* (1948, repr. with an Introduction by G. Feaver, Cambridge, 1975); *The Holmes-Laski Letters*, ed. M. de Wolfe Howe (1953); E. Eaglesham, *From School Board to Local Authority* (1956); J. Beveridge, *An Epic of Clare Market* (1960); M. Cole, *The Story of Fabian Socialism* (1961); A.M. McBriar, *Fabian Socialism and English Politics, 1884-1918* (Cambridge, 1962); E.J. Hobsbawm, 'The Fabians reconsidered', in *Labouring Men* (1964) 250-71; B. Simon, *Education and the Labour Movement 1870-1920* (1965); K. Martin, *Father Figures* (1966); K. McNaught, 'American Progressives and the Great Society', in *J. of American History 52* (1967) 504-20; P. Thompson, *Socialists, Liberals and Labour: the struggle for London 1885-1914* (1967); M. Swartz, *The Union of Democratic Control in British Politics during the First World War* (Oxford, 1971); H.V. Emy, *Liberals, Radicals and Social Politics, 1892-1914* (1973); P.F. Clarke, 'The Progressive Movement in England', *Trans Roy. Hist. Soc.* 5th ser. *24* (1974) 159-81; W. Wolfe, *From Radicalism to Socialism* (Yale Univ. Press, 1975); personal information: Dame Margaret Cole, London. OBIT. *Manchester Guardian* and *Times*, 11 Aug 1932; *New Statesman* and *Spec.*, 20 Aug 1932; *Graham Wallas 1858-1932* [LSE tributes, 19 Oct 1932] 18 pp.; *Economica 38* (Nov 1932); *Times*, 16 Dec 1972 [for May Wallas].

MARTIN J. WIENER

See also: Hubert BLAND. †Beatrice WEBB; †Sidney James WEBB.

WARWICK, Frances Evelyn (Daisy), Countess of (1861-1938)
SOCIALITE AND SOCIALIST

Frances Evelyn Maynard was born in Mayfair, London, on 10 December 1861 of distinguished parents. Four years later she inherited, under trust, estates in four counties from her wealthy grandfather, Viscount Maynard, of Easton Lodge, Essex. Frances was educated privately and grew into womanhood beautiful, spirited and intelligent. In 1881 she married Lord Brooke, heir to the fourth Earl of Warwick, whom he succeeded in 1893.

Lady Brooke experienced with delight the life of a débutante in the top rank of society. With marriage she had come into her inheritance of £20,000 to £30,000 a year; but not all her fortune was spent on lavish entertainment and luxurious living – although much of it was. Her liaisons particularly that with the Prince of Wales, for example, which lasted for most of the nineties, involved a very large expenditure of money. But in 1890 she embarked on the first of her many philanthropic schemes with the establishment of a needlework school at Easton Lodge: an attempt to alleviate the serious problem of rural unemployment. In the following year she took a shop and workshop for the school in Bond Street, and her charitable work continued in later years. In 1897, for example, she equipped a large house in Warwick as a home where fifty crippled children, mostly from poor families in Birmingham, were given treatment and care.

In 1892 Lady Brooke met the radical journalist W.T. Stead and he became a sort of mentor who exercised a strong influence on her ideas and opinions throughout the 1890s. It was less strong after the turn of the century, though their friendship lasted, with some lacunae, until Stead's death on the s.s. *Titanic* in 1912. Stead, for instance, pointed out some fields in which women could do useful social work. In 1894 she was elected to the Warwick Board of Guardians and she served for a full decade.

It is clear that from time to time at least she was dissatisfied with the inanity of aristocratic living. But more important for the future was her first contact with Socialist ideas in February 1895 when Robert Blatchford wrote a biting criticism in the *Clarion* of a spectacular costume ball she and her husband had just given at Warwick Castle. Lady Warwick, as she now was, sought out Blatchford in his office in London. Her recollections of this and subsequent meetings with Blatchford [*Life's Ebb and Flow* (1929) 89-92] need to be treated with caution, and she did not join any Socialist organisation for another nine years. There is, however, no doubt that her dicussions with Blatchford were a turning-point in her intellectual development, and she did begin to read some Socialist literature: Blatchford, William Morris, Edward Bellamy. In 1897 she discovered Joseph Arch, the pioneer of agricultural trade unionism, who lived in Barford, and induced him to write his autobiography – interfering commendably little with Arch's expression. One of the sentences in her preface to the book summarised a view she had long held and which she was at the time taking steps to satisfy: 'Adequate education, elementary and technical, is what the agricultural labourer now needs most of all' [Arch (1898) xiv]. In 1897 she had given a farm near Dunmow, in Essex, to be made into a school which for a small fee should provide boys and girls over twelve with a secondary education with a rural bias. With an eye to support from public funds, the courses were adjusted to comply with the specifications of the Essex County Council and the Department of Science and Art. Bigods School flourished for ten years and cost Lady Warwick £10,000. Then first the Board of Education – which had given a tiny grant (£113) – withdrew it in 1904 and three years later the County Council followed; and the school closed in 1907.

Lady Warwick was also occupied with another scheme of agricultural education. This one was for women, or rather for gentlewomen: she planned to open a hostel for women attached to one of the agricultural colleges for men. Her secretary and collaborator at that time, Edith Bradley, arranged the details. Reading was chosen, the Lady Warwick Hostel was opened in October 1898, and several more houses in 1899; as an offshoot from all this, moreover, the Lady Warwick Agricultural Association for Women, which already ran a registry of all women engaged in agricultural or horticultural work, started in 1899 a monthly journal called the *Women's Agricultural Times*, edited by Lady Warwick and Miss Bradley. Lady Warwick, as usual, financed everything, although the Reading hostels did charge a fee of £50. They were so successful that in 1902 Lady Warwick bought Studley Castle in Warwickshire, a forbidding mock-baronial edifice, and opened it as an independent agricultural college for women. The move from Reading was made in 1903. Miss Bradley, who was now principal, presently came to feel that Lady Warwick was not paying the College enough attention, and also that she was being ousted from Lady Warwick's confidence by her successor as secretary and collaborator, the Socialist Mrs Bridges Adams. There may have been other reasons too for frustration and dissatisfaction at the College. At all events, in August 1905 Miss Bradley and almost all the rest of the staff resigned their posts. The trouble was patched up; most of the posts were filled, the new principal being Miss Mabel Faithfull, formerly secretary to the Prime Minister's sister Miss Balfour. But the affair was bad for the College and for Lady Warwick's reputation.

When the Boer War broke out in October 1899 Lady Warwick adopted, on the whole, the conventional upper-class attitude to it. Her eldest son Guy left for the front that winter at the age of seventeen, and she had other relatives and friends in or with the British forces. Yet she had doubts. She did not share Stead's view of the war as British aggression, but in a letter to him she went so far as to call it 'a wrong war and a bad war' [Warwick (1929) 119]. Later on her doubts were reinforced by her horror at the hysteria of the London crowds over such events as the relief of Mafeking and of Ladysmith. In November 1904 Lady Warwick joined the Social Democratic Federation. Hyndman was delighted with his new recruit, who attracted curious crowds to SDF meetings but who, in her own way, worked hard for the cause. Her notion of the cause was no doubt vaguer than his, and he absurdly exaggerated the political significance of her commitment. Her main energy in these early years went into the campaign for free meals for poor children, an issue which attracted widespread support at this time. Her rapidly deteriorating finances encouraged her to begin serious writing in the few years before the outbreak of the First World War – one result was *William Morris: his home and haunts* [1912], on which she collaborated with S.L. Bensusan, a versatile writer who was a neighbour of hers at Easton. A lecture tour in America in 1911 failed after a month of exhausting publicity and diminishing audiences. In Britain she did some helpful things in the radical cause: she appointed Socialist clergymen to Essex livings of which she was patron – Edward George Maxted was appointed to Tilty in 1908 and Conrad Noel to Thaxted in 1910 – and she also actively supported industrial action; during the London dock strike of 1912 she travelled frequently to the East End to give encouragement to the strike leaders. In 1914 she gave support to the Essex agricultural labourers' strike and contributed generously to strike pay; and after the war she gave between £200 and £300 for the building of a Labour Hall at Ashdon, the village where the strike started.

When the First World War broke out, Lady Warwick did some of the conventional things: she arranged Red Cross classes, accommodated Belgian refugees, gave her park for Territorial Army training, and spoke with pride of her two sons at the front. At the same time she took a Socialist view of the war as a capitalist conflict in which the workers on both sides must lose. Moreover, she attacked certain of the effects of the war in Britain – the censorship, the Defence of the Realm Act, the release of elementary school children for work on the land (why not release instead public school boys, gillies, gamekeepers? she asked). Some of her opinions were published in newspaper articles which in 1916 were collected into a book, *A Woman and the War*. She had always argued for unity of the Socialist movement and although her views on the war differed from some of her oldest political associates – Blatchford, Hyndman and H.G. Wells – she deplored the split in the BSP, and after the war the sharp differences over Russia. She herself welcomed the Russian Revolution, even the Bolsheviks' withdrawal from the war.

Lady Warwick joined the Labour Party in the post-war years. In 1920, when she was invited to stand as Labour candidate for Walthamstow East, having first accepted she later refused, on the ground that she lacked money. But she did contest Warwick and Leamington in 1923, when her Conservative opponent, a distant relative, was Anthony Eden, and the Liberal candidate George Nicholls. She was at the bottom of the poll. Six weeks after the election her husband died and her income was reduced to a small allowance. In November 1925, with Bernard Shaw and others, she stood bail for the twelve leading Communists who were arrested some six months before the General Strike.

It was in 1923 that Lady Warwick began the first negotiations to convert Easton Lodge, her Essex home, into a permanent Labour centre. At various times the Labour Party, the ILP and the TUC were involved, but in the end all the projected schemes fell through. The story of the negotiations has been told in a number of places: *Beatrice Webb's Diaries 1924-1932* (1956) and Margaret Cole, *Growing up into Revolution* (1949).

At the end of 1927 Lady Warwick decided to give up public speaking and other strenuous political activities and concentrate, as she put it, on literary work. But Easton Lodge was still occasionally used for conferences; in the early months of 1930 what became the Society for

Socialist Inquiry and Propaganda was inaugurated there and the newly established New Fabian Research Bureau held meetings at the Lodge in the spring of 1931.

Lady Warwick died on 26 July 1938, survived by one son, Maynard Greville, and two daughters. Her estate was given as £37,100 with net personalty £7969; later it was resworn at £108,207. Easton Lodge was demolished in 1948.

Much of Lady Warwick's life lies outside the scope of the *Dictionary*. The details have been abundantly set down elsewhere. Frances Warwick was not, perhaps, a person of importance in the history of the labour movement: she was too intellectually undisciplined and emotional for that, although most of her writings, especially her articles, were sensible, acute and forcible, sometimes witty, sometimes savagely sarcastic. Her determined adherence to the Socialist cause and her willing exertions on its behalf undoubtedly had their effect. Moreover, her vitality and verve lent the movement colour and comedy. She was in the tradition of English eccentrics as well as being thoroughly warm-hearted and sympathetic: as Margaret Cole summed her up, 'an entertaining character as well as a good sort' [letter, 1 Oct 1974].

Writings: 'Technical Education in Rural Districts', *J. of the Society of Arts 45*, 6 Aug 1897, 956-9; editor of *Progress in Women's Education in the British Empire* (1898); preface to *Joseph Arch: the story of his life. Told by himself* (1898); *An Old English Garden* (1898); 'The Cause of the Children' [on new Education Bill], *19th C. 50* (July 1901) 67-76; 'Bigods' [School, Essex], ibid. (Dec 1901) 983-90; 'A Social Experiment' [Hadley Farm Colony], ibid. *53* (Apr 1903) 665-9; *Warwick Castle and its Earls from Saxon Times to the Present Day* 2 vols (1903); *Unemployment: its causes and consequences* (n.d.) 16 pp.; 'Scientific Agriculture', *N. Amer. Rev. 182* (1906) 408-13; *A Nation's Youth. Physical Deterioration: its causes and some remedies* (1906) 32 pp.; 'Physical Deterioration', *Fortn. Rev. 85* (Mar 1906) 504-15; edited with H.G. Wells and G.R. Stirling Taylor, *Socialism and the Great State: essays in construction* (1912); *William Morris: his home and haunts* [1912]; 'Race Suicide', *Hibbert J. 14*, no. 4 (July 1916) 751-9; *A Woman and the War* (1916); 'Militarism and Feminism', *Yorkshire Factory Times*, 8 Mar 1917, 3; 'Why the State should own the Land', ibid., 19 Apr 1917, 1; 'The New Religion', *Hibbert J. 15*, no. 4 (July 1917) 561-71; 'Peace – and what then?', ibid. *16*, no. 1 (Oct 1917) 19-27; 'The Need for a British Policy' [letter], *Spec. 131*, 28 July 1923, 117-18; *Life's Ebb and Flow* (1929); *Discretions* (NY, 1931); *Afterthoughts* (1931); *Branch Lines* [a novel] (1932); (with L. Reed), *The Prime Minister's Pyjamas* (1933); *Nature's Quest* [observations on natural history] (1934).

Sources: (1) MSS: Labour Party archives: LRC; for further sources see M. Blunden, *The Countess of Warwick: a biography* (1967). (2) Other: 'The Future of Village Education: Lady Warwick's plea for the village child', *Schoolmaster* (Supplement), 17 Mar 1900, 519-20; H.M. Hyndman, *The Record of an Adventurous Life* (1911); idem, *Further Reminiscences* (1912); W. Thorne, *My Life's Battles* [1925]; G.D.H. Cole, 'Bournemouth and Easton Lodge', *Highway 19* (Oct 1926) 9-10; H. Tracey, 'A very Gallant Lady', *Labour Mag. 8* (Nov 1929) 329-30; R. Blatchford, *My Eighty Years* (1931); *DNB* (1931-40); H.G. Wells, *Experiment in Autobiography* (1934); C. Noel, *Autobiography*, ed. S. Dark (1945); M. Cole, *Growing up into Revolution* (1949); *Beatrice Webb's Diaries 1912-1924*, ed. M.I. Cole (1952); *Beatrice Webb's Diaries 1924-1932*, ed. and with an Introduction by M. Cole (1956); C. Tsuzuki, *H.M. Hyndman and British Socialism* (Oxford, 1961); M. Blunden, 'The Educational and Political Work of the Countess of Warwick' (Exeter MA, 1966); T. Lang, *My Darling Daisy* (1966); G. Bennett, *Charlie B.: a biography of Admiral Lord Beresford of Metemmeh and Curraghmore, GCB, GCVO, LLD, DCL* (1968); M. Cole, *The Life of G.D.H. Cole* (1971); 'Daisy Warwick' in P. Brent, *The Edwardians* (1972) 201-24; A. Leslie, 'Daisy, Reckless Beauty and Miners' Heroine', *Sunday Telegraph*, 27 Aug 1972, 6-7; M. Cole, 'The Society for Socialist Inquiry and Propaganda' in *Essays in Labour History*, ed. A. Briggs and J. Saville (1977) 190-203; personal information: Lord Fenner Brockway; Ald. S. Wilson, Saffron Walden; Father Jack Putterill,

Thaxted. OBIT. *Manchester Evening News,* 26 July 1938; *Daily Herald, Daily Telegraph, East Anglian Daily Times, Glasgow Herald, Manchester Guardian, News Chronicle, Times* and *Yorkshire Post,* 27 July 1938; *Royal Leamington Spa Courier,* 29 July 1938; *Warwick and Warwickshire Advertiser and Leamington Gazette,* 30 July 1938; *New Statesman and Nation 16,* no. 388, 30 July 1938. The Editors wish to acknowledge the assistance given by Dame Margaret Cole in commenting on an earlier draft of this biography.

MARGARET BLUNDEN
MARGARET 'ESPINASSE
JOHN SAVILLE

See also: *Mary Jane Bridges ADAMS; †Joseph ARCH; *Henry Mayers HYNDMAN.

WELLOCK, Wilfred (1879-1972)
LABOUR MP AND PACIFIST

Born on 2 January 1879 at Nelson, Lancs., Wilfred Wellock was the eldest son of the four children of John Wellock, a textile worker, and his wife Thirza Barker, who with her brother had in 1872 left Norfolk in search of work in the expanding textile town of Nelson. Wilfred attended a Methodist elementary school, of which his father was one of the managers, and at the age of ten became a half-timer in the mill in which his father worked. This involved work from 6 a.m. to 12.30 p.m. with a half-hour break for breakfast. He went home for a midday meal and then went to school at 1.30 p.m. for three hours. The evenings were spent in vigorous exercise with his fellow half-timers, Wilfred being keen on running games and cricket. He began working full-time in 1892.

Eager to improve his education, he attended evening continuation classes and took private lessons in shorthand. He was initiated into voluntary social service at the age of eight when he spent an hour weekly in running errands for an invalid elderly neighbour. At fifteen he was teaching a class of boys in the Sunday School of the Methodist Church to which the family belonged, and at nineteen a mixed class of teenagers. He was also president of the Young People's Christian Endeavour Society. At eighteen he was invited by the church elders to prepare himself for taking services, and at twenty was preaching fifty Sundays in the year at churches within a radius of thirty miles of Nelson. For this he received no fees but, as he wrote in his autobiography, found reward in the intellectual stimulus and the rich friendships.

His political education began with attendance at meetings addressed by Keir Hardie and Philip Snowden, and he soon realised the incompatibility of the capitalist system with Christian principles. Throughout his life his teaching and conduct were based on a literal interpretation of the ethical teaching of the New Testament, but he had little love for the theological superstructure which he felt had smothered the real message of Jesus. He agreed with the Socialist criticism of the capitalist system but was not entirely happy about the Socialist remedy, which he considered too materialistic.

Although he felt no vocation for his work in the mill, he found it interesting, and his ability raised him to positions of responsibility – he became an under-manager – involving periodic increases in salary, though he never asked for these. Coming to the conclusion that his life's work was to be the exposition of the application of Christian principles to social, economic and political life, he recognised the need for further education and saved up for three years in order to go to a university. His employers deprecated this plan and offered him a partnership in the firm, which he declined. At the age of twenty-four he went to Edinburgh University for three years, selecting those studies which he felt to be relevant, but not taking a degree course.

In 1907 he returned to Nelson, to work half-time in the same mill and to devote the other half to lecturing and teaching for local Co-operative Societies and for Churches, particularly on his criticism of western industrial civilisation. At this time he met a number of Indian students in Lancashire through whom he began to write for an Indian journal, the *Modern Review.* In April 1913, his article 'Modern Industrialism: its lessons for India' was given first place in that journal. Shortly afterwards, when he was in London for journalistic purposes, he met a number of leading Indians, including Rabindranath Tagore, who thanked him for his articles. Thus began an interest in and an association with India which lasted throughout his life.

In 1913 he married Frances Wilson, whom he met when preaching in the Methodist Church in Colne, where she was a member of the choir and a Sunday School teacher. He was attracted by her fine voice and interpretation of music and she by his radical message. She subsequently gave up her work in a textile mill to devote herself entirely to music, becoming a music teacher and a popular soloist. Her earnings later made it possible for Wilfred to devote himself to his unpaid propaganda work.

The outbreak of war in 1914 made him realise that he was a pacifist and he joined the No-Conscription Fellowship in that year. He saw clearly the economic causes of the conflict and he found military service completely opposed to his interpretation of Christianity. With the support of a number of sympathisers he started an anti-war broadsheet for free distribution called the *New Crusader*, which by its third issue reached a circulation of 15,000. On the introduction of conscription, he claimed absolute exemption from the local military service tribunal, but his application was rejected. He declined to avail himself of the exemption which he might have had as an unpaid minister of religion. He was therefore arrested, court-martialled three times and spent over two years in prison (1917-19). In 1917 the *New Crusader* was taken over and issued as a weekly by Theodora Wilson Wilson, a London Quaker; Wilfred Wellock resumed the editorship on his release from prison.

In the summer of 1919 he spent three months in The Hague, trying, in co-operation with a group of continental friends, to found a multilingual peace paper, but this venture was not successful. In December 1919, at the request of a number of friends, he went to Germany for six months to study conditions there. While in Berlin in January 1920 he witnessed the Kapp Putsch, and was much impressed by the way in which an attempted military takeover was defeated, without any loss of life, by a six-day complete general strike of the Berlin workers. On his return to England he tried to arouse public opinion concerning the starvation conditions in Germany, but found no response.

Distressed by what he regarded as current materialism and self-indulgence, he sought to turn people's minds to more spiritual things, and worked for some years for the Independent Labour Party, in which he felt the ethical Socialism of Ruskin and William Morris was still a force. Challenged to enter the political arena, he contested Stourbridge at the general elections of 1923 and 1924 in the Labour interest. In the latter year he increased his share of the poll from 24.4 per cent to 35.8 per cent and came second to the successful Conservative candidate. He addressed many big meetings during the Miners' Lockout of 1926, but felt that with the growing influence of the Northcliffe Press, the odds were against him. However, he fought and won a by-election at Stourbridge in February 1927, and retained the seat at the general election of 1929. Although he found interest in serving on various Select Committees which dealt with Local Government Bills etc. and on the Joint Select Committee of both Houses on the future government of East Africa, he came to the conclusion that the back-bench member was impotent and that MPs tended to be either power-seekers or disillusioned 'yes-men'. He formed and became chairman of an India Committee of MPs devoted to furthering the cause of Indian independence, and had the opportunity of meeting Gandhi during the Round Table Conference and of arranging a meeting for him at the House of Commons. He had for many years followed Gandhi's career with interest, and had found that Gandhi's statement: 'God is Truth: Truth is God' exactly expressed his own thinking. He lost his seat at the 1931 general election and although he described his four years in Parliament as the most frustrating period of his life, he sought re-election in 1935. He was not successful and did not try to enter Parliament again.

Wellock's critical analysis of the nature of Western industrial society led him to advocate decentralisation in both economics and politics, small-scale industry and handicrafts, and co-operative organisation on the basis of small communities. His plan to form such a community with a number of friends was frustrated by the outbreak of war in 1939, but during the Second

World War he took an active interest in many of the land-based communities which were formed, particularly by pacifists allocated to agricultural work by the military service tribunals.

As a pacifist, Wellock followed up his refusal of military service in the First World War by becoming an active member of the No More War Movement (founded 1920), an elected member of its national committee and for some years its chairman. In 1921 he was one of the British representatives at a meeting in Holland at which was founded an international pacifist organisation Paco (the Esperanto word for peace), which later became the War Resisters' International. In 1923 he attended a further meeting at which the Dutch secretariat of Paco asked if the headquarters could be transferred to England. Wellock returned to London and consulted the leading members of the No More War Movement, one of whom, H. Runham Brown, offered to undertake the responsibility. Wellock maintained an active interest in the work of the War Resisters' International until his death and was at one time its political adviser.

When the No More War Movement merged with the Peace Pledge Union in 1936, Wellock was one of the negotiators and became a sponsor of the PPU. In 1940 he and John Middleton Murry were appointed by the PPU National Council to be joint managing directors of *Peace News* (then the organ of the PPU); and Wellock, who had already written for the paper, became a regular contributor. When, later, *Peace News* became an independent paper Wellock became a member of its Board of Management.

Wellock's visit to India to take part in the World Pacifist Conference in 1948 greatly increased his interest in the culture and future development of that country, to which he was to pay several subsequent visits. He now wrote frequently for Indian papers, and some of his pamphlets and ultimately his autobiography (first appearing serially in an Indian journal) were published in that country. He strongly supported Gandhi's plan, later furthered by Vinoba Bhave, for the development of self-governing village communities based on a combination of agriculture and small-scale industry.

Wilfred Wellock visited Russia twice, with his wife in 1927 and as leader of a group of English people in 1933. On the first occasion he was inspired by the faith and optimism and friendliness of the people in spite of poverty and hardship; and he had great hopes for the country's future. (He had already taken part in the 'Hands off Russia' campaign to prevent British intervention in Russia in 1920.) In 1933, during the first Stalin purge, he found fear in all faces, and hope gone, and he returned disillusioned with the Russian experiment.

His first visit to the U.S.A. was in 1926, when he was appalled by the dollar worship, the completely materialistic outlook and the rapid urbanisation. He pointed out the inevitable consequences of the path America was following. On his next visit in 1946 and on three subsequent three-month lecture tours in the States he found these evils accentuated, and never ceased to preach that the doctrine of an ever-expanding economy could lead only to conflict and ultimate disaster.

At home he was an early member of the Soil Association and practised organic cultivation in his own garden at 'Orchard Lea', New Longton, near Preston, where he settled after his period in Parliament. He grew most of the food for himself and his wife and lived on a simple vegetarian diet. He was a strong advocate of a balanced life of physical, intellectual and spiritual activity, and in addition to gardening he practised hand-spinning and knitting. He wrote only a few small books, but between forty and fifty pamphlets, and hundreds of articles for journals at home and abroad; and he must have addressed many thousands of meetings, always urging his readers and hearers to face the choice before the world today: capitalism, centralisation, expanding materialism, conflict and disaster, or a balanced and simplified co-operative economy emphasising spiritual values and quality rather than quantity – the road of hope.

His interest in workers' participation in the management of industry led to his active participation in 'Demintry' (the Society for Democratic Integration in Industry – now the Industrial Common Ownership Movement), of which he became chairman.

Declining strength in later years compelled the Wellocks to leave 'Orchard Lea', with its fairly large garden which they could no longer manage, for an old people's bungalow rented from the

238

Preston Council; later, they were cared for in an old people's home. Wilfred died on 22 July 1972 at the age of ninety-three, and his wife Frances on 4 April 1973 in her ninety-third year. No will has been located.

Writings: 'Modern Industrialism: its lessons for India', *Modern Rev.* (Apr 1913) 369-75; *Pacifism: what it is and what it is capable of doing* (Manchester, [1916]); *The Victory of Peace: three poems on the times* (1916) 15 pp.; *A Modern Idealist* [a novel] [1917]; *Godilieve: an adaptation . . . of a fable by Felix Ortt of Holland* [1917] 16 pp.; *Interest: the modern monster* (National Co-operative Men's Guild and Scottish Co-operative Men's Guild, Manchester [1917]) 15 pp.; *Christian Communism* (NLP, Manchester, [1921]) 43 pp.; *India's Awakening, Its National and Worldwide Significance* (Labour Publishing Co., 1922); *The Way Out: or, the road to the new world* (Labour Publishing Co., 1922); *The Spiritual Basis of Democracy* (Madras, 1924); *War as viewed by Jesus and the Early Church* (No More War Movement, [1924?]) 32 pp.; *No More War* (Mar 1927) [report of Stourbridge Division by-election]; 'Der Beitrag der Quäker zum Weltfrieden' [Contribution of the Quakers to World Peace] and 'Mahatma Gandhi und die Satyagraha Bewegung' [Mahatma Gandhi and the Satyagraha Movement] in *Gewalt und Gewaltlosigkeit* [Violence and Non-Violence] ed. F. Kobler (Zurich and Leipzig [1928], repr. with English Introduction, Garland Foundation, New York, 1971) 215-26 and 245-56; *Youth and Adventure: on which side shall I enlist?* (No More War Movement, [1934?]) 15 pp.; 'Labour on the Slippery Slope', [letter] *New Statesman and Nation 14*, 30 Oct 1937, 678-9; 'Revolutionary Method', *Plebs 29* (Dec 1937) 286-8; 'Inescapable Facts', *New Statesman and Nation 15*, 26 Mar 1938, 520-1; 'Labour and the Popular Front' [letter] ibid., 28 May 1938, 908; 'Fighting Fascism' [letter] ibid., 11 June 1938, 987-8; *Destruction or Construction – which? An open letter to members of the Labour Party* (PPU, [1938]) 12 pp.; *The Conscription of Youth and at what price? To what end?* (PPU, 1939) 11 pp.; *The Mystery of Germany and Russia. What does the Soviet-German Pact portend?* (PPU, 1939) 12 pp.; 'The New Situation' [letter], *New Statesman and Nation 18*, 23 Sep 1939, 427-8; 'War Aims', ibid., *18*, 4 Nov 1939, 645-6, 2 Dec 1939, 790; *Money has destroyed your Peace* (PPU, 1940) 29 pp.; 'Victory for what?' [letter], *New Statesman and Nation 21*, 15 Feb 1941, 161; *Which Way, Britain?* (1942); *A Mechanistic or a Human Society* (1944, repr. India, 1968) 32 pp.; *Non-violence and Germany* [1945] 12 pp.; *The Third Way* (Plaid Cymru, Cardiff, 1947); 'A Wider Outlook' *New Statesman and Nation 36*, 9 July 1948, 3; *Rebuilding Britain, A New Peace Orientation* (1949) 47 pp.; *Power or Peace: Western Industrialism and World Leadership* (Peace News, 1950) 23 pp.; *Gandhi as a Social Revolutionary* (1950, Tiripur, South India [1953]) 39 pp.; *The International Balance Sheet* (PPU, n.d.) 7 pp.; *The Challenge of our Times: annihilation or creative revolution?* (Peace News, 1951) 15 pp.; Twelve privately printed pamphlets: (1) *The Supreme Crisis of our Civilisation*; (2) *Economics of a Peaceful Society*; (3) *The Transition from a War to a Peace Economy*; (4) *A Spiritual Challenge to the Enslaving Fear of Russia*; (5) *The Values of the Small Community*; (6) *The Values of Work: man and the machine*; (7) *The Creative Society*; (8) *Local, National and World Government*; (9) *Education for Living*; (10) *Leisure, Waste and the Good Life*; (11) *Soil, Health and Civilisation*; (12) *The Time's Need and the Outlook* (Orchard Lea Papers, 1952-3) [These papers were published in 1954 under the title *New Horizons. Build the Future now*]; . . . *Not by Bread alone. A Study of America's Expanding Economy* (1955) 16 pp.; *Which Way America? Which Way Britain? Abundance or Abundant Life?* ('Demintry', [1957]) 52 pp. translated into German, (Vienna, 1959) 63 pp.; *India's Social Revolution from Gandhi to Vinoba Bhave* (Preston, [1958?]); *Off the Beaten Track: adventures in the art of living* [autobiography] (1961, Tanjore, India, 1963); *Gandhi and the World Crisis* (n.d.) 8 pp.; *The Tattoo exposed. Leeds Anti-Tattoo Committee* (n.d.) 12 pp.; *The Crisis in our Civilisation: reorganisation of industry a key to world peace* ('Demintry', [1962]) 23 pp.; *Deeper Implications of the European Common Market* (India, 1963) 16 pp.; *Beyond these Barren Years: towards a New Era: an appeal for a constructive revolution* (India, 1965); *India's advancing Crisis* (India, 1967) 31 pp.; *Towards*

One World – but shall we arrive? (India, 1967) 8 pp.; *Whither Western Civilisation? Can its Doom be prevented?* (India, 1968) 14 pp.; *Challenge of Materialism in the West. Can India resist it?* (India, 1969) 7 pp. Wellock also wrote articles regularly for *Peace News* and *No More War.*

Sources: *Labour Who's Who* (1927); *Dod* (1928); *Peace News*, 25 Feb 1949; W. Wellock's autobiography, *Off the Beaten Track* (1961); *WW* (1970); J. Hyatt, *Pacifism: a selected bibliography* (1972); H. Mister, 'Wellock, like Gandhi, has shown that Everyone can discover the Truth for himself', *Peace News*, 11 Aug 1972; biographical information: the late T.A.K. Elliott, CMG; personal knowledge. Obit. *Manchester Guardian*, 28 July 1972; *Pacifist* (Aug 1972).

HAROLD F. BING

See also: †Herbert Runham BROWN; †Frederick (Fred) MESSER.

WHITE, Charles Frederick (1891-1956)
LABOUR MP AND COUNTY ALDERMAN

Born at Bonsall, near Matlock, Derbyshire, on 23 January 1891, he was the only son of the family of six of Charles Frederick and Alice White (née Charlesworth). His mother was a native of Bonsall and his father, a Gloucestershire man, who was born at Tetbury in 1863, was a cobbler and dealer at Bonsall. Charles White senior was a radically-minded Liberal who played an active part in local politics and in 1918 entered Parliament as an Independent Liberal. He died during the 1923 election campaign.

'Young Charlie', as he was always known locally, was thus brought up in an atmosphere of Radical politics. He was educated at Cromford Elementary School and Wirksworth Grammar School and was apprenticed to a joiner. In 1910 he became his father's agent for the December election of that year when Charles White senior contested the West Division of Derbyshire. During the First World War he served with the Sherwood Foresters, holding the rank of sergeant, but was discharged on medical grounds in 1917. He then became a food executive officer, resigning this post in 1918 to act as his father's agent at the general election. He was again his father's agent in 1922 and in 1923, and was also agent for W.C. Mallison, the unsuccessful candidate who fought the seat after his father's death, though it was well known that he would have liked the nomination himself. For some years after, White was Liberal agent at Hereford and later in Chesterfield, but subsequently left politics. In 1928 he announced in the *Derbyshire Times* that he would fight his father's old seat as an independent Liberal but as the date of the 1929 election approached he was selected as Liberal candidate for Hanley, Staffs, where he was unsuccessful. By 1929 he had become a member of the Matlock Urban District Council and in 1928 he was also elected to the Derbyshire County Council.

After the general election of 1929 he joined the Labour Party, and was appointed Labour agent for West Derbyshire, but he resigned towards the end of 1930. Early in 1931 he was connected with Oswald Mosley's New Party for about three months, but like so many he resigned when Mosley began to show signs of conversion to a Fascist position. At this time White was in the West Midlands and for the next ten years made his living by representing transport companies in applications to the Traffic Commissioners for licences under the Road and Rail Traffic Act. By the end of 1936 he had returned to work with the West Derbyshire Labour Party, and in 1937 he was adopted as prospective Labour candidate for West Derbyshire. He was unsuccessful in a by-election in June 1938 but increased markedly the Labour vote.

During the Second World War White became food officer for Matlock. He remained prospective candidate for the West Derbyshire seat which became vacant early in 1944 with the resignation of the sitting Conservative, and White broke the wartime truce by resigning from the

Labour Party and standing as Independent Labour. His campaign received strong backing from Sir Richard Acland and Common Wealth and a great deal of help from local Labour, Liberal and Communist supporters. He defeated his Conservative opponent, the Marquis of Hartington, the son of the Duke of Devonshire, by 4561 votes. This was a great personal triumph for White, in a constituency regarded as a fief of the Duke of Devonshire, and he undoubtedly collected a large number of Liberal voters who remembered his father. In 1945 when he stood again, this time as an official Labour candidate, his majority was reduced to 156.

In 1946, the Labour Party gained control of the County Council for the first time and White, who had been an Alderman since 1937, became chairman of the County Council. Apart from a break from 1931 to 1936, he had been a member of the County Council since 1928 and remained leader of the County Council till his death in 1956. Labour's victory was sweeping and the Party filled all the aldermanic seats and committee chairmanships, an action which provoked much opposition. White was never a House of Commons man, and in 1948 he announced that for health reasons he would not stand for Parliament again. At the 1950 general election the seat was won by the Conservatives.

White aroused strong emotions locally but never made much national impact. He was proud to be called a 'county man' and was always local politician first. At home in the County Council, he was the dominating figure there until his death. He had a firm grasp of procedure, was ruthless in pursuit of his objectives and his efficiency as a chairman has been praised somewhat ruefully by those of opposing political beliefs. His reserves of acid repartee made any attempt to oppose him hazardous. The last major issue he was involved in was the County Council's move from Derby to Matlock, for which negotiations lasted five years. The move to Matlock, of which he was the originator, was a far-seeing exercise in decentralisation and undoubtedly brought back prosperity to Matlock and provided employment possibilities for young people.

White was made a JP in 1943 and a CBE in 1951. He held many appointments, the most noteworthy of which was the chairmanship of the Peak Planning Board from 1951 until his death. This occurred on 27 November 1956, and he was survived by his wife Alice (née Moore) who seems to have taken no part in his political life. In his political ideas White was obviously much influenced by his father, and his own Socialism was pragmatic rather than doctrinaire. His funeral took place at St Giles Church, Matlock, on 1 December 1956, and was attended by many hundreds of people. He died intestate, leaving effects worth £1100 net.

Sources: (1) MSS: West Derbyshire Labour Party, Minutes, 1924-56; papers relating to 1944 election: Derbyshire Record Office, ref. 602Z/18. (2) Other: *Derby Mercury*, 7 and 14 Dec 1923; 'Democracy in West Derbyshire', *Manchester Guardian*, 27 Jan 1944; *Ashbourne Telegraph*, 12 Nov 1948; *Derby Evening Telegraph*, 1 Mar 1951; A.L.R. Calder, 'The Common Wealth Party, 1942-45' (Sussex DPhil., 1968) vol. 1, 241-7; idem, *The People's War: Britain 1939-45* (1968); D.L. Prynn, 'Common Wealth – A British "Third Party" of the 1940s', *J. Cont. Hist.* 7, nos. 1 and 2 (Jan-Apr 1972) 169-79; P. Addison, *The Road to 1945: British Politics and the Second World War* (1975); biographical information: S. Borrington, formerly secretary, West Derbyshire LP; the late T.A.K. Elliott, CMG; personal information: Mrs E. Carthew, Wimbledon, sister; W. Cross, Matlock; Ald. N. Gratton, Tideswell; Mrs E. Smith, Matlock. OBIT. *Times*, 28 Nov 1956.

DAVID BARTON
JOHN SAVILLE

WOOLF, Leonard Sidney (1880-1969)
AUTHOR, PUBLISHER AND SOCIALIST

L.S. Woolf was one of the distinguished Jewish intellectuals who, born in the age of Victoria, graduated in that of her successors from a somewhat unspecified radicalism to a firmly democratic Socialist attitude from which, disappointments notwithstanding, he never diverged to the end of his long life. He never held political office, or indeed any other position of authority, but administrative ability, coupled with power of critical thought and expression and a deep and genuine altruism, gave him considerable influence.

He was born in London on 25 November 1880, one of the elder of the ten children (of whom all but one survived) of Solomon Rees Sidney Woolf, a barrister and Queen's Counsel who earned a considerable income, and Marie de Jongh; the de Jongh family were diamond merchants from Amsterdam. During Leonard's childhood the Woolfs lived in Lexham Gardens, Kensington, a neighbourhood populated largely by the respectable and comfortably-off middle class, but not so affluent as to prevent him, even in his childhood, from observing the sharp economic difference between the various strata of society. In the first, most vividly-written volume of his autobiography he put on record some of his early impressions of the horrid sights (and smells) of poverty; and these remained with him all his days.

He was educated in the manner of the time; at nine years old he was sent to Colet Court, the preparatory for St Paul's School, and five years later, in September 1894, with the aid of some private tuition, was admitted to the main school with a foundation scholarship – this was a necessity in his case, because in 1892 his father had died prematurely, which meant that the family income declined abruptly, and Mrs Woolf had to move in due course to a cheaper house in the then much less affluent suburb of Putney. They were not reduced to penury. Mrs Woolf succeeded in keeping and educating her children, but the experience had something traumatic about it. Constant economy was essential, and the foundation was then laid of an element of cheese-paring, particularly in the payment of employees, which was noticeable in the Woolf of later years.

St Paul's in 1894 stood very high in the list of English public schools; but young Woolf did not appreciate it. He was there for six years, and detested both Walker, the distinguished and formidable High Master who had come there from Manchester Grammar School, and equally the narrow and intensive classical curriculum through which he was put. Though he has a kind word for the debating society (which included in his time such well-known names as E.C. Bentley and the brothers Chesterton) he never wavered in his conviction that in the eyes of the High Master, the school existed to train up scholarship winners at Oxford and Cambridge, the rank and file being of precious little account. It is not surprising that he found his admission, in 1899, as a scholar of Trinity College, Cambridge, like a release from gaol. At Cambridge he came almost immediately into his element – into a circle of lifelong friends. The most potent influence on him (as with so many other Edwardians) was the philosopher G.E. Moore; but he also lists, almost with gloating, the names of Lytton Strachey, Clive Bell, Maynard Keynes, Bertrand Russell, E.M. Forster, Desmond MacCarthy, A.N. Whitehead, and Thoby Stephen – the last-named, who died of typhoid at twenty-six, is important because he was the son of Sir Leslie Stephen of the *Dictionary of National Biography*, and it was through him that Woolf met his sister Virginia, at a Newnham College party in 1901. Woolf became a member of the famous society of 'the Apostles', discussed every question under the sun, read enormously, and *inter alia* played a large part in the agitation over the Dreyfus Case. (It is perhaps worth observing, as a comment on those 'golden sunset' years before 1914, that he and his friends were always confident of final success in that case: like Browning's optimist, they 'never dreamed, though right were worsted, wrong would triumph'; they were 'Indignant', not 'Angry' young men.)

In 1904 Woolf took the Civil Service examination, and as he did not pass high enough for the Home Civil Service, he opted for the colonial service, was assigned to Ceylon, and in January 1905 arrived in Jaffna, 'an innocent unconscious imperialist', as he says, wearing bright green flannel collars and brown boots, which made him 'something of an eccentric', and bringing with him ninety volumes of the Baskerville edition of Voltaire and a wire-haired fox terrier. (His love of animals was always one of his outstanding characteristics.) His voyage to Ceylon on a P. & O. boat had taught him something about the meticulous class distinctions in English colonial society, and he learned more of it in the towns of Ceylon; but for some time it had little influence on him. He *enjoyed* his work; he liked, actively, the exercise of authority which fell to him – often acting alone – as the representative of H.M. Government; he felt himself on the side of law and order, liked being a judge and prided himself on being both a just judge and an efficient administrator. In 1908, when the Empress Eugénie came to visit the colony, he successfully organised her visit, and even procured for her inspection an authenticated tooth of the Lord Buddha.

This and other incidents he recounts with obvious pleasure in his autobiography; and it seems fairly established that he was an able and an intelligently sensitive imperial administrator. His understanding observation of 'the natives' comes out very well in his novel *The Village in the Jungle* (published in 1913). But clearly doubts were beginning to grow in his mind about the *de haut en bas* relationship between him and his 'clients' or 'subjects'. He was not unaffected by the general 'unrest' which began to develop in Britain after the first two or three years of the Liberal Government – he exchanged long letters with his Cambridge friends, and when in 1909 Lytton Strachey, after the termination of his own brief engagement to Virginia Stephen, wrote suggesting that he was the man she ought to marry, he replied, 'Do you think Virginia would have me? Wire to me if she accepts. I'll take the next boat home.' [Bell (1972) 142n.] But it was not until June of 1911, when he came home on leave to an England which he found delightful, secure, full of artistic ventures like the post-impressionist painters and the classical Russian ballet, and apparently becoming steadily more 'enlightened', that he laid formal siege to Virginia, and even then it was a year before the siege was successful. Before then, having applied for extended leave and been refused, he had resigned from the Colonial Service. In August 1912 they were married, and set up house in Clifford's Inn. After a brief honeymoon on the Continent, Woolf took a job as secretary to the second exhibition of post-impressionist art, organised by Roger Fry at the Grafton Galleries. By this time, according to his autobiography, what he terms 'Old Bloomsbury' had come effectively into being; the membership included, besides Fry and Forster, Keynes and Clive Bell and MacCarthy from Cambridge days, Clive's wife Vanessa Stephen and her brother Adrian, Lytton Strachey and the artist Duncan Grant. Other names were added as time went on; but though 'Bloomsbury' became widely known and discussed, sometimes with admiration and sometimes with loathing, Woolf always insisted that the group covered by the name was never propagandist of itself. It consisted simply of neighbours who happened to think alike on many if not all of the questions of the day. Really, it was much more like a London version of the Apostles, with the addition of some women.

Even before his marriage, Woolf had realised that his wife-to-be was not mentally stable; but he had little idea – and none of her relatives enlightened him – of the real seriousness of her case. Daughter of a distinguished man of letters who was himself neurotic in many ways, but whose death in 1904 nevertheless came as a great shock to her, Virginia Stephen had a long history of hysterical neurosis. Twice she had been out of her mind – on one occasion attempting suicide; and beside this her emotions were decidedly out of control. She was, for example, deeply devoted to her sister Vanessa. Yet shortly after the birth of Vanessa's son Julian she embarked on a passionate flirtation with Clive Bell; and when that was ended accepted a marriage proposal from her homosexual friend Lytton Strachey – which he himself withdrew, horrified, almost immediately after he had made it. She was trying hard to become an author; but her first book took her painful years to complete, and was not accepted for publication, under the title of *The Voyage Out*, until 1913. In the summer of that year, however, she fell ill with what turned into acute mania; in September she just failed to commit suicide – with veronal which had inadvertently been left where she could find it. For many months she was out of her mind; and thereafter, right up to the day of her final suicide, Leonard was continuously on watch and ward over her health and acting as nurse-consultant (with almost an element of gaoler) in the attacks of violent depression which were associated with all her major efforts in literary production. Few even of his close friends had any idea of the lifelong strain which he thus endured – and described with moving detachment in his autobiography; what enabled him to sustain the burden was deep love and the conviction of Virginia's genius, though it was not until 1928, after she had published several books, that this was nationally recognised by the public success of *Orlando* and the award of the Femina Vie Heureuse Prize.

Even before this trouble developed, Woolf had entered upon his life work as a Socialist. He had been interested in the Webbs's campaign to reform the English Poor Law on the lines of the Minority Report to the Poor Law Commission, had made trial of 'social work', as member of an LCC Care Committee in Hoxton – and found it as spiritually unsatisfactory as Beatrice Webb had done thirty years earlier; he had also met Margaret Llewelyn Davies, secretary of the Women's Co-operative Guild, and had learned from her (and from his experiences in the villages of Ceylon) to take the co-operative movement much more seriously as a possible vehicle for social change than did most other Socialist intellectuals. (In 1919 and 1921 he published two books on the future of the movement, which were received by Socialists and co-operators alike with massive inattention.) In the very month of Virginia's illness he lunched with the Webbs, joined the Fabian Society and visited the summer school; soon after he made acquaintance with the editor of the young *New Statesman* and some of his backers and contributors; and shortly after the outbreak of war he was engaged by the Webbs, for the sum of £100, to prepare proposals for international machinery to be established after the war, for the resolution of disputes by peaceful means. The result of his labours was issued, in the middle of 1915, as one of the once famous *New Statesman Supplements*: a little later it was combined with another of the kind to make a book, *International Government* (1916), which has been generally accepted as one of the earliest blueprints for the League of Nations. Woolf was now on the map as an authority on international affairs; and shortly after the war another book, *Empire and Commerce in Africa*, which, commissioned by the left-wing Fabian Research Department, turned out to be a detailed and blistering account of the history of imperialism in that part of the world, and established his authority in that field also. Through the Webbs he became friendly with Arthur Henderson, who when the Labour Party was reorganised in 1918 appointed him as (unpaid) secretary to the party's advisory committees on international and imperial questions, to both of which he gave long and not uninfluential service.

It was fortunate, for both his marriage and his political career, that in May 1916 Woolf was rejected on medical grounds for military service. He did a fair amount of writing for radical journals like the *Nation* and the *Manchester Guardian*, joined the National Guilds League and the 1917 Club – where he found Ramsay MacDonald 'the most egocentric and histrionic of men' – took part in left-wing politics and heartily welcomed the first and (up to a point) the second Russian revolution. More important, after Virginia had recovered her senses, he conceived the idea that the two of them might develop their common interest in printing and literature by buying a printing press and themselves producing and publishing books. Accordingly, early in 1917 they purchased a small press and installed it in Hogarth House in Richmond, which they had bought two years previously, early in 1915; they had moved their own home to Richmond Green in October 1914. The press was delivered to the house in April 1917, and in July the Hogarth Press issued its first publication, *Two Stories*, by Virginia Woolf and L.S. Woolf; the entire job – printing, binding and despatch – being performed by Leonard and Virginia. The list of Hogarth Press publications during its first three years is given by Woolf in his book *Beginning again*. From the intellectual angle it is a good list, including for example, Katherine Mansfield's *Prelude*, Logan Pearsall Smith's *Stories from the Old Testament*, E.M. Forster's *Song of the Siren*, and M. Gorky's *Reminiscences of Tolstoy, Chekhov, and Andreev*. A salesroom expert of today would be most interested in a small book dated 1919 and entitled *Poems by T.S. Eliot*, who was then barely known, though *Prufrock*, now a collector's piece, had been published two years earlier, and Virginia had made acquaintance with its author in 1918. He remained a close friend of both the Woolfs; and with *The Waste Land*, which appeared in 1923, the Hogarth Press may be said to have established its name, though its most solid venture, the English edition of the writings of Freud, did not begin to come out until the following year.

The Press was certainly a reasonably successful enterprise. If it was not quite so important in the scheme of things as it was believed to be by its founder, who devoted much thought and paper to calculating exactly the economics of its working (as well as those of himself and Virginia as authors) it nevertheless published much that was worth while, never considered a book or pamphlet that fell below its own standards, and continued to flourish until its fiftieth year, when it was linked with another firm. Nor was its output limited to the products of 'Bloomsbury': because of his political interests, Woolf's connection with that group was comparatively marginal, and he avoided the assumption of Superior Person which often exasperated its critics. As the work expanded, of course, the Woolfs gave up trying to carry it out by themselves; the actual printing was farmed out – under close supervision – and various trainee managers were taken on from time to time.

Woolf himself continued to develop politically. As a committee member of the Labour Party he was adopted in 1920-1 as candidate for the Combined Universities, and fought the subsequent election – unsuccessfully – on a Socialist programme with a strong international flavour. In 1919 he became editor of a new publication, the *International Review*, and in 1920 and 1921 edited the international section of the *Contemporary Review*; in 1923, after an unsuccessful attempt to get the still little-recognised Eliot appointed literary editor of the *Nation*, which had just undergone a reorganisation, he accepted the post himself part-time, and held it for a number of years, during which he was very successful in getting contributions from writers of standing. Other, later, journalistic jobs included joint editorship, with W.A. Robson, of the *Political Quarterly* from 1931 to 1959, which meant that for some years while Robson was absent on wartime government service, Woolf had sole responsibility. He wrote much for the *New Statesman* after Kingsley Martin had succeeded to the editorship in 1931, and was on the Statesman and Nation Publishing Company's board from November 1941 to July 1965; but though he was always a valued contributor, and was occasionally left in charge, the relationship was not consistently happy. He disagreed, sometimes violently, with John Morgan the general manager, and was quite often at odds with the editor – whom Virginia found as unpalatable as Leonard did her own friend, the strongly feminist composer Ethel Smyth.

After his first disappointment, Woolf never stood again for Parliament; but his post with the two Labour advisory committees, and his association with most of the prominent Labour and Liberal thinkers of his day (of whom, foreign and Indian as well as British, there are lively characterisations in his autobiography) gave him an assured position as counsellor to Labour on their concerns. He never revised his early unfavourable opinion of MacDonald, and the first Labour Government, of 1924, interested him little. He had higher hopes of the second, until he had occasion, on behalf of the Colonial Advisory Bureau and its clients, to approach the Colonial Secretary, who was Sidney Webb. Then he discovered that the Webb respect for expert officials was altogether excessive in the case of the department in which Webb had once served, and wrote a mordant description of the little man, flanked and supported by officials, receiving him in the vast emptiness of the Chamber of the House of Lords, and giving him nothing for his pains. It was incidents like this experienced at a time when the forces of Fascism and Nazism were so patently growing in strength, which definitely shook the foundations of his earlier optimism.

In 1933 he saw something of the Nazi regime at first hand. He had decided to tour Western Europe by car with Virginia, and was warned that as a Jew he might not be safe in Germany, and would do well to take with him a letter of support from von Ribbentrop: in the outcome, however, he made no use of the document, his welcome being assured by a pet marmoset named Mitzi, which sat on his shoulder throughout the tour and excited the eager curiosity and goodwill of the German crowds wherever he went. This experience convinced him that the political world was lapsing rapidly into a condition of lunacy, and shortly afterwards the conviction was reinforced by the war in Spain – in which his nephew Julian Bell died as a volunteer – and what he thought the disgracefully spineless behaviour of the British Labour Party.

Nor could he console himself, as many of his contemporaries did, with hopes based on 'the Socialist Sixth of the World' – the U.S.S.R. At quite an early date he became highly critical of the methods apparently adopted to establish Socialism-in-one-country; and by 1938 his disillusion had reached the point of quarrelling with the Left Book Club when a fiercely eloquent book of his called *Barbarians at the Gate* was all but rejected by the Club's controlling triumvirate of Gollancz, Harold Laski and John Strachey because it was too unkind to Stalin's Russia. (On this occasion his obstinacy won the battle; and the book was published as it stood.)

Disillusioned or not, he did not cease to write and to agitate for the causes of rationality, Humanism, and Socialism. In 1932 he collaborated with G.D.H. Cole in the creation of the New Fabian Research Bureau which six or seven years later amalgamated, with remarkable effect, with the Fabian Society; in this he had continued membership and presided expertly over its international bureau and all its troubles, pre-war, wartime, and post-war, until he resigned office at the end of 1952 because of advancing years and absence from London. He also became more directly interested in the mechanics of administration, serving as a member of the staff side of the Civil Service Whitley Council from 1938 to 1955, and being chosen by the unions as their nominee for the Civil Service Arbitration Board. This, he always maintained, had considerably enlarged his understanding as well as his experience; and he had hoped to make use of it to write a really seminal work of political philosophy. Here, however, he was again disappointed.

Like so many students of politics of the present century, he had been deeply impressed by Graham Wallas's penetrating study of *Human Nature in Politics*, and had regretted Wallas's failure to follow it up effectively. Proposing to fill the gap, he published in 1931 a book which he called *After the Deluge*, vol. *1*, which is a very interesting and suggestive study of the psychology of mankind in the mass and its political consequences up to the outbreak of war. Unfortunately, the book fell flat; its sales were poor, and Woolf was so discouraged – and also so preoccupied with immediate political issues – that no second volume appeared until 1939; and when it did it was not in any way equal in merit to the first, and gave no firm guidance to its readers. It too sold poorly; and when in 1953 Woolf gave to the world his third effort it obviously could not be entitled *After the Deluge* vol. *3*. He called it *Principia Politica*; but it had no more of finality than its predecessors. The difficulty, in fact, lay in Woolf's own mind, in that he could not really decide whether he was fundamentally a pessimist or not; his eventual conclusion was not stated until the fifth volume of his autobiography – published in 1969 and called, aptly enough, *The Journey not the Arrival matters*. In it he tries, characteristically, to evaluate his whole life and work in terms of profit-and-loss (as it might be a Hogarth Press balance sheet), and comes to the conclusion that notwithstanding the award by W.H. Smith & Son of a prize of a thousand pounds for the third volume in the series the bad outweighs the good. He has worked hard all his life, he says, and has enjoyed it; and he considers that he was 'peculiarly fitted' for the kind of political work he undertook, and did it competently. But . . . the 'invisible and probably imaginary' good results of all this work have to be set against 'the disappointment and horror and discomfort and disgust' with which he is forced to regard the world in his time; so his most cheerful last word can only be that 'the shadow of the shadow of a dream is a good enough carrot' for the virtuous striver.

He died on 14 August 1969 at his Sussex home and his funeral took place at Down's Crematorium, Brighton. He had been alone for a long while before, in Sussex. Long ago, in the 'twenties, he and Virginia had moved into Bloomsbury, taking the Press with them. In the summer of 1919 they had ventured on buying, as a summer residence, Monks House in the village of Rodmell, just south of Lewes. There, close to the banks of the Ouse, they cultivated their garden, kept their animals, made friends with villagers, and entertained their other friends from London and elsewhere (in his declining years Leonard undertook his last piece of 'public service', as Clerk to the Parish of Rodmell). As war drew nearer they, Virginia especially, spent more and more time at Rodmell; and the periods of isolation there, particularly after May 1940, while Leonard had to be working in London, probably contributed to her final tragedy. After the war became serious, Rodmell was on the flight path for the German bombers – though only one bomb fell on the village, causing Virginia to rebuke her husband for slamming the door too hard; but London rapidly became impossible. The Hogarth Press was bombed, and removed to Letchworth; bombs hit the Woolfs' flat in Mecklenburgh Square. As the winter went on Virginia was manifestly heading for another attack. Leonard did all that he could, and enlisted the help of a doctor and the novelist Elizabeth Robins; but on the morning of 28 March 1941, when he went to call her to lunch he found the room empty and a letter of love, gratitude and farewell awaiting him. Going through the garden to the Ouse he saw her stick laying on the bank; it was some days before the body was recovered from the river.

Virginia's death, and the shock of it, is recounted in simple and poignant language by her husband in the volume quoted in the preceding paragraphs; but he did not allow it to put an end to either his public or his private work. He continued all the activities which have been described above – with the *New Statesman*, the Fabian Society, the *Political Quarterly*, the Arbitration Board and the rest of it – only gradually withdrawing as his age increased. In company with friends he visited Israel and was very enthusiastic about the kibbutz as a social institution; in 1960 he spent three weeks in Ceylon, and while observing rather sadly 'the change in tempo' there since 1911 he was pleased to find that his term of office was still remembered; in 1966 he was interviewed three times, at length, on television by Malcolm Muggeridge, and noted with dry amusement that one result was to make himself and his garden more visited by people who knew nothing of his politics than ever before. Almost the last word, in his autobiography, is a reflection on a phenomenon which he calls 'senolatry' – meaning the distinction accruing to some characters merely through survival over the years. He instances Queen Victoria and W.G. Grace as examples.

In person Woolf was tall and slim, with an inherited tremor of the hands which was often taken for chorea and a long sallow face, which could occasionally break into a smile of singular sweetness. His double interest, in literature and politics, coupled with the continual anxiety over his deeply-loved wife, of which outsiders knew nothing, combined with a lack of self-importance and a critical judgement which could often be sharp, produced on others the impression of a guarded and half-withdrawn personality which nevertheless commanded great respect and real affection. On medical advice, he and his wife decided to have no children. He left an estate valued at £140,372 net. He bequeathed all copyrights in the published and unpublished books and mss of his late wife equally between his nephew, Quentin Bell, and his niece Angelica Garnett, children of Clive Bell and his wife Vanessa.

MARGARET COLE

Writings: A comprehensive bibliography of Leonard Woolf's works has been compiled by L.M.J. Luedeking and published in *Virginia Woolf Q.* [California State Univ., School of Literature San Diego] (Fall 1972) 120-40 [Copy in *DLB* Coll.]. This includes the majority of his writings, some of the works he edited, and those he helped to translate from Russian into English. It does not, however, include his political articles. Those published in the *Political Quarterly* are of particular importance and are listed below together with a selection of his principal books and other works of relevance to the labour and co-operative movements: *The Control of Industry by the People* (WCG, 1915) 16 pp.; *International Government: two reports* (1916); *Co-operation and the Future of Industry* (1918); *Economic Imperialism* (1920); *Empire & Commerce in Africa: a study in economic imperialism* (1920); *Scope of Mandates under the League of Nations* (n.d.) 16 pp.; *Socialism and Co-operation* (ILP Social Studies ser.: 1921); *International Co-operative Trade* (Fabian Tract no. 201: 1922) 26 pp.; *Essays on Literature, History, Politics etc.* (1927); 'From Serajevo to Geneva', *Pol. Q. 1* (1930) 186-206; *After the Deluge: a study of communal psychology* (1931, later eds. inc. Penguin, 1937); *The Empire in Africa: Labour's policy* (n.d.) 11 pp.; 'The Future of British Broadcasting', *Pol. Q. 2* (Apr-June 1931) 172-85; 'A Constitutional Revolution', ibid., (Oct-Dec 1931) 475-7; *The Labour Party: the Colonies* (1933) 21 pp.; 'From Geneva to the Next War', *Pol. Q. 4* (Jan-Mar 1933) 30-43; 'Labour's Foreign Policy', ibid., (Oct-Dec) 504-24; *Quack, Quack* [Essays on unreason and superstition in politics, belief and thought] (1935); 'Meditation on Abyssinia', *Pol.Q. 7* (Jan-Mar 1936) 16-32; 'The Ideal of the League remains', ibid., (July-Sep 1936) 330-45; 'Arms and Peace', ibid., *8* (Jan-Mar 1937) 21-35; 'The Resurrection of the League', ibid., (July-Sep 1937)

337-52; 'De Profundis', ibid., *10* (Oct-Dec 1939) 463-76; 'Utopia and Reality', ibid., *11* (Apr-June 1940) 167-82; 'Democracy at Bay', ibid., (Oct-Dec 1940) 335-40; 'Hitler's Psychology', ibid., *13* (Oct-Dec 1942) 373-83; 'The Future of the Small State', ibid., *14* (July-Sep 1943) 209-24; *The International Post-War Settlement* (Fabian Society Research Ser. no. 85: 1944) 21 pp.; 'The United Nations', *Pol. Q. 16* (Jan-Mar 1945) 12-20; 'Britain in the Atomic Age', ibid., *17* (Jan-Mar 1946) 12-24; 'The Man of Munich', *Pol. Q. 18* (July-Sep 1947) 199-205; 'Music in Moscow', ibid., *20* (July-Sep 1949); 'Something New out of Africa', ibid., *23* (Oct-Dec 1952) 322-31; *Principia Politica: a study of communal psychology* (1953); 'What is History', *Pol. Q. 26* (July-Sep 1955) 220-8; 'Espionage, Security, and Liberty', ibid., *27* (Apr-June 1956) 152-62; Woolf's five volumes of autobiography: *Sowing* (1960); *Growing* (1961); *Beginning again* (1964); *Downhill all the Way* (1967) and *The Journey not the Arrival matters* (1969).

Sources: The most copious source for Woolf's life is his autobiography in five volumes, of which the earlier ones are the most useful; for, as he grew older, his writing became more and more discursive and his memory slightly less accurate. Other important sources are Virginia Woolf, *A Writer's Diary* (1953) and Quentin Bell's two volumes on *Virginia Woolf* (1972); and for Woolf's political and journalistic work see E. Hyams, *The New Statesman: the history of the first fifty years, 1913-1963* (1963); idem, *New Statesmanship: an anthology* (1963) and *The Political Quarterly in the Thirties*, ed. W.A. Robson (1971). Other sources include *The Webbs and their Work*, ed. M. Cole (1949; repr. Brighton, 1974); R.F. Harrod, *The Life of John Maynard Keynes* (1951; repr. NY, 1969); *Beatrice Webb's Diaries 1912-1924*, ed. M.I. Cole (1952); J.K. Johnstone, *The Bloomsbury Group: a study of E.M. Forster, Lytton Strachey, Virginia Woolf, and their circle* (NY, 1954; repr. 1963); *Beatrice Webb's Diaries 1924-1932*, ed. and with an Introduction by M. Cole (1956) [see also the unpublished Webb diaries in the Passfield papers, section I: BLPES]; M. Cole, *The Story of Fabian Socialism* (1961); Kingsley Martin, *Father Figures* (1966); idem, *Editor* (1968); M. Cole, *The Life of G.D.H. Cole* (1971); M. Holroyd, *Lytton Strachey and the Bloomsbury Group; his Work, their Influence* (1971); C.H. Rolph, *Kingsley* (1973); *Letters of Virginia Woolf* 3 vols *1: 1888-1912 The Flight of the Mind, 2: 1912-1922 The Question of Thing's happening* and *3: 1923-1928 A Change of Perspective*, ed. N. Nicolson (1975-7); *The Diary of Virginia Woolf* vol. *1: 1915-1919*, ed. by A.O. Bell, with an Introduction by Q. Bell (1977); R. Shone, *Bloomsbury Portraits: Vanessa Bell, Duncan Grant and their circle* (1977); biographical information: A.H. Mead, St Paul's School, Barnes; J.A. Morgan, *New Statesman*. OBIT. *Times*, 15 and 21 Aug 1969; *New Statesman*, 22 Aug 1969.

See also: †Arthur HENDERSON; *(Basil) Kingsley MARTIN; †Beatrice WEBB; †Sidney James WEBB.

Consolidated List of Names

Volumes I, II, III, IV and V

ABBOTTS, William (1873–1930) I
ABLETT, Noah (1883–1935) III
ABRAHAM, William, (Mabon) (1842–1922) I
ACLAND, Alice Sophia (1849–1935) I
ACLAND, Sir Arthur Herbert Dyke (1847–1926) I
ADAIR, John (1872–1950) II
ADAMS, David (1871–1943) IV
ADAMS, Francis William Lauderdale (1862–93) V
ADAMS, John Jackson, 1st Baron Adams of Ennerdale (1890–1960) I
ADAMS, William Thomas (1884–1949) I
ADAMSON, Janet (Jennie) Laurel (1882–1962) IV
ADAMSON, William (Billy) Murdoch (1881–1945) V
ALDEN, Sir Percy (1865–1944) III
ALDERSON, Lilian (1885–1976) V
ALEXANDER, Albert Victor (Earl Alexander of Hillsborough) (1885–1965) I
ALLAN, William (1813–74) I
ALLEN, Reginald Clifford (Lord Allen of Hurtwood) (1889–1939) II
ALLEN, Robert (1827–77) I
ALLEN, Sir Thomas William (1864–1943) I
ALLINSON, John (1812/13–72) II
AMMON, Charles (Charlie) George (Lord Ammon of Camberwell) (1873–1960) I
ANDERSON, Frank (1889–1959) I
ANDERSON, William Crawford (1877–1919) II
APPLEGARTH, Robert (1834–1924) II
ARCH, Joseph (1826–1919) I
ARMSTRONG, William John (1870–1950) V
ARNOLD, Alice (1881–1955) IV
ARNOLD, Thomas George (1866–1944) I
ASHTON, Thomas (1844–1927) I
ASHTON, William (1806–77) III

ASHWORTH, Samuel (1825–71) I
ASKEW, Francis (1855–1940) III
ASPINWALL, Thomas (1846–1901) I
AUCOTT, William (1830–1915) II
AYLES, Walter Henry (1879–1953) V

BAILEY, Sir John (Jack) (1898–1969) II
BAILEY, William (1851–96) II
BALFOUR, William Campbell (1919–73) V
BALLARD, William (1858–1928) I
BAMFORD, Samuel (1846–98) I
BARBER, Jonathan (1800–59) IV
BARBER, [Mark] Revis (1895–1965) V
BARBER, Walter (1864–1930) V
BARKER, George (1858–1936) I
BARNES, George Nicoll (1859–1940) IV
BARNETT, William (1840–1909) I
BARRETT, Rowland (1877–1950) IV
BARROW, Harrison (1868–1953) V
BARTLEY, James (1850–1926) III
BARTON, Eleanor (1872–1960) I
BASTON, Richard Charles (1880–1951) V
BATES, William (1833–1908) I
BATEY, John (1852–1925) I
BATEY, Joseph (1867–1949) II
BATTLEY, John Rose (1880–1952) IV
BAYLEY, Thomas (1813–74) I
BEATON, Neil Scobie (1880–1960) I
BELL, George (1874–1930) II
BELL, Richard (1859–1930) II
BENNISON, Thomas Mason (1882–1960) V
BENTHAM, Ethel (1861–1931) IV
BESANT, Annie (1847–1933) IV
BING, Frederick George (1870–1948) III
BIRD, Thomas Richard (1877–1965) I
BLAIR, William Richard (1874–1932) I
BLAND, Hubert (1855–1914) V
BLAND, Thomas (1825–1908) I
BLANDFORD, Thomas (1861–99) I
BLATCHFORD, Montagu John (1848–1910) IV

BLATCHFORD, Robert Peel Glanville (1851–1943) IV
BLYTH, Alexander (1835–85) IV
BOND, Frederick (1865–1951) I
BONDFIELD, Margaret Grace (1873–1953) II
BONNER, Arnold (1904–66) I
BOSWELL, James Edward Buchanan (1906–71) III
BOWERMAN, Charles William (1851–1947) V
BOYES, Watson (1868–1929) III
BOYLE, Hugh (1850–1907) I
BOYNTON, Arthur John (1863–1922) I
BRACE, William (1865–1947) I
BRADBURN, George (1795–1862) II
BRAILSFORD, Henry Noel (1873–1958) II
BRANSON, Clive Ali Chimmo (1907–44) II
BRAUNTHAL, Julius (1891–1972) V
BRAY, John Francis (1809–97) III
BROADHEAD, Samuel (1818–97) IV
BROADHURST, Henry (1840–1911) II
BROOKE, Willie (1895/6?–1939) IV
BROWN, George (1906–37) III
BROWN, Herbert Runham (1879–1949) II
BROWN, James (1862–1939) I
BROWN, William Henry (1867/8–1950) I
BRUFF, Frank Herbert (1869–1931) II
BUGG, Frederick John (1830–1900) I
BURNETT, John (1842–1914) II
BURNS, Isaac (1869–1946) IV
BURNS, John Elliott (1858–1943) V
BURT, Thomas (1837–1922) I
BUTCHER, James Benjamin (1843–1933) III
BUTCHER, John (1833–1921) I
BUTCHER, John (1847–1936) I
BUTLER, Herbert William (1897–1971) IV
BUXTON, Charles Roden (1875–1942) V
BUXTON, Noel Edward (1st Baron Noel-Buxton of Aylsham) (1869–1948) V
BYRON, Anne Isabella, Lady Noel (1792–1860) II

CAIRNS, John (1859–1923) II
CAMPBELL, Alexander (1796–1870) I
CAMPBELL, George Lamb (1849–1906) IV
CANN, Thomas Henry (1858–1924) I
CANTWELL, Thomas Edward (1864–1906) III
CAPE, Thomas (1868–1947) III

CAPPER, James (1829–95) II
CARPENTER, Edward (1844–1929) II
CARTER, Joseph (1818–61) II
CARTER, William (1862–1932) I
CASASOLA, Rowland (Roland) William (1893–1971) IV
CATCHPOLE, John (1843–1919) I
CHALLENER, John Ernest Stopford (1875–1906) V
CHARLTON, William Browell (1855/7?–1932) IV
CHARTER, Walter Thomas (1871–1932) I
CHATER, Daniel (Dan) (1870–1959) IV
CHEETHAM, Thomas (1828–1901) I
CHELMSFORD, 3rd Baron and 1st Viscount Chelmsford. See THESIGER, Frederic John Napier V
CHEW, Ada Nield (1870–1945) V
CIAPPESSONI, Francis Antonio (1859–1912) I
CLARK, Fred (1878–1947) I
CLARK, Gavin Brown (1846–1930) IV
CLARK, James (1853–1924) IV
CLARKE, Andrew Bathgate (1868–1940) I
CLARKE, (Charles) Allen (1863–1935) V
CLARKE, John Smith (1885–1959) V
CLARKE, William (1852–1901) II
CLAY, Joseph (1826–1901) I
CLUSE, William Sampson (1875–1955) III
COCHRANE, William (1872–1924) I
COLMAN, Grace Mary (1892–1971) III
COMBE, Abram (1785?–1827) II
COOK, Arthur James (1883–1931) III
COOK, Cecily Mary (1887/90?–1962) II
COOMBES, Bert Lewis (Louis) (1893–1974) IV
COOPER, George (1824–95) II
COOPER, Robert (1819–68) II
COOPER, William (1822–68) I
COPPOCK, Sir Richard (1885–1971) III
CORMACK, William Sloan (1898–1973) III
COULTHARD, Samuel (1853–1931) II
COURT, Sir Josiah (1841–1938) I
COWEN, Joseph (1829–1900) I
COWEY, Edward (Ned) (1839–1903) I
CRABTREE, James (1831–1917) I
CRAIG, Edward Thomas (1804–94) I
CRAWFORD, William (1833–90) I
CREMER, Sir William Randal (1828–1908) V
CROOKS, William (1852–1921) II
CRUMP, James (1873–1960) V

CURRAN, Peter (Pete) Francis (1860–1910) IV

DAGGAR, George (1879–1950) III
DALLAS, George (1878–1961) IV
DALLAWAY, William (1857–1939) I
DALY, James (?–1849) I
DARCH, Charles Thomas (1876–1934) I
DAVIES, Margaret Llewelyn (1861–1944) I
DAVISON, John (1846–1930) I
DEAKIN, Arthur (1890–1955) II
DEAKIN, Charles (1864–1941) III
DEAKIN, Jane (1869–1942) III
DEAKIN, Joseph Thomas (1858–1937) III
DEAN, Benjamin (1839–1910) I
DEAN, Frederick James (1868–1941) II
DEANS, James (1843/4?–1935) I
DEANS, Robert (1904–59) I
DENT, John James (1856–1936) I
DILKE, Emily (Emilia) Francis Strong, Lady (1840–1904) III
DIXON, John (1828–76) I
DIXON, John (1850–1914) IV
DOCKER, Abraham (1788/91?–1857) II
DRAKE, Henry John (1878–1934) I
DREW, William Henry (Harry) (1854–1933) IV
DUDLEY, Sir William Edward (1868–1938) I
DUNCAN, Andrew (1898–1965) II
DUNCAN, Charles (1865–1933) II
DUNN, Edward (1880–1945) III
DUNNING, Thomas Joseph (1799–1873) II
DYE, Sidney (1900–58) I
DYSON, James (1822/3–1902) I

EADES, Arthur (1863–1933) II
EDWARDS, Alfred (1888–1958) IV
EDWARDS, Allen Clement (1869–1938) III
EDWARDS, Ebenezer (Ebby) (1884–1961) V
EDWARDS, Enoch (1852–1912) I
EDWARDS, John Charles (1833–81) I
EDWARDS, Wyndham Ivor (1878–1938) I
ENFIELD, Alice Honora (1882–1935) I
EVANS, Isaac (1847?–97) I
EVANS, Jonah (1826–1907) I
EWART, Richard (1904–53) IV

FALLOWS, John Arthur (1864–1935) II
FARMERY, George Edward (1883–1942) V
FENWICK, Charles (1850–1918) I

FINCH, John (1784–1857) I
FINLEY, Lawrence (Larry) (1909–74) IV
FINNEY, Samuel (1857–1935) I
FISHWICK, Jonathan (1832–1908) I
FLANAGAN, James Aloysius (1876–1935) III
FLANAGAN, James Desmond (1912–69) IV
FLEMING, Robert (1869–1939) I
FLYNN, Charles Richard (1883–1957) III
FORMAN, John (1822/3–1900) I
FOSTER, William (1887–1947) I
FOULGER, Sydney (1863–1919) I
FOWE, Thomas (1832/3?–94) I
FOX, James Challinor (1837–77) I
FOX, Thomas (Tom) (1860–1934) II
FOX, Thomas (Tom) Samuel (1905–56) V
FOX, William (1890–1968) V
FRITH, John (1837–1904) I

GALBRAITH, Samuel (1853–1936) I
GALLAGHER, Patrick (Paddy the Cope) (1871–1966) I
GANLEY, Caroline Selina (1879–1966) I
GEE, Allen (1852–1939) III
GIBBS, Charles (1843–1909) II
GIBSON, Arthur Lummis (1899–1959) III
GILL, Alfred Henry (1856–1914) II
GILLILAND, James (1866–1952) IV
GILLIS, William (1859–1929) III
GLOVER, Thomas (1852–1913) I
GOLDSTONE, Sir Frank Walter (1870–1955) V
GOLIGHTLY, Alfred William (1857–1948) I
GOODALL, William Kenneth (1877–1963) V
GOODY, Joseph (1816/17–91) I
GOSLING, Harry (1861–1930) IV
GOSSLING, Archibald (Archie) George (1878–1950) V
GRAHAM, Duncan MacGregor (1867–1942) I
GRAY, Jesse Clement (1854–1912) I
GREENALL, Thomas (1857–1937) I
GREENING, Edward Owen (1836–1923) I
GREENWOOD, Abraham (1824–1911) I
GREENWOOD, Joseph (1833–1924) I
GRIFFITHS, George Arthur (1878–1945) III
GROVES, Thomas Edward (1882–1958) V
GROVES, William Henry (1876–1933) II
GRUNDY, Thomas Walter (1864–1942) III

GUEST, John (1867–1931) **III**
GURNEY, Joseph (1814–93) **V**

HACKETT, Thomas (1869–1950) **II**
HADFIELD, Charles (1821–84) **II**
HALL, Frank (1861–1927) **I**
HALL, Fred (1855–1933) **II**
HALL, Fred (1878–1938) **I**
HALL, George Henry (1st Viscount Hall of Cynon Valley) (1881–1965) **II**
HALL, Joseph Arthur (Joe) (1887–1964) **II**
HALL, Thomas George (1858–1938) **II**
HALLAM, William (1856–1902) **I**
HALLAS, Eldred (1870–1926) **II**
HALLIDAY, Thomas (Tom) (1835–1919) **II**
HALSTEAD, Robert (1858–1930) **II**
HAMILTON, Mary Agnes (1882–1966) **V**
HAMSON, Harry Tom (1868–1951) **V**
HANCOCK, John George (1857–1940) **II**
HANDS, Thomas (1858–1938) **II**
HARDERN, Francis (Frank) (1846–1913) **I**
HARES, Edward Charles (1897–1966) **I**
HARFORD, Edward (1837/8–98) **V**
HARRIS, Samuel (1855–1915) **III**
HARRISON, Frederic (1831–1923) **II**
HARRISON, James (1899–1959) **II**
HARTLEY, Edward Robertshaw (1855–1918) **III**
HARTSHORN, Vernon (1872–1931) **I**
HARVEY, William Edwin (1852–1914) **I**
HASLAM, James (1842–1913) **I**
HASLAM, James (1869–1937) **I**
HAWKINS, George (1844–1908) **I**
HAYHURST, George (1862–1936) **I**
HAYWARD, Sir Fred (1876–1944) **I**
HEADLAM, Stewart Duckworth (1847–1924) **II**
HEATH, David William (1827/8(?)–80) **V**
HENDERSON, Arthur (1863–1935) **I**
HENSON, John (Jack) (1879–1969) **V**
HEPBURN, Thomas (1796–1864) **III**
HERRIOTTS, John (1874–1935) **III**
HETHERINGTON, Henry (1792–1849) **I**
HIBBERT, Charles (1828–1902) **I**
HICKEN, Henry (1882–1964) **I**
HICKS, Amelia (Amie) Jane (1839/40?–1917) **IV**
HILL, John (1862–1945) **III**
HILTON, James (1814–90) **I**
HINDEN, Rita (1909–71) **II**
HINES, George Lelly (1839–1914) **I**
HIRST, George Henry (1868–1933) **III**

HOBSON, John Atkinson (1858–1940) **I**
HODGE, John (1855–1937) **III**
HOLBERRY, Samuel (1814–42) **IV**
HOLE, James (1820–95) **II**
HOLLIDAY, Jessie (1884–1915) **III**
HOLWELL, Walter Charles (1885–1965) **V**
HOLYOAKE, Austin (1826–74) **I**
HOLYOAKE, George Jacob (1817–1906) **I**
HOOSON, Edward (1825–69) **I**
HOPKIN, Daniel (1886–1951) **IV**
HORNER, Arthur Lewis (1894–1968) **V**
HOSKIN, John (1862–1935) **IV**
HOUGH, Edward (1879–1952) **III**
HOUSE, William (1854–1917) **II**
HOWARTH, Charles (1814–68) **I**
HOWELL, George (1833–1910) **II**
HUCKER, Henry (1871–1954) **II**
HUDSON, Walter (1852–1935) **II**
HUGHES, Edward (1856–1925) **II**
HUGHES, Hugh (1878–1932) **I**
HUGHES, Will (1873–1938) **V**
HUTCHINGS, Harry (1864–1930) **II**

IRONSIDE, Isaac (1808–70) **II**

JACKSON, Henry (1840–1920) **I**
JACKSON, Thomas Alfred (1879–1955) **IV**
JARVIS, Henry (1839–1907) **I**
JENKINS, Hubert (1866–1943) **I**
JENKINS, John Hogan (1852–1936) **IV**
JEWSON, Dorothea (Dorothy) (1884–1964) **V**
JOHN, William (1878–1955) **I**
JOHNS, John Ernest (1855/6–1928) **II**
JOHNSON, Henry (1869–1939) **II**
JOHNSON, John (1850–1910) **I**
JOHNSON, William (1849–1919) **II**
JOHNSTON, James (1846–1928) **V**
JONES, Benjamin (1847–1942) **I**
JONES, Joseph (Joe) (1891–1948) **V**
JONES, Patrick Lloyd (1811–86) **I**
JUGGINS, Richard (1843–95) **I**
JUPP, Arthur Edward (1906–73) **IV**

KANE, John (1819–76) **III**
KELLEY, George Davy (1848–1911) **II**
KENYON, Barnet (1850–1930) **I**
KILLON, Thomas (1853–1931) **I**
KING, William (1786–1865) **I**
KNEE, Fred (1868–1914) **V**
KUMARAMANGALAM, Surendra Mohan (1916–73) **V**

LACEY, James Philip Durnford (1881–1974) III
LANG, James (1870–1966) I
LANSBURY, George (1859–1940) II
LAST, Robert (1829–?) III
LAW, Harriet Teresa (1831–97) V
LAWRENCE, Arabella Susan (1871–1947) III
LAWSON, John James (Lord Lawson of Beamish) (1881–1965) II
LEE, Frank (1867–1941) I
LEE, Peter (1864–1935) II
LEES, James (1806–91) I
LEICESTER, Joseph Lynn (1825–1903) III
LEWIS, Richard James (1900–66) I
LEWIS, Thomas (Tommy) (1873–1962) I
LEWIS, Walter Samuel (1894–1962) III
LIDDLE, Thomas (1863–1954) I
LINDGREN, George Samuel (Lord Lindgren of Welwyn Garden City) (1900–71) II
LOCKEY, Walter Daglish (1891–1956) V
LOCKWOOD, Arthur (1883–1966) II
LONGDEN, Fred (1886–1952) II
LOVETT, Levi (1854–1929) II
LOWERY, Matthew Hedley (1858–1918) I
LOWERY, Robert (1809–63) IV
LUDLOW, John Malcolm Forbes (1821–1911) II
LUNN, William (Willie) (1872–1942) II

McADAM, John (1806–83) V
MACARTHUR, Mary (1880–1921) II
McBAIN, John McKenzie (1882–1941) V
MACDONALD, Alexander (1821–81) I
MacDONALD, James Ramsay (1866–1937) I
MACDONALD, Roderick (1840–94) IV
McELWEE, Andrew (1882–1968) V
McGHEE, Henry George (1898–1959) I
McGURK, John (1874–1944) V
McKEE, George William (1865–1949) V
MACPHERSON, John Thomas (1872–1921) V
McSHANE, Annie (1888–1962) IV
MADDISON, Fred (1856–1937) IV
MANN, Amos (1855–1939) I
MARCROFT, William (1822–94) I
MARLOW, Arnold (1891–1939) I
MARTIN, James (1850–1933) I
MAXWELL, Sir William (1841–1929) I
MAY, Henry John (1867–1939) I
MELL, Robert (1872?–1941) V

MELLOR, William (1888–1942) IV
MERCER, Thomas William (1884–1947) I
MESSER, Sir Frederick (Fred) (1886–1971) II
MIDDLETON, Dora Miriam (1897–1972) IV
MIDDLETON, George Edward (1866–1931) II
MILLERCHIP, William (1863–1939) I
MILLIGAN, George Jardine (1868–1925) V
MILLINGTON, Joseph (1866–1952) II
MILLINGTON, William Greenwood (1850–1906) III
MITCHELL, John Thomas Whitehead (1828–95) I
MITCHISON, Gilbert Richard (Baron Mitchison of Carradale) (1890–1970) II
MOLESWORTH, William Nassau (1816–90) I
MOORHOUSE, Thomas Edwin (1854–1922) I
MORGAN, David (Dai o'r Nant) (1840–1900) I
MORGAN, David Watts (1867–1933) I
MORGAN, John Minter (1782–1854) I
MORLEY, Iris Vivienne (1910–53) IV
MOSLEY, Cynthia Blanche, Lady (1898–1933) V
MUDIE, George (1788?–?) I
MUGGERIDGE, Henry Thomas Benjamin (1864–1942) V
MURDOCH, Mary Charlotte (1864–1916) V
MURNIN, Hugh (1865–1932) II
MURRAY, Robert (1869–1950) I
MYCOCK, William Salter (1872–1950) III

NEALE, Edward Vansittart (1810–92) I
NEWCOMB, William Alfred (1849–1901) III
NEWTON, William (1822–76) II
NICHOLLS, George (1864–1943) V
NOEL, Conrad le Despenser Roden (1869–1942) II
NOEL-BUXTON, 1st Baron Noel-Buxton of Aylsham. See BUXTON, Noel Edward V
NOEL-BUXTON, Lucy Edith Pelham, Lady (1888–1960) V
NORMANSELL, John (1830–75) I
NUTTALL, William (1835–1905) I

OAKEY, Thomas (1887–1953) IV
O'GRADY, Sir James (1866–1934) II
OLIVER, John (1861–1942) I
ONIONS, Alfred (1858–1921) I

PALIN, John Henry (1870–1934) IV
PARE, William (1805–73) I
PARKER, James (1863–1948) II
PARKINSON, John Allen (1870–1941) II
PARKINSON, Tom Bamford (1865–1939) I
PARROTT, William (1843–1905) II
PASSFIELD, 1st Baron Passfield of Passfield Corner. *See* WEBB, Sidney James II
PATERSON, Emma Anne (1848–86) V
PATTERSON, William Hammond (1847–96) I
PATTISON, Lewis (1873–1956) I
PEASE, Edward Reynolds (1857–1955) II
PEASE, Mary Gammell (Marjory) (1861–1950) II
PEET, George E. (1883–1967) V
PENNY, John (1870–1938) I
PERKINS, George Reynolds (1885–1961) I
PETCH, Arthur William (1886–1935) IV
PHILLIPS, Marion (1881–1932) V
PHIPPEN, William George (1889–1968) V
PICKARD, Benjamin (1842–1904) I
PICKARD, William (1821–87) I
PICTON-TURBERVILL, Edith (1872–1960) IV
PIGGOTT, Thomas (1836–87) II
PITMAN, Henry (1826–1909) I
PLUNKETT, Sir Horace Curzon (1854–1932) V
POINTER, Joseph (1875–1914) II
POLLARD, William (1832/3?–1909) I
POLLITT, James (1857–1935) III
POOLE, Stephen George (1862–1924) IV
POSTGATE, Daisy (1892–1971) II
POSTGATE, Raymond William (1896–1971) II
POTTS, John Samuel (1861–1938) II
PRATT, Hodgson (1824–1907) I
PRICE, Gabriel (1879–1934) III
PRICE, Thomas William (1876–1945) V
PRINGLE, William Joseph Sommerville (1916–62) II
PRYDE, David Johnstone (1890–1959) II
PURCELL, Albert Arthur (1872–1935) I

RAE, William Robert (1858–1936) II
RAMSEY, Thomas (Tommy) (1810/11–73) I

READE, Henry Musgrave (1860–?) III
REDFERN, Percy (1875–1958) I
REED, Richard Bagnall (1831–1908) IV
REEVES, Samuel (1862–1930) I
REEVES, William Pember (1857–1932) II
REYNOLDS, George William MacArthur (1814–79) III
RICHARDS, Thomas (1859–1931) I
RICHARDS, Thomas Frederick (Freddy) (1863–1942) III
RICHARDSON, Robert (1862–1943) II
RICHARDSON, Thomas (Tom) (1868–1928) IV
RICHARDSON, William Pallister (1873–1930) III
RITSON, Joshua (Josh) (1874–1955) II
ROBERTS, George Henry (1868–1928) IV
ROBINSON, Charles Leonard (1845–1911) III
ROBINSON, Richard (1879–1937) I
ROBSON, James (1860–1934) II
ROBSON, John (1862–1929) II
ROEBUCK, Samuel (1871–1924) IV
ROGERS, Frederick (1846–1915) I
ROGERSON, William Matts (1873–1940) III
ROWLINSON, George Henry (1852–1937) I
ROWSON, Guy (1883–1937) II
RUST, Henry (1831–1902) II
RUTHERFORD, John Hunter (1826–90) I

SAMUELSON, James (1829–1918) II
SCHOFIELD, Thomas (1825–79) II
SCURR, John (1876–1932) IV
SEDDON, James Andrew (1868–1939) II
SEWELL, William (1852–1948) I
SHACKLETON, Sir David James (1863–1938) II
SHAFTOE, Samuel (1841–1911) III
SHALLARD, George (1877–1958) I
SHANN, George (1876–1919) II
SHARP, Andrew (1841–1919) I
SHAW, Fred (1881–1951) IV
SHEPPARD, Frank (1861–1956) III
SHIELD, George William (1876–1935) III
SHILLITO, John (1832–1915) I
SHURMER, Percy Lionel Edward (1888–1959) II
SIMPSON, Henry (1866–1937) III
SIMPSON, James (1826–95) I

SIMPSON, William Shaw (1829–83) II
SITCH, Charles Henry (1887–1960) II
SITCH, Thomas (1852–1923) I
SKEFFINGTON, Arthur Massey (1908–71) V
SKEVINGTON, John (1801–50) I
SKINNER, James Allen (1890–1974) V
SLOAN, Alexander (Sandy) (1879–1945) II
SMILLIE, Robert (1857–1940) III
SMITH, Albert (1867–1942) III
SMITH, Alfred (1877–1969) III
SMITH, Herbert (1862–1938) II
SMITHIES, James (1819–69) I
SOUTHALL, Joseph Edward (1861–1944) V
SPARKES, Malcolm (1881–1933) II
SPENCER, George Alfred (1873–1957) I
SPENCER, John Samuel (1868–1943) I
STANLEY, Albert (1862–1915) I
STANTON, Charles Butt (1873–1946) I
STEAD, Francis Herbert (1857–1928) IV
STEADMAN, William (Will) Charles (1851–1911) V
STEVENS, John Valentine (1852–1925) II
STEWART, Aaron (1845–1910) I
STOTT, Benjamin (1813–50) IV
STRAKER, William (1855–1941) II
STRINGER, Sidney (1889–1969) V
SULLIVAN, Joseph (1866–1935) II
SUMMERBELL, Thomas (1861–1910) IV
SUTHERS, Robert Bentley (1870–1950) IV
SUTTON, John Edward (Jack) (1862–1945) III
SWAN, John Edmund (1877–1956) III
SWANWICK, Helena Maria Lucy (1864–1939) IV
SWEET, James (1804/5?–79) IV
SWIFT, Fred (1874–1959) II
SWINGLER, Stephen Thomas (1915–69) III
SYLVESTER, George Oscar (1898–1961) III

TAYLOR, John Wilkinson (1855–1934) I
TAYLOR, Robert Arthur (1886–1934) IV
TEER, John (1809?–1883?) IV
THESIGER, Frederic John Napier, 3rd Baron and 1st Viscount Chelmsford (1868–1933) V
THICKETT, Joseph (1865–1938) II
THORNE, William James (1857–1946) I
THORPE, George (1854–1945) I

TILLETT, Benjamin (Ben) (1860–1943) IV
TOOTILL, Robert (1850–1934) II
TOPHAM, Edward (1894–1966) I
TORKINGTON, James (1811–67) II
TOYN, Joseph (1838–1924) II
TRAVIS, Henry (1807–84) I
TROTTER, Thomas Ernest Newlands (1871–1932) III
TROW, Edward (1833–99) III
TWEDDELL, Thomas (1839–1916) I
TWIGG, Herbert James Thomas (1900–57) I
TWIST, Henry (Harry) (1870–1934) II

VARLEY, Frank Bradley (1885–1929) II
VARLEY, Julia (1871–1952) V
VEITCH, Marian (1913–73) III
VINCENT, Henry (1813–78) I
VIVIAN, Henry Harvey (1868–1930) I

WADSWORTH, John (1850–1921) I
WALKDEN, Alexander George (1st Baron Walkden of Great Bookham) (1873–1951) V
WALKER, Benjamin (1803/4?–83) I
WALLAS, Graham (1858–1932) V
WALLHEAD, Richard [Christopher] Collingham (1869–1934) III
WALSH, Stephen (1859–1929) IV
WALSHAM, Cornelius (1880–1958) I
WARD, John (1866–1934) IV
WARDLE, George James (1865–1947) II
WARNE, George Henry (1881–1928) IV
WARWICK, Frances Evelyn (Daisy), Countess of (1861–1938) V
WATKINS, William Henry (1862–1924) I
WATSON, William (1849–1901) III
WATTS, John (1818–87) I
WEBB, Beatrice (1858–1943) II
WEBB, Catherine (1859–1947) II
WEBB, Sidney James (1st Baron Passfield of Passfield Corner) (1859–1947) II
WEBB, Simeon (1864–1929) I
WEBB, Thomas Edward (1829–96) I
WEIR, John (1851–1908) I
WEIR, William (1868–1926) II
WELLOCK, Wilfred (1879–1972) V
WELSH, James C. (1880–1954) II
WESTWOOD, Joseph (1884–1948) II
WHITE, Arthur Daniel (1881–1961) III
WHITE, Charles Frederick (1891–1956) V
WHITEFIELD, William (1850–1926) II

WHITEHEAD, Alfred (1862–1945) I
WHITEHOUSE, Samuel Henry (1849–1919) IV
WHITELEY, William (1881–1955) III
WIGNALL, James (1856–1925) III
WILKIE, Alexander (1850–1928) III
WILLIAMS, Aneurin (1859–1924) I
WILLIAMS, David James (1897–1972) IV
WILLIAMS, Sir Edward John (Ted) 1890–1963) III
WILLIAMS, John (1861–1922) I
WILLIAMS, Ronald Watkins (1907– 58) II
WILLIAMS, Thomas (Tom) (Lord Williams of Barnburgh) (1888–1967) II

WILLIAMS, Thomas Edward (Baron Williams of Ynyshir) (1892–1966) III
WILLIS, Frederick Ebenzer (1869–1953) II
WILSON, John (1837–1915) I
WILSON, John (1856–1918) II
WILSON, Joseph Havelock (1858–1929) IV
WILSON, William Tyson (1855–1921) III
WINSTONE, James (1863–1921) I
WINWOOD, Benjamin (1844–1913) II
WOODS, Samuel (1846–1915) I
WOOLF, Leonard Sidney (1880–1969) V
WORLEY, Joseph James (1876–1944) I
WRIGHT, Oliver Walter (1886–1938) I
WYLD, Albert (1888–1965) II

General Index

Compiled by Barbara Nield with assistance
from V.J. Morris and G.D. Weston

Numbers in bold type refer to biographical entries
and Special Notes

Scouller, Robert Elder (Bob), 17
Seamen, Committee for the Training of British, 83; Pension Fund Committee, 148
Seamen's (Tuberculosis) Advisory Committee, 83
Second World War (1939–45), 13, 17, 22, 35, 36, 50, 54, 78, 80, 85, 87, 91, 99, 115, 119, 121, 127, 133, 137, 141, 180, 196, 212, 237, 245–6; conscientious objection, 199; military service tribunals, 237
Secular Chronicle, 135–6
Secularism, 79, 89, 93, 94, 108, 135, 198, 226
Select Committees
   1890–1, Railway Servants (Hours of Labour), 106
   1906, Official Publications, 30
   1920, Work of the Employment Exchanges, 219
   1929–30, Hours of Meeting and Rising of the House of Commons, 143
   1930, Future Government of East Africa, 236
   1932–3, Local Expenditure (England and Wales) [Ray Committee], 7
Seligman, David, 15
Sexton, James, 153, 154, 155
Shaftesbury, Anthony Ashley Cooper (7th Earl of Shaftesbury), 68, 168
Sharkey, W.J., 193
Sharp, Clifford Dyce, 28
Sharp, Evelyn (*later* Baroness Sharp of Hornsey [Life Peeress]), 101
Shaw Court of Inquiry into Transport Workers: *see* Dock Labour
Shaw, George Bernard, 25, 27, 28, 129, 227, 228, 233
Shaw, Mary (Mrs George Phippen), 180
Shawcross, Sir Hartley William (*later* Baron Shawcross of Friston [Life Peer]), 125
Sheffield, 86; University, 124
Sheffield Cutlery Council, 210
Sheffield Telegraph, 127
Shepherd, George Robert (*later* 1st Baron Shepherd of Spalding), 202
Shinwell, Emanuel (*later* Baron Shinwell of Easington [Life Peer]), 116
Shipton, George, 40, 167
Shirt, Collar and Underlinen Makers, Society of, 168
Shop Stewards' Movement, First World War, 171, 172
Shrewsbury School, 1, 226
Silkin, John Ernest, 14
Silvester, Fred, 203
Simcox, Edith, 161, 168, 169
Simpson, Henry, 77
Simpson, J.T., 65
Singapore, 215
Sitwell, Sir Osbert, 101
Skeffington, Arthur Massey, **195–7**

Skinner, James Allen, **198–200**
Slutsky, Gresha, 114
Smallwood, Gertie, 193
Smillie, Robert, 61, 79
Smith, Alfred, 177
Smith, Herbert, 146
Smith, Logan Pearsall, 243
Smith, R. Tanner, 121
Smith, Sydney Herbert, 148
Smith, Walter Robert, 119, 120
Smith, William Henry & Son, 245
Smoke Abatement League of Great Britain, 122
Smyth, Dame Ethel, 244
Snowden, Philip (*later* 1st Viscount Snowden of Ickornshaw), 9, 61, 63, 79, 98, 101, 161, 215, 235
Social Democratic Federation, 2, 26, 27, 28, 30, 39, 40, 42, 65, 67, 70, 71, 79, 106, 109–10, 111, 118, 129, 130, 160, 192, 207, 227, 233. *See also* British Socialist Party
Social Democratic Party, 111
Socialist, 71
Socialist India, 134
Socialist International (1951), 36, 37
Socialist Labour Party, 71, 140
Socialist League, (1885–94), 39
   (1932–7), 198
Socialist Review, 86
Socialist Sunday Schools, 60
Socialist Women's International, 120
Society for Democratic Integration in Industry, 237
Society for Socialist Inquiry and Propaganda, 234
Society for the Oversea Settlement of British Women, 220
Society of Antiquaries of Scotland, 72
Society of Women employed in the Upholstery Trade, 167–8
Society of Women employed in Bookbinding, 167, 169
Soldiers', Sailors' and Airmen's Families Association, 166
Solidarity, 172
Somerset and Wiltshire Journal, 128
Somerset Express, 102
South Africa, 149, 185, 208
South Wales Miner, 115
South Wales Socialist Society, 112
South Wales Worker, 179
South Western Star, 41
Southall, 180; Labour Club, 180
Southall, Joseph Edward, **200–5**
Southey, H.W., 102, 103
Southwell, Charles, 135
Spalding, H.N., 193
Spanish Civil War, attitudes to, 17, 21, 24, 80, 115, 126, 244; POUM, 115
Speaker's Conference on the Franchise, 88